T0287649

# Red Cliff, Wisconsin:

# A History of an Ojibwe Community

Praise for Howard Paap's *A Northern Land: Life With the Ojibwe* (2001):

"Paap clearly has deep affection for the Indian culture and the land surrounding Red Cliff. This interesting book deserves wide readership."

—Mary Ann Grossman, Books Columnist,
*Pioneer Press*, June 16, 2002

"For those interested in Ojibwe life, the book's a winner. For anyone who appreciates what we have around here, the quiet, brooding spirit of our boreal forests, our lakeshore, Paap's book will be downright seminal."

—*The Lake Superior Sounder*, September 2003

* * *

Howard Paap's *Raspberry River* was a silver medalist for best fiction of the year by the Midwest Independent Publishers Association in 2007.

# Red Cliff, Wisconsin: A History of an Ojibwe Community

## Volume 1

## The Earliest Years: The Origin to 1854

**Howard D. Paap**

NORTH STAR PRESS OF ST. CLOUD, INC.
St. Cloud, Minnesota

For the next generation:
Mijen, Grace, Elsa, Binesi, Sawyer, and Memengwaa.
Ojibwes All
*Mino giizhigad noongom!*



Cover art: Indian Encampment on Lake Huron by Paul Kane
This piece, painted in 1845, depicts an Ojibwe camp on Lake Huron, on the shore of Georgian Bay.



ISBN 978-0-87839-557-6



Printed in the United States of America

Published by
North Star Press of St. Cloud, Inc.
St. Cloud, Minnesota

www.northstarpress.com

# Table of Contents

# 1

# Early Ojibwe Culture

THE OJIBWE PEOPLE OF THE COMMUNITY of Red Cliff, Wisconsin, often trace their origins back to a creation said to have occurred beside a saltwater sea near the mouth of the St. Lawrence River on the North American Atlantic shoreline.[1] Numerous versions of these origin teachings tell how sometime after this creation the people embarked on an epic westward migration that culminated at Madeline Island in Chequamegon Bay, near the western limit of Lake Superior. It is here, in historical time and far distant from their point of origin, that in 1854 the people eventually agreed to a treaty with the United States that led to the official establishment of several of today's Ojibwe communities in Upper Michigan, northern Wisconsin, and northeastern Minnesota. The Red Cliff Band of Lake Superior Ojibwe, found at the far northern tip of the State of Wisconsin, is one of those communities. This book will trace the early history of this community, using the written sources, and when appropriate, pertinent information from the Ojibwe oral tradition, up to 1854 with the signing of the La Pointe treaty of that year.

Much has been written about the Ojibwe people, but relatively little about Red Cliff, and until recently, most of what is written holds a perspective distant from that of the Ojibwe themselves. The present writer is not of Ojibwe descent, but for the past fifty and more years has had an intimate relationship with the Red Cliff community, and it is hoped this work will be useful to future Ojibwe scholars. Today we are fortunate to be witnessing the emergence of a community of Ojibwe writers who are offering an authentic view of Ojibwe culture and its history, and while we are still waiting for someone from this community of writers to come forward and offer an extensive and detailed history of Red Cliff, it seems likely that in time this will occur. It is hoped that until that time this present work will serve purpose to help readers understand the long and eventful story of the community, and be useful in encouraging future writers to offer their accounts of its history.

### *The Importance of Aboriginal Ojibwe Culture*

HISTORICALLY, THE OJIBWE ARE North American Indians whose home territories are located in the general Great Lakes regions, with some extending into the northern Great Plains. Their original language is of the Algonquian Language Family, and their early subsistence base is one of foraging, or as is often said, hunting and gathering, with some gardening. In earliest times they were a mobile, or at least semi-mobile community, moving with the seasons as they used the resources of their areas. As with all cultures, theirs was, and remains, deeply affected by its natural habitat—the geographical region in which the Ojibwe people chose to reside. They are a people of the northern forests, lakes, rivers and streams, and in their case are closely related to water, or, in their language, *nibi*, and so water is of great religious importance to them. Accordingly, their home bases in the Great Lakes region are situated adjacent to important water sources.

In the following pages we will present an outline of the underpinnings and main features of aboriginal Ojibwe culture, and references to this culture will from time to time be made in the chapters that follow. It is the contention of this writer that an adequate understanding of an Ojibwe community's history cannot be gained without at least a modicum of familiarity with the culture of such a community. By culture, we mean that integrated system of principles, rules, beliefs, and assumptions held by a people about their world. This system of rules for living, and the accompanying understandings, originally emerged when the peoples' forebears interacted with their natural surroundings as they struggled not just to build their world, but to carry it forth into succeeding generations. When these earliest of peoples worked to gain sustenance they established norms for living, and in the process agreed upon rules for social relationships between themselves and other life forms. As these realities were formed and understood, the people also organized values and beliefs about plausible reasons for their existence. In other words, they came to grips with their spiritual world and accepted a belief system that helped serve to motivate them to form and accept both personal and community identities.

A culture, then, has a technical, or material, base that initially was intimately connected with its natural surroundings, and as the people established rules for survival in this habitat they simultaneously built a system of relationships between their members. These were societal relationships, or social, and at base were of an economic and political nature. On the individual level, these people also established a set of understandings about their family and kinship systems within this natural setting. Finally, they agreed upon a system of beliefs about realities beyond themselves as they recognized other-than-human persons and the power these very important beings held. This complex and interconnected framework of economic, political, and social-organizational realities was interlaced with an awareness of spiritual beings that are the ultimate sources of power within the Ojibwe world.

Anthropologists, moreso than historians, recognize that culture, as this complex system of rules, principles, and beliefs, is a powerful, even causal, force in its own right. As such, it follows that a peoples' history is, to a large part, driven by events, but also by its culture. While such a written history must speak to the culture of the people it is recording, as readers of that history, we also must recognize that the culture of the person doing that recording is likewise an important element affecting the history's creditability.

Here we will present an outline of this early Ojibwe culture as it existed in the western Lake Superior region, with a focus on the Chequamegon Bay area. In this book's following chapters we will comment on how this system underwent adaptive changes over the hundreds of years of European, and later, American influence. It will be argued that throughout this long and often contentious time a viable Ojibwe culture continued to exist, and in fact, in recent years, is experiencing a meaningful growth and resurgence.

### *Subsistance Practices*

FOR THE EARLY OJIBWE PEOPLE, essentially, the man was the hunter and the woman the gatherer, but this is an overly simplified image of how food was actually procured. The sexes cooperated in the task of supplying sustenance—their specialized roles complementing each other. The principle game animals were large—white-tailed deer, black bear, moose and elk being the major species—and were solitary in their manners, that is, unlike the bison of the nearby Great Plains, they were not herd animals that required an organized group effort in their taking. A single hunter, or at most, a few hunters working together, could take these large animals. Hence, the nature of the food resource dictated not just the tools required for its use, but also the social method of human procurement.

The smaller terrestrial animals of the northern forest (rabbits, beaver, porcupine, and others) were taken for food, and some, after European contact, for their furs. The ubiquitous lakes, rivers, and streams supplied fish and other aquatic animals, and of course, birds and especially waterfowl were also taken. In earlier times the woodland bison was sometimes hunted in regions just to the south of Lake Superior, and Ojibwe communities west of the lake would seasonally take the plains buffalo for food, but these activities were not typical for those communities closer to the big lake.

Fish were a particularly important food source for the Lake Superior Ojibwe. Essentially, fishing was woman's work, and in inland locations it was the woman who kept and used a net, setting and lifting it nearly year-round. She was also the one who prepared the catch, through drying or smoking, for future use. Exceptions to this were found on the largest bodies of water where the man assumed a fisher role, sometimes using nets, but also using spears, as he joined the woman at this important task. Ice fishing, for instance, was a male activity.

An array of wild plants and fruits were used, but the main vegetal resource was wild rice, growing in inland lakes and sloughs. Maple sugar was manufactured and where practicable, the trilogy of corn, beans, and squash was grown in garden patches. While males could sometimes be involved in producing these foods, it was the woman who handled most of this work. Gardening occurred in the Chequamegon Bay Ojibwe communities, but it is not well documented in the early literature. This is unfortunate, and perhaps it shows a male bias in the early writings. As we will see, when the Jesuits arrived at Chequamegon Bay in the seventeenth century, the Huron and Odawa were keeping significant fields, or gardens, of corn and other plants, and we might assume that in time the resident Ojibwe did likewise. Ojibwe literature tells of such activities in times after the Jesuit withdrawal, particularly in the St. Croix region south of Lake Superior, and we should expect they occurred further north as well.

A seasonal round of these food-getting activities gave an annual rhythm to Ojibwe life that led to different types of villages, or encampments, being established at strategic sites and times. The year was bisected between winter and summer activities that saw the community disperse into small family-centered encampments in winter, and come back together into a single larger encampment at the bay in summer. The fall encampment was for the purpose of harvesting wild rice and although it would last only a few weeks, was of utmost importance. The spring camp was a maple sugar harvesting camp, and likewise was of short duration, but also of great importance. Sugar camps were small, holding a few nuclear families, and while it seems sometimes the white birch tree was tapped and its sap boiled into sugar, most sugar was manufactured from maple sap. It follows that sugar camps were found only where groves of sugar maple trees grew. With good harvests, enough rice and sugar could be secured and stored for use throughout the following year.

Both sexes worked in the rice and sugar camps, but in earlier times the leadership and activities involved were structured a bit differently than they are today. While both men and women labored in them, the literature shows that in earlier times these camps were the domain of the woman. In the instance of wild rice, a male political leader would declare when the rice was ready for harvesting, but once the operation began it was the woman who was usually instrumental in having the important labor carried out. She oversaw the crucial task of securing and storing the resource—both sugar and rice—for later use.

With the conclusion of the spring maple sugar manufacturing work, the various bands congregated at Madeline Island or the nearby shoreline where they more or less remained for the duration of the warmer weather. In historical time the familiar spring rendezvous of French fur buyers and Ojibwe fur trappers occurred after the sugar season when families that had been dispersed in the maple groves, congregated at places like Grand Portage, Minnesota, and La Pointe, in Chequamegon Bay. As we will see, after the arrival of the French and their market for furs, for some time the Ojibwe made this new economic activity part of their usual seasonal round of subsistence procurement activities.

### *Social Organization*

AS HUNTERS AND GATHERERS, the early Ojibwe had a series of bands—that is, clusters of related people who more or less moved together through their resource areas as the season dictated. The size of these units varied, and the range of members could be from around twenty to considerably larger amounts. After contact with the Europeans and into historical time, these bands could have a few hundred members.

Smaller descent groups would cluster with others in Chequamegon Bay in late spring to spend the summer in this locale, forming bands composed of lineages and clans, i.e., social units made up of members of the same descent line. These were exogamous, meaning an individual was required to marry a person outside his or her descent group. The clan was the largest of these kinship units and was a key element in the overall Ojibwe social organization. Each lineage, clan, and band had a political leader, the last of which was usually quite prominent within the overall Ojibwe community.

Originally the Ojibwe were patrilineal, that is, they traced their descent through the male line. William Warren, the early Ojibwe writer, recognized twenty-one clans in the early nineteenth century, but according to him there were originally only five. These were the Crane, Fish, Loon, Bear, and Marten clans.

There was no overall political leader for the numerous Ojibwe bands, but after European contact the Americans applied pressure for the people to recognize such a position. In the later years of his life, La Pointe's Chief Buffalo was said to be the overall political leader of what the American government labeled the Lake Superior Ojibwe bands.

In the times before the adoption of the use of money (the all-purpose medium of exchange) the Ojibwe used sharing and barter in their exchange system. The use of money in the process of exchanging goods and services did not come to the people until the mid-1800s, and it took some time to become widespread. Until then sharing was used, with barter (the exchange of equal-valued goods) employed with non-Ojibwe communities. In earlier times, to be Ojibwe was to have a willingness to share resources, particularly with those who were related through descent or socially close in other ways. We will see that with the arrival of the Europeans and Americans with their concept of private wealth, an immediate problem presented itself. With its social system including an economic exchange mechanism based upon sharing, when Ojibwe culture began regular relationships with Europeans, the opportunities for misunderstandings leading to conflict quickly arose.

In a political sense, early Ojibwe culture was a pure democracy. The situation of recognizing a single person holding great political power was simply unknown to the people. As we will note, in the early nineteenth century, when the Lake Superior Ojibwe first encountered American political leaders who not only seemingly held a great degree of power (and often conducted themselves in this manner), they (the Ojibwe) were put off by this unusual, and even frightening, display. In Ojibwe culture there were individuals who stood out due to their knowledge, wisdom, skills and ability to lead, but these people did not hold wide, arbitrary power. We will see that after European contact, leaders like La Pointe's Buffalo usually prefaced his speeches given before Europeans and Americans by saying he was not the all-powerful leader of his community, he was only its appointed messenger. Some of this may have been a matter of proper political presentation, even posturing at times, but at base it was legitimate. Ojibwe bands were separate, independent political units and while this said much about the freedom and liberty of these groups, it also said something about their difficulties when coming up against larger and more powerful communities.

### *Spirituality, Religion, and Worldview*

OJIBWE CULTURE POSITS A WORLD replete with spiritual forms, each holding a degree of power. While today there exists strong feelings—and some discussion—on the matter, some voices insist that originally Ojibwe culture was not monotheistic, that is, the people did not recognize a single, overriding all-powerful spiritual form that played a major, deeply pervasive role in their personal lives. These voices argue that the idea of one single powerful god was not originally part of their culture, and that the notion of such a being arrived with the Europeans. As Theresa Schenck has written, "the missionary's beliefs about sin and a Judeo-Christian God had no equivalent in Ojibwe thought."[2]

In the absence of this single spiritual being that serves as the basis for an explanation of the world, the Ojibwe perceive a world peopled by separate persons and, according to A.I. Hallowell, they use a "personalistic theory of causation."[3] Thus, the concept of persons and their actions, rather than some grand plan or design set forth and controlled by a single being, is paramount in understanding the Ojibwe worldview. Hallowell's category of "persons" includes humans and non-humans, and the interaction of these two types of persons is integral to the existence of a unified cosmos.

Key to this view is the acceptance of the notion that the universe is filled with power, and hence, this power is a life force in nature since it sustains the physical, psychological, and spiritual well being of all life forms.[4] Importantly, to the Ojibwe point of view, humans can only acquire this power through their interactions with these spiritual forms, and accordingly, they must supplicate themselves to them, and regularly offer gratitude—often through the gift of *asemaa*, or tobacco—to these spiritual persons.

In the Ojibwe view, some voices say after their initial creation the people fell upon hard times where they found themselves suffering. They were separated into a number of opposing communities, and upon seeing this unfortunate situation, Wenabozho, the Ojibwe culture hero, along with others, brought the people their major religious institution, the *midewiwin*. Thus they were able to survive and make their fabled migration to a place far to the west. A central figure in this drama was a person in the form of an otter who came to them, bringing this power.

This is a grossly simplified account of the arrival of the *midewiwin* to the people, and the origin of their long trip to La Pointe and Lake Superior, but the arrival of the gift of the *midewiwin* is a complex teaching, and there are numerous versions of the event. Let it be enough to say that today the *midewiwin* is a very important part of the peoples' lives, as it regularly allows them to be renewed as they live their lives in their northern homeland.

We see, then, that each Ojibwe person has power, or at least the potential to acquire it. To facilitate this widespread sharing of power Ojibwe culture has a network of religious ceremonies and institutions—like the sweat lodge, shaking tent, and others—beyond the *midewiwin*, and all address the matter of access to the spirit world and the proper relations, i.e., expectations and responsibilities, involved.

Ojibwe culture holds a complex religion component along with a rich cosmology and cosmogony. In the following chapters we will see how this culture, and especially its religion, came under attack with the arrival of the first Europeans, and how it struggled to survive.

*Notes*

1. Some Ojibwe hold that the creation did not occur far to the east, but instead, took place on Madeline Island. Others refer to *The Walam Olum* (The Red Score), a history including a Siberian origin, followed by a passage of the Bering Straits and an *eastward* migration to the Atlantic shore. See *The Red Record*, by D. McCutchen, 1989, Garden City, New Jersey.
2. Schenck as stated in Ely 2012:xxiii.
3. Hallowell 1964:49-82.
4. Roufs 1978:2.

# 2

# The 1600s and Red Cliff: Initial Questions

THE QUESTIONS TO BE ADDRESSED in this chapter focus on seventeenth century events concerning the western Lake Superior region. While some of the Ojibwe bands coming to Chequamegon Bay eventually moved into the lands west of Lake Superior—into what is now called Minnesota, North Dakota, Montana, Western Ontario, Manitoba, and Saskatchewan—our central concern will be with those who stayed in the immediate La Pointe-Chequamegon region. To examine these questions we will undertake an extensive and detailed literature review, including the discussion of pertinent quotations from numerous writers. In many cases it is important that the reader be aware of the actual words used by these researchers as they attempted, and in the case of contemporary times, continue to interpret the purported events of this early history.

A considerable literature for this time period exists for Lake Superior country, and it must be examined in some depth, something that has not always occurred with past analyses. In this sense we are doing what Louise Kellogg, the prominent early twentieth century Wisconsin historian, undertook when discussing the region's Jesuit literature. Kellogg said she was "blazing new ground," and likewise, we are attempting the same for early Ojibwe literature relevant to Chequamegon Bay.[1]

The labels "La Pointe" and "Chequamegon" are troublesome. While it is generally accepted they refer to the thin needle of land extending into Lake Superior from the mainland in northern Wisconsin's Ashland County near today's city of Ashland, over the last hundreds of years they have come to mean several things. For example, today the village on Madeline Island is called La Pointe, while Chequamegon often refers to the large bay of Lake Superior and its immediate environs as well as the expanse of forested land lying miles inland adjacent to the bay.[2] Historical archives identify a La Pointe Agency within the federal Bureau of Indian Affairs, an office that includes Ojibwe bands in the deep interior of Wisconsin. To complicate matters, the ethnohistorian, Harold Hickerson, mistakenly placed La Pointe in Bayfield County, Wisconsin, instead of Ashland County, or else he confused the narrow needle-like piece of land known as La Pointe with the nearby much larger Bayfield peninsula.[3] Thus, over the years these labels have had a few different referents, and this should not be understood as a problem just of the past.

Early written records tell of a La Pointe Band of Ojibwe. This reference is to the community centered on Madeline Island which utilized a wide surrounding resource area. However, it is likely there never was a single Ojibwe band residing in this large region. Instead it seems sometime after the Ojibwe arrived throughout the years a congeries of localized kin groups emerged, and by the early nineteenth century at least two distinct bands formed with ties to either Protestant or Catholic missionaries. But this oversimplified classification ignores the complexities of how Chequamegon's Ojibwe adjusted to the intense Christian mission efforts carried out in the area in the early nineteenth century. Despite this determined missionary work, early Ojibwe religious institutions and practices were extant in this wide region throughout the difficult times of the nineteenth and early twentieth centuries and such a classification denies the durability, if not the very existence, of these institutions and activities.[4]

Popular history tells that in 1854, when the treaty of that year authorized the formation of several Ojibwe reservations, most of the Chequamegon Bay Ojibwe left Madeline Island, with the Catholics going to Red Cliff and the Protestants to Bad River, but surely in the 1850s not all Ojibwe on Madeline identified as simply Catholics of Protestants. Unfortunately, a recently published visitor's guide to Northern Wisconsin adds unneeded confusion when it mistakenly reverses this denominational direction, saying that with the 1854 treaty, Red Cliff "was settled by Protestant Ojibwe while Catholic converts went to the Bad River Reservation."[5]

Important events occurred in the Chequamegon region during the seventeenth century and we need to attempt to gain an understanding of how the forebears of those who finally formed the community of Red Cliff were involved in them.

### *The Problem of Identifying the First People Named the Ojibwe*

BEFORE DISCUSSING THE EVENTS making up seventeenth century Ojibwe history for Chequamegon Bay, it is necessary to consider the problem of identifying just whom these people were that writers eventually call the Ojibwe. It is clear that the label *Ojibwe*, in its various spellings, is not what the people initially called themselves, and that they used the term *Anishinaabeg*, an Algonquian word—with a few definitions—that essentially means "humans." As we will see, in the mid-seventeenth century when the immediate forebears of the Ojibwe were mentioned in the written record they are most clearly identified with the place name *Saulteurs* (with a few spellings), because they were named by the French who found them residing beside the rapids—the *sault*—of the river at the far eastern outlet of Lake Superior. Hence, they often are referred to as The People of the Sault. Another term used by the French of the time is *Outichibouec*, (in its various spellings), also an Algonquian word. Theresa Schenck, the Blackfeet/Ojibwe writer, chooses to reserve this term for those bands centering their region in the lands just north of Sault Ste. Marie.[6] It is this name that later evolved to Ojibwe, (Ojibwa, or Ojibway), the term (but not the spelling) most regularly used in this book. As we will note below, in the eighteenth century the form *Chippewa* came into use by both British and American officials, and in some instances by the Ojibwe themselves.[7]

In the very early days the French used another label, *Outouwacs* (with a few spellings), to identify those Algonquian peoples who brought furs from the far western Great Lakes to the early fur markets at Montreal and Quebec. Conventionally, this term is said to refer to traders, i.e., those canoeists transporting their flotillas of peltries down what soon became known as the Ottawa River. We will see that in the earliest times of this trade the French commonly referred to *all* the Algonquian tribesmen using this route as the *Outouwacs*. In other words, Outouwac was employed as a generalizing term for those early tribes using the Ottawa River to effect commerce with the eastern French. Unfortunately, some later writers have assumed that the Saulteurs (Ojibwe) did not act as middlemen in the early fur trade, and that the term Outouwac refers *only* to that branch of the Algonquian tribes now known as the *Odawa* (Ottawa), when it could just as certainly have been meant to refer to any other Algonquian peoples living in the western Great Lakes who filled the role as middlemen. In the earliest literature of the trade, the term Outouwac is often synonymous with tribes acting as such mediators. As for the application of the term Outouwac to the Ojibwe, the historian Richard White understood its appropriateness when he wrote: "When the sources are specific, it is clear that the Ojibwas (particularly the Saulteurs), the Nippisings, and less often the Potawatomis, as well as the Ottawas proper, all acted as middlemen in the Great Lakes trade."[8]

More than any other writer, Theresa Schenck has investigated this problem in the extant literature, and in order to come to grips with it, she "accepted as historical records of the Saulteurs only those which name them specifically or those which are certain to include them implicity."[9] Such a stand allows a researcher to move on, but it does not solve the problem of clearly identifying the Saulteur (Ojibwe) in the earliest written records that might hold evidence of their residence in the Lake Huron and Superior regions.

Thus, when reviewing the earliest literature of the western Great Lakes fur trade, and we find the Jesuits and others using the label *Outouwacs* (and in some instances, the more inclusive *Algonquians*) to identify tribal communities involved in the trade, we face the difficulty of determining just which people are being referred to. This is not an unimportant issue since there are instances when we simply cannot ascertain specifically which tribal community is being discussed. Obviously, this is an important matter, and we will revisit it at some length below.

## *Popular Chequamegon Bay History: The Story of the Ojibwe Arrival, Their Supposed Departure and Return.*

### 1.

Over the years a popular history has formed and grown for the Chequamegon area, and its constancies and changes can be traced back through the centuries. Today, along with the written word, it is found in the verbal exchanges heard on streets, and in diverse venues like local cafés, classrooms, and pulpits. This helps make up the region's historical folklore. This story can be seen in the area's news media and local ephemera, that is, its pamphlets, advertising brochures, postcards, and the like. It is also evident in numerous forms of artwork, and more recently, expressed on film and through electronic media. At Chequamegon this colorful and rich history full of its own self-serving biases and interpretations is found in both the region's Ojibwe and non-Ojibwe communities.

Such histories have had their own origins, have taken their particular shapes and forms, and continue to serve their communities' purposes, and because of this, these popular histories are no less important than those of the best scholarly order. Both serve to help create a peoples' understanding of their time and place, and as such both affect behavior, and can play important roles in the formation of personal identities, as well as be instrumental in community decision-making processes.

In this regard, we have seen that the Ojibwe have an oral tradition that relates how the people arrived in the area in the late 1400s or earlier as they centered on Madeline Island. In the popular history of this migration it is claimed the Ojibwe intruded upon the Dakota, driving these people westward. Interestingly, in the telling of this migration, the Ojibwe early encounter with the Mesquakie people, and their subsequent withdrawal, is sometimes given minimal attention if not completely neglected. Then, the accounts go on, after staying for one or two hundred years, the Ojibwe rather suddenly "shunned" Madeline and the rest of the Apostle Islands, and some of the people undertook an eastward migration retracing their steps back to Sault Ste. Marie.

Finally, we are told the Ojibwe did not return to Chequamegon to stay until sometime after 1679, when Daniel Greysolon Duluth negotiated a treaty between the French, Ojibwe and Dakota. It was then that the Ojibwe are to have "flocked to Chequamegon" as Harold Hickerson claimed, in company with, and enjoying the added security of, the French.[10] Thus, while the Ojibwe say they were in the area for hundreds of years before the coming of the Europeans, popular history says they abandoned the region and did not return with any degree of permanence until the late seventeenth century.

The implications of this history are both interesting and important, since, among other things, they bear upon matters of land tenure and the notion of *place*. They admit that the Ojibwe may have been in Chequamegon Bay at a very early date, but, it is implied, this early arrival remains unauthenticated since it is not substantiated by written record.[11] This view argues that what *is* substantiated (put in writing) is that the Ojibwe did not come to the region and make it their lasting home until the late 1600s—decades after the arrival of the Europeans. Hence, despite Ojibwe teachings, some popular versions tell that the Ojibwe and Europeans, if not both relative newcomers, at least came to the region to stay at about the same time. Both came to, and in different ways laid claim to, the area in the late 1600s.

This history is not unrelated to the belief that except for some early instances of difficulty, the Ojibwe and French related well, right from the first days of contact. Among other things, today's abundance of French surnames in many Ojibwe communities is said to be an indicator of this positive relationship. What is sometimes added to these discussions is the supposed dependency of the Ojibwe on the Europeans, a dependency stemming from the superiority of the newcomers' material culture—their metal tools, essentially—or, as it is typically said, "their trade goods."

Taken together, popular history's accounts tell of the Ojibwe fear of the island, their respect for the military prowess of the French, and the superiority of the latter's iron tools. All this supposedly put the tribesmen in a secondary position of power in the Chequamegon region.

The account of the Ojibwe arrival in Chequamegon, their reputed departure and return will be revisited later. Here it is enough to introduce the question of what functions a *history*—whether written or oral, whether popular or scholarly—may be intended to fulfill. Historical accounts are not constructed in vacuums. A peoples' oral and written history works to serve its community. In other words, a history has a function, i.e., it is meant to do something useful, or else it would be discarded, or more accurately, not emerge at all.

History then, can be considered as something that is produced, and in this regard, it has been claimed that "History is the fruit of power,"[12] thus, it is the powerful that end up constructing the histories. In this sense, for hundreds of years both the Chequamegon Bay Ojibwe and their neighbors have been producing history, but with the exceptions of William Warren, Edward Benton-Benai, Thomas Peacock, Theresa Schenck, and a few others, it has been the non-Ojibwe who have been putting this history in writing. Among other themes, throughout this book we will explore these different mediums of producing history and the important implications of this production.

## 2.

IN THE PREVIOUS CHAPTER WE SAW that the migration teachings tell us that after years of traveling, the Ojibwe reached La Pointe and made it their homeland. According to William Warren, soon after arriving in Chequamegon and up to the early 1600s, they had a large village on the mainland, but because of the opposition from the Mesquakie, later moved it to Madeline Island. This village was the westernmost Ojibwe population center at the time but since then the tribe has fanned out to the south, west and north of the bay. The existence of this large early village has been challenged, however, an issue that will be discussed below.

Emphasizing the importance of Madeline Island in the tribe's religious ideology and in the recognition of the early Ojibwe arrival, the Red Cliff community, only two miles from Madeline, has called itself "The Hub of the Chippewa Nation." Along with the religious importance of Madeline, this characterization speaks to the centuries of time that the Ojibwe have occupied these lands and waters.

Today the island continues to be the location of ceremonies involving many Ojibwe communities, including some from Canada, and in the past several years these have become annual events. They are celebrations of the ancient and continuing role of the island in the Ojibwe origin teachings, and it is easy to recognize the similarity and cultural connections between these important contemporary gatherings and those William Warren told us were held annually hundreds of years ago.[13]

The exact nature of these ancient celebrations is not known, but it is likely they were similar to those of today's ceremonies.[14] It has been suggested that although the details of such rituals and ceremonies might be idiosyncratic, i.e., at the discretion of the individual spiritual leader in charge at the time, the underlying themes remain constant.[15]

The details of the migration of Red Cliff's ancestors to their Chequamegon Bay shoreline and islands are also difficult and often impossible to uncover. Tribal teachings indicate contacts with other peoples hundreds of years ago, but the names of communities and individuals involved are mostly gone. Yet, a present Ojibwe writer says:

> Many of the details of the ancient past lie beyond our memory or the memory provided in our stories. We will never know the stories of the people who led our ancestors on the various migrations, nor of those who led the People in war against our traditional enemies of the East, nor the stories of those who saved our communities from disease and starvation. As descendents of those great people, we carry their genetic material and fragments of ancestral memory (which are sometimes revealed in dreams or intuition), but their names and the stories of their lives are forever lost. Their lives may have been like mountains, but we know nothing of them, or only grains of sand. And that, it seems, is one of the tasks of contemporary Ojibwe writers and historians: To take these bits of historical and cultural knowledge and put them back into their proper places.[16]

Those of us in what is sometimes called the literate tradition usually cannot recall our forebears' names, occupations and so forth, for more than a few generations unless we do serious genealogical work. And even then we eventually reach a dead-end where names and events flow together into the distant unrecorded past, and at such a point we can go no further.

So we can only imagine, however soundly our imaginations are based, what occurred with these earliest Anishinaabe forebears. As Thomas Peacock suggests, herein lies a function of contemporary writers, teachers and spiritual leaders. Through these writings and teachings tribal traditions are not only reaffirmed, but as is the case in all cultures, over time they are regularly reworked as we are told how the world as we know it came to be. At these times we are asked to believe, and in fact, often admonished to do so.

In chapter one we saw how the origin teachings of the Ojibwe deal with these complex matters of cosmology and cosmogony. All cultures have such statements about their beginnings, and embedded in these are sets of rules for guiding the peoples' daily lives. In this way Ojibwe origin teachings stand beside the multitudes of others in the world as another example of a peoples' understandings of their reality and being.

### *A Note About Writing*

LINGUISTS AND OTHER SCHOLARS TELL US that the act of writing serves to change a peoples' understanding of their world. To make a written record of something, as in retelling a story, this argument claims, the writers or storytellers *interpret* and thus change the original object or event, and once written, something is locked into an unnatural stasis.

Accepting this problem, the written and oral word can work together to help a community understand its past. In this regard, to better understand their traditions some Ojibwe have attempted to move early events from their unwritten past into historical, written time. For instance, in the mid-1800s, when William Warren gathered his data at Madeline Island and its environs, he claims to have found numerous elders willing to share this information so it could be recorded in written form.

Writers of the past and of today are doing much more than giving voice to distant actors. They are going beyond simply naming the pertinent places and events of the past. As stated in the previous chapter, involved with a record of ancient origins is a system of norms—a set of rules for daily and lifelong living—and these writings and oral teachings, whether early or contemporary, help today's Ojibwe individuals construct their personal and community identities. Thus, in Chequamegon Bay, Ojibwe origin teachings can be directly tied to the contemporary Red Cliff community, and in this way, a continuum exists between the times of origin beside a distant saltwater sea and Red Cliff's shoreline and islands. Obviously, today's Red Cliff people are part of this ancient flow of existence.

### *The Earliest Written Commentary on the Ojibwe*

WILLIAM WARREN'S BOOK ON THE HISTORY of the Ojibwe in the Chequamegon area is indispensable to a serious study of the topic, but through the years it has been problematic to some history scholars. Warren gathered *oral* history, and earlier writers sometimes struggled with accepting his dates and conclusions without much substantiation from other *written* sources. He worked in the general western Lake Superior area in the mid-1800s, spending much time interviewing informants on Madeline Island and in Minnesota Territory. However, in the winter of 1852-53, he struggled with poor health and although making a trip to publishing houses in eastern cities, he was unsuccessful in getting what was essentially an unfinished manuscript in print. Warren died in Minnesota Territory in spring 1853, and his manuscript was finally published in 1885.[17]

William Warren was not the first to write about the Ojibwe, but some of the oral data he gathered from elders was from hundreds of years before. What he recorded was a retelling of the events that occurred in these earlier times. Hence, although his writings are not the first about the Ojibwe, the history he wrote covered events that occurred long before *any* writings on them were made. While his manuscript remains very important, we see that the French Jesuits were recording information on the Ojibwe about two hundred years before Warren.

William Warren's book is integral to an understanding of the historical foundation of communities like Red Cliff. For that reason it will continue to be referred to through the early chapters of this book. Warren was of Ojibwe descent, conversant in *Ojibwemowin*, and was in his day a literate scholar. He was not the only Ojibwe writer active in the nineteenth century, but he was the single native researcher working with material directly relevant to the Chequamegon Bay region. William Jones, Peter Jones, and George Copway were all Ojibwe writers from the nineteenth century but their efforts did not focus on the Chequamegon Bay area.

The *Jesuit Reports* of the 1600s help us gain a glimpse of tribal activity in the lands around Lake Superior during these early days. Sometimes ignored in the search for valid information on tribal adaptations, these missionary documents are a literal treasure of ethnographic data, and have been said to be "enormously valuable resources to anyone interested in" tribal life in northeastern North America in the early days.[18] The Michigan anthropologist, Charles Cleland, suggests that despite their biases, the early priests "were excellent observers" and thus, we should study their writing with a more accepting eye than has been done in the past.[19] However, our knowledge of the Jesuits' activities in the western Great Lakes area comes from their own reports sent from the field, or from summations of these actions made back at places like Montreal or Quebec, and these accounts are always framed with the Christian perspective of the time, not the Ojibwes'. Furthermore, we should recognize that when native persons accepted aspects of the Jesuits' religion they were doing so within the context of their own cultures. John Demos, a contemporary historian, makes this point when discussing the Jesuits' work among the Iroquois in the late seventeenth century. Demos reminds us that even when the natives would incorporate parts of Christian teachings into their lives, "the Indians were not mere imitators of an alien model; their culture, their history, their values contributed strongly to the evolving pattern [of the structure of their newly altered religious lives]."[20]

Hence, what we encounter in the Jesuit literature is extremely biased since it focuses on the thoughts and acts of the priests themselves and not on the perspectives of the tribesmen they are discussing. The tribal voice in the *Jesuit Relations* is virtually silent, and in our attempts to understand the nature of interrelations between the Catholic priests and the native communities they came into, we struggle to comprehend the second part of this relationship. We have virtually no information from this second half, and thus, our knowledge about their thoughts regarding these new black-robed men who came to them in the early seventeenth century is very limited. But as Demos points out, we should understand that the Ojibwes always related to the French priests through the lens of Ojibwe culture.

To date, the earliest mention of the immediate forbears of the people we know as the Ojibwe comes from the western Great Lakes literature of the *Jesuit Relations*. As Theresa Schenck tells us:

> Although it is likely that the Ojibwe had been encountered earlier, perhaps by Etienne Brule or Jean Nicolet, it is not until 1639 that one finds the first acknowledgement of their existence, when the Jesuit Du Peron included the 'nation of the Sault' in his list of people trading with the Huron.[21]

The next year, 1640, these people were mentioned in the *Relations* a second time, as being dwellers along the north shore of Lake Huron and at the site that later became known as Sault Ste. Marie.[22] Then, the *Relations* provides the more familiar reference when it claims that in September of 1642, Ojibwe from Lake Superior traveled the approximately 150 miles east to Georgian Bay on Lake Huron to attend a Feast of the Dead ceremony. This important religious event was held every few years. We are told that participants brought the remains of tribal members who had passed away since the last ceremony and all were interred in a mass grave.[23] Among other things, such a ceremony had great political meaning for the attending communities. On the individual level, the names of the dead could be passed on to younger tribal members, keeping family and personal identities alive. On the community level, such gatherings told of political alliances in effect between participant groups, and we can readily see that a Feast of the Dead was about much more than religion and honoring the deceased. The fact of Lake Superior's Saulteur (Ojibwe) attendance at the Lake Huron event indicates strong ties with eastern Algonquian groups.

At the 1642 ceremony, a party of Lake Superior Saulteur (Ojibwe) met two Jesuit missionaries living with the Huron and they asked these French holy men to come to their village. The priests—Charles Raymbault and Isaac Jogues—agreed to undertake the long trip and left Lake Huron at the end of September, taking seventeen days of paddling to arrive at the settlement of about 2,000 persons at Lake Superior's eastern outlet.[24] This is said to have been "the first European visit to Chippewa country of which we have a definite description."[25] The Jesuits named the river at the site the St. Marie and the community at that location became known as Sault Ste. Marie. The Ojibwe living there were called the Saulteurs, or People of the Rapids.

The Frenchmen Raymbault and Jogues did not stay at Sault Ste. Marie. They soon returned to the Huron, intending to continue their missionary work with them and to await the arrival of new Jesuits who would move westward into Ojibwe lands.

It is suggested that in 1642, the Sault Ste. Marie residents wanted the priests to come to their village in order to be taught Christianity, but we should recognize that the people were exhibiting a good degree of political astuteness by extending the invitation to Raymbault and Jogues. By 1642, Lake Superior's people had known of the French, were using French trade goods for years, and surely were interested in establishing a direct political relationship with them. It should be expected that their interest in the Blackrobes was driven by strong political and economic desires as well as by religious curiosity.

In these times of the earliest contacts, the native people seemed not to conceptualize the Jesuits as being separate from the French government and its military. And indeed, the tribesmen would have been correct in this supposition. As so often occurs with other nations in their attempts at religious mission work, the French government worked hand in hand with the Jesuits in its activities in early North America.

Although the written record shows that while in many cases the Ojibwe saw the Jesuit individuals as inept, ignorant and often pompous persons, in 1642, France must have appeared to be a very powerful nation. A political and economic alliance with the French would certainly have been something tribal leaders felt was worth working for, especially considering the threat that the Iroquois and others presented. When sitting in community councils and when consulting the *manidoog* these leaders must have been given a clear message: befriend the French because at this time we can benefit economically and politically. We could perhaps add that pragmatically, the leaders concluded that if there also was a religious benefit in this alliance of nations, then so much the better.

The complex interconnectedness of a culture's religious, economic and political systems was certainly not unknown to the people at Sault Ste. Marie in 1642, and therefore we should expect that the Jesuits were perceived not simply as religious leaders, but as officials, or at least sanctioned authorities, of the French government. Furthermore, the natives might have concluded that if the gods of the French had helped these newcomers become as powerful as the early emissaries claimed to be, then perhaps they had something to offer. We can take the invitation extended to the Jesuits Raymbault and Jogues, then, as an initial attempt at political alliance building. As is the case with other Native American nations, the desire to establish alliances with outsiders is seen in later Ojibwe history, and examples of this sort of political activity, of course, can be found today.

In the 1640s, France was embroiled with the Iroquois as well as attempting to claim new territory in the Western Hemisphere before the English did, and the Jesuits were very busy with the numerous tribal nations lying between the eastern seaboard and Lake Superior. The Iroquois, in particular, were often strong opponents of France, causing repeated setbacks to its dreams of colonization. In this regard, the missionary Isaac Jogues perhaps should have stayed with the natives at Sault Ste. Marie, for only five years later he suffered a painful and prolonged death at the hands of the Iroquois and today is considered a martyr who is celebrated in the Catholic Church.[26]

We see then, that the year 1642 is an important historical marker for the Lake Superior Ojibwe. It signals a new era for them and in obvious ways their lives were never to be the same. For this reason we need to consider these earliest written records telling of the Ojibwe. While the *Jesuit Relations* are often set in regions and times hundreds of miles distant from Red Cliff, they offer images of populations from which Red Cliff's early forebears emerged. Although, as Thomas Peacock reminds us, for the most part the names of persons and specific events have vanished, we must still recognize their Red Cliff connection.

However valuable, these earliest written accounts of Europeans coming into Lake Superior country are agonizing in their brevity and scarcity. The *Jesuit Relations* were originally published from 1632 to 1697, and while much of their effort focuses upon events of interest to historians, their pages often tell of less pertinent struggles of the priests to convert *individuals*.[27] Yet these Christian missionaries were also interested, in a literal sense, in the new lands they came into. Their descriptions of the forests and waters they traveled through and over, and how the tribal peoples used them, are very helpful in our understanding of tribal adaptations of the times.

Upon the arrival of Raymbault and Jogues, Sault Ste. Marie was a major resource center for the regional peoples, and the abundance of fish at the rapids was a powerful seasonal attractor to the area. Jacques Marquette told how fish were taken in gill nets and long-handled smaller scoop nets. Then the whitefish were smoked and dried by exposure to fire and sunlight, and stored for later use. Other foods were used, but in the diet of the Saulteurs, whitefish was the staple around which these other foods clustered.[28] In the early 1800s, Henry Schoolcraft also described the harvesting of resources at The Sault. Schoolcraft shows us that Lake Superior's whitefish were still consistently being taken at the time of his stay, some two hundred years after the visit of the first Jesuits.[29] The region was a resource magnet that attracted people back year after year for the seasonal harvest of these fish.

From about 1640 to the present time we have a continually growing literature on the Ojibwe. The earliest accounts are essentially missionary literature, and increasingly during the next two centuries we are treated to the writings of the trapper, trader and other non-clerics. In the 1800s, we find an array of documents by emissaries of the United States government, along with the start of a literature written by historians, of which some, like William Warren, were of Ojibwe descent. Journalists also begin to write about the Ojibwe at this time, leaving a considerable commentary. In the very late 1800s and throughout the 1900s came the papers and books of the anthropologists, historians, social workers, psychologists, political scientists, and more. Recently we are witnessing a proliferation of literature, films, theatrical performances, paintings, and other literary, scientific, and artistic media created by the Ojibwe themselves, and of course this is increasingly being accomplished by means of digital electronics. Along with the myriad of customs, material items and other new ideas that the Ojibwe took from the European was the written word. Today as scholars, writers, and others, they are in the forefront of this depiction and discussion of this tribal nation, and as such, they are producing their own history. Recently we have begun to see the emergence of a literature written in *Ojibwemowin*, the Ojibwe language. Through all of this oral, written and artistic expression flows an interpretation of the rich Ojibwe culture and its history.

### *The Ojibwe Come to Chequamegon Bay*

WILLIAM WARREN ESTIMATED that the Ojibwe came to Chequamegon Bay for the first time in the latter part of the fifteenth century. Warren wrote that in 1842, a Madeline Island family claimed to know the time the Ojibwe came to the island. Writing in the early 1850s, he says:

> In support of their pretensions, this family hold in their possession a circular plate of virgin copper, on which is rudely marked indentations and hieroglyphics denoting the number of generations of the family who have passed away since they first pitched their lodges at Shaug-a-waum-ik-ong and took possession of the adjacent country, including the Island of La Pointe or Mo-nig-wun-a-kaun-ing . . . On this plate of copper was marked eight deep in-dentations, denoting the number of . . . ancestors who passed away since they first lighted their fire at Shaug-a-waum-ik-ong. They all lived to a good old age.
>
> By the rude figure of a man with a hat on its head, placed opposite one of these indentations, was denoted the period when the white race first made his appearance among them. This mark occurred in the third generation, leaving five generations which had passed away since that important era in their history.[30]

Warren set the length of an Ojibwe generation at forty years and with the use of this copper plate, as well as other observations, he went on to suggest dates for important Ojibwe events. Through this method of computation he felt the migration from the eastern seaboard might have taken about 200 years and that the people could have reached Chequamegon Bay by 1490, and had their first contact with Europeans in about 1610.[31]

Edward Benton-Benai, perhaps relying in part on Warren's comments, suggests that the Anishinaabe migration from the great saltwater sea began "around 900 A.D." and that "It took some 500 years to complete." With admitted speculation, he says "if we took the lifetime of an Ojibway in these old days to be 50 years, counting backwards it would put the coming of the news of the Light-skinned Race to this area in 1544 and the settlement of the Ojibway on Madeline Island at 1394."[32]

Theresa Schenck has questioned these computations. She feels Warren was particularly generous in setting a generation at forty years, since in Schenck's words, "Warren failed to realize that a generation is more correctly analyzed according to the age of parents when children are born, and that it consists of a single cohort born generally over a period of 25 to 30 years."[33] Using her method of computing the length of an Ojibwe generation along with information gleaned from the writings of Henry Schoolcraft, Schenck feels the Ojibwe might have arrived at Sault Ste. Marie at the middle of the seventeenth century, or approximately 1650.[34]

Historian Jane Busch agrees with Schenck but goes further. She feels along with miscalculating the length of a generation, Warren:

> . . . tried to impose on Ojibwe tradition a Euro-American sense of time and a literal interpretation of the past that is alien to this tradition. The Ojibwe expect oral tradition to be dynamic, and they distinguish between events known from personal ex-

> perience and truths that transcend history. Warren's account of the history of the Ojibwe on Madeline Island reflects its importance to the Ojibwe who lived there.[35]

Although the figures the above writers use are suggestive, the realization that Ojibwe people most probably have been living at Chequamegon Bay and along the Red Cliff shoreline for about 450 years is significant. When today's reservation residents speak of *home* and the emotional notion of *place*, their remarks might be stemming from a realization of the importance of this long duration. In spite of the passing of many generations over the several centuries since the migration, and even considering the degree of out-mating and out-marriage at Red Cliff, we can recognize a connection with the distant past. Also, since the Ojibwe have buried their dead—those remains not carried to distant Feasts of the Dead—along the Red Cliff shoreline as well as in the entire Chequamegon area for this length of time, and understanding that the recurring act of burial consecrates a place, making a location a homeland, we might appreciate the importance of this long duration. For about the last 400 years an unbroken flow of "*Ojibweness*," both biological and cultural, has existed at Red Cliff.

When attempting to comprehend the importance of this we must remember that initially the people lived in bands with a hunting and gathering adaptation. Earlier we have seen how this type of culture calls for much mobility, although, to a great extent, such bands settle into a given area and are consistent in their rhythmic movement through its resource regions. Thus, a hunting and gathering band does not "roam" helter-skelter over a countryside. While Lake Superior's rich stocks of fish must have held the people close to its shores and islands at the appropriate times, as was the case at Sault Ste. Marie, Grand Island, Keweenaw Bay, Ontonagon, and Chequamegon, we know that the early people moved inland in the proper seasons to harvest the forest resources. Thus, the Ojibwe occupied a region by repeatedly—and in definite systemic ways—moving through it. At times they were assembled into population centers, and at other times their small kin-units were dispersed over a wide area. This flexible subsistence pattern along with a belief system that posits the existence of a multiplicity of spiritual beings—some able to change their forms—helps to make up what has been called "the fluidity of the Ojibwe life-world."[36]

Popular history has claimed that after European contact this Ojibwe cultural adaptation began to give way, and some voices say that at places like Red Cliff, it has practically disappeared.[37] An argument in this book will be that this flexible adaptation and "fluidity of the Ojibwe life-world" has not disappeared at Red Cliff and the rest of Chequamegon. It will be suggested that once in place it never completely left the region, and although experiencing adaptive alterations and modifications, it not only persists today, but is growing in strength.

### *The Sudden Return to Sault Ste. Marie*

1.

As we have seen, the literature tells that there was an instance when the Ojibwe left Madeline Island and the smaller islands, and did not return until approximately 1680, after Duluth established an alliance of peace between the French, Ojibwe, and Dakota in 1679. This is the time of the so-called "shunning of the islands" that is said to have occurred between 1600 and 1620, when the people left Madeline Island to disperse to several locations in the distant mainland, with some moving all the way back east to Sault Ste. Marie, and as one writer casually put it, only "visiting Chequamegon once in awhile on fishing trips."[38] We need to examine the evidence for this incident in some detail in order to bring about a better understanding of the purported event.

2.

The original written source for this exodus from Madeline Island is William Warren's 1885 publication, in which he gives two possible reasons for the Ojibwe move. The first, he implies, was offered by the tribe's "old men" as a fabrication and thus, meant to be a more palliating reason than the second, or "real" reason. In Warren's words, these informants suggested this move was "the immediate consequence to their knowledge of the white race." He explains that the "old men" (also referred to as the "old traditionalists") meant it was through this knowledge that the Ojibwe acquired guns and with this new weapon the Madeline Island Ojibwe:

> . . . all at once became formidable to their old enemies, the Dakotas and Foxes, whom they gradually drove from the vicinity of the lakeshore, and caused to retreat inland toward the Mississippi. As the war parties came less frequently to attack them, the Ojibways gained courage, and leaving LaPointe, they pitched their lodges in the adjacent Bay of Shag-waum-ik-ong, and hunted, with comparative impunity, the larger animals that abounded in the vicinity.[39]

Warren claimed that "the old half-breeds and traders" offered the second reason for the departure, and his implication is that these informants were more distant from the earlier Ojibwe culture and its traditions. Thus, they were free to speak truthfully, and therefore, we perhaps are meant to believe, they had a more objective understanding of the story. Reporting what these "half-breeds and traders" said, Warren writes,

> The Evil Spirit had found a strong foothold amongst them, during latter years of their residence on this island. Evil practices became in vogue . . . Horrid feasts on human flesh became a custom. It is said by my informants that medicine men . . . had come to a knowledge of the most subtle poisons, and that they revenged the least affront with certain death. When the dead body of a victim had been interred, the murderer proceeded at night to the grave, disinterred it, and taking it to his lodge he made a feast of it, to the relatives, which was eaten during the darkness of mid-night, and if any of the invited guests became aware of the nature of the feast, and refused to eat, he was sure to fall under the ill-will

> of the feaster, and became the next victim. It is said that if a young woman refused the addresses of one of these medicine men, she fell a victim to his poison, and her body being disinterred, her relatives were feasted on it by the horrid murderer. Such a taste did they at last acquire for human flesh, that parents dared not refuse their children if demanded by the fearful medicine men for sacrifice.[40]

Warren adds other comments to these remarks, but except for the sentence in which he said, "if a young woman refused the advances of one of the medicine men," there are no other specific indications that these men were preying upon and killing only females. He makes it clear that this reputed cannibalism was practiced on both males and females.

With the foregoing quotes in mind we have to be puzzled when in 1960, Hamilton Ross discussed this supposed Ojibwe exodus from Madeline Island. Ross wrote:

> In a severe winter, when food ran short, their medicine men resorted to cannibalism, selecting as their victims *young children, preferably female.* They continued the practice for a number of years until the enraged tribe, overcoming its fear of the *witch doctors*, put them to death.[41]

It is uncertain where Ross learned this, since he does not give a direct bibliographic reference, but it is likely he is drawing this from William Warren. Ross's suggestion that a growing population coupled with severe winters caused a diminishment of food resources is also interesting, because Warren raised the question of the possibility of such ecological causes being behind the reputed cannibalism and resulting exodus from Madeline Island. But Warren said he could not substantiate this, even though as he wrote, "he should be but too happy to give this as a palliating excuse for the horrid custom he is obliged to relate."[42]

Ross's misrepresentation of Warren's words is picked up by a more recent writer who wrote: "Tribal medicine men resorted to cannibalism, and children, *especially young girls*, were sacrificed until outraged parents finally revolted and killed the shamen."[43] These are the words of Edmund Jefferson Danziger, Jr., and while he changed Ross's dated "witch doctors" to the more acceptable *shamen*, he is still passing on Ross's incorrect embellishment of Warren's intent.

Just as interesting, a third writer, Carolissa Levi, had this to say about the troublesome sudden exodus from the island: "One reason advanced for this departure was the superstition of the natives. They had practiced cannibalism, eating the bodies of enemies slain in battle."[44] Levi gives Warren as her bibliographic source for this historical "fact," and, unfortunately, she does not offer what the other reason(s) for the departure might have been. Her phrase "superstition of the natives" is timely (she was writing in the 1950s), and it is indicative of her religious biases (she was a Roman Catholic nun, working in the Bad River Ojibwe community).

In his book on the history of Chequamegon Bay, the Ashland, Wisconsin, journalist Guy Burnham does not mention the tale of cannibalism. Instead he says simply that after initially arriving on Madeline Island the Ojibwe "remained here 'about three generations,' 120 years, but believing the island had become the home of evil spirits, moved to the mainland." Burnham claims the Ojibwe believed that all Lake Superior's islands were the abode of "evil spirits," not just Madeline and the nearby other Apostles. He writes that in 1892, Joe Caribou, of the Ojibwe community at Grand Portage, Minnesota, "voiced the feeling that still existed among his people, telling us of the presence of evil spirits on Isle Royale and the other islands of Lake Superior. According to Caribou, the time had been when no Indian would remain over night on any Lake Superior island."[45]

Joe Caribou's statement, given in 1892, suggests a particular relationship between Ojibwe people and islands, especially those in Lake Superior. He hints that a so-called "shunning" of the Apostles might not be unusual, and given the belief system of the Ojibwe, could be expected.

Hamilton Ross apparently discredited Warren's "old men's" tale that another reason for the sudden exodus from Madeline was the acquisition of firearms. His decision to embellish and change the thrust of Warren's comments on Ojibwe cannibalism is also interesting, and Edmund Jefferson Danziger, Jr.'s simple restatement of this error is likewise. Carolissa Levi's account and Guy Burnham's remarks need no further comment.

Edward Benton-Benai adds an interesting twist to this tradition of cannibalism and the Ojibwe "shunning" of Madeline Island, and suggests this was behind the spread of Ojibwe bands into adjacent regions. He feels the exodus occurred *after* the coming of the "Black Coats" (Jesuits) and that it was the result of the missionaries' attempts at causing factionalism within the Ojibwe community so that more people would convert to Christianity. Amidst this strife, accusations of cannibalism were made. Benton-Benai writes:

> At any rate the Ojibway settlement on Madeline Island began to break up. One large group left the island and journeyed south into the mainland until they came to a huge lake. On the shores of this lake they found the frozen body of an Indian. They put his body to rest with a Tobacco offering. They took this discovery to be a powerful sign, and, not far from this spot, they established a village. This place was called Lac Courte Oreille (Lake of the Short Ears) by the French. Another group left Madeline Island and settled a short way off at a place called Red Cliff. One group moved a little farther away and set up a village called Odanah. They were called the Bad River Ojibways. Still other groups left the Madeline Island Settlement. There were groups that, them-selves, split into different factions . . . The Ojibways settled all around the shores of Lake Superior.[46]

Among several interesting things about this explanation for leaving Madeline Island is that it argues the exodus was ultimately caused by the Jesuits' machinations to win converts. History shows how incoming Christian missionaries have labored to discredit traditional religious leaders in non-Christian communities.[47] In one such instance, Joseph Gilfillan, a Christian missionary in Northern Minnesota in the mid-1800s, published a novel that used this as one of its themes, and about a century later Winona LaDuke, the Minnesota Ojibwe activist and writer, published another novel that, in a critical turnabout, speaks to these efforts by Gilfillan.[48]

Another mention of the reported Ojibwe shunning of islands comes from a recent book written by Timothy Cochrane.[49] In discussing Lake Superior's Isle Royale and its importance to Ojibwe culture, Cochrane says that over the years non-Indians have not only misunderstood the meaning Ojibwe people have given to this island, but that at times they have also convoluted this meaning to their own advantage.[50]

Cochrane goes on to claim, correctly, that notions of "'islandness,' in both a symbolic and specific sense, are essential to an Ojibwe worldview."[51] He notes that our earliest known information about Isle Royale comes from Ojibwe oral narratives and that after European contact two different narrative streams developed. Of these two storylines, the earliest is the Ojibwe oral tradition, and it was this narrative that:

> . . . exerted a tremendous influence on what people thought about Isle Royale. But these [Ojibwe] narratives were not always understood or faithfully recorded. There is a tradition of Euro-Americans interpreting Ojibwe myth—in effect, asserting what they thought Ojibwe thought about Minong [Isle Royale]. These are divergent narrative streams about Isle Royale, although they are related. One narrative stream is authentic *aadizookaan*, or sacred stories. A second type of narrative is derived from the first, but has a tradition of its own in print. Non-Indian renderings of the traditional Ojibwe narratives and beliefs make up this second stream. These have moved far from the original narratives, as they often mix stories, emphasize some elements over others, and interject new concerns, characters and plotlines. These renderings have also been clipped into snippets and then retold almost like punch lines. All have had their effect on characterizing Isle Royale.[52]

In similar fashion, the early Ojibwe sacred stories (*aadizookaan*) of Madeline Island emphasize its role in the peoples' epic migration and their ongoing identity. It has been suggested that in the deep structure of Ojibwe cosmology as seen in the *midewiwin*, that Madeline Island can be viewed as a metaphoric representation of the more easterly site where Ojibwe creation occurred. Hence, Madeline, and by extension, all islands, can be said to suggest this sacred primal place where the Ojibwe came into being.[53] This relates to the notion held by some Ojibwe people today that Madeline represents the site of the initial creation of the people, and in time an eastward migration to a distant saltwater sea occurred.[54] After Euro-American contact a new narrative stream with permutations of these numerous origin narratives tells of a general Ojibwe fear of islands, and in particular for Madeline, a fear due to the appearance of cannibalism. This fear was so severe—the storyline claims—that for years the people shunned Madeline. Finally, as Timothy Cochrane insightfully points out, since "islandness" is at the center of the Ojibwe worldview, and recalling that in Ojibwe religious belief the earth is depicted as an island, we can agree that islands are primary symbols for them. Thus, given this great importance of islands in the people' origin teachings, we see that Madeline Island is best recognized as a place of reverence, and at base, a *sacred* place.

Tales of Ojibwe people shunning islands might lend themselves to Euro-American seventeenth and eighteenth century images of tribal people, but such images, with their focus on irrational fear, neglect to consider notions of sacred awe and religious reverence that are part of this fear. Thus, while Timothy Cochrane is correct when he says the Ojibwe's see islands as "sacred, not scary,"[55] we should add that sanctity and fear are not necessarily mutually exclusive. This is made clear when we understand the role of islands in the Ojibwe religious belief system, and that for these people islands can be perceived not as places to be feared, but as places of fearful reverence.

## 3.

THE REASON FOR INCLUDING this discussion of what at first glance might appear to be an inconsequential incident of a sudden departure from the Apostle Islands hundreds of years ago concerns two important points, both relating to Red Cliff. The first is the question of whether or not the departure actually occurred. Written histories can be both despotic and untrustworthy. Once recorded, if done with some authority, such a misconception can carry ill-gained weight. Some readers might actually take the "history" as fact.

The second problem is the effect such interpretations of local history can have on processes of self- and community-identity in today's Ojibwe locations like Red Cliff. Traditions of cannibalism and religious leaders preying on young girls may be uncomfortable to process. They can perpetuate unfortunate misconceptions about tribal religion, and its leaders, that can have long-term harmful personal and community effects, and when held by persons outside the Ojibwe community they could be used to help construct a false image of what tribal societies are like. Such stories of cannibalism, and in this incident with eroticism added, can live for centuries in a region's folklore.

However this may be, we cannot conclude this discussion of the "shunning of the islands" without presenting three last pieces of writing about the event. The first is the influential 1962 publication on the Ojibwe by the ethnohistorian Harold Hickerson, in which it is intimated that the early seventeenth century stories of Madeline Island and Ojibwe cannibalism have no merit because, according to Hickerson, the Ojibwe were not present in western Lake Superior at that early time.[56] In his popular 1979 historical survey of Ojibwe bands in the southwestern Lake Superior region, Edmund Jefferson Danziger, Jr. acknowledges Hickerson's conclusion as it relates to Ojibwe cannibalism on Madeline Island when he says, "Anthropologist Harold Hickerson claims that historical evidence contradicts this tradition."[57] Hickerson's work was published after the Burnham, Ross and Levi books, and here we see that even though it was acknowledged by Danziger, he offered no discussion of the controversial topic, choosing instead to refer to it in only this single, short remark.

The second writing is that of the Jesuit, Joseph P. Donnelly. Following William Warren's account of the early Algonquian migration to Lake Superior and the resultant dispersal of these diverse peoples, and also influenced by Hickerson's negative conclusion about the possibility of Ojibwe cannibalism on Madeline Island, Donnelly speculates that when Jacques Marquette arrived at The Sault in 1668, he would have been told that while some members of the Huron and Odawa tribes were living in the region along with the Ojibwe, portions of the Odawa (and likely the Huron) community had migrated westward to Chequamegon Bay, but not the Ojibwe, since:

> The Chippewa band remained [at Sault Ste. Marie], taking advantage of the abundant supply of fish, nearly always available. The remainder of the Ottawa moved further westward, disputing possession of the southern shore of Lake Superior with the Sioux, whose homeland that country was. Finally, the Ottawa settled on Madeline Island, two miles off shore, at the mouth of Chequamegon Bay. On their island the Ottawa became so prosperous that their village extended two miles in width and three in length. Security and leisure, unfortunately, brought with them vice and corruption until the all-powerful, wanton sorcerers took to practicing human sacrifices and cannibalism. At last, after years of groveling fear, the Ottawa revolted against their medicine men and, killing them, fled in horror from that bloody island which, ever after, was held to be cursed. Moving eastward, the Ottawa gradually dispersed. Some settled on Manitoulin Island while others found homes on the upper reaches of the Ottawa River. There Champlain met them and the stripling Etienne Brule dwelt with them, learning their language and customs.[58]

As we note, this interesting quotation claims it was the Odawa, not the Ojibwe, who initially penetrated into the lands west of Sault Ste. Marie and pushed the Dakota out, and later, because of "scarcity and leisure," fell into lives of "vice and corruption" that led to cannibalistic practices. Hence, according to Donnelly, historians who tell about the early removal of the Dakota by the Ojibwe have been in error, and even William Warren's accountings of Ojibwe cannibalism are incorrect.

Our final reference to Ojibwe cannibalism on Madeline Island comes from Theresa Schenck, who hints at a possible connection between Warren's undated stories and a series of incidents that unfolded over a period of years at Chequamegon Bay. We learn about these incidents from Nicholas Perrot, who was a very important figure in early Western Lake Superior history, and who we will discuss at some length later. Unfortunately, like Warren, Perrot did not offer any dates for these incidents, but in 1864—some 200 years after their occurrence—the Jesuit writer Jules Talihan edited Perrot's memoir and suggested they could have occurred in the latter 1600s, perhaps as late as 1670.[59]

Nicholas Perrot told how conflict arose between some Chequamegon Bay Huron and the Dakota, leading to both Dakota and Odawa captives being taken and eventually cannibalized by members of these two communities. Fearing Dakota retaliation, the Odawa and Huron abandoned Chequamegon Bay and moved back to sites at the eastern end of Lake Superior. Jules Talihan dated this abandonment at 1670-1671—apparently attempting to fit the time of this move with the writings of Jacques Marquette, who noted that the final exodus from Chequamegon by the Odawa and Huron took place in those years. (It is noteworthy that Marquette said nothing about the purported cannibalism incidents.)

Similar to Talihan's intent to put these incidents of cannibalism into a historical context, Theresa Schenck feels William Warren's story of Madeline Island cannibalism "vaguely corroborates" the Nicholas Perrot account, and Schenck speculates, "Such stories of cannibalism could only have originated from the Ottawa then living there, *or possibly from the few Ojibwe who may have been part of the Ottawa group*, and then these tales were magnified and rendered horrific as they were passed from generation to generation."[60] We note that Schenck agrees with Donnelly's contention that it was the "Ottawa" (except, as she suggests, a "few Ojibwe") who were the early residents of Chequamegon Bay, and as such were implicated in the cannibalism incident.

Schenck's suggestion of a possible connection between the originally undated incidence of cannibalism mentioned in Nicholas Perrot's memoir and William Warren's undated story of cannibalism is noteworthy. Likewise, her desire—and Tahihan's also—to suggest a tie between these incidents and the Odawa and Huron abandonment of Chequamegon Bay as witnessed by Jacques Marquette. But these synthesizing efforts to make literal historical connections are also interesting because Theresa Schenck is hesitant to agree to a Saulteur (Ojibwe) presence at Chequamegon in these times. As seen in our preceding paragraph, Schenck says only it is *possible* that a small number of Ojibwe may have been living at Chequamegon when the cannibalism occurred. Her hesitancy to admit an unquestionable presence of Ojibwe at Chequamegon in these years is interesting since, as we will see below, Nicholas Perrot claimed that a group of Ojibwe people was living at the bay for several years immediately prior to the eruption of the Huron, Odawa, and Dakota troubles that led to the cannibalism.

We learn of this early Ojibwe presence when Perrot tells us of the well-known 1662 military encounter between a band of Saulteur and other fighters, and a group of Iroquois warriors at a site just northwest of Sault Ste. Marie now called Iroquois Point. Perrot clearly said that after soundly defeating the Iroquois, the Saulteur returned to their homes at Keweenaw and Chequamegon Bay where, in Perrot's words, "They dwelt there in peace always, until some Hurons who had gone to hunt on the borders of Scioiux country" captured some Dakota, an indiscretion that began the above mentioned conflict. Importantly, we note Jules Talihan, Perrot's editor, indicated these live Dakota captives were taken to Saulteur villages at Chequamegon Bay (note the plural). Unlike Schenck, Perrot is not equivocal in saying the Ojibwe were residing at Chequamegon. He says they were living there, and Talihan concurred.[61] Furthermore, the 1662 date for the Iroquois Point conflict is supported by a 1663 entry in the *Jesuit Relations*,[62] but despite this, Theresa Schenck hesitates. As we saw above, she says only, that some Ojibwe "possibly" could have been at Chequamegon in these times.

We will return to the question of an early Ojibwe presence in Chequamegon Bay below, but for now it is enough to note that the final validity of stories of Ojibwe cannibalism on Madeline Island remains uncertain, but such stories, whether historical misconceptions or not, can linger on over the years and become part of a region's popular history, and unfortunately, the emotional aspects of accounts of cannibalism including the sacrificing of young girls can have long-term retentive qualities. Today, in the popular history of communities in the environs of Chequamegon Bay, the story of cannibalism and "witch doctors" preying on young girls lingers on, and can function to support self-serving beliefs about the early nature of tribal communities in the region.[63]

*Notes*

1. Kellogg 1968[1925]:139.
2. Busch 2008:77.
3. Hickerson 1988[1970]:56.
4. Schenck 1997:10.
5. Bewer 1999:1.
6. Schenck 1997:19-20.
7. Busch 2008:40-1; Vizenor 1984:13-36; Schenck 1997:17-27.
8. White 1991:105-6; Kellogg 1917:73; *Jesuit Relations* 51:21-47; Schenck 1997:45.
9. Schenck 1997:19.
10. Burnham 1974:8; Danziger 1979:31; Hickerson 1988 [1979]:57.
11. Benton 1986[1972]:4.
12. Trouillot 1995:xiv.
13. *Ashland Daily Press*, 3 September 2009, p.5.
14. Paap, H.D., fieldnotes, 9 July 2001.
15. Paap 1985:11.
16. Peacock and Wisuri 2002:121-22.
17. Buffalohead 1984[1885]:xiv; Williams 1984[1885]:18; Schenck 2007:vii-xv.
18. Dean 2003:6.
19. Cleland 1992:81; Parkman 1963[1887]:v-vii.
20. Demos 1995[1994]:131, brackets added.
21. Schenck 1997:18.
22. Schenck 1997:18.
23. *Jesuit Relations* Vol. 23:207-223.
24. *Jesuit Relations* Vol. 23:225-7.
25. Danziger 1979:26.
26. Parkman 1963[1887]:394-403.
27. Busch 2008:38-9.
28. *Jesuit Relations* Vol. 54:129-130; Cleland 1982.
29. Schoolcraft 1992[1953]:96.
30. Warren 1984[1885]:89-90.
31. Warren 1984[1885]:90.
32. Benton-Benai 1988:102-105.
33. Schenck 1996:250.
34. Schoolcraft 1851:250; Schenck 1996:250-1.
35. Busch 2008:36-7.
36. Smith 1995:17.
37. Vecsey 1983:22-3; Hickerson 1970:17; Godfrey 1998:32-3.
38. Burnham 1974[1929]:8.
39. Warren 1984[1885]:108-9.
40. Warren 1984[1885]:109.
41. Ross 1960:11-13, italics added.
42. Warren 1984[1885]:109.
43. Danziger 1979:27, italics added.
44. Levi 1956:15.
45. Burnham 1974[1929]:7-8.
46. Benton-Benai 1988:106-7.
47. Lewis 1988.
48. Gilfillan 1904; LaDuke 1999.
49. Cochrane 2009.
50. Jesuit Relations Vol. 54:153-161.
51. Cochrane 2009:42.
52. Cochrane 2009:43-4, brackets added.
53. Paap 1985; Smith 1995.
54. Paap 2012: fieldnotes of 24 June 2012 (Speech by Rob Goslin in Bayfield, WI.).
55. Cochrane 2009:176.
56. Hickerson 1988[1970]:55-7.
57. Danziger 1979:27.
58. Donnelly 1985[1968]:133-4.
59. Blair 1996[1911]:I, 181-2.
60. Schenck 1997:46, emphasis added.
61. Blair 1996[1911]:I, 181-2.
62. *Jesuit Relations* 47, 1663, Ch. iv.
63. Brody 1998[1981]:xvii-xxv; Feldman 2008:72-82; Paap 2005, field notes of 10 June.

# 3

# Seventeenth Century French in Chequamegon Bay

### *The French Come to Chequamegon Bay*

ETIENNE BRULE MAY HAVE BEEN the first Frenchman to come to western Lake Superior. He is thought to have arrived in the area about 1620, but Europeans could possibly have been there before Brule, and surely they were regularly on Lake Superior from Brule's time onward, although their presence was not always documented.[1]

Brule was sent by Champlain and is said to have passed through Chequamegon quickly, intent on searching for a Northwest Passage to the Orient, and we should feel that Chequamegon peoples knew about the Europeans by Brule's time.[2] Benton-Benai is justified in calculating an early Ojibwe awareness of the "Light-skinned Race," much earlier than the date of the first actual physical appearance in Chequamegon Bay.[3]

It seems likely that the French were in the area before Etienne Brule and that although at his time the Saulteur (Ojibwe) may not yet have entered into regular trading relationships with them, they were at least familiar with French trade goods brought to the region by others. Regarding the fur trade, the Ojibwe probably did not become involved as active traders until sometime after 1642 (after the Jesuits first came to Lake Superior), but they likely were aware of, and using French material items, before that date.[4]

William Warren wrote that sometime after becoming aware of the desirability of European trade goods, the Ojibwe:

> . . . commenced the custom of yearly visiting Quebec, and afterwards Montreal, taking with them packs of beaver skins, and returning with the firearms, blankets, trinkets, and firewater of the whites. This custom they kept up for many years, gradually curtailing the length of their journeys as the whites advanced toward them step by step, locating their trading posts, first at Detroit, then at Mackinaw, then at Sault Ste. Marie, till at last the smoke of their cabins rose from the island of La Pointe itself, when these periodical journeys came comparatively to an end.[5]

Warren could not offer a date for the beginning of this trade, but this is still an important quote for it points out an image of early Ojibwe society often overlooked. It was not just the Odawa and Huron who were serving as trading mediators between the French and more westerly nations. The Ojibwe too, were traders and, in time, said to be quite serious ones. Harold Hickerson pointed this out when he noted that: "In 1681, Jacques Duchesneau, the Intendent of Canada, characterized the Chippewas, along with the Hurons and Ottawas, as a trading people." This remark is supported by the early French explorer La Salle, when he wrote in 1682 that "the Saulteurs . . . go and trade in the country of the Nadouessioux, distant about sixty leagues to the west of Lake Superior."[6]

These references point to the 1680s, the years immediately after the peace negotiations between the Dakota, Ojibwe, and French, brought about by Daniel Greysolon Duluth, and, importantly, Harold Hickerson uses them to suggest it was these negotiations that allowed this trading to exist.[7] However, as we will see below, we know that trading relationships between the Dakota and Ojibwe existed over twenty years earlier, at least by 1661, when Radisson and Grosilliers and the Ojibwe went into Dakota country. This early date is supported by Reuben Thwaites, when he noted that the first Ojibwe voyage—recorded in writing—to Montreal for trade was in 1659.[8] This date is significant, but Rueben Thwaites notes that it is quite possible the Ojibwe were bringing furs to Montreal five years earlier. According to Thwaites, "Father Mercier, in a letter of September 21, 1654, alludes to a flotilla of canoes, guided by two traders, loaded with furs, belonging to Indians who had come 400 leagues from the west."[9] The *Jesuit Relations* writers also say that in 1656, a fleet of canoes with three hundred Upper Algonquians arrived at Montreal to trade.[10] Considering that these large trading parties likely held some Saulteur canoes, it appears that by at least the 1650s, natives from western Lake Superior—possibly including the direct ancestors of the Ojibwe—were making the long trips to Montreal. This tells us that it is probable that it was not the 1679 Duluth peace negotiations that suddenly allowed the Ojibwe to assume a trader's role.

This image of the Ojibwe as a trading people was pointed out by an early student of the writings of Pierre Esprit Radisson when he wrote: "Among the characteristics of the Ojibways which we discern in Radisson's writings is an aptitude for commercial enterprises, as they came yearly with their furs to Montreal and Quebec."[11]

This point has important implications in understanding the relationships that existed between these nations long before the French themselves regularly came to Chequamegon Bay. The several Algonquian bands in the western Great Lakes were constructing social and economic alliances with neighboring groups well before the arrival of the French. We should expect that these relationships involved the trading of material goods and therefore worked to maintain peace between these communities, and after European contact this practice of building alliances was extended to the newcomers.[12] However, the arrival of a French presence in the Lake Superior region was relatively late, occurring only after a century or more of European exploration and trading in North America.

Long before the arrival of Brule at Chequamegon, European ships were visiting the North American coast, from the Hudson Straits to Florida. After the Vikings arrived in North America others soon attempted to explore the new land and reap whatever benefits it had to offer. John Cabot was here in 1497, and the Portuguese sailor Cortereal came about 1501. By this time Norman, Breton and Basque ships were regularly crossing the northern Atlantic and setting up fishing stations in Newfoundland. According to Reuben Thwaites, Jacques Cartier was in the St. Lawrence Valley in 1535, and in 1541 his fellow Frenchman, Roberval, without any input from the native residents of the new land "was commissioned as viceroy of the new country beyond the Atlantic, with Cartier as his chief pilot and captain-general, and a choice selection of jail-birds for colonists."[13]

Reuben Thwaites did not hold any favor for the sort of individuals France intended to use to populate its new colonies. Somewhat surprised by the thinking of France's colonizing leaders in the early 1600s, Thwaites felt that:

> It is difficult for us today [Thwaites was writing in 1896] to realize that at any time in the world's history, enlightened folk should have thought good colonists could be made out of the sweepings of the jails and gutters of the Old World. But in the sixteenth and seventeenth centuries that delusion was quite generally entertained by would-be-founders of states across sea; it required the lessons of more than a hundred years of disastrous experiments to teach discerning men that only the best of middle class and the masses, can successfully plant a new community in the wilderness.[14]

Of importance here is that according to Thwaites, at least, the New World's native people had to deal with Europe's "sweepings of the jails and gutters" as this light-skinned force invaded their lands. Of course the "hundred years of disastrous experiments" may have been a century of disasters largely to the Europeans. To the native North Americans these encounters were gratuitous—because of the bounty of trade goods—but at times were troublesome, if not tragic, in their negative effects. Therefore, to the tribal peoples, at times they may have been viewed as victories, not disasters, in which the invaders, if not repulsed, were at least successfully delayed.

The Ojibwe forebears' migration from the eastern saltwater sea appears to have preceded this European invasion of the northeastern seaboard, but with a closer alignment of the dates involved, for both the invasion and migration, it is plausible that such an invasion could have been just cause for precipitating the momentous and monumental westward trek Red Cliff's early forebears made. Recalling the Ojibwe teaching of the start of the migration, we see that before the visit by *Wenebozho* and The Otter, that the people were estranged and suffering. Surely, for some east coast Native communities such unfortunate conditions were counterparts of the European invasion and could easily have caused westward migrations.

Such migrations are not unknown in the history of Native America. For example, in the early days of their dispersal after European contact, a band of Wisconsin and Illinois Kickapoo people trekked westward in their desire to be distant from the new Americans, finally settling in safety just south of the border in Mexico.[15] Likewise, a community of Creeks, as late as the early 1900s, in their dismay with the persistent negative treatment received from the United States, discussed the possibility of moving to South America in order to finally be free from their invaders.[16] The Ojibwe ancestral relatives, the Lene Lenape (Delaware) also discussed how they could move to an area where they would be freed from contact with the troublesome Euro-Americans,[17] and in the early nineteenth century some Wisconsin Territory Ojibwe families grew tired of hardships brought by Euro-Americans and moved back east to a Canadian Ojibwe community to try to isolate themselves from the stress of this contact.[18]

Certainly the European activity on North America's northeastern seaboard brought changes in tribal adaptations that were upsetting and in some cases acted as a catalyst for early westward migrations, and it was not long after the earliest European contacts that the volume and intensity of such encounters greatly increased. We are told that "by 1578 one hundred and fifty vessels from France" were employed in the northern New World fishing trade and by that time "a good trade with the mainland Indians had now sprung up." During 1600 to 1663, the Frenchmen Chauvin and Pontgrave made trading voyages to the St. Lawrence. In 1603, Samuel de Champlain came to Montreal and in 1609, set a permanent post at Quebec. From this base the French quickly pushed westward, and in only thirty-two years the black-robed Charles Raymbault and Isaac Jogues stepped from their canoes at the eastern outlet of Lake Superior to be greeted by the Saulteur.[19]

It was Champlain who moved west from the St. Lawrence valley in 1615 and met the Huron. In this year a Catholic mission to this nation was established. This "great Huron mission" existed for thirty-five years but was abandoned in 1650, because of the inability of the French to deal with the Iroquois.[20] In 1616, Champlain contacted the Odawa. Then in 1618, he sent the young Jean Nicollet to live among the Odawa and study them, and Nicollet did this, writing about them and others in the lands to the west of Lake Superior's eastern outlet. He described groups in Upper Michigan and along the nearby south shore of Lake Superior, and from Nicollet's remarks it has been concluded: "It is clear that these people living near Lakes Superior and Michigan were ancestors of the modern Ojibwe or Chippewa."[21]

In 1634, Champlain sent Nicollet back to the northwest to explore and reconnoiter with the tribesmen and to look for a way to China. Again, Nicollet visited the country at the eastern outlet of Lake Superior before going down to Green Bay, Wisconsin. Very importantly, it is during these times—the mid-1630s—that "the first outbreaks of European disease appeared among the Great Lakes Indians." Estimates of sixty to seventy percent died, or at least two out of every three Indians perished within several decades.[22] We do not know enough of the tragic and potentially devastating effect these illnesses had on the peoples along Lake Superior's southern shore. These diseases appeared suddenly and killed quickly, and this extreme loss could have reduced population levels at Chequamegon so drastically that when Radisson and Groseilliers arrived in the middle of the seventeenth century, although the tribesmen were still in the area, these Frenchmen might have seen few people. In this light, it has become conventional for historians to say, "In 1659 [with the arrival of Radisson and Groseilliers] Chequamegon By was fairly deserted."[23]

Extreme death tolls could also have given credence to the tales of the "abandonment" of Chequamegon. The newly acquired firearms were no help against these invisible pathogenic killers. At this time, the region's residents were perhaps recovering somewhat from this wave of disease when Rene Menard and Claude Allouez arrived in the western lakes in the 1650s and 1660s. We are told the Ojibwe associated these early missionaries with the coming of the disease and death of the time. Thus, as Cleland writes, "It is little wonder that the Jesuits were regarded as witches and sorcerers and were greatly feared,"[24] and the depictions by Menard and Allouez of their harsh treatment received at Keweenaw and Chequamegon becomes understandable when set in this wider context.

For these Ojibwe forebears, these times—the early decades of the 1600s—must have, indeed, called for contemplation. The people desired some of what the French had, and as seen in Warren's statements of the annual marathon canoe trips to distant French trading centers, they soon were quite willing to extend considerable effort to establish and maintain a friendly relationship with these wealthy and powerful newcomers, but still there were the doubts. Why had disease raised havoc with the Ojibwe, and did the Black-robes and their companions bring it? Just who were these haughty, proud, light-skinned foreigners roaming through the land? Why weren't they content to stay in one place and settle down? Why did they keep pushing further and further into the countryside?

Even though the early Ojibwe had heard about them well beforehand, used some of their tools for decades, and had battled their diseases, it must have been newsworthy to have the new white-skinned race in their midst. Most of the human features of the French were different. And it was not just their skin, the shapes of thier faces, the forms of their bodies, or the clothes they wore that were so unusual. Their very voices sounded strange, and the way they related to spirits—they insisted there was only a single great god—was unusual.

The forebears of the Ojibwe processed all this information and experience. But the newcomers were not just strange in their physical behavioral and linguistic differences—they were indisputably the possessors of a new degree of power. Their tools were made of iron, a material new to the Ojibwe, and often far superior to the stone, wood and native raw copper they were using, and although at first these iron tools were not felt to be essential for the Ojibwe to acquire, in time they became valuable to them.[25] And the French kept coming. Their numbers must have seemed endless.

It is important to understand that these newcomers were related to in the age-old Ojibwe manner: initially they were greeted with a reserve-filled respect, and their coming was interpreted within the context of the Ojibwe world of the time. In the early years of contact the Catholic priests were sometimes understood to be *manidoog*—that is, spirits—and were shown the deference demanded of such personages.[26] Because of this, the Ojibwe turned to their own spirits for guidance on how the people should work out the details of this new relationship. As so often happens when two heretofore-unrelated communities come in contact with each other, an alliance was attempted. These Europeans had things the tribesmen could use. Hence, relationships of a political and economic nature were established.

It is just such alliance building that was attempted by several nations when in the seventeenth century Pierre Esprit Radisson and his brother-in-law, Chouart Sieur Des Groseilliers, traveled to Chequamegon.

### *Pierre Esprit Radisson and Medart Chouart, Sieur Des Groseilliers in Chequamegon Bay*

SURELY THERE WERE EUROPEANS in Chequamegon soon after Etienne Brule's visit and they must have come regularly for the next few decades, but no written documentation has surfaced. As we will see below, some French paddlers likely came to the bay after leaving the Jesuit, Rene Menard, at Keweenaw Bay, but we have no clear testimony to document such a visit.[27] It seems very unlikely that for the nearly four decades following Brule's supposed arrival up to the coming of Menard that no French visited the bay.

Historians have said it was in 1659 that both Radisson and Groseilliers paddled the length of Lake Superior, arriving at Cheuamegon Bay late in fall, but the validity of this date remains troublesome. Arthur Adams and others claimed that the trip was made in 1661, not 1659.[28] In my discussion of the time of Radisson and Groseilliers in western Lake Superior, it is, finally, unimportant which date is used for their arrival. For my purposes, I will agree with Martin Fournier, who uses the 1659 date.[29]

Pierre Radisson published a memoir of his travels, a manuscript that Grace Lee Nute spoke highly of, but which has been troublesome for some historians to interpret.[30] Jane Busch calls the memoir "evocative,"[31] Harold Hickerson called it a "strange and wild account,"[32] and until very recently, it has been underused, if not neglected, ignored, and humorously belittled.[33] For instance, the early Minnesota historian, Warren Upham, had this to say about Pierre Espirit Radisson: "His narration, besides being very uncouth in style, is exceedingly deficient in dates, sometimes negligent as to the sequences of events, and even here and there discordant and demonstrably untruthful. Therefore much discussion has arisen concerning its significance and historical value."[34]

Today this troubled view of the Radisson memoir is giving way as students of historical discourse are beginning to approach selected manuscripts with new questions stemming from an interest in social, cultural and historical context.[35] For instance, the Canadian researcher, Germaine Warkentin, feels that we need to understand that throughout his time Radisson was very familiar with life as lived in the French court, yet in stark contrast, as a youth he was captured and tortured by Iroquois people "and had spent 17 months first as their victim and then as the adopted member of a Mohawk family."[36] Thus, he experienced life as an Iroquois of his times, but he also saw himself as a contemporary European, and as such was part of the economic, political and "civilized" intrusion into North America in the seventeenth century.

He carried, then, two vantage points with which to interpret his world, and, Warkentin argues, "All Radisson's accounts of his voyages have to be read with his adoption—and the consequent interaction in his experience of two radically opposed ways of seeing—constantly in view." The matter of these two points of view has been part of the controversy over his memoir, and, while today we still wait for further analyses of the Radisson memoir, we are witnessing a new willingness to accept the historical validity of the document. Accordingly, it is only now, as Germaine Warkentin says, that we are "Discovering Radisson."[37]

Theresa Schenck wrote that the journal of Radisson "stand[s] out as essential to any study of the Ojibwe during the French period,"[38] and Martin Fournier's work on Radisson argues strongly for our acceptance of the importance of Radisson's writing to a study of the earliest Ojibwe history.[39] Letting this preliminary discussion serve as an indication of the significant contribution Radisson's memoir makes to our understanding of Lake Superior's Chequamegon Bay Ojibwe in the 1600s, we can examine the memoir's contents. For this purpose I will focus on several or its incidents.

TO BEGIN, IT WAS IN 1659, when the Iroquois were disrupting the flow of trade from the western lakes to the eastern fur merchants, that Radisson and Groseilliers were in Quebec, hopeful of making an attempt to break the Iroquois blockade.[40] Their plan was to travel with two Hurons who had been captured by the Iroquois, but escaped, and now desired to return to their Lake Huron homes. Then, according to Radisson, in August word came of "a company of the nation of the Sault' that had just arrived and would immediately start its return voyage. Radisson wrote that there were seven canoes in this fur trading party, and that he and Groseilliers were successful in joining it for its return trip. Although the exact tribal identity of all the members making up his "company of the nation of the Sault" goes unstated, it seems most were Saulteur. This conclusion is supported when we note that weeks later upon arriving at The Sault, Radisson remarked, "This rapid was formerly the dwelling of those with whom we were," meaning his party was composed of Saulteur persons, but who no longer lived at Sault Ste, Marie. In the fall of the year, Pierre Radisson and his brother-in-law accompanied these individuals back to their homes, now located in the proximity of Chequamegon Bay.[41]

Initially, some time after departing Montreal, Radisson and Groseilliers and their companions skirmished with some parties of Iroquois along their route, but eventually arrived at The Sault and for a few days enjoyed its wealth of resources.[42] However, we understand that upon their arrival they found the area deserted. As an early writer said: "When Groseilliers and Radisson came to the Sault Ste. Marie in 1659, the country was deserted, the Ojibways formerly there having fled westward before the fury of Iroquois rangers."[43] Radisson's remarks about the people he was traveling with show that while they were known as being from "the nation of the Sault," their residences were located in the Chequamegon Bay region, some few hundred miles distant from The Sault.

Thus, Radisson tells us that in the fall of 1659, the Saulteur were not at Sault Ste. Marie because they had moved westward. We know that in the mid-1600s, and for decades after, Sault Ste. Marie was a magnet for many peoples who regularly came to harvest the area's whitefish. Some Ojibwe forbears, for instance, residing in the Lake Huron regions, came up to The Sault to seasonally take large stores of this fish. Other bands that used the lands west (and north) of the Sault traveled back each season for the same purpose.

These periodic movements were driven by resource harvesting demands, but other movements toward, or away from, Sault Ste. Marie were driven by desires to avoid military strife. The Odawa, Huron, and we should assume, some other bands, at times moved westward from Sault Ste. Marie to avoid the Iroquois. At other times some moved eastward—to the Sault—to avoid the Dakota.

Upon leaving Sault Ste. Marie, Radisson and his party encountered signs of human activity along almost the entire southern shore of Lake Superior. Some of these people using this shoreline certainly were Saulteurs, but there were others. For instance, soon after leaving The Sault his party came upon what Martin Fournier interprets to be an "allied band" that was known to Radisson and Groseilliers, having met them on another of their trips.[44] Writers have implied these people were Odawa, but their identity is uncertain. Then, after passing the Keweenaw Peninsula Radisson said his group came upon "a company of Christinos (Cree)" and from his remarks we infer they paddled to Keweenaw from an island to the northwest, presumably Isle Royale.[45]

In a recent study of western Lake Superior's Apostle Islands, historian Jane Busch offers this commentary about the 1659 trip of Radisson and Groseilliers:

> It is clear that from the beginning of their journey Radisson and Des Groseilliers were accompanied by people of the 'nation of the Sault,' i.e. the Saulteur, or Ojibwe. Originally Radisson and Des Groseilliers had planned to travel with two refugee Huron, but it is not clear whether this plan materialized. Early on in their journey the traders and their companions were joined by a group of Ottawa, increasing the size of their party to fourteen boats. As the trading party approached Chequamegon Bay, many of the Indians left to go to their families. The remainder left shortly after the group arrived at Chequamegon Bay.[46]

We see that while there may have been a few Huron in the Radisson-Groseilliers party and that some Odawa were later included, Ojibwes were present from the start. Later, upon nearing Chequamegon, Radisson tells us some persons left the group to join their families—Theresa Schenck feels they departed at the Bad River to begin a long paddle to their village at the headwaters of the Chippewa River, far inland[47]—but exactly who these travelers were, and where they were headed, is unclear. In Radisson's words, after their departure, "Seaven (sic) boats stayed of the nation of the Sault (Ojibwe),"[48] and only after arriving at the westernmost portion of the bay did some of them leave to join nearby relatives.

Thus, a careful study of Radisson's words shows that when approaching the proximity of the bay his fellow travelers began to drop off—to leave his immediate group as they headed to their final destinations. For some of these parties we cannot be certain where in the Chequamegon region these places were situated; we know only that they were somewhere in the proximity of the bay. As we have mentioned above, today what is considered to be the Chequamegon Bay region encompasses a rather large land and water mass. For example, even when referring to only the actual portion of Lake Superior that makes up the bay, it is approximately fifteen miles from the bay's westernmost extremity eastward to the mouth of the Bad River, and a full twenty-three miles to the easternmost land boundary of today's Bad River community. In 1659, when traveling was accomplished by canoe or foot, these distances were not insignificant.

Radisson does not tell us enough about the region and its people to allow us to learn just who was living there and in which specific parts of the region they situated their encampments. Contrary to what we have been led to believe about Chequamegon Bay being "empty" of residents at Radisson's arrival, it seems in 1659, Saulteur (Ojibwe) and possibly some Odawa or others, were residing near, if not actually at the bay.

Soon after arriving in Chequamegon Bay, the two Frenchmen erected a fort, of sorts, and stayed twelve days before venturing down to a southerly location to acquire furs. After the "fort" was built, Radisson says, "we had the company of other wildmen of other countreys that came to us admiring our fort and the workmanship."[49] Even though these people brought the Radisson party a quantity of food[50]—a gesture that could be interpreted as one of friendship—he suggests he and Groseilliers had some trepidation about the motives of these newcomers, since they could have been desirous of taking the stores the Frenchmen brought from the east. Accordingly, Radisson tells of the handguns and knives he and Groseilliers displayed at this time to inform these visitors of their ability to defend themselves. We do not know the identity of these visitors, and just what Radisson meant by "countreys," but Theresa Schenck feels "it is hardly likely they were Saulteurs, Ottawa, or Hurons, all of whom were on friendly terms with the two Frenchmen."[51] Schenck may be correct in this assumption, but we should not be certain all the region's Saulteur, Odawa and Huron were friends of the Frenchmen. These were autonomous band systems, each with their own leaders, and they may not have ever seen Europeans and might have stood aloof, reserving their trust until Radisson and Groseilliers proved themselves as friends. After nearly two weeks, this initial posture of reserve seems to have given way a bit, for Radisson wrote that on the twelfth day as they prepared to leave the area, "There came above foure hundred persons to see us goe away from that place."[52] This seems a rather large gathering and could be interpreted as a sendoff party of friends instead of enemies.

We should be interested in these brief comments by Radisson because popular history has told us that upon their arrival in autumn 1659, he and Groseilliers found a bay devoid of humans, or at least "fairly deserted."[53] Since it was late autumn—recall that Radisson and Groseilliers did not leave Quebec until sometime in August and did not reach the bay until the end of October[54]—we must expect that the bulk of the regional tribesmen were away, or at least at the nearby Kakagan Sloughs on the Bad River finishing the annual rice harvest, if not already departed to establish their winter hunting camps. But Radisson tells that people were, if not in the actual bay, in its environs, and if we can accept his numbers, then on the last day of their visit there were "above foure hundred persons" that gave him and Groseilliers a sendoff. He does not tell us if these four hundred persons were residing at the bay at the time, or if they came from regions away from the bay, but it is apparent they were not overly distant from the immediate area. The close proximity of this many people suggests Chequamegon Bay was anything but "deserted" when Radisson and Groseilliers arrived in October of 1659.

Thus, we should question just how unpopulated Chequamegon Bay—and its surrounding region—really was in the fall of 1659, and this point is seen in the remarks of a recent writer. She wrote that when Radisson left Chequamegon Bay to go down to Lac Courte Oreilles that "his party left *the Odawa* living at Chequamegon."[55] After her study of the Radisson memoir, Warkentin feels some people *were* residing at the bay, and we might agree that they could have been Odawa, but they also could have been Saulteur.

Another incident of interest in the Radisson memoir is the 1659-60 fur-trading expedition he and his brother-in-law made inland, south of Chequamegon Bay to what is often thought to have been an Odawa village (Lac Courte Oreilles) where the Frenchmen wintered-over. For years historians have been telling us these people were Odawa,[56] but more recent writers are not so certain. Martin Fournier feels they were predominately Menominee,[57] and Theresa Schenck refers to them as "ancestors" of the Ojibwe who were residing at Chequamegon Bay in William Warren's time.[58] Jane Busch feels that when coming back to Chequamegon Bay in the spring of 1660, Radisson and Groseilliers were "accompanied by Ojibwe," and that "[s]ome of their party had gone ahead of them, so that when they arrived at the bay they found at least twenty lodges full. It seems likely that these cottages were occupied by Ojibwe, Ottawa, or a combination of the two."[59]

We see, as Jane Busch writes, that after arriving at the southern site, "Radisson recounted that at first the two traders lodged with a chief who came with them from Quebec, but they did not like the chief and moved in with a family of Menominee."[60] Radisson's identity of his family as Menominee fits well with the geographic spread of this tribe at the time. Into the late seventeenth century the Menominee used land, along with the Dakota and Ojibwe, in what is now northwestern Wisconsin and eastern Minnesota, as far west as the Mississippi River.[61]

It seems then, that the Ojibwe chief whose lodge Radisson and Groseilliers left in favor of a Menominee lodge came with the party from Quebec and was one of the original "company" of traders from The Sault that Radisson mentioned at the onset. This conclusion would indicate that this chief was Ojibwe, and that in late fall of 1659, while there was a village of Menominees at the site we are told was Lac Courte Oreilles, there were others who most likely were Ojibwe, and perhaps not primarily, or even *all* Odawa, as many writers have suggested.

Another important event Radisson recorded is his involvement in a Feast of the Dead ceremony held with the Dakota, Ojibwe, Cree and several other nations, somewhere in Chequamegon Country south of Lake Superior in the winter of 1659-60. This was no little gathering, for Radisson claims at its opening "500 were in council" and that over the several days, likely approximately 2,000 persons took part. Although we should not take these figures as a hard and accurate counting, it still indicates an important coming-together.[62] When we consider the logistics for such a large gathering, and perhaps more importantly, that these were not communities who were overly friendly with each other at the time, we can appreciate the complex and sensitive political, social and emotional nature of the event and of what Radisson said the ceremony accomplished.

He writes of this gathering at some length, and despite his troublesome writing style, gives us a considerable degree of rich detail. An example of the color of his remarks is his noting that when a particular group came forward to announce itself and offer gifts to the leaders present, "Every one had the skin of a crow hanging at their girdles."[63] Although such remarks leave us with questions of interpretation, and always yearning for more, we still are enriched by his discussion of this multi-day ceremony. His descriptions of ritualistic behaviors such as solemn gift giving, rites of personal and community recognition and identity validation, and the usual obligatory pipe offerings and other religious acts, give us a window through which to see native life in the region at the time. It is a small window, but this was in the middle of the seventeenth century in western Lake Surerior Country, and anything we can learn about native life in that location at that early time is valuable.

The fact that the two Frenchmen had no dead to bring to the feast, yet were integral players in the ceremonial, is significant. Radisson and Groseillers were as interested in taking part in the event as were the Dakota, Ojibwe, Cree, Odawa and others. However, Radisson's account of this major multi-day event is neglected by some early writers, and downplayed, if not misinterpreted, by others.[64] For example, Harold Hickerson's discussion of the event has been criticized by a recent writer because Hickerson concluded that the two Frenchmen "ran the show," when a more appropriate understanding would be that the numerous communities involved were orchestrating the event just as much as were Radisson and Grosielliers.[65] As Germaine Warkentin notes, in 1660:

> A political opportunity offered itself to the Saulteaux [Ojibwe] in the arrival of Radisson and Groseilliers; by involving them in the meeting with the Sioux the French were invited to trade, and they were also in a position to act as ambassadors of peace to the "Christinos" [Cree] which they were in any case anxious to do.[66]

What Warkentin is suggesting is that while Radisson and Groseilliers were clearly intent upon having the complex ceremonial occur—an intent stemming from their commercial interests (they wanted peace in the region so they could trade for furs)—the tribal nations involved (including the Ojibwe) were also manipulating the setting-up and unfolding of the event. Interestingly, we are told that a band of Cree were "hovering nearby" and were strategically included in the ceremony.[67] It seems these northern visitors were intentionally "hovering," i.e., hoping to be part of the important ceremonial. Finally, indicating that this feast was a significant one, Radisson wrote that "Eighteen severall nations" took part in the ceremony.[68]

As we noted, this major event took several days to complete and involved extensive gift giving, calumet smoking and alliance building. To help seal the alliances, Radisson told that as the Feast of the Dead concluded, along with "the renewing of alliances, the marriages according to their Countrey Coustoms are made," and finally, when "This feast ended, every one returns to his Countrey well satisfied."[69]

The phrase "according to their country's customs" was commonly used in Great Lakes fur trading days to describe the manner of marital unions within and between tribes and also between tribal and European partners.[70] In the latter case, such marriages were consummated according to the rituals and rules of the tribal nations—not the Europeans'.

Harold Hickerson sees the Radisson instance of marriages as evidence for their use to bind *already related* kinship groups. As in the case of his argument about the origin of the Ojibwe *midewiwin*, his contention is that such feasts were, partly, ceremonial devices to restabilize a disintegrating clan system among tribes like the Ojibwe. Thus, he feels the marriages were intra-tribal, not inter-tribal. According to Hickerson:

> . . . [marriages] must be interpreted as an endemic feature of the Feast of the Dead, which attracted related people living separately for most of the time, to a central location where they encamped as separate units. Although non-related allies, in this case Dakota and French, in other cases such peoples as Huron and Cree, would be invited to sanctify alliances these outsiders would not normally be expected to intermarry with the hosts.[71]

Harold Hickerson's reason for writing about marriages at Feasts of the Dead was to discuss matters of social structure within Saulteur and related tribal societies in the Lake Superior region in the seventeenth century. However, after the coming of France, the importance of these marriages was partly to create or maintain alliances between *non-related* social systems. In the western Great Lakes region of the seventeenth century—the time from which most of our knowledge about the feasts comes—such ceremonial marriages between groups not already related by blood likely was more common than Hickerson wanted us to believe.[72] Therefore, after European contact the single function he attributes to these marriages is overly restrictive. If marriages were endemic to the Feasts of the Dead, then more likely their importance would have extended to non-kindred groups in attendance in order to support the primary purpose of the ceremonies—to wit, to initiate or enforce positive relations between attending groups. We will see in the following pages that according to both Nicholas Perrot and Daniel Greysolon Duluth, just such inter-tribal marriages were effected at two major Chequamegon alliance-setting gatherings.

To conclude, Radisson's Feast of the Dead held in Chequamegon somewhere off of Lake Superior's south shore in 1659-60 contained the usual elements found in such a complex ceremonial of alliance-making: gift giving, the scripted display of ritual paraphernalia, feasting, the prescribed handling of the remains of the recently deceased, pipe offerings, and marriages between the participant nations. When the tribes departed, peace was effected. The French were able to proceed with their trading for furs, and concomitantly, the tribal nations were able to proceed with their trading for the French goods. It is significant that such a large and complex ceremony occurred just a few years after the first Jesuit came to western Lake Superior, and a full twenty years before the coming of Daniel Greysolon Duluth.

The last incident of note in the Radisson memoir is the trip he and Groseilliers made into Dakota lands far west of Lake Superior at the conclusion of the ceremony in 1660. Radisson said that at the ceremony he and Groseilliers had agreed to go even further into Dakota lands to do some trading, and thus, "To be as good as our words we came to the nation of the Beef, [the Dakota], which was seven small journeys from that place [the place of the Feast of the Dead].[73] A trading expedition, this important trip may have been the first visit of Europeans to Dakota country, and it was also a venture to reinforce the alliances made at the Feast of the Dead. On this trip Radisson and Groseilliers "counseled peace [between the Dakota], the Crees and other tribes."[74] Of this trip, Radisson said, "We stayed there 6 weeks, and came back [with] a company of people of [the] nation of the Sault, [that] came along with us loaden with booty."[75]

This is a very interesting comment, although still troublesome. Radisson does not tell us that he and Groseilliers traveled with anyone when heading west into Dakota lands for this trading expedition, although it might seem that at least a small party of Dakota, or others, would have accompanied them to show the way. We are only told that *on their return* Radisson and Groseilliers somehow joined a party of Ojibwe who also were burdened with a load of beaver skins, acquired presumably from the Dakota.

Warren Upham had this to say about Radisson and Groseilliers' return from this trading trip: "On the return to lake (sic) Superior, Groseilliers and Radisson accompanied a party of Ojibways who had been trafficking with the Sioux, probably buying furs, under the advise of the French traders, for their trip back to Lower Canada the next summer."[76] As we see, Upham concluded that after Radisson and Grosseilliers completed their trading, it was *on their return* that they came upon a group of Saulteur who had also been trading with the Dakota, and only then, together, did these trading parties proceed to make their way back to Lake Superior.

Theresa Schenck, however, has a different understanding of how the two Frenchmen and the Saulteur trading party met. She says that after the Feast of the Dead ceremony, which included some Dakota, that "Radisson and Groseilliers tarried six weeks longer with the Sioux, and a company of Saulteurs stayed with them," an interpretation seemingly not borne out by Radisson's memoir, or by Warren Upham's remarks.[77]

This incident of an Ojibwe trading party going into Dakota lands west of Lake Superior in the fall of 1660 is another example of the Ojibwe in their role as a trading people. Warren Upham's remark that it was probably "French traders"—it is unclear if he meant Radisson and Groseilliers—who had advised these Ojibwe to buy Dakota furs is puzzling when it seems more likely that by 1660, the Ojibwe needed no advise to learn that trading for furs with the Dakota was good business.

Theresa Schenck's assumption that the Ojibwe trading party was, from the beginning, traveling with the Radisson and Groseilliers party is also puzzling. Recalling that the earliest written recording of Ojibwe canoes carrying furs to Quebec was made in 1659—a full year earlier than the Radisson and Groseilliers fur-trading excursion just discussed—and that there is evidence to suggest they likely were making these long trips at least several years *before* 1659—we see, again, that the Ojibwe were trading for furs with the Dakota *before* the 1661 Radisson and Groseilliers trip to western Lake Superior.

Radisson's memoir then, causes us to reconsider the popular history stating that in 1659, the Ojibwe did not have a presence in western Lake Superior lands. We saw how his rich account of the Feast of the Dead tells us the Ojibwe were role players in this event, and since it contained a peace agreement with the Dakota, Cree, and others, the Ojibwe were able to more easily use the far western Lake Superior region as they moved over its lands and waters to harvest its resources. This view is supported by their trading activity in lands west of the bay. Thus, the Radisson memoir challenges the notion posited by Harold Hickerson that until the 1679 peace agreement Daniel Greysolon, Sieur Duluth, negotiated between the Dakota, Ojibwe, and French, the Ojibwe essentially resided in the more easterly portions of Lake Superior, no further west than Keweenaw Bay.[78]

Finally, when Radisson and Groseilliers returned to Quebec, their trip stimulated others to attempt similar journeys to Lake Superior country, so the western lakes Ojibwe were soon to encounter more Europeans.

*Notes*

1. Ross 1969:14-16; Isherwood 2009:109 in Pure Superior by Jeff Richter, 2009. Isherwood erroneously claims Brule was a Jesuit priest and that he came to the lake to convert tribesmen to his Christian religion.
2. Smith 1973:6; Fisher 2008:498-501.
3. Benton-Benai 1988:105-106.
4. Ross 1960:18.
5. Warren 1985[1885]:126.
6. Hickerson 1974:18.

7. Hickerson 1974:29-33.
8. *Jesuit Relations* 45:105; Schenck 1997:40; Warren 2009[1885]:77.
9. *Jesuit Relations* 40:11; Ross 1960:18.
10. *Jesuit Relations* 46:75.
11. Upham 1905:529.
12. Schenck 1997:37-38, 85.
13. Thwaites 1896:1-2.
14. Thwaites 1896:3; brackets added.
15. Goggin 1951:314-327.
16. Wilson 1998:324.
17. Weslager 1991[1972].
18. Johnston 1999:10.
19. Thwaites 1896:3-4.
20. Thwaites 1896:25.
21. Cleland 1992:86.
22. Cleland 1992:88-89.
23. Danziger 1979:28.
24. Clelland 1992:89.
25. Schenck 1997:85.
26. White 1991:9-10; Hall 1997:3.
27. *Jesuit Relations* 45:161-163.
28. Adams 1961; Davidson 1895:4; Schenck 1997:41.
29. Fournier 2002.
30. Nute 2000[1944]:21-23.
31. Busch 2008:37-38.
32. Hickerson 1988[1970]:38.
33. Adams 1961:i.ii.
34. Upham 1905:450.
35. Adams 1961; Warkentin 1996:43-70; Fournier 2002; Busch 2008.
36. Warkentin 1996:46.
37. Warkentin 1996:43-70.
38. Schenck 1997:11.
39. Fournier 2002.
40. Fournier 2002:99.
41. Adams 1961:111-112, 120.
42. Adams 1961:120-121.
43. Upham 1905:529.
44. Fournier 2002:105.
45. Radisson 1885:193.
46. Busch 2008:38.
47. Schenck 1997:41.
48. Radisson 1885:193.
49. Radisson 1885:196.
50. Fournier 2002:106.
51. Schenck 1979:41-42.
52. Radisson 1885:196-198.
53. Danziger 1979:28.
54. Fournier 2002:101.
55. Warkentin 1996:58; italics added.
56. Ross 1960:20; Danziger 1979:28.
57. Fournier 2002:101-106.
58. Schenck 1996:253.
59. Busch 2008:38.
60. Busch 2008:38; Radisson 1885:201.
61. Beck 2002:73.
62. Radisson 1885:210.
63. Radisson 1885: 212.
64. Ross 1960:20.
65. Warkentin 1998:60-66.
66. Warkentin 1998:66
67. Warkentin: 1998:63-4; Radisson 1885:217.
68. Radisson 1885:209.
69. Radisson 1885:219.
70. Brown and Peers 1988:139.
71. Hickerson 1970:48-49.
72. Hall 1997:74-5.
73. Adams 1961:142.
74. Upham 1905:531.
75. Radisson 1885:220.
76. Upham 1905:502.
77. Schenck 1997:43.
78. Hickerson 1974:16.

# 4

# The Jesuits in Chequamegon Bay

BY THE START OF THE SEVENTEENTH CENTURY, France desired to undertake serious exploration efforts in North America. In 1603, Pierre du Gast, Sieur de Monts, was granted a trade monopoly by King Henri IV to begin this process. Along with this monopoly and the establishment of a permanent French colony, de Mont's charter, and those of later companies, stipulated that the firm "provide for the instruction of the aborigines in the knowledge of God and the Christian religion."[1] The French Jesuits were engaged to carry out this missionary work.

From early times, as Joseph P. Donnelly writes, "French kings had treated the Church as an arm of the state," and this relationship was in place during the seventeenth century when the Jesuits were working in the upper Great Lakes region.[2] However, in these times the arm of the state struggled to effectively reach into the heart of the North American continent, resulting in the trading companies'—and especially their field agents'—ability to have a relatively free hand in their *modus operandi*. The early missionaries, therefore, were forced to work under both the sometimes-conflicting aegis of the Crown, and that of the field personnel of the profit-seeking companies.

Beaver pelts made up the commodity at the base of the trade monopoly, and as we will note, the cooperation of North America's "aborigines" was necessary for their acquisition. The ultimate goal of trading companies was to generate profits for their stockholders and thus, company personnel worked to acquire as many pelts as possible. This soon led to traders dispensing alcohol to native trappers in order to help increase the number of pelts taken, even though it often resulted in conflict within the native community. As Donnelly says, "From the very onset, traders and other company officials in New France learned that debauching the Indian was the most effective means of compelling the native to gather a rich harvest."[3] This use of alcohol troubled the early Jesuits and was something they argued against, and French Crown authorities may similarly have spoken out against the use of alcohol in the fur trade, but their voices had little effect in distant North America. This inherent conflict between the profit motive of trading companies and a nation's governmental concern about humane treatment shown "aborigines" may not have been as acute in the mid-seventeenth century as it became later, but it still was something the early Jesuits had to confront.

We have already spoken of the first Jesuit missionaries to come into Lake Superior's Ojibwe country. Here we will look again at the arrival of these French religious men in Chequamegon Bay, hoping to discover information that will help us understand events that although far distant in time, may have left their effects on today's Red Cliff.

Writers sometimes have said these early Jesuits were not successful in their attempts to bring Christianity to the Lake Superior nations.[4] While it seems some sincere religious conversions were made, the words of the Jesuits themselves indicate a goodly portion of the baptisms were of sick children and seriously ill adults, rather than the otherwise healthy portion of the population.

It also has been suggested that behind many of the baptisms was a desire on the part of the natives to align themselves with the French trading and political system rather than French religion. For example, in 1669, the *Jesuit Relations'* writers trumpeted Claude Allouez's conversion of an entire Odawa village at Chequamegon Bay, while what triggered this mass conversion was the priest's threat to move back to the more thriving mission at Sault Ste. Marie if this group did not start attending his religious meetings with any regularity.[5] Given the nature of relationships with the Dakota at the time, as well as the importance of French trade goods, it is likely that political and economic concerns were important factors causing this "mass conversion," not simply a sincere attraction to Allouez's religion. When mentioning this particular group baptism, Hamilton Ross intimates that such extra-religious motives were behind it,[6] and the contemporary Jesuit writer, Joseph P. Donnelly, suggests likewise.[7] Given this, it is interesting that Harold Hickerson used the example of this mass conversion to support his contention that the Great Lakes Jesuits were successful in their work to bring their religion to the area's tribal people.[8] In the early days of contact it was not unusual for tribal leaders to enter relationships with Europeans and Euro-Americans ultimately based on economic and political goals rather than matters like religious preference.[9]

We are told that in the mid-1600s, the non-Ojibwe tribes were congregating at Chequamegon Bay due to their fears of the Iroquois, but we need to understand that they soon were also concerned about the Dakota, who were centered about 135 miles to the west and were known from time to time to visit Chequamegon. Unfortunately for the people residing at Chequamegon, soon after the Huron came to the area, they (the Huron) ventured westward and skirmished with the Dakota.

In a very interesting passage about the Dakota, Claude Allouez said, "These people are, above all the rest, savage and wild—appearing abashed and as motionless as statues in our presence. Yet they are warlike, and have conducted hostilities against all their neighbors, by whom they are held in extreme fear."[10] However, while the Dakota were, at times, feared by their neighbors, they (the Dakota) had fears of their own, for they greatly feared the French. Jacques Marquette felt this fear was due to the French having iron, something the Dakota lacked. At Chequamegon, Marquette had this to say about these "abashed" people who stood "as motionless as statues' in the presence of the French: "I wish that all the Nations had as much love for God as these people have fear of the French; Christianity would soon be flourishing."[11] Hence, given this fear the Dakota held for the French, and knowing that the Chequamegon tribes understood this, it was clearly in these tribes' interests to keep Allouez (i.e., to keep the French) at Chequamegon Bay. Considering this, when Allouez threatened to leave Chequamegon and go back to Sault Ste. Marie, we see that there were serious non-religious motives for submitting to the ceremony of religious conversion, motives that involved political alliances and their economic relations.

Like missionaries everywhere, the seventeenth century Jesuits brought more than religion to native people. In reality, they brought a new culture with its particular worldview.[12] For example, at Chequamegon when Claude Allouez admonished the Odawa and Hurons to give up polygamy, polytheism, and other customs and beliefs, and to adopt *his* customs and beliefs, he was introducing them to what at the time were important aspects of French culture. Other points of interest were the incidents when priests acted as medical curers, an example being when Allouez practiced bloodletting on some ill natives. The tribesmen were familiar with medical treatment involving the removal of a foreign object—a practice not completely dissimilar to bloodletting—and it seems Allouez's attempts at bloodletting were appreciated.

It has been said the more noteworthy gains of the Jesuits were in areas other than religion. According to one writer, "The most lasting contributions of the Jesuit fathers were not what they had hoped for. Rather than great numbers of Christian converts, the priests left detailed and accurate descriptions of the land, sympathetic accounts of the Indian inhabitants, and scholarly studies of various Indian languages."[13]

While we could debate how sympathetic these accounts of the natives really were, the Jesuits *did* leave us with some early geographic and geological descriptions as well as valued linguistic studies. These were major contributions to the Western scientific study of North America, and have had a value far superior to the Jesuits' efforts toward religious conversion.

Hamilton Ross remarked about the difficulty the Jesuits faced in attempting to gain religious conversions in western Lake Superior communities. He claimed that upon arriving at the Huron and Odawa villages in Chequamegon, "Allouez had hoped to find some evidence of Christianity among the Huron; thinking that the work done by earlier Jesuits, when the tribe lived near Georgian Bay, might make his own task easier. In this he was disappointed, and recorded that both tribes were primitive pagans."[14]

These European Christian missionaries were active in Chequamegon Bay two hundred years before Chief Buffalo was able to have land set aside for his community in 1854, so the connections between Red Cliff and these early French visitors of the seventeenth century may appear tenuous, if not non-existent. However, these early missionaries were writers, and their record of encounters with native residents of the region help to compose its history, and therefore, they command our attention. For this reason we will discuss the Jesuits' time in western Lake Superior.

### *Fr. Rene Menard at Lake Superior*

RENE MENARD WAS THE FIRST JESUIT to arrive and the story of his time in the region is relatively brief. The *Jesuit Relations*' writers say he and an assistant named Jean Guerin were in Chequamegon Bay, where they ministered to the Kiskakon Band of the Odawa a few years before the arrival of Claude Allouez,[15] and some recent writers concur.[16] However, others feel he never traveled as far west as Chequamegon.[17] Be that as it may, we know he traveled as far as the Keweenaw Peninsula where he spent a difficult winter with a large contingent of native people and a few French.

In his popular book on the Lake Superior Ojibwe, Edmund Jefferson Danziger, Jr., gives Menard only three short sentences, saying:

> The first Jesuit to visit the homeland of the Lake Superior Chippewa was feeble, fifty-six-year-old Father Rene Menard, one of the survivors of the decimated Huron mission and an expert in Indian languages. He accompanied Groseilliers on his return trip to Kitchigami in the fall of 1660. Shortly thereafter he perished on a charitable trek south to rescue some starving Huron on the Black River.[18]

In what appears as a self-fulfilling prophesy, Rene Menard felt he would meet his death while doing his missionary work in the forests of Lake Superior, and die he did. Perhaps here was a man who truly believed in martyrdom, for in a letter to a close friend back in France, written on 27 August 1660, before he left Three Rivers (Montreal) he said:

> This is probably the last word I should write you, and I wish it to be the seal of our friendship until eternity . . . In three or four months you may include me in the memento for the dead, in view of the kind of life led by these peoples, of my age, and of my delicate constitution.[19]

The *Jesuit Relations* give a few clues to what was occurring on Lake Superior's south shore about the time of Menard's stay. For example, one informant, a baptized "Savage" named "Awatanik" said, "The whole length of its coast is lined with Algonkian Nations, fear of the Iroquois having forced them to seek there an asylum."[20] The people of these tribal nations, as well as the French and native people in Menard's immediate party, are said to have treated the Jesuit poorly. According to Ross, "the priest seemed to have been the victim of insults and hardships at the hands of rather vicious *coureurs de bois* and their Indian companions. This might serve as another example of the hatred which the *coureurs de bois* bore the Jesuits in general."[21]

At Keweenaw Bay, Menard and a small group of French and others stayed behind to spend the winter of 1660-61 before moving west to their ultimate destination, Chequamegon Bay. There were native people residing at Keweenaw that winter, but we do not know exactly who they were since Menard refers to them only as Algonquians. At Keweenaw the priest says that "some Algonkians stole a part of our provisions,"[22] and we are told that during that winter Menard baptized "three hundred little children of the Algonkian Nation," but that "These children were the victims of disease and famine; and forty went straight to Heaven, dying soon after Baptism."[23]

For this priest to baptize three hundred sick children at Keweenaw Bay in the winter of 1660-61, a sizeable community of "Algonkian" residents must have been in the area and disease must have been rampant. In a letter Menard wrote from Keweenaw Bay (he named the bay "Bay Ste. Therese") to his superior back in Quebec, he lamented about how poor the tribesmen at that village were. According to him, they had little to eat and were decimated with sickness. Yet:

> The savages are living on moose-meat, which came very opportunely. The supply of fish failed, and those [in his party] who wished to keep lent suffered greatly; those who did not keep it, did not suffer. The savages invite us every day to their feasts.[24]

Finally, Menard wrote:

> I must push onto the last post, the Bay of St. Esprit [Chequamegon Bay] 100 leagues from here. There the savages have their rendezvous in the early spring, and there we must decide to either leave the country entirely, or to settle permanently in some place where we may hope to grow wheat. I pray the Father of Light to direct the purposes of these poor people toward his own greater glory.[25]

Menard hoped to reach Chequamegon Bay in time for spring rendezvous, and his words show us that in his time Chequamegon Bay was a gathering point for peoples, more than a permanent residence. Menard's remark touches on a subject—the nature of "settlements" and "permanent residences" for hunting and gathering societies—that we will discuss at length later.

Here we can leave Rene Menard. This European, who has been called "feeble"[26] and "a kindly and retiring individual"[27] and who identified himself as having "a delicate constitution" soon passes out of the literature. He was another of the European zealots who came to western Lake Superior and was given a troublesome reception. Perhaps it is a wonder parents let him baptize their children at all, for in the early days of European contact some of the natives felt baptism killed children.

Menard was a linguist and a man of letters who although may have reveled in the sea of heretofore-unrecorded languages in northeastern North America, perhaps was out of place in the Lake Superior country of the 1600s. He described the people he found as poor, but we see that they had moose meat when the usually abundant supply of fish "failed." And very interestingly, amidst this hunger and poverty, these people were able to invite Menard and his party to *daily* feasts. One must wonder what Rene Menard really saw at Keweenaw.

This European perception of natives suffering in poverty is readily found in the early literature from Lake Superior, and when we recall that in these years the people likely were struggling with recurrent occurrences of smallpox, we might agree that an element of truth is seen in these passages, yet some Ojibwe in their relations with Europeans purposely emphasized an image of poverty. For example, students of Ojibwe discourse used in the fur trade say that:

> In Ojibwe speech, expressions such as 'pity us' or 'we are starving,' as uttered to a European fur trader, commonly betokened the speakers' caution, respect, or efforts to manipulate the trader rather than standing as statements to be taken literally, at face value.[28]

A similar instance of perceived poverty is found in the writings of Alexander Henry who, when traveling in Ojibwe country west of Grand Portage in 1775, over a full one hundred years after Menard, wrote about a group of people he found at Saganaga Lake. He said, "I found only three lodges filled with poor, dirty and almost naked inhabitants, of whom I bought fish and rice, which latter they had in great abundance."[29] We are left to wonder how poor, dirty and naked these people really were if they had fish and a "great abundance" of wild rice to sell to the European.

Surely Rene Menard was at Keweenaw Bay in times of disease, probably from the first waves of pathogens brought to the New World by the Europeans decades earlier. If this was the case, he witnessed a community that was struggling, not just with the militarism of the Iroquois (and perhaps with the Mesquakie and Dakota), but also with the devastating effects of these invisible killers.

Lastly, we note Menard's mention of his hope to plant wheat in what he perceived as the wilderness at Chequamegon Bay. A few years later, in 1668, his fellow Jesuit, Jacques Marquette, also mentioned his hope to plant wheat—in Marquette's case, at Sault Ste. Marie.[30] These priests might have been speaking metaphorically, using *wheat* as a referent for the "truth" of their religion and way of life. Taken literally, these remarks could have been stemming from their hope to have grain from which to prepare bread to be used as the Christian host during their ritual of Holy Communion.

If these reasons for the remarks were not the case, then the priests' penchant for having wheat as a food source shows their being bound to cultural expectations they carried from their homelands in France. The Jesuits valued this grain, and perceived it as a staple of the Western world. They apparently missed their homeland's familiar bread, and two hundred years later this yearning for bread made from wheat is also seen in the journals of missionary Edmund Ely, when he was among the Ojibwe people in 1833 and 1834 in western Lake Superior.

Perhaps wheat, as a symbol of the settled agrarian, marked a yearning on the part of these men for the Lake Superior tribesmen to "stop the chase and settle down." If anything, it might have been felt that the absence of wheat in their cultures was yet another instance of the depravation of these "savages".[31]

Two things seem certain. One is the death of Rene Menard in a still unidentified location in inland northern Wisconsin in 1661, when he journeyed to minister to a group of Hurons he felt were in need. The second is that the party of French that came with Menard to western Lake Superior quickly returned to Montreal in 1661, and even though it did not gain a significant financial reward from the trip, it did help create strong interest in the pursuit of a Lake Superior fur trade. As Hamilton Ross writes, the party's trip "inspired others to such an extent that thenceforth there was a steady stream of adventurers heading westward."[32] Rene Menard with his Montreal party was a catalyst that worked to bring more French to Chequamegon.

Just as importantly, while Rene Menard doubtless was a sensitive, caring human being who felt his mission was to bring a better life to Lake Superior's native people, it was still *his* mission. It was *his* Euro-centric notion of what constituted a proper life. Like all the early Jesuits, he evinced a strong ethnocentrism in which the way of life of the Odawa, Huron, Iroquois, Ojibwe and others was seen as decidedly inferior to that of the French.

### *Fathers Jean Claude Allouez and Louis Nicholas at Chequamegon*

THE NEXT CATHOLIC PRIEST TO FOLLOW was Jean Claude Allouez. He left Quebec on 8 August 1665, and arrived at Chequamegon either later that year, or in early 1666.[33] Writers have been confused on the dates of the exact departures and returns of this priest's several canoe trips between Quebec and points west, and perhaps it is enough to say that Fr. Allouez was on the water often, traveling to and from various points between Quebec and western Lake Superior. Like the other Jesuits in North America of his time, he was truly *a man with a mission*, and perhaps this characteristic of this "Blackrobe" was part of the allure he presented to the tribal people. In the mid-seventeenth century the French Crown's representatives in New France were busy, moving over a large expanse of new lands, hurrying to make discoveries and political contacts. There was a *frontier excitement* in the new European community in North America. We have already referred to Fr. Claude Allouez and his accounts of the Odawa and Huron villages at Chequamegon, and here we can add a few details from his reports back to his superiors.

It had been four years since the loss of Rene Menard, and by 1665, the French were quite busy with plans to continue expanding their economic and political reach into the western Great Lakes. The new fur trade was an opportunity to garner wealth for the Crown and its representatives in North America, and the Jesuits were an integral part of this venture. It was a busy time for the French in the New World, as they were in the forefront of exploration of the continent's eastern regions and along the river valleys extending up and over the Appalachian watershed, along the St. Lawrence River and into the Great Lakes areas. They viewed Chequamegon Bay as a doorway to the north and west where they could reach tribes like the Cree and Assinniboine, and after evangelizing these communities move further west in search of a pathway to the Orient.[34]

Fr. Claude Allouez was caught up in this excitement and although we at times struggle to piece together the exact details of his travels into the western Great Lakes, we can be certain his intent was clear: he desired to evangelize the many native communities being discovered as the French moved westward. In time he encountered rumors of large rivers flowing south and west, and although he is not usually associated with the intriguing notion of discovering a Northwest Passage to the Orient, we should not think he was uninterested in this idea.

We know that from 1665 well into the 1670s, Fr. Allouez was one of an increasing number of Frenchmen who made repeated canoe trips from Quebec and Montreal to Sault Ste. Marie and the far western reaches of Lake Superior, and in the latter years down to Green Bay and its environs. However, the historical literature on men like Allouez can be troublesome since at times it portrays them in a heroic and even triumphal light, and thus might cause us to focus, largely, on the words and acts of the man, to the diminishment of the voice and acts of the native people he was encountering.[35] In the seventeenth century in North America, European men like Allouez entered a world foreign to anything they had ever experienced, and it should be recognized that their understanding of their new surroundings always included the primacy of the region's native peoples. This social and cultural environment that the Jesuits came into did not cease to exit upon their arrival. Its daily and seasonal rhythms, although under stress due to the political and economic changes of the times, were ongoing throughout the Jesuits' short stay. In the mid-1600s, the subsistence patterns and all related activities of the tribesmen in Lake Superior country did not cease to function with the arrival of the Jesuits.

We recall that the entire purpose of the Jesuits' presence in North America at the time was to minister to these people, (but always of course, to the advantage of the French), so Allouez, like his fellow missionaries, was preoccupied with his relationship to them. Yet, at times the Euro-centrism of the literature does little more than portray these people as deficient and whose way of life held little inherent value.

An example related to this depiction of tribal culture is an account of the incident wherein soon after arriving at Chequamegon, Claude Allouez built a small chapel on the west side of the bay. Hamilton Ross says: "Here he built his chapel, the first house of worship west of the Appalachians except those in French or Spanish territories to the far south and southwest."[36]

These remarks are an instance of *the production of history*, and they are a statement about the final value Ross seems to have put on tribal religions. If we agree that the verb,"to worship" can be justifiably applied to aspects of human behavior evident in displays of reverence, veneration and so forth found in rituals and ceremonies of many of the non-Christian tribal religions, and not exclusively to Christianity, then we should also agree that this bark chapel was not the first "house of worship west of the Appalachians." William Warren told of a large *midewiwin* lodge the Ojibwe erected on Madeline Island in the early days of their residence, and we might agree that such a structure was "a house of worship." For that matter, the ubiquitous sweat lodge of North American tribal communities is another example of an early structure that can also be called "a house of worship." In this sense houses of worship were spread all through The Americas long before the coming of the European. Remarks like Ross's can reinforce a majority group's negative understanding of these important institutions.

Despite this troubling characteristic of the early literature we see that Claude Allouez was observant, energetic, and it seems, a strong force. He appears to have enjoyed writing for he gives considerable detail of what he saw. However, we wish he had written more, for when studying the English translations of the *Jesuit Relations* we find too few pages attributed to this colorful priest. As was true for all the field reports in the *Relations*, his communiqués back to his superiors were edited, at times leaving us with uncertainty about the original content, and sometimes the focus, of his writing.

For example, chapter five of volume fifty-one of the *Relations*, which is given the interesting title, "Of the False Gods and Some Superstitious Customs of the Savages of that Country," opens with this introduction: "Following is what Father Allouez relates concerning the customs of the Outaouacs *and other peoples*, which he has studied very carefully,—not trusting the accounts given him by others, but having been himself an eye witness and observer of everything described in this manuscript."[37]

It is not always clear if the remarks that follow this validating introduction are referring to Sault Ste. Marie or Chequamegon Bay, and once again we are left with the question of exactly who "the Outaouacs and other peoples" were. Could some of these have been Ojibwe, or at least the immediate forebears of them? Although early writers felt the people Allouez was with at Chequamegon were Odawa and Huron, another conclusion is offered by a present day Ojibwe writer who states that in 1666, Allouez established what became known as the Mission of St. Esprit at Chequamegon Bay "for the Ojibwe."[38] This question of exactly which peoples early observers like Claude Allouez were speaking of has troubled students of early Ojibwe history for years.

Regarding "the False Gods and Some Superstitious Customs," Allouez says:

> There is here, . . . a false and abominable religion, resembling in many respects the beliefs of some of the ancient Pagans. The Savages of these regions recognize no sovereign master of Heaven and Earth, but believe there are many spirits—some of whom are beneficent, as the Sun, the Moon, the Lake, Rivers, and Woods; others malevolent, as the adder, the dragon, cold, and Storms. And in general, whatever seems to them either helpful or hurtful they call a Manitou, and pay it the worship and veneration which we render only to the true God.[39]

In reference to our above remarks about houses of worship, here we see that Fr. Allouez recognized that the early residents of Chequamegon Bay did, indeed, offer "worship and veneration" to spiritual forces. But, perhaps more importantly, throughout his writings Claude Allouez gives us a rich description of religious beliefs and practices he found when first coming among Lake Superior's people. He points out in the above quote, for example—as we have discussed in an earlier chapter—that monotheism was not a central part of early Algonquian religion; instead these people saw a universe of spiritual forms. Just as importantly, he tells of numerous details of religious practices he observed, including public and private offerings of tobacco, dogs, and other "presents." When leaving Sault Ste. Marie and moving along the southern shoreline of Lake Superior he notices many pieces of raw copper found in the shallow waters and he relates how people treasure them as spiritual objects, placing some of the smaller pieces into their personal medicine bags. He describes a pipe ceremony—one of the first descriptions found in the Lake Superior literature. And, as the Western world tends to do, he berates polytheism, as if monotheism is the only way to understand the spirit world. Finally, however, the rich religious beliefs and practices he witnesses are "false and abominable," and he hopes to destroy them, replacing all with *his* nation's religion.[40]

Much has been made of Claude Allouez's time at Lake Superior, even though, as with his predecessor Rene Menard, it was for a relatively brief period. He came to the western Great Lakes in the times when the Iroquois Confederacy was undergoing serious military challenges from the French, and when England and France were beginning to compete for what they considered open lands south of the Great Lakes.[41] Allouez's stay at Chequamegon Bay is best understood within this larger geo-political and historical context.

He arrived at Chequamegon at the time when the Marquis de Tracy, the French Crown's viceroy in North America, successfully led a large military force against the Iroquois at Lake St. George. The Iroquois had caused a four-year blockade of the canoe route from the western lakes to Montreal, a problem, as we saw, that Radisson and Groseilliers tried to rectify, and de Tracy's military attack was meant to end. De Tracy's victory was followed by a peace agreement in the summer of 1667 between the French and the Iroquois that re-opened the trade, bringing great joy to the eastern merchants and the line of fur depots reaching back to Sault Ste. Marie. This agreement was followed by the beginnings of an eastward migration of tribal communities desiring to return to their earlier homelands. These were peoples who, in previous days, had moved west to the Sault and, for some, on to Keweenaw and Chequamegon to avoid the Iroquois.

Allouez claimed that immediately upon his arrival at Chequamegon he noted two large villages of bark lodges with several fields of corn and other crops nearby. He said there were about 800 men able to bear arms in these villages and that the overall community likely held 2,000 or so persons. These large villages with their fields of corn were located on the mainland at the furthest reaches of the bay and have become part of the earliest written imagery we have of the region. Jane Busch feels these may have composed the village community at the environs of Chequamegon Bay witnessed by Pierre Radisson just a few years previously, an interpretation that suggests, as we noted, that the bay was not devoid of human residents in 1659.[42]

In the summer of 1667, about a year after he came to Chequamegon, Allouez and a cadre of native paddlers traveled to the far southwestern point of Lake Superior and up along its northern shore to Lake Nipigon to visit a band of Nipissing people, who, it is said, had accepted Jesuit missionary efforts about twenty years earlier when residing with the Huron at the lake of that name. The Iroquois had driven the Nipissing from that site when they attacked this mission in 1649-50, and Allouez was anxious to renew the Christian faith of these people after such a long hiatus from any contact with the Jesuits. But when reaching Lake Nipigon, he found a community with little interest in his missionary efforts, and after only two weeks he returned to Chequamegon Bay. It has been claimed that when leaving Nipigon, Allouez followed the northern shore of Lake Superior to Sault Ste. Marie, thus making him the first European to circumnavigate the big lake,[43] but the Jesuit scholar, Donnelly, has shown this supposition to be incorrect since upon leaving Nipigon, Allouez paddled back down to Chequamegon Bay—this was in the summer of 1667—where he later joined a flotilla of canoes loaded with furs headed for Sault Ste. Marie to do its summer trading at Montreal.[44]

On this trip Allouez went on to Quebec, where he contacted his superiors to try to convince them to provide more Jesuit workers for western Lake Superior conversion efforts. He was successful, and Fr. Louis Nicholas, who was at Montreal at the time, was assigned to work with him at Chequamegon. Fr. Jacques Marquette and Br. Louis Boehme, both also at Montreal at the time, were assigned to Sault Ste. Marie where Marquette would work to convert the resident tribesmen while Boehme engineered the construction of a permanent mission station, complete with palisade and required buildings. Apparently Marquette and Boehme remained in Montreal, busy preparing for this new assignment, and did not leave for The Sault until the *next* year, in 1668.[45]

In the summer of 1667, Allouez, Nicholas, and a Christian brother and two lay workers left Montreal for Sault Ste. Marie. After arriving and before going on to Chequamegon Bay, they spent time laying plans to Christianize the region's tribal people. Joseph Donnelly discusses the likely subject of these conversations and tells how Allouez and the other Jesuits saw the rapids at the St. Marie River as "a herald's platform from which to broadcast the word of God."[46] Likely, the plan was to work hard at converting the resident Saulteur (Allouez called them the *Outchipouec's* [Ojibwe]), who would then influence the site's many seasonal tribal visitors.

According to Donnelly:

> As for the Chippewa themselves, they were a shrewd, canny lot who understood quite well their economic and geographic importance. Instinctive business men, they were quick to realize that it was good business to maintain friendly relations with the French, who could supply them with French goods, which could in turn, be exchanged at a profit to the nations beyond the Sault . . . . Christianizing the Chippewa at the Sault was the first crucial step toward winning the West to the doctrines of Christ. If the Chippewa became staunch Christians all the Indians who visited them would be influenced to do likewise.[47]

This characterization of The Sault's Ojibwe as "instinctive businessmen" is extreme but still hints at the early awareness held by Europeans like Radisson—as we have already noted—that these early people were adept traders in the western Great Lakes region.

In late fall, 1667, Allouez, Nicholas, and the others left Sault Ste. Marie for Chequamegon Bay where they undertook efforts to bring Christianity to the region's tribal people. However, it seems Fr. Nicholas soon became disheartened with the rigors of missionary work at the near-wilderness site, and after only one year he left the field to return to Montreal.[48] Claude Allouez also left Chequamegon Bay in the spring of 1668—to make what Donnelly calls "a flying trip to Quebec"—returning in the fall of that year.[49]

During these times, as he wrote in the *Jesuit Relations*, Fr. Allouez identified three bands of the *Outaouacs* (Odawa) residing at Chequamegon Bay. These were the *Keinouche*, *Sinagaux*, and *Kiskakon*. The latter were an Illinois band of the Odawa, and it is these people, who in 1668 were said to convert *en masse* to Christianity after Allouez threatened to abandon them unless they began to pay attention to his admonishments to change their behavior and to worship his god. This threat involved the scene wherein he removed one of his shoes and knocked the dirt from it to show that when he left Chequamegon Bay—the home of the Kiskakon—to return to Sault Ste. Marie he would not want even the dust of its land to remain with him.[50]

Except for this reputed conversion of the Kiskakon, Allouez's reports indicate he did not hold much hope for the tribal residents of Chequamegon, for it is apparent that, by and large, they paid his religion little heed. For example, about the Keinouche and Sinagaux, he said, "These peoples have very little inclination to receive the faith, since they are extremely addicted to idolatry, superstitions, legends, polygamy, unstable marriages, and every sort of licentiousness, which makes them renounce all natural shame."[51] We do not know what finally became of the Keinouche band, but Fr. Jacques Marquette, who followed Allouez at Chequamegon, claimed when he arrived at the mission in 1669, these people declared themselves not yet ready to convert to Christianity.[52] Like the Keinouche, the Sinagaux band also refused to listen to Claude Allouez, but a few years later, sometime during 1672-73, apparently out of a fear of the Dakota and after Fr. Marquette worked hard to convince them to come back east, some left Chequamegon Bay and moved to the new mission station at St. Ignace south of Sault Ste. Marie, across the channel between the mainland and Mackinac Island.[53]

After having some initial success in gaining religious conversions with the Kiskakon people, things took a downturn. Allouez wrote that in 1667, after he moved his chapel from its distant site west of the bay to a more central location in a village, an altercation erupted during which the chapel was set afire and destroyed. The priest claimed he barely escaped from this melee with his life, and Hamilton Ross suggests this incident throws doubt on just how successful Claude Allouez was in his mission work at Chequamegon Bay.[54]

Alloucz left the bay in spring of 1669 (we assume his lay assistants left with him) and returned to Sault Ste. Marie. We might think he was following through on his threat to abandon the Odawa and Huron, but he left because his missionary interests were being redirected to the lands of the Potawatomi at Green Bay. He had learned of these lands from the Kiskakon, and from the Potawatomi themselves, who made periodic appearances at Chequamegon Bay.

After he arrived at Sault Ste. Marie, a group of local Odawa returned from an excursion far to the south of Lake Superior where they came upon a band of about forty Iroquois who were passing through after attacking a Shawnee village. With these Iroquois was a single Shawnee captive, whom they apparently intended to use as a slave.

Even though the Odawa were considered allies of New France and supposedly committed to maintaining a peaceful relationship with the Iroquois through the Marquis de Tracy's peace agreement of 1667, they captured this group of Iroquois with its prisoner. Fearing the Odawa might put these Iroquois to death, and thereby rupture the recent peace agreement, Allouez interceded and insisted they be freed. This was done, except for three who were held as a safeguard against any Iroquois reprisal for the Odawa indiscretion. Fr. Allouez argued the three Iroquois be put into his custody and taken to Quebec to be turned over to French authorities for final disposition, and this was agreed upon. The Shawnee was released, and in ensuing conversations with Allouez he told of the rich lands south of Lake Superior with many native communities and a large southerly flowing river. This sparked Allouez's interest, and soon he was speaking of the need for an expansion of Jesuit mission work in that area.[55]

In late summer of 1669, Allouez and the three Iroquois joined a trading flotilla setting off from Sault Ste. Marie for Quebec where, upon arrival, the "captives" were received by Governor Courcelle, and it is assumed, summarily released.[56] When in the city, Allouez updated Fr. Le Mercier, his Jesuit superior, of the mission activities on the upper lakes and of his thoughts about opening a new mission among the Potawatomi on the west side of Lake Michigan at Green Bay. Le Mercier approved of Allouez's plans and appointed Fr. Marquette—who had come to The Sault in 1668—to replace him at the Mission of St. Esprit at Chequamegon.

This transfer of Claude Allouez from Chequamegon Bay to Green Bay was part of the Jesuits' desire to extend their evangelizing efforts to southern lands, but there was another reason for this move. When on their periodic visits to Chequamegon, the Potawatomi had won the favor of Claude Allouez. They treated the priest with respect, and recalling the difficulties he was experiencing with some of the bay's Odawa bands, the visits of these well-mannered southern tribesmen must have been a welcome change.

Perhaps just as important in trying to understand why Allouez moved to Green Bay was that the Potawatomi asked him to come, but as the priest wrote in the *Jesuit Relations*, they were not asking for religious instructions because they were not interested in becoming Christians. Instead, at the time—the late 1660s—they were asking Allouez to help them with troublesome French traders. They were upset with the way these men were treating them and wanted Claude Allouez to help rectify this problem.[57] At this time, French traders were coming to the western lakes from Montreal and Quebec in attempts to garner wealth through direct trade with the tribes and their aggressiveness was causing difficulty, even physical conflict.

Allouez brought Fr. Claude Dablon to Sault Ste. Marie from Quebec in the summer of 1669, before departing for his work at Green Bay. At The Sault, Fr. Dablon began overseeing the work meant to lead to the conversion of the Saulteurs (Ojibwe) and any other bands residing at that location, as well as those who continued to come to the rapids to harvest whitefish and to trade. He also was to supervise preparations for receiving the Odawa and Huron people who were expected to arrive from the Mission of St. Esprit. During the previous year—1668—some of these bands had begun leaving Chequamegon Bay to return to their former eastern homes, and the Jesuits hoped to entice them to settle into a region close to Sault Ste. Marie where attempts at their religious conversion could be undertaken.[58]

It is noteworthy that during his approximately three years at Chequamegon Bay, Claude Allouez wrote hardly anything about the Ojibwe. One instance, however, is his brief paragraph on what he called "The Mission to the Outchibouec." This is a particularly important quotation because it suggests a band of Saulteurs (Ojibwe) may have been spending much time, or even residing permanently, in the region of far western Lake Superior during 1666-68.

In his reporting of this mission "to the Outchibouec", Allouez said:

> They are called the sauters by the French, because their abode is the Sault [rapids] by which Lake Tracy [Superior] empties into the Lake of the Hurons. They speak the common Algonquian, and are easily understood. I have proclaimed the Faith to them on various occasions, *but especially when I sojourned with them at the head of our Great Lake for a whole month.* During that time, I instructed them in all our mysteries; I also baptized twenty of their children, and an adult who was sick; this man died on the day after his Baptism, bearing to Heaven the first fruits of his nation.[59]

In this instance, Claude Allouez was writing back in Quebec, after he left Chequamegon the last time. He was summing up the tribes under the umbrella Sault Ste. Marie Mission, called "The Mission to the Outaouaks." We do not know if his month-long "sojourn" in western Lake Superior was a fishing trip, spent generally on or beside the water, or if it was a hunting and gathering expedition into the woodlands west of the big lake. The differences in such trips become important because if they were in the western forest lands then the existence of a peace agreement with the Dakota, or even the Assiniboine, who often used these regions should be expected, and of course, we recall just such an agreement made in 1660 with Pierre Esprit Radisson.

The problem of correctly understanding this quotation of Allouez is seen in a remark of Christosytom Verwyst, the late nineteenth and early twentieth century Catholic priest who worked in Chequamegon Bay. Verwyst felt that in this case, Allouez was "probably at Fond du Lac where he met some Chippewas and Sioux."[60] This early remark of Verwyst suggests he felt Allouez could have paddled to Fond du Lac at the westernmost extremity of the lake from his base at Chequamegon Bay to minister to a band of Ojibwe who, at the time were *residing* at Fond du Lac, not merely visiting it from their home at the far eastern end of the lake.

At a first reading, Allouez's important passage might be interpreted to mean that he traveled *to* Lake Superior's western shore with a band of Ojibwe from Sault Ste. Marie. And it might be assumed that both the priest and these Ojibwe spent one month on this trip, then returned home to The Sault. These understandings would fit if we started with the assumption that in the 1660s, *all* Ojibwe resided at the Sault. However, we have seen that the historical record does not indicate this was the case. Thus, a different set of conclusions must be drawn from this passage.

Allouez said he traveled with them *at* the far western end of Lake Superior, not that he traveled with them *to* this location. He "sojourned" with them for a month, but the Ojibwe might have been "sojourning" in that region much longer, or even residing "at the head of our great Lake," i.e., at Fond du Lac as Verwyst felt, or elsewhere along Superior's western limits, or perhaps even at the Chequamegon Bay area, *permanently*. Put another way, while the abode of the Saulteurs was said to have been at the Sault, it seems that for this particular band—these "Outchibouec" Allouez was with—*their* permanent abode was far to the west.

Another reason this Allouez quotation is interesting is his use of the label "Outchibouec" for this band of Saulteurs. Unfortunately, the priest does not tell us why he uses it, but according to Claude Dablon[61] "Outchibous" was the name for the community that seasonally came to Sault Ste. Marie from an area north of The Sault. As such, "Outchibouec" is a label for one of Harold Hickerson's several "proto-Chippewa" bands that, he claims, originated in areas surrounding Sault Ste. Marie. It seems strange that these people would have been "sojourning" at the head of Lake Superior, an area to the west and far distant from their northern homeland. While spending time at The Sault in the whitefish harvesting season, it is more likely that in other seasons this band would have returned north to its traditional hunting, ricing, and sugaring grounds, rather than venturing to new and perhaps unknown grounds a few hundred miles to the west. Either this band was unusually far from home or else they were actually residents of the Chequamegon region, a more plausible conclusion.

A supporting interpretation could be that this band *was* earlier associated with the Sault Ste. Marie area, hence, were "Outchibouec," but during Allouez's time on Lake Superior was beginning to spend some of its time of open water on Lake Superior's western shore. This conclusion is plausible since Radisson has shown that as early as 1659, Saulteur bands were residing in western Lake Superior. Finally, the instance of Allouez's "sojourning" with this band does much to place the Saulteur in far western Lake Superior during his time in the same region.

The problem this incident and these questions raise is whether or not writers have assumed that through most of the early and mid-1600s, the significant portion of the Ojibwe nation headquartered at Sault Ste. Marie and nowhere else. The Sault allowed for a regular clustering of larger groups of people due to the abundance of whitefish, but at times when the fish were not available and groups of Ojibwe left that region to fish other areas, hunt in the forest, harvest wild rice, or manufacture maple sugar, they were doing so in much smaller groups—kin groups that we have already said adopted a more diffuse and at times mobile and *less easily seen* foraging settlement pattern. It seems that in the very early years Ojibwe people resided in most of the bays and coves of the lake's southern shore. One area, for instance, was Grand Island, just west of The Sault,[62] and as we have noted, in the years immediately previous to 1679-80, the written record indicates that there were Ojibwe groups using Keweenaw Bay, Ontonagon and Chequamegon Bay, but these rarely are referred to in the literature.

This quotation from Claude Allouez helps us answer the question of what happened to the Saulteurs (Ojibwe) Pierre Radisson and Nicholas Perrot showed us were residing at, or in the vicinity of Chequamegon Bay in 1659-60, and the ensuing several years—only five or so years preceding the arrival of Allouez. The *Jesuit Relations* writers tell us that in the mid-seventeenth century the bay was a center of many native communities, and wrote that "More than fifty villages can be counted, which comprise diverse peoples, either nomadic or stationary, who depend in some sort on this Mission, and to whom the Gospel can be proclaimed, either by going into their country or waiting for them to come to this to do their trading."[63] At another point in the *Relations* we are told that at Chequamegon, "We had to do with twenty or thirty nations, all different in language, customs and policy."[64] We should not take these numbers of villages and nations as exact, but we are still left to ponder, as we noted some writers do, if it was not possible for a few Saulteur bands to be in the mix of this relatively large amount of different peoples regularly visiting, or actually residing at Chequamegon Bay during the few years Claude Allouez was himself—to use a phrase Pierre Radisson would have understood—"coming and going" from this strategic site.

### *Fr. Jacques Marquette in Chequamegon Bay*

FATHER JACQUES MARQUETTE and the Jesuit Brother Louis Boehme, both in their thirties, came to Sault Ste. Marie from Montreal in 1668 to assume their new assignments.[65] At that date Marquette reported there were approximately 2,000 tribal persons regularly coming to, or residing at, The Sault, and out of this number only 150 were Saulteurs (Ojibwe).[66] This seemingly small number of Saulteurs hints at the possibility that by Marquette's time the greater amount of these people had left The Sault in favor of more westerly sites, a notion supported by Nicholas Perrot when he claimed that in 1662, and for several years following, communities of these ancestors of today's Ojibwe were, as we noted above, living in western parts of Lake Superior, principally in regions of Keweenaw and Chequamegon Bay.

While Marquette addressed the matter of the religious conversion of tribesmen at The Sault, Louis Boehme and a few French assistants set to work constructing new mission buildings at that site, completing them in late 1669 or early 1670.[67] Soon after this work, French builders were pressed into service erecting a second mission station at St. Ignace where, it was hoped, the Odawa and Huron residents of Chequmegon Bay who were beginning to migrate back to their eastern homelands would be enticed to settle. After de Tracy's French and Iroquois 1667 peace agreement, increasing numbers of these tribesmen were leaving western Lake Superior, and when a Jesuit attempt to have some of them settle on Mackinac Island failed, the priests decided to use the nearby new St. Ignace site.[68]

At this time, things were moving fast at Sault Ste. Marie. As we have noted, after Claude Allouez and Fr. Dablon arrived in 1669, it was announced that Allouez would immediately travel to Green Bay to begin a new southern mission, and Jacques Marquette would replace him at Chequamegon Bay. Apparently eager to begin this work, it was in late autumn of that year that Marquette left The Sault for this new assignment. The *Relations* writers note that Br. Boehme accompanied Marquette to Chequamegon, and in 1670, wrote that, "Within a year they have Baptized eighty children," but the written record is unclear just how long Boehme stayed at the bay.[69]

Marquette told that the canoe trip to Chequamegon was a difficult one because of the amount of ice and poor weather his party encountered due to the tardiness of its departure. He obviously was happy to conclude his trip safely, and claimed that the Huron villagers residing at Chequamegon showed great joy with his arrival.[70] We should contemplate this journey, and as was true of those made by Menard and Allouez, how when on the water these priests were in the company of other Frenchmen and native tribesmen. In seventeenth century Lake Superior country the Jesuits did not take solitary canoe trips. Even though the written record is usually silent, by the time of Marquette's first paddle to Chequamegon Bay, such trips likely were a regular part of tribal life, and for the French in Marquette's time they probably had become quite common as well. As we will see below, a century later the Ojibwe were making canoe trips from Lake Superior's western to its eastern shores on a regular basis.

More is known of Jacques Marquette in the times after he left Chequamegon then during his brief stay at the bay, and as is the case with Claude Allouez, the early literature portrays him as a solitary and heroic figure laboring among "the savages." We know Fr. Marquette did not work alone at Chequamegon, and it seems he was there intermittently, for only two years (and never in the summertime)—a time that was interrupted with regular canoe trips back to Sault Ste. Marie and points beyond. Since 1608, Jesuits were obligated to make annual retreats "of eight or ten days" for solitary prayer and meditation away from all distractions, and it is thought when at Chequamegon Fr. Marquette made his retreats to Sault Ste. Marie, but he could have gone back as far as Montreal or even Quebec, as Reuben Thwaites claims. Such long canoe trips would have reduced his time at Chequamegon considerably.[71]

An example of this martyr-like and heroic depiction of Marquette at Chequamegon is written by Reuben Thwaites when he said, "For four years he labored alone in this wide wilderness, hoping against hope, varying the monotony of his dreary task by occasional canoe voyages to Quebec, distant over a thousand miles by water, to report to his superior-general."[72]

Writing in 1976, Walt Harris parrots this view when he comments on Jacques Marquette's first winter at Chequamegon Bay:

> Like Allouez, this 32-year-old Jesuit found the Chippewas, Ottawas, Hurons and other half-starved Indian malcontents unfriendly and aloof. That winter he had no white man and no halfbreed with him. However, he understood the Algonquin and Huron languages. Agriculture was unknown here. So was the cow, the chicken and the horse. The only liquid was water, but it was crystal clear, tasty and fresh. Ever present for the faithful agent of God was the constant threat of scurvy, dysentery and scabies. In zero and subzero weather, also, life in a hut of pine, balsam and maple branches was such that draft was a hazard along with smoke from a wood fire at night. Pneumonia was a death sentence. There was no medicine to ease pain, and the faking medicine man, if in the vicinity, could do no speck of good.[73]

This colorful quotation shows that even as late as 1976, we find a writer with little apparent positive sensitivity to cultural differences as evinced in the seventeenth century in western Lake Superior. Harris ignored the reports by Claude Allouez of the Odawa and Huron corn fields in the bay, and he seemingly was unaware of Marquette's comments on the warm and friendly reception the Huron gave him upon his arrival. His derogatory remarks about Ojibwe medical practitioners are also telling, and it is informative that while other writers of Harris's time were saying the Ojibwe were not present in the bay during Marquette's stay, he claims the "Chippewas" *were* residing there. Finally, Walt Harris erroneously stated that Marquette came to Chequamegon without the company of another Frenchman. The image of the solitary white man laboring in the *savage* wilderness, *alone*, that Harris constructs for Jacques Marquette and his time at Chequamegon Bay fits well the notion of *the heroic age* of early European exploration in North America.[74]

While Jacques Marquette was in Chequamegon, the Huron and Odawa were headquartering in the area. Except for his success with the Huron and the Kiskakon band of the Odawa, Marquette struggled to bring his religion to the others. In a letter to his superiors in Quebec, he said this about these other tribesmen: "[They are] very far from the Kingdom of God . . . They turn prayer to ridicule, and scarcely will they hear us talk of Christianity; they are proud, and without intelligence."[75]

When Marquette hurried to Chequamegon Bay in the late fall of 1669, he left Sault Ste. Marie with the understanding he would be staying at the far western mission for only one year. His superiors had told him that in 1670, he was to leave Chequamegon and go to the southern land of the Illinois where he was to open a new mission. This intent to go to the Illinois is particularly important in understanding Marquette's brief time at Chequamegon Bay. Writers have left us with the image of Marquette's work at the bay being abruptly interrupted by military attacks of the Dakota, but the written record shows that from the time of his first coming, this priest was under orders to stay at Chequamegon no longer than a single year. Parties of Illinois came to Chequamegon Bay to trade, and as was the case with Claude Allouez and the Potawatomi, Jacques Marquette was drawn to these southern people by their cordial demeanor. Marquette had this to say about the Illinois:

> The Illinois are warriors and take a great many Slaves, whom they trade with the Outaouaks for Muskets, Powder, Kettles, Hatchets and Knives. They were formerly at war with the Nadouessi [Dakota], but made peace with them some years ago, which I confirmed, in order to facilitate their coming to la Pointe,—where I am going to await them, that I may accompany them into their Country.[76]

What also increased the priest's interest in the new southern lands was that sometime after Marquette's arrival at the bay, a Kiskakon man gave him an Illinois youth who had been a slave, and through the balance of 1669 and into the early months of 1670, this young man told Marquette of his southern homeland and the great river found there. Then, only several months later—probably on 8 May—Fr. Marquette was back on the water, returning to Sault Ste. Marie.[77] Upon arrival, however, he did not immediately depart for his new station in Illinois country. Instead, he remained at Sault Ste. Marie through the summer of that year, where like the other Jesuits, he was caught up in the pressing matter of political unrest along Lake Superior's southern shore.

Due to the reduced threat of the Iroquois, some Odawa and Huron tribesmen were beginning to migrate from the western region of the lake back to their eastern homelands, and the Jesuits hoped to encourage these people to establish bases close to The Sault in order to facilitate attempts at religious conversion. However, some of Chequamegon's residents were not interested in returning to the eastern end of the lake. Instead, they contemplated going to war against the Dakota, perhaps as part of the lingering conflict caused by the earlier instances of cannibalism we have already discussed, but most likely there was a more encompassing reason. This was the growing problem of the relationship between the tribesmen and the French.

By this time—the late 1660s—this relationship was showing signs of stress. For years most of the contacts between the tribesmen and the French occurred at the annual trade fairs held in Montreal, where, even though they were carried out in a major French city, the Europeans conducted themselves within an *Algonquian* model of exchange. This involved ample amounts of ritual and ceremony, including obligatory gift-giving within a "familial" setting—we will discuss this below—and as stressed by the historian, Richard White, this setting was of utmost importance to the tribal people. At first these Montreal trading fairs worked well, but as the decade of the 1660s passed, things began to deteriorate and incidents of conflict erupted.[78]

Part of the reason for this downturn in relations was that individual French traders began to make the long trips out to the tribal communities where they "transferred the site of exchange" from Montreal, with its overriding control of French officialdom, to the freer context of tribal villages. These individual traders, and their unlicensed counterparts, (the famous *coureurs de bois*) penetrated the western lakes regions, and by the 1660s, in some instances, as we noted with the Potawatomi and their interest in Claude Allouez, there were growing complaints about the poor behavior of the French. Desiring to increase their profits, these independent traders demanded more furs for their merchandise, and in some cases because of "cupidity" and simple "greed," caused adverse reactions from the tribesmen. These reactions sometimes involved physical conflict, and of course, such incidents threatened the overall seasonal patterns of trade, something the Montreal fur merchants became concerned about.[79]

Thus, by the time Jacques Marquette came to Lake Superior this overriding matter of the relationship between the French and the western tribal communities was a point of concern. Drawing upon the written documents of the time, Joseph Donnelly discusses this problem and reconstructs an imaginary, but still important, scene wherein some western tribes were debating whether or not the French, with their troublesome traders, might become as serious a threat as the Dakota, and that perhaps instead of moving east, "into the clutches of the scheming French," the people should stand firm against the Dakota, even to the point of undertaking military excursions into their country.[80]

Due to this potentially volatile political climate, in the late fall of 1670 Fr. Marquette left Sault Ste. Marie, not for the lands of the Illinois as he and his superiors had planned, but to paddle back to Chequamegon Bay. There he tried to convince the Huron and Odawa still residing there not to attack the Dakota, but to come back with him to the eastern part of the lake where it was hoped they would settle at the new Jesuit site at St. Ignace.[81] From all indications the fall and winter of 1670-71 were uneasy times at Chequamegon Bay.

We do not know for certain what occurred at the bay during these last months of Jacques Marquette's stay, but it is likely that after what had to have been an uncomfortable winter, his final departure took place sometime in the late spring of 1671, and although he left, it seems certain that some unidentified Algonquians, and others, stayed.[82] Perhaps some of the most familiar remarks about this exodus were written by Reuben Thwaites, who declared that a year previous to Marquette's departure, "the Huron and Ottawas of Chequamegon Bay foolishly incurred the fresh hostility of the Sioux and the following year *were driven eastward like Autumn leaves before a blast.*"[83] In Thwaites' colorful metaphor, the blast, of course, was a Dakota war party.

However, the details of Marquette's departure from Chequamegon are unclear. We simply do not know exactly what happened. While it is suggested his leaving was due to the fears of the westerly Dakota, the descriptions of the actual circumstances leading to the Jesuits' abandonment of the bay are uncertain. For example, Edmund Jefferson Danziger, Jr. says Marquette and his party left "when an intensification of the Sioux-*Chippewa* war drove the priests east to the Sault."[84] Danziger's remark, of course, is in error and not supported by the early literature of the time, since in these years the Saulteur and Dakota were trading partners, enjoying a peaceful alliance.

Hamilton Ross disagrees with Danziger. When speaking to the difficulty Marquette experienced in his attempts to Christianize the people at Chequamegon Bay he says, "either he or the nearby villages had, in some manner, incurred the enmity of the Sioux who by their continuous raids, disrupted his labors. Marquette left the mission in 1671 and probably in that same year the Sioux forced the natives of the two villages to abandon them and to retreat eastward."[85]

We see that Danziger mistakenly uses the familiar image of a long-standing enmity between the Ojibwe and Dakota as the reason for the departure, and while Hamilton Ross more correctly attributes the exodus to troubles brought about by the Huron and Odawa instead of the Ojibwe, both these writers turn to the popular history image of tribal warfare for their explanations.

This, however, does not adequately explain what was occurring during the winter of 1670-71, when Jacques Marquette was struggling to convince the Huron and Odawa to put down their weapons and join him in the long paddle back to Sault Ste. Marie. To better understand the event we should place Marquette's situation within the wider political context of the western Great Lakes at the time.

When Jacques Marquette first arrived at Sault Ste. Marie changes in the focus of the western fur trade were underway. North American French leadership desired to gain a greater share of the trade for their own private wealth, and to this end it was hoped to bypass the Odawa, Ojibwe, Iroquois and other middlemen so the bulk of western furs would not be taken to the private merchants at Montreal, but to the new Fort Frontenac on Lake Ontario. This initiative was part of the emerging French interest in more southerly lands, a gesture that saw La Salle being sent south where his understudy—Henri de Tonty—oversaw the construction of another new fort, this time in Illinois country—a trading station meant to draw furs from more northerly tribal traders. Thus, during Marquette's time on Lake Superior the thrust of the trade was shifting somewhat from Chequamegon Bay back to Sault Ste. Marie, Mackinac, and Green Bay, and this commercial shift was a factor behind the eastward movements of western Algonquians that Marquette met when he first arrived at The Sault.[86]

As we noted, when Marquette initially came to Lake Superior the Iroquois threat had just subsided somewhat allowing western Lake Superior people to migrate back to their eastern homelands, and the Jesuits were trying to influence this relocation by having some of these people settle at sites near Sault Ste. Marie. At the same time the matter of the eroding relationship with French traders was growing more serious, along with hostile contacts with the Dakota, resulting in a dilemma: should the people move back east, where the Jesuits might serve as protectors, or at least powerful advocates, even though by making this move the people would be closer to the Iroquois and troublesome French? Or should they stand firm and strike back at the Dakota, possibly exacerbating the situation on their western boundaries even further? It is in this sense that in the late seventeenth century at Chequamegon Bay, the Huron and Odawa were in a *betwixt and between* situation.

The *Jesuit Relations* show us that sometime after his arrival at the Mission of St. Esprit, likely in the spring of 1670 before he departed for The Sault, Jacques Marquette wrote a report to his Jesuit superior. (The *present* he refers to was a few Christian missionary pictures of some sort included with a request that the Dakota consider letting him tell them about his religion.) Referring to the Dakota, he said:

> I sent them a present by the Interpreter, with a message that they must show due recognition to the Frenchman wherever they met him, and not kill him or the Savages accompanying him; that the Black Gown wished to proceed into the country of the Assinipouars [Assiniboines], and into that of the Kalistinaux (Cree]; that he was already among the Outagamis [Mesquakie]; and that I should set out this Autumn to go to the Ilinois [Illinois], the passage to whom they were to leave free. To this they consented; but, as for my present, they were waiting until all their people would have come back from the chase; and that they would be at la Pointe this Autumn, to hold council with the Ilinois and talk with me.[87]

Reuben Thwaites claims the Dakota returned the pictures Marquette sent them, "and then declared a general war against the people of La Pointe" and that "It was thought impossible in this fateful spring of 1671, for the La Pointe savages, who had been the aggressors, to overcome the threatened onslaught of the indignant Sioux" and that "A retreat was decided upon."[88] This picture of Fr. Marquette hurrying to flee the Dakota has stayed in the account found in the popular history of the event.

Whether or not the Dakota, as claimed by Thwaites, "declared a general war against the people of La Pointe" is uncertain, because it seems unlikely that in 1671 they intended to attack *all* tribesmen who were residing in the vicinity of La Pointe, or at least periodically coming to the bay. Instead of this declaration of a *general war* against all La Pointe people, if the Dakota made any declaration to go to war at all, it is more likely they expressed their intent to attack the Huron—"the aggressors" Thwaites mentioned—instead of everyone who used the bay, because at the time the Dakota were enjoying a trading relationship with some of these people (the Saulteurs).

However this may have been, Marquette's letter mentioned above shows a side to the seventeenth century presence of the Dakota in Chequamegon Bay that we rarely see offered in the literature. Jacques Marquette claimed the Dakota "never attack until they have been attacked," and that they "keep their word inviolate,"[89] characteristics not usually associated with these people by later writers of the history of Chequamegon Bay. We know delegations of Dakota were peacefully visiting the bay during the time of Claude Allouez, and in 1670, we see that they agreed to come—again in peace—to parlay with the Illinois and the Jesuits. We saw this peaceful image of the Dakota in their contacts with Radisson and Groseilliers about a decade previous when they partook in the Feast of the Dead, and later when they traded in their own country with these two

Frenchmen and the Ojibwe, but it is far different from the militaristic description of the Dakota the literature gives us in the early decades of the *eighteenth* century, and in later historical accounts like those of Reuben Thwaites.

We know Jacques Marquette left Chequamegon Bay in the spring of 1671, never to return, and that he likely was in the company of some Huron and Odawa who had agreed to migrate to Sault Ste. Marie, St. Ignace, or other eastern sites.[90] We also know that the Jesuits planned Marquette's departure two or more years previous, and while the fear of strife with the Dakota was apparently a factor in the 1671 move, it likely was not the prime cause, nor was the move brought about, as popular history tells, by Dakota-*Ojibwe* warfare. Marquette's often-noted departure from Chequamegon Bay must be understood as part of the larger scene, wherein French authorities maneuvered for a greater share of personal wealth from the lucrative fur trade, not simply as Reuben Thwaites felt, a fearful response to Dakota raiding parties.

Jacques Marquette left no specific mention of any Saulteur presence in Chequamegon Bay, although we must remember that he was in the bay for less than two years, and most importantly, he was there only during late fall to early spring, a time when foraging communities like the Ojibwe were usually in, on their way to, or returning from, their winter hunting territories. In the mid-1600s, the Saulteurs were a foraging society that may have done a minimum of gardening. Their culture was composed of mobile autonomous bands, and even at Sault Ste. Marie, where the fall run of whitefish offered an apparent plethora of food, when this harvest was completed they broke camp and repaired to the adjacent forests for their winter hunting. This was, more or less, the case all along the southern shore of Lake Superior from The Sault to Chequamegon Bay, and later to the mouth of the St Louis River, a site the French would name Fond du Lac. For a few summer months some of these bands periodically clustered at lakeside sites, but the *Jesuit Relations* and related literature shows at such times Jacques Marquette was not in the western parts of the lake, having returned to Sault Ste, Marie, or other points further east. Except for the gatherings at The Sault—gatherings that he spoke to in 1668, when he initially came to Lake Superior—he would not have witnessed these larger congregations of the Saulteurs. Therefore, we should not expect that Fr. Marquette's writings would hold extensive information about the Saulteur at Chequamegon Bay.

In the next chapter we will discuss what other historical evidence exists for an Ojibwe presence in western Lake Superior in the seventeenth century. In these years the fur trade continued and the Ojibwe and French were both deeply involved.

*Notes*

1. Donnelly 1985:73.
2. Donnelly 1985:75.
3. Donnelly 1985:73.
4. Gara 1962:22-3.
5. *Jesuit Relations* 52:201-207.
6. Ross 1960:31.
7. Donnelly 1985:104-105, 122.
8. Hickerson 1970:61.
9. Kugel 1998:12; Weslager 1991[1972]:237.
10. *Jesuit Relations* 51:53.
11. *Jesuit Relations* 54:193.
12. Tinker 1993.
13. Gara 1962:22-3; Danziger 1979:30; Kellogg 1968[1925]: 177-178.
14. Ross 1960:30.
15. *Jesuit Relations* 52:203-204; Kellogg 1968[1925]:146-152.
16. Donnelly 1985:135-36; Ross 1960:29; Larson 2005:45.
17. Harris 1976:20-21; Holtzheuter 1974:16-17.
18. Danziger 1976: 29-30.
19. *Jesuit Relations* 46:81.
20. *Jesuit Relations* 45:219.
21. Ross 1960:28.
22. *Jesuit Relations* 46:141.
23. *Jesuit Relations* 45:233-235.
24. *Jesuit Relations* 46:139-141, brackets added.
25. *Jesuit Relations* 46:141, brackets added.
26. Danziger 1979:29.
27. Ross 1960:28.
28. Brown and Peers 1988:137.
29. Henry as quoted in Nute, *The Voyaguers Highway*, page 24.
30. Donnelly 1985:119.
31. Donnelly 1985:119-120; Ely 2012:51, 96, 114.
32. Ross 1960:30.
33. Donnelly 1985:136.
34. Donnelly 1985:129-30, 137.
35. Trigger 1985.
36. Ross 1960:30.
37. *Jesuit Relations* 51:285, italics added.
38. Loew 2001:57.
39. *Jesuit Relations* 51:285.
40. Smith 1995:98.
41. Donnelly 1985:125.
42. Busch 2008:38.
43. Ross 1960:31.
44. Donnelly 1985:107.
45. Donnelly 1885:115.
46. *Jesuit Relations* 59:131; Donnelly 1985:117.
47. Donnelly 1885:118.
48. Kellogg1925:153; Ross1960:31; Donnelly 1985:108-112.
49. Donnelly 1985:136.
50. *Jesuit Relations* 52:205, 207; Donnelly 1985:122-123.
51. *Jesuit Relations* 51:21.
52. Donnelly 1985:141.
53. Donnelly 1985:180.
54. Ross 1960:31.
55. Donnelly1985:122-23, 142.
56. *Jesuit Relations* 52:199.
57. *Jesuit Relations* 54:197.
58. *Jesuit Relations* 52:197-199; Donnelly 1985:124-126.
59. *Jesuit Relations* 51:Ch.XIII; italics added.
60. Verwyst 1895:440.
61. *Jesuit Relations* 54:133.
62. Graham 1995:11-22.
63. *Jesuit Relations* 54:165.
64. *Jesuit Relations* 58:259.
65. Donnelly 1885:116-117; Smith 1985[1973]:26.
66. Donnelly 1985:121.
67. Donnelly 1985:118-119.
68. Donnelly 1985:172.
69. *Jesuit Relations* 58:261.

70. *Jesuit Relations* 54:169.
71. Donnelly 1985:160.
72. Thwaites 1925:72.
73. Harris 1976:24.
74. Trigger 1985:5-7.
75. Thwaites 1925:74.
76. *Jesuit Relations* 54:173; brackets added.
77. Donnelly 1985:147-151.
78. White 1991:108.
79. White 1991:109-110.
80. Donnelly 1985:161-167.
81. Donnelly 1985:158:159.
82. *Jesuit Relations* 52:199; Donnelly 1985:170.
83. Thwaites 1896:33; italics added.
84. Danziger 1979:30; italics added.
85. Ross 1960:32.
86. Smith 1985[1973]:33-35.
87. *Jesuit Relations* 54:193; brackets added.
88. Thwaites 1916[1902]:89-91.
89. *Jesuit Relations* 54:191.
90. Ross 1960:32; Donnelly 1985:169-170; Busch 2008:38-40.

# 5

# Events and Issues Closing Out the Seventeenth Century at Chequamegon Bay

### *Other Voices and Views*

1.

ASIDE OF DAKOTA-SAULTEUR RELATIONS pertinent to our better understanding of the Jesuits' 1671 abandonment of Chequamegon Bay is found in Bacqueville De La Potherie's writings about the early allies of France in North America. La Potherie was using portions of Nicholas Perrot's memoir that tell of an early Saulteur presence at Chequamegon Bay. However, as is true of most of Perrot's memoir, because he offers few dates we struggle to determine the exact time of this presence, but as Richard White noted, by contextualizing Perrot's information, we might better place his writings in their proper historical periods.[1]

In a long quotation La Potherie discussed how in his memoir, Perrot said the Saulteur used the whitefish at Sault Ste. Marie, but that:

> This [Saulteur] tribe is divided: part of them have remained at home to live on this delicious fish in autumn, and they seek their food in Lake Huron during the winter; the others have gone away to two localities on Lake Superior, in order to live on the game which is very abundant there. Those who left their natal soil made an alliance with the Nadouaissioux, who were not very solicitous for the friendship of any one whomsoever; but because they could obtain French merchandise only through the agency of the Saulteurs, they made a treaty of peace with the latter by which they were mutually bound to give their daughters in marriage on both sides. That was a strong bond for the maintenance of entire harmony.
>
> The Nadouaissioux, who have their village on the upper Mississippi about the latitude of 46°, divided their territory and their hunting-grounds with the Saulteurs. The abundance of beaver and deer made the latter gradually forget their native land. They spent the winter in the woods to carry on their hunting; and in the spring they visit Lake Superior, on the shore of which they plant corn and squashes. There they spend the summer in great peace, without being disturbed by any neighbor, although the Nadouaissioux are at war with the people of the north [Cree]. The Saulteurs are neutral; and the tribe that goes to war always takes care beforehand that there is not Saulteur [involved in it]. Their harvest being gathered, they return to their hunting-grounds.[2]

We might think that the Dakota-Ojibwe peace La Potherie was speaking of was the familiar agreement arranged by Duluth in 1679, but we recall the 1662 alliance Radisson and Groseilliers were part of between these tribes that was made in the Feast of the Dead. If our understanding of Dakota-Ojibwe trading relations preceding the Radisson and Groseilliers expedition into Dakota lands we discussed above is correct, as well as including Hughes Raudin's peace mission into the western Lake Superior region after the 1674 incident at The Sault (we will discuss this below), then there were at least three incidents of Dakota-Ojibwe-French peace agreements occurring *before* Duluth's well-known alliance, and therefore, La Potherie's remarks could be referring to any of them.

Harold Hickerson used this La Potherie quotation to support his contention that the two western Ojibwe communities (Keweenaw and Chequamegon Bay) it mentions were formed only after the Duluth peace of 1679-80, but this denies the importance of these earlier alliances.[3] We have shown that Ojibwe bands were using, if not actually residing in, the western Lake Superior region decades before Duluth's 1679-80 peace agreement, and that these earlier agreements also included marriages between the two tribes, and doubtlessly, as La Potherie said, these marriages caused "a strong bond for the maintenance of entire harmony."

Another point of interest raised by this long quotation is that La Potherie correctly noted how the Ojibwe spent summers at Chequamegon Bay, but they dispersed into small kin groups for their winters spent elsewhere, presumably in the bay's wooded environs. It is important to recall that in the seventeenth century this foraging movement was at the heart of Ojibwe culture and its existence is *a priori* in any consideration of early Ojibwe life on Lake Superior. Even after the advent of the fur trade, this seasonal adaptation was ongoing right up into the nineteenth century during the treaty-making years, and for some groups, into the latter decades of that century.

By now we are familiar with the trading role of the Ojibwe in the mid-seventeenth century, and also with the importance of marriages regularly made to help solidify alliances.

Even allowing for its serious deficiency in dates, we can see that La Potherie's quotation resonates with the notion that by 1671, the Saulteur not only may have been seasonally residing in the area of Chequamegon Bay, but that at the time, they and the Dakota were enjoying a *peaceful* relationship, and thus, when the Huron, Odawa, and the Jesuits made their departure, the Saulteur had no pressing reason to leave with them.

Except for a few of Jacques Marquette's comments about his early time at Sault Ste. Marie, the *Jesuit Relations* writers tell us little about efforts to convert the Saulteur. Sometime after arriving at The Sault in 1668, when Marquette spoke of his attempts at religious conversion, he wrote that "the harvest . . . is very abundant," but his superiors were skeptical of the sincerity of these conversions, and decided the priests should focus their energies on working at giving instructions instead of rushing into baptisms, and only "baptizing the dying, who are a surer harvest."[4] Similarly, in a quote given above, we saw how Claude Allouez claimed he baptized some children and an aged, very ill man when he traveled with a band of Saulteurs at the head of Lake Superior. We learned that this man died soon after baptism, and Allouez remarked that he was the first of the Saulteurs "to enter heaven." We never learn, even at Sault Ste. Marie, where the Jesuits desired to convert these people so they would have a direct influence on the several other tribes that regularly came to the region, that the Saulteurs converted in any great numbers, and it is apparent that in their several years on Lake Superior the Jesuits had practically no success in converting these people. Thus, we might conclude that in 1671, when Jacques Marquette left Chequamegon, any Saulteurs residing in the area essentially were not Christians, and therefore, would not have had a religious motive for leaving with him.

## 2.

AT ABOUT THE TIME OF MARQUETTE'S final departure from Chequamegon Bay, a major event was occurring at The Sault. Nicholas Perrot says Jacques Marquette arrived from the bay in time to be part of it, and that he signed a document as a witness, but it seems due to all that was involved in his departure from Chequamegon that he was delayed, and was not present for the ceremony.[5] The event took place on 14 June 1671, and had to have been an elaborate affair in which a representative of the French monarch laid claim to the surrounding lands, including—as a written version of the proceedings phrased it—"all countries discovered or to be discovered between the Northern, Western, and Southern Seas."[6]

The stated reason for this claim of territory was to locate and acquire the copper Fr. Claude Allouez reported to have seen when first coming to Lake Superior, as well as any other minerals the French could find, although it is likely the underlying motive was to acquire these lands before the British claimed them. In time, Nicholas Perrot held a similar ceremony at Lake Pepin on the Mississippi River, Duluth held another west of Lake Superior at the Dakota community at Mille Lacs Lake, and La Salle held a third at the mouth of the Mississippi River.[7] Jean Talon, the intendant of New France, initiated preparations at Sault Ste. Marie, and appointed Sieur de St. Lusson to officiate. Runners were sent out to notify tribal leaders to assemble on the scheduled date, and fourteen nations sent delegates.

Both Nicholas Perrot and the *Jesuit Relations* writers give us a description of this event, a ceremony filled with the requisite pomp and ritual of the times.[8] Perrot was involved in the gathering's organization and execution from the onset, and Claude Allouez was called upon to give a testimonial to its legitimacy. At the event's beginning, a Christian cross was positioned on a hilltop near the rapids at The Sault, both the King's and a Christian standard were raised beside it, and the throng of onlookers gathered around. A cedar pole was set into the earth nearby with a French escutcheon attached. Then, religious and patriotic songs were sung, followed by shouts of "Long live the King," before the loud reports of several muskets added their martial approval. Only after a long and purposeful spate of silence flooded the site did Fr. Allouez rise to sanction the event, and with his spiritual presence he praised the king and told the tribesmen they were submitting to the control of the French sovereign. Finally, de St. Lusson rose to officially take charge of the lands. Several of the French men who were in attendance signed a document testifying to what had transpired, and at the end of the day a bonfire was lighted and Christian hymns were sung.

We are left to imagine the preparations for this colorful bit of seventeenth century pageantry. Certainly the tribal representatives who came to the event did not travel alone. Their contingents must have been lodged in a nearby encampment and it is likely that French authorities made arrangements for the proper reception and hosting of such a large body, including the matter of providing a few days food for the entire congregation.

William Warren claimed informants at La Pointe told him that in 1670, "a messenger of the 'Great French King' visited their village at Shag-a-waum-ik-ong [Chequamegon], and invited them to a grand council of different tribes to be held at Sault Ste. Marie" in spring of the next year. Writing approximately two hundred years after the ceremony, Warren went on to say, "Some of the words of his messenger are still recollected and minutely related by the Ojibways." He said a group from La Pointe attended the ceremony, and that "*Ke-che-ne-zuh-yauh*, head chief of the Crane family, headed this party, and represented the nation of the Ojibways."[9] (Interestingly, Warren also said the early La Pointe patriarch, Michel Cadotte, told him that "his great-grandfather, a Mons. Cadeau, on this occasion first came into the Ojibway country in the train of the French envoy Sieur du Lusson."[10]

Warren's statement of the involvement of the Ojibwe from La Pointe in the Sault Ste. Marie ceremony supports the contention that at least one band of the Saulteur were residing in, or regularly frequenting, the region of Chequamegon Bay in 1670-71, and it corroborates the words of Nicholas Perrot that tell of Ojibwe people being in this location during the bulk of the 1660s. It also lends credence to the suggestion, made above, that the literature holds a historical line of evidence for the existence of a band, or bands, of Saulteur people living in the area of Chequamegon Bay at least from the time of Radisson and Groseilliers up through the Jesuits' years. The long quote of La Potherie, given just above, fits this conclusion well, and disagrees with the contention of Thwaites, and more recent writers, that Chequameon Bay was abandoned when Marquette departed in 1671.

Although the Jesuits departed, we should conclude that *the French* and some tribesmen did not cease using Chequamegn Bay in that year.[11] Despite any problem with the Dakota, it was still a rich and strategic region for securing beaver pelts, and the Europeans desired to go on benefiting from this harvest. Certainly, French traders continued to visit at times of the spring rendezvous, or when passing through to go inland to native villages. The words of William Warren and La Potherie (and Nicholas Perrot) support this presence.

3.

AT THIS POINT WE MIGHT PAUSE to ponder the effect the seventeenth century Jesuits had on the tribal people of Chequamegon Bay. As we already noted, some writers feel the priests were not successful in bringing their religion to these people, and taken overall, these writers seem to be correct. In this regard, some relevant remarks about the difficulty the Jesuits had in their attempts to win converts at La Pointe were made by Claude Dablon in the *Relation* of 1668-69. The Wisconsin historian, Reuben Thwaites, writing in 1899, translated Dablon's French into English, and in this translation, Thwaites gives the following about these problems:

> Dissimulation, which is natural to those Savages, and a certain spirit of acquiescence, in which the children in that country are brought up, make them assent to all that is told them; and prevent them from ever showing any opposition to the sentiments of others, even though they may know that what is said to them is not true. To this dissimulation must be added stubbornness and obstinacy in following their own thoughts and wishes; this has obliged our Fathers not to admit adults so easily to Baptism,—they being, moreover, brought up in idolatry and licentiousness.[12]

This quotation is an articulate example of what the Jesuits, and from the opposing stance, the tribal people, were confronting. What the Jesuits saw as *dissimulation*, (the propensity to feign, or pretend), and *acquiescence* (to passively comply without showing agreement or dissent) can be understood as an adaptive behavioral mechanism employed by the tribesmen in settings where the French Jesuits demanded compliance. In tribal culture, where an outward show of respect for the other is paramount, we can envision the scene wherein a Jesuit, after explaining his religious notions to a tribesman—and the tribesman neither nodding assent nor dissent, but silently seeming to accept what is being said—later witnesses the tribesman ignoring what he had just been told. Nicholas Perrot seems to have been referring to this characteristic when he said, "The savage's mind is difficult to understand. He speaks in one way, thinks in another."[13]

La Potherie, drawing upon the memoir of Nicholas Perrot, remarked about these characteristics when he wrote: "The savages are sufficiently politic not to seem to distrust one another; and in regard to news that is announced to them they always suspend their opinions, without letting it appear that often they think the informant is not telling the truth."[14]

As we will see below, over a century after the Jesuits' time in Chequamegon this propensity for "dissimulation and a certain spirit of acquiescence," as Father Dablon (and Reuben Thwaites) phrased it, was witnessed in the early days of the coming of the Americans to Lake Superior country, but in time—when making land-cession treaties, for example—this outwardly respectful behavior could turn to open anger when tribal leaders recognized obvious duplicity on the part of the Americans.

4.

THE HISTORIAN EDMUND JEFFERSON DANZIGER, JR. argues that the Jesuits did not work to introduce "civilization" to the tribes because these Frenchmen felt the policies of civilization and assimilation "always seemed to lead to debauchery with liquor and white men's vices and to exploitation by unscrupulous traders." Instead, Danziger claims, "Simply stated, the goals of the blackrobes in the Northwest were to preserve the pine forests and native inhabitants in their rustic seventeenth-century state and to Christianize the Indians." Danziger goes on to say: "Jesuits therefore did not introduce red men to the French language, French customs, French habits, or to Frenchmen (including *coureurs de bois*—and commandants), except for themselves, of course whom they regarded as the eventual supreme authorities on the upper Great Lakes."[15]

Danziger's view is an oversimplification of what was finally involved in the seventeenth century contacts between the tribal people and the French Jesuits. When Claude Allouez admonished the Odawa to cease taking multiple spouses, or to stop making sacrificial offerings to the *manidoog*, and even to cease going into Dakota territories for the purpose of acquiring war trophies, he was insisting they give up some of their most important customs and adopt *his*. Like the other Jesuits, Allouez was working to bring important aspects of French culture as it existed at the time to these tribesmen. The historian David R. M. Beck was speaking of the seventeenth century Jesuits working among the Menominee, the Ojibwes' neighbor to the south, when he said one of the reasons the Jesuits were in Menominee territory was the advancement of French culture, but he could have said the same for the seventeenth-century Jesuits working amidst the residents of Chequamegon Bay.[16]

The argument that the Jesuits did not attempt to introduce French customs in Lake Superior's communities is specious, since, as we already pointed out, religions can never be meaningfully separated from their overall cultural context, and therefore, although we might associate the Jesuits' efforts primarily with the notion of bringing the religious ideology of Christianity to the people, in the final analysis, they were working to destroy an existing cultural system and replace it with their own.[17]

It is true, however, that the Jesuits did not work to quickly and completely change the way of life for the tribesmen, as was the case over a century later with the coming of Protestant missionaries, but we are naïve if we feel the Jesuits did not work to bring important aspects of French culture to Lake Superior. Perhaps the most basic change the priests hoped for was for the tribesmen to cease their seasonal migrations and to settle at one location all year long.[18] As was witnessed with the coming of the reservation system in the middle of the nineteenth century, this change forced major changes throughout the rest of tribal life.

Marquette's 1671 departure ended the seventeenth century Jesuits' attempts at Christian conversion in Chequamegon Bay. The priests withdrew and the bay was not to see a permanent mission effort until the 1830s, when the first Protestant missionaries arrived. The Catholic faith was not brought back until 1835, with the arrival of missionary Frederic Baraga. Thus, we see that from 1671 to 1835, a period of 164 years, Catholic missionaries were not in Chequamegon Bay.

5.

THE 1671 ABANDONMENT OF THE MISSION of St. Esprit at Chequamegon disrupted the Jesuits' plans to enter lands west and north of the bay and to go on in search of the famed Northwest Passage. Then in 1674, only three years after the abandonment, and the land-claiming ceremony at Sault Ste. Marie, a serious altercation occurred at The Sault that further delayed all such plans. This confrontation was initiated when a band of warriors from Sault Ste. Marie—it seems certain they were Huron, Odawa, or both—traveled into lands west of Chequamegon Bay and captured eighty Dakota persons. We recall that at this date there were Huron and Odawa bands from Chequamegon that had moved to the area of Sault Ste. Marie eager to attack the Dakota. When telling of this capture, even though the *Relations* writers say only that "a band of warriors from Ste. Marie du Sault, having surprised them [the Dakota] in their country and taken eighty of them prisoner"[19], Theresa Schenck concludes that these prisoners were captured by a group of *Saulteurs* who had gone into the western lands to hunt, since at the time they were using the area in common with the Dakota, as Nicholas Perrot told us they were doing.[20]

Schenck's conclusion about what tribe captured the eighty Dakota seems at odds with what the historical record tells us about the state of relations between the Dakota, Cree, and Saulteurs in 1674. Schenck opines that the Saulteurs captured the Dakota because the Saulteurs were allies with the Cree, and because the Dakota were at war with these northern people, the Saulteurs were compelled to support these northern allies. However, we recall that at that same time the Saulteurs were allied with the Dakota—witness their ability, as Schenck admits, to share a common hunting territory—and thus, we must ask why in 1674 the Saulteurs favored one ally over another. Just as importantly, we recall that at the time, the Saulteurs were serving as middlemen in the trade between the Dakota and the French, and the Saulteurs desired to continue benefiting from this important relationship. Therefore, it seems more likely that the eighty Dakota were captured by Hurons, Odawa, or both, who at the time were residing at the eastern end of the lake, if not at, then at least in the proximity of The Sault, and clearly were in a state of conflict with these westerners.

At the time of their capture, the Dakota sued for peace, agreeing to send ten of their people back to Sault Ste. Marie, along with a female slave, for negotiations. However, soon after paddling to The Sault and before any parley could commence, a band of Cree arrived and since these people were still at war with the Dakota, one of them assaulted a Dakota warrior, resulting in a general melee. A report claims that in this fight several Dakota were quickly killed, but that two fled to the nearby Jesuits' house where they took refuge, and finding arms inside, began firing at their adversaries. In this fracas, the slave escaped, but Louis Boehme—Fr. Marquette's earlier assistant—who was by then "the armorer and blacksmith of the mission" allowed a canon to be fired at the house, an act that killed the remaining Dakota and started a serious fire, causing the destruction of important mission and trading center structures. Along with the Dakota, at least twenty others died in this fight and resulting conflagration, among them being some Huron, Odawa and some Saulteurs. These latter (the Saulteurs), the *Relations* writers say, were "*inadvertently*" caught up in the unfortunate struggle, a significant comment. We are not told however, that the Huron and Odawa deaths, were *inadvertent*, thus, we can only conclude that these two tribes were implicated in this altercation from the very beginning, i.e., that they were involved in the original capture of the Dakota.

The Jesuits were greatly shocked by this tragedy and at a temporary loss as to what could be done to correct things.[21] Given the fear that this incident might seriously disrupt the peaceful relations the French were enjoying with the Dakota, and apparently fearing the Ojibwe might take action against these people for their loss, therein causing a disruption of the peace between them and the Dakota, Governor Frontenac took action. He had Louis Boehme sanctioned for allowing the canon to be fired—the act that began the disastrous fire—but Frontenac wanted to do more, so he sent Hughes Raudin, a Frenchman the literature refers to as his engineer, "to the extremity of the lake with presents to conciliate the Sioux and Ojibways."[22]

This incident of Governor Frontenac sending Hughes Raudin to western Lake Superior with presents for both the Dakota and Ojibwe, if mentioned at all, is given as a minor event in the history of relationships between the French, Dakota and Ojibwe in the late seventeenth century in western Lake Superior lands. At the time, the 1670s, France and England were competing for control over the western fur trade, and Frontenac was worried that the Sault Ste. Marie killings would lead to more strife, seriously harming the French cause. Unfortunately, the written documentation of Raudin's trip has not survived or has not yet surfaced, so writers do not have access to the details of his meetings with the two tribes.[23] It seems however, if Raudin had been unsuccessful in his attempts to appease these people, writers of the time would have made comment on this important turn of events. Also, if Raudin had failed in his mission and if the Saulteur had sought revenge for the deaths at The Sault, then the Dakota-Saulteur-French alliance might have been severely tested, if not actually broken, as Frontenac feared. But there is no record indicating such an important breach occurred. Thus, in the absence of any literature on the matter it appears Raudin was successful in meeting with both tribes and in carrying out Frontenac's goal of appeasement.

Raudin's was a peace-making trip, its function being to effect expiation rites. These are meant to cleanse a wrong committed between involved parties, and since in this case killings occurred, these rituals were meant, as was said in that time, "*to cover the graves of the dead.*" Expiation rites occur in a ceremonial setting in which goods (i.e., the presents Raudin took with him) are given to the aggrieved parties to symbolically compensate them for their losses. And in the instance of the Raudin trip, we should assume that pipe ceremonies were used to sanctify and solemnize the event. We should also understand that the "presents" transferred to the aggrieved in a rite of expiation are understood as symbols. This points to the aggrieved party's acceptance of the importance of the resolution of the potential breach in relationships the deaths could cause. By accepting the presents—hence, foregoing the undertaking of revenge killings—the aggrieved publicly acknowledge the importance of upholding the peaceful relationship, in this case, between the Dakota and the Ojibwe.

However the details of this may have been, the importance for us is that the trip of Hughes Raudin to western Lake Superior immediately after the 1674 Sault Ste. Marie fire and killings is another instance of the French making a peace agreement—an alliance—with both the Dakota and Ojibwe in the years prior to Duluth's more publicized 1679-80 alliances, and we are reminded that the Ojibwe and Dakota made a few such alliances in the two decades preceding the Duluth agreement. Furthermore, since Raudin is said to have traveled to "the extremity" of Lake Superior to meet with these tribes, it shows that in the years immediately following 1671, an Ojibwe community was situated in that far western location. This challenges Harold Hickerson's contention that the Ojibwe had no significant presence in western Lake Superior until after Duluth's 1679-80 alliance.

It is significant that *Relations* writers say the Saulteurs killed in 1674 at Sault Ste. Marie were unintended victims of an unfortunate altercation. The use of "inadvertently" here is important since it shows the Saulteurs were not causal players in the original capture of the eighty Dakota that precipitated it. They were *inadvertent* victims of the following melee, an act that was originally caused by Sault Ste. Marie residents other than the Ojibwe. The *Relations* writers say some Odawa and Huron were also killed at Sault Ste. Marie in 1674, but they do not say these individuals were unintentionally killed, thus we can conclude that unlike the Ojibwe, the Odawa and Huron may have been involved with the origination of this melee, that is, with the capture of the eighty Dakota. Given all this, it follows that in 1674, the Ojibwe were still at peace with both the Dakota and the Cree.

After this conflict the Jesuits moved their area headquarters to St. Ignace, although the Sault Ste. Marie mission continued to function until 1689, when it was moved to Michilimackinac.[24] It is unclear what happened with those Saulteurs residing in the Sault Ste. Marie region at the time of this 1674 incident, but it seems likely, due to the continuing largesse of whitefish at the site, and to the Saulteur's presence today, that they stayed in the area.

Generally, historians do not acknowledge any significant presence of the Saulteur people in the western portion of the lake, especially at Chequamegon Bay, until after Duluth's often-mentioned 1679-80 peace negotiations between the Dakota, Ojibwe and French. It is probable this is partially because of the nature of Ojibwe settlement patterns of the time. They had a mobile foraging society, and such systems were troublesome for Europeans of the day to witness or to accept as legitimate human systems worthy of mention except in a fleeting manner. This problem of perception will be discussed below.

### *The Problem of Tribal Settlement Patterns on Lake Superior's South Shore in the 1600s*

THE JESUIT LITERATURE ON THE EARLY tribal peoples of Lake Superior shows how these European priests were drawn to what they called large villages at Sault Ste. Marie and later at Chequamegon Bay. In the mid-seventeenth century each site was said to hold up to 2,000 individuals, with the Huron and Odawa example at Chequamegon being occupied nearly year-round by the Huron due to the presence of agriculture. The Sault Ste. Marie village was formed only in the summer months and into fall when whitefish ran the river's rapids. It is perhaps easy to envision these villages, with curls of blue smoke from wood fires lazily rising through exit holes in the roofs of their bark-and-mat lodges during the cold months, and lifting from outdoor cooking fires in the warm times.

The remarks of Claude Allouez that described what he saw when first coming to Chequamegon Bay in 1665 help capture this image. According to Allouez:

> It is a beautiful bay, at the head of which is situated the great Village of the Savages, who there cultivate fields of Indian corn and lead a settled life. They number eight hundred men bearing arms, but are gathered together from seven different nations, living in peace, mingled one with another . . . This large population made us prefer this place to all others for our usual abode that we might apply ourselves advantageously to the instruction of these infidels, build a chapel, and enter upon the functions of the Christian religion.[25]

Such sites of concentrated populations were sought out by the Jesuits since they made it possible for the priests to reach a greater number of persons with much less effort than would be the case in a community of smaller kin units widely dispersed over a resource area. The Jesuits also favored these large villages because these Frenchmen understood them more readily than they could the small, mobile, hunting and gathering bands.

Virtually the entirety of the Jesuit literature from Lake Superior concerns time spent within these large villages, the exceptions being the month Claude Allouez was with a Saulteur band at the head of the lake—discussed above—and perhaps when he paddled to Nipigon. The priests did not live with the tribesmen when they dispersed into smaller kin units during their long months of winter hunting, and thus we learn virtually nothing of life in these smaller dispersed communities. Jacques Marquette was at Chequamegon Bay in the wintertime, but at that time he was with the more sedentary Huron (and possibly some Odawa people) who wintered at that site.

For information on life as lived by dispersed small kin groups we must wait for writers in the nineteenth century—John Tanner, for example—who actually lived and traveled with such small hunting bands.[26] Until these later writers bring this literature to us, we have only the information from the large villages and the implications of this should concern us.

Fr. Allouez spoke of these smaller, mobile bands that periodically visited Chequamegon Bay, and in a telling quote, he commented on his understanding of the reasons for their coming: "These peoples' motive in repairing hither is partly to obtain food by fishing, and partly to transact their petty trading with one another, when they meet. But God's purpose was to facilitate the proclaiming of the gospel to *wandering and vagrant* tribes."[27]

This quotation epitomizes the Jesuits' understanding of these small, mobile band systems, and discloses the bias these Frenchmen held toward them. Such communities were perceived as "wandering and vagrant," i.e., as *roving*, and *unorganized* in their intent. In a word, they were seen as being *homeless*. Their "vagrancy" meant they had no *base*, no *settlement*. This is how the French perceived mobile hunting and gathering band systems in the seventeenth century, and our point of interest here is the effect this bias doubtless had on the production of history in the Lake Superior region, not only during the seventeenth century, but in following times as well.

The ready recognition of large villages at Sault Ste. Marie and Chequamegon Bay experienced by the Jesuits hindered any reasonable understanding of these smaller and less settled adaptations. This predisposition for focusing on large villages hampered their ability to register—to be cognitively receptive to—the adaptive settlement patterns of the foraging Saulteur bands that we saw existed to the west of The Sault in the mid-1600s. Although these smaller communities were periodically present at places like Chequamegon, they were far less significant, if not simply unappreciable to the Jesuits.

Basic to the major reason for this difficulty in recognizing these types of adaptations is the nature of their resource procurement structures. As we have been noting above, these were what anthropologists have called hunting and gathering cultures with a *foraging* adaptation, and the nature of foraging cultures is far different from that of more sedentary systems. Thus, these foraging peoples were not well understood in the seventeenth century, and sometimes even today Euro-American writers have difficulty in recognizing their sophistication. At base, this difference is primarily due to the nature of a foraging culture's economic system. Centuries ago such a system was deemed non-existent, and more recently, at least in the western world, a foraging culture and its accompanying economic system is often seen as *undeveloped*, i.e., as an anachronism that will eventually give way to "settled" adaptations such as those of agricultural communities with more concentrated population centers like villages, towns, and in the case of the most complex instances, even cities.

Today when states and foraging cultures must meet for political purposes, the relationship between these two types of communities is often labored.[28] For example, about recent negotiations concerning land-use issues between First Nations communities and the Canadian government, Hugh Brody says:

> Concessions are made to Indian leaders as long as they do not demand a recognition of the Indian economy. Pluralism is a North American ideal, but in practice it does not have room within it for a multiplicity of economic systems. Exotic languages do not get in the way of pipelines: hunting and trapping economies might . . . *The white man's inability or refusal even to see the existence of Indian economic systems is the one theme that threads its way through the story of the New World.*[29]

The fact that the Jesuits who came to Lake Superior in the mid-1600s were unable to recognize that tribesmen even *had* economic systems is a problem at the base of the region's recorded history. The Jesuits' culture was so different from that of the tribesmen they came amongst that any initial points of commonality were minimal. For the Jesuits to accept the existence and legitimacy of these tribal economic systems could have caused questions about the acceptability of the rest of the components of these cultures, and this would have called to question the underlying motives for the very presence of the missionaries in the New World, for ultimately, the French desired to destroy these tribal systems.

So the French saw what they could. And when they saw large villages they felt comfortable, for this was a social form they were familiar with. It was a context they understood. Some 200 years after the Jesuits, William Warren may also have had an inability to conceptualize foraging systems as anything but archaic, and therefore, in need of transformation. As we will see below, in the nineteenth century when the Ojibwe were under great pressure to give up their foraging way of life, Warren became an advocate for their transformation through the adoption of agriculture. And when the pressure to change became extreme, Warren developed a plan to have the small, disparate Ojibwe bands form a single, large village community to better deal with the Americans.

Thus, like the Jesuits, Warren's readiness to be drawn to large village settlements is quite evident. Partly because of Warren, over the generations the image of a large Ojibwe village at Chequamegon Bay has become integral to the popular history of these people, but Harold Hickerson, and more recently, Theresa Schenck, challenged the historical existence of this large village, arguing that until at least the latter nineteenth century, the Ojibwe never had such large settlements. And this, of course, means the foraging systems they *did* have were difficult for Europeans to understand, if even just to *see*.

Schenck points out that according to Warren, "Chequamegon was once a vast settlement, and that [Warren assumed before-his-time Ojibwe] bands were formerly much larger and more concentrated." However, she goes on to say that such accounts of large villages are not "borne out in the historical or the archeological record; they were rather beliefs which grew firm in the telling, exaggerations which resulted from a natural desire (perhaps on the part of both narrator and recorder) to glorify the past." Schenck sees that in the Western mind of Warren's time the size of a community was deemed important—larger and more concentrated populations were accepted as the eventual outcome of human endeavor.[30]

William Warren overstated the size and duration of the early Ojibwe village at Chequamegon, and in the years after his book was published it became *the* written source for this earliest period of written Ojibwe history. Going further, Theresa Schenck says, "More recently, many Ojibwa themselves have come to regard Warren's *History* as sacred tradition."[31] When we recognize the importance and strength of our cultural bias for larger, concentrated settled populations, then we might agree that small, foraging communities slip into the shadows of relative insignificance.

This predisposition to focus on the large, to the detriment of the small, could have had ramifications for our understanding of an early Saulteur presence in western Lake Superior. For instance, when Harold Hickerson says, "Chippewa did not permanently occupy Chequamegon (La Pointe), the peninsula jutting out into Lake Superior on the south shore in Bayfield County, Wisconsin, until about the year 1680," we should ponder what is being claimed. Could Harold Hickerson have been influenced by the same predispositions—although centuries removed—that affected earlier observers? Like others, Hickerson struggled with the referents of concepts like *occupy*, *reside*, *permanent*, *village* and *encampment*.[32]

We have shown that other writers told how the Ojibwe were in Chequamegon Bay from time to time, perhaps living in small gatherings of short or long duration. Yet we must ask, is this a *permanent* or perhaps only a *temporary* occupation? Is it acceptable to understand the recurrent seasonal use of a resource area by a nomadic hunting and gathering culture as a permanent occupation? Do recurring short seasonal encampments in a region indicate a permanent occupation, or does "permanently occupy" mean a day after day, week after week, month after month, year after year *physical* occupation of an area? We must ask, finally, are occupation areas different from use areas?

These are the sorts of questions raised in the late nineteenth century when the Ojibwe people sued to try to reclaim rights to harvest resources in ceded territories in Wisconsin and Minnesota, and they need to be raised again when analyzing an Ojibwe presence in Chequamegon Bay in the *seventeenth* century.

When reading the writings of historians and others from more than a decade or two ago, we should be troubled by just such questions, since the subtle appearance of cultural bias is a problem for all writers of history. Human settlement patterns are complex in their sophistication and diversity, and we expect such sophistication in what we have for long considered the most complex of human adaptive systems—the urban center—but we struggle with a *settlement-centric language* to understand, in a positive manner, hunting and gathering adaptations. Our language fails us as it predisposes us to see these cultural systems in a negative way, i.e., too often we see such worldwide foraging adaptations as *undeveloped*, and finally, as *deficient*. This was the case in the above quotation from Claude Allouez when he said such foraging cultures coming to Chequamegon Bay in the mid-seventeenth century were "*wandering and vagrant* tribes." According to Allouez, these were people who did not stay put, who did not "settle" into a single space, and to a European of Allouez's time, such a lifestyle was not acceptable. As Hugh Brody has shown, this is a problem of cognition and conceptualization that remains as troublesome in the twenty-first century as it was for the Lake Superior Jesuits in the seventeenth.

To conclude, in 1642, Raymbault and Jogues, it appears, did not venture westward beyond The Sault and we have no written documentation of Saulteur settlement patterns in these western areas until Radisson and Groseillors arrived almost ten years later. Unfortunately these two adventurers were not greatly interested in the settlement patterns of "Savages." Of course, the paucity of European written documentation of a Saulteur presence along the hundreds of miles of forested shoreline from Sault Ste. Marie westward to Chequamegon does not obviate the possibility of such bands occupying this vast region, and as we have argued, the written record indicates Saulteur bands were residing in this region from the 1650s up to the 1670s.

*Notes*

1. White 1996:4, in Blair 1996[1911].
2. Blair 1996[1911]:275-279.
3. Hickerson 1974:17.
4. *Jesuit Relations* 52:213.
5. Donnelly 1985[1968]:170.
6. Margry, Pierre: New York Colonial Documents, IX. 803-804; Wisconsin Historical Collections, 1888: XI, 26-28.
7. Smith 1985[1973]:29.
8. Blair 1996[1911] Vol. 1:220-225; *Jesuit Relations* 50:105-115.
9. Warren 1984[1885]: 130-132, brackets added.
10. Warren 1984[1885]:131.
11. Donnelly 1985[1968]:170.
12. *Jesuit Relations* 52:203, 205.
13. Harris 1976:39.
14. Blair 1996[1911]:I, 340.
15. Danziger 1979:29.
16. Beck 2002:34.
17. Tinker 1993.
18. *Jesuit Relations* 54:137-138.
19. *Jesuit Relations* 58:255-263; brackets added.
20. Schenck 1996:48.
21. *Jesuit Relations* 58:255-263; italics added.
22. Neill 1885:408-409; Smithsonian Miscellaneous Collections 1917, Vol.66:6.
23. Kellogg 1968[1925]:201.
24. Neill 1885:417.
25. *Jesuit Relations* 50:273.
26. Tanner 1994[1830].
27. *Jesuit Relations* 50:37; italics added.
28. Perry 1996.
29. Brody 1998:273; italics added.
30. Schenck 1996:253; brackets added.
31. Schenck 1996:253.
32. Hickerson 1988[1970]:56.

# 6

# The Final Decades of the Seventeenth Century in Chequamegon Bay

### *Nicholas Perrot and Daniel Greysolon Sieur DuLhut: Two Role Players in Early Ojibwe History*

1.

NICHOLAS PERROT AND DANIEL GREYSOLON Sieur Duluth (I will use the more recent spelling of his name) were both in western Lake Superior lands in the late 1600s and were deeply involved in political matters of the area at the time. We have already given considerable discussion to Perrot's memoir and its importance in helping establish a Saulteur presence in the Chequamegon Bay region in the mid-1600s, and here we will revisit part of this discussion to help better understand Perrot's importance to early Ojibwe history.

Both Perrot and Duluth are said to have been well-received by the native peoples, and there can be no doubt that these French patriots were important and very influential persons of their time, and as such, they seem to have been easy for later writers and scholars to relate to. For example, the descriptions and analyses of the activities and writings of both these men done by historians like Jules Talihan, Bacqueville De La Potherie, Emma Helen Blair, Louise Phelps Kellogg, John Davidson, Walt Harris, and Reuben Thwaites all show a degree of enthusiastic approval.

As with all members of the species, Perrot and Duluth were products of their time, and therefore, these Frenchmen carried the ideologies of Christianity and the emerging free-enterprise capitalism found in their Europe, and New France, of the day. Both saw the New World tribal nations as undeveloped and inferior to their own. And of course, both worked for France, their intent being to extend French control into the western Great Lakes region and beyond. Beside the hope for any possible personal aggrandizement, their ultimate purpose was to manipulate the tribal peoples for the benefit of France.

The last one hundred years (and more) of scholarship concerning these two men has sometimes portrayed them as *heroic*. The Wisconsin historian Louise Phelps Kellogg for instance, writing in the early 1900s, had this to say about Duluth:

> He annexed an empire to the colony, had secured it by forts on Lake Superior, Lake Nipigon, and the River St. Clair; he had treaded the portages from Lake Superior to the Mississippi, had discovered the headwaters of that stream and the sources of Lake Winnipeg; he had turned back the threatening English invasion of the Northwest, and by firmness, decision, good judgment, and sacrifice had saved to New France a seventy years' tenure of the Upper Country. Singularly modest in the midst of boasters, always a nobleman in his treatment of both friends and rivals, this 'gentleman of the King's Guard' was equally at home in the haunts of pleasure, or the savage wilderness, in the palace of Versailles, or the council house of the Sioux. His memory is perpetuated by the noble city that bears his name at the head of the mighty lake he delighted to traverse.[1]

Kellogg goes on to mention how Duluth, Perrot and other French colonial leaders met at Fort St. Joseph in 1687, between Lakes Huron and Erie on the St. Clair River. Here they were involved in assembling a military force drawn from "the wild tribes of the West" for the 1687 attack against the Iroquois. Of this meeting Kellogg says: "Great must have been the satisfaction of these explorers and governors of the great Western hinterland to meet and relate tales of adventures and plan for future growth and progress."[2]

Even today it is still interesting to conjure in our minds such a meeting of these adventuresome personages of the time. From their point of view these men saw themselves in the midst of empire building, and their conversations at Fort St. Joseph must have been filled with a colorful recounting of their adventures with "the Savages." Perhaps they sat in a log long-room of the fort, lit by a warm and glowing fireplace, and talked long into the night. Since no lengthy accounts of this meeting remain, we can only, as Kellogg did, imagine such a scene.

One last quote from Kellogg adds a meaningful note to her accounts of Perrot and Duluth. She says: "Like Nicholas Perrot, Duluth was a master of the art of Indian domination. Mingling sternness with kindness, and always meting out a rude justice, he secured an ascendancy over the savage mind that proved of vital importance to the colony of New France."[3]

We need to remember that we are reading these quotations more than one hundred years after their writing. As a renowned historian of her time, Kellogg was using culturally constructed concepts and a writing style prevalent in her day. In her time the United States was concluding its westward expansion to the Pacific and it recognized the important early role persons like Perrot and Duluth played in laying a foundation for this expansion.

By using the concept "Indian domination" and by labeling it an "art" that brought about "an ascendancy over the savage mind," Louise Kellogg suggested that Perrot and Duluth were working to advance what was in her day called *progress*. We can conclude that in her time Kellogg produced a history useful to her community and culture.[4]

With these introductory remarks we can now go on to examine for ourselves what might have occurred in the travels of Perrot and Duluth that is relevant to our purposes, and particularly what the activities of these men may tell us about the forebears of Red Cliff.

2.

NICHOLAS PERROT IS A COMMON NAME in the written historical accounts of the western Great Lakes region from about 1665 to the late 1690s. He is said to have learned tribal languages easily and generally to have won the respect of the people in regions he operated in. One writer feels he was so prominent that, "He became what might be called a French chief—an equivalent of the medal chiefs who arose among the Great Lakes Indians and gained influence through their dealing with Europeans."[5]

As we have already seen, we know something about Perrot because he left a relatively lengthy memoir published in French in 1864, and translated into English in 1911 by the Wisconsin historian Emma Blair. Perrot came to New France at about age fifteen as a servant for the Jesuits, but after only a few years he left them and became an independent fur trader who eventually was called upon to be a French emissary to tribal nations. Among other things, he is known for negotiating "an important peace between the Fox and neighboring Ojibwas."[6]

Past writers were impressed with Nicholas Perrot. He is portrayed as a colorful, knowledgeable and very capable frontiersman, who was at home in a canoe, struggling over difficult portages and confidently striding into tribal villages where he sometimes issued lengthy harangues.[7]

We do not have all of Perrot's writings, some not surviving the approximately three hundred years from his time to ours. However, we have the Emma Blair translation of his lengthy memoir—written for the purpose of, we are told by Jules Talihan, "enlighten[ing] confidentially the intendant of Canada" in the regime's dealings with the tribesmen (brackets added). And, as we have already mentioned, we have another Perrot manuscript as found in the French historian La Potherie's publication on early North American history. We have enough of his writings to agree that Perrot identified with the goals of French leadership and labored to carry out its desires regarding western Lake Superior country. It is clear Perrot knew the tribal nations could hinder and even deny the accomplishment of these goals, and thus Native nations were integral in matters of political and economic importance in the region. Nicholas Perrot did not see the tribesmen as non-entities, and was certain they had to be taken seriously.

Of this, Richard White, writing in 1996, says:

> Perrot's purpose is important. In both his account and La Potherie's Indians are not objects of study but rather active participants in a larger common history. They not only fascinate Perrot and La Potherie, they irritate them, deceive them, and actively pursue interests of their own that sometimes coincide with those of the French and sometimes oppose them. The authors are practical men interested in giving accounts that will allow Indians to be manipulated and put to French uses, but this very practical bent reveals how independent and different these peoples remain. Indians emerge at once exotic and *sauvage* and yet also as critical participants in a common politics and economy with the French.[8]

As Richard White claims, Perrot's purpose was always to successfully achieve *French* political and economic goals. However, when Perrot was manipulating the tribesmen, they were also manipulating him—and through him, they were finally manipulating the French. For example, while Perrot labored to establish a degree of peace between the Mesquakie and Ojibwe, from the tribesman's perspective, it was just as much a peace that the Mesquakie and Ojibwe negotiated between themselves and the French. In other words, the leaders of these two tribes negotiated the peace just as much as Perrot did.

With this understanding, when we read Perrot we can force our way through his European ethnocentrism and form a more acceptable image of the western Great Lakes tribesmen of the latter decades of the 1600s. While they, too, were ethnocentric, we need to understand that they also had political and economic goals, and that they worked hard to achieve them.

3.

WE HAVE ALREADY REFERRED to Perrot's discussion of the 1662 battle at Iroquois Point and its importance in placing a Saulteur community in the areas of Keweenaw and Chequamegon Bay in that year. We have also discussed how these people "dwelt there in peace always," until this peace was broken by some Huron and Odawa who disturbed the western Dakota.

We have also noted how this early Ojibwe presence at Chequamegon Bay was corroborated by further commentary of Perrot. He claims the peace was broken when some Hurons went to hunt west of Chequamegon where they captured a few Dakota "whom they carried away to [Saulteur] villages alive" (brackets added by Talihan). These captives were not killed but remained at Chequamegon for some time. They returned to their own lands in 1665 or 1666 (Talihan's date), in the company of an Odawa chief named Sinagos, his men, and four Frenchmen. Back in the Dakota village an attempt at restoring peaceful relations was made. To do this the Chequamegon visitors and their Dakota hosts carried out a pipe ceremony. Of this important ceremony Perrot says, "All the chiefs were present, and gave their consent to an inviolable peace. After that solemnity, Chief Sinagos, with his people and the Frenchman who had gone with him, returned to Chagouamikon."[9]

We see that Perrot correctly recognized the pipe ceremony as a solemnity, and his statement that through it an agreement was made to keep "an inviolable peace" is very important. When speaking of this incident, Richard White remarked that Perrot knew a violation of a pipe ceremony "was a crime that could not be pardoned."[10] This reminds us that the pipe ceremonies with the Dakota, Ojibwe, Radisson, Raudin, Duluth, and any others through the latter decades of the 1600s in western Lake Superior were serious matters that supported peaceful relations between the involved parties. At times, breaches of the peace could occur for numerous reasons—the unsanctioned acts of "young men" for example—but all parties knew of the overriding influence of the sacred pipe. For politically decentralized societies this was a powerful deterrent for social control.

There were, of course, other means of enforcing social convention. The rite of expiation called *covering the graves of the dead*, just mentioned, being an example. Here the perpetrator of a breach of peace would be ordered to make a payment of some sort to the afflicted person(s), an act meant to wash the infliction away.

In the 1660s, a few tribal nations were struggling to establish proprietary rights in the western Lake Superior area. The region was rich in resources, but perhaps more important was the role of traders played by the Chequamegon tribes like the Odawa, and to some extent, the Ojibwe.[11] As we noted, in these early times of the fur trade they were mediators between the French and the western and northern tribes like the Dakota and Assiniboine.

We recall that William Warren wrote about the early Ojibwe trading flotillas that went as far east as Quebec and brought back the desired European trade goods, and we understand that the conflicts between the Dakota and more easterly tribes were battles for resource territories, but just as importantly, struggles for rights to establish and maintain trading relationships either directly with the French or with these mediatory tribes that had direct access to the French. Considering this, the incidents of the Dakota coming to Chequamegon Bay in the mid-1660s become even more significant. The Jesuit Allouez told of his gift of wild rice from the Dakota at the bay and Marquette's remarks about the Dakota being in awe of the technology of the French suggest these western tribesmen came to the region seeking trade goods.

The politically astute Nicholas Perrot knew this and saw how important ceremonial pageantry could be in establishing political and economic alliances. No doubt he smoked many pipes with tribal leaders during his tenure in the western Great Lakes and he knew that in the eyes of the tribesmen such sacred ceremonies were used to seal important negotiated agreements. Doubtless, in the economic and political times Perrot was writing about, these ceremonies were not uncommon.

Just as important, we note that Perrot's 1864 editor, Jules Talihan, understood that the Dakota captives in the incident mentioned above were brought back to *Saulteur* villages at Chequamegon. Odawa and Huron clearly were present in the bay at the time, but by stressing that the captives were brought back to Saulteur villages, Talihan tells us that the Saulteur were also present.

Perrot goes on to tell that in 1669 or 1670 (Talihan's dates), the Huron once again went west into Dakota country to hunt, but this time were themselves taken captive by young warriors and held in Dakota villages. He says a Dakota chief who had been part of the earlier peace agreement protected the Huron captives. This chief sent one of them back to Chequamegon to tell its residents that it was not this particular Dakota chief who had broken the peace pact, but it was the fault of "some misguided young men," and that "in a few days he himself would conduct to their homes the captives whom he had retained in his village." However, Perrot tells us, through the deceit of the Hurons, when this chief arrived at Chequamegon he was killed by the Odawa, who then, along with the Hurons, feared retaliatory raids by the Dakota. Thus, they abandoned their villages and moved eastward to Sault Ste. Marie.[12] (According to Donnelly's reading of the Marquette literature, as noted above, not all the Chequamegon Huron and Odawa left with Marquette at this time—some chose to stay and stand firm against the Dakota.) As we have seen, Jules Talihan set this abandonment of Chequamegon (by the Odawa and Huron) at 1670-71, the dates the *Jesuit Relations* give for Jacques Marquette's abandonment of the St. Esprit mission in the bay.[13]

What these latter episodes of the Huron and Dakota conflict tell us is that while some of the Huron and Odawa at Chequamegon left the region in 1670-71, it is not clear if the Ojibwe residing in the area also moved back east out of fear of the Dakota. However, if we use what the historian Harold Hickerson called "negative evidence" we must conclude that since no writers of the time tell about the Ojibwe leaving, they did not go with the Odawa, Huron and the Jesuit Marquette.[14]

It should be expected that like the other tribal nations, there were times when the Saulteur smoked the calumet with the Dakota—times not recorded in the extant literature—and in these solemn ceremonies made agreements which worked, at least for a time, to maintain a degree of peace between their nations. This peace was periodically tested by incidents when both Dakota and Ojibwe individuals, or "parties of young men," might impulsively or surreptitiously enter each other's territories to gain personal trophies—that could include scalps—for reasons of enhancing prestige, for example, or relieving burdensome mourning obligations. Such breaches of the overall peace could be resolved with rituals of "covering the graves of the dead" or other agreed upon mutual efforts. In other words, peace agreements made sacrosanct with a pipe ceremony could generally prevail, despite these periodic breaches. Such crises-rectifying customs were built into decentralized tribal political systems like those of the seventeenth century Dakota and Ojibwe. With this in mind, while many of the Odawa and Huron abandoned Chequamegon because they felt they were in danger from Dakota retaliatory attacks, it is likely the Ojibwe remained, their security somewhat ensured by their more amiable relations with the Dakota. As we have seen, Pierre Radisson's memoir suggests this is precisely the type of relationship the Dakota and Ojibwe had a full twenty years before the coming of Duluth.

## 4.

We see that Nicholas Perrot (in some cases with the aid of his editor, Jules Talihan) tells us that the Ojibwe were present at Chequamegon Bay in the early 1660s and into the later years of the decade. Also, while he says the Odawa and Huron left the area to take sanctuary at The Sault, he tells us nothing about the Ojibwe leaving Chequamegon, and they were not mentioned as instigators of conflict in the above incidents. This is particularly significant, considering the validity some historians attribute to Perrot's memoir.

Given this, it is still plausible that some Ojibwe might have moved eastward with Marquette in 1671. Those who feared the Dakota, or for other reasons recognized a strong affinity with the Odawa and Huron (due to intermarriage, for example) may have left with these peoples. Yet Pierre Radisson has shown there were Dakota-Ojibwe marriages that worked in an opposite way, to strengthen peaceful relations between these nations. Therefore, it is possible that the bulk of Ojibwe people who Perrot says were using Chequamegon in the 1660s might have remained, continuing to use it as a headquarters as they seasonally moved over the numerous resource areas in the region. If so, Nicholas Perrot's writing supports the notion of a continual seasonal presence of Ojibwe people at Chequamegon Bay from the time of Radisson and Groseillier through the 1660s.

With this suggestion we leave Nicholas Perrot and consider what the historical record can tell us about Daniel Grayselon Sieur Duluth and the Ojibwe in the Chequamegon region.

5.

DULUTH WAS BORN IN A PARISIAN SUBURB into a family that included members connected to the French court. From the start we see that unlike the young Nicholas Perrot, he had a degree of wealth and political connection that, even granting Perrot's success on the western frontier of New France, Perrot never did acquire. As a young man, Duluth was chosen to be a member of the King's Guard and in this role apparently saw military action in Europe in 1674.[15] He made two trips to New France, where he learned, as he tells us:

> . . . everyone believed that it was impossible to explore the country of the Nadouecioux [Dakota], nor to have any commerce with them, both because of their distance, which is 800 leagues from our settlements, and because they are at war generally with all sorts of tribes, this difficulty made me resolve to go among them.[16]

While Duluth was busy with military matters in Europe in 1674, as we saw above, the Dakota and Cree were scheduled to hold a peace meeting at Sault Ste. Marie. However, this turned into a bloody melee and signaled that Lake Superior country was still not safe for French missionaries and traders. It was only four years later, in 1678, that Duluth made his third trip to New France. In September of that year he set out from Montreal intending to put his plan for pacifying the frontier into effect.[17] For our immediate purposes we will examine Duluth's two major negotiation sessions that impinge directly upon the Ojibwe. The first is the often-mentioned peace agreement between the French, Dakota, and Ojibwe.

In working to bring a degree of peace to the frontier, in autumn of 1678 he left Montreal for Sault Ste. Marie, where he wintered over while befriending the community's Ojibwe. Then, Louise Kellogg says, in the spring of 1679, with some Ojibwe, he set out from Sault Ste. Marie "to seek the Sioux." She continues, saying:

> They went forward to a rendezvous arranged with the Sioux at the western end of Lake Superior. This fierce tribe received the French messengers graciously, and after making peace between the two most powerful tribes of the Northwest, the Chippewa and the Sioux, the explorer was escorted in triumph to the home of the latter tribe on the headwaters of the Mississippi.[18]

Kellogg's characterization of the Dakota and Ojibwe as "the two most powerful tribes of the Northwest" is interesting because Harold Hickerson has argued that at this time the Ojibwe were largely centered at The Sault, and they were a collection of disparate proto-Ojibwe bands that emerged as a more identifiable tribal unit only after the Duluth peace agreement of 1679-80. The suggestion that in 1679 such loose, autonomous bands could be one of the most powerful tribes in the Lake Superior region is puzzling. Writing in 1925, Louise Phelps Kellogg may have been working under the assumption commonly held at her time, one that portrayed the Dakota and Ojibwe as fierce adversaries who were finally brought to the negotiating table at the far western end of Lake Superior by the very capable Duluth, who after this difficult feat, in Kellogg's words, "was escorted in triumph" to the Dakota's western homeland.

Although Duluth suggested it was a major personal accomplishment, we should understand his negotiations as a renewal of the French-Dakota-Ojibwe peace alliances both Radisson and Raudin were part of in the immediate years. As far back as the early 1660s, the Dakota were eager for a direct trading relationship with the French, but political unrest in the area kept interceding on their attempts to achieve this. Duluth's peace was driven by his strong desire to quell this unrest, and approved by Frontenac, the Canadian governor at the time, but Radisson did not have the sanction of the French leaders in Quebec when he took part in the 1661 Feast of the Dead we discussed above. Therefore, this event—as is the case, apparently, with Raudin's negotiations—did not receive the notice given to the later activities of Duluth.

Unfortunately, the frequency of the mention of the Duluth 1679-80 meeting in the written historical record is not matched by the telling of the details of the meeting's proceedings. We know virtually nothing of these important events. We assume the parties all wanted peace and relations conducive to trade, but just what did the Dakota, Ojibwe, and Duluth agree to in order for this to happen?

The second peace agreement Duluth negotiated was in September of the same year (1679). About this meeting Duluth himself wrote:

> On the 15th of September, having made with the Assenipoulaks [Assiniboine] and all the other nations of the North a rendezvous at the extremity of

> Lake Superior to cause them to make peace with the Nadouecioux [Dakota] their common enemy, they all appeared there, where I had the good fortune to gain their esteem and their friendship, to bring them together, and in order that peace might last longer among them, I believed that I could not better cement it than by causing marriages to be made mutually between the different nations. This I could not carry out without much expenditure. During the following winter I caused them to hold meetings in the forest, at which I was present, in order to hunt together, feast, and thus draw closed the bonds of friendship.[19]

Here we find the use of marriages again, and interestingly, according to Kellogg, at these latter negotiations the Assiniboine and Dakota agreed "to send delegations to visit Frontenac the coming summer. An epidemic of smallpox in the colony, however, frightened them away."[20] In these important years the specter of smallpox and other European diseases, relatively new to tribes in western Lake Superior country, was always something the tribesmen were concerned with.

These, then, are the two major peace agreements Duluth was part of: in spring of 1679 it was one between the French, Dakota and Ojibwe, and in fall of the same year it was the French, Dakota and Assiniboine agreement. Both were said to have taken place at the far western end of Lake Superior, and both are important in that they seemed to, at least temporarily, affect events in Lake Superior country. Yet both are troublesome because of their lack of details.

## 6.

DANIEL GREYSOLON SIEUR DULUTH was instrumental in bringing about the 1679 peace agreements and he continued to be a prominent figure for Lake Superior Ojibwe for some years thereafter. He is portrayed as a peacemaker who quieted Chequamegon country, then moved up the Brule River and over to Mille Lacs where he supposedly freed a Dakota captive, the Catholic missionary Louis Hennepin. He also went inland west of Lake Superior to the headwaters of the Mississippi to Dakota villages. And he traveled north to Cree and Assiniboine lands, at what is now called Grand Portage at the Minnesota-Ontario border. Among other things, he was for a time the commandant at the French fort at Michilimackinac. After all these accomplishments for the French Crown, and more, he died in Montreal in 1710.[21]

A roving ambassador for France, it is clear that Duluth's intent was to work toward freeing the western Lake Superior region of tribal military strife in order to keep the area from English influence and control. Like Perrot, Duluth realized that if he was to achieve the goals of the French crown he had to go to the tribal villages and negotiate. As he sought to bring about, in the words of Louise Kellogg, "an ascendancy over the savage mind," we need to view him as less *peacemaker* than an *alliance* maker.[22] If it can be said that much of the basis for intertribal strife in the Lake Superior country of the mid-to-late 1600s was the struggle for positive relations with the French, then we must agree with the historian Edmund Jefferson Danziger, Jr. when he stresses the role of Duluth as alliance maker.[23] Popular history has portrayed Duluth as a peacemaker coming among warring tribes and successfully settling age-old disputes. This story feeds the early image of tribal society as a life of tooth and claw, where one tribe is regularly in strife with its neighbors, but by seeing Duluth as an alliance maker it shifts the reader's orientation from "warlike savages" to one of tribal leaders using rational thought to improve their peoples' political standing.

When we recall that Dakota, Cree, and Saulteur peoples were in contact with each other for a considerable length of time before the coming of Duluth, then we need to expect that these nations regularly, or irregularly, met to resolve questions of how they would relate to one another. Essentially, these were hunting and gathering societies which moved over the land in a fluid manner, headquartering at appropriate times at strategic resource locations, and dispersing at other times. The presence of the Ojibwe at Chequamegon Bay, for example, must have been one of changing population levels as one season gave way to another and as resource availability demanded.

While hunting and gathering adaptations call for a community to more or less settle in and lay claim to a given resource area, it is still accepted that these types of communities repeatedly *move over* such a region. Competing human communities then, interact along the boundaries of these regions, as they probe for stable relationships. There could be long peaceful times, even amiable relations, but these could be broken now and then because of various exigencies.

Considering this, the "traditional" warring between communities like the Dakota and Ojibwe that popular history tells us about might be overdone. The reasonable response to conflict over resource areas would have been negotiation rather than long-term warfare, and we should expect that this was the case for the Dakota and others. With the coming of the European, though, this relationship was exacerbated by the desire for trade relations. This desire on the part of the Dakota to negotiate is witnessed by the trip of Tioscate, the prominent Dakota leader, to Montreal in 1695, when he argued for a direct trading relationship with the French. We will discuss this trip below, so here it is enough to suggest the Dakota were desirous of such a direct relationship in the years preceding Tioscate's 1695 trip, and that the strong desire for a direct trading relationship helps explain the friendly welcome Duluth said the Dakota gave him back in 1679, particularly with his account of how after the conclusion of that year's meeting he was transported joyfully to the Dakotas' western lands.

With this in mind we can see Duluth and even Perrot as persons who first of all mediated between France and the different tribal nations. The 1679 peace agreement between the Dakota and Ojibwe, therefore, needs to be seen as having a *tripartite* nature, with France being the third member. This Dakota-Ojibwe- *and* French peace agreement left all three nations with access to trade. Such a perspective shifts the historical focus from one stressing perpetually warring tribes to an image of tribal nations negotiating for political advantage. This perspective offers a more realistic image of the western Lake Superior Ojibwe in the early days.

7.

ONE LAST INSTANCE OF RELATED historical interpretation for this time period is from Guy Burnham, a journalist in Ashland, Wisconsin, in the late nineteenth and early twentieth centuries. This quotation is journalism and needs to be accepted as such. It uses the old image of Dakota-Ojibwe warfare as the prime cause for the event. However, while it is historically inaccurate—it denies the role of the Huron and Odawa as the original perpetuators in the 1670-71 strife with the Dakota—its historical impact should not be denied. These sorts of writings came before a vast regional readership when first written, and in this particular instance remain before this readership. After originally appearing in the Ashland newspaper in the 1800s, it was republished in 1891-92, has been reprinted in 1972, 1986, and in 1988, and will probably be reprinted again.[24] This particular piece reviews the early history of Chequamegon Bay, but it says nothing about the Duluth alliance negotiated between the Dakota, Ojibwe and French. According to Burnham:

> The hunting ground of Northern Wisconsin were (sic) abandoned by the Hurons and Ottawas only because they were compelled to it by the incoming of more powerful and numerous tribes of the Sioux and the Ojibwas (properly spelled Od-jib-ways). Through the trade of these new-comers, Chequamegon Bay became the emporium for a vast territory including for a time the largest part of what is now represented by the states of Wisconsin and Minnesota.[25]

Summary in nature, condensing many years into a sentence or two, and not meant to be taken as rigorously documented historical research, this quotation nevertheless is significant. Here is popular history at work. For centuries the "traditional warfare" between the Dakota and Ojibwe has been at the foundation of the early story of Chequamegon Bay. And Guy Burnham's interesting comment on the Dakota and Ojibwe being behind the growth of trading at Chequamegon fits well with the discussion of Nicholas Perrot and Daniel Greysolon Sieur Duluth given above. That is, that in the 1660s and the years immediately following, both Dakota and Ojibwe interests concerned the maintenance of a *peaceful* relationship between their nations since they both wanted an open door to trading with the French at Chequamegon. Therefore, while much of the regional written history characterizes Dakota-Ojibwe relations as filled with warfare, we see that the desire for peace runs deep.

To summarize, writers have said the Huron, Odawa and Jesuits abandoned Chequamegon Bay in 1671, but we have argued the Ojibwe did not, and surely the French continued to come for trade. The Chequamegon fur trade went on, and history shows that in the last decades of the seventeenth century the Ojibwe were major actors in the drama that was this trade.

## *The Ojibwe at Chequamegon Bay from 1680-1700*

1.

BY THE LAST TWO DECADES of the seventeenth century Chequamegon Bay's Ojibwe were major players in Lake Superior's fur trade. They had allied themselves with the Dakota, Cree, Assiniboine and French, and in their strategic position at Lake Superior's western terminus they assumed a new importance in the fur trade economy. Things seemed to be going so well for the Ojibwe that a later writer felt this time period at Chequamegon was the start of "the Chippewas' Golden Age."[26]

Throughout these years the people continued to live as they had been doing for some time. They fished, hunted, gardened, and gathered resources from their territories as, in the words of the Minnesota Ojibwe writer Ignatia Broker, they enjoyed life in their "Manito World."[27] Their social and cultural institutions were in place, but a new element was added to this system when their winter trapping activities were intensified with their participation in the fur trade. Through this trapping they acquired new material items that sometimes served to increase the efficiency of their labors.

From the French perspective this was a time of some prominence for the Crown. France had established itself as the European power in the Lake Superior region, and as we saw through the ceremonial at Sault Ste. Marie, laid claim to the entire area. A number of outposts were set up to ring this new possession, and although small and minor, were still enough to announce a French presence, and as Danziger put it, "Lake Superior became an integral part of the French Empire."[28]

We noted that at the 1671 Sault Ste. Marie ceremonial the Ojibwe, along with several other tribal nations had, in the words of Nicholas Perrot, "placed themselves under the protection of the king, and in submission to him."[29] When we look again at this event more than two hundred and thirty years later, some interesting imagery comes to mind. Such a major ceremony must have included the usual rituals like feasting, gift giving and the invocation of the spirits through calumet smoking. Nicholas Perrot tells of a mock battle and a lacrosse game that were part of the colorful event. We noted that Ojibwe leaders from Chequamegon Bay were present, as were others of the Potawatomi, Sauk, Menominee, Mesquakie, Mascouten, Kickapoo, Miami, Illinois and Cree.[30]

Three prominent Jesuits were involved—Gabriel Dreuillettes, Claude Dablon, and Claude Allouez—and a fourth priest would have been there, but he—Jacques Marquette—was busy, like some Huron and Odawa, making his way to The Sault from Chequamegon Bay. The inclusion of the Jesuits is another indication of this religious order's deep political involvement in France's colonial ventures in the New World.

This proceeding was meant to counter the attempts of England to garner territory and wealth in Lake Superior country, and soon these activities erupted in open warfare when the English-French War of 1689 (King William's War) broke out.[31]

In the years immediately preceding this war, France's role in the New World was challenged when the Iroquois, British, Mesquakie, and their allies turned their combined interests to the fur trade of the western Great Lakes. According to Louise Kellogg, this attempt to displace the French became so serious that it threatened to drive the French from the Northwest. She noted that "three times flotillas of English traders accompanied by their Iroquois customers penetrated to the upper Great Lakes," and "more than once the western tribesmen formed embassies to arrange an Iroquois alliance—an alliance that meant death to every Frenchman in the western country."[32]

France worked to nullify these threats and proceeded with its plans to explore the territories west of Lake Superior, still hoping to find the desired passage to the Orient. With this purpose in mind Duluth came to Michilimackinac in 1683, and, in Kellogg's words "found the West seething in revolt." French traders had recently been killed on Lake Superior and for such traders, Kellogg claimed, "The route through Lake Superior was especially dangerous."[33] Apparently this political strife was not unrelated to that we mentioned earlier, found on Lake Superior between the tribal communities and the French back in 1671, when Fr. Marquette and some Odawa and Huron persons left Chequamegon Bay.

While historians have told how the Ojibwe and French enjoyed a particularly friendly relationship from the early days of the fur trade, the 1670s and 1680s were a different story. By the 1680s, Governor Frontenac had fallen out of favor with the French monarch and was called back to France, and Le Febvre de LaBarre was sent to New France to replace him. LaBarre immediately made plans to prevent an Iroquois-English takeover of the western region. Under the new governor, Duluth, Perrot, and another Frenchman—de la Durantaye—were summoned to Michilimackinac to assemble fighting forces of native warriors to enter battle with the Iroquois. LaBarre himself took a unit of native fighters to Lake Ontario to engage the Iroquois but was not successful and was recalled to France.[34]

By the summer of 1687, the Iroquois kept French traders from getting past Lake Erie, causing economic havoc for the Montreal and Quebec business community.[35] English traders were coming into the upper lakes region and, with better trading rates than the French, were winning some of the trade away. Michilimackinac became the springboard for French efforts to stop this, and it was from this post that Perrot and de la Durantaye left to reestablish French alliances with the tribal nations at Green Bay, Wisconsin, the very important passageway to the Lake Pepin area and the rich Dakota lands beyond.

In June 1688, Duluth came to Sault Ste. Marie from western Lake Superior with forty Ojibwe warriors—presumably some, if not all, from Chequamegon Bay—and joined his force with the Odawa.[36] In late June he left Michilimackinac with "400 vigorous warriors to begin the long paddle to Lake Erie, where they engaged a group of Iroquois.[37] Duluth's force lost four of its members, but killed three, wounded five and took prisoners of the rest of the Iroquois party. This Lake Erie incident surprised the Iroquois with its show of force and indicated that the northern Algonquian nations would no longer retreat, but were ready to stand and resist future military incursions."[38]

A year earlier, on 4 July 1687, Nicholas Perrot organized a fighting force at Lake Pepin in western Wisconsin, traveled to Michilimackinac where he met a larger force—surely with Ojibwe fighters from the entire region, including Chequamegon Bay—and went on to Lake Ontario to battle the Iroquois. These were significant events since they served to offer initial checks on the Iroquois-British initiative into the upper lakes. Also, Louise Kellogg said of the Duluth trek to Lake Erie, "[it] was the first war party of Indians to traverse the Great Lakes at the behest of the White man."[39] No records exist to tell exactly who the warriors were, but it is possible that ancestors of some of today's Ojibwe residents of western Lake Superior were in the groups that made these long paddles to Lakes Ontario and Erie, and some that died in these early skirmishes with the Iroquois.

The written record shows it was in 1688 that Duluth's post on the far northwestern shore of Lake Superior—*Kaministiqwuia*, as it was then called (now Grand Portage)—was closed, but the French presence at Chequamegon was ongoing.[40] This was of some importance to the French since with King William's War (1669), the Mesquakie—allies of the English—had sealed off Green Bay, making Lake Superior the only passageway to the rich fur lands of the Upper Mississippi.[41]

For a few more years France continued to have difficulty reaching this rich region. Finally, Governor Frontenac—reinstated as governor after LaBarre's failure to quell the Iroquois—sent a party to Michilimackinac determined to bring the amount of furs in storage there down to Montreal. Nicholas Perrot was in this force and in August 1690, he and "five hundred of the Upper Indians arrived at Montreal to trade, and the merchants rejoiced, as so large a number had not appeared for a long time." Again, it is likely that Ojibwe from western Lake Superior were in this group, and if so, they doubtless took part in a feast of gratitude Frontenac presented on 25 August 1690. According to the written record, "On the 25th, Count Frontenac, the Governor, gave them a grand feast of two oxen, six large dogs, two barrels of wine, some prunes, and plenty of tobacco to smoke."[42]

With this, France hoped trade would resume between Montreal and the western Great Lakes, but it still experienced restrictions due to Iroquois, English and Mesquakie activities. Furs continued to be warehoused at Michilimackinac, due to the difficulties in getting them through to Montreal. Then, in May 1692, Frontenac sent another group of canoes up the waterways to secure another load of furs, in Louise Kellogg's words, "at any cost."[43] This was successful, resulting in two hundred French and Indian canoes arriving at Montreal, an event that brought great joy to the community. That fall, on 6 September, Frontenac came to Montreal from Quebec where at a gathering of tribal leaders he "entertained the principal chiefs, and the next day distributed presents and made preparations for the reoccupation of the Northwest." No doubt Ojibwe leaders from the western lakes were at Montreal for this celebratory occurrence.[44]

It was in these years that Nicholas Perrot was at the French post on Lake Pepin on the Mississippi River in far western Wisconsin, working to win the favor of the Dakota. He was successful and able to see the movement of Dakota furs from this location up to La Pointe in Chequmegon Bay. With Green Bay still closed to the French, La Pointe continued to be an important fur post for the entire western region. France wanted to trade with the Dakota in order to benefit from the lands of the headwaters of the Mississippi and needed a viable post in western Lake Superior to serve as a northern doorway to this wealth. Of course, the Ojibwe of the Chquamegon region were integral in these plans.

To strengthen its presence in the western Great Lakes, in 1692, the French Crown decided to send the first of a line of officials to Chequamegon Bay to establish a garrison at that site. The next year—1693—Pierre LeSueur arrived with a detachment of French military and had a fort built on Madeline Island. Hamilton Ross felt that Frontenac sent LeSueur "to maintain contact with the Indians in the hope of enlisting them as allies in his war against he British."[45] According to another writer, LeSueur's task was "to endeavor to maintain the peace lately concluded between the Saulteurs and the Sioux," a reference to Perrot's ceremony at Fort St. Antoine on Lake Pepin in 1689, in which he not only reinforced earlier alliances between the Ojibwe, Dakota, and French, but also, in the grand style of European expansionistic desires of the time, laid clam to the entire region for France.[46]

LeSueur was no stranger to the Chequamgon area, having a long history of trading in the west during which he spent time with the Dakota in the upper Mississippi territories. This is a major point, for his lengthy and politically active presence suggests a serious involvement of France in western Lake Superior country in the latter decades of the sixteenth century. Among other ventures, LeSueur investigated the colored soil at Blue Earth, a location in what is now south-central Minnesota, for it's copper mining possibilities. He was also with Perrot at Fort St. Antoine in 1689.[47] For two years after his arrival at Madeline Island he spent time in the immediate region, as well as traveling to more distant Dakota and Ojibwe communities, exploring for economic possibilities and trying to strengthen tribal relations with the French. To this end, in 1695 he joined the La Pointe Ojibwe leader, Chingouabe, and the western Dakota leader, Tioscate, and their joint Ojibwe-Dakota entourage on its long canoe journey to Montreal where they reaffirmed their threefold alliance with Governor Frontenac. It was at this meeting that Chingouabe spoke of the Ojibwe's friendship with the French and his desire to continue their peaceful relationship—to include the presence of a French trader at Chequamegon.

Tioscate was the first Dakota to travel to Montreal, and he gave a moving plea for the French to bring their trade goods to these westerners, especially their metal weapons and other tools. Unfortunately, he took sick in the French city, and died there the following winter. Chingouabe was admonished by Governor Frontenac to have his warriors cease their depredations on the Dakota, after which the Ojibwe leader, in an oft-quoted passage, reminded the governor that the Ojibwes' political system was far different from that of the French, and while he would attempt to comply with the governor's wishes, the issue was much more than he could easily control. In his speech he stressed that the political organization of Ojibwe culture was complex—a system involving patri-clans and other social control mechanisms—and not designed in a manner that allowed for a single leader to easily command control.[48] Chingouabe's remarks hint that at the close of the seventeenth century, the French struggled to understand the democratic political system of the Ojibwe. But as we will see, by the early nineteenth century, William Warren argued that the French had acquired a good understanding of this system and had made accommodations that allowed them to successfully work with it.

With the Green Bay outlet closed by the Mesquakie, France intended that La Pointe would become the post through which all western furs flowed to Michilimackinac and on to Montreal. It has been stated that during these times—the 1690s—large contingents of Ojibwe began to leave their Sault Ste. Marie home to come to Chequamegon to partake in this renewed fur trade activity.[49] Neill claims that in this decade "the Ojibways began to concentrate in a village, upon the shores of Chagouamigon Bay. It was in the interest of the French to draw them as far away from the influence of English traders, who had appeared in the vicinity of Mackinac."[50] Neill's suggestion that this purported move was set in motion out of a French need to shield the Ojibwe from the British demands commentary.

We have argued that by the 1690s, the Ojibwe were already in western Lake Superior and had been there for many decades. To suggest they moved because of a French desire—perhaps deviously acted out—to keep them from trading with the British not only gives undue emphasis to the French influence over the tribes, but also ignores the evidence in the historical record that establishes an earlier Ojibwe presence in the western region of the lake. Neill's remarks furthermore suggest that the French were manipulating the Ojibwe, when we could argue that the Ojibwe were manipulating the French, as they played one European power off against the other. In this view, it can be suggested that the decision to send LeSueur with a military detachment to Madeline Island in 1692 was forced by the Ojibwe (and Dakota) overtures made to the British. When we reconsider Chingouabe's 1695 speech to Governor Frontenac, we might agree that it was less of a "dependent" tribal leader pleading for French trade goods than a clever pose made by an Ojibwe leader with deeper political and economic motives in mind. These motives involved a desire to have *direct* trade with the French, in a setting in the heart of Ojibwe territory instead of in a distant French city.

Whatever the ultimate reason for Chingoube's plea for a French trader, his attempt to inform Governor Frontenac of the deep difference between the Ojibwe and French political systems is noteworthy. Chingoube was a high-level diplomat of the times negotiating with the highest ranking French official in North America and certainly understood the important context of his speech. His words show that the Ojibwe political organization was functioning properly at the time, and suggested how difficult it was to adapt to the pressures of French demands. Clearly, Chingoube was reaching out to Frontenac, asking him to at least understand the Ojibwe, if not to actually accept the legitimacy of their differences.

However, by the late 1690s, so many furs were being taken in Lake Superior country "that French prices plummeted . . . and for the next twenty years official operations above The Sault were suspended."[51] The year after the Montreal meeting, on 21 May 1696, the French "king issued a royal ordinance revoking all licenses for the fur trade, violation of which edict would be punished by condemnation to slavery in the galleys."[52] But there was more to this suspension of the French trade than a glut of furs. Missionaries had been complaining of "the abuses that French traders and *coureurs de bois* inflicted on the Indians."[53] The 1696 suspension of trading licenses was, in part, a gesture by the French Crown to quell this unrest on the frontier. Fur trappers unhappy with their treatment by French traders might have taken their pelts to the British. The British, who in these times not only had better trading rates, but also treated the trappers better than the French, were eager for this to occur. In any event, the 1696 royal edict removed the official French trading activity from Chequamegon.

What actually occurred at Chequamegon can only be surmised since with the 1698 exit of LeSueur and his military force the written record is scant until the second decade of the 1700s, when the French officially returned. Quite interestingly, it is claimed that by 1695, La Pointe was a major Ojibwe fishing and trading village, with its population—by 1697—estimated to be 1,000 persons. By 1700, it was the center of Ojibwe territory and called "the main gathering place" for summer *midewiwin* ceremonies.[54] Such a large amount of persons would have offered a desirable market for fur traders and with the 1698 exodus of French officialdom we should expect that other traders moved in, and of course, some of them were *coureurs de bois*.

A colorful literature has grown up around these French traders.[55] The *coureurs de bois* worked for themselves[56] and depending on the writer's bias, are often depicted as predatory, if not even cheating, and ruthless exploiters who seriously mistreated the tribal trappers, or else as adventuresome individuals who turned away from a restrictive colonial life to seek their fortunes in the wilderness. Numerous of today's Ojibwe families in part stem from these early fur traders, and certainly by 1700, the Ojibwe community at Lake Superior's western limits had some of them as permanent residents.

The seventeenth century closed in Chequamegon Bay without an official French post on Madeline Island. However, this did not greatly affect the Ojibwe community. Each winter season, furs were still being taken, and traders were active in the region as the vast lands to the west of Lake Superior witnessed an increase in this trade. The Ojibwe were in the midst of this and saw few serious changes, leaving their culture essentially the same as prior to the coming of the French. Their social, political, religious and economic systems were functioning as they continued to use the plants and animals of their region, but now they had added commercial fur trapping to their economy.

As Edmund Jefferson Danziger, Jr., suggests with his characterization of the last few decades of the 1600s as the start of a "Golden Age" for the Ojibwe, perhaps it actually was a good time for them. The fur trade brought a degree of wealth to the people and "acted to regularize peaceful relationships between the Ojibwe and Dakota."[57] After the Dakota-French-Ojibwe peace agreements of 1661, 1674, 1679, and 1689, in Chequamegon Bay the Dakota were visiting as traders, not raiders, and the flow of trade goods was continuing. This important point is not usually made in the historical written literature. Instead, we find a literature stressing warfare between these two tribal nations. The lake still held fish, the forest held deer and other animals, in spring the maple sap still flowed, and each fall *manoomin* still stood in its places in the area's waters, so at the end of the old century and the start of the new, it likely was felt that the *manidoog* were favoring the people.

### *The 1600s and Red Cliff: Final Questions and a Summing-Up*

WE HAVE SEEN THAT OJIBWE ORAL TEACHINGS tell of the peoples' coming to Lake Superior hundreds of years ago and initial settling along its southern (and northern) shores, possibly reaching Madeline Island by the fifteenth century or earlier. However, the written historical record tells of these people residing in the general area of the eastern limits of the lake only by 1640 or so, and while some remained in this region, others moved westward to utilize resources along the length of the lake's southern shore. These bands may have reached Chequamegon Bay by 1650.

However, the written record is, at most, suggestive, and the problem stems from three areas. The first concerns the historical penchant for some writers to focus on settled villages rather than foraging bands. The second is the overdue emphasis some researchers have put on Duluth's 1679 peace agreement between the French, Dakota, and Ojibwe. The third concerns a stress put upon warfare, especially between the Dakota and Ojibwe. Here we will offer a brief discussion of these three topics as we close our commentary on the Ojibwe and the seventeenth century.

The first area is that of the early French observers' expectation of large villages. This has been discussed above and we argued it is a serious impediment to research because of its subtlety. The negative perception of mobile foraging adaptations held by the early French—a view still held by some westerners today—made a serious consideration of the complexities and subtleties of mobile systems difficult, if not impossible. This predisposition may have rendered these communities absent in the early days of western Lake Superior. Hence the presence of Ojibwe communities as foraging band systems was downplayed and ignored, if not actually deemed non-existent.

The second problem, the undue emphasis put upon Duluth's peace agreement of 1679, was also discussed. Duluth's negotiations were deemed significant from the perspective of New France because of their importance to the economy of the time. Harold Hickerson, in particular, also stressed Duluth's negotiations as a causal factor in the westward movement of the Ojibwe. Historical perceptions of Duluth too often have been couched in an early triumphalism that tells of the glory of civilization over the "Savages." This misconception supported the image of "savages" as a lawless people who were not able to live in peace with one another, a misunderstanding that made the Europeans' purpose in the New World a humane responsibility, one undertaken for moral reasons, and thus, not driven simply by desires for the acquisition of materialistic wealth.

The third problem, that of warfare, is part of the second, but needs discussion on its own right. In the seventeenth century, "savage" societies were seen as lawless and so the earliest French writings about Lake Superior's peoples can be expected to speak to matters of war. This continues through the *Jesuit Relations*, the first fur traders' memoirs, and into the earliest of some historians' writings as well. Perhaps surprisingly, this can be seen, although more subtly, in some recent historical writings also.

It is in this sense that we must challenge Harold Hickerson's conclusion that the peace-making efforts of Pierre Radisson in 1660 were unsuccessful. Hickerson's refusal to adequately address how at times inter-tribal relationships may have turned upon cultural norms that essentially derived not from purely economic needs—such as access to food resources—but from less primary causes, is unfortunate. The threat of hostility between tribes may have been constant in the region in the mid-1600s, but this intertribal hostility would have taken a different character when viewed from within the tribal communities. Theresa Schenck has reminded us that in the early days the Ojibwe and others held a warrior ethic that saw inter-tribal hostility as a positive means for securing status and recognition. Hostile acts against an outsider could be used to advance a person in tribal political standing, and obligatory mourning rituals could call for such hostility as well, since a mourner could shorten the prescribed grieving period by heading out in search of someone from a distant nation, and returning with war relics that could be used in prescribed ways to reduce lengthy mourning periods.[58]

Intertribal strife between the Dakota and Ojibwe can certainly be seen as part of the struggle of these two nations to claim resources in the Lake Superior region, but warfare, or simply the threat of its occurrence, also functioned to serve as a means for individuals to fulfill various cultural goals. In other words, warfare was not used simply for resource procurement. For example, it has been shown that the existence of an out-group can be useful in boundary identification and the psychological functions of such hostility can serve religious leaders as they attempt to project a community's problems and fears outward onto a real or imagined adversary. Just such functions have been proposed for some aspects of Ojibwe shamanism.[59] Viewed this way, Dakota and Ojibwe warfare was not only a matter of gaining use rights to a resource territory—as some writers contend—but also a cultural device for maintaining its identity and internal functioning.

Such uses for inter-group hostility, when expressed, for example with the energy said to have been seen in the wars of the Iroquois, was startling to the Jesuits and their French companions. This was a type of warfare far different from that of the marching legions of European monarchies they were familiar with.

A final problem is the dogmatism that can take form in scholarship. Historical researchers use the work of those who have come before. This is not unique to literate societies but is also the case in communities with an oral tradition where information is passed from one generation to the next without writing. Properly done, such scholarship—whether in written or oral forms—is accomplished with all due consideration.

What has occurred for Chequamegon Bay has been a heavy reliance upon the writings of early scholars like Wisconsin's Reuben Thwaites, Louise Kellogg, and of course, William Warren. Warren's nineteenth century accounting of Ojibwe history remains for some such a primary source. More recently, the work of ethnohistorian Harold Hickerson has also been used as an initial source, especially with writers focusing on the early Ojibwe in the southwestern Lake Superior region, and a few very recent writers continue to rely upon Hickerson for their synoptic accounts of Ojibwe history in this area.[60]

Fortunately, we are now seeing research calling some of these early key sources into question. For example, some of Harold Hickerson's conclusions are being challenged, and likewise William Warren's. What is starting to take form is a suggestion that the supposed "flocking" back to Chequamegon Bay from Sault Ste. Marie, done by the Ojibwe in 1680 and immediately thereafter that Hickerson based so much of his understanding of early Ojibwe culture and society on, may have been over-emphasized. We have suggested a greater presence of the early Ojibwe in the western regions of Lake Superior than has been posited before. The implication for this to help us understand important aspects of Ojibwe culture and history are only now starting to be examined.

With this we can leave the 1600s and move to the next century. The 1700s offer a challenge to Ojibwe cultural persistence from its earlier times. By the end of the one hundred years that followed we will see that the Ojibwe people had witnessed a century of great importance.

*Notes*

1. Kellogg 1917:328.
2. Kellogg 1917:327.
3. Kellogg 1917:326.
4. White 1996:6-7 in Blair 1996[1911].
5. White 1996:2 in Blair 1996[1911].
6. White 1996:23 in Blair 1996[1911].
7. Hickerson 1988[1970]:56.
8. White 1996:3 in Blair 1996[1911].
9. Blair 1996[1911]:181-187.
10. White 1996:5 in Blair 1996[1911].
11. Schenck 1996:49.
12. Blair 1996[1911]:Vol.I,187-188.
13. Blair 1996[1911]:Vol.I,190-191.
14. Hickerson 1970:51.
15. Kellogg 1968[1925]:208.
16. Kellogg 1917:329.
17. Kellogg 1917:330.
18. Kellogg 1968[1925]:209.
19. Kellogg 1917:330-31; brackets added.
20. Kellogg 1917:211.
21. Kellogg 1968[1925]: 208, 237.
22. Kellogg 1968[1925]:326.
23. Danziger 1979:28-29.
24. Burnham 1974[1929];Benton 1972.
25. Burnham 1974[1929]:4-5.
26. Danziger 1979:27.
27. Broker 1983.
28. Danziger 1979:29.
29. Blair 1996[1911]: Vol.I, 220-225.
30. Blair 1996[1911]:Vol.I, 220-225, 342-348.
31. Ross 1960:37.
32. Kellogg 1968[1925]:221.
33. Kellogg 1968[1925]:225.
34. Kellogg 1968[1925]:223, 229.
35. Neill 1885:415-17.
36. Neill 1885:416.
37. Kellogg 1968[1925]:299.
38. Neill 1885:416.
39. Kellogg 1968[1925]:229; brackets added.
40. Neill 1885:416-17.
41. Ross 1960:37.
42. Neill 1885:417.
43. Kellogg 1968[1925]:250.

44. Neill 1885:418.
45. Ross 1960:40.
46. Neill 1885:419.
47. Kellogg 1968[1925]:251.
48. Neill 1885:25; Upham 1908:249-50; Schenck 1997:72; Harris 1976: 420; Kellogg 1968 [1925]:42; Bieder 1995:68; Blair 1996 [1911]: Vol.I, 269.
49. Hickerson 1988[1970]:56-7.
50. Neill 1885:420.
51. Danziger 1979:29.
52. Kellogg 1968[1925]:257.
53. Beider 1995:51.
54. Roufs 1975:46-47.
55. Harris 1976; Kellogg 1968[1925]; Nute 1969[1941]; Parkman 2001 [1948].
56. Treuer 1988:57.
57. Roufs 1975:45.
58. Schenck 1996:252.
59. Grim 1983.
60. Jordahl 2011:14-5.

# 7

# The Start of the Eighteenth Century in Chequamegon Bay

THE EIGHTEENTH CENTURY WAS A GOOD TIME for the Chequamegon Bay ancestors of Red Cliff, one in which their culture continued to provide them with a full and meaningful life. Throughout these one hundred years the essential structure of this ancient foraging adaptation remained intact, with the overlay of the fur trade. As they did in the seventeenth century, the people had a continued role in this trade and also took part in considerable military activity. In this new century, Chequamegon Bay was a busy place and Madeline Island continued to be important in Ojibwe religious teachings. Throughout most of the century the European powers of France and England sought to exploit the western Great Lakes region for its wealth in furs, and in the latter decades Spain also attempted to garner wealth from the region from its main outpost in New Orleans and others far to the north on the Mississippi and Missouri Rivers.

In the early decades the Chequamegon territories saw France continue to share a major position in this international economy. However, by mid-century Great Britain became the prominent European nation in this industry and despite the desires of the new government of the United States to limit England's involvement, the British were a power in the fur trade well into the 1800s, even after the War of 1812. However, we should not overemphasize the roles of these European powers. Too often historians have told of the control these nations had on the trade while underplaying the integral role of the tribal peoples. Without the willing compliance of tribal leaders and the enterprise of the native trappers, pelt preparers, and fur traders the industry would not have existed.

It is in this sense that from the beginning of the fur trade the Europeans were dependent upon the tribal nations.[1] The Canadian historian Ian Steele has written that back in the late 1600s, in the earlier days of the trade, in some cases tribal leaders quickly understood this "and came to fathom and profit from some of the insatiable appetites of European consumers on both sides of the Atlantic."[2] This dependency soon became acute, and the Europeans understood that their dreams of empire in the western regions were only dreams without the cooperation of tribal peoples.[3] The Lake Superior nations were integral in this economy, and the Ojibwe, in their roles as traders and trappers, were in the midst of this industry.

The fur trade has been labeled an extractive economy, since its purpose was to remove the fur pelts from North America and ship them to Europe, where they were usually transformed into items of personal adornment. Perhaps we are familiar with visual accounts of the movement of beaver furs in this trade. Step by step, we are shown drawings and photos of live beavers at their lodges, their trapping, the preparation of the pelts, so forth and so on, to the finished product of a stylish beaver hat worn by a citizen on a London street, but we see less of what happened with the items exchanged for these pelts. The trade goods the tribal trappers received also moved along paths of transformation and use, all dependent upon tribal customs, but we are seldom treated to such colorful depictions.

Therefore, to label the fur trade as strictly an extractive economy is needlessly one-sided because it was at once extractive and intrusive. The furs were extracted from North America as the goods exchanged for them intruded into the tribal communities. However, as we will see later, even this view is harmfully incomplete. For it was not simply to exchange furs and trade goods that the tribesmen and Europeans entered the trade. As the historian Richard White argues, the fur trade was first of all about political alliances, and these were facilitated through *mediation*. The European nations entered North America with notions of empire, not furs, and the tribal nations entered the trade with goals of such alliances. White suggests that from this view, it was not the furs or the trade goods at the center of the trade but the political negotiations and alliance building that was always the first order, and at the crux of these was *mediation*, i.e., the ability of both tribal and French leaders to interact and form meaningful social, political and economic relationships. From a Western view with its concern for material commodities this might seem questionable, even ludicrous. But from both a tribal and European leader's administrative view it does not. In the historical literature a Western technocentrism has given a false shape and understanding to the fur trade.[4] This complex matter will be addressed later in this discussion.

In this new century, tribal affairs at times hindered the movement of furs from Lake Superior country to the European market. This resulted in disruption in cash flow for the French Crown and from time to time officials were dispatched in attempts to negotiate new alliances or restore the old to allow the trade to continue. In this way the fur trade can be said to have been reliant upon these periodic negotiations that began in the seventeenth century and, as we will note, continued throughout the eighteenth. Later in this new century as competition between England, France, and Spain became contentious, considerable amounts of European money were spent on goods used as gifts (usually called "presents" in the literature) for tribal leaders as trading post commandants tried to keep tribes loyal to particular monarchies. We saw how in the previous century intra-tribal relations also sometimes grew contentious as tribes struggled to gain a direct trading access to the French rather than go through other mediatory tribes.

As Ian Steele stated, the Europeans' hunger for material wealth fed their dependency. In the later 1600s and throughout the 1700s, they were virtually helpless in Chequamegon country without the willing compliance of the Ojibwe. Written historical accounts however, generally downplay this relationship, as early writers stressed the supposed dependency of the Ojibwe upon the French.

The question of an Ojibwe dependency is one issue we will explore in the following narration. Others are the Ojibwe movement from Chequamegon Bay into areas west and south of Lake Superior that continued in the 1700s; the Ojibwes' ongoing alliance with the Dakota and French that finally was ruptured because of the French in 1736; Ojibwe involvement in French military battles with the British in mid-century; the appearance of the British in Chequamegon; Ojibwe contacts with international tribal leaders like Pontiac, Neolin, Tecumseh and his brother, Tenskawatawa; the emergence of the new government of the United States of America, and how this affected Chequamegon country; and lastly the persistence of the foundations of a strong Ojibwe culture through this century of often volatile economic and political activity.

A considerable literature exists for events in Chequamegon country for this next century. While some of the early French documents and manuscripts have been irretrievably lost, many are still accessible and have been made available in English translation, and at mid-century we are treated to a British literature for the area, as seen in the journals of Alexander Henry, for example. However, this writing is done from the perspective of the Europeans and Euro-Americans and must be understood in this manner. Importantly, some of this literature speaks directly to affairs at Madeline Island and the Red Cliff shoreline, and it continues to present names of local Ojibwe leaders of the time.

As we did in the last chapter, we will peruse the written and oral accounts of the history of this new century as played out in the Chequamegon Bay region, always noting instances of importance to Red Cliff. The community's forebears were in the region in the 1600s, and right from the start of the 1700s they were not only residents of the area, but were here to stay. As was done in the last chapter, their presence will be traced through this next century.

### *1701: The Michilimackinac and Montreal Meetings for Peace Between the Ojibwe, French, Iroquois, and Others*

AN IMPORTANT PART OF THE CONTEXT for understanding the history of western Lake Superior's Ojibwe communities at the start of the eighteenth century is the state of diplomatic relationships between France, England, the New York colonies, and the Iroquois tribes (The Five Nations) at the time. In Europe, King William's War between England and France had recently ended, and in New France the long conflict between the Five Nations and France was struggling to a conclusion. By 1700, a growing factor in this important matter of French, Iroquois and British relationships was the increasing power of New York colonists, who were backed by the British, and their threat to lands claimed by New France and the Iroquois nations. Writers sometimes suggest that by this time the Iroquois were reevaluating their long positive relationship with the British and beginning to see the French more as a friend than adversary. This change in political sentiment is supported when we note that from 1693 to 1700, France and the Iroquois tribes periodically met to discuss ways of establishing peace between themselves, and for the Iroquois, peace with their several tribal adversaries—a move that would free both France and The Five Nations to more successfully deal with the increasing power of the British and their aggressive North American colonies.

In this atmosphere, it was in 1701, at a large international meeting that "The Great Peace of Montreal" was agreed upon by the French and Iroquois. This familiar peace agreement was several years in the making and is a marker for major changes in political relationships between New France, the Iroquois and their tribal allies, and the emerging British colonies. This peace signaled the end of the Iroquois's long role as military power in the Old Northwest and Eastern Great Lakes, and had a major impact on French and British policy in North America, as well as many tribal nations in the region.

Geographically, the Chequamegon Bay Ojibwes were on the periphery of this military, political and diplomatic activity, but written records show they were, nevertheless, involved. We have argued that for previous decades western Lake Superior Ojibwe were regularly included in meetings at Sault Ste. Marie and Michilimackinac, some of which saw contingents of tribal leaders, and on occasion military units that included Ojibwe fighting personnel departing the eastern Lake Superior sites for more distant eastern destinations. By 1701, the new peace between France and England gave a renewed impetus to the desires of both these nations to continue exploratory and land-claiming initiatives in North America. As historians have noted, it was when these two European powers were at peace with each other that they could turn the bulk of their energies to the matter of relationships with tribal nations, and in the early years we are discussing, peace between European nations often meant difficult times for North American tribes.

With this background in mind, when we turn to a study of Chequamegon Bay in the very early 1700s, we might better understand what was occurring in the local communities. 1701 is usually taken as a very significant marker for the end of warfare with the Iroquois, a phenomenon that meant the Europeans could more easily advance their economic and other agendas for North America.

The French understood the strategic importance of the Ojibwe community at Chequamegon Bay for European hopes of gaining control of lands and their resources, not only at the bay but also in the rich lands lying to its west. As we noted, over the several decades before 1700, there had been several years of unrest in Lake Superior country—unrest that saw the deaths of French traders. To make matters worse, some Huron bands began agitating to send military units into Iroquois country to attack them, a situation that could have disrupted current attempts to bring peace to the entire western region. Through French and Algonquian intervention these plans were thwarted, and further plans for peace were able to proceed.

It was in this milieu that a major peace conference was held at Michilimackinac and, at its completion, the attendees went on to meet the new French governor at Montreal. Frontenac had died on 28 November 1698, and Louis-Hector de Calliere was appointed to replace him. Chingouabe, the same Chequamegon Ojibwe leader who had gone to Montreal with Tioscate, the Dakota leader, in 1695, was in the large Michilimackinac conference and with the group that went on to meet Governor Calliere in Montreal. Approximately 1,300 representatives of upwards of forty tribal nations met with the new governor to finalize the Iroquois peace, and Nicholas Perrot was commissioned to be one of the interpreters at this important conference.

The preliminary Michilimackinac meeting shows the Lake Superior Ojibwe were part of the collaboration of western native nations involved in the negotiation of this important peace agreement. Chingouabe must have been a busy Ojibwe leader at these times, one the French knew they had to work with in order to be successful in not only western Lake Superior but the lands of the Upper Mississippi River as well. The withdrawal of LeSueur and his military contingent from Madeline Island in 1698 saw, for a time, the ending of an official French presence at La Pointe, but it did not signal the final end of French political and economic hopes to be involved in the region. Chingouabe's apparent strong alliance with the French at both Michilimackinac and Montreal indicates his willingness to continue working with this European ally, but the Ojibwe's positive relationship with the British seemed to be an emerging possibility.

The famed 1701 Montreal "Great Peace" also shows the renewed opportunity for the Ojibwe to continue supporting their alliance with the Dakota, a peaceful relationship that would continue for over thirty more years. For both these western tribal nations the role of the British in all this remained a question of great importance, and in time this European power began to have a greater presence in the western lakes regions.[5]

### *The Ojibwe Dispersal from Chequamegon Bay and the Continued Symbolism of Madeline Island*

1.

THE EIGHTEENTH CENTURY OPENED with Chequamegon Bay serving as a headquarters for the Ojibwe as they continued their seasonal movement into lands north, west, and south of Lake Superior. Their alliance with the Dakota and French allowed them to spend more time in the western region, and they soon reached the headwaters of the Mississippi River and areas to the north. The southern regions were opening up to them because the Mesquakie were being weakened by warfare with the French. As the Mesquakie pulled away from the headwaters of the Ontonagon, Chippewa and St. Croix River regions in what is now northern Wisconsin, the Chequamegon Bay Ojibwe were more easily able to use these southern territories.[6]

In his 1885 publication, William Warren gave an accounting of these numerous movements as told him by his Madeline Island informants. However, as noted, Warren has come under recent criticism for his methodology and biases, but aside from this his work still remains a valued source for students of Ojibwe culture and history. As a recent writer noted:

> He knew his subject well, and he experimented with an approach to oral history methodology that produced impressive results. No one can ever duplicate this feat, and it makes his work all the more valuable as a primary source. In fact, Warren might well have come closer than any other writer to describing Ojibway tribal history from the inside.[7]

Warren claimed that in the more northerly regions some Ojibwe began using the Rainy Lake lands and at times would join the Assiniboine and Cree for excursions onto the Great Plains to fight the Gros Ventre and Arikara. On more peaceful westward trips he said Ojibwe would trade for tobacco grown by the Gros Ventre people.[8] Apparently, despite these distant forays, the Ojibwe would generally return to Chequamegon Bay each season for rendezvous and for *midewiwin* ceremonies. In this way, Madeline Island remained a central symbol representing a homeland for the people.

As we recall, William Warren's claim that in the earliest days the Ojibwe had a large village settlement on Madeline Island was questioned in the 1970s by Harold Hickerson,[9] and more recently by Theresa Schenck.[10] They suggest that in the early times Madeline Island was not a headquarters for the Ojibwe, as Warren felt, but that it did achieve such prominence in the eighteenth century. Today, the spiritual symbolism of the island and the nearby shoreline and hills, especially in the immediate Red Cliff-Bayfield area, is clear.[11] It represents a center of great importance in Ojibwe religious and geographic awareness, and along with the surrounding islands and the nearby shoreline, remains integral to an understanding of the concept of an Ojibwe homeland.

In early times the forays out from this center seemed to be regular events, driven by the Ojibwe foraging culture. The people would return to the bay, but for some, eventually the frequency of these returns lessened. The alliance with the Dakota was ruptured in 1736, opening up the western lands for Ojibwe village sites, and the Mesquakie were routed from northern Wisconsin, allowing the Ojibwe to establish village headquarters south of Lake Superior. In time, these communities started holding their own annual *midewiwin* ceremonies, and for some the trips to Chequamegon Bay were greatly diminished, if not halted completely. However, Ojibwe teachings still told of the primacy of Madeline Island. Today families in distant Ojibwe communities such as White Earth in Minnesota, and Turtle Mountain in North Dakota, trace their ancestry back to the island.[12] Interestingly, some of Montana's Blackfeet people, another Algonquian nation, claim Madeline Island as their origin point, and this radiation from Madeline is not just a westward and southern phenomenon. Today there are Ojibwe people in eastern Canada that also trace their ancestry back to Madeline Island, claiming their forebears made an eastward migration from this Lake Superior homeland.

The significance of this for Red Cliff (and for the nearby Ojibwe community of Bad River) is obvious. These are the present-day communities that were the immediate Madeline Island-Chequamegon Bay Ojibwe community in the very earliest of times. In this sense the Red Cliff shoreline, the Bad River area, and Madeline Island together represent this symbolic homeland for many distant Ojibwe families today. Over the years some Red Cliff households have been surprised by a knock at the door from descendents of these early migrants. They return to Chequamegon Bay to La Pointe to make contact with this homeland, and in an interesting fashion, as doubtless long before the present time, the Ojibwe people of the region play host to these visitors. Today, because of renewed interest in Ojibwe identity, a deep, powerful sentiment is making this connection with Red Cliff, Bad River and Madeline Island even more important to distant Ojibwe people.

We should understand that the depths of this connection stem not just from ancient Ojibwe teachings about the westward migration, wherein Madeline Island marked the symbolic terminus for this long trek. While the island and the entire La Pointe-Chequqmegon Bay region stands as a symbol of the completion of this migration, it also represents hundreds of years of ongoing Ojibwe survival through adaptation since that distant time. Much has occurred in this region since the migration and these historical events, with their varied interpretations, have become part of what is today's Ojibwe history.

In an attempt to become familiar with this history we will offer a brief summary of the unfolding of events related to the Ojibwe of Chequamegon Bay throughout the 1700s, starting with a look at Ojibwe involvement in France's military battles with the Mesquakie (Fox). We will then consider the matter of Ojibwe and French political leaders at La Pointe. Other sections highlighting the major events for the Ojibwe during the early years of the century will follow. Finally, we will conclude with discussions of questions concerning these happenings. Since these are the years of the major part of the European fur trade, there is ample literature on this topic and the interested reader can pursue the details in the many sources available. Here we will focus on Chequamegon Bay and Red Cliff.

### *The Ojibwe and Mesquakie in the Early 1700s*

1.

AS THE OJIBWE MOVED INTO THE REGIONS south of Lake Superior they encountered the Mesquakie nation. Their involvement with these Algonquian speakers was at times as intense and contentious as with the more westerly Dakota, but except for the writings of William Warren, the historical written record has not consistently offered a discussion of this relationship. At the time of the French contact in the late 1600s, the Mesquakie were residing in what is now northeastern Wisconsin, and would make regular forays into the regions immediately adjacent to Lake Superior's southern shore. The Jesuits reported their visits to Chequamegon Bay in the 1660s, but with the intrusion of other groups into the western Great Lakes regions they eventually headquartered in lands further south, in what is now central and southern Wisconsin. Their subsistence base relied to a considerable extent on agriculture, and this may have been part of the reason for their move south, but it seems that the move occurred also because of the influx of the Huron, Odawa, and others, when these tribes were trying to avoid the Iroquois.

The Mesquakie became a strong military force in these southern regions and were more allied with the British than with the French. Due to their southern location it is generally felt that the Lake Superior Ojibwe had little later significant contact with them. William Warren tells us about their earlier trips to the lake's south shore when they engaged in military conflict with the Ojibwe, and they continued to have a military presence in southern Lake Superior country for some decades.[13] We see that La Pointe Ojibwe were at times in battle with the Mesquakie and at other times called by the French to help when such conflicts appeared imminent. In the 1680s and 1690s, the Ojibwe would sometimes work with the Dakota on military campaigns against the Mesquakie in regions south of Lake Superior.[14]

Along with these actual military confrontations there was the potential for an even greater impact upon Chequamegon Bay's Ojibwe people partly due to the Mesquakie. This involved the French and their struggles to keep the British out of the western fur trade in the 1690s and early 1700s. All through these times the Mesquakie were troublesome for the French. In 1696, France attempted to gain a better hold on the trade by reducing the number of trading stations, the hope being that this would stop a growing British influence.[15] At least three French centers were to be established—one at New Orleans to block British attempts to move up the Mississippi River, another at Detroit to block attempts to move into the western lakes region, and a third to handle the Chicago region and the western Illinois country at St. Louis. (French plans for this last site are unclear. Louise Kellogg felt it was headquartered at St. Louis, but Robert Beider claims there were two sites in this general area, one at Chicago, the other on the Mississippi at St. Louis.) These were to be agricultural settlements, all garrisoned with troops, and it was expected they would grow into centers of French civilization that would initially block British intrusion but soon develop into thriving French colonies.

The tribal communities in this large area were to move to these centers and begin a process of assimilation into French society. This is an interesting concept since it suggests a French willingness to accept the tribal peoples as potential French citizens. Although it was grounded in a certainty that tribal societies would disappear through biological and social absorption, it is still a far more accepting stance toward the tribesmen than that of early British commanders in North America. Lord Jeffery Amherst, for example, suggested the spreading of smallpox amongst the tribal communities. Another case of British thoughts of genocide for the natives is found in remarks of Henry Bouquet, the British commander at Fort Pitt, who "suggested hunting them with English dogs."[16]

Under this new French policy of Indian concentration, some Illinois, Kickapoo, Mascouten and Potawatomi communities moved south in the area of the Chicago-St. Louis center. At Michilimackinac the French commander, Antoine la Mothe de Cadillac, was successful in having a Huron group, and others, move south to Detroit.[17] Then, in 1711, Cadillac also enticed a Mesquakie community from west of Lake Michigan to move to Detroit, hoping they and the other tribes would reside in peace. However, the Mesquakie, Huron and Odawa had been at war for decades, and Cadillac was not able to establish peace at the site. At Detroit, in 1712, this old tension erupted into intertribal war and:

> When forced to choose sides, the French clearly favored their own Huron, Ottawa and Potawatomi allies and did not protect the newcomers. The Fox surrendered, only to have an estimated one thousand warriors systematically butchered. From a fortified base at Green Bay, those Fox who had not migrated to Detroit took revenge on their Amerindian enemies and on the French.[18]

Cadillac's poor decision to bring the Mesquakie to Detroit and his inability to resolve their old disputes with the Huron, Odawa and Potawatomi already resident at the new settlement led to the French decision, in historian Beider's words, "to chastise" the Mesquakie, and soon "the French . . . became embroiled in an extensive though sporadic frontier war."[19] France soon gave up its plan for Indian concentration, and in 1714, entered an inter-colonial war against England (Queen Anne's War).[20]

France's late seventeenth century policy of moving tribal populations to agricultural and "civilizing" centers did not reach the La Pointe Ojibwe because of the outbreak of this open warfare with the British. We can only speculate on what might have occurred in Chequamegon country if this concentration policy had been successful. It seems questionable whether the La Pointe Ojibwe would have been enticed to move south. More likely, because of France's interest in economic opportunities west and north of Lake Superior and because of a growing British presence in that region, an "agricultural-civilization" center would have been attempted at Grand Portage or even at La Pointe itself.

La Pointe's Ojibwe are not said to have been involved in these political and military machinations, but it is clear that they were affected by them. For example, France made the decision to reopen the Madeline Island post in 1718, in order to keep La Pointe's Ojibwe (and Keweenaw's as well) from going into battle with the Mesquakie at that time. Such warfare could have hindered France's attempts to develop a strong presence in the region in order to keep the British at bay. Also, a few years earlier, in 1711, when a large British naval force appeared at the mouth of the St. Lawrence River, causing French authorities to fear an attack, they sent a message to Green Bay and Lake Superior for help. A large force was assembled and reached Quebec sometime that summer, only to learn that the British fleet had been destroyed by a severe storm, thus ending the threat. The French governor at Quebec staged a festive council at which he thanked his western friends for coming such a great distance for his aid.[21] Certainly, some Ojibwe from western Lake Superior were in attendance at this council.

## 2.

THE MESQUAKIE HAD FURTHER INFLUENCES in Lake Superior country throughout the first several decades of the 1700s. These may not always have touched the La Pointe Ojibwe in a direct military manner, but their significance to an understanding of the times is important. The historical record suggests that Chequamegon country was geographically removed from the years of bloodshed occurring in the 1700s, in regions like the Ohio valley and later in Indiana, Illinois and southern Wisconsin. Yet the Ojibwe in Chequamegon Bay certainly experienced the pervading effect of these years in North America.

There is a lasting feeling of togetherness, or *camaraderie*, among tribal people in North America today, and this shared sentiment must have been evident in the 1700s, in what is now Wisconsin and Illinois. By that time the tribesmen were becoming aware of the strength and determination of the Europeans. As the decades of the eighteenth century passed it must have been increasingly evident that these newcomers were here to stay, and that their presence would have long-term effects on tribal nations. The early decades of the 1700s immediately preceded attempts of select tribal leaders to form a united front against this European intrusion. Doubtless there were long harangues in Indian communities in which political and religious leaders discussed what was occurring throughout the land and importantly, how to deal with it. The history of astute political leadership among the Ojibwe suggests that such discussions were going on in Chequamegon country in those years.

When France and Great Britain ended their Queen Anne's War by signing the Treaty of Utrecht in 1713, it allowed France to turn its energies to quieting the Mesquakie, and almost immediately a French force engaged them in battle in eastern Wisconsin.[22] A year later this was over, and for a period of about thirteen years open hostilities between the Mesquakie and French were minimal. However, those years following 1713 were not times of complete quiet on the frontier. Louise Phelps Kellogg tells of fears of a "vast conspiracy," probably led by a Mesquakie leader named "Kiala." This plan was extensive, supposedly including "the Abenaki of the East, embracing the Iroquois of Lake Ontario, and extending to the Sioux at the northwest and the Missouri and Oto tribes to the southwest."[23] This "Amerindian confederacy against all Europeans"[24] could have devastated the French in North America. According to Kellogg:

> It was a resurgence of barbarism against civilization, a rebellion of a brave, independent people against the demoralization of white influence and the invasion of their lands. Like barbarians, however, they were un-able to plan with sufficient foresight, or to hold together their allies against the influence of the French or of intertribal rivalries.[25]

Putting Kellogg's biased colonial imagery aside, we can at least appreciate her awareness of a strong anti-European sentiment among tribal nations of the times. Regarding La Pointe, she says it was the work of the French commandant at Chequamegon who caused the Dakota to refuse to take part in this Mesquakie "conspiracy." In 1728, France again began a major military thrust into Wisconsin, which Kellogg called an "armed invasion." It started in Montreal with 400 French and 800-900 Indian fighters. At Michilimackinac another 300 tribesmen joined the force before leaving that fort on 10 August to go south into Mesquakie country.[26] It is not improbable that some of those 300 persons at Michilimackinac were from western Lake Superior. In October of the following year, an Odawa and Ojibwe force attacked another Wisconsin Mesquakie community. Then in 1733, the Mesquakie leader, Kiala, came to the French post at Green Bay to settle for peace. He and fifty or so people surviving in his community were apprehended and while his colleagues were said to have been distributed among eastern French communities as slaves, Kiala himself was sent to the West Indies as a prisoner.[27]

But the French were still not finished with the Mesquakie. By this time the few remaining Mesquakie survivors had sought refuge with their neighbors the Sauk, and together they withstood further clashes with the French in east-central Wisconsin. Then in 1724, another French invasion of Mesquakie lands was undertaken but was not successful. One suggestion for its failure is that it was composed largely of Iroquois from French settlements in the St. Lawrence valley, and that these "mission Iroquois" were not willing to engage the Mesquakie in battle. Another reason offered is that the French commandant at Michilimackinac "had been unable to induce the Indians of that post to reinforce Des Noyelles" [the leader of the French force].[28] This suggests that the tribesmen of the north were no longer eager to respond to a French beckoning for military aid.

By the late 1730s, the number of surviving Mesquakie is felt to have been drastically low. Importantly, in 1727, a group of tribal leaders from the western Great Lakes traveled to Montreal to ask the French governor to cease his destruction of this tribe. Apparently fearing the tribes might abandon the French in favor of the British, the governor considered this plea. Then in 1740, when another group of western tribal leaders traveled to Montreal again to seek an end to the French policy of what was looking more and more like Mesquakie extermination, the wars ended.

The importance of this for the Ojibwe at La Pointe is hinted at by Louise Kellogg when she suggests that while some tribes "secretly dreaded" the Mesquakie, they, paradoxically, were admired. In their persistent refusal to bow to the French, the Mesquakie had helped to hasten the downfall of this European colonizer in the New World. By the 1730s, perhaps tribes held common understandings of the changes sweeping their homelands. Writers like Kellogg insist that the tribes had become dependent upon the French, yet these writers intimate that these tribes desired the native way of life and deeply resented the French invasion.[29]

Such a deep-seated sentiment was hinted at in a 1924 outdoor theatrical production at the Ojibwe community of Red Cliff. According to an eyewitness to the stage show, after a group of Ojibwe actors took part in a patriotic ceremony celebrating the coming of the French to Lake Superior country, the actors filed off stage led by the French and followed by the Ojibwe. At the very end of the line was an Ojibwe man shaking a fist at the French tricolor being held aloft at the head of the line. According to Hale O'Malley, who participated in this outdoor pageant as a seven-year-old boy, the crowd watching this show understood the poignant sentiment of the shaking fist.[30]

## *Ojibwe and French Leadership at La Pointe*

1.

An important question to ask at the start of an analysis of a century of historical events in Chequamegon Bay concerns the underlying matter of human motivation. Why did the Ojibwe and French act the way they did in these early years? What motivated them to make the decisions they did? These are the sorts of questions raised by political, economic, social and cultural theorists, all students of human behavior who use the underlying assumption that such behavior is systemic, i.e., that no matter how idiosyncratic historical events might sometimes appear, it is agreed that the motivations behind the behavior of individuals are largely influenced by the social and cultural systems in which they are situated.

Accepting this, we can focus upon the nature of the Ojibwe and French political organizations extant at Chequamegon in the late 1600s and early 1700s. When doing so, we immediately see that these were two very different systems. The Ojibwe, as we saw in a previous chapter, had a society with a hunting and gathering culture. They were not Christians (although the record indicates there may have been a few legitimate conversions to Christianity under the Jesuits) and their political and economic systems were complex. Kinship was set within a network of patrilineal clans, and sharing and barter were at the base of their economic system. They had an unstratified egalitarian society, one in which wealth was to be shared, and leaders had to work within this structure. As we saw, there were several types of leaders, among which two were major: a civil leader and a military leader. However, both of these positions existed only with the approval of the entire society, and therefore, neither had anything that approached a totalitarian sense of power. As we saw in an early chapter, it can be argued that this Ojibwe political organization was, finally, a democratic one.

In contrast to this Ojibwe decentralized political system, the French were operating under a stratified paternalistic society in which great power was in the hands of a monarch. The overall French system was based on agriculture, and at least in the urban centers, worked within the structure of a cash economy. The French Revolution changed much of this, but during the years of the Ojibwe-French alliances in North America, political power and decision-making was essentially in the hands of the Crown. Political positions were embedded within a patronage system, one where positions were given to individuals who pleased the Crown and at times were purchased through the Crown.

The important point to be made here is that a system like that of the French did not allow for a conceptualization of the political system of the Ojibwe as anything other than a lawless entity, that by its "undeveloped" nature did not qualify as meaningful, except to see it as a "savage" society. And as such, no matter how empathic and friendly the French leaders were, at times, toward the Ojibwe, in the last analysis the French saw the Ojibwe political system as they saw the entire Ojibwe world: as a primitive, archaic form, meant to give way to a superior European civilization.

The Ojibwe had a system with a multiplicity of leaders who assumed responsibilities within the context of clans, age grades, religious institutions, and other social constructions within the culture. In times this demanded diplomacy with societies outside the Ojibwes', and a dual system of leadership was activated: the civil and military structure we already discussed.

Earlier literature, as noted, stressed the military leaders of the Ojibwe. Essentially this is due to the popular writings of William Warren, in which military leaders at Chequamegon were mentioned to the virtual exclusion of other tribal leaders. So we are generally unfamiliar with the names of the numerous non-military leaders integral to Ojibwe politics all through the 1600s and early 1700s. Their leadership was important in those years, and although for most, their physical remains lie in the earth of the region, their names are no longer with us.

What we do have are several names of Ojibwe leaders involved in relations with the French in the times we are discussing. The Jesuits left few such personal names in their records and even William Warren offers few, or if he does mention names he often gives the person's community but not the times or the actual years they were alive.

2.

BY THE LATE 1600S, LA POINTE was a busy fur-trading center. France was trying to keep England influence out of the region and had appointed Pierre LeSueur as commander of a military detail to go to Chequamegon and secure it for the Crown. After erecting a fort on Madeline Island, LeSueur traveled down the St. Croix River to Prairie Island near Hastings, and then went westward in an attempt to secure this vast area for the French.[31] There was extensive French contact in this territory at the time, and La Pointe was a strategic site for the Crown. In these years the Mesquakie, with English involvement, had closed off the Green Bay, or southern route, for moving furs from the Upper Mississippi River regions to Montreal, causing all French furs to be funneled through La Pointe. In the latter years of the fur trade huge rendezvous were held north of La Pointe at Grand Portage, where large French canoes arrived from Montreal, laden "with their loads of trade goods, to return with furs." Hamilton Ross suggested that in earlier times at Madeline Island, "No doubt the same kind of rendezvous was held every year, with the Indians assembled from all directions, the *coureurs de bois* from their lonely stations of the interior, the important men from Montreal and the soldiers of the post."[32]

We can imagine the festiveness of these events at Madeline, perhaps grown quite large with the increasing French interest in garnering as many bundles of furs as possible. These large rendezvous were a continuation of the annual gatherings of tribesmen at the bay reported by Menard, Allouez, Marquette, and told about by William Warren, in the early decades of the 1600s. For the Ojibwe, the rendezvous were recurrent annual homecomings.

However, the Madeline Island post was closed by the French in 1698, only five years after the arrival of LeSueur and his small military force. It seems the Ojibwe and other trappers and traders had been too successful, for the eastern warehouses were glutted with furs, causing their value to plummet and the European market to suffer. So the Madeline Island post was abandoned by the Crown and fur trading licenses were cancelled. Another reason—mentioned above—for the sudden downturn in the trade was the poor treatment of the tribesmen by the French. According to one writer, "Missionaries complained of the abuses that French traders and *coureurs de bois* inflicted on the Indians," and this resulted in the Crown's restriction of the trade.[33]

For the Ojibwe at Chequamegon, even though the French officials were withdrawn, fur trapping and trading continued, but not through official Crown channels. Without licensed traders, the Ojibwe were supposedly at the hands of the "lawless" *coureurs de bois* who still worked to gather furs.[34] When the Treaty of Utrecht of 1713 officially ended inter-colonial warfare between France and England, both nations were to have equal rights to trade with the North American tribesmen, but such an ideal did not materialize in the western Great Lakes area. In 1714, France returned to its system of licensing fur traders and once again looked to western Lake Superior country for wealth through furs.[35]

Attempting to recoup its control of the trade, in 1718, twenty years after LeSueur left, the Crown sent Paul Le Gardeiur, Sieur de St. Pierre, to reopen the Madeline Island post. It has been said that St. Pierre found the Ojibwe in Chequamegon in poor condition because they had become dependent upon French trade goods only to suddenly have their availability greatly reduced in 1698. As we will see below, Hamilton Ross stressed this purported poor condition of the island's people.

Part of the problem at Chequamegon is thought to have been the continuing conflicts between the Ojibwe and the Mesquakie in the trapping regions south of Lake Superior. To calm this region, St. Pierre negotiated a peace with the Mesquakie. Importantly, as French trading relationships were officially reestablished in Chequamegon country, alcohol became an important commodity in the arsenal of French trading goods.[36]

Our understanding of approximately the next forty years of events at La Pointe is minimal because many records of these activities were destroyed in France during the French Revolution. We know St. Pierre was at Madeline Island for only two years, being replaced by Rene Godefroy, Sieur de Linctot in 1720, and that Linctot was at La Pointe for six years—suggesting his leadership had a degree of success—but we know little about the details of his tenure. In 1727, the next French official to command the La Pointe post was Louis Denis, Sieur de la Ronde. We know much more about La Ronde's time at Chequamegon because although many of his official documents are gone, some of his personal letters have been preserved. Louis Denis La Ronde was interested in the copper found along Lake Superior's south shore, and is said to have investigated the possibility of having it mined.

For the next twenty-two years,—from 1727 to 1749—the La Pointe post was in the hands of the La Ronde family. For most of these years, from 1727 to 1741, Louis Denis La Ronde led the post, but when he fell ill and died, his son Philippe took charge until 1743. Philippe was called back east to fight in the French and Indian War against the British and was killed. At this point his mother took command at the La Pointe post, as she "was given the position as a pension in reward for her husband's services." According to Hamilton Ross, we do not know if Mrs. La Ronde took an active role in managing the post, or if her leadership was only titular, but as Ross says, "It is notable that a woman should have been charged with the responsibility of administering such an important post in those times."[37]

The next commandant at La Pointe was Joseph de la Margue, Sieur Marin, who took charge in 1749. Marin and his father were both said to have been deeply involved in political corruption evident in the government of New France at the time. About Marin the younger, Ross wrote, "he and his kind were largely responsible for the rotten core which spelled the downfall of the French in Canada." Apparently to gain financial advantage, Marin was successful in having the governor of New France "abolish the old leasing system which had been in force since LeSueur's time, and substitute for it the still older licensing method. The governor lent a sympathetic ear since he would receive a generous cut." Marin was at La Pointe for only two years, leaving to resume command at the Green Bay post in 1750.[38]

The next La Pointe commandant was Joseph Gaultier, Chevalier de la Verendrye, who commanded from 1751 to 1755. A dispute between Marin and La Verendrye about the boundary between their trading territories caused problems to these two French businessmen. La Varendrye was a son of Pierre Gaultier de Varennes de Verendrye, a French explorer and entrepreneur of whom we will hear more later.

From 1756 to 1758, La Pointe's French commandant was Pierre Hertel de Beaubassin. These were the years of open conflicts between France and England in eastern North America and interestingly, as a military officer, Beaubassin "left La Pointe in 1758 with a company of Indians which he had trained, to aid the hard-pressed French forces against the British."[39] We assume this company was composed of Chequamegon Bay Ojibwe who went east to fight the red-coated British.

With Beaubassin's departure, the new commandant was Sieur Corne de la St. Luc. There is a question of St. Luc's official status since he was a military officer but seemed to serve at La Pointe as a civilian. Ross suggests it would have been unusual for the French to send a capable military officer to distant Lake Superior country when such a person was obviously needed to assist in the war against the British in the eastern portions of the continent, and thus it might have been possible that St. Luc "had been temporarily banished on account of the fiendish work of the Indians under his command, upon the surrender by the British of Fort William Henry the year before."[40]

Like most of his predecessors, St. Luc's time at La Pointe was relatively brief—only for four years—from 1758 to 1762. France's struggle with England in North America was not going well and it finally ended in 1763. It seems, as was the case with those who came before him, that St. Luc intended to reap considerable financial reward through trading furs while at Madeline, but we do not know how successful he was. In fact, we know nothing of the details of his four years in Chequamegon country.

*A Summary of French Commanders at La Pointe*
(taken from Ross 1960:57)

| | |
|---|---|
| Pierre LeSueur | 1693-1698 |
| Paul Le Gardier, Sieur de St. Pierre | 1718-1720 |
| Rene Godefroy, Sieur de Linctot | 1720-1726 |
| Louis Denis, Sieur de la Ronde | 1727-1741 |
| Philippe Louis Denis de la Ronde | 1741-1743 |
| Madame La Ronde (Wife of Louis) | 1743-1748 |
| Joseph de la Marque, Sieur Marin | 1749-1750 |
| Joseph Gaultier, Chevalier de la Verendrye | 1751-1755 |
| Pierre Hertel de Beaubassin | 1756-1758 |
| Sieur Corne de la St. Luc | 1758-1762 |

3.

FOR ALMOST SEVENTY YEARS, the Chequamegon Bay Ojibwe saw a series of French officials come to the station at Madeline Island. With few exceptions, each stayed for only a few short years. Each came as a representative of the French Crown and as such was intended to hold an authoritative presence in the region, with the task of commanding the military trading station, and from the French perspective, as said by Louise Kellogg, "to control the natives."[41] What is often not stressed is that these French government officials were also private businesspersons. They were fur traders, and looked upon their government appointment as a business opportunity, i.e., a chance to garner private wealth through buying and selling furs, a fact that must be considered whenever we attempt to understand their time on Lake Superior. The Ojibwe knew this, of course, and while it might seem unusual for us—considering how we value what we call "a separation of private business and public service"—tribal leaders related to these French officials for what these French persons were: government officials *and* fur traders.

This point warrants further consideration since the literature does not usually discuss it. What we do find in the written record, at least during the treaty making and annuity-payment days, are remarks concerning deferential treatment shown to tribal leaders who accept cash and goods payments seemingly aside from the public transfer of the same to other tribal annuitants. Tribal leaders, for instance, are sometimes given cash and other gratuities for their efforts to win approval of treaty articles desired by government treaty officials.

So tribal leaders were familiar with the matter of personal "profit" as a counterpart to holding public leadership positions, and at early La Pointe it seems both French and Ojibwe leaders accepted this as normative, since it was built into both French and Ojibwe culture.

Given this, we must ask what effect the combined roles of French government official and private businessperson might have had on French-Ojibwe relations at Chequamegon Bay. Also, did the fluid French presence (the almost rapid change of leaders) have an effect on the Ojibwe? And lastly, to what degree, if any, were the Ojibwe, as Kellogg claims was the French intent, "controlled" by these French fur-trading officials?

Like the Jesuits who came decades earlier, these French officials had an almost rapid turnover. A French commandant arrived and began a period of adjustment in which the names of Ojibwe leaders and the nature of politics at La Pointe were learned, and in a few short years, he (or in the case of Mrs. La Ronde—she) would leave. And likewise, the tribal people adjusted to a particular commandant only to have him (or her) leave, then had to start the adjustment to the next French leader, a process that would have worked to keep politics at La Pointe on edge. Yet, it is likely the regular turnover of French leaders would have helped the Ojibwe to look *inward* for stability, i.e., to remain absorbed in the regular rhythm of their culture. The seasonal round of Ojibwe subsistence practices discussed in a previous chapter may have been affected negatively by the intensity of the fur trade, but the tradition of moving in season to the different resource areas did not cease. Trapping was done essentially during the winter hunting season, when the fur-bearing animals were wearing their finest pelts. The French—and in turn, the British—did not work to disrupt the Ojibwe cultural system, only to add commercial fur trapping to it.[42]

France brought no schools to Chequamegon Bay, so there were none of these European institutions to assimilate the Ojibwe into French culture, and, with the departure of the Jesuits in 1671, Christian mission work ended. We see then, that all through the years of a French presence at Chequamegon—going back to the coming of Radisson and Groseilliers in 1659 (or even earlier with Etienne Brule), and concluding with the abandonment of the La Pointe trading station in 1762—the Chequamegon Bay Ojibwe were able to continue enjoying their mobile foraging adaptation. They hunted, gathered, fished, did some gardening, and in winter worked hard to get furs for trading at the spring rendezvous. Their clan leaders, as well as the religious and other leaders, continued to aid them as they had been doing since the earliest times. In fact, their several tribal leaders were at work in these years, using their language, knowledge and beliefs to help guide the people. The herbalists and other healers, family and clan members, and hunting, fishing and gathering specialists were all working to keep the Ojibwe cultural system operable.

At rendezvous the people bartered the furs for trade goods. The notion of a cash economy was to come in force after the European fur trade ended. Bartering, an economic exchange method in which trade good is exchanged for trade good, does not use an all-purpose medium of exchange (money). This is important in understanding the long French-Ojibwe relationship in Chequamegon. Usually, the introduction of a cash economy into a culture without one precipitates major cultural change. However, for the Ojibwe, the European fur trade was a cashless system, based instead on a barter system. This meant their traditional economic system had to keep functioning because it allowed for the production of furs—the item desired by the French.

All through the years of the fur trade the Ojibwe continued their age-old method of producing furs. The steel traps introduced by the Europeans increased the efficiency of the trappers but they did not, in a fundamental way, change the Ojibwe tradition of trapping fur-bearing animals. The introduction of guns did have an important effect on the way animals were taken, but regarding the fur trade, it was the beaver that was the pelt of choice, and while on rare occasion a beaver could be taken with a gun, the bulk of them had to be trapped. The long French presence in Chequamegon Bay, with its explorers, Jesuits, *voyageurs*, *coureurs de bois*, military and civilian commandants, had not caused a rupture in Ojibwe culture. To the contrary, even accepting the obvious changes that occur with a hunting and gathering culture when it comes into extended contact with a centralized state system, Ojibwe life at Chequamegon Bay stayed on course and was even encouraged *not* to make major altering changes.

Historians have told us that the Ojibwe enjoyed their long relationship with the French traders. Writing in the mid-1800s, and using the style of the time, William Warren said:

> The Ojibways learned to love the French people, for the Frenchmen, possessing a character of great plasticity, easily assimilated themselves to the customs and mode of life of their red brethren. They respected their religious rites and ceremonies, and they 'never laughed' at their superstitious beliefs and ignorance. They fully appreciated, and honored accordingly, the many noble traits and qualities possessed by these bold and wild hunters of the forest. It is an acknowledged fact, that no nation of whites have ever succeeded so well in gaining the love and confidence of the red men, as the Franks. It is probable that their character in many respects was more similar, and adapted to the character of the Indian, than any other European nation.[43]

Warren may have been correct in saying the character of the Ojibwe and French probably was similar and that this is what allowed for their positive relationship. Such relations, however, can also be driven by a similarity in cultural motivations. In the seventeenth and eighteenth centuries, it was to the benefit of the French that Ojibwe cultural adaptations not be significantly altered. To be fur trappers the Ojibwe had to continue to move with the rhythms of the seasons, and so the French encouraged the continuation of traditional tribal economic, political, and other cultural systems. Herein lies a deep, structural reason for the generally amiable Ojibwe-French relationship in Chequamegon country, but this very important point has not adequately been addressed in the literature.

However, William Warren recognized this factor underlying Ojibwe-French relations. After writing at some length about the similarities in what he called Ojibwe and French character, Warren went on to note that:

> The French early gained the utmost confidence of the Ojibways, and thereby they became more thoroughly acquainted with their true and real character, even during the comparative short season in which they mingled with them as a nation, than the British and Americans are at this present day, after a century of intercourse. The French understood their division into clans, and treated each clan according to the order of its ascendancy in the tribe. They conformed also to their system of governmen-

tal polity, of which the totemic division formed the principal ingredient. They were circumspect and careful in bestowing medals, flags, and other marks of honor, and appointing chiefs, and these acts were never done unless being first certain of the approbation of the tribe, and it being in accordance with their civil polity.[44]

It can be suggested then, that as the long line of French commandants moved through their rather short terms at La Pointe from1693 to 1762, the question of the French "controlling" the Ojibwe became a moot point. Both nations were getting what they sought in their relationship. From its perspective France was able to go forward with its imperial activities (at least until the British stepped in) and the Ojibwe were able to enjoy their chosen way of life. In this sense the Ojibwe were "controlling" the French and the historian Edmund Jefferson Danziger, Jr. may have been correct when he called this period in Ojibwe history a "Golden Age".

### *1700-1736:*<br>*Chequamegon as an Ojibwe Headquarters;*<br>*The End of the Ojibwe-French-Dakota Alliance*

1.

WHEN THE 1700S BEGAN, CHEQUAMEGON BAY was serving as a springboard from which Ojibwe bands moved further and further into the resource areas south and west of Lake Superior. For the Ojibwe this was nothing new, since for the previous century Sault Ste. Marie had served in a similar fashion. The Ojibwe community at Keweenaw—about halfway between Sault Ste. Marie and Chequamegon—likewise was a base for the Ojibwe as they grew, always moving westward.

To some extent this is probably the overall pattern of adaptation that occurred as the Ojibwe ancestors moved from the eastern seaboard through the eastern Great Lakes, to Lake Superior, and beyond. This fluid east to west flow, like the daily movement of the sun overhead, is a deep pattern of much of Ojibwe ritual expression.[45] It is in this context that Madeline Island takes on its central characteristic—as the center point of the Ojibwe Nation. The island, with its nearby Red Cliff shoreline and hills, is more than a terminus of the migration in Ojibwe origin teachings; as we have already noted, it is a *central* place in the peoples' spiritual belief system.

As William Warren wrote, for some Ojibwe the migration went far beyond Madeline Island. Numerous bands continued their trek hundreds of miles west, and north to the Great Plains. Writers have suggested it was the European fur trade that after 1680, caused the Ojibwe to leave Sault Ste. Marie and move westward along both the north and south shores of Lake Superior, and when the people reached the western parameter of the water to eventually push into lands west, north and south of the big lake. Yet, a study of the structural underpinnings of Ojibwe culture, and especially its religious ideology and ceremonial expression, suggests such a movement was more than a yearning for material possessions gained through the fur trade. Earlier writers, by understanding early Ojibwe history only within the context of the fur trade, have given us a misdirected interpretation of this history. As we have seen, this point is hinted at by Theresa Schenck, a more recent writer. The earlier view of Ojibwe history as a history driven by the European fur trade involved conclusions that sometimes are not only controversial, but to some Ojibwe people, are absurd.[46] For example, when stating that the *midewiwin* took form in response to this westward migration from Sault Ste. Marie, Harold Hickerson pointed to the fur trade as the cause for this "new" religion.[47] To today's Ojibwe *midewiwin* members, this conclusion is not simply an absurdity, but also an insult.

As we have already mentioned, the Chequamegon Bay Ojibwe negotiated numerous alliances with the Mesquakie and Dakota that helped facilitate these movements. As was the case in the latter decades of the 1600s, these alliances of the early 1700s often involved the French. The Mesquakie and French were adversaries at this time, and as we have seen, due to numerous military conflicts that began to take their toll, the Mesquakie finally headquartered in west central Wisconsin with the Sauk Nation and in time ceased to be a problem to both the French and Ojibwe.

But the French continued to dream of a Northwest Passage to the Pacific as well as nurturing visions of expansion into lands west of Lake Superior. France struggled to keep British influence away from the western Great Lakes, but with the abandonment of La Pointe in 1698, French officialdom did not have a direct presence in western Lake Superior country. When the Iroquois were quieted at about 1701, all this changed, and the northern waterway was once again open from Montreal to the Upper Lakes. With the Treaty of Utrecht in 1713 that brought a halt to the English-French war, others would turn toward these northern British outlets for trade. It has been written that because of these events, "for some time after the year 1700, the French had little intercourse with the Ojibways."[48]

There was no French official at La Pointe from 1698 to 1718, but one must wonder about the importance of this to the Ojibwe. We are familiar with the roles of the independent traders in Lake Superior country. Sometimes working outside the realm of French law, these traders were often considered to be illegal, and as such were troublesome to Crown authorities who sought personal wealth through their official positions. But these "illegal" traders still were French, and through them a European presence existed in Chequamegon. We recall that Nicholas Perrot was on occasion appointed by the Crown to carry out official tasks, but we know he was trading in furs and often acted in an unofficial capacity and in this role enjoyed considerable influence with tribal nations. The Jesuits, as well, were not officials of the Crown but in some cases had a Crown-related influence with tribal peoples. Writers like Louise Kellogg and Grace Lee Nute have told us about the success of the *coureurs de bois* enjoyed in trading relations with the Ojibwe.

Given this, we must ponder the above statement of Reverand Neill, in which he suggests that when colonial authorities closed the La Pointe post in 1698, the Ojibwe had little contact with the French. We see that among colonial documents for 1717 is a message from a French lieutenant at Grand Portage to a trader at "Chequamegon Point." The document was a statement about the Dakota seeking peace with the Cree but for our interests it shows the presence of the French at

Chequamegon Bay at the time.[49] This helps suggest that French traders must have regularly been in Chequamegon Bay all through the late 1600s and right up to 1718, when the Crown sent St. Pierre to take command of the region. We know an Ojibwe community was at Chequamegon Bay at this time because historical documents tell that one reason St. Pierre (and Ensign Linctot) were sent to Chequamegon in September, 1718, was "because the Ojibway chief there, and also at Keweenaw, were threatening war against the Foxes."[50]

These historical details are significant because they suggest that for some time previous, contrary to what historians have been telling us, it is likely the Ojibwe were enjoying the trade goods of unlicensed traders at Chequamegon and were strong enough to contemplate taking military action against the (at that time) still powerful Mesquakie. Therefore, when pulling together the bits and pieces of historical documentation and commentary for the late 1600s and early 1700s, we can conclude there must have been much activity at Chequamegon Bay in these times. Even though France had a minimal official presence in the area, its eagerness to control the taking of furs from the rich lands south and west of the big lake and its dreams of political and economic growth in lands stretching west to the Rockies and beyond must have affected the Ojibwe.

William Warren tells us about some of the events of these times in Chequamegon as Ojibwe bands ventured further and further into lands of the St. Croix, the Ontonagon, the Chippewa, the Wisconsin, and even the Mississippi River systems. These were regions rich in all the traditional foods and other resources of the people, and fur-bearing animals—especially the beaver—were found in abundance. However, despite the wealth of these regions, and the readiness of *coureurs de bois* and *voyageurs*, as traders, to follow the various Ojibwe bands into the rich lands of these waterways, a recent writer notes that these Ojibwe excursions were not one-way trips. They were circular in the sense that the people did not permanently leave Chequamegon Bay. According to Danziger, "The menace of lingering Fox and Sioux war parties forced Chippewa hunters to return each spring to La Pointe, where they bartered their winter pelts and participated in unifying *Midewiwin* rites."[51]

This is a puzzling statement, especially as it pertains to the Dakota, because in these years (at least those previous to 1736), the Ojibwe, French, and Dakota were allies in the fur trade, and at times Ojibwe and Dakota military units would work together on forays against the Mesquakie.[52] Certainly, as we have noted, this Dakota-Ojibwe-French alliance was a tenuous one, perhaps even allowing for a skirmish here and there. But given this, we also should understand that while an Ojibwe war leader could speak of the need to resolve international conflicts with force, the civil leaders were counseling their followers to work for peace. In an earlier chapter we saw how this tension between Ojibwe war and civil leaders was built into the political infrastructure of the tribe. And we are familiar with recorded incidents of other cultural devices, such as inter-tribal marriages (with their accompanying pipe ceremonies and other ritual prescriptions), that worked against this tendency for the alliance to waver.

Edmund Jefferson Danziger, Jr.'s remark shows the ease with which some analysts have used warfare as an ever-ready explanation for some tribal activities and relations. A century and more ago, warfare was a common explanation historians used for understanding behaviors and customs of non-Western, or "uncivilized" peoples. Such peoples were often said to be "warlike." An alternate explanation stems from two well-known features of Ojibwe society. One is the gregariousness of the people and the other is the ritual prescription of the *midewiwin*.

After a winter spent in the forest hunting or trapping animals, perhaps in quite solitary circumstances, Ojibwe families desired to go to the spring rendezvous. For matters of courtship and arranging marriages, attendance at these annual social gatherings was a prerequisite to the successful functioning of Ojibwe society. Such spring treks to a central location to meet other Ojibwe bands was a constant in early Ojibwe times. In an earlier chapter we saw that each spring small hunting groups met in the sugarbushes and after a few weeks of manufacturing sugar and completing their spring fishing, they moved, along with numerous other such smaller kin-based units, to summer village sites. These returns to Chequamegon Bay were an ongoing aspect of traditional Ojibwe culture and unlike Danziger's contention, need not be understood simply as something "forced" by the threat of military activity from the Mesquakie or Dakota.

The second reason for such annual moves back to Chequamegon Bay concerns the *midewiwin*. Only certain leaders are qualified to officiate at the complex *midewiwin* initiations, and these annual rites at Chequamegon were precisely such large initiation ceremonies. For the earliest years, at least, when the different Ojibwe bands left Chequamegon Bay to harvest resources in distant regions, they may not have had the trained religious leaders needed to officiate at an annual initiation ceremony. Thus, except for times of emergency due to the illness of a child or other family member that demanded an immediate initiation into the *midewiwin*, religious prescription required that the various bands go back to Chequamegon for these rites.

Danziger's comment then, leaves the reader with questions. While the Ojibwe traded furs with *coureurs de bois* and *voyaguers* at sites distant from La Pointe, it is likely the people preferred to return to the bay each spring for the distinct pleasures of rendezvous. The French felt seasonal trips to the trading stations were not popular with the Ojibwe, but the British felt the tribesmen were not concerned about these regular treks.[53] Rendezvous was much more than a meeting with French officials at the main trading station. Just as important, perhaps even more so, was the sociality of meeting with kin and other Ojibwes not seen for months. Furthermore, it was spring, a time that called for celebration, and importantly, it was when courtship typically took place. Individuals that might have spent the entire winter in the company of only their own clan members were now in contact with those from other clans. Given this, along with the inability of these small winter hunting and trapping kin units to perform *midewiwin* initiation ceremonies, we see that the people likely were not forced to return to La Pointe primarily by marauding Mesquakie and Dakota military units. Rather, they returned because of the demands of the Ojibwe cultural system.

To summarize, instead of turning to warfare to explain some patterns of Ojibwe population movements in the early 1700s, we can consider the nature of Ojibwe culture with its rules, expectations and prescriptions. In this way, important aspects of Ojibwe history might be better understood as functions of the characteristics and demands of the Ojibwe cultural system itself, rather than suggesting it was something external to this complex system that caused particular events. For example, military strife between societies like the Mesquakie, Dakota and Ojibwe—warfare often ultimately caused by the machinations of an intrusive European society—may not have been as causal in many Ojibwe historical events as has sometimes been said. Explanations that start with an understanding of tribal sociocultural systems as proactive entities, systems that took their own initiative, rather than passive, reactive entities that were simply responding to Europeans, can offer a more acceptable view of Ojibwe history—and by extension, European history—in Chequamegon Bay in the busy times we are considering.

2.

EVENTS IN REGIONS WEST, NORTH AND SOUTH of Lake Superior in the 1730s serve to show such proactivity on the part of tribal systems as they interacted with the French. These are the events leading to incidents like the rupturing of the Dakota-French-Ojibwe alliance in effect since at least the 1660s. The termination of this alliance had far-reaching effects on all the nations involved.

The long Dakota-French-Ojibwe peace alliance is often said to have begun in 1679, with the efforts of Duluth, but as we recall, the written record indicates peaceful relationships between the Ojibwe and Dakota were in place in the early 1660s, likely before Radisson's ceremony of the Feast of the Dead. This long-standing peace was broken in 1736. The reason for the fracture involves the French, Cree, Assiniboine, Dakota and Ojibwe, and is obviously complex. Through the past several decades of historical research, the conclusions of the ethnohistorian Harold Hickerson emerged as perhaps the seminal argument, at least in the Western literary arena, for what occurred in this important event. For years, Hickerson's writings were repeatedly used as the prime source for interpreting events of the time. In this section I will consider Hickerson's interpretations while offering commentary from other pertinent writers, including Carolyn Gilman and, most recently, the Minnesota Ojibwe historian Anton Treuer.

In the early eighteenth century, Sieur de la Verendrye was desirous of finding the Northwest Passage, and after some efforts gained a government commission for this purpose. However, Charles de La Boische, marquis de Beauharnois, the governor of Canada, would not finance his exploratory efforts, but as a means to cover his expenses, he did grant la Verendrye a monopoly on fur trading in the region of the Pigeon River at Grand Portage. With this agreement, in 1727, la Verendrye was sent to the French post at Lake Nipigon on Lake Superior's northwest shore as its commandant. Here, along with four sons, a nephew, and a contingent of French military personnel he put his plans for exploration into effect.[54]

After settling in at Nipigon and doing some initial exploration in the region, la Verendrye reached Rainy Lake in autumn of 1731, where he established a new successful trading station. Previous to his coming, the Cree and Assiniboine in this region were able to acquire French trade goods only through intermediate traders and they welcomed la Verendrye, hoping that through him they could trade directly with the French.

Both area tribesmen and la Verendrye saw the opportunity before them and, according to custom, established a kinship bond in order to facilitate a peaceful relationship. La Verendrye allowed his eldest son to be adopted by the Cree, an act that cemented an alliance between the parties and carried serious reciprocal responsibilities. At the time, Rainy Lake and its border country was a strategic crossroads for the fur trade that could draw a few thousand people at peak seasons, and it also was an area of some contention between the northern tribes and the more southerly Dakota, and to some extent the Ojibwe. In order to establish his presence in the region, la Verendrye began supplying these northern tribes with arms, even though France was desirous of maintaining its peaceful relations with their southern neighbors, the Dakota and Ojibwe. Of considerable importance to our purposes is what these relations and events meant to Lake Superior's Ojibwe, who were allied with both the French and Dakota, but at the time were having periodic conflicts with the Cree. In 1733, la Verendrye was at his Fort St. Charles on Ontario's Rainy Lake when a force of over three hundred warriors of the Monsoni (a band of the Cree) came to the fort on their way to La Pointe to fight the Ojibwe, while another band headed westward to fight the Dakota. Recognizing the negative impact such attacks would have on his efforts to trade in these regions, la Verendrye was able to persuade the party at Fort St. Charles not to go on to La Pointe and attack the Ojibwe found there.[55]

La Verendrye feared his opening of direct trade with the northern tribes and supplying them with arms would alienate the Dakota, so to appease them, he urged French officials to reopen Fort Beauharnois, a trading post on the Mississippi River at Lake Pepin that the French Crown had opened in 1727, but subsequently closed. The French hoped by reopening this southern post it would not siphon off Dakota trade from Chequamegon Bay, where French allies—the Ojibwe—were acting as trading intermediaries between the Dakota and French. However, as Robert Beider says, the new Lake Pepin post "drew many Sioux who had formerly traded with the Ojibwa [at Chequamegon] and so eventually undercut Chequamegon trade."[56]

As the Dakota began to receive goods—including military supplies—through this southern post they became a more serious adversary to the northern tribes, and in 1724, the Cree reacted by pressuring la Verendrye to fulfill his kin ties by allowing his son, and other Frenchmen, to join them on war parties. Under great personal pressure, la Verendrye consented. Consequently, the French began taking part with the Cree on raids against the Dakota, and in 1736, his son Jean-Baptiste de la Verendrye and his party of twenty French soldiers were killed by a Dakota war party—a war party that included Ojibwe warriors.[57]

The killing of these Frenchmen was a particularly egregious act because of the relatively high number of deaths, the victims' beheading, and the symbolic staging of the corpses. The bodies were found arranged in a fashion interpreted as a council circle, and each had been decapitated, each severed head wrapped in a beaver fur. Historians feel this was a clear reaction to la Verendrye's supplying arms to the Dakotas' and Ojibwes' enemies, and even more, to the willingness of French soldiers to physically enter the fray.[58]

The unvoiced message of the symbolism of the circle of bodies and the severed heads wrapped in beaver pelts is not clear, but interpretive attempts suggest the scene was a statement on the French extreme penchant for desiring beaver furs—something that in this case caused them to "lose their heads over it"—and particularly that the French consciously planned to attack the Dakota, hence the council circle. The fact that Ojibwe were included in the military party that did the killing suggests this tribe was sending a message to the French as well: you need to reconsider your arming of our enemies, the Cree.

As Carolyn Gilman notes, because rules of kinship and alliance-making were involved that included the Ojibwe, this incident had major ramifications for long-term political relations in western Lake Superior country. With the re-opening of the Lake Pepin fort, the Ojibwe role as intermediary traders between the Dakota and French was seriously affected and the usually amiable Dakota-Ojibwe relationship that we traced back to the mid-1600s began to give way. Eventually, the Dakota no longer welcomed the Ojibwe on their lands, but the Ojibwe, after enjoying this resource use for "almost three generations, were not about to leave. They decided to fight for territory they had originally entered as guests."[59]

In 1736, soon after the killing of the younger la Verendrye and his party at Rainy Lake, an event occurred that is directly related. Some Ojibwe from La Pointe killed a party of Dakota at the southern French station at Lake Pepin, an incident that some historians interpret as a symbolic attack on the Dakota, and as such, a clear example of the Ojibwe seeking revenge for the Dakota killing of their allies—the younger la Verendrye and his French companions. Such revenge killings are examples of tribal justice, and in this case, seen as a function of a serious breach of kinship bonds and political alliances.

However, when we recall that some Ojibwe (as allies of the Dakota) took part in the northern killings, and that the Lake Pepin conflict was not just a matter concerning the Ojibwe and Dakota, but involving the French as well (the Dakota were at Lake Pepin because of the French decision to reopen the post), it seems clear that both the northern and southern attacks can also be understood as statements from the Ojibwe to the French. That is, these attacks were statements about the French decision to arm the Cree, (who, it is important to recall, at the time were in conflict with the Ojibwe), to send French men into war against the Dakota (who were allies of the Ojibwe), and finally, to reopen Fort Beauharnois, with its serious negative effect on Ojibwe trade at La Pointe.

This interpretation of both the Rainy Lake and Lake Pepin 1736 killings serves to remind us that while eighteenth century tribesmen like La Pointe's Ojibwe lived within what Carolyn Gilman called "the Indian system of kinship and justice," tribal people were at the same time proactive participants in a system of relationships with European outsiders. At Lake Pepin, the La Pointe war party did not go as far as the Dakota-Ojibwe party did in the Rainy Lake incident with its symbolic manipulation of the dead, but as was the case at Rainy Lake, the Lake Pepin attack was, nevertheless, a strong statement to the French concerning their relationship with the Ojibwe. The Ojibwe were saying they continued to stand with their European ally, but just as importantly, they were signaling the French that they (the Ojibwe) did not appreciate French decisions that negatively affected Ojibwe-Dakota trading relationships.

Anton Treuer offers a slightly different interpretation of some of these events. He argues that the senior la Verendrye was so affected by the killing of his son that he "expended all French resources to avenge his son's death. He armed the Cree and their allies for war against the Dakota, whom he held exclusively responsible—in spite of Ojibwe participation in his son's death. The Ojibwe had to choose between their alliance with the French, Ottawa, and Potawatomi and their entente with the Dakota."[60]

It is evident that while la Verendrye was the French official directly involved in these incidents, it was much more than this one expansionistic-minded Frenchman and his strong desire to revenge his son's death that precipitated the tragic events. It is likely la Verendrye had been supplying the northern tribes with arms and ammunition a few years before the 1736 killing of his son. It was in the 1720s that France started to vigorously expand exploration and trade to the west of Lake Superior, posing a potentially troublesome threat to existing relations between the area's tribes. However, la Verendrye was not the only French trader operating in the area. To the southeast of his Rainy Lake installation were French posts at Grand Portage and La Pointe that had been open years before la Verendrye's arrival. After the reopening of the La Pointe post by St. Pierre in 1718, this Madeline Island site was integral to French interests in western Lake Superior lands, and although La Pointe's surviving historical records do not stress them, we should expect that arms and ammunition were sometimes among items traded with the Ojibwe and Dakota. During this decade of the 1720s, and certainly immediately after it, Ojibwe and Dakota relations started to decline.[61] Thus, the 1736 incidents of the killing of the young la Verendrye followed by the Ojibwe attacking the Dakota at Lake Pepin are best seen as a capstone on these several previous years of deteriorating Ojibwe-Dakota relations.

For the Ojibwe of Chequamegon Bay, the ending of their long alliance with the Dakota had serious repercussions. In 1736, before the Lake Pepin attack, the French commandant at La Pointe, Denis La Ronde, counseled tribal leaders not to attack the Dakota. He claimed such an act would cause hardship at La Pointe the following winter due to the Ojibwe need for the food resources they relied on from Dakota regions south and west of Lake Superior. This is the official stance La Ronde took, but we must remember, like other French post commandants on Lake Superior of the times, he was also a private business person involved in the fur trade, and a renewal of Dakota-Ojibwe conflict would be detrimental to his profits. However, even the arguments of someone as influential with the Ojibwe as La Ronde is said to have been did not deter their resolve to carry out their plan of action. By attacking the Dakota at Lake Pepin, the Ojibwe were ostensibly attempting to revenge the recent deaths of their French allies, but at the same time they were sending a double message to these allies: we stand with you against the Dakota, but we also want you to know of our disappointment in your decision to reopen Fort Beauharnois, with its serious negative effect on our trade at La Pointe.

Thus, we see that tribal and French relations in western Lake Superior in the early eighteenth century were a complex matter, filled with multi-vocal signals. There must have been much political posturing and innuendo in ongoing personal contacts between French and Ojibwe leaders at La Pointe and other stations in those years. After 1736, as a result of both the Rainy Lake and Lake Pepin killings, Ojibwe war leaders rose to positions of prominence in their communities, as shown by their frequent mention in William Warren's writing, and Ojibwe military parties became more active in lands west and south of Lake Superior. This military activity helped make this region less desirable for Dakota use, and soon permanent Ojibwe headquarters sites began to appear in these important areas.

In the years after 1736, some of the bands that left Chequamegon Bay each fall to hunt and trap the surrounding regions did not return in spring. New strategic headquartering sites appeared in northern Wisconsin and Minnesota, bringing about a decentralization of the previous Chequamegon community. In time, new *midewiwin* leaders emerged, and this meant some of the people began spending less and less time at the bay as they settled into a year-round existence in their new regions.

### *1736-1762: Ojibwe Expansion from Chequamegon Bay.*

WITH THE END OF THE LONG Dakota-French-Ojibwe alliance in 1736, almost suddenly the regions south and west of Lake Superior were opened up for Ojibwe occupation, but not without a price. When the Dakota and Ojibwe became adversaries instead of allies, historians suggest this area became a region of many military conflicts, and according to anthropologist Tim Roufs, "At this time La Pointe became a base village for hunting and war."[62]

The displacement of the Mesquakie and Dakota in these regions has been understood as a result of the Ojibwe desire for resources, since according to popular history, by these years the Ojibwe were dependent upon the fur trade, and due to this dependency they sought the wealth of furs in these areas. If warfare was a correlate of this wealth seeking, then that was acceptable, since these tribal nations held a "war ethic" in their complex of customs. With this reasoning the movements into these Mesquakie and Dakota territories might have been eagerly undertaken by the Ojibwe because they offered both economic and military rewards.

In this argument, warfare is used once again as a prime factor in explaining events and their motivating forces. Writers have characterized the Ojibwe years after 1736 at Chequamegon as times preoccupied with war. Puzzlingly, this readiness to go to war is even said to have taken precedence over the desire to trap animal pelts for the fur trade. For example, while the Ojibwe were said to have expanded into areas south and west of Lake Superior in order to harvest the rich fur resources of these regions, at the same time it has been stated that once in the area their concern with military actions threatened the fur trade. Their propensity to "chase the Sioux"[63] could affect the amount of furs taken and be troublesome for the Europeans. It might seem unusual that for a people as dependent upon the fur trade as the Ojibwe are said to have been, that they would be willing to abandon this activity, with its valued trade goods, to "chase the Sioux."

The late seventeenth century and early eighteenth century movements outward from Madeline Island certainly have economic underpinnings, but as we have suggested, they can also be understood as an aspect of the long migration from the east and its accompanying religious ideology. From this perspective the motivations for these movements resonate with the overall spiritual nature of the Ojibwe world. By considering Madeline Island (the Red Cliff shoreline hills, and the entire La Pointe region immediately contingent to it) as a metaphor for the sacred *migiis* shell, we move beyond economic or obvious material causes that guide human behavior, and can see Chequamegon as a geographical and spiritual center with its beams of influence radiating out in a sun-like manner. This resort to a partial religious symbolism to explain important aspects of Ojibwe history offers the interesting awareness that, as is the case with all human societies, some Ojibwe historical events must be understood as having been affected by more than material needs, a point I will discuss later in this book.

The written details of the process whereby the Ojibwe displaced the Mesquakie and Dakota in lands that are now northern Wisconsin and central and northern Minnesota come to us largely from William Warren. From time to time Warren mentions that during the turning of the seasons the typical Ojibwe subsistence practices and religious ceremonies were carried out along with the taking of furs. But these activities are a backdrop to the prominent theme of warfare Warren uses.

I will not give a synthesis of Warren's comments on these events—domestic or military—but instead offer a simple chronology of the major Dakota-Ojibwe battles along with the approximate times and places where Ojibwe village sites were established. The exactness of the dates is not a prerequisite to our understanding of this important dispersal from Chequamegon. Nevertheless, an acceptable consensus in agreement on the appropriateness of the dates exists among the writers of Ojibwe history.

The significance for us is simply that these movements were initiated through Chequamegon Bay. As a result, most of today's "satellite" Ojibwe communities west and south of Lake Superior stem biologically and culturally from that original source.

As we saw, after the 1736 incident in which the Dakota killed members of the Cree and la Verendrye party in the boundary region north and west of Grand Portage, the La Pointe Ojibwe attacked a group of Dakota at Lake Pepin. We noted above that La Ronde, the French commandant at La Pointe at the time, counseled the Ojibwe against this act, but was ignored. This Ojibwe attack on a community of people that had been an ally is taken as a marker for the start of a long period of open warfare between these two nations. However, it is evident that for some years the relationship between the Ojibwe and Dakota was a fractious one that required periodic renewal. For example, William Warren told how intertribal marriages were ceremoniously used to help solidify international relations. We have also seen how Pierre Radisson, Nicholas Perrot, and others told of such politically driven institutional attempts to shore up alliances.

There is evidence that in these years the Dakota were being pulled more and more in a westerly direction toward the Great Plains—a pull that caused a diminishment in Dakota determination to fight the Ojibwe for lands to their east.[64] If this were an important factor in the Dakota world of the time, it would help explain what has for long appeared as a quick takeover of these Dakota lands by the in-rushing Ojibwe. This "push-pull" question, along with the fact that the Ojibwe were being supplied with French guns while, in the earliest days at least, the Dakota had weapons of stone and wood, would help explain the Ojibwe success.

The Ojibwe were moving into lands south of the big lake with such regularity and intensity that by 1745, they had a solid base at Lac Courte Oreilles, a site about seventy-five miles south of Chequamegon Bay. The establishment of this base may actually have begun much earlier, as we suggested in the above discussion of Radisson and Groseilliers and their 1660 trip to that region, but by 1745, it had become a strategic headquartering base for the Ojibwe. Warren says he was told this site was a village for the people of the Bear totem, even though the Ojibwe leader named Shadawish, whose father was Tugwangaune, a Crane clan descendent, established it. This latter leader was present at Sault Ste. Marie in 1671, as a representative from La Pointe. Soon after 1745, another Ojibwe village was established northeast of Lac Courte Orielles, at Lac Du Flambeau.[65]

In approximately 1744, they fought the Dakota at Big Sandy Lake, southwest of Lake Superior, and soon established a base at that important location. At about the same time—1745 or 1746—La Pointe's Ojibwe engaged the Dakota in a three-day battle at Kathio, on the southwest edge of Mille Lacs Lake in central Minnesota. Then, in 1748, at the site called Cut-Foot Sioux, another battle with the Dakota took place. In 1755, La Pointe Ojibwe traveled far to the south, to Prescott Point, and attacked a Dakota village, killing several persons. From the 1760s to the 1780s, the Ojibwe moved westward into the Dakota sites at Vermillion River, Rainy Lake, Leech Lake and the Red Lakes.[66]

These are the major battle and village sites, but in these years there were numerous smaller skirmishes and site occupations through both the Wisconsin and Minnesota regions. Danziger and Treuer remind us that large and extended military campaigns were not the norm.[67] Other than the injuries and deaths these battles and displacements caused to both the Dakota and Ojibwe communities, the importance of all this is that the Dakota (and Mesquakie) saw the loss of much territory and the Ojibwe witnessed the gain of these important resource regions. For the Chequamegon Bay Ojibwe community the years from 1736 to 1762 continued to be busy with arrivals and departures of canoes filled with people, furs and trade goods, but they were also times of important demographic changes. The outflow of Ojibwe families to the distant new population centers had to have been a loss to the region.

Just as importantly, these were the times when England tried to make new inroads into the rich fur trading lands around Lake Superior. British traders kept trying to reach the Ojibwe, offering their trade goods at better exchange rates than the French. The resulting strain of the escalating friction between these European powers certainly reached the tribal nations. This competition between the Europeans may have been behind the remarks of the historian Neill, when he wrote that in 1746, the Ojibwe "became unfriendly to the French."[68]

We do not know enough about the details of these sorts of political and economic pressures the Ojibwe were witnesses to in these important years. However, we are told that whatever the feelings, emotions and sentiments were, the Ojibwe agreeably aided the French in their efforts to throw off the British.

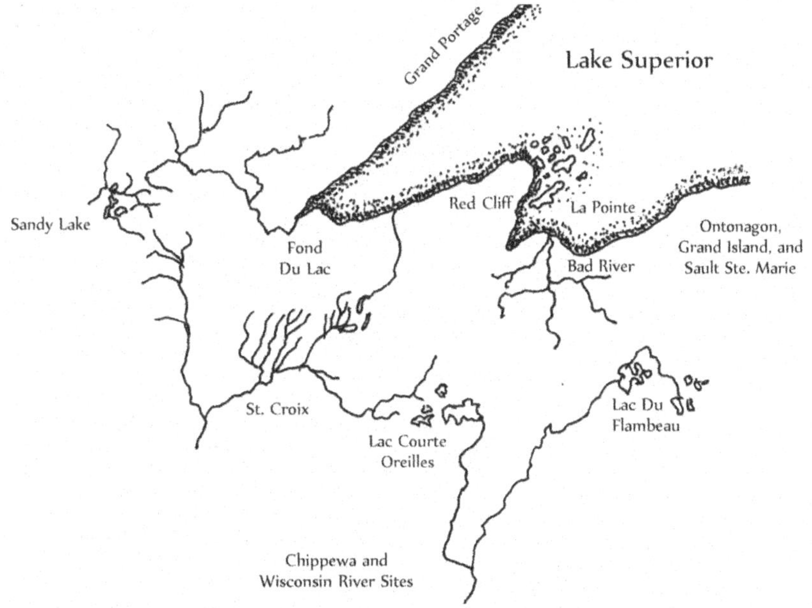


**Ojibwe communites in the Lake Superior region during the eighteenth century.**

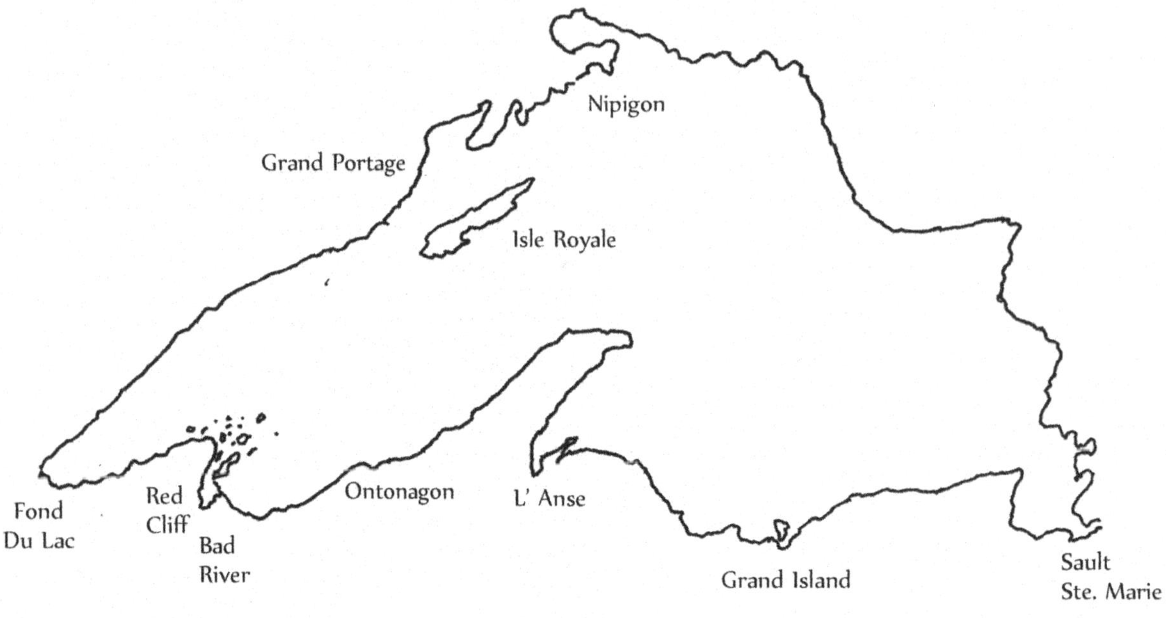


**Modern-day Ojibwe communities on Lake Superior.**

*Notes*

1. Ray 1998[1974]:xix; Treuer 2012:12-14.
2. Steele 1994:21; Axtel 1992:130.
3. Axtell 1992:130-134.
4. White 2000:33-40.
5. Blair 1996[1911,1912]:Vol.I, 269, Vol.II, 136,255; Kellogg 1968 [1925]:264-267; Steele 1994; 147-150; Harris 1976: 42-4.
6. Danziger 1979:33.
7. Buffalohead 1984:ix
8. Warren 1984[1885]:178-182.
9. Hickerson 1970:56.
10. Schenck 1997:14-5.
11. Paap 1986.
12. Erdrich 1999: Forward.
13. Warren 1984[1885]:104-107, 126-129.
14. Beider 1995:67.
15. Beider 1995:51; Kellogg 1968[1925]:268-289.
16. Beider 1995:79.
17. Kellogg 1968[1925]:272.
18. Steele 1994:163.
19. Beider 1995:51.
20. Kellogg 1968[1925]:268.
21. Kellogg 1968[1925]:279.
22. Kellogg 1968[1925]:288.
23. Kellogg 1968[1925]:316-17.
24. Steele 1994:163.
25. Kellogg 1968[1925]:317.
26. Kellogg 1968[1925]:193-323.
27. Kellogg 1968[1925]:323.
28. Kellogg 1968[1925]:335.
29. Kellogg 1968[1925]:340.
30. Paap 2001:Field Notes of 3-18.
31. Ross 1960:43-5.
32. Ross 1960:45.
33. Beider 1995:51.
34. Harris 1976:40.
35. Kellogg 1968[1925]:290-1.
36. Ross 1960:49.
37. Ross 1960:46-53.
38. Ross 1960:53.
39. Ross 1960:55.
40. Ross 1960:55.
41. Kellogg 1968[1925]: 291.
42. Danziger 1979:39.
43. Warren 1984[1885]:132.
44. Warren 1984[1885]:135.
45. Paap 1986.
46. Treuer 2010:11-13.
47. Hickerson 1970:51-63.
48. Neill 1885:422.
49. Neill 1885:423.
50. Neill 1885:423; Rathburn and Vennoy 1987:34-36.
51. Danziger 1979:33.
52. Beider 1995:52.
53. Kellogg 1935:39.
54. Gilman 1992:35-42; Danziger 1979:36.
55. Lund 1984:35.
56. Beider 1995:67; Gilman 1992:142.
57. Treuer 2010:20-1.
58. Gilman 1992:37-8; Lund 1977:12-3; Crouse 1956:107-8.
59. Gilman 1992:37-38.
60. Treuer 2010:21.
61. Busch 2008:79-82; Rathbun and Vannoy 1987:16, 34-6.
62. Roufs 1975.
63. Danziger 1979:38.
64. Holtzheuter 1974.
65. Warren 1984[1885]:192.
66. Warren 1984[1885]:155-190; Hickerson 1974:25-31; Treuer 2010: 20-23.
67. Danziger 1979: 37; Treuer 2010:21.
68. Neill 1885:430.

# 8

# Wars and Dependencies

### *Chequamegon Bay Ojibwe in the Seven Years War (1752-1759) and The Defeat of the French*

1.

BOTH THE WRITTEN AND ORAL LITERATURE shows that Lake Superior Ojibwes had, and continue to have, a history of involvement in military affairs that sometimes occurs very distant from their homeland. We have discussed regional military skirmishes with the Iroquois, Mesquakie, and Dakota, but Chequamegon Bay's Ojibwe have also left their homes to serve at sites hundreds and even thousands of miles away. This is not simply a fact of early Ojibwe history. It has occurred in every century since the 1600s. Here we will review these events as they took place in approximately the first half of the eighteenth century.

The literature tells of Ojibwe military encounters with several tribal nations. Conflicts with the Dakota and Mesquakie quickly come to mind when thinking of Ojibwe warfare, but several other nations have been involved. Earlier, we noted the 1662 battle at Iroquois Point in today's Upper Michigan in which Chequamegon Bay Ojibwe fought a band of Iroquois warriors. In July 1687, Nicholas Perrot led a group of Lake Superior fighters east to engage the Iroquois, and Duluth did the same. These fighting units were assembled at Sault Ste. Marie, but most likely included persons from Keweenaw and Chequamegon.

In both the Duluth and Perrot cases the Ojibwe were acting in company with the French, an alliance that continued into the 1750s, when the struggle between France and England in North America erupted into warfare. It was in 1752 that the French openly resisted British intrusion into the western fur trading regions with an attack on Pickawillany, a British and Miami community in what is now west-central Ohio. It was "on June 21, 1752, when Charles de Langlade, a French-Ottawa of mixed blood, attacked Pickawillany with 30 Frenchmen, 30 Ottawa, and 180 Chippewa from Michilimackinac."[1] Pickawillany was "a center of British commercial activity" and an important post that anticipated further English advancement in the west.[2] Charles de Langlade was originally from the Sault Ste. Marie area, but it is not unlikely his fighting force included persons from the western end of the lake. Of de Langlade one Chequamegon Bay historian wrote:

> In the Mackinac-Sault Ste. Marie area a hardship-trained Frenchman, Charles le Langlade, was sending word to Indians of the Chequamegon country, Green Bay and Fox River Valley concerning Indian volunteer-military service. He was depicting Indian doom unless the English were soon halted. In the technique of stirring emotions, he excelled.[3]

For the next eight years, military units from Lake Superior were likely involved in such long paddles to the east. According to Louise Kellogg, in the summer of 1755, "large detachments of Indian auxiliaries" from the western regions traveled east to aid the French in battles with the British. Kellogg notes that in this year, at Mackinac, de Langlade formed a force of "600 Indians, 70 regular French soldiers, and 50 Canadian solders and paddled to the Ohio River at Fort Duquesne. It was here that Britain's General Braddock was surprised by the extent of resistance his forces encountered. His defeat and death were shocking to the British."[4]

Writers suggest that in this case, de Langlade's force was probably composed of eastern Ojibwe and others—that is, those Ojibwe, Odawa and Potawattomi from areas east of Lake Superior. However, we do not know exactly where de Langlade's fighters originated. Given the importance of the French stations at the eastern end of Lake Superior at the time and the recurrent movement of flotillas of trade goods, along with both French and Ojibwe persons that must have occurred between the eastern and western ends of the lake, it is likely that Keweenaw and Chequamegon fighters were in de Langlade's force. Writers often say these fighters were from "Lake Superior," and we should expect that this could mean both eastern and western regions of the lake. Wilfred A. Rowell, writing in the 1930s, is even more specific when he claims warriors from Madeline Island were with the French back in 1755, when they went against the British forces at Fort Duquesne.[5]

In 1757, "again hundreds of miles from their homeland, Lake Superior Chippewas fought beside the French at Lake Champlain" in upstate New York,[6] and as we have noted, in 1758, Pierre Hertel de Beaubassin, the French commander at La Pointe, assembled and trained a company of Ojibwe fighters and traveled with them to the eastern Great Lakes to engage the British.[7] This instance of a force of Ojibwe from La Pointe being formed and trained and then traveling hundreds of miles east to fight the British is important since it shows that Chequamegon Bay Ojibwe did indeed take part in these distant French-English battles, but its significance is also seen in its hint at the regular involvement of La Pointe Ojibwe in the formation of such military units at Sault Ste. Marie and Mackinac.

As we suggested in our discussion of Ojibwe culture in an earlier chapter, today it is customary for us to conceptualize an eastern Ojibwe region—a collection of Ojibwe communities in the eastern Great Lakes, to include the region of Lake Huron, northern Lake Michigan and far eastern Lake Superior. It is conventional to agree that to a great extent, this eastern region is geographically and culturally separate from the Ojibwe communities resident along the southern shore of Lake Superior and at its far western reaches. However, in the late 1600s and early 1700s, such a separation may not have been so readily evident. In earlier times economic, social and ceremonial intercourse occurred more regularly between these regions than it did in the 1800s and early to mid-1900s, when outside historians first turned their attention to the Ojibwe. We see that today these communities are once again interacting as they periodically meet to discuss common economic, political, and language-recovery concerns, and to carry out religious ceremonies. In fact, such relationships are also increasingly occurring between Ojibwe communities from Lake Superior's southern shore and those along its northern shore in distant Canada.

In 1759, this combined Ojibwe-French military activity against the British was coming to an end. It was in this year that the French general, Montcalm, was defeated on the famed Plains of Abraham at Quebec, and once again La Pointe's Ojibwe were involved. A fighting force from Chequamegon Bay, led by the war leader Mamongesida, was in the battle.[8] The next year, 1760, the French surrendered to the English at Montreal, and a final peace was agreed upon in 1763.

2.

As for our understanding of direct Chequamegon involvement in these conflicts, with few exceptions history has left no details of who these people were: their names, clan identities and the like. If any were killed it seems likely their remains lie at or near the battle areas. For all of these military skirmishes so distant from Red Cliff we can only imagine the days of paddling through the Great Lakes and on the eastern rivers, the nighttime encampments, the fires, the meals taken on the trips, the recurrent ceremonies, and other typical incidents involved in such military treks. Certainly most of these people returned to Lake Superior, finally to be put to rest on its shores, but again, we can only imagine such events. They were the descendents of the Sault Ste. Marie, Keweenaw and Chequamegon Bay Ojibwe which the Jesuits were amongst and wrote about a hundred years prior. Assuming that some of these warriors were in their twenties in the 1750s, if they returned to Chequamegon Bay to live out their lives, they may have been among the elders in the community in the early 1800s, when writers like Henry Schoolcraft occasionally visited the bay. Even though we know virtually nothing about these people, a regional connection with them exists. The men (and possibly women) with Pierre Hertel de Beaubassin who paddled to the east in 1758 were from La Pointe. Two years later, Mamongesida and his fighting force were also from La Pointe. These Chequamegon Bay warriors, their long trips, and their battles with the Red Coats, are part of the area's history.

3.

It may be useful to ponder why the Lake Superior Ojibwe willingly put themselves in harm's way in these distant conflicts with the British. We saw that one writer claimed that a few decades before the French left that in the 1740s, the longtime Ojibwe-French alliance was being strained in the western Great Lakes due to the expansionist desires of the French. With French movement into lands west of Chequamegon Bay the Ojibwe trade relations with the Dakota were threatened, since the Dakota could have traded directly with the French instead of using the intermediary Ojibwe. Another reason for the strain on Ojibwe-French relations was that through these years a growing English presence was developing in Lake Superior country, certainly from the north and east. English traders were working to encourage the Ojibwe to trade with them instead of the French, and there is evidence that the English offered superior trade goods at a lesser bartering rate than the French.[9] Also, as friction between England and France increased in the eastern regions of North America, more and more of the French detachments in the western Great Lakes regions were called back east to give assistance.

A discussion of this is found in the literature, and among other things, once again we see how an early writer offers an account of events along with an interpretation, and then how this becomes a prime source in historical research, and is used, and reused, in this case, over a span of more than a hundred years. To begin this discussion we must go back to the Minnesota writer Reverend Edward D. Neill and his *History of the Ojibways*. Neill's interesting short manuscript is a collection of random events in Ojibwe history, as recorded in French colonial documents from the 1700s. However, it is not Reverend Neill we are directly interested in here. Instead it is the Wisconsin historian, Reuben Thwaites, who, while writing some fifty years after Neill, used Neill's manuscript and the collection of colonial documents he refers to as major sources. The validity of these documents, while apparently unquestioned by Thwaites (and Neill), has been called into question by Hamilton Ross, when he suggests, "These, for the most part, express opinions and describe events through the eyes of persons unfriendly to France."[10]

Thwaites speaks of the 1750s in Chequamegon country when he says, "For several years past, wandering English fur traders had been tampering with the Chippewas of Lake Superior, who in consequence frequently maltreated their old friends, the French." To support this statement he offers the words of the French Governor Galissoniere (who was writing to the colonial office at Paris) in a document from October 1748. In Galissoniere's words: "Voyageurs robbed and maltreated at Sault Ste. Marie, and elsewhere on Lake Superior; in fine there appears to be no security anywhere."[11]

This report from Governor Galissoniere calls into question the alliance and reputed deep friendship said to be found between the Ojibwe and French in Lake Superior country in the late 1600s, which we discussed above, and during the first fifty years of the 1700s—a friendship to be addressed below. Here we must go back to the above quote of Reuben Thwaites where he tells of English traders "tampering" with the Ojibwe of Lake Superior. Thwaites continues his sentence with:

> . . . but now the tribe were (sic) summoned for actual fighting in the lower country, with extravagant promises of presents, booty, and scalps, they with other Wisconsin Indians eagerly flocked under the French banner, and in painted swarms appeared on the banks of the St. Lawrence, with no better result than to embarrass the French commissariat and thus unwittingly aid the ambitious British.[12]

The image of Indian people as "savages" presented in this writing of the 1890s tells much about the perspective held by such learned historians as Rueben Thwaites—who a recent writer calls "a fastidious Victorian."[13] While it is important that we keep in mind the bias of Reuben Thwaites, what is of more importance to us here is his saying that the Ojibwe and others were "summoned" to travel hundreds of miles east to join the French in their war against the English. This agrees with his earlier assertion that in the late 1750s, the commandant at La Pointe, Hertel de Beaubassin, was also "summoned to Lower Canada with his Chippewa allies, to do battle against the English."

Thwaites' words suggest what could be, perhaps, a very important reason for Ojibwe involvement in these eastern battles with the British. They were asked, or more strongly, ordered to go east. If we insert such an official French summons into formal Ojibwe-French discourse of the times we might appreciate the significance of this important call for help. After nearly one hundred years of interacting with the Ojibwe, and after an apparently similar length of time for studying the linguistic manuscripts pertaining to native languages and customs—some provided by the early Jesuits who worked at Lake Superior—the French apparently knew what they were doing.

This is not to suggest the French were manipulating the Ojibwe in this instance. For long, they had used a formal address system when relating to French authorities, a system graphically shown in the literature, for instance, in the accounts of the colorful pageantry at the Sault Ste. Marie ceremony back in 1671. This use of honorific titles in the Ojibwe language is well known. William Warren told how the people referred to their local French commandants as "Father,"[14] but we should be assured that when doing so they were applying rules of Ojibwe etiquette in displaying respect to someone whom they had chosen to receive this honorific label. An Ojibwe worldview with its linguistic categories, its rules and expectations, was alive and well in the 1750s, when the French asked for assistance in fighting the British. The politics of Ojibwe alliance-building and -maintaining was always at play in Ojibwe-French relations, and continued, for instance, as Rebecca Kugel has shown, at White Earth, Minnesota, all through the nineteenth century.[15]

Considering that all successful cultures are viable systems of adaptation, we can understand that in the case of Ojibwe relations with the French in the 1700s, the entirety of the Ojibwe social and cultural system was at work, and of course worked to aid the Ojibwe community. Their political maneuverings were intertwined with felt economic needs, and the discourse called for in the actual playing-out of these maneuverings was applied to the task. The French request—or in Thwaites's terms, *summons*—was considered and replied to in the proper manner. The Ojibwe interpreted the request through their cultural system and acted accordingly.

When in the early decades of the 1700s the French were distracted from their goals of empire in the western Lake Superior country by English intrusions in the continent's eastern regions—a distraction resulting in the lessoning of the French official presence in Lake Superior country—the English "tamperings" with the Ojibwe may truly have presented the tribesmen with economic advantages. But again, it seems economic advantage was not the only variable the Ojibwe considered in such instances, and as we should expect, their entire cultural system came into play.

## 4.

WHILE ECONOMIC ADVANTAGE FOR TRADE with the British may have existed, writers also tell that the British character was different from the French. Despite an early appearance of friendship for the Indian, the British generally could not establish the warm, caring relationship for the Indian that the French—especially the *coureurs de bois* and *voyageurs*—are said to have offered. There were times of strife, of course, but all in all, the French and natives got along well. At risk of using stereotypes of national character to explain the difference in the French and English relations with the Ojibwe, perhaps it is enough to suggest that traditional English Victorian society, as brought to the forests of Lake Superior by Britain's authorities in the 1700s, did not allow for a free-flowing melding of Ojibwe-British relations—a melding that so often occurred with the French.

William Warren told of the Ojibwe being emotionally close to the French, when he claimed that, "The fact of their love and adherence to the French people cannot be gainsaid . . ."[16] For the Ojibwe, regarding the choice of trading either with the French or the English, Edmund Jefferson Danziger, Jr. writes: "the Northwest tribes had a personal preference for the French, especially the lusty *coureurs de bois* and *voyageurs* dwelling among them."[17]

This Ojibwe friendship, trust and loyalty toward the French, then, is said to have been the major reason why some warriors willingly left Chequamegon to travel so far to the east to fight the British. If indeed the French were accepted as close friends, and in many cases as family members, then Ojibwe cultural norms allowed no options. The tribesmen had to help fight this common enemy. Ojibwe warriors had to step into their canoes and undertake the long paddle to places like Quebec.

However, two other reasons for this willingness to fight the British are offered by the historian Edmund Jefferson Danziger, Jr. (who obviously is drawing upon the imagery of Reuben Thwaites). One was the chance for the "plunder of war" and the second was the obvious concern about maintaining the favored trading relationships with the French.[18] Underlying the usual accounts of Ojibwe-French friendship the literature so often offers us, we find pragmatic statements, such as Danziger's, about the Ojibwe desire for the French trade. We recall how Pierre Radisson, back in the mid-1600s, noted this Ojibwe interest in trade. No doubt, as is the case with the desire for plunder through warfare, the economics of trade was also an underlying factor in the Ojibwe's fighting the British.

One other comment can be found on these Ojibwe involvements in France's eastern battles with the British. This is the implication seen in the writing of Reuben Thwaites given above, that in North America the European powers used the tribal nations not as truly equal allies, but as pawns in a larger battle whose outcome always would mean the destruction of the tribes.[19] Writers sometimes pose the tribesmen in these situations as the unknowing *sauvage*, a person meant to eventually pass out of existence when civilization came in its full glory to remake the land. In this context the Indian is seen as one who is duped to do the work of the "superior race." Such a perspective was popular in the 1800s and earlier, when the paradigms Europeans and Euro-Americans used to understand the non-western world were grounded in the assumption of the certainty of the superiority of Western biology and culture.

5.

MUCH HAS BEEN WRITTEN about the "lusty *coureurs de bois* and *voyageurs*" Edmund Jefferson Danziger, Jr. spoke of above. These Frenchmen did, indeed, at times dwell with the Ojibwe—sometimes as husbands (or more simply, as mates). The colorful mystique in this writing is seen in the following quotation from a popular writer of over sixty years ago:

> The voyageur sang when he was happy, when he was in danger, when he got up in the morning, as he sat by his campfire at night, when passing through 'white water,' when at his fort, and especially while he was paddling. He was an effervescent being who took life easily, worked hard, took orders well, assumed little responsibility, got on admirably well with the Indians, especially the native women, and gave a fine loyalty to his bourgeois. He was an excellent canoesman—better, in fact, than the Indian. His ability to live in the wilderness, make canoes, erect forts, manage huskies, and procure furs made him the mainstay of the trade.[20]

This romantic image of the Frenchman coming amongst the Ojibwe and being sincerely welcomed and, in a fashion, accepted as part of the community, is a familiar one. This was the *voyageur*, not the *coureurs de bois*. The *voyageur* operated all through the years of the French fur trade, but the *coureurs de bois* is said to have been part of this trade for a much lesser time, and in a smaller geographic region. And the *coureurs de bois* is often seen in a far different light than the *voyageur*. Walt Harris writes: "The despicable *coureur de bois* plied his lechery and his theft only in the Upper Mississippi-Great Lakes area, and only at one particular time—when the licensed trade of New France was abandoned by the government because of the Iroquois or other wars."[21] (Harris is in error here, since the *coureurs de bois* came back into the scene in the several years after the French withdrew from Lake Superior in 1760.[22]

The *coureurs de bois* lived and worked in a fashion deemed to have been a step or two removed from acceptable French behavior of the times. Writing in the 1860s, the United States historian Francis Parkman saw such a person as reprehensible—as an outlaw who did not operate by the accepted rules of propriety.[23] About one hundred years later, the writer Walt Harris still echoed this view.

It is interesting that when William Warren wrote about the Ojibwe love for the French, he did distinguish between, in his words, "the jovial hearted *'Coureur du Bois'* and open-handed 'Marchand *voyageur*'," but when speaking of them he had only positive comments to offer.[24] It seems likely that he may finally have seen only a single overall category of these mobile fur traders, and despite his intentionally glorifying remarks of the French, we are left feeling his 1830s informants at Madeline Island harbored warm sentiments for both types of traders.

Is the difference between the *coureurs de bois* and *voyageur* a distinction made largely by the non-Ojibwe observer who is using a point of view different from the Ojibwe of Warren's time? Once the technical difference between these two traders is set aside (the *coureurs de bois* were unlicensed traders), the difference between these two types of French fur traders, as seen in the quote from Danziger (above), is not made. Both types of traders are depicted to have been "lusty" (Danziger's word) and feeling quite comfortable in an Ojibwe lodge. We can only surmise whether the Ojibwe of two hundred or more years ago made a distinction between them. However this might be, it seems certain that both the *coureurs de bois* and the *voyageurs* were prominent figures in the background of today's western Lake Superior Ojibwe communities.

The literature then suggests that in the 1750s, the Ojibwe joined their French allies in their eastern battles with the British because of economic and other reasons. Friendship, gifts, the opportunity for the plunder of war, and the desire to maintain trade relations with the French are said to be these concerns. Writers sometimes stress the latter, saying that after more than a half-century of involvement in the fur trade, the Ojibwe had become *dependent* on trade goods, and willingly agreed to help the party that brought these goods to them.

### *The Question of an Ojibwe Dependency on European Fur Trade Goods*

1.

THIS THEME OF AN OJIBWE DEPENDENCE on the material goods they received through the European fur trade is easily found in the historical literature. Richard White feels "The classic statement" of this purported dependency is seen in the writings of Wisconsin's Louise Phelps Kellogg.[25] The influence of the very prominent Kellogg, who wrote the early seminal accounts of the French and British involvement in the North American fur trade, was widespread. However, she was drawing upon the work of Reuben Thwaites, also at the Wisconsin Historical Society. The archeologist George Irving Quimby agreed with these two early historians when he claimed that, "by 1760 every Indian in the [upper Great Lakes] was in some way dependent upon the fur trade and thus in a sense was working for the white man."[26] Some writers give this "dependency" as common knowledge with no bibliographic references offered in its support. For the Ojibwe this dependency was said to have been so acute that it threatened the very survival of the people.

This is a contentious issue because it is a conclusion about Ojibwe history that has been accepted as *a priori*, and as such, unquestioned by historians because of its presumed obviousness. In this section I will review this dependency argument, especially as it is found in writings on the Ojibwe of Chequamegon Bay. The reader should keep in mind that the assumption of this dependency is situated squarely in other aspects of the popular history of the Chequamegon Bay region, not just in its written scholarly literature. For example, a quick perusal of local newspapers from the 1800s and into the twentieth century in Chequamegon country shows editorial commentary that at times mocks the Rousseauian image of the noble savage. These editors jokingly tell of stories of "the good old days" of the "local Indians" before the coming of the white man, when the tribesmen struggled to survive using a Stone Age technology. As is the case throughout North and South America—but really anywhere on the planet where Europeans have colonized tribal peoples—the assumption of the superiority of Western technology is deeply embedded in local popular histories.

However, our interest in this dependency is more than a concern about the methodologies and untested assumptions of past writers. This dependency upon trade goods has been said to be behind the reason the Ojibwe initially left Sault Ste. Marie and moved westward into Lake Superior country.[27] Hence, the desire for trade goods is seen as the underlying cause for their lengthy period of hostilities with other nations like the Dakota, Mesquakie, and to a lesser extent, the Cree and Assiniboine, and at times even with the Ho-Chunk and Menominee.[28] As we see, the Ojibwe "dependency" upon European trade goods has been accepted as a major factor underlying practically all of earlier written Ojibwe history.

It is not merely the reality of historical events that is supposedly driven by this dependency. It is also said to have been a causal factor in deep changes in the Ojibwe social and religious order. For example, as we saw above, Harold Hickerson has argued that the Ojibwe clan system and religion both were seriously affected by the coming of the French. Ultimately, these were deep structural and ideological responses to this supposed need for French trade goods. We readily see that the notion of the Ojibwe quickly becoming dependent upon the French for their trade goods is indeed a matter of great importance.

Recent writers are offering new ideas on this supposed dependency. One writer is Richard White, who in a well-reasoned argument, has concluded that by the middle 1700s, "There is no denying that European goods had become an integral part of Algonquian life, but by the end of the French period there was not as yet, material dependence."[29] White's important argument will be presented below and its relevance to the ancestors of the Ojibwe of today's Red Cliff will be discussed.

Here we begin by reviewing the early literature's major examples of writing about this supposed dependency, and it is important that the reader be provided with the actual words indicating the certainty of the writers' assumptions. To this end I will present what I consider proper examples of relevant writing on the subject, then discuss their importance.

We can begin by asking what evidence exists for this purported dependency presented in the literature of over the last one hundred years. Perhaps there are those who might easily conclude that the issue is manifest and needs no further contemplation, since it should be obvious that iron and brass are superior to stone, bone and wood as weapons for warfare and as materials for making implements for hunting, trapping, fishing, gardening, and so forth. And perhaps we will agree that woven wool or other cloth made from vegetal fiber, offered in bright colors from European dyes not available to the Ojibwe in Lake Superior country at the time, is more aesthetically pleasing and amenable to the making of clothing—it is easier to clean, for instance—than tanned hides. The reader might easily conjure other material possessions of the Ojibwe that were assumed to have been quickly replaced by European items brought by the early traders.

Students of cultural change have argued that a human society's material culture, that is, the implements and their use-patterns its people create as they live out their lives can change more easily and quickly than the non-material aspects of their socio-cultural system. In other words, their tools might change, but their beliefs, values, and numerous rules of life in which the use-patterns for these objects are embedded might not, or at least might change much more slowly. Therefore, the adoption of a new material item could have few far-reaching ramifications for non-material aspects of a cultural system.[30]

Unfortunately, the detailed changes the introduction of French trade goods had on the Ojibwe socio-cultural system are not well-known. Early writers of Ojibwe history used the notion of cultural change to understand the Ojibwe, but the model for these researchers was from nineteenth century cultural evolutionists—a model long since discredited.

The quotation from Hamilton Ross, given below, stands as a powerful statement of drastic change brought to the Ojibwe by European trade goods. If a non-discriminating reader reads Ross's words, and no others, she or he might be left with an image of the Ojibwe as a people who in the late 1600s and early 1700s were so seriously affected by the lack of French trade goods that their very lives were threatened. Ross's desperate image of Chequamegon Bay Ojibwe in 1718 can linger in a reader's mind long after reading it, and since his manuscript was first published in 1960, this scene of a helpless and dependent tribal community has been in the literature for over fifty years. The recent reprinting of Ross's 1960 book means that his image is ongoing—and that some of today's readers might be accepting it as a statement of fact.

When we ask where Hamilton Ross learned about Ojibwe dependency, we must go to the references he offers. What we find is a single manuscript—the somewhat brief 1895 publication of Reuben Thwaites entitled *The Story of Chequamegon Bay*. Numerous historians have used Thwaites's document as a major synopsis of early Chequamegon history. We have already noted that Thwaites was the editor of an important translation of the *Jesuit Relations* referred to in an earlier chapter. As a prominent Wisconsin historian of the time, he used the relevant written sources available to him—in the instance of *The Story of Chequamegon Bay*, a major one was Rev. Neill's short manuscript—but he also colored this particular piece of writing with sentiments and assumptions common for his day. In Thwaites's time, European-American writers were certain the Indian would disappear as the tide of Western civilization swept over the continent.

This example shows how at times the written historical record can be seen as a series of references, one pointing back to the other. In this instance we will begin with the long Thwaites quotation, then offer three subsequent quotes that play out as a string of evidence, each referring to the previous quote. These quotations will be followed by an analysis.

According to Thwaites:

> At first an agriculturist in a small way, and hunter and fisher only so far as the daily necessities of food and clothing required, the Indian was induced by the white man to kill animals for their furs,—luxuries ever in great demand in the marts of civilization. The savage wholly devoted himself to the chase, and it became necessary for the white man to supply him with clothing, tools, weapons, and ornaments of European manufacture—the currency, as well as the necessities, of the wilderness. These articles the savage had heretofore laboriously fashioned for himself at great expenditure of time; no longer was he content with native manufactures, and indeed he quickly lost his old-time facility for making them. Soon he was almost wholly dependent on the white trader for the commonest conveniences of life; no longer tied to his fields, he became more and more a nomad, roving restlessly to and fro in search of fur-bearing game, and quickly populating or depopulating a district according to the condition of trade. Without his trader, he quickly sank into misery and despair; with the advent of the trader, a certain sort of prosperity once more reigned in the tepee of the red man. In the story of Chequamegon Bay, the heroes are the fur trader and the missionary; and of these the fur trader is the greater, for without his presence on this scene there would have been no Indians to convert.[31]

Sixty-five years later, Hamilton Ross used this quotation as his bibliographic source when he was writing about the string of French commandants who served on Madeline Island. He noted that the first one was Pierre LeSeuer, who was in Chequamegon Bay from 1693 to 1698, a period of five years. LeSeuer's tenure was followed by a span of twenty years when no French commandant was stationed on the island. Then, in 1718, the French government sent St. Pierre to reopen the trading post. According to Ross:

> During LeSeuer's regime in the district, the Indians had become dependent upon the French for such articles as needles, blankets, shirts, axes, kettles, and the almost endless variety of trade goods which were offered them. During the twenty year absence of the French, these items had worn out or become lost, and the natives, in that time, had forgotten their old arts of making substitutes. Thus, upon St. Pierre's arrival, he found the Indians in desperate straits, all half starved and poorly clad. He hastened to remedy their condition by advancing trade goods against the further take of furs.[32]

Nineteen years later, Edmund Jefferson Danziger, Jr. offered the above Ross quote as his reference for his own quote, given below. Danziger was describing and attempting to explain the Ojibwe "dependency" upon fur trade goods, and he concluded his discussion with the following:

> Their dependence upon European goods at times produced tragic results. In 1718, when Captain St. Pierre arrived at Madeline Island to revive the fur trade after a twenty-year absence of licensed traders, he discovered starving and ragged Indians who obviously had forgotten the traditional skills of making stone, bone, and wood substitutes for worn-out or lost iron and brass weapons, tools, and utensils.[33]

Interestingly, we see that the situation of the Ojibwe has become more extreme: Ross's "half-starved" people have now become "starving" and they are "ragged" rather than merely poorly clad. Today the above information from Edmund Jefferson Danziger, Jr. lives on as the source for a recent quotation by a contemporary cultural geographer who wrote about the earliest historical views of Chequamegon Bay. Regarding the influence of the fur trade on Ojibwe culture, Eric Olmanson claims that: "By the time France's dominance of the fur trade ended with the surrender of Montreal to the British in 1760, all tribes had essentially abandoned their woodland material culture and become dependent on European tools and weapons and fund of European luxury items, including ornaments and liquor."[34] Thus, Reuben Thwaite's information—in this case passed on by Hamilton Ross and Edmund Jefferson Danziger Jr.—remains before today's readers in these troublesome conclusions of Eric Olmanson.

For a number of reasons these are all fascinating quotations, and they beg for an in-depth analysis. However, since the latter three derive directly from the first, we will focus primarily on the comments from Reuben Thwaites.

This quotation by Thwaites is an excellent example of the understanding of Ojibwe society and culture (and by extension, perhaps an understanding of most other tribal systems as well) held by learned writers of Thwaites's time. And we may be correct in suggesting it is an understanding held by much of United States non-Indian society of the time as well. In other words, the quotation might be taken as what was, in non-Indian society in the late 1800s, "common knowledge" about the nature of early Indian society and culture.

The image of a pervading *present orientation* in Ojibwe culture underlies this long quotation. Quite interestingly, Thwaites suggests the Ojibwe were agriculturalists, although only minimally, and as such they were enjoying at least a modicum of economic stability by caring for their "fields." He implies that any serious future orientation, i.e., preparations for winter, that this subsistence practice allowed was quickly cast aside with the advent of the fur trade. This conclusion is puzzling since he must have been familiar with the well-documented harvest of whitefish at Sault Ste. Marie by the Ojibwe—a harvest described in the *Jesuit Relations*, and later by Nicholas Perrot and others.

For some Ojibwe bands, these harvests were large community undertakings precisely because they were a major complement to the supply of food put away for winter use. Certainly Thwaites was familiar with the mid-1800s writings of Henry Schoolcraft, in which the Sault Ste. Marie harvest was described again as a major event still occurring in Schoolcraft's time. Reuben Thwaites chose to ignore the serious preparations the Chequamegon Bay Ojibwe took for winter, such as the caching of dried meat, fish, berries, and the seasonal manufacture of surpluses of maple sugar and wild rice that we know generally continued all through the years of the fur trade.

Thwaites's emphasis on *the chase*—an old European image of foraging societies—and how with the advent of the fur trade, the Ojibwe turned from their traditional seasonal round of subsistence activities to a life "wholly devoted . . . to the chase," is fundamental in his understanding of tribal society. He would have us believe that, by and large, the Ojibwe cast major components of their earlier material culture and traditional subsistence economy aside as they hurriedly worked to acquire furs in order to gain the esteemed European trade goods. Such an event, if true, would have brought about the virtual destruction of the Ojibwe socio-cultural system, an outcome sometimes erroneously said to have been the final result of the fur trade. For example, the Ashland, Wisconsin, writer Walt Harris claimed that when becoming involved in the fur trade, the Ojibwe "gave up a way of life" for something new.[35]

The vast bulk of furs were taken during the winter, a time when the Ojibwe communities were traditionally broken into small nuclei of immediate family members who worked their own hunting territory. Before the fur trade this was the season in which large animals like deer, elk and moose were taken for food. Therefore, the fur trade did not directly affect the subsistence activities of the Ojibwe in spring, summer and fall, the three remaining seasons for food production. It has been argued that the food producing activities of these other seasons continued to be important to the Ojibwe all through the fur trade,[36] and thus when Reuben Thwaites states that the people became "wholly devoted . . . to the chase," he is in error.

When, at the start of his discussion, he turns to agriculture, Thwaites implies that being sedentary for at least a portion of the year was part of Ojibwe life. Thus, he offers an image of "the savage" contrary to what was otherwise held in the days of the fur trade. In those times, and even into the late 1800s, western Lake Superior Indians were said "to roam" through the countryside, moving from one region to another to acquire food, and the notion of being tied to one place by farming—even if for only a portion of the year—was not readily thought to apply to them. Yet, Thwaites began his discussion by stressing farming as a prime aspect of their culture. Although arguing that the Ojibwe used agriculture only "in a small way," he claims that through "the chase" he (and she) became even more nomadic, since the Ojibwe were "no longer tied to their fields." This is an interesting imagery. Unless Thwaites is using "fields" loosely here—he might have been employing metaphor by suggesting the Ojibwe fishing and hunting grounds, their ricing areas and other harvesting regions were their "fields"—we might conclude that he is choosing whatever stereotypical images of "the savage" were useful to him at the time. Such picking-and-choosing of images of "savages" is not uncommon. According to Reuben Thwaites, the Ojibwe assumed the posture of a somewhat-settled "savage" (with fields) who discarded the more sedentary strictures of an agrarian life to take up "the chase."

Thus, the Ojibwe was "roving restlessly to and fro in search of fur-bearing game," and in the process was "no longer content with native manufactures, and indeed he quickly lost his old-time facility for making them." This was so extreme and accomplished in such a short period of time that "Soon he was almost wholly dependent on the white trader for the commonest conveniences of life." In this process the traders became "the heroes," and in Chequamegon Bay they were more important than the missionary, for if there had been no traders "there would have been no Indians to convert." The irony of this conclusion is that according to past writers, the Jesuits in Chequamegon Bay failed miserably in their attempts at conversion, and after they left no other missionaries were in the area until the 1830s, long after the peak of the fur trade.

That the Ojibwe would forget how to manufacture age-old tools, items of clothing, and so forth, in the span of a single generation or less (Ross said this loss of knowledge occurred during a period of twenty years) seems unlikely. A culture's material expressions such as tools and items of clothing, jewelry and the like do not exist in vacuums. Their manufacture and use are bound within a complex network of beliefs, values, and norms that is part of the infrastructure of the culture itself. To take Thwaites's statement about this loss, and Ross's, Danziger's and Olmanson's reiteration of it as fact, we would have to conclude that within a very short span of time the Ojibwe of Chequamegon Bay were living in a near socio-cultural void, an existence lacking much of its past underpinnings. This is not to say that a culture's tools and so forth are at the very heart of the peoples' notions of their world, but only to suggest that a way of life is *systemic*—one aspect being functionally related to another—and if a component of this system is altered or removed, the remaining aspects of the system will be affected.

With this in mind, we cannot agree with the historian Danziger when he wrote that a major impact of the fur trade on tribal nations in the upper Great Lakes was that "By about 1760 all tribes had scrapped their woodland material cultures for the superior tools, weapons, ornaments, and liquor introduced by the ingenious French traders."[37] If such a wholesale discarding of material cultures actually occurred, deep and wide ramifications should have been evident in the other aspects of these tribal cultural systems. Yet, after saying the tribes "scrapped" a major component of their cultures, Danziger goes on to say that in total, both the French and English fur trade did not cause major change with tribal cultures. He says both these European powers worked to keep tribal socio-cultural systems intact, for such systems were essential to the success of the fur trade. After all this, we are left to ponder the troublesome conclusions writers like Edmund Jefferson Danziger, Jr. have drawn about the effects of the fur trade upon the Ojibwe.

If the Ojibwe of Chequamegon Bay were as forgetful as Thwaites, Ross and Danziger suggest, we should be interested in the comments offered on these very same people some forty years after 1718. These are the remarks of Alexander Henry. This Englishman, as we will see below, came to the bay in 1765, and although he claimed he was beseeched by the community's leaders to advance trade goods (because of recent interruptions in the trade), he nevertheless was impressed with the physical appearance and social demeanor of the Ojibwe he found at Chequamegon. Interestingly, Henry noted that their clothing "was chiefly of dressed deer-skin."[38] According to Henry, it is apparent that by 1765, the Ojibwe were not only well fed, but they were once again plying their ancient, and considerable, knowledge and skills of leathercraft, something they were to have forgotten some forty years ago.

One more set of short quotations needs to be given before we move on. These are from Louise Phelps Kellogg, the prominent Wisconsin historian of the early 1900s. Commenting on the coming of Alexander Henry to Chequamegon Bay, she says, "When an English trader reached Chequamegon Bay in 1765 where the trade had been interrupted for several years, he found the Indians almost naked and clamoring for firearms and ammunition to hunt for food and clothing." We will examine her (and Henry's) remarks further below, but for now we note that the situation Kellogg indicated was due to the Ojibwe dependence upon trade goods. "For the French," she went on, "had so accustomed the tribesmen to the use of white men's goods that they had lost their primitive economy and could no longer clothe and feed themselves without the help of the traders."[39]

We see that Kellogg's claim that the Ojibwe were in this situation because their "primitive" economy was no longer functional conflicts with the later conclusion of Danziger, who claims that all through the 1700s, the Ojibwe had not seriously altered their culture (to include, of course, their economy). As we have argued above, both the French and English needed to keep the Ojibwe culture working as it was before the coming of the Europeans, i.e., the people needed to continue as mobile hunters and gatherers in order for the fur trade to exist.

Another difficulty in accepting the purported Ojibwe dependency on trade goods is seen in the latter decades of the 1700s, after the removal of the French, when the English were attempting to acquire the rich bounty of furs from the western Great Lakes. We will speak to this time period below, so here it is enough to point out—as we mentioned above—that in the latter 1700s, we are told the Ojibwe became preoccupied with military skirmishes with the Dakota, a preoccupation so severe they chose not to trap significant numbers of fur bearing animals, and for periods of time the fur trade languished in the rich regions south and west of Lake Superior. Such a serious turn of events might seem unusual for a people said to be as dependent upon European trade goods as the Ojibwe. The ability to turn away from the traders in these decades might point to an alternate source of trade goods—an unlikely conclusion—or else it might hint that the fur trade was not, finally, as important to the tribesmen as writers like Thwaites, Kellogg, Ross, Harris and others, would want us to believe. If this were the case, we would be left with the suggestion that during the late 1700s, the Ojibwe were still relying on their own methods of gaining a livelihood: they were still, essentially, a culture with a foraging adaptation, and as such were able to meet their needs without regular economic exchanges with fur traders.

The suggestion that, even though they were laboring under a severe dependency on European trade, the Ojibwe were able to neglect the trade in order to focus their energies on military skirmishes with the Dakota is not completely dissimilar to an event occurring some forty or more decades earlier. Reuben Thwaites noted that the reason St. Pierre was dispatched to Chequamegon Bay in 1718, as we noted, was that "the Chippewa chief there was, with his fellow-chief at Keweenaw, going to war with the Foxes."[40] The French commandant at Montreal intended that St. Pierre would work to quell these overtures of warfare, which threatened the trade. While telling us of the coming of St. Pierre to Chequamegon, Ross neglects to mention this. We are left to contemplate the unlikely scene wherein a Chequamegon Bay community of Ojibwe, according to Hamilton Ross, "all half starved and poorly clad" is still able to plan and prepare to enter serious battle with an adversary as powerful as the Mesquakie.

## 2.

A QUESTION NOT YET RAISED in this discussion concerns what, if any, evidence comes down to us from the French commander at Madeline Island in 1718. Is it possible to actually deduce the condition of the Ojibwe that Captain Paul Le Gardier, Sieur de St. Pierre met upon his arrival in La Pointe? This is integral to an understanding of our discussion of eighteenth century Ojibwe dependency, since it is with St. Pierre that the dependency argument begins. Hamilton Ross noted that we know very little of the details of the times at Chequamegon in the early 1700s, because many related documents were destroyed during the French Revolution.[41] Also, unfortunately, William Warren has left nothing specific about Pierre's arrival at Madeline.

We can set the context for the situation at Madeline, as witnessed by Captain St. Pierre, by recalling that in the late seventeenth century the region's rich fur-bearing areas were in the Ojibwe-Dakota borderlands south and west of Lake Superior, and at that time the earlier glut of furs on the French market was easing somewhat. With this welcome change, by the few years prior to 1718, the French were desirous of reviving the flow of furs from western Lake Superior. To accomplish this it would be necessary to strengthen peaceful relations between the Ojibwe and Dakota nations. This goal was important to French officials since many of them, including Governor Frontenac himself, were directly involved in the trade as private investors. Thus, in 1693, when Frontenac sent LeSueur, who was also an investor, to command the post at Madeline, LeSueur was to work to keep this peace, while at the same time it was to his financial advantage to encourage the advancement of the Ojibwe into Dakota lands in order to increase the harvest of furs. This advancement threatened the Dakota-Ojibwe peace alliance, or entente, as Anton Treuer says, helps explain the delicate peace between the Dakota and Ojibwe in the early days of the eighteenth century, and points to the underlying role of the French in how this uneasy relationship was played out. It did not take long before this peace was ruptured, and as we noted, it was the French who had a major hand in causing this outbreak of hostilities.

In 1718, when Captain Paul Le Gardieur, Sieur de St. Pierre traveled to Lake Superior to revive the post at La Pointe, he came as another French investor in the fur trade. Surviving documents show that "On 26 September 1718, St. Pierre entered into a partnership with several merchants who financed the trip and provided two canoes with goods. In exchange for these goods the merchants received one quarter of the profits of the post until such time St. Pierre paid for the original supply of goods." The written agreement for this transaction is dated 28 September 1718, and lists the typical items a western Great Lakes fur trader of the time would offer as trade goods for exchange with Ojibwe fur trappers, and testifies to St. Pierre's financial involvement in the La Pointe trade.[42]

This calls into question the underlying motive for St. Pierre's immediate advancement of trade goods to La Pointe's Ojibwe who, we recall, according to Hamilton Ross, were "in desperate straits, all half starved and poorly clad." It suggests that when St. Pierre quickly distributed goods to the La Pointe people he was partially doing it out of his desire for personal monetary gain, and not for purely humanitarian reasons. Also interestingly, we noted that another Frenchman who came to La Pointe with St. Pierre was Rene Godefroy, Sieur de Linchot, who assumed command at the post in 1720, immediately after St. Pierre returned to Montreal, and who was a partner with St. Pierre in the above mentioned trading business venture. The efforts of both de Linctot and St. Pierre worked to renew the fur trade at their post, an outcome they, their official superiors, and their financial backers doubtlessly were pleased with.

This example of early eighteenth century French commandants at La Pointe being directly involved in the fur trade as private investors is not unusual. In a similar instance, it seems a few years later Louis Denis, Sieur de la Ronde, when in charge of the Madeline Island post, formed an association of investors who exploited the issuance of canoe permits granted to traders for "Point Chagwamigon." Documents show that La Ronde took one-half the profits from this venture, with the rest being divided between his associates.[43]

These instances of private enterprise operating hand-in-hand with government officials was the norm in the earliest days of the fur trade at outposts like La Pointe, and because of them, it is unlikely the resident Ojibwe made any great distinction between French government representatives and those of private enterprise. To the tribesmen, these often were one and the same.

Finally, the upshot of this discussion is that when we read early writers who tell of the extreme unfortunate conditions of Ojibwe tribesmen caused by their "dependency" upon European fur trade goods, we must be suspect. Reuben Thwaites and those writers who unquestioningly used his pronouncements of such "dependency" were influenced by their own "dependency" on assumptions regarding the nature of early tribal life and its supposed innate inferiority to that of the incoming Europeans. The result is that such writers wrote a version of Ojibwe history that served the writers' needs, to the detriment of those of the Ojibwe.

## 3.

As WE SAW, THE QUESTION of an Ojibwe dependency on European trade goods has been linked with Ojibwe expansion into lands west, south and north of Sault Ste. Marie. Harold Hickerson has been the major proponent of the notion that it was because of the trade that the Ojibwe left Sault Ste. Marie in the late 1600s. Other writers concur, using Hickerson's work as the source of their conclusion. As already noted, Hickerson felt it was not until 1680 that the Ojibwe left The Sault, and the reason for this exit was to move further into prime trapping lands.

We have already suggested that in the written historical record there are claims this Ojibwe expansion is related to the military hostilities between the Ojibwe, Dakota, Mesquakie, and others. Thus, two major events of Ojibwe history—the expansion during the 1600s and 1700s, and warfare with other tribal nations in these years—were results of the fur trade. The reason the Ojibwe entered the trade was to receive trade goods, thus, supposedly, their dependency on these material items was at the base of this chain of inter-related events.

Perhaps it was easy for earlier writers to assume the supremacy of European culture over that of tribal societies. Writers before the very late 1800s did not have the culture concept to use as an analytical tool in their work as they described events such as the European colonial expansion into North America. So, the notion of a tribe's attraction to trade goods that included, as Danziger stated, "tasty wines and brandies," might have been seen as obvious. Whatever the cause, the result is that to a great extent the written historical record posits Ojibwe history through the 1600s and 1700s essentially as a reaction to the Europeans. Read this way, Ojibwe history is an accounting of responses to European initiatives.

An interesting take on this view is seen in Richard White's discussion of Nicholas Perrot's memoir. As noted above, White feels that in Perrot's (and La Potherie's) writing, "Indians emerge as at once exotic and sauvage and yet also as critical participants in a common politics and economy with the French."[44] In other words, according to White, Perrot understood that in his time the Western Great Lakes fur trade held aspects of both the tribal and French cultures. To Perrot, both the tribal and European nations were role players in this economic intercourse. This appealing voice of Perrot is a major reason why his memoir, despite its many problems, is a refreshing document. Perhaps paradoxically, even though Perrot seemed to always have been certain of the superior position of the European in matters of French-Indian affairs, he still accepted the validity of tribal people, their nations, and their way of life.

Given this, we still might agree that "a common politics and economy" was not so common after all. While the tribal nations acted as equals to the Europeans in the fur trade, each did it from the perspective of their own cultural systems. The Europeans operated from their seventeenth and eighteenth century market economies, and the tribesmen from their foraging adaptations with their economies using sharing and barter as distributive mechanisms. In other words, the Europeans and Ojibwe both participated *in common* in the fur trade, but from very different cultural points of view.

Precisely such an acceptance of tribal peoples as Nicholas Perrot's is beginning to appear in more recent discussions of Ojibwe history.[45] Integral to these are two important ideas. One is the matter of voice—with the attending aspects of discourse such as posturing, bias and perspective. The truly basic importance of language in international relationships is now accepted as having a major significance. The second idea is the culture concept. After over a century of increasing use, the culture concept is now regularly being employed in legitimate discussions of historical events. For example, the importance of the culture concept is evident when Theresa Schenck discusses William Warren's ideas on Ojibwe-Dakota warfare and the fur trade. Schenck says:

> Although he recognized that it was competition for hunting grounds that led to the Ojibwa-Dakota warfare, Warren concluded that it was competition in the fur trade that led the Ojibwe into Dakota hunting grounds . . . However, while the Ojibwa were not averse to acquiring items which made their life easier, and they most certainly did participate in the fur trade, there was a limit to how many axes, guns, knives, kettles and clothes they could take with them as they moved on their seasonal rounds. *It is more likely that they engaged in the fur trade because it fitted into their way of life, and that their first concern was to feed and clothe their families. Thus competition for food more than furs led the Ojibwe westward.*[46]

From this understanding, the proposed westward movement of the Ojibwe out of Sault Ste. Marie and the resulting competition and warfare with the Dakota become less a matter of reacting to the European desire for wealth through furs, and more a matter of a people having motivations and making decisions that stem from their world rather than that of the outsider. As Richard White intimated, Nicholas Perrot understood this. Viewed this way, the question of an Ojibwe dependence upon trade goods begins to fall away. The Ojibwe expansion into Lake Superior country, the resulting struggles with the Dakota, and the involvement in the fur trade are then seen as coming out of the reality of the westward migration taught by their spiritual leaders and the reality of their own cultural needs. This interesting imagery was seen decades ago, when Claude Levi Straus, the prominent French anthropologist, said that after studying the depths of the available published accounts of Ojibwe teachings of their origins and movement into the Great Lakes area and the related tribal literature, he concluded it was as if Ojibwe culture was the story of a people in a canoe, on water, and always moving westward.[47]

If there was a dependency, it was the peoples' "dependency" upon their cultural system. It was their recognition and acceptance of themselves as Ojibwe people—and the deep ramifications of this recognition and acceptance. Their identity was as a nation of hunters and gatherers who followed the *miigis* to Chequamegon Bay. Theresa Schenck says their first priority was to feed and clothe their families, so it follows that their underlying task was to acquire food and shelter. Their recognition that the material items they acquired by taking part in the fur trade, as Schenck also notes, "made their life easier," not only indicates their humanness, but also indicates their adaptability. This deep adaptability of the people—an ability to make changes as they stayed the same—is a major aspect of their involvement in the fur trade.

## 4.

THE IMAGERY AND CULTURAL ASSUMPTIONS used in 1895 by Reuben Thwaites served to help produce a history eminently useful to the non-Ojibwe of the times. It was felt that doubtless the material possessions of the Europeans were far superior to those of a Stone Age culture such as the Ojibwe had in the seventeenth and eighteenth centuries, and when given the opportunity, the tribesmen would choose to replace their inferior materials with those of the European. Hence, it was assumed, since the tribal people immediately saw the superiority of the European goods, and given that they could get these treasured items only through the fur trade, they became dependent upon this new activity.

In Thwaites's time this conclusion was not questioned. It helped support the image of the deficient savage. This primitive person was not simply lacking the "light" of the Europeans' religion, a situation the Jesuits tried unsuccessfully to rectify, but he (and she), as examples of earlier, less developed forms of the human species, was also destined to give way to "civilization." To thinkers like Thwaites, an initial step in this entire process was the taking on of new material possessions. The replacement of stone, wood, and bone implements (along with animal hides, numerous vegetal materials and other Stone Age items) with a European material culture was an obvious and necessary change that would lead to many others. Furthermore, in the Western mind, an Ojibwe dependency upon the trader was fortuitous. Once this dependency was in place, the European entrepreneurs would be assured of a steady supply of furs, and eventually the divinely formed script of manifest destiny would be played out. With a solid dependency on the trader, the rest of the primitive tribal world would soon give way to that of the European.

It is important to ponder the impact of a scholar as prominent as Wisconsin's Reuben Thwaites. Certainly in his time and for many decades following 1895, his pronouncements were used by classroom educators, including history professors and secondary education instructors who trained future teachers. These were the early 1900s, a time when a self-assured industrialism was sweeping across America. And as we will note below, this meant something very important in the daily lives of persons in Ojibwe communities of the time as they interacted with non-tribal people.

A conclusion that can be drawn from this consideration of the Reuben Thwaites's 1895 quote about an Ojibwe dependency on the fur trade is that Thwaites's remarks are not based upon factual evidence, i.e., historical documentation for the dependency, but upon Thwaites's late nineteenth century unquestioned assumptions about the nature of tribal society and culture. We have seen that over sixty years after the Thwaites writing, we find a connecting thread through Ross to the writings of Edmund Jefferson Danziger, Jr., and after another twenty-eight years, the writing of the cultural geographer, Eric Olmanson. Nineteenth century assumptions held that "savages", because of their very nature, would eventually disappear as they took on the "superior" trappings of a Western way of life. In the western Great Lakes of the 1600s and 1700s, a dependency upon the fur trade was only a necessary first step in this change. In the following discussion we will see how more recent historians are calling these assumptions and conclusions into question.

### *Further Thoughts on an Ojibwe Dependency on Fur Trade Goods*

CULTURAL ANTHROPOLOGISTS HAVE REMINDED US that a culture's technology, i.e., its *material* culture, or tools, is meaningful because it is functionally integrated within a particular cultural system. As Marshall Sahlins insisted, "A technology is not comprehended by its physical properties alone. In use, tools are brought into physical relationships with their users. On the largest view, this relationship and not the tool itself is the determinate historical quality of a technology."[48] We see then, that when the Ojibwe people accepted items of seventeenth century French material culture through trade, ultimately it was not the nature of the tool that was the attraction, but the nature of how the tool fit into, or altered, existing social styles and patterns of tool use within Ojibwe culture. In other words, the new tool had to fit existing social patterns, or be adjusted in some manner to fit such patterns in order to find widespread acceptance. The material items brought by the early French, then, were confronted with a new social and cultural milieu—that of Ojibwe culture—and for these trade goods to be successful they had to fit into this system. If they did not fit, they would not be accepted, or if they were accepted even with their lack of initial fit, they would have to change the tribal system.

Given this, since we know Ojibwe culture did not witness significant changes through the seventeenth and much of the eighteenth centuries due to its participation in the fur trade, the question of a dependency on these new trade items is unimportant. In other words, we might agree that for many decades at the start of the fur trade in North America, European trade goods did not radically alter existing social patterns within the tribal world. In fact, in the seventeenth century, the reason the fur trade was almost immediately successful was because the French found trade goods that fit the needs of tribal trappers, and conversely, the tribesmen found products—among them beaver pelts—that the French could fit into theirs.

With this in mind, we should agree when the historian Richard White says past discussions of the North American fur trade generally set it into a purely *economic* parameter, to the exclusion of other social aspects. The actual trading for furs was only one part of a wide spectrum of exchange relations that *were* the relations between the tribal nations and the French. The point here is that these two foreign nations made contact *through exchange*, i.e., by *mediation*, and hence, the prime variable in understanding how the French and tribal nations related to each other was *exchange* itself, not the actual material goods or other gratuities passing between them.

It follows that if there was a dependency involved in this exchange relationship it was the dependency upon exchange itself, for it was through the medium of an exchange relationship that the two heretofore unrelated parties established a bond, and obviously a bond is what both parties sought, for without it there could have been conflict, even war. Richard White argues that, "Colonial and early-American historians have made Indians marginal to the periods they describe. They treated them as curiosities in a world that Indians also helped create."[49] Such an interpretation opens up the matter of the history of the Ojibwe and Chequamegon Bay in a way the Ojibwe themselves always have recognized, but was not given voice in the written literature until now. In his manuscript, White focuses upon a geographic triangle encompassing the area between Sault Ste. Marie on the northeast, Chequamegon Bay on the west and a point between present-day Chicago and St. Louis in the south. He reviews the coming of the French to this region, followed by the English, during a period from approximately the early 1600s to the early 1800s. While most of his energies are devoted to the interaction of the non-Ojibwe Algonquians and the Europeans in this triangle, at times he speaks directly to the Ojibwe and Chequamegon, and importantly, his conclusions generally apply to all tribal communities in the region.

White posits the notion of a "middle ground" set up between the tribal and European nations. This is not an actual geographical territory but instead a system of rules and understandings to guide relationships between the different communities involved. Both the Algonquians and Europeans established a *modus operandi*, a mutually accepted means of interacting with each other, even though both started from cultural assumptions of their own worlds. He insists that the middle ground emerged not out of an Indian dependency or "some mythical affinity towards the French"—an affinity writers like William Warren felt existed—but because both the Algonquians and Europeans understood that if they were to have an amiable relationship, a *middle ground* was something they needed to construct.

Central to this new system of relationships was *mediation*. A peace of some sort was needed between the French and the tribal communities and also between the tribesmen and their non-European allies. Without regular and recurrent mediation sessions the fur trade likely would not have existed. Through ritual and ceremony, these meetings worked to restore and renew relationships when needed, and through this regular, or irregular, process, the ongoing exchange relationships at the core of the trade was maintained. This point is a key to Richard White's argument. Mediation rather than coercion is perhaps a novel concept to posit as the causal factor in the fur trade. Yet, White argues, it was precisely mediation that allowed the French to quell the military threats of the Iroquois, for example. With much effort, (both military and mediatory), the French were able to mediate with non-Iroquois groups in order to bring the Iroquois to an acceptance of peace, and similarly, mediation was at the core of the numerous alliances in the upper Great Lakes its fur trade literature tells us about. The underlying importance of mediation in this trade, and the alliances mediation sessions worked to maintain, was stated by a contemporary historian who writes that for the French in the late 1600s, the trade "had been supported as much to maintain Native American alliances as to generate profits."[50]

According to White, in the middle ground a merger occurred between "the French politics of empire and the kinship politics of the Indians."[51] In this arena of international diplomacy each side used its own norms, and those of the other party, to manipulate each other. Contrary to the views of many early writers, White feels the Europeans did not simply overwhelm the Indians with a superior material culture (the word used by some writers was *overawe*), backed up with the threat of military force, but instead both sides worked to achieve their own goals as each manipulated the other. This is the point Theresa Schenck makes, for example, when she notes that in the early days at least, the Ojibwe people used the fur trade to keep their cultural system functioning.

Woven through this system of relationships was the metaphor of father and child. In this metaphor the French assumed the position of the "father" and the Indian assumed that of the "child." According to White, this metaphor was at the base of the fur trade. The assumed roles of "father" and "child" were as integral to the trade as was the desire for mediation. Put another way, it was mediation through the guise of a father-child relationship that allowed trade to occur. Set in a context of ritual and ceremony based on this metaphor, the two countering flows of tribally generated goods and French merchandise was allowed to proceed. These rituals and ceremonies were not just "decorative covering" for the trade, but White insists were the very "sinews" of the trade. The mutual acceptance of rituals of authority accruing to the role of the "father" and of his acquiescence to the demands of the "child" involved the regular movement of gifts (in the literature often called "presents") between these parties. White stresses that what is important here is that this model of exchange was primary—not secondary—to the actual material items, and other things, exchanged.

Imbedded in this model of exchange was the posture of begging (sometimes including claims of starvation) on the part of the "child," and the posture of the powerful and respected "father," with its attending responsibilities. In other words, the Ojibwe person presented himself as a starving child as he begged for sustenance from his father, who, in turn, had the responsibility to minister to his child's needs. Very importantly, the pose of the Ojibwe person in this exchange was the same he took when seeking power from the *manidoog*. (And it is not irrelevant that in the earliest days of French and Ojibwe contact the tribesmen related to the Jesuits and other French authorities as if the French *were manidoog*.) A just "father" had the obligation to care for his children, and conversely, a "child" needed to expect such care—in fact, could demand it. A French term that can be translated simply as "needs," used in the times to label what was to flow from father to child, is *besoins*. Broadly defined, the noun *besoins* refers to the proper treatment of a child by its father, to include protection and sustenance. Thus, the Ojibwe could expect they would receive their *besoins* from the French authorities, but this was a reciprocal relationship. For their *besoins* the Ojibwe had to give friendship, respect, and goods to the French, or in other words, in its own turn a child must give to a father that which is expected of him.

Richard White's point is that when considering that the fur trade was an exchange relationship, its reciprocity comes to the fore. Something flowed in *both* directions, and we see that "the orientation toward besoins rather than profits" was at the heart of the trade. If we see the trade only from the perspective of the European with his "superior" goods, we might see only the profit motive. When the tribal peoples and their cultural realities and expectations are admitted into a wider and more complete view of the trade, then we appreciate the importance of motives other than what the Europeans understand as economic profit. When accepting this more encompassing view of the trade, tribal rules and expectations of kinship rise to a new importance. The French were forced to accept their responsibility to give proper *besoins* to the Indian, and conversely, the Indian accepted their obligation to give *besoins* to the French. With this understanding, the core role of mediation in the fur trade becomes clear.

One obligation of a "father" is protection of his "child." White feels it is mediation, perceived in this case as a trade good, that flowed from the French to the Indian, and again, from the Indian perspective, furs, other valued possessions, and, sometimes intangibles, were to be passed on to the French. Thus, in the minds of the Ojibwe and others, as long as the people continued to trade with the French, they could expect this protection. Richard White stresses that this relationship extended to the Crown authorities' obligation to work to resolve disputes and other more serious conflicts between the various tribal societies. To bring this around full circle, mediation was carried out in a context of exchange rituals that involved both French and Ojibwe trade goods. (We need to understand that it was not just furs tribal people passed on to the Europeans. They also traded items like food, canoes, knowledge, and at times personal companionship, which includes sexual intercourse.)

To support his argument, White offers three areas of research that suggest an absence of an early dependency on French trade goods, the first being archeological evidence. Work done at sites in Michigan and elsewhere indicate that non-European tools were relied upon in a major way, right up to the end of French involvement in the trade. Obviously, this should not have been the case if we believe the conclusions of early writers about the complete acceptance of French trade goods. We recall Edmund Jefferson Danziger, Jr.'s certainty that early in fur trade times the Ojibwe "scrapped" their material culture for that of the French.

A second area of research is the matter of cargo space. A study of commercial shipments between eastern ports and their western destinations indicate there simply was not enough cargo space to fill the supposed needs for tools and other goods people like the Ojibwe were said to have. Thus, they were relying on their own material culture, not that of the French.

Third, estimated population levels at places like Chequamegon Bay were such that the purported needs for tools, clothing, and related French items could not possibly have been met by French commerce. Furthermore, there is evidence to suggest that in the early times of the trade French goods like metal axes, kettles and the like were not primarily desired for their purely utilitarian functions. Instead, they were sought for symbolic reasons. Trade goods like simple metal mirrors were desired for use as decoration and for ceremonial purposes, and even in the case of metal kettles there is evidence to suggest the worth of these was more in their use as items primarily used as gifts passed on to other tribesmen in ceremonial contexts, and it is apparent some of these items may never have been used in a utilitarian fashion. Therefore, it is proposed that the supposed immediate acceptance of French trade goods due to their obvious superiority over the tribal material culture may be a fiction. Early French metal tools were accepted in trade, but were not immediately used to replace their stone, bone, horn, and wood counterparts. Such French trade goods were accepted into Ojibwe culture because they could be used in ceremonial contexts, not utilitarian ones. White feels such "decoding" of the meaning of early European trade goods is essential to a proper understanding of their role in Indian and French relations.[52]

The conclusion Richard White draws, and one supported by Ian Steele and Theresa Schenck, is that up to the mid-1700s, when France surrendered to England, the Ojibwe were not helpless without French trade goods, i.e., they were not dependent upon them. We are left with the awareness that the writings of the earlier historians who told of "starving and naked" Ojibwe and other tribal peoples in the early 1700s, and in many cases well into the eighteenth century, at Chequamegon must be reconsidered. In fact, when we recall that it has been concluded there would have been no fur trade without "the willingness of the Indians to trade with the white man,"[53] we could say that it was the white man who was dependent upon the Indian. And, importantly, as argued, in these early decades of the trade the Indians welcomed the trade as another method of maintaining their particular cultural systems, not to eagerly relinquish those systems in favor of that of the French.

The Euro-centered models early writers used to interpret the events in the seventeenth and eighteenth centuries precluded their acceptance of the validity of these tribal social and cultural systems. This bias is evinced in the writings of historians like Reverend Neill, Reuben Thwaites, Louise Phelps Kellogg, and their colleagues, and it is significant that it carried on as late as the 1960s and 1970s, with others like Walt Harris, Hamilton Ross and Edmund Jefferson Danziger, Jr.

To conclude, we might agree that the label *fur* trade is unnecessarily restrictive, and, finally, a *misnomer*. In the larger picture the furs exchanged by the Ojibwe and Europeans were only a single aspect of a very important exchange relationship that far transcended the economic value of the pelts of the beaver, and other fur-bearing animals, passing between the traders.

*Notes*

1. Carter 1987:34.
2. Danziger 1979:38-9.
3. Harris 1976:47.
4. Kellogg 1968[1925]:425.
5. Rowell 1932:1-15.
6. Danziger 1979:39.
7. Burnham 1974[1929]:86; Kellogg 1968[1925]:429-433; Ross 1960:55.
8. Harris 1976:49-51; Quaife 1921[1809];Warren 1984[1885];195.
9. Danziger 1979:38.
10. Ross 1960:48.
11. Thwaites 1895:412, as taken from N.Y. Colonial Documents, page 182.
12. Thwaites 1895:412-3.
13. White 1991:392.
14. Warren 1984[1885]:195.
15. Kugel 1998:19-53.
16. Warren 1984[1885]:196.
17. Danziger 1979:38.
18. Danziger 1979:38.
19. Harris 1976.
20. Nute 1988[1941]:50.
21. Harris 1976:45.
22. Thwaites 1895:413.
23. Parkman 1867 as noted in Harris 1978:45:
24. Warren 1984[1885]:195.
25. White 1991:23.
26. Quimby 1969:147, brackets added.
27. http://www.everyculture.com/northamerica/ojibwa-history-and-cultural-relations.html.
28. Warren 1984[1885]:127; Armour and Widder:1986:81-2.
29. White 1991:140.
30. For a contrary example, one showing drastic cultural change brought by the introduction of a single, comparatively simple item into a tribal society see Lauriston Sharpe's classic work on the Australian Yir Yorant. (Sharpe 1952).
31. Thwaites 1895:409-10.
32. Ross 1969:48.
33. Danziger 1979:31.
34. Olmanson 2007:40.
35. Harris 1976:41-45.
36. Danziger 1979:32-3.
37. Danziger 1979:38.
38. Henry 1921:190.
39. Kellogg 1935:10.
40. Thwaites 1895:411.
41. Ross 1960:46,48.
42. Rathbun and Vannoy 1987:16-34[copy at U.S. National Park Service archives at Bayfield, WI].
43. Rathbun and Vannoy 1987:36.
44. White 1996:3, in Blair 1996[1911].
45. Treuer 2010; McNally 2009; Gray 2006; Angel 2002; Spielmann 1998.
46. Schenck 1996:251, italics added.
47. Levi Straus 1981:453.
48. Sahlins, Marshall, as given in *The Culture of Wilderness* by Frieda Knobloch, 1996:49.
49. White 1991:xiv.
50. Ward 2009[2005]:20.
51. White 1991:33.
52. White 1991:103.
53. Smith 1985[1973]:35.

# 9

# The Coming of the British

### *The Years of Transition from a French to a British Alliance*

1.

THE THREE YEARS BETWEEN THE FRENCH surrender in 1760 and the final peace agreements signed in 1763 are said to have been difficult times for the Ojibwe and many others involved in the North American fur trade. From the European perspective, a vacuum of leadership existed—the French had been defeated and were withdrawing from the scene, but as victors the British had not yet officially taken over as the new leaders.

What is overlooked in this argument is that all through these years, people in nations like the Ojibwe in western Lake Superior went on with their lives. Their foraging adaptation had not been irrevocably altered by French contact, so they continued with their routine of seasonally moving through their different resource regions. As some writers point out, during the century of the Ojibwe-French alliance, the fur trade did not alter the essentials of Ojibwe culture. For the Chequamegon Bay Ojibwe, the years from 1760-1763—from the end of the Seven Years War to the time of the official peace agreement—may have presented some challenges for their fur trapping and trading regimen, but did not seriously disrupt their way of life.

The economics of the fur trade, we recall, had been added to the traditional Ojibwe subsistence pattern of foraging. Contrary to what some writers have stated, it had not completely replaced this system. However, to writers like Louise Phelps Kellogg, with her European-American orientation, these years were understood as a very unsettling *interregnum* between the reigns of two European monarchies. This is essentially the way the early 1760s have been interpreted in the popular history of Chequamegon Bay. The defeat of the French in 1760 has been seen as an emotionally and economically troubling event for the Ojibwe.[1] As noted above, readers have been told of the extreme dependency of the tribesmen on trade goods and how when the flow of these goods was halted the people fell into times of poverty, i.e., "starvation and nakedness."

There was much more going on in the western Great Lakes communities in the mid-1700s than a change in European monarchies. In this section we will look at these times and how the Ojibwe at Chequamegon were involved.

2.

FOUR YEARS BEFORE THE FRENCH SURRENDERED at Montreal, the British Crown instituted a new plan for its relations with North American tribal nations. In 1756, the Crown set up two Indian superintendencies, a Northern and a Southern. These were meant to provide a structure for English and tribal relations that would work toward a peaceful expansion of British colonies into the continent. Sir William Johnson was appointed Northern Superintendent and he oversaw British policy as played out in Chequamegon.

With the death of the French commander, Montcalm, at Quebec in 1759, France's North American forces were put into the hands of Brigadier Francois-Gaston de Levis, but his tenure lasted only until 1760, when he surrendered to the British at Montreal. Importantly, the surrender agreement at Montreal included two articles that had long-term effects on Ojibwe communities in the western regions. First, French officers and soldiers were to go to the nearest port and take a vessel back to France, but French non-combatants could remain at regional posts "and have free exercise of their religion."[2] Second, any French who remained were allowed to take part in the fur trade with the same privileges as the British.

The second agreement gave official sanction to those French who had become intimately involved with tribal communities and wanted to stay in their regions. A different agreement could have seen the forced removal of many French persons out of areas like the Chequamegon region, and although such an edict would have been difficult to enforce, it nevertheless could have affected significant historical events for the Ojibwe. When the 1760 peace settlement allowed French citizens to stay in the western Great Lakes regions, there may have been several of these French persons who remained at Chequamegon, or at least migrated to the region over the subsequent years from more eastern French locales and stayed.

Edmund Jefferson Danziger, Jr. has written that after the withdrawal of the French from western Lake Superior in 1760, "There were no permanent white settlers above the Sault."[3] While there may have been no such "settlers" in Chequamegon Bay, we should not assume there were no French persons who remained in the region after 1760. In fact, when French military troops were recalled from the fort at La Pointe in 1759, some French persons remained at the post until 1762.[4]

When Pierre Hertel de Beaubasin left La Pointe in 1758, it was Sieur Corne de la St. Luc who arrived that same year to assume the position of resident trader. St. Luc stayed until 1762, a period of four years. By then the French government restored the earlier system of leasing trading districts, and St. Luc paid for the La Pointe lease. He acted as a civilian during his four years at the post, but had been a French army officer who led troops in the eastern wars only a few years previous.

The written record is silent about his success at La Pointe, and it is suggested since the British closed off the St. Lawrence waterway to French furs moving east he had difficulty getting any furs out of Lake Superior. However, we know British traders at Albany were accepting cargo from the French, so St. Luc's La Pointe furs, like others from western regions, might have reached New York via Albany in those years. In any event, since he was at Chequamegon for four years—up to the pending arrival of the British—it is suggested that he was successful as a trader in those years. There may have been no white settlers west of the Sault when the French officially withdrew in 1760, but at Chequamegon we see that a regular French presence remained right up to 1762. Also, it seems highly likely that over the preceding one hundred years the French had been coming to the region, some French males had easily adapted to the way of life of the Ojibwe and decided to stay in these communities after the French surrender. Even more likely is the presence of a few generations of tribal members who were of Ojibwe and French descent by 1760.

Ojibwe and French relations in the Chequamegon area, as elsewhere in the western lakes region, were contentious well before 1760, as France and England competed to capture the bulk of the fur trade. As we noted, French and Ojibwe relations in the Lake Superior region suffered as British traders tried to reach into the area in the mid-1700s. This unrest was exacerbated with the defeat of the French and the withdrawal of an official French presence in the Lake Superior country, and it continued for several years after 1760, until England established itself in the region. While it appears that in some tribal communities the transition from French traders to British went smoothly enough, there is evidence that for some British, the entrance into the western lakes was not a welcome one.[5]

The Canadian historian Ian Steele made an important point concerning relations between France and England in North America, a point alluded to above, when he suggested that the tribal communities may have been better off when these European powers were at each other's throats than when there was peace between them. He feels that when France and England were fighting each other, they needed the tribesmen to aid in these wars and the focus of European energies was directed less at the tribes than at the European adversary. Steele suggests it was when the Europeans were at peace with each other that they could direct their attention to the tribal communities, i.e., could get back to their underlying intent to exploit and colonize these people, and it was during such peaceful times that the tribal systems suffered most.

This is an interesting perspective from which to view the mid-1700s in the western Great Lakes region. From this stance, perhaps the few years when France and England were struggling with each other, to include Kellogg's "interregnum" of 1760-1763, were years when tribal nations were able to confer with each other about their common European problem. And this is precisely what occurred for the tribal societies. It was in the mid-1700s that pan-tribal meetings took place and a so-called "Northwest Rebellion" erupted.

## 3.

THE TERMS OF THE 1760 SURRENDER of the French included no mention of the tribal nations who had aided them in their conflicts with England, leaving the question of tribal-European relations uncertain. Those who considered themselves allies to the French expressed their anger, and although this reaction is justifiable, historians who were writing as late as the 1930s did not acceptably understand it. For example, Louise Phelps Kellogg said the "primitive minds" of the Indians could not understand the French capitulation to the British, the natives insisting that they were still free, "never having surrendered."[6] While Kellogg, writing in 1935, used the early European notion of "primitive Indian minds" to understand the tribal anger, Ian Steele, writing in 1994, sees another aspect of this anger. Steele feels the omission of tribal nations as legitimate actors in the French-English peace settlement of 1760 is another example of the French and English "arrogance" that allowed the Europeans to look upon the North American tribal peoples as "subjects" rather than as independent, full-fledged allies.[7]

The anger of the tribes at being omitted from the peace agreement between the two European powers sheds light on another topic concerning tribal-European relations in North America at the time. This is the use of a formal discourse with the Europeans in which the natives assumed the posture of "children" in the presence of their "father", as discussed above. This ritual posturing is clear: it was a *formal* (hence, ritual) form of discourse, or political maneuvering, meant to serve desired ends for *both* the tribal and European nations. For the Ojibwe this discourse stemmed from their perceptions of reality, as set forth in their cultural tenets concerning their place in the universe, and especially with their relations with other powerful persons. Such discourse was not a literal acceptance of themselves as submissive to, or actual *children* of the European *fathers*. Instead, it was used as a mechanism to establish and continue meaningful relationships between otherwise equal persons and sovereign nations they represented. Thus, the anger Kellogg attributes to a "primitive mind," is instead an indication of a mind holding alternate understandings of how human societies should work, and also a mind rich in political astuteness.

Perhaps Carolyn Gilman said it best when she spoke of the opening of trade between the French and tribesmen. Gilman argued:

> In Indian society, trade was a public ceremony. To open trade was to cement an alliance—a relationship imbued with many mutual obligations, including political and military aid, social duties such as food sharing, and intermarriage. Politics and trade were inseparable, as the French soon found out . . . . They also found themselves enmeshed in a fabric of kinship. In native American society, family was a civil body as well as a biological one. It was, in fact, the Indian equivalent of a legal and judicial

system . . . . It was to both the trader's and the Indians' advantage to be considered each other's kin.[8]

At any given time even their most determined enemies could be recognized as *kin* (sometimes due to inter-tribal marriages), so generally speaking, the Ojibwe saw themselves living in a world of kin—a universe filled with forms of life they (the Ojibwe) were related to. Primary of course, in this world were the *manidoog*, those powerful spirit forms who, finally, were relatives. And the tribes saw themselves, rightfully, as sovereign nations, independent self-chosen allies of the Europeans, and the fact of their being omitted from the French surrender and following peace negotiations with the British was an insult to this sovereignty.

France recalled troops from its La Pointe post in 1759, and in 1760, evacuated Michilimackinac and Green Bay. We have noted that the Jesuits (and other French leaders) shifted their headquarters at the eastern end of Lake Superior from Sault Ste. Marie to Michilimackinac in 1689, an important move, as we will note below. In 1760, the French left that post in the hands of Charles de Langlade, who had successfully led Indian-French forces in several skirmishes against the British in the 1750s. This is the same de Langlade who, as a British officer, later led tribal forces against the new United States military in the late 1700s.[9]

Doubtless the Chequamegon Bay Ojibwe watched the political activities of the French and British from 1760 to 1763 very carefully. Officially their long alliance with France was no longer functional but the presence of St. Luc in the bay must have alleviated a degree of uncertainty. Under the French-English peace agreement, he was allowed to trade in the region and should have been able to bring trading goods to La Pointe regularly, so any Ojibwe who cared to could have continued to trade during the four years he was there. The British were in the general region, but no officials had yet come forward to establish an alliance with the Ojibwe, so St. Luc apparently had little competition in his trading activities.

In 1758, Great Britain appointed General Jeffery Amherst as its commander-in-chief in North America, and under his leadership British-tribal relations took a decided downturn. Jeffery Amherst had a clear disdain for Indian people, calling them "vermin" and is said to have had smallpox germs "spread by infected gift blankets" among them.[10] (Such genocidal acts by the British toward tribal peoples were not unprecedented in North America. In 1623, Britains served poisoned wine to a community of Pamunkey, murdering 200 persons.[11])

In 1761, Amherst stopped the policy of ceremonially feasting and giving presents to native tribal dignitaries. Such feasting and gift giving was a custom used successfully by the French and tribesmen for over a century.[12] The ceremonial act of gifting carried out between diplomats throughout the world continues as an important aspect of international protocol today, and as we have seen in the discussion of Richard White's notion of the *middle ground*, it had great importance within the context of tribal cultures in the seventeenth and eighteenth centuries as well. It is likely such a custom has a long history—and doubtless a prehistory—in North America, and as such was simply extended to the Europeans upon their arrival in the fifteenth century.

Jeffery Amherst's discontinuance of this ritual was a serious affront to the tribal leaders who had to meet with British authorities on a regular basis in the late 1700s. Earlier writers failed to recognize the importance of Britain's sudden refusal to embellish such meetings with the usual lavish servings of food and the ritual presentation of presents. The tribesmen expected these events to be imbued with a proper ceremonial importance and dignity. Such political theater was integral to the success of these meetings and indeed, was necessary to continue alliances. Instead, these writers portrayed tribal leaders as "savages" who, in their "childlike" ways were interested more so in the opportunities to gorge themselves with free food and to acquire "gaudy" minor trinkets. From the European perspective the fact that Indians were upset with Amherst's decision supported the notion of what "savages" were like.

His act flagged a significant alteration in what was considered proper protocol by the tribesmen, but just as importantly, it halted what may have been seen as an integral economic relationship. It has been suggested that "these gifts may have been regarded by Amerindians as ground rent for forts, payment for permission to trade, tokens to sustain an alliance, or even as tribute." Furthermore, such presents often did not stop moving when given to a tribal leader, for a successful leader was usually obligated to share them with his followers. Therefore, the "presents' given to such leaders by Europeans can in many cases be considered in a wider context that included more than the persons doing the initial gifting and receiving. Thus, "Favored 'medal' chiefs . . . reinforced their own and the donor's standing in village and tribal politics by distributing impressive gifts to warriors, followers, and allies."[13]

General Amherst's and other British authorities' certainties about the worth of tribal peoples, along with the increasing threatening presence of British civilians in the eastern portion of the continent in the 1760s, worked to heighten anxiety for tribes in the region. It may be felt that because of the distance, this friction had few repercussions in western Lake Superior lands, however, we should not conclude that in those times the Ojibwe of Chequamegon Bay were untouched by all this unrest to the east. We know Ojibwe military units were on the fighting fields of several eastern regions in the immediate preceding years, and even though historians have suggested few of these fighters came from Chequamegon, we should not think that the bay's people knew nothing about distant British activities. In 1762, British troops arrived at the old French post at Grand Portage, northwest of Chequamegon Bay. Surely, the Ojibwe at La Pointe were aware of this close British military presence and pondered its implications for the future.

The direct negative effects of British arrogance shown toward tribal peoples in North America may have been a reality essentially avoided by many Ojibwe at Chequamegon Bay in the 1760s, and the American Revolution of 1776 may have removed its threat. Yet for the Ojibwe residing north of the Canadian border it was another matter. Here this British sentiment continued to be troublesome, even to very recent times. This is significant, since from the earliest times, Lake Superior's Ojibwe people have traveled over what is now the border region between Canada and the United States with regularity, and this continues today.

4.

WITH THE EXIT OF ST. LUC FROM CHEQUAMEGON in 1762, when the Ojibwe were left without their old French allies with which to relate economically, and with their awareness of a new, but still unauthenticated presence of the British, there must have been a degree of uncertainty in the Chequamegon communities. It is likely unlicensed traders were visiting the region but the matter of an official European alliance was left open. On a more personal level, those families who lost members as French allies in battles with the British must have struggled with France's final defeat on even a deeper level. As Theresa Schenck has suggested, we should expect that such deaths may have strained things even further for the Ojibwe if affected persons sought relief from obligatory mourning rituals by taking trophies from other tribal communities that may, at the time, have been at odds with the Ojibwe. All this could have made for new levels of anxiety throughout the Chequamegon region.

It has been suggested that these immediate years after the French surrender saw a serious disorganization to the fur trade.[14] However, with the presence of St. Luc at La Pointe, we should not conclude that the Ojibwe were left helpless to care for their needs. St. Luc was in business for four years. Kellogg tells that in 1760, with the end of French-English hostilities in North America, the fur trade in western regions was suddenly opened up to the British, and wealth seekers from eastern British colonies rushed to the upper lakes with this "opportunity to enrich themselves." She claims "traders of all types from the several colonies hurried into the Northwest in order to reap rich harvests."[15] Understandably, it may have taken a length of time for some to reach Chequamegon Bay, but British traders were active for several preceding years in the immediate regions north of Lake Superior. British in this northerly region could have moved south into lands just to the west of the big lake. The major fur entrepot at Grand Portage was available to the Ojibwe, and there was nothing to prevent them from transporting their furs to Michilimackinac and on to the eastern centers. We should not conclude that with the fall of France in 1760, Chequamegon Bay's Ojibwe were not actively participating in the trade until the arrival of the first licensed British traders a few years later.

There is another point to be made about this. As we have stated, writers note that all through the fur trading years the French and British desired not to seriously disrupt the culture of the Ojibwe because their mobile adaptation was required for the fur trade to exist. Therefore, we could expect that through the years of transition from a French to an English alliance that the Ojibwe continued to live as they had for centuries, that is, to move with the seasons, hunting, fishing, gardening, and otherwise harvesting the produce of the land and waters. Surely while the disruption in the trade may have been acutely felt in some European quarters its effects were of a different, if not actually less severe nature to the tribesmen.

Louise Phelps Kellogg's interregnum may have been unsettling to the Europeans in North America and may have been viewed as a time of conflict and upheaval by early writers, but to the Chequamegon Bay Ojibwe its three years were not a time of great change.

Yet by the mid-1760s, the Ojibwe of the bay did see a shift from an alliance with France to one with England, and over the next forty years they would be challenged to shift again, this time to the new government of the United States. Through these decades these four nations—Ojibwe, France, England and the United States of America—witnessed many conferences and some military skirmishes, but through it all the trade went on. By the end of these years the geographic heart of the trade had moved to regions north and west of the Mississippi. By 1800, the Lake Superior Ojibwe were witnessing the new challenges of the impending end of this trade, a trade that had flourished for over 150 years.

## *The 1760s: Pontiac and Alexander Henry*

1.

THE CESSION OF FRANCE'S CANADIAN LAND holdings to the English that occurred in 1763 marked a distinct change in the direction of Ojibwe history. France's "ownership" of most of this vast territory was a paper ownership since the region's tribal peoples still held the land. We recall the pretentious ceremony of French officials and Jesuits at Sault Ste. Marie in 1671, when a proprietary claim was made on the vast region beyond The Sault. As we know, after one hundred and fifty or so years most of this region did fall from tribal hands, but in the 1700s, this had not yet occurred. In any event, the exit of France eventually played out in major ways for the Ojibwe at Chequamegon. For them, France would never again have a meaningful official presence in their region. And even though their foraging culture was still intact and its social and religious institutions were solid, their future had taken a decided turn. The French were gone and now they faced the British.

Almost immediately after France's exit, the British Crown issued the Proclamation of 1763. In an attempt to undo the harm Jeffery Amherst's program to stand firm in relations with tribal nations brought about, Sir William Johnson sought to have the new proclamation put into effect. Amherst desired to use the European market exchange system in all dealings with the tribes, in other words to function only in a business-like fashion, where the profit motive drove the international relationships. As we saw, the giving of presents to tribal emissaries was curtailed, and father-child rituals based on the giving and receiving of *besoins* came to a halt. Jeffery Amherst's negative view of Indian people, and his new policy of diplomatic relations, along with the reality of the steady increase of European settlers moving further and further west, all added to the stress and frustration felt by tribal communities.

It was Johnson's hope to restore the western alliances with the tribes and to once again use presents in meetings with leaders. Under the proclamation, the Appalachian watershed was to be a boundary for British westward expansion. Settlers west of the range were to remove back east and no more land was to be acquired without Crown approval. In all, the Proclamation of 1763 was meant to restore at least a semblance of peace in the old northwest so that eventually the colonizing desires of England could continue to achieve fruition. It was finally meant to control both the growing North American colonies as well as the Indian communities. According to Louise Phelps Kellogg, the proclamation "was merely a temporary expedient to quiet hostile Indians and to secure time for the consideration of the best methods to regulate trade."[16]

However, the proclamation was a failure. The British government's financiers resisted the expense of outfitting the English posts with presents, and British settlers refused to move back east. Across the ocean, the ultimate seat of British authority was too far-removed to be effective and any attempt to increase its forceful pressure on the new continent was precluded because of monetary expense.

For the people at Chequamegon all this is said to have meant little, but we cannot be so sure. The written record is generally non-committal on the details of sentiments on these events as felt at Chequamegon Bay. But given the history of the bay's Ojibwe peoples' involvement in eastern commercial and military affairs, we should expect the Ojibwe in western Lake Superior were not simply uninformed distant bystanders. The record shows they were aware of the unrest in the eastern Great Lakes communities, an awareness that included attempts of an Odawa-Ojibwe leader named Pontiac to have the Chequamegon Bay Ojibwe join him in his struggle.

## 2.

OVER THE YEARS SINCE THE 1760S, an extensive literature has grown on the man Pontiac and "his war." In the nineteenth century, this man, who came out of the Odawa-Ojibwe communities of eastern Lake Superior and the Detroit region, had become a person symbolizing the unfortunate tribesman who for a period of time stood fast in the path of European colonization only to falter and give way. Frances Parkman, the early prominent historian, posed Pontiac as a lone figure who led a handful of dissidents in activities that they should have seen could only lead to their destined demise. Through Parkman's pen, Pontiac was portrayed as the leader of a small faction of reactionary tribesmen who resisted the inevitable. He was a tragic primitive hero—an idealistic "savage" figure standing against the "advance" of civilization.[17] Today we understand Pontiac in another way. His "war" is now seen as part of a widespread resistance throughout the Great Lakes region and in some cases, in lands more distant.[18]

For some years in the early decades of the 1700s, a new type of politico-religious leader was emerging in Indian country. In the 1750s, for instance, along the Susquehanna River (in a region called the state of New York today), the Assinsink Prophet, a member of the Munsee tribe, started preaching an anti-British message. In the 1760s, a prophet named Neolin, in the Deleware nation, started to acquire a considerable following. Neolin preached a message of revival for tribal peoples that quickly became militant. Pontiac took inspiration from Neolin and soon had his own following.[19]

By the 1760s, Pontiac and his emissaries were busy visiting communities with his message: strike down the British invaders and establish a more meaningful existence. Today we recognize this as not simply the preaching of a single visionary but as the widespread "Midwest Rebellion." Early writers suggest all this was too distant to have any important effect at Chequamegon. Yet there is evidence to suggest that this conclusion may have been unwarranted.

## 3.

ONE YEAR AFTER FRANCE FELL TO ENGLAND in 1760, French-Canadian emissaries came to Detroit to try to get support from tribal leaders for a military assault against the British. This was a last, gasping effort to save Canada for the French. This meeting convened in the summer of 1761 and it is likely Chequamegon Bay Ojibwe were in attendance. According to George Croughan, a powerful trader in the region and at times an important British official, the meeting involved those tribes in the immediate Detroit area as well as "some other tribes who live amongst those Indians on Lake Superior, above Mechelemackinac and Fort Le Bay."[20] We might think that Croughan was referring only to the Ojibwe community at Sault Ste. Marie, but he could just as easily have been speaking of places like Keweenaw and Chequamegon. In the 1760s, these two western Ojibwe centers were maintaining their old commercial ties with The Sault. Even today families at Red Cliff recall how in the early times an ancestor migrated to Chequamegon from The Sault. Kinship ties between eastern and western Lake Superior Ojibwe communities must have been strong all through the 1700s. Apparently the Canadian Frenchmen at Detroit were not successful in seeing any immediate positive response to their efforts, but we should expect their message became part of the political dialog between tribal communities in these years.

The Odawa, and ancestors of the Ojibwe, had used the Michilimackinac site for years but the French did not use it as a regional headquarters until about 1715. Its commanding position over the Mackinac Straits made it a contested site for the French and British for decades. We recall that in Fr. Marquette's time a station had been built at nearby St. Ignace where, it was hoped, the Odawa and Huron returning from La Pointe in those years would settle, but after a time of little success in this venture, the French moved their installation to the Michilimackinac site. It was here that Alexander Henry arrived when first coming to the upper Great Lakes in 1761, and it was this fort that members of Pontiac's Rebellion attacked in 1763. The British used this fort from 1761 until 1779, when they decided to move their fortification to nearby Mackinac Island (a move that took the larger part of two years) to better withstand any attacks from colonial forces after the beginning of the American Revolution.[21]

With the exit of the French there were attempts on the part of some tribes to establish new alliances with the British, but other tribes still held hopes of a return to power by the French. This "disarray of the Algonquians" witnessed in the lower Great Lakes may have aided the British as tribes sought stability in their trading relationships,[22] nevertheless, "conspiracies" against the British are said to have been fomenting. The Iroquois in the eastern areas, the Algonquians in the Old Northwest region, and the French-led initiatives at Detroit are three major examples. The Algonquians "disarray" was exacerbated by "crop failures, epidemics and famine" visiting the Indian communities in the lower Great Lakes regions in these years.[23]

It is in this unsettled milieu that Pontiac began to operate. By the 1760s, he was already known as a capable military leader, having successfully led a combined Odawa-Ojibwe defense of Detroit in 1746, when the Dakota and Mesquakie attacked. These two western tribes were angered by the French act of providing the Odawa and Ojibwe with arms to use in their skirmishes with them.[24] For our purposes it is not necessary to review the entire span of years and major events now known as the Northwest Rebellion, but instead to concentrate on the events most closely related to Chequamegon Bay.

Today in Lake Superior country, Pontaic is perhaps best remembered for his efforts to strike British posts in the Great Lakes in 1763. This was a well-planned effort which saw thirteen such posts simultaneously attacked. Success was such that by 1765, only four posts remained.[25] One fort that fell to the tribal nations was the post at Michilimackinac. We have an eyewitness account of this attack, recorded by a British trader who was at the site in 1763.

4.

ALEXANDER HENRY LEFT HIS NATIVE New Jersey with the surrender of the French and quickly made his way west. He had served as a British soldier in battles against the French[26] and was one of the many wealth-seekers Louise Phelps Kellogg speaks of who "hurried into the Northwest in order to reap rich harvests from the needs of the Indian."[27]

As we have argued, Kellogg felt these "needs" came about because of the "dependence" of the native peoples on French trade goods, but this is an unfortunately biased view of the matter. Henry made his way to Albany where he was successful in getting a trading permit from British General Gage, outfitted himself with a cargo of trade goods, hired a crew of paddlers and soon was on the old Ottawa River-Lake Huron canoe route, heading westward. He arrived at Michilimackinac late in the open water season of 1761.[28]

Henry remained at the fort for some time, involved in the fur trade from that location, and was still there two years later when the attack occurred. It was set for 4 June 1763, the date of the British king's birthday. This was a day of festivities and celebration and military personnel would not be especially vigilant in their task of defense. The colorful details of the day are well known, so here it is enough to offer an outline of the events. Henry's memoir tells of the lacrosse game staged by local tribes, how it was held just outside the fort's open gates, how the Indian women secreted weapons into the fort under their clothing while the game went back and forth. Then the ball was intentionally tossed over the wall and the teams surged through the open doors of the fort, were quickly handed their weapons and proceeded to attack the British. The attack was very successful and soon the fort was in the hands of the tribesmen. Henry was hidden away by Indian friends or he most likely would have perished like most of the other British. Later, under cover of darkness, he was taken to safety.

Historians have written that the Chequamegon Ojibwe communities were not directly involved in the attack at Michilimackinac. As one writer tells it, "The Michilimackinac Chippewas took the fort at the straits, but there the revolt halted,"[29] the message being that those tribal communities beyond the Straits of Mackinac such as Sault Ste. Marie and westward did not join in the attack against Britain. It is pertinent that in 1763, no British forts existed for some distance beyond Michilimackinac, so as a revolt designed to attack British forts, it had to stop there. The documented degree of anti-British sentiment in Algonquian communities in the early 1760s hints that if any forts had stood at Sault Ste. Marie or Chequamegon Bay it is likely that they would have been included in the attacks. However, there is evidence to the contrary.

We are told that the La Pointe Ojibwe refused to take part in the attack at Michilimackinac, due to the influence of a single person. William Warren wrote that:

> It is true that the war-club, tobacco, and wampum belt of war had been carried by the messengers of Pontiac and his lieutenant, the Mackinac chieftain, to LaPointe, and the principal villages of the tribe on Lake Superior, but the Ojibways listened only to the advise and the words of peace of a French trader who resided at Sault Ste. Marie, and from this point (with an influence not even surpassed by that which his contemporary, Sir Wm. Johnson, wielded over the more eastern tribes), he held sway, and guided the councils of the Lake Superior Ojibways, even to their remotest village . . . . The name of this man was John Baptiste Cadotte, and he was a son of the Mons. Cadeau who first appeared in the Ojibway country, as early as in 1671, in the train of the French envoy, Sieur du Lusson, when he treated with the delegates of the northwestern Indian tribes at Sault Ste. Marie.[30]

Today, representatives of the Cadotte family are found in several Lake Superior Ojibwe communities, and William Warren tells, at some length, the story of their forebear, Jean Baptiste Cadotte. He was a fur trader who traveled extensively into Ojibwe lands, married a woman of the Crane clan, and they had a daughter and two sons, John Baptiste, Jr. and Michel. It is of no little matter that Mrs. Cadotte was a member of the Crane clan, since traditionally this is the clan that provided tribal leaders. Later in our discussion we will see how Jean Baptiste Cadotte's descendents continued this tradition of leadership on Lake Superior's southern shore.

Alexander Henry wrote that "M. [John Baptiste, Sr.] Cadotte enjoyed a powerful influence over [the Sault Ste. Marie Ojibwes'] conduct. They considered M. Cadotte as their chief, and he was not only my friend, but a friend to the English. It was by him that the Chippeways of Lake Superior were prevented from joining Pontiac."[31] William Warren drew upon Henry's memoir when he said that Lake Superior Ojibwes, those on lands between Lake Superior and the Mississippi, and those on the Upper Mississippi itself were not at Michilimackinac on the day of the attack. Yet, about these Lake Superior and westward Ojibwe communities, Warren offers an interesting exception. He says, "at most, but a few of their old warriors who have all now fallen into their graves, were noted as having been accidentally present on the occasion of this most important event in the history of the tribe."[32]

From Warren's remark we see that some Chequamegon Bay Ojibwes were at Michilimackinac on 4 June

1763, and although Warren wanted us to believe their number was negligible, we do not know exactly how many were there. Given the political climate of the time Warren did his fieldwork, we might assume both he and his informants may have desired to downplay any presence of La Pointe Ojibwe at the fort on that day. Furthermore, in Warren's time, they desired to project themselves as friends of the Americans. Therefore, while he claims only a few La Pointe men were at Michilimackinac on the day of the attack, and that they were not part of the attack, we cannot be sure. What we should be certain of is that in the nineteenth century there existed a tradition of ongoing social and economic intercourse between the Ojibwe communities along the entire length of Lake Superior. All through this time these native communities, like the Europeans who were in their midst, kept in contact with each other.

What also comes through in the writings of Warren and Alexander Henry is the strong influence of John Baptiste Cadotte in Lake Superior Ojibwe communities from Sault Ste. Marie westward, including areas of the Upper Mississippi. Pro-British Cadotte was a force in these communities, and if we can believe William Warren, even more powerful than Sir William Johnson was in tribal communities far to the east. Cadotte's wife was a power in her own right, working in these same communities, according to Warren, "to further the interests of her husband."[33] As a member of the Crane dodem, his wife would have added much to his efforts, or perhaps more correctly, it was due to her kinship connections that his leadership carried credibility, making his fur trading efforts especially successful.

We are told that in the 1760s, due to France's downfall, Ojibwe communities, "in particular, were hostile to the English."[34] This is what makes Cadotte's success especially noteworthy. His pro-British sentiment was likely not what the Lake Superior people welcomed in these times, and their acquiescence to the will of Cadotte became more important at Chequamegon as the last decades of the eighteenth century played out, and in the early years of the 1800s, it continued to be of some significance for them.

5.

THE NORTHWEST REBELLION—OR "PONTIAC'S WAR"—is said to have failed. A contemporary historian suggests that soon after the 1763 attacks the "Indian resolve was ebbing," and "running low on supplies, the Indians were forced to negotiate for peace and return to the task of supplying their people with food."[35] Here the notion of tribesmen dependent on the European trade for survival is hinted at, and this harks back to the writings of historians over a century ago. As we noted, earlier writers like Francis Parkman posed the Northwest Rebellion as a futile, albeit pathos-laden gesture by "The Savage" to throw off his civilized adversary despite the supposed inevitability of the outcome. More recently, Richard White argues differently. To White, the rebellion was more complex than earlier writers—and even some more recent ones—recognized. He sees it as an attempt to return to customs that existed before the coming of the European, and as an attempt to bring back the old kin-based exchange relationship as held with the French. In this view the tribesmen are accepted as perceptive actors on a much wider international stage. The powerful Delaware leader, Neolin, and his followers wanted a return to somewhat "native" ways, but other tribes yearned for a return of an alliance such as they had with the French. According to White, "the genius of Pontiac" was to understand the long-term implications of the coming of the European for tribal society and to formulate plans to meet this problem. Pontiac understood the complexities of this and set as his goal the merging of the two different tribal desires into a movement that to some degree brought back both.

Richard White argues that Pontiac's efforts led the tribes and the British to reestablish an acceptable relationship. In other words England moved back into "the middle ground."[36] As we saw, the tribal nations were struggling with Jeffery Amherst's program of putting profit—in terms of a market exchange system—before all other relations. The fort attacks of 1763 were the catalyst that moved England back onto White's middle ground. The very next year, Sir William Johnson worked to have tribal leaders confer with him at Fort Niagara to establish the guidelines for the new alliance, and historians have interpreted this meeting as signaling the defeat of Pontiac. For example, Louise Kellogg saw the meeting at Oswego, New York, between Johnson, Pontiac and other tribal leaders as a council where the Indians "made (a) complete submission."[37] But White chooses to see this as a victory for Pontiac, since through it he was able to have the British move back onto the middle ground. From this perspective it was Johnson who submitted to the tribesmen.

Envoys of Sir William Johnson came to Sault Ste. Marie early in 1764 to invite the Ojibwe to the summer meeting at Fort Niagara. The written record is silent on the matter of delegates from Chequamegon Bay being present at Niagara, but it is unlikely that the bay's Ojibwe leaders would have missed this important affair. According to Henry Schoolcraft and William Warren, at this time an Ojibwe war leader at La Pointe was Mamongazida (the literature gives various versions and spellings of this man's name), a descendent of the legendary Mudjikiwis (also called Waishki), who was the community's leader in earlier times. Mamongazida was a major political figure for the Ojibwe in the middle of the eighteenth century and was originally from a division of the Northern Ojibwe in the Grand Portage region, but as a young man had relocated to La Pointe. According to William Warren, Mamongazida's wife had previously been married to a Dakota man, and a son from this marriage was Wabasha, the famed Dakota leader. Mamongazida was part of the La Pointe force that fought the Dakota at Prescott Point on the St. Croix River in approximately 1755.[38]

We recall that Mamongazida had been an ally of France, and Warren claims that in earlier times he "was noted for the frequency of his visits to Montreal and Quebec, and the great love he bore to the French people, whose cause he warmly espoused against the British . . . . He actively aided them in their wars with Great Britain, and on one occasion he took a message from Gen. Montcalm to the Lake Superior Ojibways, asking them to come to his aid in Canada." This Ojibwe political leader was with a contingent of La Pointe fighters in the French ranks on the Plains of Abraham when Quebec fell to the British in 1759. However, even given this strong loyalty to France, Warren claims that due to the diplomacy of Sir William Johnson, in 1764 Mamongazida "became a fast friend of the

English."[39] This seemingly quick political switch likely was not due solely to the diplomacy of Johnson, but also to Mamongazida's political acumen and surely the reality of his situation. By 1764, France was out of the picture and not likely to return as a powerful ally, so it was the English or nothing. After what had to have been an active political career, upon Mamongazida's death he was succeeded by his son, Waubojeeg. This brief synopsis of the life of Mamongazida indicates the extent of the involvement of Ojibwe communities from western Lake Superior in distant international affairs in the middle of the eighteenth century. Like tribal leaders that preceded and followed him, Mamongazida was a very busy person, able to operate on the highest North American political planes, and in this role often found himself being called to lands distant from La Pointe.

Warren claims that twenty tribal representatives from Sault Ste. Marie were present at the 1764 Niagara meeting, and since by that time most Lake Superior Ojibwe were residing in areas west of The Sault, it is likely that such a large contingent included leaders from Keweenaw and Chequamegon Bay. The conference was a lavish affair, with about a total of 2,000 tribal leaders in attendance. Although anti-British sentiment was not immediately quashed in all quarters, the conference was successful in establishing acceptable relations between the British and the western tribesmen and almost instantly, as occurred with the peace negotiations ending the Seven Years War in 1761, Europeans from the eastern regions started moving west with the intent to enter the fur trade. Many congregated at Michilimackinac but could not go further without a license. At the time it still was the British policy to allow trading only at garrisoned posts, but under the mounting pressure at The Sault, its commander issued licenses to a few traders, and Alexander Henry, who had been in the area since 1761, won one of these. His license gave him the exclusive right to trade on Lake Superior for three years. Most importantly, during his three years at The Sault, Henry and Jean Baptiste Cadotte became business partners in the trade.[40]

Alexander Henry's memoir has served as a major source for historians of the fur trade of the period. While Henry had considerable success in the Lake Superior trade for the three years he held a license, by the late 1760s, the Lake Superior region saw many more traders entering the business.

6.

THE POPULAR HISTORY OF ALEXANDER HENRY'S time at Chequamegon tells how he and his crew of paddlers left Sault Ste. Marie with several canoes loaded with trade goods and their own provisions in July 1765, heading west for La Pointe. Our knowledge of Henry's time in western Lake Superior comes largely from his own telling, as found in his familiar memoir. While this important document is rich with valued descriptive accounts of native people and how they related to this first English trader to come among them, it also is a prime example of what I have been calling *fur trade theater*.

On the way to Chequamegon Bay, Henry writes that he and his colleagues encountered a group of "nearly starving Ojibwe" who joined them after agreeing to trap for Henry during the upcoming season. Upon touching land at Chequamegon, he said he found a community of fifty Ojibwe lodges in which the people were "nearly naked and starving." These people pleaded with Henry to give them supplies so they could start hunting and trapping in order to feed their families. As with the party of Ojibwe he met on the water, he issued provisions with the agreement that at the end of the season they would return with their furs.

Henry is said to have found the same situation at the bay that the Frenchman St. Pierre found upon his arrival in 1718. In both cases we are told the people had been without the benefits of a European trader—in Henry's case it was only three years and in the case of St. Pierre, we recall it was twenty years—and since they no longer had the knowledge and skills to meet their food and clothing needs, they were facing serious problems of survival. In a word, the Ojibwes' dilemma was due to their dependency upon European trade goods.

This popular history storyline for Henry's experience at Chequamegon in 1765 can be traced through the writing of Neill, Kellogg, Ross, Harris, and Danziger, in serial order.[41] In all cases, sometimes more extreme than others, the native people were depicted as suffering from a lack of food and clothing. Without burdening the reader with the descriptions of Henry's arrival given by all the above writers, perhaps the imagery used can be appreciated by reviewing the words of only one. That is the Ashland, Wisconsin, writer, Walt Harris. According to Harris:

> When British traders first arrived on Madeline Island to replace the French, they learned that the Chippewas had been in a desperate flight. Naked, thin of flesh and frightened by war losses and French collapse, these savages had abandoned the zeal they once had in the original way of life. Confusion and frustration had harmed them immensely.[42]

This synoptic telling of Henry's arrival at Chequamegon must be compared with Alexander Henry's own words of that arrival. The following is his account as he wrote in his memoir:

> On my arrival at Chaqouemig I found fifty lodges of Indians there. These people were almost naked, their trade having been interrupted, first by the English invasion of Canada and next by Pontiac's War. Adding the Indians of Chagouemig to those which I had brought with me, I had now a hundred families, to all of whom I was required to advance goods on credit. At a council which I was invited to attend, the men declared that unless their demands were compiled with their wives and children would perish; for that there were neither ammunition nor clothing left among them. Under these circumstances I saw myself obliged to distribute goods to the amount of three thousand beaver skins. This done, the Indians went on their hunt, at the distance of a hundred leagues. A clerk, acting as my agent, accompanied them to Fond du Lac, taking with him two loaded canoes. Meanwhile, at the ex-

> pense of six days' labor I was provided with a very comfortable house for my winter's residence.[43]

Alexander Henry also said the following about the Ojibwe:

> The Chipeways of Chegouemig are a handsome well-made people; and much more cleanly, as well as much more regular in the government of their families, than the Chepeways of Lake Huron. The women have agreeable features, and take great pains in dressing their hair, which consists in dividing it on the forehead and top of the head, and in plaiting and turning it up behind. The men paint as well their whole body as their face; sometimes with charcoal, and sometimes with white ochre; and appear to study how to make themselves as unlike as possible to anything human. The clothing, in which I found them, both men and women, was chiefly dressed deer skin, European manufactures having been for some time out of their reach. In this respect, it was not long, after my goods were dispersed among them, before they were scarcely to be known, for the same people. The women heightened the color of their cheeks, and really animated their beauty, by a liberal use of vermillion. [44]

At first glance these two quotations might seem to be at odds with each other, and what seems to have occurred is that early historians have misread Alexander Henry's account of his arrival at Chequamegon. Writers like Neill, Thwaites and Kellogg labored under their assumptions of tribal life, i.e., its innate inferiority, and this caused them to embellish Henry's remarks with imagery of "starving and naked savages."

Henry told how, upon his arrival, the people were wearing clothing of animal skins. In 1765, an English person accustomed to wearing clothing made of tailored wool or cotton who comes upon people in deerskin garments might easily conclude they are in need of clothing, if not actually "naked." And if these same people assume the ritual stance of "the child" as they beg for his food, cloth and other trading goods, he might conclude that they are starving, or at least, as Hamilton Ross and Edmund Jefferson Danziger, Jr. more discreetly put it, "in precarious circumstances."

For a number of reasons, Henry's eyewitness account and later writers' interpretations of it are troublesome. Henry arrived in July, when fifty lodges were in a village on the shore of Chequamegon Bay. It was summer, the time when the Ojibwe traditionally returned to the bay after the early-spring season of sugar-making and late-winter spear fishing. And it was a time for another round of initiation ceremonies for the *midewiwin*, something which alone could explain the high number of lodges. Summer was also a time of little serious hunting. Instead, energies were given over to gardening, gathering wild food-plants, minimal fishing, and generally socializing with those who people had not seen for many months. And despite the lake effect, summers can, at times, be quite warm in Chequamegon Bay, at least in mid-day—for the Ojibwe, this was a time when little clothing need be worn. July was also the time for anticipating preparations for the community's movement to their places for harvesting wild rice.

Fifty lodges make a large village, and such a congregation of persons does not allow for a lack of food. If these people were facing a serious food shortage, they more likely would have dispersed to reduce the strain on their food sources. (This sort of population dispersal due to food shortages is graphically shown in the writings of John Tanner.[45]) Therefore, the fact that Alexander Henry came to Chequamegon Bay and found a village of fifty lodges suggests its supply of food was secure, not nonexistent as he would have us believe. Despite popular history's interpretation of Henry's memoir, we might conclude that these people had experienced another successful spring with its stores of maple sugar and dried fish. Also, it is very interesting that in this community, supposedly one witnessing an extremely serious shortage of food, that soon after his arrival Henry had his house erected and, in time, his personal winter food needs addressed. In his words Henry says:

> My house being completed, my winter's food was the next object; and for this purpose, with the assistance of my men, I soon took two thousand trout and whitefish, the former frequently weighing fifty pounds each and the latter commonly four to six. We preserved them by suspending them by the tail in the open air.[46]

This obvious abundance of fish readily taken by Henry's party in the weeks after arriving at the bay is a bit puzzling, and suggests that the "handsome, and well-made people" he claims to have found at Chequamegon Bay were not "naked and nearly starving," as later writers tell us.

Also, given that the people were wearing clothing of "dressed deer skin" we see Ojibwe leatherworking skills were still being practiced, so we must conclude that they had not forgotten all of their old technical arts, as later writers claimed. And they acquired these deer hides from somewhere, more than likely from hunting them, and since they were said to be bereft of European metal tools, they had to have worked the hides into finished leather with their old, traditional tools. Furthermore, Henry was impressed with the appearance of these people—the women took "great pains in dressing their hair" and the men were not averse to fueling their own vanity since they were painting most of their bodies with charcoal or white ochre. (This could help explain any actual nakedness Henry may have witnessed since Ojibwe men willingly showed off their painted bodies.) In fact, Henry pronounced the Ojibwe at Chequamegon Bay as "a handsome, well-made people." Soon after he distributed his goods among them, they put on the new European clothing and the women dabbed his vermillion onto their cheeks. Such behavior harks to the festiveness and carnival nature of the earlier accounts of rendezvous passed down by the French.

Henry's description of these people sounds like the antics of a well-fed community celebrating the arrival of a new trader, not the behavior of Walt Harris's "confused" and "frustrated" people who had "abandoned the zeal they once had."

Furthermore, these were Mamongazida's people, and he himself could have been in the village, having returned from his meeting with Sir William Johnson at Niagara only the summer before. Such an experienced diplomat as Mamongazida would have been aware of the proper protocol with which to meet a trader who was the first licensed Englishman to reach the west end of Lake Superior. For the Ojibwe, central to this diplomatic protocol was the stance of the dependent child who begged for sustenance.

At first the deep importance of this theatrical context of the ritual stance of father and child may not have registered with Henry to the degree it needed to because of his unfamiliarity and inexperience with the cultural details and unspoken rules of the trade, but by 1765, Henry had had a few years of experience in the fur trade from his time at both Michilimackinac and Sault Ste. Marie. When starting out on his fur-trading venture Henry was admittedly inexperienced in what was involved, but by the time of his coming to La Pointe his success tells he must have learned at least the basic manner, and ceremony, of trading.[47]

Thus, Henry, who has been described by one writer as an aggressive businessperson, surely was eager to lock the Ojibwe into a trading obligation, as St. Pierre was at La Pointe back in 1718, in order to help ensure his receiving their season's catch of furs. At the time, it was expected the amount of their furs would be large. In other words, Henry's description of the Ojibwe likely was driven by his desire to achieve a significant economic gain from them. In this regard, it is important to recall that his memoir was written some years after 1765, back east when he was "summing up" his life, and he may have been attempting to pose himself as a moralistic benefactor who came to Chequamegon in time to give relief to a troubled "savage" community rather than arriving as a wealth-seeking opportunist.

Recalling the importance of kinship and its role in the ceremony of the actual trading setting between the tribesman and the European in the seventeenth century, and if the reader approaches Alexander Henry's own account of his arrival at Chequamegon Bay with an understanding of what I have been calling *fur trade theater*, then an image contrary to what Henry tells us emerges. Henry says a council was held, one he "was invited to attend." In this staged meeting the men "declared that unless their demands were complied with their wives and children would perish." This encounter has all the features of the ceremonial father-child relationship in which both the child and the trader demanded their *besoins*. Both the trader and the Ojibwe were acting properly, i.e., they were demanding that each party provide something for the other. The new British "father" was to meet the needs of his "children," and they were to meet his. The trader would provide the trade goods and the tribesmen would provide the furs and other possible items.

Some eighteenth century Europeans who invested in the fur trade in North America actually stepped into a canoe and traveled to tribal communities to engage in face-to-face trading with the tribesmen, and some of these traders—in official documents, or in personal memoirs—suggested there was a humanitarian side to their trading. They claimed the tribesmen *depended* upon the traders' goods, and therefore, traders were doing more than seeking financial wealth. As Carolyn Gilman wrote:

> Traders made many claims of dependence when reporting on trade rhetoric, where the Indians were attempting to rouse "pity," and in polemical documents, where traders were trying to convince government officials they were performing a public service.[48]

In 1765, upon Henry's arrival, Chequamegon Bay's Ojibwe had supposedly been without any European fur trade contacts for only three years, but given the number and type (both legal and illegal) of traders who came to Lake Superior all through the time of the trade, this isolation is unlikely. The Ojibwe seem to have been doing well up through the departure of the Frenchman, St. Luc, in 1762, and we need to ask if three years is enough time to allow the Ojibwe to fall into such a difficult situation as Henry and later writers claimed. We have already seen that there is evidence suggesting that as late as the 1760s, the Ojibwe were still relying on aspects of their pre-European material culture, so we must ponder whether they could have fallen into the serious, even life threatening situation that writers have said Henry found them in.

It is interesting that Alexander Henry says that after he distributed his goods among the people, they set off for a hunt to a distance of about "a hundred leagues." Over the years the definition of a league has changed from anywhere between 2.4 to 4.6 miles, so if we agree that in 1765, a league was comparable to three miles, then according to Henry they traveled 300 miles.[49] He says the people first went to Fond du Lac, so they most likely traveled to resource territories directly south and west of Lake Superior. Three hundred miles would have taken them deep into Dakota country, either far south on the Mississippi, or possibly more westerly onto the distant prairie. It is unlikely that in 1765, the Ojibwe of Chequamegon Bay would have had to travel that far for either food or furs, and most importantly it is unlikely, given their current fractious relationship with the Dakota, that they would have gone so far into Dakota lands. Was Henry exaggerating the distance in order to portray the severity of the peoples' situation?

One last detail gleaned from the Henry quote needs to be considered. He said the men demanded ammunition, supposedly, as popular history claims, to kill animals for food. Given the discussion above about the Ojibwe retention of their early pre-European tool-kit, along with the fact that it was unusual for the Ojibwe to do much serious hunting in summertime, this hints at the possibility that the ammunition was desired for military use rather than for hunting. This was 1765, some years after the long Ojibwe-Dakota-French alliance had been broken. By this time the Ojibwe conflicts with the Mesquakie had largely ceased, but such encounters with the Dakota were becoming troublesome. Could the Ojibwe men have been demanding ammunition from Henry to better equip themselves against the Dakota rather than to hunt meat for their families? In other words, upon Alexander Henry's arrival in 1765, perhaps the Ojibwe were not really in such need of food as writers have claimed.

Even more so than with the arrival of St. Pierre at Chequamegon Bay in 1718, early writers have depicted the coming of Alexander Henry to the bay in 1765 as the arrival of someone bringing badly needed relief. The image in Western literature of the missionary explorer—or in this case, the enterprising trader—who arrives in time to save a downtrodden people in an old one. What is ignored in accounts using this image is the fur trade theater prevalent through the 1600s and most of the 1700s in North America. Richard White's middle ground was the stage on which this theater was acted out. It seems these performances were so successful that they caused early writers to suspend their disbelief, and write as if the scenes involving St. Pierre and Henry at Chequamegon were not scripted, but real. These writers saw no actors among the Ojibwe and early French and English traders. Their ethnocentrism did not allow it. They saw only needy tribesmen who begged for aid from the goods-laden newcomers. However, the Ojibwe actors in this fur trade drama knew the script, for in fact, they had helped to write it.

The French were familiar with the theater of the French court in their homeland and upon coming to North America immediately saw the existence of the script. Radisson's ready ability to maneuver in a tribal setting is an example of this, but the British were apparently not as readily adapted to it. After Amherst's failure, however, Sir William Johnson easily learned his part and was a successful player in this theater. Amherst recognized no script except that of the "naturally superior" Englishman coming amongst "the Savages," but as Richard White tells us, even Jeffery Amherst eventually learned his role.[50]

White suggests that those persons in North America—the tribesmen and the Europeans—who personally met each other on a regular basis to negotiate alliances and to facilitate the trade could suspend their disbelief and act out their roles in this theater. It was the British back in England who did not easily recognize these North American relationships as being scripted. They were distant from this frontier, and like early historians who had minimal direct contact with Indian cultures, did not experience the regular personal face-to-face contact with native peoples, and consequently, saw no script. What they did "see" was "The Savage" as a starving, naked person, in need of help.

7.

Despite its surrender to England in 1760, France still played a role in the Lake Superior fur trade. After the 1763 peace settlement, France officially withdrew from the Canadian territory, but unofficially its traders were still active. As we saw, one of the peace agreements was that French persons could participate in the trade, and some did this, especially in the western Great Lakes regions. Recognizing this, England attempted to gain control over the western trade. Fearing that French armed resistance might still be possible in outlying regions it sent a detachment of troops to Madeline Island at Chequamegon in 1765, to destroy the old French fort at that site.[51]

Another move to bolster its control of the trade was to abolish the trading monopolies of the French and to assign traders to British posts. These posts, garrisoned with troops, were to serve as a check on fur traders since under this new program the traders were to stay at the posts rather than travel inland to the tribal villages. This meant that unless Chequamegon Bay's Ojibwe trappers willingly dealt with unlicensed traders who irregularly appeared in their spring villages, they themselves had to transport their furs to Michilimackinac.

This was an important change for at least two reasons. One was that it meant at least some of Chequamegon's Ojibwe were probably seasonally making the long paddle across the breadth of Lake Superior to The Sault, then traveling down to Fort Michilimackinac.

We saw that when the French Jesuits and others moved their post from Sault Ste. Marie to Michilimackinac back in 1689, the latter post took on a new importance to the Chequamegon Bay Ojibwe. As was the case with Sault Ste. Marie before 1689, people from western Lake Superior became oriented socially, politically and at least partially economically to the post at Michilimackinac. This hints that when France was assembling native military units at the latter site to battle the British at more easterly sites, that these units might certainly have included persons from Chequamegon Bay. We should also expect that in the last of the French years of power in the region, that when Ojibwe leaders like Mamongazida made their trips to Montreal and Quebec, they passed through Michilimackinac. It is likely that Mamongazida, the busy politician, also made regular shorter trips between Chequamegon and Michilimackinac.

A second reason for the new importance of Michilimackinac to the Chequamegon Bay Ojibwe was that after the French left, for several years it was a major post for the British, and important meetings between tribal leaders and the British were held there.

In these years Michilimackinac was the only northern post beyond Detroit. It was a military post with troops, officers, Indian agents, various government officials and the complete cadre of other British governmental staff persons of the day. British troops came to the site in 1764 and stayed for thirty-two years, leaving in 1796 when the post, as well as the one at Detroit, was turned over to officials of the new United States. Even after 1796, British traders remained active in the area for another sixteen years, until after the War of 1812.[52]

The Michilimackinac post, along with the one at Green Bay, was integral in maintaining a British presence in the western lakes regions. According to Kellogg, it was essentially through these posts that "Wisconsin Indians were enrolled as efficient auxiliaries of the British army." Surely, over the years a significant number of these enrollees were from Chequqmegon.[53]

In 1766, Robert Rogers, an experienced military officer from New Hampshire, became the British commandant at Michilimackinac.[54] Rogers had expansionist plans that involved the extension of the fur trade. He reinstituted trading monopolies and awarded the Michilimackinac region to the Alexander Henry-Jean Baptiste Cadotte partnership. In 1767, intending to push the trade westward, Rogers held a conference at the site to attempt to establish peaceful relations with western tribal leaders. It was at this meeting that the Dakota and Ojibwe agreed to renew their old alliance, and there can be no doubt that Chequamegon Bay Ojibwe leaders were present. Immediately, Rogers sent four canoes to La Pointe and according to Kellogg, "the western trade opened up."[55]

But Robert Rogers sought more than furs. He was one of the proponents of the old search for a northwest passage to the Orient. It was during this time that Jonathan Carver, also a passage enthusiast, paddled up the Mississippi River to the St. Croix and Brule, and on to Lake Superior's north shore to Grand Portage.[56] There is no evidence that Carver came to La Pointe on this voyage. At Grand Portage, he waited in vain for replenishment of his provisions before abandoning his trek. Interestingly, it was on a later paddle up the Chippewa River to Lac Courte Oreilles in north central Wisconsin that Carver noted the presence of woodland buffalo in this region. This sighting suggests that the Chequamegon Bay Ojibwe hunted this animal.

The visionary Rogers had plans for a major government seat at the confluence of the Wisconsin and Mississippi Rivers—a dream that if brought to fruition could have greatly affected the path of history at Chequamegon. Growing unrest in the eastern colonies forced the British Crown to focus its energies on these easterly trouble spots instead of assuming new expenses with expansion in the west, and in only a few years warfare erupted between the colonies and the Crown. This quickly curtailed British plans for any development in the western lakes region, and Chequamegon would be left to itself for some decades to come.

## 8.

ALEXANDER HENRY'S MEMOIR GIVES US a few details of Ojibwe people residing at Chequamegon Bay in the mid-1760s, but for the next several decades the written record offers little. The sons of Jean Baptiste Cadotte became active fur traders in the western Lake Superior region in the late 1700s, but except for a few business records and brief commentary by William Warren, their paper trail of these early years is minimal.

Warren's writings remain a major source for Chequamegon Bay's history during these years although his reporting was heavily biased toward military activities, leaving other community events relatively unrecorded. It is not until the early 1800s, when the United States government began showing interest in the geography and natural resources of the western lakes regions, that we see the writings of persons like Henry Schoolcraft and others who came to the area. With the arrival of Christian missionaries on Madeline Island in the 1820s, we find detailed written accounts of persons and activities in the bay. This literature grows, although with troublesome gaps, up to the present day, and in post-World War II becomes voluminous.

The unfortunate sparsity of written documents telling of persons and events on the Red Cliff shoreline in the last three decades of the eighteenth century is troublesome. All through these years the western fur trade was active, and although Grand Portage became the major post in western Lake Superior, La Pointe still played an important role. Ojibwe communities were also busy with recurrent military encounters with the Dakota and these decades were especially important since they saw the emergence of a new government in North America—the United States.

Interestingly, despite this new government, in these last years of the 1700s, the British were still an important factor in the lives of Chequamegon Bay's Ojibwe people. In fact, the people are said to have been strongly pro-British all through these years. After the peace agreements concluding the Revolutionary War, the new United States government made several important gestures toward forming an administrative policy for tribal people, and while it seems true that these did not immediately affect Chequamegon Bay, they established a foundation for future relations. In the nineteenth century their effects became very important to the bay's Ojibwe people.

*Notes*

1. Warren 1984[1885]:194-209.
2. Kellogg 1935:4.
3. Danziger 1979:39.
4. Ross 1960:55-6.
5. Quaife 1921[1809].
6. Kellogg 1935:6-7.
7. Steele 1994:246 .
8. Gilman 1992:26-7.
9. Kellogg 1935:135-6.
10. Steele 1994:239;White 1991:288.
11. Steele 1994:47.
12. Steele 1994:236; White 1991:252.
13. Steele 1994:236.
14. Ross 1960:56-8.
15. Kellogg 1935:8-10,19.
16. Kellogg 1935:29.
17. Parkman 1963[1867].
18. Dowd 1993.
19. Dowd 1993:32-3.
20. Croughan as quoted in White 1991:278. Croughan was referring to the site at the northernmost tip of what is now the lower peninsula of the state of Michigan, where the French had built a substantial fort on the straits between Lakes Michigan and Huron. Unfortunately, in the literature we are considering, this site and that on nearby Mackinac Island are sometimes confused, and often referred to interchangeably. To complicate matters further, "Michilimackinac" is sometimes shortened to consider the date of the historical incident under study. Incidents after 1779-1781 and using the term "Mackinac" may be referring to Mackinac Island, after the British moved their fort from Michilimackinac. Today, as was done during William Warren's time, the entire region—the straits, the site at the tip of Michigan's lower peninsula, and Mackinac Island itself—is often referred to as simply "Mackinac."
21. Armour and Widder 1986:4,13.
22. White 1991:274.
23. White 1991:275-277.
24. Warren 1984[1885]:148-9.
25. Dowd 1993:34.
26. Harris 1976:58-60.
27. Kellogg 1935:10.
28. Kellogg 1935:9.
29. White 1991:287.
30. Warren 1984[1885]:210-12.
31. Henry as quoted in Warren 1984[1885]:214, brackets added.
32. Warren 1984[1885]:210.
33. Warren 1984[1885]:213.

34. Ross 1960:58.
35. Beider 1995:81.
36. White 1991:269-314.
37. Kellogg 1936:4.
38. Harris 1976:50,61-2; Schoolcraft 1993[1958]:11; Warren 1984 [1885]:218-220.
39. Warren 1984[1885]:220.
40. Warren 1984[1885]:217; Ross 1960:59.
41. Neill 1855; Thwaites 1895; Ross 1960; Harris 1976: Danziger 1979.
42. Harris 1976:58-9.
43. Quaife 1921[1809].
44. Quaife 1921[1809].
45. Tanner 1994[1830].
46. Quaifc 1921[1809]:191
47. Gilman 1992:44-52.
48. Gilman 1992:141.
49. Webstcr 1959:478.
50. White 1991.
51. Ross 1960:61.
52. Kellogg 1935:36-7; Armour and Widder 1986.
53. Kellogg 1935:xi.
54. Ross 2009:364.
55. Kellogg 1935:47.
56. Carver 1956[1781].

# 10

# The British Regime and the New United States

### *British Attempts to Control the Colonies and the Western Fur Trade after the French Defeat in 1763, and their Effects at Chequamegon Bay*

1.

AFTER THE DEFEAT OF FRANCE, the British quickly experienced the growing difficulty of controlling the eastern seaboard colonies, and their rapid spread into the Ohio Valley and adjacent regions. The far southeastern reaches of the continent were also demanding attention since for some time France remained a force in the areas surrounding the mouth of the Mississippi River. Military expeditions and the maintenance of alliances with tribal nations demanded financial outlay—a cost the Crown at times felt ill equipped to undertake. It struggled with decisions about how to oversee and control this growth, and the southern threat of the French, while at the same time stabilizing the western fur trade.

By the late 1760s, Britain was not pleased with the benefits it was witnessing from the fur trade and felt something had to be done. The amount of furs reaching London was dropping while the financial costs of maintaining the posts in the west kept increasing. It was clear that the restrictions put into effect in 1764 (under the Proclamation of 1763) to control the trade were not working. These restrictions had been intended to resolve this problem, or at least forestall it while the Crown could come to a more permanent solution.[1]

There were two solutions proposed for the problems of the Ohio and northern Mississippi River valleys. Sir William Johnson supported the notion of what was called an Indian preserve. Among other things, the Proclamation of 1763 called for the removal of all European colonizers west of the Appalachia watershed. They were to remain east of the mountains, allowing the western lands to be temporarily left to the tribesmen. This would supposedly bring a degree of peace to the frontier and would have allowed the fur trade to be sustained, at least as long as the furbearing animals remained in numbers sufficient enough to make it profitable. This plan would have retained the centralized control of British tribal relations that the northern and southern superintendents held for several years previous.

Opposed to this plan was the notion that since the furbearing animal populations in the region would eventually be depleted, it was best to immediately throw the entire region—including the Mississippi Valley—open to British colonization. In 1766, Lord Sherburne became secretary of state for the Crown's department that included the colonies, and he argued that Britain would see a greater benefit from the establishment of white colonies in the western areas than from a policy that allowed the continuation of the fur trade.[2] This trade demanded ongoing alliances with tribal nations and this meant considerable cost for presents for tribal leaders, an expense the British homeland officials felt would be difficult to sustain. This second option would have decentralized the control of relations with the tribal nations, placing this authority into the hands of the various colonies.

Lord Sherburne's plan was not received well in England and soon he was removed from office. With Sherburne's dismissal, Lord Hillsborough of the Crown's board of trade and plantations set forth a new plan that allowed the trade to continue. To lower Crown expenses, Hillsborough reduced the budgets for the Indian superintendents and ordered the dismantling of some of the western fur trading posts. Those at Niagara, Detroit and Michilimackinac were retained, and to prevent any incursions of the French from Canada, a naval force was established on the Great Lakes. No new colonies were to be started in the west out of fear that through French influence they could become uncontrollable.[3]

Thus, in these years—the mid-to late 1760s and early 1770s—a serious British attempt to increase its profits from the western fur trade was made, and the Chequamegon Bay region, although not central to these activities, nevertheless played an important part. The province of Canada accepted the new Crown regulations regarding the trade—including the restriction of trading to the posts—but because of the opportunity to garner large amounts of wealth, individual traders clamored for a lifting of some restrictions. They asked the governor of Canada to extend trade beyond the British posts and "offered to establish and maintain at their own expense additional posts; this they did at Sault Ste. Marie and somewhat later at La Pointe and Grand Portage." It was at this time the first British post was established at Chequamegon Bay. Britain brought large amounts of trading supplies up to Michilimackinac, then moved them to other posts at Green Bay, Prairie du Chien, Sault Ste. Marie, Grand Portage and La Pointe. On Lake Superior the goods were transported in large canoes, most going to Grand Portage, but some to La Pointe. Through such activities, these years soon saw a wealth of furs flowing to London, but the fur trade was not the only extractive industry the Europeans attempted.[4]

2.

DURING THE LATE 1760S, THE BRITISH became interested in mining for minerals in the Sault Ste. Marie area. There is a Chequamegon connection in this venture, since the Alexander Henry-Jean Baptiste Cadotte partnership is involved.[5] Initially, it was Cadotte who took a sample of a huge copper boulder at Ontonagon for an assay. The local Ojibwe were troubled by the Europeans' interest in copper and especially in this large boulder, and Cadotte's willingness to take the sample suggests he thought little of these concerns. Writing of this incident in the 1930s, using the assumptions and imagery of her world of that time, Louise Phelps Kellogg remarked that Cadotte "knew all the traditions and superstitions" of the Ojibwe and he "appeased the Indians' suspicions by the gift of a few presents."[6] We recall that the early missionaries had noticed pieces of raw copper in the eastern end of Lake Superior back in the late 1600s, and how this metal had spiritual significance to the Ojibwe. The La Ronde family, while serving as the French authorities at the La Pointe post, had taken a turn at mining at The Sault, and other names of speculators—some quite prominent—are mentioned in the literature. Sir William Johnson and Britain's General Gage were two from North America who, although they initially showed interest, apparently did not follow through to invest in the venture.

As part of its intent to establish a naval and commercial shipping fleet on the Great Lakes, in 1770, the British set up a shipyard at Sault Ste. Marie and a few ships were built. According to Louise Phelps Kellogg, "An assaying furnace was also begun and men sent out to collect ores." Fur traders were troubled by this mining activity, apparently fearing that wealthy British investors would assume control of the Sault area and that the traders "were to be shut out of Lake Superior." Some mining was done but by 1773, it ceased to be an important activity.[7]

Perhaps this early British mining incident is a minor note of passing interest in the history of the Ojibwe. Yet it speaks to the difference in worldviews between the Ojibwe and Europeans of the time. In this way we see again that these two cultures harbored deep and opposing assumptions about the world. For purposes of understanding events at La Pointe, it shows how an individual like Jean Baptist Cadotte was able to use both these cultures to his personal advantage. He was by blood one-half Ojibwe and one-half French. The written record does not tell us much about him or his parents, except to say he was the son of a Frenchman named Cadeau and his Ojibwe wife. Of this couple we know little except that their son became a person of some influence in Lake Superior country. Alexander Henry saw this and he, apparently eagerly, took Cadotte on as a business partner, and Jean Baptiste Cadotte's wife was able to function in a fashion similar to her husband. As we have seen, she was a prominent person in the Ojibwe community and was able to use both the Ojibwe and French world to her, and her husband's, advantage. Such cultural brokers were not uncommon in the fur trade. Successful leaders needed to have some acceptable understanding of the culturally based assumptions of leaders from other societies. These are the sorts of persons Richard White feels were especially adept at maneuvering in the sometimes precarious middle ground, and in western Lake Superior country, over the ensuing years after the late 1700s, numerous of these successful leaders emerged.

As was the case with the fur trade, the European interest in mining at Sault Ste. Marie in the 1700s foreshadows similar activities that were to occur in the region in the succeeding two or more centuries. Prehistoric people did some mining for copper in the same region a few thousand years before the coming of the Europeans, and as the Jesuits noted, the Ojibwe of the area were interested in raw copper in the late seventeenth century. Some of this early copper was used for trading—it is found in archeological sites far distant from Lake Superior—but perhaps most was used locally for ceremonial or spiritual purposes. This latter use is in stark contrast to the Europeans' interest in the mineral in the 1700s. They immediately saw its possibility for use as a commodity for amassing personal wealth. Like the fur trade, Lake Superior mining was hoped to be another extractive industry. In similar fashion, about one hundred years later the Americans would come to remove the timber of the region, and of course, they also mined the region's minerals.

3.

IT WAS DURING THESE SAME YEARS, immediately after 1763, that Robert Rogers, the commandant at Michilimackinac, authorized additional expenditures for presents to tribal leaders in order to win their favor so he might better maneuver for further British expansion into the regions at the Mississippi River headwaters. These financial outlays were felt to be exorbitant by crown officials, and for this initiative Rogers was removed from office, suffered humiliating court defeats, and eventually spent time in debtor's prison back in England.[8]

The Rogers incident is part of the political debate in these years concerning Britain's problems regarding control over the colonies and the trade. As we noted above, the Proclamation of 1763 failed largely because European colonists who had moved west of the Appalachians refused to move back east. The Ohio Valley, for instance, was seeing the establishment of a number of growing European settlements that began to resist Crown attempts at control. A preponderance of the western European communities had more French residents than British, so French influences were still strong, especially in the far western and northern regions. Some crown officials felt a decentralization of the administration of tribal affairs could have meant an overall loss of British control. However, Britain soon learned that it was not the French that were their main problem. In 1775, colonial forces attacked Quebec, opening the military hostilities that preceded the colonies' declaration of independence on 4 July 1776. For the region below Canada, the English problems of tribal administration and the fur trade would soon end. These events were major occasions to the British colonists, but historians have told us that for the Ojibwe at Chequamegon Bay, all of this meant little.

Images of late eighteenth century British settlements in the northern Mississippi Valley are interesting to ponder since they would have had a considerable effect on Ojibwe history. If a British colony had been established at the western end of Lake Superior, what would have been the fate of the Ojibwe in that region? Lord Hillsborough had called for the establishment of white colonies in the Mississippi Valley, and if this had come to pass, what would the resident tribal people have experienced? Would the British have removed them like they did the French in Arcadia? The policy of population removal was not unknown in the times of British colonization in North America, and it quickly became a policy for the young United States government in the 1800s. In a later chapter we will see how just such a policy was attempted with the Ojibwe of Chequamegon Bay in the 1850s, an attempt that led to tragedy.

The reality of the matter is that the British never established these western colonies. It took until several years after the American Revolution, but eventually the British were removed. Although many western Ojibwe bands carried a positive British sentiment well into the nineteenth century, the British and these American Ojibwe communities had ceased being political allies.

4.

HISTORIANS TELL US THAT NO OJIBWE from the western end of Lake Superior fought as allies of the British in the revolutionary war, yet we know that on several occasions military forces were formed at Michilimackinac and led eastward to do battle with the Americans, though the names of the rank and file of these groups are unknown. We are told these Michilimackinac units were composed of the *eastern* Ojibwe and other tribesmen like the Odawa, who resided in communities in Michigan and nearby Canada. However, given the social, economic and political importance of Fort Michilimackinac to western Lake Superior, it is not improbable that persons from Chequamegon were in some of these military units.

In 1776, when the American force was still besieging Quebec, Canadian governor Carlton ordered the commandant at Michilimackinac to send an Indian military force to that city for assistance. Charles de Langlade, who was now a British officer, assembled 200 fighters and set out only to arrive after the Americans had been driven off. In 1777, de Langlade led another force from Michilimackinac—this time we are told it was composed of Odawa and Menominee persons—and went east to take part in the battle at Lake Champlain against the Americans. In 1778, Col. Arent Schuyler DePeyster, the British commandant at Michilimackinac who had replaced Robert Rogers, assembled a force of 500 fighters and sent them off to aid the British at Montreal. The large number of individuals this latter force held suggests it was composed of many more persons than just those residing in the immediate Mackinac Straits area, since by that date most Ojibwe were living in the western Lake Superior regions.[9]

In 1779, the British held a council at Mackinac meant to recruit help in their battle with the Americans, and Walt Harris claims "Lake Superior savages" were in attendance. These persons could have been only from the Sault Ste. Marie community, but they also could have been from other Ojibwe communities along the south shore. Again, we cannot know, but it is likely that given the strong pro-British sentiments people in these communities are said to have held in these years, that some of these warriors were from places like Grand Island, Keweenaw, Ontonagon, La Pointe and possibly even Fond du Lac. The next season, in 1780, a large expedition was started at Mackinac that was meant to go against the Americans and Spanish along the Mississippi south of Prairie du Chien. In this incident Jean Baptiste Cadotte, Sr., who was at the time a British lieutenant, set off from Sault Ste. Marie, moving westward along the southern shore of Lake Superior soliciting persons for a military force to move down the Mississippi.[10] Cadotte's mission was to take this unit south and meet with Wabasha, the Dakota leader who was a British ally at the time, at his village on the river. Together they were to take their forces down the Mississippi and join the British operating in the area.

There is no evidence that this force actually engaged the Spanish or Americans, and the final role of Jean Baptiste Cadotte and his unit from the Ojibwe communities on Lake Superior's south shore is unknown. The record tells that Wabasha and the Ojibwe leader from the Mackinac area—Matchekewis—were with British forces at Cahokia (the early large community on the east side of the Mississippi River near the site of today's St. Louis) in 1780. According to Louise Phelps Kellogg, this entire venture did not achieve the goal the British intended. At these times, even given the reportedly strong pro-British stance of Lake Superior's western Ojibwe communities, Kellogg suggests these people still harbored the hope that France would return and rout both the British and Americans or at least, together with Spain, halt their westward expansion so the days of the French alliance would be brought back.[11]

Edmund Jefferson Danziger, Jr. claims the Ojibwe, at places like Chequamegon Bay, were not interested in joining the British in its struggle with the rebelling colonists, and that the military activities of George Rogers Clark, the American, who with his troops was moving through the Ohio Valley in those years, meant little if anything to them. Danziger feels the Ojibwe were too busy trapping furs—the British reaped much wealth from the western fur trade in the 1770s—to become involved in these distant battles. In these times, there was also the matter of skirmishes with the Dakota that demanded their time and energy.[12] Danziger's conclusions may be valid but the reality of several pro-British military units being formed at Mackinac and of Jean Baptiste Cadotte's influence in Chequamegon Bay means we cannot be certain that the bay's Ojibwe did not take part. In fact, it would appear highly unusual if they did not.

## *1775-1800: The Chequamegon Bay Ojibwe During the Years of the American Revolution*

1.

ALMOST IMMEDIATELY AFTER THE AMERICAN REVOLUTION, the new United States government was confronted with problems in its northwestern territories. Great Britain was still a powerful participant in the fur trade and to complicate matters, American citizens surged into the area, a region they perceived as rich in resources and often vacant of human habitation. The years from 1775 to 1800 were when significant military action occurred in the northwest, and political decisions for new policy were made by the fledgling United States. In some cases the Chequamegon Bay Ojibwe were involved in this military activity, and just as important is how policies the United States enacted at these times would come to have long term effects on the Ojibwe people.

In the decade of the 1770s, Europeans reaped significant monetary profits from the expanded fur trade. The increase in furs that began flowing eastward across Lake Superior to Sault Ste. Marie and eventually on to London after 1765 continued into the next century. The traders attempting to reach into the lands of the headwaters of the Mississippi River and those more northwest of Lake Superior, including the Lake of the Woods, were beginning to see large monetary returns. To more easily facilitate the harvest of furs from this vast region, the site of Grand Portage became the major fur trading depot in the western lakes. Far to the east in 1775, when rebelling colonists moved north and besieged the British headquarters at Quebec, they began the American Revolution but they did not disrupt this trade.

The license issued to the Alexander Henry-Jean Baptiste Cadotte partnership expired in 1768, and almost immediately other traders flooded into Chequamegon and regions to its north and west. Until these years the Hudson Bay Company controlled most of the trade, but in 1779, a group of Montreal investors formed the new North West Company. As this organization grew it absorbed numerous smaller independent traders and became a major power. The operations of the Henry-Cadotte partnership would eventually be absorbed by this new company, but that did not occur until about 1787.[13]

What is significant for La Pointe is that in these times Jean Baptiste Cadotte's two sons—Jean Baptiste (the younger) and Michel—assumed active roles in their father's business, and in 1782, Michel became the factor at Madeline Island. He had initially stationed himself inland at Lac du Flambeau and Lac Courte Oreilles where, in large part due to his fluency in both French and Ojibwe, he moved through the region with ease. In the late 1780s, when his father's firm joined the North West Company, he became a North West factor and in 1793, was put in charge of the post at La Pointe. Both Cadotte sons were members of a fur trading expedition into the region of the headwaters of the Mississippi River a year earlier, and with the help of these brothers, this 1792 expedition opened up this western region for the British.[14]

After this expedition, the North West Company expanded throughout Ojibwe country in western Lake Superior. Four departments were established: Fond du Lac, at the head of Lake Superior and the St. Louis and Mississippi River sources; Folle Avoine, at the St. Croix River area; Lac Courte Oreilles, in the region of the Chippewa River; and Lac du Flambeau, in the upper Wisconsin River region. This organization allowed for significant amounts of furs to be taken from this vast and rich land. In these years—approximately 1792 to the early 1800s—the colorful spring rendezvous at Grand Portage and elsewhere continued and were even expanded upon. This was a very active time for the fur trade, and the British-allied Cadotte brothers were key players in it.[15]

In 1783, the Treaty of Paris was signed by England and the United States to officially end the hostilities brought by the revolution. This treaty set the western boundary of the United States at the Mississippi River and its northern boundary through the Great Lakes, the Lake of the Woods and further westward. This western territory was still solidly in the hands of tribal nations but their occupancy was of little accord to the British and American treaty negotiators. As they had done from the beginning, in 1783, the Europeans viewed tribal society as an archaic way of life that would, in time, give way. Like the peace settlement between France and England in 1763, the 1783 treaty was between two major powers only. The leaders of the tribal nations which played prominent roles in the war were not present at Paris. Edmund Jefferson Danziger, Jr. stated it in an interesting way when he said that at the Paris treaty signing, "Twenty-five unsuspecting Indian tribes, including the Lake Superior Chippewas, were . . . . turned over to the United States."[16]

The United States and England signed the Treaty of Paris in 1783, but military encounters recurred over the next several years in the western lakes region, and the British remained active in its fur trade for over twenty years. These were the decades when the trade was carried out in a particularly aggressive manner, and it is important to note how early historians presented this competition. Edmund Jefferson Danziger, Jr., for example, claims that all through the years of the revolution the North West Company continued to send its pelts to the London market and in the process "controlled the Lake Superior fur trade and was a formative force in Chippewa country." This same writer concluded that as North West aggressively sought to control the take of furs it "tightened its grip on native peoples south and west of Lake Superior," and that in the 1780s, "None could deny that enterprising fur interests dominated the land of the Chippewas."[17]

This sort of popular history writing is troublesome. Writing almost two hundred years after 1780, throughout his book Danziger shows the increasing sensitivity and understanding of cultural diversity, and especially tribal society, learned over these two centuries. However, at times his writing is still unnecessarily unilateral in its perspective. While not denying the existence of a strong Ojibwe culture extant in the 1780s, Danziger fails to directly include it in his orientation toward the times. Instead of considering the presence of both a strong tribal culture and an aggressive European trade, he orients his discussion on the monetary profits of the market system of Europe and the machinations of the trade's representatives in Ojibwe lands. One wonders if in the 1780s at La Pointe when Waubojeeg was a prominent Ojibwe political leader, if he would have said he felt the "grip" of the North West Company, and if he would have agreed that the Ojibwe were being "dominated" by European fur trade interests. And just as importantly, would the bulk of the members of the La Pointe Ojibwe community, as they went about their yearly activities—securing food, interacting with kin and others, and working to maintain a proper relationship with the numerous *manidoog*—have felt dominated by European fur trade interests?

There can be no denying that the North West Company was very active in Chequamegon country in those years, but the record also tells that the Ojibwe were just as active. Among other things, they continued to stand firm militarily, and this implies their communities were fulfilling their basic needs. i.e., they were still harvesting necessary resources and successfully raising their families. The rhythm of the seasonal movement through their harvesting regions was ongoing. Hunting territories, sugarbushes, fishing places and ricing areas were still in use and therefore, of great importance to them.

Surely, after the coming of the fur trade there were troublesome disruptions caused by increased military conflicts and new anomalies like alcohol abuse—some of this is graphically shown by John Tanner in his memoir of the late 1700s and early 1800s, and by the young French trader, Francois V. Malhiot, in his journal of 1804—but at base the people were still living as Ojibwe had for ages.[18] They continued to utilize an economy built upon hunting, fishing, gathering, and gardening. Their kin groups remained integral to their social organization and their world was still a *manido world*. These aspects of Ojibwe participation in the fur trade have essentially gone unreported. Instead, the history of the trade has too often focused on the activities of individual European persons in the trade, and on events of the market and their supposed immediate far-reaching consequences. It is as if once the trade was in place in North America, these annually recurrent cultural activities of the Ojibwe were inconsequential to it. In the extreme, it is suggested the tribal peoples ceased living as they had been doing before the fur traders' coming.

When Danziger writes that the British were "lavishing enough gaudy presents upon the Chippewas to keep them within the economic sphere of the Union Jack," he neglects to mention that the tribesmen were still in their own economic sphere as well.[19] Assuming the viewpoint of the Ojibwe, it could be stated that they "were lavishing enough furs upon the Europeans to keep them within the economic sphere of the Ojibwe Nation." In the 1780s, and for years to follow, the old Ojibwe economic system did not cease to exist. Furthermore, from the Europeans' (and early American historians') point of view some of England's trade goods may be deemed as relatively worthless, or as Danziger says, *gaudy*, but such a view is unnecessarily restricted. Danziger's imagery is unfortunate. We know the Ojibwe were astute traders, so if they might have perceived the British goods as gaudy they would not have accepted them.[20] When we understand the trade for what it was—a relationship *between* parties—we remember that it was a *reciprocal* relationship. And most importantly, during the first one hundred years or so of the trade, it was an exchange of goods between two very diverse cultures. What one party might perceive as gaudy might have been viewed as quite sophisticated and valuable by the other. This is, finally, a comment not upon the inherent worth of the trade good, but a comment upon different cultural viewpoints. A small pyrite mirror and a swatch of red cloth might have been deemed inexpensive, even gaudy trade items to the Europeans in the same way a large London hat made of beaver fur might have been viewed by the Ojibwe. Perhaps the Ojibwe saw such hats as *tawdry*, that is, perhaps they saw them as ostentatiously showy and in poor taste, even decadent. The worth of what the Ojibwe gave to the European and what the European gave back was a matter of differences in the use-patterns of the trade objects rather than the inherent value of the physical objects themselves.

This is a major point not usually made in the early Chequamegon historical literature. If it is, it is made quickly, even in passing. It is so primary that we must pause to contemplate it. Danziger, Kellogg, Thwaites and other writers were knowledgeable, informed and respected in their times, but they also were writing from the point of view of their culture, not from that of the Ojibwe. And as already stated, their views were passed on in classrooms and lecture halls and perhaps, were canonically accepted.

The Ojibwe were puzzled and even amused by the European penchant for beaver pelts. They especially sought *castor gras*, those few pelts that the tribespersons had used as clothing to the point that they became worn and greasy. These garments had been worn with the hairs inside, next to the human body, causing the pelts' outer hairs to wear away, exposing the smooth inner hairs that the hat-makers desired.[21] These used, often soiled, and worn pelts were considered to hold little value and the Ojibwe felt it was strange that the European traders eagerly accepted them, at times even asking for them.

Before the coming of the Europeans, the Ojibwe would at times take and use the fur of some animals, but such fur seems never to have been a particularly important economic item to them. Animal fur was not a food commodity, and although rabbit skins were used for blankets and robes, a few other kinds for ceremonial purposes—otter and a few other furs for medicine sacks in the *midewiwin*, for example—there seems to have been no great utilitarian demand for furs before the Europeans arrived.

## 2.

EVEN THOUGH THE TREATY OF PARIS officially ended the hostilities between the colonists and the British, in the northwest regions this new peace did not readily take hold. The Ohio Valley, for instance, saw military encounters between American and tribal forces for some time after 1783. From their Canadian strongholds, the British were encouraging these skirmishes, if not actually being involved in more direct ways. The British wanted to continue their participation in the fur trade and enjoy their influence with the region's tribal nations, and the new United States government was, for some years, unable to successfully halt such activity. England controlled the northern waterways from its Quebec headquarters and kept producing and delivering trade goods to the tribes. The United States was occupied with its organizing problems further east and was hindered in the fur trade because it was unable to provide trade goods in comparable amounts and value.

In 1782, Patrick Sinclair, the new British official at Mackinac, wrote that "all was quiet on the Mississippi," but only a year later, Captain Daniel Robertson, the next Mackinac commandant, reported that things were not well. At Mackinac, the Ojibwe were upset about the British leaving them out of the negotiations of the Treaty of Paris, and the Ojibwe leader, Matchekewis, expressed this displeasure, at times openly "insulting" Robertson.[22] To add to the unrest, smallpox was spreading through the tribal community. Too little is documented about these scourges that visited Lake Superior at these times but we should be sure that their toll was devastating, affecting the lives of survivors for a generation or more.[23] From the European view, these sweeping diseases were also a danger to the health of traders and officials in the western regions, and just as importantly, they caused a reduction of furs brought to the posts.

While this was occurring, from their bases in Canada the British pondered ways to reach into the United States and influence the trade. The annual shipments of furs to London continued to provide an important amount of revenue for the Crown, and it did not want to lose this money. Britain unsuccessfully worked to have the United States do what some British leaders argued for a few years previous—that is, to keep settlers out of the western region of tribal territories so that military conflict would be reduced, and the area could then serve as a buffer between the colonies and the far distant lands beyond the Mississippi. It was in these years that Joseph Brant, the Mohawk who sailed to England and spent several years there, returned and formed a new confederacy of tribal nations that worked against the United States. In this confederacy were the Odawa, Potawatomi, and Ojibwe from the Detroit, Mackinac and other communities east of Chequamegon Bay. Writers have said the Ojibwe in this confederacy were from the "Eastern Chippewa" communities in Michigan and eastward, but once again we meet the question of any possible western Lake Superior Ojibwe involvement.

With the heightened activity of the fur trade, tribal nations in the rich trapping lands just south of Lake Superior witnessed increased strain in their relationships. In the more southerly area the Ho-Chunk, Sauk, Mesquakie and Menominee at times were involved in hostilities with the Ojibwe and further north it was the Dakota. These outbreaks of hostility caused enough difficulty to individual traders that finally, in 1786, several of them—including Alexander Henry—sent a memorandum to Sir John Johnson, the Superintendent General of Indians in Quebec, asking for assistance. This communiqué is particularly interesting for what it says about the Ojibwe. It is claimed that:

> A few of them are around Lake Huron & at Michilimackinac, but by far the most numerous and warlike part (and to whom the present remark more particularly alludes) inhabit the south side of Lake Superior, from the Falls of St. Mary to the west end of that Great Lake with the Country adjacent, and a very numerous tribe of them occupy the sources of the Mississippi with all the Country on the East side of that famous River.[24]

This is a particularly important document for three reasons. The first is that only a decade or so earlier these Ojibwe people were supposed to be struggling with disease, starvation and the like. Their assumed dependency upon the material goods received through the fur trade had caused their previous food harvesting techniques to be "forgotten" and their old tools discarded. This popular history would have us believe that in only a decade or so these "apathetic" people made a near miraculous recovery.

The second reason for the memorandum's importance is that it states some Ojibwe people lived in the regions of Lake Huron and Mackinac, but stressed that most bands resided along the length of Lake Superior's south shore, from Sault Ste. Marie to the far western reaches. The traders wanted to make this clear when they wrote that "by far the most numerous" of the tribe were along this shoreline. This is significant since it suggests that the military units formed at Michilimackinac by the British in the last decades of the 1700s up through the War of 1812 were likely drawing upon these distant Ojibwe communities. By these years, most Ojibwe were residing between The Sault and Fond du Lac, *not* at the Mackinac Straits and Lake Huron. Therefore, as we noted above, there is evidence in the written record that shows Chequamegon Bay's Ojibwe may well have been in some of these military units and would have fought against the Americans in these years.

The third important point in this document is that these Ojibwe along Gitchigami's southern shore—including Chequamegon Bay—were, in the traders' eyes, "the most . . . warlike" of the Ojibwe communities. This was the time that Waubojeeg was the military leader at Chequamegon, and again, it indicates the community was viable, i.e., contrary to what some historians have written, there was no life threatening shortage of resources to fulfill basic needs.

Sir John Johnson responded to this 1786 memo by sending his agent, John Dease, to Mackinac. Dease called for a council with tribal leaders for the following summer, and in August 1787, about 200 tribal delegates came to Mackinac. For the few days of the council there was "much ceremony and gifting" and all tribal delegates pledged to cease hostilities—except the Ojibwe and Dakota. It is noteworthy that a year later, a military force was formed at Mackinac and traveled to the Ohio valley where it skirmished with American soldiers, killing several.[25] Such acts throughout the 1780s and 1790s indicate the strong pro-British sentiment among the Ojibwe. At La Pointe, this continued on into the new century, and as we will see below, was very evident as late as the 1840s. However, there is evidence that this strong pro-British stance was not found in some Ojibwe communities in the earlier days.

## 3.

After the exit of the French, the early British traders and officials coming to the western Great Lakes experienced the anger and frustration of the Ojibwe, who felt that unlike the French, they had not surrendered to the Redcoats. An instance of this is shown in the speech the Ojibwe leader at Michilimackinac, Minavavana, gave to Alexander Henry in 1761. Since this long speech insightfully, and candidly, shows the sentiment of the Ojibwe, it is offered in its entirety:

> Englishman, it is to you that I speak, and I demand your attention. Englishman, you know that the French king is our father. He promised to be such; and we, in return, promised to be his children. This promise we have kept. Englishman, it is you who have made war with this our father. You are his enemy; and how, then, could you have the boldness to venture among us, his children? You know that his enemies are ours. Englishman, we are informed, that our father, the king of France, is old and infirm; and that being fatigued, with making war upon your nation, he is fallen asleep. During his sleep you have taken advantage of him, and possessed yourselves of Canada. But his nap is almost at an

end. I think I hear him stirring, and inquiring for his children, the Indians; and when he does awake what must become of you? He will destroy you utterly! Englishman, although you have conquered the French, you have not yet conquered us! We are not your slaves. And, these lakes, these woods and mountains, were left to us by our ancestors. They are our inheritance; and we will part with them to none. Your nation supposes that we, like the white people, cannot live without bread and pork and beef! But, you ought to know, that He, the Great Spirit and Master of Life, has provided food for us, in these spacious lakes, and on these wooded mountains. Englishman, your king has never sent us any presents, nor entered into any treaty with us, wherefore he and we are still at war and until he does these things, we must consider that we have no other father, nor friend, among the white men, than the king of France, but, for you, we have taken into consideration, that you have ventured your life among us, and supply us with necessaries, of which we are in much want. We shall regard you, therefore, as a brother and you may sleep tranquilly, without fear of the Chippeways. As a token of our friendship, we present you with this pipe, to smoke.[26]

Minavavana's speech is another example of fur trade theater, with its assumed roles of father and child and their resultant responsibilities and compensations. It also tells of the ignorance, inability or refusal of British authorities to engage as active players in this theater. As Charles Cleland noted,

> As Minavavana's speech clearly states, the western Indians, through mostly firm allies of the French, were neither dependent upon Europeans nor did they believe themselves defeated in the recent wars. In tribal tradition, peace could have soon been concluded with payment of reparations in the form of gifts. Being ignorant of this fact, the British regarrisoned the western posts but neglected to supply these detachments with Indian presents. This greatly angered local tribesmen, who viewed the same arrangement with the French as a form of rent on the land where the forts were erected.[27]

While Minavavana said his people desired to receive trade goods that Henry and other British traders offered, he made it clear that the people were not, as Cleland stated, dependent upon them. The Ojibwe felt their lands and waters held ample food resources, and while the people were in "much want" of the labor saving devices found among European trade goods, if necessary they could still do quite well without them. They did not agree with the British ethnocentric assumption that tribal people "cannot live without bread and pork and beef."

A statement as insightful and candid about the economic and political independence of tribal societies in the mid-1700s in Lake Superior country as this Mackinac Ojibwe leader's is refreshing, although extremely rare in the written historical record. No doubt, however, such commentary was a lively part of oral tradition in the Ojibwe community not only during Minavavana's lifetime but for a generation or more to follow. Unfortunately, those of us in the literate tradition rarely have access to this rich Ojibwe storyline. And, importantly, Minavavana's speech was given in 1761, only four years before Alexander Henry moved on to La Pointe, where he supposedly found people "naked and starving" because they had been without trade goods. If the Ojibwe were standing firm at the eastern end of Lake Superior at this time, as indicated by this speech, it seems likely it was a similar case at La Pointe. As has been argued above, Minavavana's telling admonition suggests that historians' interpretations of Alexander Henry's account of his 1765 arrival at La Pointe must be reconsidered.

As Charles Cleland intimates, in 1761, the Ojibwe at Mackinac were giving the British the opportunity to step into the middle ground of the fur trade and assume the role of "father" previously held by the French. As we have seen, in time the British learned their role and began to assume it. In this way, after a period of uncertainty, Ojibwe leaders and the British agreed to an alliance, and at La Pointe this lasted for several decades.

The Crane clan had been providing civil leaders for the Ojibwe, but during this transition of alliances the Chequamegon Bay community saw this leadership shift to the Loon clan. Sometime in the mid-1700s, Gaagaawiiyaas (Raven's Meat, or Crow's Flesh) became the civil leader and, possibly as early as 1765, he, in turn, was superseded by a son (or grandson), named Gichibizhiki (Great Buffalo).[28] Buffalo was with the Ojibwe forces that took military action against both the United States and the Dakota, but written popular history has generally portrayed him as a peaceful leader who was a good friend of the Americans. During his later years as the civil leader at La Pointe, he worked with tribal war leaders like Waubojeeg.

In 1786, when Alexander Henry put his signature to the memorandum sent to Sir John Johnson in Quebec, he was familiar with Waubojeeg. The latter was a son of the famous Mamongasida, the previous war leader at La Pointe who, as we noted, made several trips to eastern sites both to meet with British officials and to lead Ojibwe forces against the French. During the last two decades of the 1700s, La Pointe's Ojibwe leaders were allied with Great Britain. In these years the Chequamegon Bay Ojibwe were doubtless aware of the growing strength and presence of the government of the new United States.

In 1788, the Continental Congress was dissolved and the next year the United States government was officially formed. What is important for us at this point is that in the constitution of this new government was a paragraph that has become known as the Commerce Clause. This paragraph holds the single reference to tribal nations in this famous and significant document, and as we will see in the following chapters, is of some importance to the Ojibwe. This clause was made part of the constitution because of the economic strength of the tribes. It gave the federal government the sole right to enter into commercial relationships with them and was clearly a maneuver to restrict British involvement in the fur trade. Obviously the formation of the new government and its constitution would have major ramifications for Lake Superior's Ojibwe.

Little is known about the direct involvement of La Pointe Ojibwe fighters in the battles with American forces in the Ohio Valley in the important years just after the American Revolution, and historians have intimated that Chequamegon Bay was too distant for its residents to be interested in these battles. From its Canadian strongholds, the British were still very active in the Ohio valley, and it is apparent the tribesmen expected British assistance in efforts they took to repel the Americans. The years from 1786 to 1794 saw several major American military expeditions into the region, with most ending in disaster for the United States forces.[29] The Miami war leader, Little Turtle, was one of the reasons for these defeats, due to his brilliance in leading forces from several tribes.[30]

For us it is enough to note that while these actions were distant from Lake Superior and as such are typically omitted from a discussion of the history of communities like Red Cliff, their long-term effects for Ojibwe peoples in western Lake Superior lands cannot be neglected.

At least two writers suggest that La Pointe Ojibwe were in some of these Ohio Valley military encounters. Mark Diedrich feels Chief Buffalo may have been one of the signers of the Treaty of Greenville in 1796, with Major General Anthony Wayne, that ended these Ohio military conflicts. He says that on this early treaty the signature, Peshawkay, or Young Ox, appears with ten other Indians, some from Lake Superior. If, as generally stated, La Pointe's Buffalo was born in 1759 or so, he would have been in his thirties in 1795, and if Peshawkay is a poor phonetic translation for Bizhiki, the Ojibwe word for Buffalo, or ox, then at the time of the Greenville meeting he likely would have been known as Young Ox.[31]

All of this is conjecture, of course, but a little-used written source states unequivocally that La Pointe's Buffalo was not only at Greenville in 1796, but was one of the principal speakers at the treaty convention. Sister M. Carolissa Levi, F.S.P.A., writes: "Chief Kish-ke-tug-wug, a Chippewa, was present at this treaty. As an old man, Kish-ke-tuh-wug, related the story of the treaty to his grand-nephew, Chief James Stoddard (died in 1933), who in turn gave the following account of it to his friend, James M. Scott:

> 'It was in the early part of May, 1775, that a group of Ottawa braves appeared at Madeline Island. They were delegated by Wyandot chiefs to invite the chiefs of Lake Superior Chippewa to a grand council to be held in the near future at Greenville, Ohio. The Chippewa accepted the invitation. The Wyandot chiefs and Buffalo, the Chippewa chief, were the principal speakers for the tribes who participated in this treaty.'[32]

It follows that if Buffalo's name is on the Treaty of Greenville, then it is quite likely that the several units of military personnel from Mackinac in some of the Ohio battles included La Pointe people.

Once again, the implication of this for present-day Red Cliff is clear. Ancestors of today's community have been active in these eastern battles, and we should note that in some cases these were serious encounters. For example, in 1794, at Fort Recovery, Ohio, "a force of about 1,600 warriors (with) at least half (being) Ottawa and Ojibwe from northern Michigan" went against Anthony Wayne's forces.[33] This was no minor battle since considerable numbers of Odawa and Ojibwe fighters were killed. Louise Kellogg puts it this way:

> The Mackinac Indians led the van and attacked with great impetuosity, but they were received by the garrison with showers of bullets, and even canon balls . . . . The tribesmen were mowed down in droves, neither courage nor skill availed against the secure fort, the hail of bullets, and the death of their comrades. During the night they withdrew and while the dark hours lasted were employed in carrying away their dead.[34]

Such was the involvement of at least some of the military units from Mackinac, and the battle at Fort Recovery serves to show that the people took their alliance with England seriously. And before this alliance, the Ojibwe had one with the French. It too, saw military units formed at Mackinac, Sault Ste. Marie, and La Pointe. The loss of these warriors certainly affected family and clan members back on Lake Superior for some time. Regarding their willingness to aid their French allies in these distant battles with the British, it has been claimed that "This was a pattern . . . repeated for several generations, as son followed father east to fight in the service of the French father."[35] First the Ojibwe (as allies of the French), fought the British, then (as allies of the British) fought the French, and later the Americans. And of course, Ojibwe fighting personnel have been in uniforms of several colors and types in many of the wars of the United States ever since.

The Treaty of Greenville is one of the very important early documents in North American history. In its aftermath it had a major effect on Chequamegon country. This treaty set up boundaries between the United States and tribal nations to the west and most importantly, in it the United States "relinquished claim to native possessions south and west of the upper lakes and east of the Mississippi." In doing so, the United States government recognized the legitimacy of tribal land ownership in this large region, and within this area future land sales by the tribes could only be made to the United States. Importantly, about these lands, the Treaty of Greenville says the Ojibwe "are quietly to enjoy, hunting, planting, and dwelling thereon so long as they please, without any molestation from the United States."[36] If the young Buffalo was present at the signing of this treaty, and *if* he was informed of this passage, he surely registered these words and likely was accepting of their sincerity.

However, even though the United States recognized tribal land ownership in the Old Northwest, to include Ojibwe lands in the western reaches of Lake Superior, it was helpless to prevent a virtual invasion of these lands by citizens eager to do business with the resident tribes, or simply to move into the regions to farm. The Ohio valley was soon overrun with traders, farmers and others, causing disruption in tribal communities. In discussing this period of time, the historian Robert Beider felt that with the intrusion of its military forces in the Ohio valley, the United States government caused much disruption to the fur trade and to the tribal communities in the area. He stresses the resultant social breakdown of tribal organization, but feels traders were also a factor in this disruption. Beider says, "The traders, also, however, must share in the blame for the social disruption in Indian communities. Supplying liquor, traders proved just as damaging to community survival as warfare did."[37]

This turmoil in the Ohio valley in the late 1700s, as tribal communities struggled with the transition of alliances from England to the United States, is well known. The political decisions made by leaders in Washington, D.C., and elsewhere were played out locally by traders and others. In 1795, Chequamegon country perhaps did not immediately witness this turmoil, but soon its time would come.

In 1790, the United States took further action to restrict England's participation in the western fur trade by establishing what is known as the Trade and Intercourse Act.[38] This involved a series of requirements for American citizens who wished to engage in trading in Indian territories and was meant to improve the new country's business interests while restricting British activity in the region. A few years later, in the very early 1800s, the United States itself entered the Indian trade by establishing what is known as the factory system. (The importance of both the Trade and Intercourse Acts and the *factory system* for the Ojibwe will be discussed in following chapters.)

Chequamegon seems to have been relatively unaffected by these attempts to manipulate the fur trade, and records indicate that the North West Company continued to operate virtually unhampered in the entire region. The two Cadottes were present, working for North West and sending their furs to the British, but independent traders still visited the region, some being antagonistic to England. In 1791, when the Scotch and Irish John Johnston came to Madeline Island to trade for furs, he was given an unfriendly reception by French-Canadian trappers.[39]

Upon coming to La Pointe, Johnston met Ozhawguscodaywayqay, a daughter of Waubojeeg. They married in 1793 and moved to Sault Ste. Marie, where they raised a family of eight children. Throughout the region Mrs. Johnston was known for her intelligence and civility.[40] While spending her married life at the eastern end of Lake Superior, she still maintained a connection with the Chequamegon Bay Ojibwe communities. The marriage of a trader like John Johnston to the daughter of a prominent tribal leader was a practice repeated throughout Indian country, and such a union created a valued relationship between the communities of both parties. Another such marriage at Chequamegon Bay was that of Michel Cadotte to Equawayway (Traveling Woman), a daughter of Waubijejauk (White Crane), who resided "on the mainland near present day Bayfield, Wisconsin."[41]

The growing struggle between Britain and the United States led to diplomatic negotiations that culminated in 1796, with Jay's Treaty. In it the British agreed to give up their posts south of the new border between Canada and the United States, but the British could still enter the United States to trade. To try to end Britain's control of the western lakes trade, the American Major Henry Burback, with two companies of soldiers, was sent to Fort Mackinac in 1796, where he remained until 1800, when he was called back east. Despite this move to enhance an American presence in the region, the western lakes trade was essentially still in the hands of the British through all these years.

Mostly, this trade was carried out by the North West Company, but in the latter years of the 1700s, a growing number of independent traders became a serious threat to North West. In 1798, some of these traders formed the X Y Company, and its traders "trailed NorWesters, built posts near them and dispensed rum and presents" and in this way "secured much of the Ojibwe peltry."[42] The new X Y Company presented such a threat that in 1804, North West merged with it, ending the hostilities.

### *Summary: The 1700s and Red Cliff*

AT CHEQUAMEGON BAY, THE CENTURY OPENED and closed in similar fashions. At its onset the people were living as they probably felt they always had. That is, they worked to harvest the resources necessary to raise their families, at times went to war against those they felt were enemies, and they interacted with the *manidoog* in a manner that allowed for these activities to be carried out successfully. The French were their European allies at the start of the century, and at its close they were allied with the British. Throughout the century several tribal nations, at differing times, were allies of the Ojibwe as well. The new United States had formed, but at the close of this century it had not yet reached into Chequamegon country with any degree of authority. This would soon change when the War of 1812, between Britain and the United States, saw the removal of British posts south of the new boundary between Canada and the United States, leaving the western Great Lakes areas open for American intrusion.

Several major themes can be identified in Ojibwe history in the 1700s in Chequamegon country. Most will carry over into succeeding centuries and will be discussed throughout the remainder of this book. Here we will present these themes, and for now, offer summary comments.

IT IS READILY APPARENT THAT THE NATURAL habitat of the Ojibwe was not seriously altered throughout the 1700s, except for one major resource. Populations of fur-bearing animals, especially the beaver, were heavily exploited, and by the close of the century their mere survival was sometimes threatened. However, these species generally were not among those included in the diet of the people so their diminishment was not a direct threat to human survival.

Throughout the century the land itself was not seriously altered. There were no large human construction projects, like river dams, and there was no logging. Commercial fishing on Lake Superior had not yet begun, and other issues we struggle with today, such as environmental degradation, the depletion of fossil fuel resources and the like, were very minor, if not nonexistent.

Writers have offered little comment about the overall biology of the Ojibwe population throughout the 1700s, even though the Ojibwe gene pool experienced an influx of new genes through the entire century. Certainly this brought about significant change. Gene flow must have been a reality in Ojibwe life all through the century preceding the 1700s, when several tribal nations visited and even resided for extended lengths of time at Chequamegon Bay. The ceremonial marriages already mentioned in the 1600s, as well as the marriages of Ojibwe women to European traders since then, are cases in point, but there must have been many other exchanges of genetic material between the diverse linguistic and cultural communities of those times.

It is clear that the gene pool at Chequamegon, like most human gene pools, experienced a regular and continuing influx and outflow of genes. As we will see in following chapters, this continues at Red Cliff into the present time.

The ability to defend themselves militarily continued for the Ojibwe all through the 1700s. As we saw, in the century's later decades some Europeans characterized them as "warlike." Earlier writers generally stressed this all through the century. Louise Kellogg, for instance, referred to them as "the Great Chippewa," intimating that they were a major military force, and Danziger stressed the continuance of their "bloody skirmishes" with the Dakota. As already stated, this characterization of the Ojibwe has been overdone. This bias in the literature continued all through accountings of the history of the 1700s.

Ojibwe interest and involvement in matters of international economics, politics and diplomacy remained all through the century. As we saw, the 1700s opened with regular canoe trips to eastern centers like Quebec and Montreal, and such treks to distant sites were still occurring at the century's close. Chequamegon Bay's Ojibwe leaders were having nation-to-nation relationships with many tribal peoples all through the century and were, of course, regular actors in such relations with Europeans as well as with the new United States. Clearly, throughout the 1700s, the Ojibwe were thinking continentally and even inter-continentally.

Related to this interest in international matters, we saw that in the 1700s, perhaps for the first time the Ojibwe, like many other tribal nations in the Americas, began to be concerned with a new feeling of unity with other tribal people. Perhaps this first emerged when Ojibwe leaders joined other tribal representatives who traveled to Montreal to argue that the French should stop their genocidal warfare against the Mesquakie, and it clearly appeared with Ojibwe involvement with Pontiac's attempts to repel the British. If this trans-national tribal sense of unity was new, and perhaps therefore halting or uncertain for some, in the 1700s and in the times to follow it quickly became much stronger. The belief of some early writers that the Chequamegon Bay Ojibwe were not concerned with matters distant from their immediate world is a fallacy.

All through the century, Ojibwe culture at Chequamegon Bay continued to function. This point has been stressed by some writers but not by others. Europeans needed to keep tribal cultures relatively intact in order to receive a constant flow of furs, and conversely, once an alliance was in place with a European nation, the Ojibwe desired that it be maintained. Generally, the deep-rooted contradiction in the image of a successfully functioning tribal cultural system, as the Chequamegon Ojibwe had in the 1700s, that was at the same time seriously dependent upon Europeans, has been lost on some historians. Only recently are some writers recognizing the ethnocentrism of this earlier view, and the deep reciprocal complexities of this dependency argument. At the close of the 1700s, at Chequamegon, the Ojibwe worked to maintain their economic and political alliance with the British, but they were still living within the sphere of their own traditional cultural system.

No Christian missionaries worked at Chequamegon through the 1700s. Catholic missionaries were active at the eastern end of Lake Superior intermittently throughout the century, and doubtless given the regularity of contacts with persons from the lake's western reaches and beyond, they had an influence with some community members. Yet, as we will see in the next chapter, the next Christian missionaries to arrive at Chequamegon came in the 1820s, and they found a deep resistance to their preaching. The *midewiwin* and other aspects of Ojibwe religion were an integral part of the peoples' lives in the bay all through the 1700s.

This continuance of the traditional religion was a very important factor in the tribe's overall cultural persistence. Another was the presence of the community's civil and war leaders. Waubojiig was there, and by 1800, Buffalo was emerging as a respected younger leader.

All in all, the century had been a successful one for the Ojibwe. However, at its close they must have had foreboding thoughts about the growing presence of the *Gichi-mookomaanag* (The Long Knives, or Americans) looming on their eastern and southern horizons.

*Notes*

1.Kellogg 1935:98.
2. Kellogg 1935:98.
3. Kellogg 1935:100.
4. Kellogg 1935:102-3.
5. Armour and Widder 1986:17.
6. Kellogg 1935:107.
7. Kellogg 1935:110-11.
8. Rogers 2009:411; Armour and Widder 1986:16-7.
9. Armour and Widder 1986:54-56,62-3, 81-2.
10. Harris 1976:61-64.
11. Kellogg 1935:176.
12. Danziger 1976:59.
13. Ross 1960:63.
14. Ross 1960:62-7.
15. Warren 1984[1885]:279-282.
16. Danziger 1979:60.
17. Danziger 1979:59-60.
18. Malhiot 1910; Tanner 2000[1830].
19. Danziger 1979:60.
20. Steele 1994:69.
21. Beck 2002:32-3.
22. Kellogg 1935.
23. Clelland 1992:161.

24. Danziger 1979:61.
25. Kellogg 1935.
26. Henry as quoted in Cleland 1992:129-30.
27. Cleland 1992:130-31.
28. Warren 1984[1885]:316; Diedrich 1999:69.
29. Cleland 1992:154.
30. Carter 1987:88-124.
31. Diedrich 1999:69.
32. Levi 1956:52-3, 320.
33. Cleland 1992:155.
34. Kellogg 1935:222.
35. Cleland 1992:128.
36. Satz 1991:5.
37. Beider 1995:85.
38. Cleland 1992:176.
39. Ross 1960:64.
40. Soetebier 2000.
41. Ross 1960:65.
42. Danziger 1979:62.

# 11

# The Start of the Nineteenth Century

WITH THE DAWNING OF 1800, the Chequamegon Bay Ojibwe began a century that would see the coming of several major threats to their way of life. The previous century saw them make adaptations that changed their lives in important ways but still allowed them to continue living as they had for hundreds of years. However, the new century would see even more challenges to this long-term stability. These challenges came from many quarters, all emanating from the arrival of the Europeans.

Initially, the removal of the British below the Canadian border and the emerging power of the new United States forced the Ojibwe to shift alliances once again. By mid-century, it became apparent the fur trade was a dying industry. At the same time, several decades of treaty negotiations with the United States began, and such political events always forced difficult decisions to be made. With these years came Christian missionaries and a serious influx of the next wave of non-Ojibwe residents. In the early 1850s, the La Pointe Ojibwe had to deal with a tragic attempt to force their removal to distant western lands. Then followed an abortive attempt to have the people become full time agriculturalists, and the new exploitative industries of commercial fishing and logging soon followed.

The foraging culture of the Ojibwe continued through these 100 years of challenges but it was seriously altered and at times greatly diminished, and by 1900, the effects of a cash economy were deeply felt in Ojibwe homes. The people were submitted to endless pressure to cease using *Ojibwemowin*, their language, and to stop respecting and interacting with the *manidoog*. Through all of this, most importantly, deep inside they were challenged to take on new personal identities.

In the beginning of the 1800s, the community's leaders were in regular contact with British officials, who desired to continue the lucrative fur trade and halt further incursions by Americans into prime fur-taking lands. The Ojibwe considered British requests for aid with these endeavors, and from time to time sent military units eastward to help in these conflicts. Major decisions, like that of going to war, were handled democratically, and community-wide ceremonies and discussions occurred in which elders and the proper *manidoog* were consulted. The shaking tent ceremony, for instance, must have been used often in these times, and through its invocations the spirits would have been asked to interpret signs and dreams, as well as to divine the future.

In these years, distant voices telling of new problems began to be heard. In the late 1700s, prophets and their messengers from tribal communities far to the east began appearing in Ojibwe country and continued to come in the early years of the 1800s. These voices told of the growing threat of the *Gichi-mookomanag* (Americans).

Soon the Americans would cause the final exodus of the British below the Canadian border and force a new alliance with the Ojibwe. The United States would replace England, and with this new alliance would come mounting frustration and change. Yet, as we will see, when the Chequamegon Bay ancestors of present day Red Cliff closed out this century, they may have been using new clothes, foods, and tools, and even though they may have layered their beliefs, ceremonies and knowledge with that of the Euro-Americans, they still identified as Ojibwe people and in important ways still lived in a *manido* world.

### *The Buildup to the War of 1812*

1.

THE FIRST DECADE OF THE NEW CENTURY was a time of political and economic posturing by the nations carrying out the fur trade in the western Great Lakes and upper Mississippi regions. The Ojibwe were pivotal in this maneuvering since they held the lands along Lake Superior's south and north shores as well as the rich regions immediately west of the lake. As the populations of fur-bearing animals in the eastern portions of the continent began to be depleted, the geographic center of the trade shifted further and further westward. The upper Mississippi country became increasintly important to these traders as the Ojibwe, British and Americans set their sights on this region.

For some time the British had been sending their traders into the riverine territories far to the south and west of Lake Superior. In the later 1700s, they already were taking furs on the southern reaches of the Wisconsin River and even operating as far south as the Des Moines and the Iowa. Soon they were in the trans-Mississippi region along the eastern tributaries of the Missouri, where they competed with Spanish traders coming up from St. Louis.[1]

Perhaps all this activity had little direct effect on the Chequamegon Bay peoples, but what it did accomplish was to assure the Ojibwe that Britain was a powerful and very valuable ally. The French had withdrawn, and the United States, at least in the immediate post-revolution years, had no significant presence in Chequamegon country. Historians have shown that for decades after the American Revolution, the British moved with ease through these western regions, and when William Warren wrote that in these years the La Pointe Ojibwe were strongly pro-British, we can easily agree. The economics of the fur trade shows that it made sense to ally with this new foreign power.

Chequamegon Bay's Ojibwe peoples were aware of the interest the British had in regions far to their south. English supporters attempted to enlist them in efforts to halt the intrusion of the United States and the Spaniards along the Mississippi, but it was the fur trading activity in the upper Mississippi region that was more directly relevant to the Ojibwe community. Chequamegon Bay was a funnel through which many people who migrated into these northern upper-Mississippi regions flowed. William Warren has chronicled this movement and we need not review it here except to note the early role of Chequamegon Bay's Ojibwe people in this migration.[2]

Native trappers were integral in the fur trade. Both England and the United States were dependent upon them, but this did not keep earlier writers from overlooking their importance, or from portraying them as reactive participants. Louise Kellogg, for instance, who wrote in great detail about these times, posed the native peoples as auxiliaries, who would bring their furs and other goods to the British as long as their traders continued to exchange worthwhile commodities for them. The British themselves, like the French before them, and the early Americans later, understood the tribesmen were essential to success in the fur trade, but they still saw the native people as *savages* who, while useful, would eventually give way to *civilization*. In one instance, when describing military units of Wisconsin's western lakes' warriors mustered to aid the British in battle with the Americans, Kellogg suggests the British saw them as "savage hordes from the Northwest." While essential to the British, the tribal peoples were still troublesome. Their "insatiable appetite" (Kellogg's words) for more and more presents was not only annoying, but a burdensome drain on the Crown's finances.[3]

2.

IN 1800, THE VAST LANDS WEST of the Mississippi River were quietly transferred from Spain to France, and only three years later this large western expanse was transferred again to the United States. These were paper transfers since the lands were still held by many tribal nations, and when the Louisiana Purchase removed Spanish and French authority from the upper Mississippi and western Great Lakes, it left the fur trade in the hands of the tribal nations, the British, and the Americans.[4]

Soon after 1803, the United States began an aggressive campaign to wrest its new western purchase from tribal ownership. Washington leaders had an immediate interest in keeping the fur trade operating in a way that benefited America, but they were ultimately after land. Under the orders of President Jefferson, Lewis and Clark departed St. Louis on their famous trek in 1804, and in 1805, Lt. Zebulon Pike was sent up the Mississippi River to force another peace between the Dakota and Ojibwe so the furs of this rich region would come into American trading posts rather than those of the British. A year later, Pike set off on a much more expansive trip to the far west, sent by national leaders who were certain it was America's destiny to claim this land.

Such expansionistic acts were topics of discussion in political centers of the United States in these years as the country's population grew and its business leaders foraged new pathways to wealth. In this regard, the natural resources west of the Mississippi were, in Americans' minds, beckoning to them. The fact that communities of human beings inhabited this land was deemed important and was a matter that would have to be dealt with, but at the start of the nineteenth century the leaders of the country, like its masses, plunged ahead. There was a great opportunity for individuals to achieve private wealth, notoriety and acclaim, and the opportunities offered in the fur trade were part of this. By 1800, competition in this trade became intense.

3.

THE RIGOR OF THIS COMPETITION is graphically shown in the personal journals of four fur traders in the region immediately south of Lake Superior. While Thomas Jefferson was sending Lewis and Clark off to the Pacific and Zebulon Pike to the upper Mississippi, these four men were laboring to earn their share of this new wealth. George Nelson, Francois V. Malhoit, Michel Curot, and John Sayer kept personal journals that give us a glimpse into their lives during these difficult years of 1802 to 1806, and these writings offer insights into the fur trade as it was played out at posts in Chequamegon country.[5]

By 1800, the financial success of the fur trade saw sharp competition between the older North West Fur Company and newer, competing firms. This led one of the early North West Fur stalwarts, Sir Alexander MacKenzie, to leave the firm to start his own, but he soon joined what by then was known as the X Y Company. Traders for this new firm were dispatched into the rich fur-bearing lands south of Lake Superior, where they set up stations in the immediate vicinity of North West's posts in order to draw trade away from the older firm.[6]

This fierce competition involved the free dispensing of liquor to regional Ojibwe fur trappers and soon led to conflict. Much has been written about these difficult times, and often the image of Ojibwe people shown in these writings is one of social breakdown and debauchery.[7] Alcohol became a fur trader's tool, readily used to outdo one's rival in the quest for more and more furs. As Peers and Schenck tell us:

> Competition in the fur trade increased alcohol use by Native peoples in the western Great Lakes to an unhealthy point; alcohol came to be used as a weapon by rival companies so that during very competitive periods . . . . traders offered far more of it, and more readily, and more often, to entice hunters to leave former business partners.[8]

However, while this extreme alcohol use raised havoc with the Ojibwe—and the trading post personnel—the underpinnings of tribal culture generally remained secure. The heavy consumption of alcohol dispensed by the traders was usually done in spring or fall, when the trappers either brought their winter's catch to the post and were compensated for it, or when the new season was about to begin as they took goods on credit before leaving for their winter grounds. These drinking times were followed by long periods of sobriety, and this "binge drinking," with its imposed patterns of periodicity, could be called ceremonial. In this sense, it has been suggested these drinking times were similar in function to other customs of wealth and commodity-sharing held by the Ojibwe. Thus, these fur trading era bouts with alcohol might, in part, be said to mirror patterns of economic exchange between band leaders, kin groups and other social and political units. In fact, in this sense we could agree that the fur traders—and the entire institution of the trade itself—were accepted by the Ojibwe because these new ideas were adapted to the pre-existing structure of the tribal social and cultural organization. As the Ojibwe did in the case of other trading goods—various utensils, items of personal adornment, cloth, and such—alcohol and the accompanying norms for its use were made to fit into the existing structure of the Ojibwe world. In this way it has been said: "Whatever they took from the traders, the Ojibwe made theirs."[9]

Along with informing us about struggles with liquor, the journals of the four fur traders show that in the first decade of the nineteenth century, the people living in the Lac du Flambeau, Chippewa River, and adjacent regions of interior Wisconsin Territory, as well as those in the Yellow and Snake River areas of the St. Croix bands, were practicing other traditional Ojibwe customs. Accounts of pipe offerings as part of preparations for going to war with the Dakota, of the activities requisite for the manufacturing of maple sugar, of using nets for fall fishing, and the *midewiwin* ceremonies, can be found in virtually all the journals. While increased alcohol consumption was taking its toll, these other, more important activities went on.

4.

IN 1806, SEVERAL MONTREAL MERCHANTS who were struggling under the far-reaching power of the North West Company formed their own firm. The Michilimackinac Company came into being, and to avoid rivalry, North West agreed to a partitioning of fur trapping lands.

Of interest to us is that the North West Company gave up its Lake Superior posts along the south shore, from Sault Ste. Marie to Chequamegon Bay and inland from Lac du Flambeau westward to Lac Courte Oreilles. The St. Croix River posts, however, were retained. Thus by 1806, most fur trading posts in what is now northwestern Wisconsin were run by the Michilimackinac Company. At the onset this was a lucrative business, but soon the trading competition became more intense due to the start of open hostilities between the United States and England. These events came to have important effects in Chequamegon Bay.

At this point we need to note that two of the organizers of the new Michilimackinac Company were Ramsay Crooks and Robert Stuart. In 1806, these were not familiar names in Chequamegon country, but only a few decades later these two aggressive businessmen would play major roles in Ojibwe history.

The United States was not standing by simply observing these Montreal-based British business transactions. America had its own share of businessmen who were anxious to reap profits from furs but in these times the western trade was largely in the hands of the powerful British. As noted in a previous chapter, America instituted its factory system back in 1796, but at that time it was operating only in the southeastern parts of the country. This trading system involved annual legislative appropriations to purchase and supply goods to government posts in Indian country. The intent was to civilize the tribesmen while making them allies of the United States. A network of trading posts was set up, each run by a factor who was a political appointee. These persons were able to purchase trade goods at cost, putting British traders at a distinct disadvantage.

When Thomas Jefferson became president he wanted this system expanded and in 1802, new factories were established at Detroit and other western sites. In 1809, one was opened at Mackinac, clearly to take most of the fur trade from the British. Montreal merchants struggled to compete, and fearful that the United States had plans to restrict British trading even further, pressured Canadian authorities to work for the establishment of an Indian barrier state. This was an early British idea and soon was presented to American authorities at Washington, D.C.

Britain was aware that voices in Washington wanted more than furs. Ever since the revolution there was a call to push the nation's northern boundary far to the north, even to rout England from the continent.[10] Consequently, Canadian authorities were concerned with territorial security and argued that the area north of the Illinois and Missouri Rivers all the way up to Hudson's Bay should be preserved as a zone for fur trading, not for farming or other non-fur trapping pursuits. Such a barrier would have allowed the tribal people to continue trapping furs and would have kept the United States from pushing its boundary closer to British lands, but once again the United States rejected this buffer state suggestion.

Even though Jay's Treaty of 1796 allowed British traders to operate south of the border, in some regions the fact of their disadvantage became overly troublesome. Trading goods brought into the country were to move through customs houses where a fee was extracted. The Mackinac post presented a barrier to the British, but the western lakes and the Upper Mississippi lands were open to them. In these times there were comparatively few American traders operating north and west of Detroit, leaving British traders with a virtual monopoly in this western lakes region,[11] and since this was troublesome to the Americans, they immediately undertook steps to remove them. We should expect that the Chequamegon Bay Ojibwe knew of these activities.

While the British and tribesmen were still allies, when the United States exerted its influence through Mackinac and elsewhere, this alliance was put under stress. The Ojibwe knew of the aggressive westward expansion of the Americans, since in these years international economics and politics certainly were topics of discussion in tribal communities. According to Edmund Jefferson Danziger, Jr., the British worked hard to convince the Ojibwe that the Americans were seeking more and more territory, to include that of western Lake Superior.[12] Also, if Mark Diedrich is correct in suggesting that La Pointe's Buffalo was a signer of the Treaty of Greenville in 1795 with General Anthony Wayne, then we should agree that not only was Buffalo there, but that he was accompanied by other La Pointe leaders. Furthermore, if Buffalo was a signer of this treaty, it suggests he and his military units were participants in the conflict that preceded these negotiations for peace. This points to a strong presence of western Ojibwe people in the Ohio Valley when these important activities occurred.

Of these times, Louise Kellogg said "the northwestern Indians were reminded that they had 'two fathers,' an American one as well as a British one, and that the former was more land hungry than the latter."[13] Pushing these metaphors of fur trade theater further, we can add that from the tribal perspective, England and the United States were being reminded that they had responsibilities toward the same "child." In these years just prior to the War of 1812, the middle ground was becoming a crowded stage where tribal leaders met the Redcoats and the *Chimookomaanag* as they attempted to negotiate with both.

The North West Company was headquartered in Canada and continued to enjoy a successful trade north and west of the Great Lakes, but the Michilimackinac Company's trading regions were south of the border, where it struggled to carry out a successful business. Things became desperate and the company's leaders turned to John Jacob Astor, the wealthy American fur magnate, for aid. In only a few years, Astor had nearly monopolized the trade in the United States and along the west coast of North America. He formed the American Fur Company in 1808, with a twenty-five year charter from the New York legislature, and by working with traders in St. Louis he began efforts to establish a string of posts along the Lewis and Clark trail.[14] To achieve this end he joined with a group of North West Company leaders from Montreal. Two members of this new Astor organization were Robert Stuart and Ramsay Crooks.

In 1811, Astor agreed to work with the Michillimackinac organization and formed the new South West Company. Included in the articles of formation for this new firm was the proviso that if the American factory system ended, Astor's share of South West profits would greatly increase.[15] John Jacob Astor used his influence in Washington to relax federal restrictions on the fur trade, but soon these restrictions were of secondary importance when the beginning of the War of 1812 added serious complications to fur trade activities.

These hostilities broke out in 1812, but their precipitating pressures built for years. As we have seen in the journals of George Nelson and others, the literature of this history tells that tribal people were witness to an increasingly aggressive fur trade as the 1700s came to a close and the 1800s opened. Traders dispensed more and more alcohol in order to maintain relationships with tribal trappers, and in the lands where the furs were taken, the result was community strife in all quarters. As happens in such circumstances, spiritual leaders emerged to help put things right again.

## *The New Religion and Chequamegon Bay*

1.

IN THE MID-1700S, WHEN THE BRITISH in North America defeated the French, a Delaware visionary named Neolin was active in working to improve the lives of tribal people. He admonished them to stop using European trade goods, alcohol and other items, so they could regain their former lives. Neolin was not alone. Prophets emerged in numerous tribes all through the decades of the mid-1700s and into the early 1800s. This widespread phenomenon is testimony to the unrest and stress tribal peoples in the eastern half of North America witnessed in those times. Handsome Lake, the well-known prophet of the Seneca, began such a movement among the Iroquois in 1799, and in 1807, in Michigan territory, an Odawa spiritual leader named Trout was preaching for cultural change.[16]

Chequamegon Bay's Ojibwe heard such voices. Like their forebears, the bay's leaders were in regular contact with communities in the eastern parts of Lake Superior and they still took long paddles to points even further east. The descendents of Mamongasida and other such busy diplomats who knew the importance and rigors of these trips had not turned a deaf ear to the east. That they kept themselves and their people informed can be seen in the published memoir of Henry Schoolcraft, the United States Indian agent at Sault Ste. Marie and Detroit in the mid-nineteenth century. The reader of Schoolcraft's memoir quickly learns that, especially in the decades Schoolcraft resided at the eastern end of Lake Superior, he was regularly visited by Ojibwe persons from the far western regions of the lake and beyond, even from distant Sandy and Leech Lakes in Minnesota Territory. Like the fabled *Wenebozho*, these early Ojibwe people were travelers who apparently did not hesitate to undertake what to us today must seem as long treks that could cover hundreds of miles, usually in canoes, for social, political and economic reasons.[17]

In the first decade of the 1800s, two Shawnee brothers began to work for a widespread union of tribal peoples that would throw off harmful behavior learned from the newcomers. Tecumseh and Tenskwatawa (The Prophet) operated in tandem to achieve their purpose. Tecumseh traveled from one village to another with a political message that included, among other things, the refusal to sell any more land to the Americans. Tenskwatawa, the spiritualist, preached about morality and the importance of regaining a proper religious life. He was influenced by years of contact with Quaker missionaries and his message reflected this. For example, farming was to be part of the way of life at Prophetstown in Indiana Territory, the settlement he and his brother established for followers of the new religion, and adding something novel to the cultures of many tribes, he insisted it was the *males* who were to do the bulk of this agricultural work, not the women.[18]

Native American military leaders have been favored subjects in past histories of the United States, and the list of these leaders is long, but until recently writers have posed them as fighting men who led their warriors in battles not only against overwhelming odds, but against destiny. Tecumseh, Pontiac, and later leaders like Black Hawk, Crazy Horse, and Geronimo, for example, were often seen as militarists who fought to maintain an old way of life. In the earliest of these writings they were portrayed as "proud savages" standing opposed to "the advance of civilization." Their causes were tragic because of the assumed inevitability of the outcome.

Recently we are seeing a more balanced and complex interpretation of their struggles.[19] We now understand that these were thoughtful, contemplative men who maneuvered in a complicated world calling for more than gun, spear, arrow and bow, and instead of fading into oblivion, or *vanishing*, their people were persisting as they adapted to ever-changing circumstances. With the more recent interpretations of the lives of these tribal leaders, we are beginning to understand that while they advocated the use of force when needed, more importantly, they crafted new, creative methods of survival that went far beyond military action.[20]

While Tecumseh and Tenskwatawa wanted tribal people to build a united resistance to Americans, it is overly simplistic to characterize their movement as simply a military one, and more specifically, only as "anti-American." The messages of these brothers were complex, and were sometimes interpreted differently by disciples who carried them far from Indiana Territory. Nonetheless, from about 1805 to 1811, these Shawnee activists won and held many followers. Together their voices offered a powerful argument for native peoples to reconsider their life situations and to forge a new and better way.

Their message was carried to Lake Superior and westward to the Red River and beyond,[21] and importantly, William Warren tells us that Buffalo, the leader at La Pointe in these times, was a disciple of this new religion. According to Warren, "The venerable chiefs Buffalo, of La Pointe, and Esh-ke-bug-e-coshe, of Leech Lake, who have been men of strong minds and unusual intelligence, were not only firm believers of the Prophet, but undertook to preach his doctrines."[22]

The popular history of Chequamegon Bay written and told for the past 150 years or more typically neglects to mention Buffalo's attraction to the religious and political activism of the Shawnee brothers. Instead it tells of his strong character, his late conversion to Catholicism, and his firm pro-American stance. William Warren's image of Buffalo, at La Pointe, and Eshkebugecoshe at Leech Lake, preaching the doctrines of Tenskwatawa is telling. It shows that in the very early 1800s, at both La Pointe and about 160 miles west in the Ojibwe community of Leech Lake, there was considerable concern with the strife tribal peoples were experiencing.

It is difficult to accept the suggestion of a recent writer that among Wisconsin Indian communities "Only the Winnebago from southern Wisconsin and northern Illinois, who encountered the effects of an increasing American population, eagerly embraced the Prophet's message."[23] Such a conclusion is unappreciative of the efficiency and effectiveness of intertribal communication networks extant in North America long before the 1800s.[24] It also suggests that the pathways of new travelers into the western regions wound around the southern extent of Lake Michigan before moving into what is now known as Wisconsin. Such a view neglects to recall that much early travel was accomplished on water and therefore, the rivers and lakes of the land were the "pathways." In the early nineteenth century American newcomers were using water travel to reach points like Green Bay, and of course, to the north, others used the St. Mary's River to reach Lake Superior. We should conclude that if Wisconsin's southern tribal communities were under threat from encroaching non-native settlers, communities a few hundred miles to the north eventually learned of this problem. Certainly news traveled more slowly than today, but communities like the La Pointe Ojibwe were not isolated from the news of the day. We have seen how regular lines of communication were extant from the western to the eastern ends of Lake Superior for centuries and how news was funneled through La Pointe to Fond du Lac, Sandy Lake and points west.

We recall that the written record tells of a long tradition of Ojibwe interest in commercial trade, an interest that from time to time took them to distant Canadian trading centers. Likewise, lengthy trips for more diplomatic purposes were made to French, English, and later, American political centers. Sometimes these trips may have been shorter, such as to sites like Sault Ste. Marie, Michilimackinac, and later Mackinac Island, but the point is that they attest to an interest in affairs distant from the peoples' homeland. At first they focused on Canadian governmental centers, and later they shifted to those of the United States. And these were trips undertaken by Ojibwe leaders from western Lake Superior, not just from the eastern Great Lakes. In fact, a serious study of Ojibwe history shows the continuation of commercial and political contact through such long treks up to the present day. Today, Red Cliff tribal officials can expect from time to time they, like Chief Buffalo in the early 1800s, will need to travel to Washington, D.C., and other distant points for tribal business.

William Warren wrote at some length about the new religion at Chequamegon Bay. He said:

> It is astonishing how quickly this new belief obtained possession in the minds of the Ojibways. It spread like wild-fire throughout their entire country, and even reached the remotest northern hunters who had allied themselves with the Crees and Assiniboines. The strongest possible proof, which can be adduced of their entire belief, is in their obeying the mandate to throw away their medicine bags, which the Indian holds most sacred and inviolate. It is said that the shores of Sha-ga-waum-ik-ong were strewed with the remains of medicine bags, which had been committed to the deep. At this place, the Ojibways collected in great numbers. Night and day, the ceremonies of the new religion were performed, till it was at last determined to go in a body to Detroit, to visit the prophet.[25]

Warren claims that at this time 150 canoes filled with followers of the new religion set off for Detroit to meet with Tenskwatawa—it seems likely that Buffalo was in one of them—but that they were turned back by Michel Cadotte, who was returning from a trip to Sault Ste. Marie.[26] Cadotte had great influence at Chequamegon, and his act does not deny the strength of the new religion at the time. Other stories of The Prophet's influence in the western Great Lakes telling of hundreds of followers making the trip east, some never to return—dying of disease and starvation—may have been exaggerated, but as a recent writer suggests, "Somewhere behind these doubtlessly exaggerated stories lay a kernel of truth."[27]

When gathering data on Madeline Island for his history of the Ojibwe, Warren claimed he had difficulty getting information about the new religion. When speaking with elderly men who, some forty years previous, had been followers of Tecumseh and Tenskwatawa, he said these informants desired "to conceal the fact of their once having been so egregiously duped." Warren was writing four decades after the fact, in a time of intense missionary activity at La Pointe, and at the time the United States was experiencing a fervor of religious revivalism. Protestant missionaries had come to the community in 1831, and the record tells that they were unsuccessful in cultivating much Ojibwe interest in their religion. But in 1835, the Catholic, Frederic Baraga, arrived and in a fury of activity was soon making mass baptisms.[28]

In Warren's time the community was confronting an oppressive colonial situation. The fur trade had essentially moved westward, wealth-seeking Americans were coming to Ojibwe lands in increasing numbers, Washington officials were laying the groundwork for more and more treaty-making sessions, and Christian missionaries and school teachers were demanding deep cultural change. For some Ojibwe it was no longer meaningful, or even possible, to stand firm and reject white ways. There were families to care for, and in order to provide for them adaptations had to be made. This was the situation at La Pointe when Baraga appeared, and this was the social, economic, religious, and political context into which missionary Baraga set to work, and this was the same scene into which William Warren came when he gathered material for his historical manuscript.

It is pertinent to consider what Warren brought with him as he interviewed his Madeline Island informants. Raised as a Christian, he spent one year in the protestant missionary school at La Pointe, then was sent to a similar school at Mackinac for three years. At age nine he was taken to his grandfather, Lyman Warren, Sr., in Clarkson, New York, where he was enrolled in Clarkson Academy. In 1837, he was switched to the nearby Oneida Institute at Whitesboro, New York. Oneida was a missionary preparatory school that enrolled students of all races and was known for its anti-slavery stance. When the institute closed in 1840, William was enrolled back at Clarkson until 1841, when at age sixteen he came back to Lake Superior.[29]

By this time, William Warren was living in a personal world far removed from that of the earlier 1800s at La Pointe. A few years later when undertaking his fieldwork, what questions did he ask his informants, and how did he interpret the responses he witnessed? During his lifetime in western Lake Superior, like others of his mixed racial and cultural composition, William Warren did not consider himself an Indian. When studying his manuscript the reader quickly grasps the degree of Warren's assimilation into the American mainstream of his time, and might begin to recognize the extent to which Warren considered himself as part of the greater non-tribal community. Within this context, his view of the new religion and its followers those few decades before might be better understood.

The new religion was dealt a serious blow in 1811, when Tenskwatawa's village of Tippecanoe was attacked by a force of American soldiers led by William Henry Harrison, the governor of Indiana Territory. While the Americans took heavy casualties in this battle, the native force was defeated, although Tenskwatawa survived. Tecumseh was not involved since he was in a distant southern state on a recruiting mission for his cause. This battle was a setback to the new religion but William Warren suggests it was still active at La Pointe where, another writer claims, Buffalo "preached the Prophet's doctrines for a time during the War of 1812."[30]

### *The War of 1812 and the Ojibwe*

IN 1812, GREAT BRITAIN AND ITS TRIBAL ALLIES entered a war against the United States. Hostilities continued until December of 1814, when peace was finalized in the Treaty of Ghent in the Belgian city of that name. It has been conventional for historians to argue that the western Lake Superior Ojibwe communities had no significant involvement in this war.[31]

In the summer of 1812, the American fort at Mackinac was surrendered to tribal and British forces led by John Johnson, and in the next two years military encounters occurred throughout the northern regions of the United States, as well as in lower Canada. During the war a British naval force entered Chesapeake Bay allowing foot soldiers to reach Washington, D.C., where they plundered and burned the White House, the Capitol building, "the treasury, and the building housing the war and state departments." Historians tell us that after a year or more, the Americans and British were eager to look for ways to end hostilities and negotiate a peace, although the written record says nothing about the eagerness of the tribal nations to call a halt to the combat. After initial pretensions to inclusion, these nations were excluded from the negotiations which ended a war in which they took a very active part.[32]

This war was no little matter. It is likely thousands of tribesmen were in it, and for a period of time at least, Tecumseh's confederacy threatened the United States. Great Britain was engaged in the Napoleonic wars with France in the early years and was convinced its priorities were in the European theater rather than in America, but in March of 1814, Napoleon was defeated and British troop reinforcements were sent to Canada. By the end of 1814, almost 40,000 British troops were in North America. However, land and sea battles took their tolls and by late 1814, Britain and the United States negotiated a peace settlement.[33]

2.

WILLIAM WARREN TRIED TO CONVINCE his readers that western Lake Superior's Ojibwe did not fight on the British side in this war. He insisted that when making inquiries on Madeline Island, apparently in the late 1840s, "not more than one or two warriors are mentioned as having joined the British," and while there were other Ojibwe warriors who fought under the British flag they were from the "several villages of Indians in Upper Canada," and from "small bands who lived among the Ottaways at Mackinaw, and who were scattered in Michigan among the Pottawatumies and other tribes."[34]

To support his claim of neutrality for the western Ojibwe he offers a lengthy account, told to him by Michel Cadotte, of the meeting between Keesh-ke-mun, a civil chief at Lac du Flambeau (Wisconsin), and British officials at Mackinac in 1812, after the fort was taken from the Americans. When a British agent insisted Keesh-ke-mun join the British against the Americans he refused. Warren's point is that this man was influential in Ojibwe country and served to show that western Ojibwe communities refused to enter the war. However, Keesh-ke-mun was a civil leader, not a war leader, and he was from Lac du Flambeau, the inland community south of Lake Superior. As a civil leader his role was to speak to peace, not war. Just how far his influence reached is unknown, but we do know that in 1808, it was not enough to keep the new religion out of the Lac Courte Oreilles community just to his west.[35]

Warren goes on to say:

> The main body of the tribe occupying Lake Superior, and the waters of the Mississippi firmly withstood every effort made by the British to induce them to enter into the war, and it is thus they have succeeded in holding their own in numbers, and in fact, gradually increasing, while other tribes, who have foolishly mingled in the wars of the whites, have become nearly extinct.[36]

In previous chapters we have shown that Lake Superior's Ojibwe warriors have indeed "mingled in the wars of the whites," at first as allies of the French and later of the British. And it seems likely that in the War of 1812, more than a few fought alongside their British allies once more.

Warren told how Jean Baptiste, and Michel Cadotte, Jr., did indeed fight for the British in the war. He says:

> Of the Ojibway half-breeds, John Baptiste and Michel, sons of Michel Cadotte, Sr., of La Pointe, were captured or enticed by the British of Isle Drummond, and there given the option, either to go into confinement during the war, or act as interpreters, and use their influence to collect the Ojibways. They accepted the latter alternative, and were actors *in all the principal Canadian battles*, and were present on the occasion of Tecumseh's death. John Baptiste was severely wounded, and is now a pensioner on the British government. Michel is also living, minus one arm, at La Pointe, on Lake Superior.[37]

Guy Burnham, the nineteenth century Ashland, Wisconsin, writer, concurs with Warren, and adds that *both* of Michel Cadotte, Sr.'s sons were wounded while fighting on the side of the British at Thames.[38]

What are we to make of this writing? Since the Cadotte brothers "were actors in all the principle Canadian battles," it seems they were successful in their charge to "use their influence to collect the Ojibwe," and, it follows, lead them to battle the Americans. The written record is virtually silent on the matter of any La Pointe Ojibwe being in the military force that captured Fort Mackinac at the start of the hostilities, yet this force "of about a thousand Indians and Canadian wood rangers" was led by John Johnston.[39] This is the same John Johnston who worked as a trader at La Pointe after Alexander Henry left the post. We noted that Johnston's wife was the daughter of Waubojeeg, the prominent La Pointe war leader, and it seems this kin relationship was a major factor behind the economic and political success Johnston achieved during his life on Lake Superior. Previous to the outbreak of the war, Johnston actively recruited his force, and given his tie to the Ojibwe in Chequmegon, it would have been unusual that no military personnel from that community were with him in his march to Fort Mackinac.

Louise Kellogg has written that from the time of the fall of Mackinac in 1812 to the ratification of the Treaty of Ghent, the Wisconsin tribes were strongly pro-British. As she puts it: "Wisconsin, during this period, was even more British than Canada."[40] However, Edmund Jefferson Danziger, Jr., writing in 1979, said of Lake Superior's Ojibwe that "Their strong dependence on the Canadian fur trade doubtless made them pro-British, but . . . British appeals could [not] arouse them to war on the United States."[41]

Drawing largely on the words of William Warren, Danziger, like others before him, felt it was the eastern Ojibwe who joined the British to fight the Americans, not the Lake Superior communities. His emphasis on an assumed Ojibwe dependence on British trade goods and how this predetermined the peoples' motives for their acts in these years runs contrary to their supposedly firm stand against joining in the fight against the Americans. If they were so dependent upon the British why did they refuse to help them in their new fight with the Americans?

It seems more likely that if this dependency upon British trade goods was as pronounced as writers like Danziger claimed, then, coupled with the support for the strongly pro-British new religion of Tecumseh and Tenskwatawa, the Ojibwe would readily have agreed to help their allies in the new war with the United States.

Recalling the great influence Jean Baptiste Cadotte, Sr., had with the Ojibwe back in the latter 1700s, when he was a trading partner of Alexander Henry, and in turn, the influence his two sons, Jean Baptiste, Jr., and Michel had with the Ojibwe people in both the eastern and western Lake Superior communities, it is difficult to agree that Michel Sr.'s sons failed in their attempts to recruit warriors to join them in this war against the *Chimookemaan* in the early 1800s. We are told that in the latter years of the eighteenth century, their father moved westward along Lake Superior's south shore to convince the Ojibwe to join him in battle against the Americans, but unfortunately, the written record does not tell how successful he was in this endeavor. Cadotte traveled south in the Mississippi valley to the Dakota village led by Wabasha and was able to have that prominent leader join the cause, but the record is not clear if he had a force of Lake Superior Ojibwe with him on that trip.[42]

We also recall that for some time, Mackinac, as was the case earlier at Sault Ste. Marie, was a congregating place for people from the western portions of Lake Superior when they formed fighting units to paddle east or south to go to war. It seems strange, despite what Warren has stated, that in the early 1800s, when so strongly allied with the British, that Chequamegon Bay's Ojibwe community would not have answered Britain's call for help. We are told that in the late 1700s and early 1800s, Col. Robert Dickson, who was working for the British at Grand Portage and other points north and west of Lake Superior, had no influence at Chequamegon. John Tanner tells of his encounters with this red-headed British official in areas west of the lake in these years, and of his pronounced distaste for the man, but he does not suggest that the Ojibwe with which he was living in these times felt the same animosity for Col. Dickson.[43]

One contemporary writer hints that British recruiters like Jean and Michel Cadotte and Robert Dickson may have been successful in having western Lake Superior Ojibwe forces join them in battles with the Americans. After a study of related documents and literature of the time, Mark Diedrich says La Pointe's Buffalo "apparently was one of the Indian leaders in the Battle of the Thames (October 5, 1813), where Tecumseh was killed. He also seems to have been included in a delegation of chiefs which visited Sir George Prevost at Quebec in March 1814."[44] These suggestions are controversial however, due to the great difficulty to correctly identify personal names on some of these early treaties. A prerequisite to do this work with even a small degree of credibility is to hold a solid grasp of the Ojibwe language, something few non-Ojibwe researchers have.[45]

Perhaps we have difficulty in envisioning La Pointe's Buffalo as a younger man involved in military encounters since we typically think of him as an elderly civil leader. We do not know him as a young man during the important years when he was earning the respect of his contemporaries, a respect that would, of course, allow him to rise to the prominent position of a civil leader. Years of successful war exploits were normally requisite for a warrior to advance to the position of civil chief, and we would expect that Buffalo went through this early time of what we can call "leadership apprenticeship" that included being challenged by warfare.[46]

After the death of Tecumseh, the tribes wanted assurance of Britain's support in a continuation of the conflict, and the British sought a similar assurance from the tribes. Prevost's 1814 meeting was an attempt to reinforce the alliance between Britain and the tribes.

The possible involvement of Buffalo in distant battles against the United States in the early 1800s resonates with the image of the La Pointe leader given by Benjamin Armstrong. Armstrong left a valuable manuscript that is not readily accessible today. His dates are sometimes approximate rather than exact, but it is not the veracity of his dating that is important. His voice offers another eyewitness account of life in Chequamegon in the early to late 1800s, and given his prominence in both the Ojibwe and non-Ojibwe worlds of the times, we are obligated to study him. Also, his apparent fluency in the Ojibwe language lends credence to his account.[47]

According to Armstrong, "Buffalo . . . never went on the warpath and would only agree to fight when it became actually necessary to repel an invasion."[48] This characterization of Buffalo as a leader standing for peace rather than war has come down through the years in the popular history of the man. Yet we should understand that Benjamin Armstrong only knew Buffalo during his (Buffalo's) later years, by which time he had been established as a civil leader. If Buffalo did go to war beside the British against the Americans he did it as a much younger man, before Armstrong's time at Chequamegon. And when joining the British, he would have been working "to repel an invasion." This activity would have been good preparation for his later years as an Ojibwe civil chief. Furthermore, his involvement in distant eastern battles would have broadened his vision and provided training for his role as a diplomat with a far reaching grasp of complex and threatening issues affecting his people, a trait we will see he clearly had in the decades following the War of 1812.

Buffalo's participation in the distant Canadian battle that caused the death of Tecumseh is entirely possible and his presence at the 1814 meeting with British officials in Quebec would plausibly follow. And if Buffalo was present in these events we should conclude he was leading a military force from La Pointe at Thames and possibly a smaller contingent of Chequamegon Bay diplomats at the Quebec meeting. These conclusions are speculative, of course, and are contrary to William Warren's claim of neutrality for the La Pointe Ojibwe in the War of 1812, but if plausible, they support the suggestion of other evidence, discussed below, that in these early years of the nineteenth century, Chequamegon Bay's Ojibwe had not yet switched from their long alliance with Britain to one with the Americans.

Perhaps Warren's image of Buffalo rejecting British overtures to join them in war against the Americans can be understood by recalling the time in which his fieldwork was done at La Pointe.[49] William Warren was interviewing elders on Madeline Island only a decade or two after the War of 1812, and in those years his informants had been in regular contact with Americans for some time, and importantly, these Americans were *change agents* who were working hard "to civilize" the resident tribesmen, and perhaps most significantly, these government agents, missionaries, teachers and traders were all representatives of a very powerful and aggressive society. Doubtless, even though he was partially of Ojibwe descent, Warren's informants saw him as part of this American community and were surely sensitive to their own precarious political and economic situation. At the time of Warren's fieldwork they might have felt that to disclose that their immediate forebears had been deeply pro-British would not have been politically wise.

## 3.

IN 1813, THE BATTLE OF THE THAMES marked the breakdown of Tecumseh's confederacy and suggested that the western tribes might be amenable to entering into treaty negotiations with the Americans. The United States saw an opportunity, and quickly returned to its attempts to divest these tribes of their landholdings. This divestment was initiated by a set of four meetings. Unfortunately, the written record does not tell us about the internal discussions that doubtlessly occurred in and between Ojibwe communities in western Lake Superior at this time—discussions at which no non-native persons were present—nor does it inform us of any such meetings that might have ensued after Tecumseh's death. We have only the written record provided by non-native participants in the negotiation sessions, and the interpretations of American writers in succeeding years, so our knowledge of these times is extremely limited.

According to the historian Francis Paul Prucha, with the death of Tecumseh:

> Very quickly the pressure on the Indian landholdings was renewed with a vengeance. The extinguishment of so many parcels of the Indians' landed estate that proceeded inexorably was due to the inordinate demand for lands that came after the defeat of the Indians in the War of 1812, fueled by an explosive spirit of nationalism that marked the period. And the subjugated Indians were in no po-

> sition to forcefully resist the new onslaught. Treaties poured into Washington and were sent in batches to the Senate for what was almost always unanimous approval of their ratification.[50]

Such was the political atmosphere in which Buffalo and his people were immersed in the early years of the 1800s. It must have been clear to them that the Americans were intent on pushing further and further westward, threatening life as the Ojibwe had known it for generations.

The United States' near frenzy of activities Prucha wrote about was well organized. It was essential to the Americans that the western frontier be quieted, so the decision was made to immediately negotiate peace treaties with the resident tribes. Land cession treaties could then follow. To this end, in the summer of 1814, Governors Harrison and Cass, of Indiana and Michigan territories respectively, were sent to Ohio to meet with regional tribes that had remained friendly to the United States throughout the conflict. In July, they signed the Treaty of Greenville with the region's tribal leaders. The next month, Andrew Jackson signed a similar peace treaty with the Creek peoples in the southeast. Immediately the following month, two last treaties were signed at about the same time. One was with the western tribes at Portage Des Sioux at the mouth of the Missouri River on the Mississippi, and the other at Spring Wells, near Detroit. This latter treaty was signed "with the Chippewa, Ottawa, and Potawatomi Indians, who had been hostile to the United States during the war." It is conventional to understand that in both the treaty of Greenville and Spring Wells—the two treaties in which Ojibwe people were involved—that these Ojibwe were from the eastern Great Lakes, not from western Lake Superior. We are left to conclude that Chequamegon Bay's Ojibwe communities were not part of any of these four negotiation sessions. Yet, much diplomatic activity occurred from 1813 to 1815, and as we have seen, the record shows La Pointe's Buffalo, as well as other western Lake Superior leaders, could have taken part in some of it.[51]

There is no reason to doubt William Warren's assertions about the Cadottes' taking part in British battles distant from La Pointe. Given Buffalo's pro-British stand, as evinced by his participation in the new religion of Tecumseh and Tenskwatawa, it would follow that he was with the Cadottes in 1813, at the Battle of Thames. If he was there, it shows his support for the British and it follows that it would be possible for him to be in the contingent of western tribal leaders who met with Sir George Prevost only a few months later in February of 1814, in Quebec. The death of Tecumseh was a blow to tribal enthusiasm, and the British feared they would break their alliances with England, leaving it unable to continue its conflict with the United States in the western lakes region. Thus, Prevost was attempting to avoid this by reassuring his western allies that Britain would continue to stand with them in the ongoing war. At the time of this meeting Britain was routing the French in the Napoleonic Wars and had reason to feel it would soon be able to devote many more troops to its North American conflict.

Assuming that Buffalo was in Quebec in March for the Prevost meeting, he could have been back in Chequamegon Bay in June, 1814, when the British held a conference at Mackinac to rally support from Dakota and Ho-Chunk leaders from southern Wisconsin and Minnesota. Little Crow and Wabasha, the two famous Dakota leaders, and Tomah, the Menomini, along with Carmaunee, the Ho-Chunk leader, traveled to Mackinac to meet with the Redcoats. To date, no written documentation of Ojibwes from western Lake Superior being at this meeting has surfaced. Later in June, a force led by Robert Dickson left Mackinac for Prairie du Chien to drive the Americans from that strategic post. Given the long tradition of communication between Mackinac and western Lake Superior, news of this meeting likely reached Chequamegon, where it would have assured Buffalo and his community that Britain was still engaged in conflict with the Americans.[52]

The next month, the United States started holding the peace treaty meetings with western and northern tribes. So far no indisputable record of western Lake Superior Ojibwe leaders attending any of these four meetings has surfaced, suggesting they were not included. Thus, the record hints that the strong pro-British stand from 1812 to 1815 that has been attributed to Wisconsin tribes may have been left to linger on for some time in the far northern portions of the territory, and it is not insignificant that five years later, as discussed below, in 1820 at Sault Ste. Marie, the members of the Cass Expedition to the sources of the Mississippi witnessed a strong pro-British sentiment in at least a portion of that Ojibwe community.

In concluding this discussion of the War of 1812, we have seen that over the years writers have not hesitated to offer their assumptions on the question of Chequamegon Bay's involvement. While earlier historians claimed that except for a very few individuals, western Lake Superior's Ojibwe peoples were not participants in the conflict, we have suggested that the literature may show otherwise, and therefore, we should be suspect when reading the claim of a mid-twentieth century writer that Lake Superior's Ojibwe have "never engaged in armed conflict with the United States Army."[53] Such declarations likely rose from a desire to project what at the time may have been felt to be a positive image of the Ojibwe, and thus, tell more of the political sentiments of the writer than of the people she was writing about.

As we will see below, a favorable British sentiment remained at western Ojibwe sites long after the War of 1812. La Pointe's Buffalo expressed such a sentiment in 1826, at Fond du Lac and again, twelve years later in 1838, at La Pointe. Four years later, in 1842, and again in 1852, Black Bird, a Bad River leader, did the same. This shows the existence of a strong British sentiment in western Lake Superior lands all through the first half of the nineteenth century, and suggests the region's tribal leaders held positive political ties with England during those years.

After 1815, Britain's posts were officially removed from south of the Canadian border, and even though any actual personal visits between the British and these Ojibwe leaders may have been few, it is clear that at La Pointe, a pro-British sentiment remained. However, it was soon countered by visits from American emissaries when several years after the War of 1812, Buffalo and other La Pointe leaders witnessed the power and intent of the government of the United States as its representatives began to arrive in Chequamegon country.

*Notes*

1. Kellogg 1935:248.
2. Warren 1984[1885]:108-112.
3. Kellogg 1935:176, 270, 297.
4. Calloway 2006:170.
5. Curot 1803-4; Larson 1989; Malhiot 1804-5; Nelson 1802-4.
6. Ross 1960:76-8; Thwaites 1910:169.
7. Harris 1976:63-71.
8. Peers and Schenck 2002:15.
9. Peers and Schenck 2002:14-5; Waddell 1985.
10. Hickey 1989:289.
11. Williams 1992[1953]:3, in Schoolcraft 1992[1953].
12. Danziger 1976:67.
13. Kellogg 1935:264.
14. Schoolcraft 1978[1851]:115-117.
15. Kellogg 1935:268.
16. Calloway 2006:29,70; Dowd 1992:33-5, 127; Edmunds 1985[1983].
17. Schoolcraft 1978[1851].
18. Dowd 1992:135.
19. Chute 1998; Dowd 1992; Edmunds 1985[1983]; Sugden 1997; Trask 2007.
20. Peyer 1997:101.
21. Tanner 2000[1830]:147.
22. Warren 1984[1885]:324.
23. Bieder 1995:85.
24. Turner 1970[1891]:10-1.
25. Warren 1984[1885]:322-3.
26. Diedrich 1999:71; Warren 1984[1885]:323.
27. Sugden 1997:144.
28. Warren 1984[1885]:324.
29. Schenck 2007:11-19.
30. Diedrich 1999:71.
31. Danziger 1979:66-7.
32. Hickey 1989:199; Borneman 2004:216-235.
33. Hickey 1989:182-3, 300; Borneman 2004; Langguth 2006.
34. Warren 1984[1885]:368-377.
35. Warren 1984[1885]:372-6.
36. Warren 1984[1885]:369.
37. Warren 1984[1885]:372, italics added.
38. Burnham 1974[1900]:117.
39. Harris 1976:74-5.
40. Kellogg 1935:285.
41. Danziger 1979:66, brackets added.
42. Harris 1976:64.
43. Tanner 1994[1830]:250-1.
44. Diedrich 1999:71.
45. Paap 2004, field notes with comments from David Bisonette of Lac Courte Oreilles, Wisconsin.
46. Chute 1998:13.
47. Armstrong 1892.
48. Armstrong 1892:197.
49. Schenck 2007:ix.
50. Prucha 1997[1994]:135.
51. Prucha 1997[1994]:132-134.
52. Kellogg 1935:317.
53. Levi 1956:33.

# 12

# 1814-1825: The Cass Expedition

### *1814-1820: Adjusting Ojibwe Alliances*

1.

IN 1814, WHEN THE UNITED STATES and Britain negotiated the treaty to end hostilities, the British initially insisted upon "the inclusion of Indian nations in the peace conference and the establishment of a definite boundary and security guarantees for their lands."[1] The inclusion, however, did not come to pass, and this request to involve the tribal nations was self-serving for the British since they wished to safeguard their northern and western boundaries from further threats of American invasions. To this end, British negotiators asked that an Indian buffer zone be established in the western lands between Canada and the United States, but the Americans rejected this old idea. The historian Donald R. Hickey feels that the notion of such a barrier was anathema to the United States because it "undermined American sovereignty, ran counter to a tradition of national control over the Indians, and threatened the westward movement."[2] By 1814, America had surely developed its "tradition of national control over the Indians" and by this time its policies directed toward tribal governments were constructed with this tradition in mind. But it is doubtful that the Ojibwe, as we have already discussed, would have agreed this tradition had, in practice, become reality. In 1814, the underlying institutions of Ojibwe culture were still functioning in Chequamegon Bay and although the Americans may have felt they were controlling the tribesmen, it is likely the Bay's Ojibwe felt otherwise.

The tribal land barrier was not formed but both Britain and the United States agreed to settle a peace with the tribes and "to restore . . . all the possessions, rights, and privileges" they had before 1811, when conflict began.[3] This agreement, of course, was a "dead letter from the beginning" and today we understand that both the British and Americans had no intent of following through on it.[4] Perhaps by making this agreement the negotiators were doing little more than telling each other that they were, indeed, concerned about the welfare of tribal peoples, even though both parties understood the pretense of such an act.

Once again, regarding this peace agreement for a war that included tribal nations, we find another example of delegates from powerful nations making decisions that in a very direct way concerned communities they perceived to be less powerful. The British demand that initially the tribal nations be present at the Ghent meeting did not, finally, derive from a gesture of concern for these nations, but out of its own interests. Despite this overture to the tribesmen, in 1814, when British and American authorities met to settle this peace, it was deemed unnecessary for the tribal nations' representatives to be present. This practice of the European and American authorities ignoring their Indian allies when going to the peace settlement table was common in early North America, a point lamented by a number of tribal leaders.[5]

After the signing of the Treaty of Ghent, the United States quickly returned to its long-time goal of civilizing the western tribes. This is something it was trying to accomplish through its factory system before the War of 1812. This trade system was, among other things, meant to quiet the western frontier so the fur trade could continue. As we have already seen, America's factory system was a network of trading posts—called factories—run by the federal government. Right from the beginning a pervading purpose of the system was to economically attach the tribesmen to the Americans, or as George Washington put it, to "engross their Trade, and fix them strongly in our interests."[6] The trade of the Indians was a lucrative endeavor and the new United States wanted its share.

Beyond this purely material intent, the factory system had three other goals. First, it was meant to remove British traders still found at certain locations along the northern and western frontiers. By subsidizing the trade, federal traders were able to offer goods at rates far lower than the British. Second, the system was intended to counter what some non-tribal voices felt was the damaging effect of private traders on the Indians. The sentiment that private traders projected a demoralizing and uncivilized image to tribal peoples was widespread. Federally hired and paid factors could be screened for moral and other more acceptable traits. Third, underlying all of this was the constant goal of assimilating the tribal people into the way of life of the new Americans. Federal traders were to work at implementing this cultural change through their regular trading contacts with the tribesmen. This goal of *civilizing the savage* was always central to federal policy directed toward the Indian throughout the nineteenth century.

The fur trade was still lucrative and with a peaceful frontier the country could benefit financially as well as continue its efforts to push its border westward. After 1815, the excitement of the Lewis and Clark expedition and Zebulon Pike's western explorations was fueling the national desire for this expansion. Even though the war was over, British traders were still legally able to operate below the Canadian border, but sentiment to remove them was strong. The American businessman, John Jacob Astor, was applying pressure to halt this British involvement and in 1816, Congress responded by outlawing foreign fur traders within American lands when it passed a bill requiring traders to be licensed. Astor's political influence not only worked to remove his major competitor and thus, bring him increased profits, it also effected a change in Ojibwe fur trading relationships. To a great extent, it was due to him that after 1816, Ojibwe fur trappers began to deal almost exclusively with the new American traders rather than the British. This was an important change since the Americans were ultimately after more than furs.

2.

THE YEARS IMMEDIATELY FOLLOWING the peace settlement after the War of 1812 are particularly important for understanding later events in Chequamegon country. What was occurring in more eastern portions of the continent would soon have its effect on life in the region. The new United States was stirring with nationalistic desires that focused on expansion to the west, and the question of an international border to the north was also a concern. Desires to expand in this direction were not put to rest for some time.[7] The country's pride in American nationalism was intense, and as more and more immigration from Europe occurred the demand for more land grew. The victory by the colonists over Great Britain in the revolution of 1776 had fueled this pride, and although the Americans did not have a clear victory in the War of 1812, their ability to at least fight a world power to a standstill along the Canadian and American border allowed the colonists to be certain they were meant to form their new country in what had been perceived as the wilderness of the North American continent.[8]

Manifest destiny was a solid reality to them. As we have already discussed, the Americans felt they were destined to move west. They were certain the natives were inferior to them, and that as a people the new Americans were obligated to carry out their god's plan to build their nation.[9] We should suspect that contrariwise, some Ojibwe were questioning what was occurring.

Western Lake Superior country is sometimes said to have been outside the main stream of this movement to the Pacific, but the Chequamegon region and the area at the headwaters of the Mississippi drew its own share of interested wealth seekers. We have seen this expressed in the literature of the fur trade, but in the early 1800s, the new nation's leaders wanted this western lakes region for more than the extraction of furs. The United States saw itself as a role player in the spreading industrial revolution coming from Europe and as a still "undeveloped" nation, was felt to hold resources destined to be utilized. This northwest region was known to hold some of these resources.

The spirit of these times is perhaps best seen in the ideas and acts of Thomas Jefferson. As a national leader he was instrumental in sending several expeditions to western lands and his interests as a scientist gave added validity to them. These expeditions were given a fact-finding character, and clearly, were expeditions to discover natural resources useful to an industrializing nation. The fact that this territory was the homeland to numerous tribal nations was troublesome, but felt to be something that would be overcome. As we have seen throughout the previous chapters, America's religious and legal discourse had already been put into place to address this problem.[10]

3.

EDMUND JEFFERSON DANZIGER, JR. WRITES that after the meeting of the Americans and the pro-British tribes in the old northwest at Spring Wells, the Ojibwe "dealt with two powerful but different groups of White Americans," each having its own agenda. The first was the fur traders of John Jacob Astor's American Fur Company. This group worked to keep the Ojibwe and their lands as they were when first encountered by the Europeans, that is, to leave the land relatively unaltered so tribal systems could continue functioning as foraging cultures. The second group was composed of "agents of civilization—white miners, lumbermen, farmers, townbuilders—[that] sought to subdue Kitchigami land."[11]

These two powerful groups had opposing goals and at times the tension between them must have been troublesome, if not excruciating, to the Ojibwe. It was not long before the fur trade showed signs of weakening. While this in itself would not have forced a wholesale cultural change, since in the early 1800s they were still enjoying their age-old hunting and gathering way of life, the increasing numbers of the second group, along with its intensity and determination, soon became a major threat. When using Danziger's image of this group determined "to subdue Kitchigami land" we see the severity of the times for the Ojibwe people.

On their seasonal round when they increasingly encountered members of this second group cutting trees, building homes, fencing off newly cleared fields, removing minerals from the earth, and so forth, the Ojibwe must have taken pause to recall the warnings the British were still giving them about these aggressive Americans. Eventually it was these agents of change, who in Danziger's words, "elbowed the natives off most of their hunting grounds and had them assigned to small reservations" who were the greater threat to their way of life.[12]

4.

ALONG WITH THE AGENTS OF CHANGE who increasingly came into the western lakes region were officials of the new American government, who began to appear almost immediately after the Treaty of Ghent was signed. Accounts of their expeditions are heavy with descriptions of the natural landscape and its potential resources, but they also tell of the area's tribal communities. Members of these parties filed reports and kept personal journals or other papers that in most cases were published, or at least deposited into numerous archives. Today these are invaluable for what they show about the Ojibwe people met along the way, but just as importantly, for what they tell about the writers' points of view.

In the sections below we will begin a discussion of these latter references found in the documents of these expeditions by presenting material from the 1820 trip to the head of the Mississippi led by Lewis Cass, then governor of Michigan Territory. Writing in 1958, an editor of a collection of documents from this trip remarked that it was a "relatively uneventful expedition," but eventful or not, for our purposes it is quite significant.[13] What is important in virtually all the literature of such excursions is twofold. First, it offers a glimpse of Ojibwe life in the western Great Lakes during a time from which little written or oral detail has come down to us. Secondly, it lays bare the perspectives these writers held when describing and interpreting tribal life. By studying this point of view, we understand what native people were confronted with. Furthermore, since the printed words of these writers were sometimes given wide dissemination, they were a major source of information on tribal societies for the country's reading public.[14] For a number of years immediately after 1820, newspapers, academic journals and the popular press published this material to the effect that it, among other things, fed images and assumptions about tribal communities held not only by the general public but also by business and governmental leaders. As part of the national literature of the time it fueled the fires of westward expansion and reinforced the country's biases toward Indians.

With the end of the War of 1812, a national cry arose for what President James Monroe called an "active western policy."[15] The British were still a concern in the northwest and there were new rumors of another Indian war in that region. Consequently, the Secretary of War, John C. Calhoun, gave directives for a line of military forts meant to halt British intrusions into the region and to quiet any Indian unrest as well as to establish an American presence along this frontier. New military posts were to be set up on the Yellow River (North Dakota) and at St. Peters (Minnesota). Other posts at Mackinac, Green Bay, Chicago, and in southern Wisconsin (on the Rock River) and at Prairie du Chien (on the Mississippi) served to complete this military line.

In his annual address of 1818, President Monroe spoke of his desire for a western policy. He addressed the issue of Native Americans and his fear that if a strong policy was not put into effect the country's native communities along the western frontier would cease to exist. According to Monroe:

> To civilize them, and even to prevent their extinction it seems to be indispensable that their independence as communities should cease, and that the control of the United States over them should be complete and un-disputed. The hunter state will then be more easily abandoned, and recourse will be had to the acquisition and culture of land, and to other pursuits tending to dissolve the ties which connect them together as a savage community and to give a new character to every individual.[16]

Monroe's words capture the sentiment of manifest destiny held by national leaders of the time, and he was using the "provisional race" theory to understand the situation. This theory held that a community could justifiably use its land but when another "race" came along that could put it to a better use, the original landholders had to relinquish their right to it.[17] The recognition of native sovereignty in the carefully worded treaties Monroe's government had been signing with Indian nations was, with this statement, called into question and its pretense exposed. The goal was clear: Indian communities had to cease existing as self-sustaining and self-containing systems, and their constituent individuals were to take on new personal identities as they melded with what was then the mainstream of United States society. Agriculture was to replace "the chase," as cultural evolution moved forward. The Indians' *savage* state was to leapfrog over the *barbarian* state directly to *civilization*. And of course, in this evolutionary process, the tribesmen were to embrace Christianity as their new religion. There could be no uncertainty in this. The tribes had to change and do it quickly, or, as Monroe feared, they would come to extinction.

With today's hindsight we can appreciate the enormity of the problem that faced both the Indians and those persons bent upon changing them. The emerging American academy, the clergy, the government, and powerful voices in the business community were in unison on this issue. The situation the tribesmen found themselves in became known as their "plight," and a familiar phrase that began appearing in the press and in literary tracts at the time was "Lo, the Poor Indian."[18] From the perspective of the non-Indian, there often was a definite sadness in the situation, and images of pathos involved began to appear in literature and other art forms of the day. Voices such as President Monroe's decried the possibility of the Indians' physical extinction but applauded the cultural and social extinction they were working for.

## *The 1820 Cass Expedition to the Headwaters of the Mississippi*

1.

In the several years after the War of 1812, both the British and the United States were consciously on edge in the western Great Lakes region. The northwest boundary was still a matter of contention, especially as it meandered westward from the headwaters of the Mississippi River, and both countries feared the influence of the other in this region. Soon after the close of the war, the United States maneuvered to show its sovereignty at the eastern end of Lake Superior by stationing military troops at Mackinac and making plans to build a fort to the north at Sault Ste. Marie. In 1816, the British countered by reinstituting its practice of distributing presents to the upper Great Lakes bands and the communities at the western terminus of Lake Superior responded immediately. In a letter to Lewis Cass dated 20 August 1817, W. H. Puthuff, the Indian Agent at Mackinac, said, "Potawatamies and other tribes from the Illinois and Chippewas from Lake Superior and intervening Country bordering on the head waters of the Mississippi . . . have visited this Post and Drummund's Island during the present season."[19] As late as 1832, the British were still dispensing gifts as told by the Catholic missionary Frederic Baraga, who was at Arbre Croche, Michigan, where he wrote:

> The English, a nation so generous in its rewards, bestow great benefits on our poor Indians. The Indians were allies of the English in the war with the United States, and because of that the English government still continues to reward the Indians. There are certain places in Canada that belong to the Eng-

> lish, intended for the annual presents that are distributed to the Indians in July and August, and each Indian who comes there receives considerable presents every year: clothing, utensils, rifles, and the like; and if he comes with his family, his wife and each of his children also receive considerable presents. Nearly all my Indians go annually to Canada. Although it is far, however, all the way there in their light canoes.[20]

As Baraga witnessed at Arbre Croche, Lewis Cass—from his vantage point in Detroit—saw the flow of western tribal leaders coming annually to the British post at Fort Malden located across the river in lower Ontario on Lake Erie. In 1818, Cass informed John Calhoun, the Secretary of War, that the British were dispensing various sorts of goods—including guns and ammunition—to western Indians at this site. In 1819, Cass claimed three thousand Indians came to Fort Malden that summer and "a large portion of these Indians live on the Mississippi."[21] The fact that sizable contingents of people were traveling on water and on foot from the Mississippi River to the shore of Lake Erie in 1819 tells something about the political and economic interests of the western tribesmen at the time. Given these remarks of Lewis Cass, we should conclude that some, if not all, of these travelers from the Mississippi were Ojibwe tribesmen.

Further north, and of greater importance for our consideration of activities in Chequamegon Bay, the British were also dispensing goods, this time south of Sault Ste. Marie, on Drummond's Island, and after 1828, at Penetanguishine on Georgian Bay, below Manitoulin Island. According to George Boyd, the American agent at Mackinac, in June of 1819, it was at Drummond's Island where "the Duke of Richmond was distributing presents to some six or seven hundred Indians."[22] Nineteen years later when Boyd was the Sub-agent at Green Bay he again told of this annual trek of Wisconsin Territory's Indians to Drummond's Island. In a letter to Acting Wisconsin Territorial Governor William B. Slaughter, dated 28 June 1838, in which Boyd was responding to the House of Representatives of the United States' call for information about any involvement of British agents with Wisconsin's Indians, Boyd said:

> [I]t is within my certain knowledge that the Winnebagos, Sacs & Foxes, Ottawas & Chippeways from the extreme north of Lake Superior and the Menomonees, have been in the yearly habit of visiting Drummond's Island . . . with a view, no doubt, to draw their regular allowances for Services performed by them to the British Government, during the last War.[23]

We might think 1838 is overly late for the British to have any influence with western Lake Superior's Ojibwe people but as we will see, in that year this influence was present at La Pointe, as well as westward into the headwaters of the Mississippi, and there is evidence it reached as far as the Red River Valley. William Warren and others since him have intimated this was not the case, but their suggestion that these western Ojibwe communities turned aside British political and economic overtures is not borne out by the documents of the time. For instance, in his memoir, Henry Schoolcraft remarked that in 1822, La Pointe's Buffalo was known as "a Chief decorated with British insignia,"[24] and ten years later, in 1832, Schoolcraft said the La Pointe Ojibwe were making regular trips to Georgian Bay on Lake Huron for British presents. In fact, he identified the La Pointe band as "the *British* band." According to a letter written by Schoolcraft in August of 1832, "the British band of the Chippewas of La Pointe, Lake Superior have made their usual journey to Penetanguishine, during the present season."[25] Henry Schoolcraft was stationed at Sault Ste. Marie, Michigan Territory, and he used the label, "the British band" to identify the Ojibwe band residing across the Canadian border from his station, but in his August 1832 letter he was using it to identify the Ojibwe at La Pointe in the far western end of Lake Superior. By labeling them the *British* band we see the extent to which Schoolcraft felt the La Pointe people were still being influenced by the Crown.

Similarly, almost a dozen years later, Alfred Brunson, when at La Pointe in 1843, claimed that "among the Indians bordering on this lake there was a lingering attachment to the British, and presents had for many years been bestowed upon them to retain their friendship . . . which had the effect to draw hundreds of [them] annually to Drummond Island."[26]

Further evidence of British influence in the western Lake Superior region is seen in a letter from Wisconsin Territorial Governor James D. Doty of 19 May 1843, to Bureau of Indian Affairs Commissioner Crawford, in which he said La Pointe's Sub-agent Brunson asked for thirty-five American medals and flags to be exchanged for British medals and flags held by chiefs in Ojibwe bands affiliated with his agency.[27] Two months later, Robert Stuart as Acting Superintendent of Indian Affairs in Michigan said Brunson "asked for more [medals] than there were head chiefs in his whole subagency," and reduced the number to "12 flags & 6 or 8 medals (half large & half small)," while accusing Brunson of having "ideas of grandeur and large expenditures."[28]

By the summer of 1843, Robert Stuart was growing displeased with Alfred Brunson and may have been responding to his request in an unnecessarily negative manner, but the fact that *any* British medals and flags were still held by La Pointe band leaders in 1843 throws new light on the politics of the Ojibwe in those times. By this date leaders had repeatedly pledged loyalty to American officials and the notion that British medals and flags were still held by them suggests that the authenticity of these pledges should be suspect.

To conclude, recalling the interest Chequamegon Bay's Ojibwe had in the Shawnee Prophet only a few years previous to 1819, and given the remarks of observers like George Boyd, Henry Schoolcraft and Alfred Brunson, for the time period from 1819 to 1843, we can appreciate the lingering period of British influence at areas like Chequamegon Bay. In these years the British were still important to these western Ojibwe people since they offered an alternative to the increasing presence of, and pressure from, the Americans.

A related issue is how in telling of the long trips of western people to Fort Malden and Drummond Island, Lewis

Cass stressed the attraction of the British material goods. According to Cass, by dispensing presents at these sites, the British "appeal directly to the love of property, one of the strongest & most active passions which influence and guide the Indians."[29]

This is an interesting remark for a number of reasons. Early Euro-Americans were struck by the "nakedness" of the "savages" they encountered in North America—a characterization about the way of life of the natives—a way of life that showed their lack of the "truth" of the Christian religion, but also a way of life that evinced little need for a wealth of material possessions. Yet at the same time, these free, *non-materialistic*, "naked savages" supposedly clamored for the *material* property the British were giving them.[30] This contradiction in reasoning seems lost on writers like Lewis Cass. Like other early American writers, he condemned the tribal people for their communal orientations, a way of life that supposedly held little desire for private property. Yet, contradictorily, these writers also noted that a "love of property" was "one of the strongest & most active passions which influence and guide Indians." When it came to describing Indians, such illogical thinking was common in early American culture, and remains so today.[31]

Cass used this British influence along the eastern border of Michigan Territory to support his argument for the 1820 expedition to the Mississippi. He told Calhoun of his desire to visit the western tribes to admonish them not to make these trips and how the regional Indian agents should reinforce this message. Also, he used this British threat to argue for the establishment of a strong military force at the Mackinac post. Of great importance to Cass was the posture of the United States government being presented to the tribes. Again and again he spoke of his government in the eyes of the "savage." He insisted that all along its frontier America needed to strike a powerful and dignified pose, with an added emphasis on the latter. According to Cass there were enough persons of a less than dignified character on the frontier who, through their uncouth demeanor, harmed the image Indians held of Americans. Accordingly, Cass felt that dignity and power went hand in hand, and there was to be no doubt in the Indian mind about the new country's power and its willingness to use it.

This then, was the background for the 1820 Cass Expedition. To clinch his argument for Calhoun's approval of the trip, Cass listed six reasons for its undertaking: First, the United States needed to familiarize itself with the Indians of the western Lake Superior regions; second, to acquire land for military installations at Sault Ste. Marie, Prairie du Chien and Green Bay; third, to determine the extent and value of copper deposits at Ontonagon; fourth, to explore attitudes of tribes in the Chicago area on the possible move of the Iroquois Six Nations from New York to that region; fifth, to demand that western tribesmen stop making the eastward treks to Drummond Island and Fort Malden; sixth, to discern the amount of British trade being carried out in the western area.[32]

An additional purpose that Cass felt strongly about was both literal and symbolic. This was to carry the flag of the United States to this large territory and display it to tribal people. The importance of this was not to be underplayed. Lewis Cass wrote again and again of the need for the government of the United States to present a commanding posture to the tribes. The *savages* needed to learn to respect this new flag and its government and to understand that America's best intentions were to help them. Using the phraseology of the times, Indians were to stand "in awe" of the American government, as they became "subdued" in its presence. In the following paragraphs we will discuss the written accounts of the trip to determine what, if anything, they can show us about the Ojibwe people encountered along the way, particularly those in Chequamegon Bay.

## 2.

THE EXPEDITION WAS WELL-PLANNED and organized, due largely to the efforts of Lewis Cass himself. He was a determined national politician who had served as an officer in the early days of the War of 1812, to include leading a force of 300 men against a British unit that had entered American soil near Ft. Malden. Cass succeeded in driving the enemy back into Canada and received positive national notice for this action. This militaristic background fused with a deep patriotism helped make him a strong advocate of expansion into western lands.[33]

Cass was known for his interest in and knowledge of American Indians. Interestingly, it is claimed that he was respected and even admired by native people. This admiration, however, was not reciprocated. Apparently Cass made a distinction between a native person as an individual and the culture that individual carried. A biographer wrote that Cass did not hold "any admiration for Indian culture. In fact, he felt repugnance toward what he regarded as their low estate."[34] He was convinced he had the responsibility to have them accept his version of *civilization*.

Lewis Cass was a teetotaler and took a firm public stand against traders bringing liquor into native communities, but the record shows that in 1818, he authorized a government factor to dispense it to his clients in order to compete with a North West trader.[35] It is also significant that liquor was included in the inventory of goods taken on the 1820 trip, and that it was periodically given to Indian people along the way.[36]

Included as members of the expedition were Robert A. Forsyth (private secretary for Cass), Capt. David B. Douglas (cartographer and natural scientist), Charles C. Trowbridge and Alexander Chase (both assistants to Douglas), James D. Doty (journalist), Dr. Alexander Wolcott (physician), Henry R. Schoolcraft (mineralogist), Lt. Aeneas Mackey (artillery), a small group of soldiers under Lt. Mackey's command, and a group of Indians. The makeup of this expedition is interesting for what it shows of the times. Extensive mapping was to be done, and the presence of important natural resources noted. A written account of the trip was to be made, hence the need for a journalist, and for a show of military force the small detachment of soldiers was included. The inclusion of Indians presumably was to do the bulk of the paddling, to provide food by hunting and fishing, to serve as guides and possibly to ease the introduction of the party into native communities. An interpreter was the last member of the party. The papers of several of this group's members survive today, but it is the writing of Henry Schoolcraft that stands out. He kept a daily journal which today serves as the major account of the trip.[37]

## 3.

HENRY ROWE SCHOOLCRAFT IS ONE of the most important non-Ojibwe persons in early Ojibwe written history. He was a prolific writer and considered himself an authority on Ojibwe culture. However, we must remind ourselves that his literary efforts, like those of William Warren, were directed to the non-Ojibwe public, a public distant from Lake Superior country. Schoolcraft attempted to establish himself as a major figure in the then new literary community of the United States.

Among other things, he was a naturalist, an ethnologist, Indian agent, a writer and an explorer. His writings were readily published and through them he gained notoriety within the budding scientific community in the new country. One of his major works was the six volume series published from 1851 to 1857, entitled *Historical and Statistical Information Respecting the History, Condition and Prospects of the Indian Tribes of the United States*. Like most other Euro-American thinkers and writers of his time, he subscribed to the prevalent view that the continent's indigenous peoples were a separate race, one deficient in comparison to the Euro-Americans. He was particularly interested in the mind of the Indian, feeling it was locked into a darkness that could only be altered by "civilization."[38]

In 1825, Henry Schoolcraft married Jane Johnston, whose parents were Oshaguscodaywayquay (Woman of the Green Glade)—whose English name was Susan—and John Johnston, Sr.[39] Susan Johnston was the daughter of Waubojiig, the well-known military leader at La Pointe in the late eighteenth and early nineteenth centuries. John Johnston, Sr. was a fur trader who first resided at La Pointe but spent his later years at Sault Ste. Marie.

As was the case with many other traders and government personnel on the frontier, Schoolcraft's marriage to a woman who was a member of a prominent Ojibwe family served him well in his relationships with the Ojibwe. Mrs. Schoolcraft emerged as a dignified and popular member of the Sault Ste. Marie community. As a younger person she had been sent east for a formal education.

Even though Henry Schoolcraft was intimately related to the Ojibwe people, he did not applaud their way of life. An editor of his account of the 1820 expedition said of his narrative, "There is neither warmth nor appreciation in his handling of Indians as people."[40] Like other Europeans and Americans who came to Indian communities in that time, Schoolcraft was certain the Indians' culture was inferior. For example, like the Jesuits about one hundred and fifty years before him, he felt tribal people had no religion and that their entire culture was less than his. About their ability to comprehend what he claimed was real religion, he said, "The savage mind, habituated to sloth, is not easily roused into a state of moral activity, and is not at once capable of embracing and understanding the sublime truths and doctrines of the evangelical law."[41] When observing the *midewiwin's* complex initiation rite, he said, "the spectator finds a difficulty in restraining his laughter."[42] Such arrogance is at times difficult to struggle through today, but if we stay with his narrative we come to understand the seriousness of the situation the Ojibwe faced and the accommodations they eventually had to make in the world of the early nineteenth century in Lake Superior country. The Americans were coming to stay, and from that time forward the Ojibwe people were forced to accommodate them.

Men like Henry Schoolcraft, while being products of their own culture and bound by its biases, were, however, also able to show self-criticism, but even this is troublesome. About his opinions of the worth of tribal culture Schoolcraft said, "Much allowance, however, is to be made on account of our ignorance of their language,—on account of bad interpretation, and the unfavorable sentiments we may entertain from early prejudices, or from other causes, which are apt to influence our opinions and views." He was, like several other members of the 1820 expedition, a trained scientist, and therefore, sensitive to the need for objectivity in his observations and recordings. When we remember this, his conclusions about Indian people and their way of life become even more troublesome because he saw himself as a highly educated person and hence to him, his pronouncements about Ojibwe culture *had* to have merit. Surely for Schoolcraft and others, they were logical conclusions arrived at through objective analysis, and as such were supported by solid factual evidence. Thus, writers like Henry Schoolcraft knew they wrote the truth about Indians.[43]

Expedition members were assembled at Detroit and embarked on 24 May 1820. They moved up to Lake Superior, then west to Sandy Lake where some members paddled up to Leech Lake and searched for the headwaters of the Mississippi River before rejoining the others back at Sandy Lake for the trip down to St. Peters. From St. Peters it was down to Prairie du Chien, where Schoolcraft, with eight *voyageurs*, paddled south to Dubuque to examine its lead mines, before coming back to rejoin the group for the long trip to Green Bay. Then it was down Lake Michigan to Chicago and back up to Mackinac before paddling to Detroit. The expedition arrived at Detroit on 23 September 1820, after traveling approximately four thousand miles in one hundred and twenty-two days.

Our purpose is not to discuss the entire expedition but only to note its references to Ojibwe life in western Lake Superior and to draw out any importance the trip may have had in that region's future. With this in mind, we begin by examining the journal of Henry Schoolcraft.

## 4.

OSTENSIBLY THE EXPEDITION CAME to learn about the native communities but we immediately note that most of his narrative concerns the natural world. However, upon leaving Detroit, native people are almost regularly encountered. These are usually mentioned with minimal commentary, and we yearn for more, but there is enough to show a definite native presence in the land. Between Detroit and Mackinac the party meets several groups of Indians and we see how in most incidents stops were made for the common inquiries about weather, upstream travel conditions and the like. Schoolcraft claims that in virtually all cases the natives asked for whiskey and that this quickly became burdensome. Accordingly, he said, "We have generally found it the *first* thing and the *last* thing enquired for."[44]

The ritual bracketing of these requests hints at the ceremonial aspects of similar encounters between natives and government officials that Richard White speaks to in his discussion of the middle ground, considered in a previous chapter. If we interpret these encounters in the context of the middle ground, then we could understand them as a requirement of proper frontier protocol. This is what we find in the writing of James Doty where he said, "We were . . . hailed as very dear and pleasant friends by every band we met, and invariably their speeches commenced with a statement to their good Father who they had long expected to see, of their extreme distress for a little *tobacco* and a little of his generous *milk*, and concluded with a most earnest prayer that the tobacco and liquor might not be refused them."[45]

Schoolcraft noted that such requests were common in the early days of the trip, but as the expedition made its way westward this changed. Later, in retrospect, he said that the Lake Superior communities and those at the head of the Mississippi were different. He claimed, "we found them far less eager for whiskey than the more contiguous tribes [those closer to Detroit], and . . . cases were presented, in which it was not relished."[46]

We yearn to learn the reasons behind this different attitude toward liquor. These communities distant from Mackinac and Detroit surely were familiar with the drug, and recalling the remarks of Francois Malhoit, George Nelson and other western lakes traders, at least for regions south of Lake Superior, there was no lack of desire for it fifteen or twenty years before the expedition's visit. Perhaps this reticence to accept alcohol in 1820 signals the lingering determination of these Ojibwe communities to respect the teachings of the Shawnee religion they accepted during the time of the War of 1812. If this was the case, then despite how warmly the expedition's journalists say the people greeted them, they may still have recognized their relationship with the British—their annual trips to Drummond Island would have reinforced this feeling—and we might suspect that the greetings the expedition encountered may have been more superficial than genuine.

The expedition arrived at Mackinac Island on 12 June, and we are treated to more lengthy accounts of native people at this site. According to Schoolcraft:

> Since our arrival here, there has been a great number of Indians of the Chippeway and Ottaway tribes, encamped near the town. The beach of the lake has been constantly lined with Indian huts and bark canoes. The savages are generally well dressed, in their own costume, and exhibit physiognomies with more regularity of features and beauty of expression, than is common to find among them . . . This is probably attributable to a greater intermixture of blood in this vicinity. These savages resort to the island for the purposes of exchanging their furs, for blankets, knives, and other articles. Their visits are periodical, being generally made after their spring and fall hunts, and their stay is short. Some of the tribes also bring in for sale, several articles of Indian manufacture, particularly a kind of rush mat of a very handsome fabric, bark baskets filled with maple sugar, called *moke-ocks*, with quilled moccasins, shot pouches, and other fancy goods of Indian fabric, which are generally in demand as articles of curiosity.[47]

Here is witness to the continuation of significant aspects of Ojibwe culture nearly two hundred years after the advent of the fur trade. We see that the age-old Ojibwe technology for manufacturing material objects necessary for their foraging life was still solidly in place. Such technological persistence is noteworthy, especially when we have been told that by 1820, the peoples' dependence upon European and American trade goods was supposed to have been severe. And it is interesting some of the objects brought to Mackinac were sought after as *curios* by the outside world at this early date. Perhaps this was a foreshadowing of the era of the "Indian Trading Post" that was to come to Ojibwe country much later, with the advent of the American tourist.

At Sault Ste. Marie, Schoolcraft found about forty lodges which he speculated held 200 individuals—Ojibwe residents of the general Sault region. He described the way they took whitefish from the rapids and stressed the harvest's importance to the diets of these Ojibwe. We are also told of strong British sentiment that surfaced in a meeting between Cass and particular Ojibwe leaders, followed by the well-known incident wherein the British flag was hoisted before an Ojibwe lodge, and the expedition members were threatened with physical violence. Schoolcraft tells how Cass immediately came forward, boldly pulled down the banner and in the process reiterated his show of the United States' sovereign right in the region.

This incident has been understood differently by different writers, but perhaps it has been conventional to describe it as a matter of local Ojibwe leaders acting out the wishes of British officials, traders and others who hoped to keep the eastern region of Lake Superior open to their commercial interests. In other words, it has been interpreted as an incident showing how in areas near the Canadian border the British were able to have their political interests readily taken up by self-interested local Ojibwe leaders.

Recently, the Canadian writer Janet Chute feels "This view depicts the Native people merely as extensions of British military commercial policy along the northern frontier," and focusing on the melding of spiritual and political power, she feels a more detailed analysis of the incident suggests it shows how in 1820, the major Ojibwe actors were enmeshed in a dynamic of relationships involving the use of traditional Ojibwe spiritual power, not for self aggrandizement, but for the benefit of the entire community.[48]

We recall that one of the reasons for the expedition was to secure a cession of land at Sault St. Marie for a site for what was to become Fort Brady. In his written account of the incident, Henry Schoolcraft claims that in a council soon after the expedition's arrival, Lewis Cass told the resident Ojibwe leaders their right to the land had been relinquished to the French decades ago, and following the Treaty of Greenville signed in 1795, it now, rightfully, was in the hands of the Americans. Upon hearing this, Sassaba, a Crane chief, grew upset and drove a lance into the earth at his feet before angrily striding off to his nearby lodge where he raised the British colors and called for a force of fighting men to attack Cass and his group.

According to Schoolcraft, in an attempt to diffuse the matter, other Ojibwe leaders went to the home of John Johnston, the powerful trader at The Sault, where in her husband's absence, Mrs. Susan Johnston took decisive action and was able to quiet the incident. She did this by having her son George call another council of the chiefs in which he commanded them to intercede with Sassaba. These leaders chose another Ojibwe leader, Shingwaukonse, (Little Pine), as the person to confront Sassaba and demand he not attack the Americans. This was accomplished and a treaty was signed wherein the Americans received sixteen square miles as a site for their new fort, and the Ojibwe received a perpetual use-right to harvest fish from the nearby rapids.

Janet Chute feels from the Ojibwe view, a key to this incident concerned the differences between Sassaba and Shingwaukonse. Both men were war leaders, but Sassaba was young and not yet at the point in his life where he was experienced enough to adequately handle matters of power for the benefit of the entire band. His demand that the Sault Ste. Marie Ojibwe's join him in driving out the Americans was not accepted by the band, but Shingwaukonse, who was older, a war leader, and had the experience to use spiritual power correctly, was accepted by the people, and therefore able to provide the leadership needed to defuse the threatening confrontation.[49]

In a recent publication, Anton Treuer, the Minnesota Ojibwe writer, offers another interpretation of this 1820 Sault St. Marie incident. According to Treuer, one reason the Cass Expedition came to The Sault when they did was "to intercept a British trade shipment to the Ojibwe." Along with these trade goods was a quantity of "annuities" (presents) the British annually dispensed to those Ojibwe bands that allied with Britain in the War of 1812. Lewis Cass claimed between two and three thousand people were encamped at The Sault, waiting for the arrival of these goods, and that a British flag flew over their lodges. Seeing this, "Cass stormed into the camp, tore down and trampled the British flag, hoisted the American flag, and demanded that Indians loyal to the United States step up and help him defend the Stars and Stripes."[50]

A contingent of Ojibwe from Sandy Lake, Minnesota Territory, apparently made up of persons who had *not* sided with Britain during the recent war, but did not prefer to trade with the Americans over the British, were present. They had come to the Sault to trade with the British, but were aware of the growing serious presence of Americans in the region of their immediate homeland (the upper Mississippi headwaters area) and saw an opportunity. Treuer tells how the Sandy Lake men rushed to aid Cass, creating a standoff that soon dissipated the uncomfortable scene. Quick not to lose an opportunity, Lewis Cass had goods from his expedition's stores distributed to these Sandy Lake Ojibwe as a token of his gratitude and friendship.[51]

Of related interest is that some writers claim a young Ojibwe leader from Sandy Lake may have been in this party of western Ojibwe people who paddled to Sault Ste. Marie to meet the British. Years after 1820, Bagone-giizhig the Elder (Hole-in-the-Day), who was a young warrior at the time of the Sault incident and went on to become a very prominent Minnesota Ojibwe leader, is said to have held a chief's medal and an American flag given out by Lewis Cass that day of the confrontation in Sault Ste. Marie.

LEAVING THE SAULT, THE EXPEDITION encountered a Fond du Lac trader on his annual trip to bring in the season's furs, and further along Schoolcraft said, "we met eighteen or twenty canoes of Chippeway Indians on their way to the Sault Ste. Marie and Michilimackinac." By these remarks we see that the eastern end of Lake Superior was still the important economic center for the western communities that it had been for over two centuries.[52]

Then, moving along the south shore the expedition arrived at Grand Island, where an Ojibwe community was visited. Schoolcraft said, "We found these Indians very poor, both as to clothing and provisions, but were struck with their manly figure and beautiful proportions." The Grand Island people told the familiar story of how their band had been accused of not taking an active part in the long-running conflict with the Dakota and how a few years before 1820, a party of thirteen warriors traveled far to the west to engage the Dakota and remove the stigma of this accusation. Twelve of them were killed, and Schoolcraft claimed the sole survivor of the war party was in the village during the expedition's visit. Schoolcraft said, "He was a tall and beautiful youth, with a manly countenance, expressive eyes, and formed with the most perfect symmetry,—and among all the tribes of Indians I have visited, I never felt, for any individual, such a mingled feeling of interest and admiration."[53]

At Ontonagon, the question of copper deposits was explored and in the process the party came upon several Ojibwe people at a fish weir where sturgeon were being taken. Then, later, along the river a live black bear was found in a deadfall trap and the killing of this animal was witnessed. Of this event Schoolcraft wrote, "By the joy which was evident upon the countenances of the savages upon this occasion, it is a rare occurrence among them to kill a bear. But perhaps this animal is never killed without exultation, as it is universally considered the noblest object of the chase."[54]

By the second of July, the expedition reached Chaquamegon Bay. Unfortunately, comparatively little is written by any of the group's members about the stay here. There is no mention of Buffalo or other leaders being in the bay. Bad River was noted but the party did not pause to venture up the river. A stop was made on Madeline Island, where it was learned that Michel Cadotte, the resident trader, was away on a trip to Mackinac. According to Schoolcraft:

> Six miles beyond the Mauvais [Bad River], is point Che-goi-me-gon once the grand rendezvous of he Chippeway Tribe, but now reduced to a few lodges. Three miles further west is the island of St. Michael which lies in the traverse across Chegoimegon Bay, where M. Cadotte has an establishment. This was formerly an important trading post but is now dwindling to nothing. There is a dwelling of logs, stockaded in the usual manner of trading houses, besides several out buildings, and some land in cultivation. We here also found several cows and horses, which have been transported with great labor. On this island two pieces of native copper were found some years ago, one of which was a foot long, and

> weighed twenty-eight pounds. It is also stated that a silver mine exists on the mainshore southwest of the island, but during the short time of our stay, we could procure no satisfactory information on the subject. The Indians appear very jealous of every attempt to explore the mineralogy of their territories, and are loth to communicate any information that would lead to a discovery.[55]

The party did not stay long on Madeline but continued on its journey to a mainland beach Schoolcraft said was seven miles to the west. He does not speak to what occurred on that campsite, but his next two entries tell of sites important to today's Red Cliff, so both are given below. Schoolcraft said:

> We had rain during the night and it continued until six o'clock in the morning, when we embarked, and proceeded northwest eight miles to Raspberry River,—then southwest six miles to Sandy river, where a head wind and an approaching storm compelled us to land. Before we could unload our canoes, or pitch a tent, rain commenced and it continued down in torrents for an hour or more, during which there was no alternative but to stand patiently upon the said. If we had lain at the bottom of the lake, we could not have been more completely drenched. When the rain ceased, the wind arose from the southwest, and confined us to that spot during the remainder of the day.

On the fourth of July he wrote:

> We passed the forty-fifth Anniversary of American Independence until two o'clock, at the mouth of Sandy River. The wind continued to blow unfavorably a great part of the day. In the afternoon it changed so that we were able to put out, although the lake was still agitated: on going three miles we turned a prominent point of land called De Tour, which lies at the foot of the great Fond du Lac, or, West Bay. Here we changed our course from N. W. to S.S.W. and continued it with little variation, to the mouth of Cranberry River, where we encamped at eight o'clock, having progressed thirty-three miles. The evening was clear and calm and twilight was observable all night.[56]

Schoolcraft then goes on to describe the paddle to the Brule River and on to Fond du Lac on the St. Louis River, where the expedition began its trip to Sandy Lake. In the days after leaving the Cranberry River Schoolcraft mentions Ojibwe met along the way. The process of harvesting wild rice is briefly described and other aspects of the peoples' life receive some commentary. Since these remarks pertain to areas beyond Chequamegon Bay we will not present them. Instead, we will review the comments about the Ojibwe that appear in the narratives of other members of the expedition.

## 5.

David Bates Douglas never published his narrative of the trip. His writings offer many more observations of native people than Schoolcraft's, and generally, they are much more detailed. Most importantly, they carry a degree of acceptance and understanding that is lacking in Schoolcraft's. Douglas was a captain in the United States Army, an engineer, a mathematician, a topographer and natural scientist. In these ways he came from a world not completely dissimilar from Henry Schoolcraft's, but unlike him, Douglas does not judge the Indian. In 1953, Mentor L. Williams compared the Douglas journal to those of other expedition members. Accordingly, he said, "it has a liveliness the others do not possess. He should have been the one to take up the study of Indians and their lore; he should have presented the public with his memoir. It would have been most readable."[57]

We will encounter other writers like Douglas in the early years of Red Cliff's history, and we might wish they had written more and published what they wrote. As we have noted in preceding chapters, the literature speaking to Chequamegon Bay and its Ojibwe residents in the seventeenth and eighteenth centuries is a literature of bias. However, in the early decades of the nineteenth, with the journal of David Douglas we begin to hear a more accepting voice.

On the third day of the trip, Douglas, like Schoolcraft, entered the names of the expedition members in his journal, with one major difference. While Schoolcraft noted that there were ten Indians "of the Ottaway and Shawanee tribes"[58], Douglas listed the names of these men and gave their tribal identities as Shawnee, Potawatomi, Ojibwe and Odawa. His willingness to not only be more specific about their tribal identities, but to actually offer their names, tells something about his approach to these people that is lacking in Schoolcraft's.

On 9 June at Mackinac, Douglas reports having dinner with Robert Stuart, the resident official employed by John Jacob Astor's South West Company. At Sault Ste. Marie, he records the British flag incident, and also shares considerable details of a *midewiwin* initiation ceremony some members of the expedition witnessed. Several more sightings of Indian people west of the Sault are mentioned, and at Ontonagon he gives us a lengthy account of pipe and buffalo dances. Unfortunately, his journal entries skip from the Montreal River to the St. Louis, so we are told nothing of Chequamegon Bay and Madeline Island, nor are we given any reason for the absence of these entries. However, later in his journal Douglas gives detailed accounts of Ojibwe at other villages. For example, at the portages along the St. Louis River from Fond du Lac to Sandy Lake he tells how Ojibwe men and women who were hired at a village just south of the mouth of the Brule River worked to transport the expedition's baggage and how they took great pride in doing the heavy labor.[59]

The journalist, James D. Doty, included several remarks about native people met along the way. Interestingly, while Cass and a few others paddled up to Leech Lake to attempt to discover the source of the Mississippi River, he stayed at Sandy Lake and gathered information about Ojibwe subsistence practices, inter-village communications and trade. At the completion of the trip he composed a lengthy letter to Lewis Cass in which he relayed this information. Unfortunately for our purposes this unusual letter speaks to communities at Fond du Lac, Sandy Lake and Leech Lake, but not specifically of La Pointe.

As is the case with Schoolcraft's and Douglas's, Doty's journal speaks fleetingly of Madeline Island and the campsites at Raspberry and Sandy River. However, he does say "several Indians" on Madeline spoke of copper found in the region, and that they mentioned an Englishman—probably Alexander Henry—who was there some sixty years earlier. Upon leaving Sandy Lake the expedition visited the Ojibwe community at Rice Lake, several miles to the south. These Ojibwe, he said, annually made a trip to Drummond Island to receive presents from the British. This suggests that surely the La Pointe Ojibwe made such trips as well.

Charles Trowbridge, the last writer to record a journal of the expedition, wrote sparingly of the natives, but he did note the party's coming to Chequamegon Bay. Mistakenly, he said that Michel Cadotte's trading post was on Oak Island, not Madeline, and that although Cadotte was absent, "the Indians however were very pleased to see us, particularly our old pilot Monsieur Roi, whom they knew; they fell on his neck and wept for joy." Then, he went on, "After distributing a little tobacco among our Indian friends we proceeded on about 5 miles and landed, having made 39 miles."[60]

6.

WHAT DOES THE LEWIS CASS EXPEDITION of 1820 tell us about the Ojibwe, and especially about those at La Pointe? We recall that one of the reasons Cass undertook the trip was to gain knowledge about the region's resident tribes, and accordingly, even though the greatest amount of information recorded was about the natural habitat, to some extent this goal was achieved. This information is framed in the perspective Americans used in 1820, that is, the tribesmen were considered to be *savages*, and as such, were felt to be on the first evolutionary level of human existence. The notion of *culture* as defined in an earlier chapter would not be developed and generally accepted until after 1870, so the expedition writers did not have this tool to use in their observation and interpretation of native life. To Cass, Schoolcraft, and the others—with the possible exception of David Douglas—the natives' way of living was not simply rudimentary, but was felt destined to evolve into a "higher" level of human existence.

What we see from the various journals is that in 1820, the Ojibwe people of Lake Superior were living in a world driven by the changing seasons and overseen by the *manidoog*. They had been trapping and trading furs for over 175 years, and yet their culture was essentially unchanged from before the advent of the fur trade. Their world was a place of forest, stream, lake and sky, and for the residents of Chequamegon Bay, Gichigami—the Big Lake, was the centerpiece. Today many Ojibwe still live in a *manido* world, but it is a world far changed from the one Lewis Cass, Henry Schoolcraft and their companions visited.

The expedition occurred in summer and accordingly, its written accounts tell that the Ojibwe people were present from Detroit to the far western reaches of Sandy and Leech Lakes and were busy with activities required at that time of year. Fishing was going on, and trips to trading posts were being made. Ojibwe gardens were not mentioned although we can assume some were encountered. Summer ceremonies were underway, including the important *midewiwin* initiation rites.

The sparseness of information from Chequamegon Bay is unfortunate, but enough is given to tell that the Ojibwe were there. A few lodges were seen on Chequamegon Point, Ojibwe people were met on Madeline Island, and the American Fur Company's post is mentioned. We are told nothing of whether or not an actual village was evident on Madeline, and no tribal leaders are mentioned. Summer was a busy time for Ojibwe people in the early 1800s, and for most it demanded traveling. Furthermore, the expedition's officials were products of *their* culture, and as such would have been oriented toward *its* physical manifestations, not those of a hunting and gathering adaptation as the Ojibwe had at the time. If a collection of empty, or near-empty, wigwams were evident they may not have felt it was significant.

The expedition passed through a land occupied by tribal people who were at work in their traditional ways and, we might assume, who intended to continue enjoying their way of life. Lewis Cass and his group came to gather information needed to carry out a plan to destroy this existence and replace it with their own. We should expect that if this underlying motive for the trip had been known, Cass and his companions would not have been welcomed in the friendly way they were. If we can imagine the expedition's canoes moving along, stopping to visit at Ojibwe villages—and at other sites for its members to take topographic measurements, to collect mineral and plant specimens, and so forth—we might envision a far-less amiable meeting of the Ojibwe and Euro-American worlds than seems to have taken place.

## *Ojibwe Culture and the Historical Context of the Cass Expedition*

1.

UNTIL RECENT YEARS, THE WRITTEN HISTORY of the western Lake Superior region has essentially been a history of how Europeans, and after 1776, Americans, entered the land and exploited it. With little exception the resident Ojibwe communities were portrayed as impediments that eventually would give way. The literature on the fur trade necessarily includes the Ojibwe people, but with the end of this trade their role in this written history is greatly diminished. The reader who is sensitive to an ongoing Ojibwe presence in this vast region from the time of its earliest recording discovers that at approximately 1840, with the end of the fur trade, a *narrative shift* occurs wherein the Ojibwe communities slip into the distant background, or even worse, disappear. It is a history written first by the European, then by the American, (and north of Lake Superior, the Canadian). This is the history that has been taught in the region's schools from their beginning in the mid-nineteenth century, and to a great extent continues to be taught today.[61]

At the time of the Cass Expedition, this written history presents the resident native people as anachronisms, that is, as persons whose time has passed. In these early decades of the nineteenth century we find the start of a paper trail that increasingly ignores the Ojibwe as it moves along, telling of the *reduction* of the land. Soon after 1820, the historical events of this vast region begin relating the story of the failing fur trade and the coming of the *settlers* with their farms, villages, railroads and more. By the 1830s and 1840s, the Ojibwe start being portrayed as poverty-stricken onlookers, if they are portrayed at all. This image goes on to be the prevailing image for the next century or more.

When Cass, Schoolcraft and the others came to Chequamegon Bay, the fur trade was still a major part of the Ojibwe economy, and John Jacob Astor's American Fur Company had by that time taken over most of the trading areas south and west of Lake Superior. According to the historian, it was at this time that the American Fur Company began "to dominate the fur trade and, consequently, the native peoples of the upper lakes and upper Mississippi region."[62] This notion of *domination* of Ojibwe people rises repeatedly in fur trade literature. Apparently their supposed dependency upon European trade goods led to an outright domination of their lives by the Euro-American business world. In above paragraphs we have raised the question of the appropriateness of this assertion, and will speak to it later.

The American Fur Company divided Ojibwe country into "outfits" based upon band territories. Each outfit had a resident trader who exchanged his furs for goods at Mackinac in summer, and the northern outfit was headquartered a La Pointe, where Michel Cadotte was the trader. Cadotte had sub-outfits at Lac du Flambeau, Lac Court Oreilles and St. Croix. Nearby outfits were headquartered at Grand Portage, Fond du Lac, and Keweenaw. Over time, the resident traders at these large stations acquired considerable influence in Ojibwe communities.[63]

John Jacob Astor was an astute and aggressive businessperson who yielded considerable influence with governmental leaders. In 1816, he benefited from federal legislation prohibiting unlicensed traders to enter the business, and in 1822, he benefited again when Congress abolished the federal factory system. These acts left practically no competition for his traders. The factory system had been strengthened back in 1806, when the office for the Superintendent of Indian trade was established, and ten years later, with the appointment of Thomas L. McKenney to that position, it gained a strong and vocal supporter.

Lewis Cass was a powerful opponent of the factory system, arguing that it demeaned the status of the American government in the eyes of the Indian. In typical fashion, Cass worked to convince government leaders that when engaging in mercantile exchange on the frontier, the dignity of the United States was compromised. He insisted that when the government needs to come in contact with Indians such engagement must always occur within a proper setting, one that evinces the lofty bearing officials of the United States needed to present to the "savages."[64]

Thomas L. McKenney spoke eloquently about the importance of the factory system as a civilizing agent, and worked to have it assume a major role in federal Indian policy, but Congress disagreed and voted to privatize the Indian trade, a vote Astor worked hard for. The discussion over the factory system is recorded in the literature but we hear nothing from the native voice in this debate. Surely there was a discussion extant in the Ojibwe community regarding the merits and demerits of private versus government traders. Discussions about status, demeanor, official bearing, and so forth occur in these communities today and we should assume they did so in the early nineteenth century as well, but today we can only imagine what they were.

In 1818, Chequamegon Bay saw the arrival of two young easterners who would go on to play a major role in the area's history for the next several decades. Truman and Lyman Warren were brothers who came from Massachusetts to make their fortune in the still lucrative fur trade and they soon settled in as private traders in the rich lands south of Lake Superior.[65] They are said to have related well to the Ojibwe people and in return garnered a considerable portion of the trade. They took their furs to British buyers north of the border for the higher prices offered there and in time emerged as such serious competitors to Michel Cadotte and his American Fur Company that he hired them to work for him. This became more than a business relationship when, in 1821, they married two of Cadotte's daughters. Truman married sixteen-year-old Charlotte, and Lyman married twenty-one-year-old Marie. Three years later the brothers bought out their father-in-law's interest in the American Fur Company and in 1824, it appears Lyman became the chief factor at La Pointe, a position he filled until 1838. Truman Warren met an early death when he succumbed to pneumonia in 1825, but Lyman went on to trade for some time.[66]

2.

IT WAS DURING THE DECADE OF THE 1820S that the American Fur Company's northern outfit at La Pointe absorbed the outfits at Grand Portage, Keweenaw, and Fond du Lac. Initially it was Michel Cadotte who assumed leadership over this large region, but this responsibility soon passed to his son-in-law, Lyman Warren. When these outlying trading centers were merged into the post at La Pointe, Madeline Island regained some of the commercial importance it held in earlier times before Grand Portage rose to prominence.

Sometime after the War of 1812, the frequency of military skirmishes between Ojibwe from the immediate western Lake Superior regions and the Dakota began to diminish. In these years the Ojibwe community at Leech Lake assumed the role of the vanguard against the Dakota. By the early 1830s, La Pointe's leaders used runners to garner information about military activities far to the west, and we might conclude that its warriors were still occasionally involved in these skirmishes, but such conflicts seem to have been few.[67] Accordingly, in these times as the Ojibwe political organization demanded, it was Buffalo, a *civil* chief, who became the leading political figure at La Pointe. He would hold this responsibility for the next twenty or so years.

After the Treaty of Ghent, officials of the United States were anxious to defuse this hostility between the Dakota and Ojibwe in order that the country could more easily extend its borders westward. To bring peace to these western lands they arranged for a gathering of tribal leaders at Prairie du Chien in 1825. Warfare between the Dakota and Ojibwe, as we have seen in earlier chapters, was something that sporadically occurred throughout the previous two hundred years, and was a theme historians of the Great Lakes have stressed. What these writers have not always made clear is that by the early nineteenth century, the persistence of conflicts between the Ojibwe and Dakota was a detriment to the movement of Americans into the western lakes region, and hence, the United States hoped to end this warfare so it could eventually treat with the tribes for this land.[68] With this as an ultimate motive, numerous American officials soon entered into a series of treaty meetings with the western Ojibwe and their neighbors.

*Notes*

1. Borneman 2004:267.
2. Hickey 1989:291.
3. Hickey 1989:296.
4. Borneman 2004:267.
5. Parker 1998[1952].
6. Prucha 1997[1994]:35.
7. Trask 2007:125.
8. The notion that North America was a vast land, devoid of a meaningful human presence when Europeans first arrived lingers on today. For example, during his campaigns for the presidency, Ronald Reagan twice stated he thought there was a divine plan that the early Europeans were to come to North America and "develop this empty continent."
9. Stephanson 1995.
10. Williams 1992[1990].
11. Danziger 1979: 68.
12. Danziger 1979:68.
13. Mason 1993:xiv.
14. Jenkens 2004:30-1; Mason 1993: xi.
15. Schoolcraft 1992[1953]:277.
16. Schoolcraft 1992[1953]:283.
17. Williams, in Schoolcraft:1992[1953]:278.
18. Jenkens 2004:37-8.
19. Puthoff 1817 in WisHistColl, Vol. XIX, p. 472.
20. Baraga letter of 8 March 1832, to sister, Amalia Gressel. In Baraga Bulletin,Bol. 59, No. 1, Spring 2007, pp.5-7. (Quarterly publication of the Bishop Baraga Association, Marquette, Michigan.)
21. Schoolcraft 1992[1953]:292.
22. Schoolcraft 1992[1953]:290.
23. Boyd 1838, in WisTerrPap, Vol. 27, p. 1025.
24. Schoolcraft 1975[1851]:103.
25. Schoolcraft 1832:149, italics added, in Mason 1993[1958].
26. Brunson 1879:192, brackets added.
27. Doty 1843: 542-3, in WisTerrPap, Vol. 28.
28. Stuart 1843:561-2, in WisTerrPap, Vol, 28, brackets added.
29. Cass 1819:293, in Schoolcraft 1992[1953].
30. Williams 1990:1239.
31. Berkhofer 1979.
32. Cass 1819: 302-305, in Schoolcraft 1992[1953].
33. Dunbar 1970:16; McLaughlin:1980[1899]:53-87.
34. Dunbar 1970: 25.
35. Schoolcraft 1992[1953]:320.
36. Schoolcraft 1992[1953]:421.
37. Schoolcraft 1992[1953].
38. Bellin 2008.
39. Soetebier 2000: 1-6. (The spelling of Susan Johnston's Ojibwe name used here is what was used in the Soetebier biography.)
40. Williams 1992[1953]:23.
41. Schoolcraft 1992[1953]:70.
42. Schoolcraft 1992[1953]:69.
43. Schoolcraft 1992[1953]:69.
44. Schoolcraft 1992[1953]:74, italics added.
45. Doty 1820, in Schoolcraft 1992[1953]:448.
46. Schoolcraft 1992[1953]:75.
47. Schoolcraft 1992[1953]:87-8.
48. Chute 1998:31, 34.
49. Chute 1998:34.
50. Treuer 2011:39.
51. Treuer 2011:39-40.
52. Schoolcraft 1992[1953]:103.
53. Schoolcraft 1992[1953]:110; Graham 1995.
54. Schoolcraft 1992[1953]:127.
55. Schoolcraft 1992[1953]:133.
56. Schoolcraft 1992[1953]:134.
57. Williams 1953, in Schoolcraft 1992[1953]:364.
58. Schoolcraft 1992[1953]:61.
59. Douglas 1820, in Schoolcraft 1992[1953]:375-6.
60. Trowbridge 1820, in Schoolcraft 1992[1953]:478.
61. Schenck 2007:xv.
62. Danziger 1979: 68.
63. Danziger 1979:68-9.
64. Ross 1960:73.
65. Ross 1960:73.
66. Ross 1960:73-4. Hamilton Ross says Truman Warren died in 1835, but that is incorrect.
67. Schoolcraft 1993[1958]:117-8.
68. Cleland 2000:18-9, in McClurken, *et al*, 2000.

# 13

# The 1825, 1826, and 1827 Treaties and the Arrival of Protestant Missionaries

### *The 1825 Prairie du Chien Treaty*

1.

During the summer of 1825, a few thousand people gathered at the site on the Mississippi River known as Prairie du Chien, in the far southwestern corner of what would become the state of Wisconsin. This meeting was initiated by representatives of the United States with the intent of establishing boundaries between regional tribal peoples, and hopefully to bring peaceful relationships between all. Moreover, it was an official initiative signaling the desire of the United States government to begin a concerted effort to claim lands in the western Great Lakes, and to stabilize the boundary between the United States and Canada in that region. William Clark, of the Lewis and Clark Expedition, and Lewis Cass officiated for the Americans, and leaders from the Dakota, Ojibwe, Sac and Fox, Menominee, Iowa, Ho-Chunk, Odawa and Potawattomie nations represented their respective communities.

This was a major gathering and foreshadowed the many treaty meetings that would soon come to the region's tribal peoples. As occurred at these political sessions, a strict protocol for issuing formal greetings and farewells was followed with the arrival and departure of each attending delegation, and these ceremonial events were colorful and lengthy with their required pomp. An actual meeting ground was set up and consecrated where the requisite ceremonies were carried out. Eyewitness accounts tell of pipe offerings, drumming, singing, dancing, formal orations, intertribal games, lively orations, and the other usual ritual activities held at such large and important events. The Americans slaughtered upwards of 100 head of cattle, and along with this beef, quantities of pork, flour and other foods, as well as several barrels of whiskey were provided.

The first Ojibwe signature on the treaty is that of "Shinguaba W'ossin" (Spirit, or Image Stone) identified as the leading chief of the Ojibwe from Sault Ste. Marie. The second Ojibwe signature is "Gitspee Jiauba, 2nd Chief, [Lake Superior]," and the third is "Gitspee Waskee, le boeuf of la pointe lak Superior," which obviously is referring to La Pointe's Buffalo.[1] All signers agreed to respect the call for peace between the tribes, to refrain from hunting on another's territory without permission, and to accept the overall control of the United States Government. In particular, the Dakota and Ojibwe pledged to honor the demarcation line to be surveyed and set up between their territories. Since the northern Ojibwe bands resided a great distance from Prairie du Chien, and few of their members were present, northern Ojibwe leaders asked for a second meeting during the following year on Lake Superior, where the agreements in the 1825 treaty would be explained to them.[2]

While the literature holds ample details of the proceedings of this early treaty gathering, it tells relatively little pertaining to the La Pointe members in attendance, and particularly about Buffalo, or "le boeuf." This is unfortunate, but since Shinguaba W'ossin of Sault Ste. Marie was the first Ojibwe leader to sign the treaty, he was deemed the most prominent Ojibwe leader present. Today, with the historical importance of La Pointe's Chief Buffalo, usually expressed in the regional literature, we might wonder about the personal relationship between these two Lake Superior Ojibwe leaders. Shinguaba W'ossin was decidedly the senior Ojibwe political leader in the Lake Superior Ojibwe communities in 1825, and since La Pointe's Buffalo would probably only have been in his sixties at the time, he would have deferred to the more senior leader. Doubtless they knew each other, but the literature discloses virtually nothing about this important relationship.

Today we might ask why this treaty was necessary, and what effect the reality of rigid geographic boundaries might have had for the tribes involved. Until 1825, the geographic boundaries between these communities surely was recognized by the tribal people, but the nature of these demarcations seemingly had an amorphous—or fluid, i.e., *changing*—character. The social and cultural effect of this change imposed by the Americans could have been significant, and perhaps we can see it as the very early advent in the western Great Lakes of what we now understand as "property lines"—an ownership concept that, in 1825, must have been novel to the tribal people involved, but a notion that would become more and more significant with passing time.

More importantly, perhaps, is the treaty article in which the tribal leaders agreed to accept the overall control of the Government of the United States. By 1825, the American's concern about British "meddling" with tribal peoples located below the Canadian border was not nearly what it had been a decade earlier, so today we might wonder about the implied ramifications of this agreement, and whether or not the tribal leaders who put their mark to this treaty understood what was involved. In the important years preceding 1825, they had made many formal intra-tribal alliances, and also with the earlier Europeans, but these were not agreements that recognized a political dependency on the part of the tribes. (Chief Justice John Marshall's famous 1832 decision about *domestic dependent nations* and the matter of tribal sovereignty would become very important in Ojibwe Country, but in 1825, that would have to wait for a few more years.)

In 1825, the large and formal gathering of several of the region's tribal leaders and American officials at Prairie du Chien was a foreshadowing of what was to come for the tribal people. The new government of America was on the move, and this treaty gathering was only the beginning of many future meetings between American officials and tribal leaders.

### *The 1826 Fond du Lac Treaty and the Thomas McKenney Manuscript*

1.

IN 1826, THOMAS L. MCKENNEY was into his third year as head of the Office of Indian Affairs in Washington, D.C. He had been appointed to this position by John Calhoun, Secretary of War, and held it until 1830, when incoming president Andrew Jackson dismissed him. McKenney is said to have been "tall and slender, outgoing but aristocratic, fastidious in dress," and to have had a "military bearing," all characteristics he apparently used to good effect when dealing officially with tribal people. Unfulfilled with his life as a dry goods merchant in Georgetown, he joined the army at the start of the War of 1812, and at its end sought employment in government service. Said to have been "politically and socially ambitious," he rose to a position of some importance with the Calhoun appointment. After Jackson's dismissal, he struggled with personal disappointments until 1859, when "[h]e died alone and penniless in a Brooklyn boarding house."[3]

There is some poignancy in the fact that after several years of public service in which he apparently found a degree of comfort in representing the United States government to tribal people—and doing so with a certain lofty aplomb—McKenney spent the last twenty years of his life struggling, and finally, dying in poverty and isolation. The nature of the last few decades of his life resonates in some way with images of the "wretched and poverty stricken" way of life he claimed the Ojibwe of western Lake Superior had in 1826, when he came among them.

When reading McKenney's manuscript about the Fond du Lac treaty gathering we see the same perspective held by Cass, Schoolcraft, and others of the time. He was certain that *his* religion and way of life had to be taken up by the Indian. Like the others, McKenney posed himself as a willing and empathic friend of the *savage*, but always as their learned superior. This self-righteousness strikes a note of disharmony with the style of his prose. Literate, and with an obvious flair for the written word, his pages of description and commentary about native life are at times colorful and lively. If it were not for his extreme ethnocentrism, his manuscript could be an enjoyable read. In the following paragraphs we will do as was done with the Schoolcraft journal from 1820. We will note McKenney's references to native people to help us understand the nature of Chequamegon Bay's Ojibwe community at the time of his visit.

2.

MCKENNEY'S MANUSCRIPT IS LITERALLY a near-daily accounting of his trip from Washington, D.C., to Fond du Lac, the Ojibwe site on the St. Louis River at what is today Duluth, Minnesota. He covered the early distances by carriages until near Detroit, where he stepped into a canoe. This mode of transportation was to be the method of his conveyance for the rest of the trip.

His writings are really letters written to his wife, and perhaps because of this, are at times personal and heartfelt accountings of what he witnessed and how he interpreted what he saw. On 19 June 1826, an incident occurred that indicates the manner in which native peoples were related to throughout the entire trip. McKenney was at the farm of Governor Cass at Detroit, and remarked about some Indian burial mounds being destroyed by cattle, the weather, and by horse drawn carriages that were from time to time driven over them. He claims to have picked up and examined portions of human remains eroding from one of the mounds and of being promised a large human skull that had been removed sometime earlier.[4] He offers no comments on the inappropriateness of this—on the sanctity of human burial sites, and the like. This was 1826, and to mainstream Americans, Indian burial mounds were deemed little more than curiosities.

After leaving Detroit, he reported encounters with native people repeatedly all the way to Fond du Lac. As seen in the Schoolcraft journal of six years earlier, an Ojibwe presence was very evident along the entire length of the southern shore of Lake Superior. While both observers spoke of occasionally coming upon people that displeased them—either from an overindulgence of alcohol or merely from being in desperate need of food—McKenney, more than Schoolcraft, counters this image with one of not only well-fed people who were doubtlessly experiencing success in meeting their needs, but with instances of healthy, and physically very handsome people found all along the way. In other words, we see that while in 1826 there were Ojibwe who struggled with problems of food procurement and alcohol abuse, there were those who not only were free from these concerns, but also were healthy and physically attractive. This contrast is a striking feature of the McKenney manuscript and is vividly shown in incidents that occurred immediately below Mackinac at a point called the Detour, where the party came ashore to spend the night across from Drummond's Island.

They landed just before nightfall on the second of July, when a whiskey trader who had set up shop on a small adjacent island was experiencing a lively trade. McKenney seemed fascinated with what he observed, enough so that he went back after dark to witness it a second time. He told of the island being "filled with Indians—drunk, noisy and naked!" They were Ojibwe and Odawa who earlier had received their presents from the British only to exchange them for this trader's whiskey. McKenney claimed,

> It is not possible to give a description of the looks of those staggering and besotted Indians, when seen by torch light. The torch is made of birch bark, and emits a large flame, and much smoke. The glare from one is livid, but a hundred all lighted at once, and flaring about in all directions, and reflecting

> upon naked and painted savages, with bells rattling from their long plaited locks, and who every now and then fall into a thicket and letting go of their grasp of the torch, send it flaming and smoking along the ground, produced an effect which is not easy to describe, whilst its fittest resemblance is that hell of which we read, and from whence the smoke of their torment ascends![5]

In striking contrast, McKenney tells of how that same evening, he visited the nearby encampment of approximately six hundred people and said, "Their lodges were in fine order, and filled with many comforts; and themselves well clothed." Later he and Lewis Cass "walked around looking at the Indians," when they heard the alluring notes of a wooden flute. They came upon a solitary youth sitting on a rock, serenading his lover who was in a nearby lodge. It was a calm, moonlit night and the tones of the flute added to the idyllic scene.[6]

The juxtaposition of the loud party on the nearby island with these apparently clean and comfortable lodges, their well-clothed inhabitants, and the courtship scene involving flute music is compelling. Despite the raucous behavior caused by the whiskey, it seems many others were spending the beautiful summer moonlit night in a—to McKenney at least—quite acceptable manner.

When McKenney's party reached Sault Ste. Marie we are told of a busy morning at the military post including an inspection of the troops' barracks and equipment, some close order drilling, the firing of guns, and so forth, all observed by the local community of native people. McKenney said:

> The Indians who live about here in summer, and who subsist on fish taken in the rapids, but who go in winter into the interior to hunt, assembled to witness these maneuverings. It was easy to see that they had yielded the contest for supremacy. They looked as if they believed the white man got the ascendancy. They sat in groups on the green, upon their hams, as is their custom, their bodies naked, with a blanket round their hips, smoking their pipes—silent, but watchful . . . The little naked Indian boys, and hardly better clad girls, were meanwhile sporting over the green, playing ball—*bag-gat-iway*, caring more about the military, than the military cared about them . . . These boys and girls are nimble as fawns, and fleet as the wind.[7]

While at the Sault, McKenney attended a *wabeno* ceremony held in a tent not fifty yards from the house of Henry Schoolcraft. He describes this in some detail, to include the preparation of a dog to be cooked and eaten during the night-long event. Interestingly, the entire ceremony is presented without the negative remarks Schoolcraft uttered when he told of watching a similarly complex *midewiwin* rite in 1820.

Between Sault Ste. Marie and Chequamegon Bay the party had numerous encounters with Ojibwe people including the sightings of lodges, the taking of passenger pigeons for food, a visit at the Ojibwe village at Grand Island, and another at Ontonagon. It was at the latter site where McKenney noted a family with a pet crow "as tame as a chicken," and reported the presence of a sweat lodge nearby. About a family at the Black River he said, "I have not seen a family of Indians so well dressed in all this tour. The man shows in his countenance and by his manner that he is more provident than Indians usually are, and no doubt he is a successful hunter." However, later at the Montreal River they visited a lodge where a man, several women and children were in desperate need of food. These unfortunates had powder but no shot, and no canoe. McKenney's party fed them and told how they would have provisions sent from Madeline Island, eighteen miles distant.[8]

A recent writer feels that when the party reached the Keweenaw Peninsula, Thomas McKenney experienced "homesickness, a sense of loneliness, and a growing anxiety at being separated from family, friends, and familiar society", and it was here where he began to form an image of the land and of the Ojibwe people residing therein. According to Eric D. Olmanson, for McKenney,

> . . . [t]his territory was different. It was *baffling*, and he did not quite know what to make of it. But encountering groups of Indians who were obviously hungry and poor convinced him that it was an essentially barren land—barren not just in resources but also in terms of society. Without a sophisticated knowledge of the complex associations and expectations of the middle ground and of its seasonal round, McKenney perceived the hungry Indians simply as beggars. He misunderstood their relationship with him, believing that they depended on him, while in fact, the opposite was closer to the truth. If the Cass party had suffered a mishap and lost the provisions they were carrying to Fond du Lac, the consequences would have been much more serious for them than it would have been for the Indians. The Indians were far more adept at living off the land. Even though most of the Chippewa McKenney described seem to have been doing just fine, and in some cases prospering, it was the apparently starving or drunken Indians that stuck in his mind.[9]

Once reaching Chequamegon Bay McKenney wrote:

> Arrived at Michael's island, a trading post about an hour by sun, having come seventy-five miles since twelve o'clock last night, and visited several Indian lodges by the way. On nearing the shore, (which was grateful to my feelings beyond the power of language to express; for it looked green, and had the evidences of civilized life, in houses, horses, and cattle, and fences, which I had not seen since I left the Sault) the Indians, to the number of seventy, set up a whooping and yelling, and ran down to the beach, each armed with a rifle or gun, and fired a salute of several rounds. Never were poor starving

> creatures more overjoyed. They had been here, on their way to the treaty, for six days, and had taken in that time but forty fish! . . . I was struck with the mute appearance of the Indians, after the first expression of joy was over, and at their manner of grouping about against the sides and ends of the houses. Always sitting on their hams, with their feet drawn close under them, watchful, silent, and smoking. We fed them with flour and pork—and made them happy. They had but one want more, and that was whiskey. This we chose not to gratify.[10]

The party stayed on Madeline Island two days, leaving the morning of 26 July. When moving through the channel beside the hillside where the town of Bayfield now stands, he remarked about the spot once holding the residence of John Johnston. This was the location of the village of Johnston's father-in-law, the famed Ojibwe war leader, Waubojiig.

The cliffs, bays and beaches of the Red Cliff shoreline were passed and after rounding the point at Eagle Bay he wrote that:

> At about two o'clock we ran alongside of an immense flat rock, which projected out of the hill; got upon it, kindled a fire, and fried our fish for our lake meal. The day, which an hour ago promised to be windy, has grown calm. The water is still, transparent, and glassy, and no sound is heard but its motion in the crevices of the rocks . . . . Just as we were embarking, a canoe full of Indians, naked and painted—naked, except a certain covering made of a quarter of a yard of cloth, which they call *Auzeum*, and which is fastened before and behind to a string which goes around their bodies just above their hips—and immediately after, the whole fleet of barges and canoes, bearing the greater part of the seventy Indians we found at Michael's island. The men were all naked except the quarter of a yard of cloth. They had a blanket, or pieces of blanket, but these were not needed at this season. The women, generally, had a petticoat of strouds, and a peculiar dress for the back of the arms, and breast, and shoulders, which I mean to have sketched.[11]

Later that day, McKenney's party put in at the Brule River where he noticed the framework for a *jiisakaan*, or shaking tent. Then it was on to the St. Louis River and upstream to Fond du Lac. At the direction of Lewis Cass the party did not immediately paddle up to the landing site, instead pausing out of sight downstream to assemble itself into a military squadron for a ceremonial, if not pretentious, arrival. The canoes of officials were placed at the head of a column, followed by the barges of provisions and military personnel, and in turn, the canoes of Indians they met on Madeline Island.

While the squadron moved along with its flags aloft, its few military musicians played "Hail Columbia." McKenney added that "The Indians all naked, painted and silent; glided over the surface in their birch canoes, eyed this, to them, wonderful display, as a new creation, and as something beyond their comprehension." When coming to shore the band played "Yankee Doodle."[12]

They arrived at the treaty grounds on 28 July, and stayed until 9 August. McKenney felt that over seven hundred individuals were in attendance and we have little difficulty in imagining the festiveness of the large gathering. The day before the council was to open there was concern that some of the attendees were getting restless since they had been at the treaty grounds for a few days, and in the process Lewis Cass directed that "brooches and various little ornaments" be tossed into their midst. After the scrambling for these was over, a few games were played to entertain the Indians. These involved racing for prizes placed on distant goals and similar contests of speed.[13]

It was summertime, traditionally the season for social gatherings. The participants had a full year to prepare for the event, and we know that leaders from fifteen bands were signatories to the treaty, so this was no small gathering. The numerous groups arrived at different times, so detailed customs of protocol had to be carried out with each arrival. This involved what McKenney said the people called *pipe dances*, but which he claimed were really *begging* dances because they invariably concluded with the line of dancers standing before the Americans asking for presents. Ritual tobacco smoking, gift giving and drum playing were all part of these events. Once again if we interpret them in the context of *fur trade theater*, they are elevated to a level beyond one of merely begging for gifts from the Americans.

Thomas McKenney's writings covering the ensuing thirteen days of the gathering are a literal treasure of information about Ojibwe culture. He was an astute observer and has left us with numerous comments that demand discussion. Like other writers of his time, he was bound by his culture and was certain of its superiority. To him, Ojibwe culture was inferior and would in time give way. He was convinced he had a moral obligation to bring Christianity and what he called *civilization* to these *savages*, in the process destroy their foraging way of life. All of this aside, we must still speak to a few of his observations and reactions to what he encountered at Fond du Lac. They help depict Ojibwe life as exhibited throughout the days of the treaty gathering, and they show that in 1826, important aspects of the culture were successfully functioning.

At Fond du Lac more *wabeno* and *jiisakaan* ceremonies were held and female mourning rituals were observed. He noted a burial ground where both non-Indian and Indian graves were covered with wooden houses, but while the former held structures of hand-worked logs with roofs made of boards, the Indian burials had grave-sized wigwams built over them. Dogs were apparently ubiquitous throughout the days of the gathering and McKenney was struck with the fact that, in his words, the Ojibwe held "a strange union of respect and contempt" for them. Recent writers noted this paradoxical role of dogs in Ojibwe culture almost two hundred years after McKenney made this early observation.[14]

McKenney lamented that although they were said to exist, he did not witness what he called an Ojibwe *man-woman*. This was a male who, because of a sign from the *manidoog*, assumed the role of a woman for a length of time until released from this obligation. Ojibwe methods of treating illness were witnessed, and since Governor Cass desired a new canoe for his return trip, a group of Ojibwe men, women and youngsters built one—a task McKenney observed and described.

He tells of the account wherein the trader at Fond du Lac stuffed a moose hide, stood it upright like a living animal, and kept it indoors as a curiosity. When seeing the reconstructed moose, the Ojibwe expressed their uneasiness with its indignity and held a pipe ceremony to appease the spirit of the animal. Not wanting to upset them, the trader dismantled his trophy. Such an incident candidly exhibits the radically different approaches the trader and the Ojibwe took in relating to their worlds.

3.

TWO OJIBWE LEADERS NAMED BIZIKI (BUFFALO) were in attendance at the gathering. (A number of phonetic spellings are used in the literature for this man.) One was from the St. Croix band and the other from La Pointe. A third Ojibwe leader named Biziki—a member of the Leech Lake community—was living at the time but seems not to have been present at the Fond du Lac gathering. Unfortunately, in some cases the McKenney manuscript is not clear on which man it is referring to. One reference is obviously to St. Croix's leader and another to La Pointe's, but the others are uncertain.

On 31 July, two days before the treaty session was officially opened McKenney wrote:

> A young man, son of *Pe-chee-kee*, came in to-day with a British medal around his neck. I heard some of our company talking about it. On going up to where the young man stood, he folded his blanket over his breast and walked away—manifestly a good deal confused. I called him, and asked him (through an interpreter of course) to let me look at it; but he was loth to show it. *Pe-chee-kee*, his father, was near, and spoke, saying, "It is my medal, he only wears it for ornament." The young man came to me. I told him not to think I was hurt with him. I knew he was too good an American to wear the medal as a token of partiality to the British king. He said that was so. Well then, I continued, as you are an American *inside*, I will make you one *outside* too. I will give you a medal with the likeness of your great Father at Washington, in exchange for this. He consented. But when I brought it out, he was very particular in wishing one as large in all respects. He was very shrewd in bargaining.[15]

It would not have been unusual for this incident to be referring to La Pointe's Buffalo. In 1826, he would have been approximately sixty or more years old, so the young man could have been his son. Also, it would have been very *un*likely that in 1826, La Pointe's Buffalo was not a holder of a British medal. By that time he had several contacts with British authorities and as noted in the previous chapter, he was known as an Ojibwe leader who was "decorated with British insignia."

As was the case on the 1820 trip of Lewis Cass and his company, one purpose of the 1826 gathering was to discourage Ojibwe allegiance with the British and to insist they aligned themselves with the Americans. To this end, at Fond du Lac American silver medals, with an image of George Washington or Thomas Jefferson cast into them, were distributed to tribal leaders and when found, British medals were confiscated. When a member of the party attempted to present an American medal to La Pointe's Buffalo he is reported to have said, "What need I of this! It is known from whence I am descended."[16]

Despite expected issues of translation, for a number of reasons this is still a very important remark. Among other things, it suggests that the *father-child* relationship was quite complex and must be considered with some care. Even though tribal leaders might assume the ritual subordinate role of *child*, they never relinquished their position as powerful international political persons. Buffalo was proud of his forebears and his remark can be understood that even though he accepted his new alliance with the United States, he did so with a degree of disfavor. He was not relinquishing any of his political and personal independence and reminded the Americans that he did not need their medal to provide him with an identity. It is very unfortunate we have no other reference to this medal incident other than Schoolcraft's single sentence, and that it was recorded a long six years after the event. Buffalo's remark suggests that despite the open display of grateful hospitality the Ojibwe showed to the American officials in 1826, there existed an undertone of begrudging discontent. This will be made clear below, when we consider the important speech La Pointe's Buffalo made at Fond du Lac, and again when we discuss the letter of 1838 he sent to Shingwaukonse the Canadian Ojibwe leader. Likewise, when discussing the 1845 attempt of La Pointe's Black Bird and Neokoma to contact Canadian authorities about moving their people north, and also when considering the petition of 1852, which several Wisconsin, Michigan and Minnesota Territory Ojibwe leaders sent to Canadian authorities at Sault Ste. Marie. Through all these events we see the continued positive presence the British had in western Lake Superior lands in these years.

4.

ON AUGUST NINTH, THE DAY AFTER the treaty was signed, one last ceremony ensued before McKenney and his party departed. This involved the placement of a barrel of whiskey in the center of the gathering ground where it was distributed to the tribesmen. Accordingly, McKenney wrote:

> The morning is fine and calm. The barrel of whiskey was in the square at sun-rise, and around it the Indians were gathered, in close and firm order, every Indian pressing in to this common centre, and stretching his neck between the heads and over the shoulders of others who had the happiness to be nearer it; whilst those within bent over to inhale the fumes from this barrel; which contained the object, of all others in this world, the most to be desired. Each brought his bark bowl, and in this received his portion. *Pe-chee-kee* came to me with his, to complain that it was so small—told me his wife wanted some, and his children. I answered they

> were better without any, as he would be himself. He seemed to think this was very strange; for all his notions upon the subject had always resulted in the conclusion that there could not be too much of any thing so good.[17]

It was the custom at such events that if a man coming forward for a ladle of whiskey had a family, he could receive additional servings for each of its members. These extra portions he could drink himself. Once again we cannot be certain it was the La Pointe leader referred to in this instance, but we see that the Buffalo McKenney told about was not only fond of whiskey, he also was determined to receive his just share. We should not believe that in 1826, La Pointe's Buffalo was a teetotaler. We see at the very end of his opening speech given at Fond du Lac, when he addressed the American officials and said, "Give us a little milk, *Fathers*, that we may wet our lips," that he clearly asked for whiskey. Even though La Pointe's Buffalo may have refused to drink alcohol when he was espousing Tecumseh's New Religion some fifteen years earlier, by 1826, like other Ojibwe leaders, in all probability he cherished it for its intoxicating, ceremonial and symbolic aspects.

Another reference to Biziki appears in the entry for the morning McKenney and his party departed Fond du Lac. The incident of dispensing the barrel of whiskey over, the party readied their canoes and pushed off from the landing at the trading post. McKenney tells of how his canoe, heavily loaded and with its eight *voyageurs*, had its "awning up and flag flying" as it moved out into the river beside that of Lewis Cass, likewise heavily loaded. With typical gusto, the *voyageurs* in the two vessels had a short race before settling down, then, with the military barges joining them they "all were in motion to the tune of Yankee Doodle." McKenney tells us:

> It was at this moment Pe-Chee-kee's canoe came along side, that his squaw might give me a mocock and a terrapin shell. It was the most valuable present she had to give, and was, of course, accepted. The river was alive with canoes. On looking back we saw the members of the Fur Company's establishment standing on the shore, silent, and looking sad, nothing moved around them, save a cow, and beside them, sitting on his hind legs was one of their dogs.[18]

This quotation may be referring to La Pointe's Buffalo, since the Biziki from St.Croix most likely would have taken another route to his southern home rather than the much longer and more difficult one down the St. Louis River to Lake Superior, then many miles east to the Brule River—a notoriously difficult river because of its many windfalls blocking a canoe's way—before ascending the Brule River with the long portage to the St. Croix River. In the incident McKenney describes, we are given a glimpse into the domestic world of Ojibwe husband and wife. If McKenney is indeed speaking of La Pointe's Buffalo, then here they were, in the same canoe, heading out to their Chequamegon Bay home after the festive days at Fond du Lac. Unfortunately, McKenney fails to give us any more information about this woman except that she was offering a gift of departure. Admittedly, this scene may have more to it than depicted in McKenney's little vignette, since a recent researcher writes that in his long life La Pointe's Buffalo is said to have "acquired five wives and had numerous children."[19]

One last lengthy reference to La Pointe's Buffalo is found in the appendix to McKenney's manuscript. This is the speech already referred to above, and given on August second, during the opening ceremonies that preceded the presentation of the treaty to the assembled group. We are given an English version, so should expect something was lost in the translation from the Ojibwe language. Here we see Buffalo rising before the crowd to introduce himself, then appropriately assuming the humble role of messenger. He said he was only a speaker, relaying the wishes of his people. He framed his speech in the father-child idiom demanded by the setting, coming before his father and asking for sustenance not only for himself but for his women and children as well. At one point he spread a map before the commissioners but unfortunately, we are told nothing of the document and must surmise its purpose. It seems he was marking band territories to make the point that he knew what land was his, and that he was asking only that his boundaries be respected.

He told of his truthfulness and sincerity, and remarked that while he was willing to listen to what the commissioners had to say, he could not guarantee that the younger men would do the same. Without speaking directly to the difference between the political organizations of the Ojibwe and American society, Buffalo reminded the audience that in the Ojibwe community, the sacred pipe was the ultimate mechanism of social control available to tribal leaders. He implied that unlike in the commissioners' society, there was no police force or standing military to enforce leaders' decisions.

Here he may have been alluding to a demand from the commissioners that the Ojibwe men who killed four Americans at Lake Pepin in 1824, and after arrest escaped from confinement at Mackinac, be surrendered so they could be tried in an American court. This demand had been issued at Prairie du Chien the previous year, and at the end of the Fond du Lac gathering it was brought before the assembled group again. In a stern threat McKenney told the tribesmen, "we expect you to deliver these men to us by the time the traders come in, in the spring. If they are not surrendered then, destruction will fall on your women and children. Your father will put out his strong arm. Go and think of it. Nothing will satisfy us but this." The next morning a contingent of Lac du Flambeau leaders came forward and agreed to have the men delivered to Green Bay or Sault Ste Marie in spring. This was never done, however, and apparently the matter was dropped.[20]

At mid-point in his speech Buffalo said, "*My Brothers.*—Why is it that we are in difficulty? It is because you have deserted your country. Where your fathers lived, and your mothers first saw the sun, there you are not. I alone, am the solitary one remaining on our own ground."[21] Here is another strikingly important statement from the La Pointe leader. At the time in his late middle-age, Buffalo was offering a tragic comment about recent Ojibwe history. The difficulty he spoke to seems not to have been the matter of warfare with the Dakota, since by this time for Chequamegon Bay peoples, this was to a great extent no longer a major concern. Instead, Buffalo more likely was referring to the overall serious changes occurring in his country.

By 1826, he had to be cognizant of the diminishing returns from the fur trade, and of the ominous threat posed by the new and aggressive Americans. Apparently he felt compelled to remain on the land his ancestors inhabited for hundreds of years, instead of moving westward like so many others had done, hence his statement can be read as a lament for a world slipping out of his control. This conclusion is supported by William Warren, who, when writing some twenty-five years after the signing of the Fond du Lac treaty, marked 1826 as the time when the traditional Ojibwe leadership structures began to break down.[22] The perceptive William Warren saw what was occurring to Ojibwe culture and certainly saw this change in political organization as a foreshadowing of even more serious changes yet to come.

Perhaps Buffalo's words were referring to what the British had been warning him about for years—that the Americans would not be content until they had all of Ojibwe territory. It was only eleven years later that the Treaty of 1837 was negotiated, through which they lost a huge piece of land in northern Wisconsin and central Minnesota. This was quickly followed by the Treaty of 1842, which saw the loss of all their land south of Lake Superior. With the signing of these treaties the Ojibwe had entered a new and very trying time.

As noted above, Buffalo concluded his speech with a final reference to his role of the *child*, reminding the Americans of their obligations as *fathers*. He asked for liquor by saying, "*Fathers*,—You have many children. But your breasts drop yet. Give us a little milk, *Fathers*, that we may wet our lips."

Although by now we are familiar with the metaphors, they are still striking. Buffalo is asking for alcohol, while in a deeper way he is acting out the prescribed role of the child by demanding sustenance from the Washington authorities. He has agreed to cease his former alliance with Britain and to replace it with a new one with the United States, and in return he reminded the commissioners of their responsibility to provide sustenance for their "children." In this way liquor became more than an intoxicating beverage. It was transformed into an important symbol used by both the Americans and the Ojibwe to aid in the mediation of their alliance.[23]

In the 1820s, Buffalo and the other western Ojibwe leaders were still in contact with the British at the eastern end of Lake Superior, and this fact plays a role in understanding the Ojibwe uneasiness with the 1826 Fond du Lac treaty. It is significant that in the new treaty they—the Ojibwe—agreed to cease their contacts with the Crown, although as history shows, a British influence remained with these bands for some years. What seemed to have been happening at the time of the Fond du Lac treaty was that Buffalo and his co-leaders were adapting to the American presence while still not relinquishing their possibilities with the Crown. By 1826, Shingwaukonse, the Sault Ste. Marie leader, and friend of the Ojibwe at the western reaches of Lake Superior, was emerging as a powerful person in his own right, and a relationship between him and his people with the western Ojibwe communities was something that could have benefited both parties. It has been suggested that in the years immediately previous to 1826, Shingwaukonse may have been acting as a fur trade mediator between the Sault Ste. Marie Johnston family, or even the North West Company itself, and the western Ojibwe bands reaching as far west as the Red River. In this regard he was periodically making trips to these western locations and in the process establishing positive relationships with Ojibwe leaders along the way. It is clear that in the 1820s, the Ojibwe communities at the eastern and western extremities of Lake Superior were regularly in contact with each other as they attempted to manage their relationships with both the British and American authorities.[24]

The persistence and new power of the Americans was frustrating to Buffalo and the other western leaders, and the alliance between them was an uneasy one. In the decades after 1826, the Ojibwe would be confronted with demands to make land cessions, and by that time in these negotiations they would find that their options for refusal were few, if existing at all. The frustration this awareness must have caused for Buffalo is hinted at in an incident at La Pointe involving anti-American sentiment and occurring in 1827, less than a year after the signing of the Fond du Lac treaty. Henry Schoolcraft felt it was due to the contacts Mesai, a La Pointe co-leader and brother of Buffalo, had been having with British traders at Sault Ste. Marie, but George Johnston claimed it was because of Shingwaukonse, who was attempting to strengthen his ties with the Crown by developing strong political ties with western American Ojibwe bands.

In May 1827, George Johnston, the government Subagent at La Pointe, informed Henry Schoolcraft he had been told by a man named Tugwaugaunay (this person could have been Peter Marksman, the Ojibwe who went on to become a Methodist missionary) that Shingwaukonse recently threatened the south shore Ojibwe, saying they would be harmed if they did not come east to meet with the British. This threat was an obvious reaction to the recently signed Fond du Lac treaty, in which the Ojibwe pledged to turn away from any influence the British may have had with them. According to Johnston:

> Kaw go dah eway said Shing wah konce . . . told Missi if you do not listen and come to your English father . . . he is determined to fire four shots, and there will not be left, one single man, woman or child living on the south shore of Lake Superior and throughout the interior country, within the limits of the United States, the power of his shots will be great inasmuch that he will not leave a tree standing.[25]

The Canadian writer Janet E. Chute feels this unusual threat could indicate Shingwaukonse "may have been involved in a minor stress-induced revitalization cult," hence the use of the extreme imagery, but also he was clearly reacting to Great Britain's recent decision to leave Drummond's Island, and in so doing, negatively affect his political standing. By issuing the threat to the south shore groups, Shingwaukonse was attempting to align the Ojibwe leaders at the three powerful centers of Mackinac, Sault Ste. Marie, and La Pointe with the Crown, and in that manner offset the increasingly powerful role of the Americans along that shore. However this may have been, it is clear that in early 1827, the Ojibwe on both sides of the Canadian-American border were attempting to manipulate political relationships as they struggled to successfully adjust their connections with both the Americans and the British.

As Mark Diedrich says, we do not know Buffalo's response to the stylized admonishment from Shingwaukonse, but as shown below, within the next decade it is clear these two prominent Ojibwe leaders and their families maintained a friendly relationship.[26] This strong mid-nineteenth century connection with the Canadian Ojibwe community at Sault Ste. Marie, and hence with the British Crown, has not been stressed in earlier accounts of Chequamegon Bay Ojibwe history and as we will see, this relationship continues on for at least another twenty-five years.

5.

THE FOND DU LAC TREATY HAS NINE ARTICLES, along with an addendum. In summary, its articles stipulate that: one, the chiefs and warriors of the Ojibwe tribe assent to the Prairie du Chien treaty; two, the Ojibwe shall be represented the following year at Green Bay (Butte des Morts) to negotiate a treaty setting the southern boundary line between their lands and those of the Menominee and Ho-chunk nations; three, the American government is granted the right to take any metals or minerals found in Ojibwe territory; four, plots of land at Sault Ste. Marie shall be set aside for certain individuals of mixed Ojibwe and non-Indian blood (this article was not approved by Congress); five, an annuity of two thousand dollars shall be paid the Ojibwe at Sault Ste. Marie (this article was not approved by Congress); six, an annual sum of one thousand dollars shall be given to the Ojibwe at Sault Ste. Marie for the education of their youths; seven, the fourth, fifth and sixth articles can be rejected by the President and Senate without affecting the other articles; eight, the Ojibwe tribe accepts the authority and jurisdiction of the United States and disclaims any connection with any foreign power; nine, after ratification by the President and the Senate the treaty shall be binding to both parties. (The addendum states that the Lac du Flambeau leaders shall turn the suspects of the Lake Pepin murderers over to American authorities in spring.)

The Treaty of 1826 is a major document even though it is not a land cession treaty. As we have stated, taken together with its companion treaties of Prairie du Chien (1825) and Butte des Morts (1827), it set the stage for the next step in the Americans' plans to acquire more lands in the western lakes region. At Fond du Lac, the new alliance between the Ojibwe and the United States was affirmed, and the Ojibwe repeated their agreement to sever any connections with Britain. However, as we will see below, a dozen years later La Pointe's Buffalo will give cause to question his sincerity in pledging to sever these ties with the Crown. The fur trade was still going on, and at the time the western Lake Superior communities were not yet feeling the immediate pinch of Americans encroaching on their hunting, fishing, gathering and trapping lands, so the Ojibwe probably still felt a degree of confidence in their ability to sustain themselves.

However, in Buffalo's speech we find his concern about this when he admonished his fellow tribesmen who migrated out of Chequamegon Bay for leaving their homeland. Buffalo was troubled that his was the only community of Ojibwe left still on its native lands, and seemingly, he was uncertain of his ability to hold these lands in the future. In this regard, William Warren's remark about 1826 being the time when the traditional Ojibwe political structures began to give way seems to be correct.

Perhaps Buffalo's words were referring to what the British had been warning him about for years—that the Americans would not be content until they had all Ojibwe territory. It was only eleven years later that the Treaty of 1837 was negotiated, through which they lost a huge piece of land in northern Wisconsin and central Minnesota. This was quickly followed by the Treaty of 1842. which saw the loss of *all* their land south of Lake Superior. With the signing of these treaties the Ojibwe had entered a new and very trying time.

6.

RECENTLY, THE AMERICAN MIXED-BLOOD (Ojibwe-German) writer Gerald Vizenor has portrayed Thomas McKenney as a pretentious, if not domineering, representative of the United States.[27] McKenney's threat that if the jail escapees from Lac du Flambeau were not brought forth, Ojibwe women and children would be harmed, was doubtless calculated to register his government's resolve, but today it sounds like an unnecessarily egregious threat from an abusive overseer. At Fond du Lac, Thomas McKenney and Lewis Cass were influential government leaders who took their task to heart. They were the powerful representatives of the "Great Father" who resided in distant Washington, and together with their contingent of armed military personnel must have presented an officious and formidable front to the tribesmen.

Throughout his entire manuscript, Thomas McKenney speaks of the "poverty, nakedness and wretchedness" of the Ojibwe people, and these three concepts become the prominent theme of his description of them. While at times he was dismayed when witnessing those who were suffering from a lack of food and clothing, he ultimately was saying the Ojibwe were poor, naked and wretched because they did not espouse his religion and culture. The fact that they were not Christians and did not live according to his notions of religious, social, economic and political proprieties *made* them poor, naked and wretched.

Today we can easily castigate him for his tirades against a way of life at odds with his own, but we should understand that his biases were those of his people, and as such, were *cultural* in their origins. McKenney was viewing tribal people from his cultural perspective and concluded they were deficient. He judged them and found them wanting. While we can find fault with Thomas McKenney for his personal reaction to Indian people in 1826, it is his way of life, with its overriding assurance of its own superiority, that is the deeper source of McKenney's sentiments. This refusal of mainstream Americans to accept the legitimacy of foraging peoples like the Ojibwe, found in the literature of 1826, is tenacious in its persistence from one century to the next.

7.

AN ADDED BIT OF HISTORICAL INTEREST about the Treaty of 1826 is that along with the cadre of specialists Lewis Cass brought with him from Detroit to Fond du Lac was James Otto Lewis, a young painter. An American citizen whose parents had immigrated to the United States from Germany, Lewis entered the world of art as a stage actor and an engraver. His image of Daniel Boone caught the public's eye and soon Lewis was successfully selling framed prints of the piece for three dollars each, a considerable sum at the time. This business of printmaking took him to Detroit, where in 1823, he was commissioned by Lewis Cass to do a portrait of Tenkswatawa which Cass sent to Thomas McKenney in Washington, D.C. McKenney wanted more paintings of Indian leaders and Lewis was invited to join Cass on his 1825 Prairie du Chien, 1826 Fond du Lac, and 1827 Butte des Morts trips as a portraitist.

James Lewis made about 330 portraits and drawings on the first two trips, and while at Fond du Lac rendered one of Biziki. We cannot be completely certain this is an image of La Pointe's Chief Buffalo, since in publications of Lewis's work it is identified only as *Pe-Schiek-Ee—A Celebrated Chippewa Chief*, but since Leech Lake's Chief Buffalo was not present at the Fond du Lac treaty gathering, and because St. Croix's Buffalo seems not to have been known as a "celebrated" Ojibwe chief, it is very likely the painting depicts Lewis's version of La Pointe's leader. Only a very few drawings or paintings said to be of La Pointe's Chief Buffalo have been passed down to the present, so this 1826 image is of particular importance. This matter of artists' renderings of images of La Pointe's famed leader will be revisited later.[28]

8.

IN THE SUMMER OF 1827, LEWIS CASS and Thomas McKenney (and James Otto Lewis) once again were in Indian Country. This time they journeyed to a site called Butte des Morts on the Fox River in southeastern Michigan Territory, now part of the state of Wisconsin. Here, on 11 August, they signed another boundary-establishing treaty, on this occasion with representatives of the Menominee, Ho-Chunk and Ojibwe tribes. This treaty determined the southern boundaries of territory held by the Lake Superior Ojibwe, and except for the lingering uncertainty of the national boundary between Canada and the United States running westward from Lake Superior, the Ojibwe peoples' land was now circumscribed by firm lines imposed by the Americans. This attainment allowed American authorities to focus on these lands with some exactitude as plans were laid for the next steps needed to acquire this vast tribal territory.

Forty-four tribal leaders signed the Butte des Morts treaty, sixteen of them identified as being Ojibwe. The first was "Shinguaba W'Ossin," the second was "Wahishkee," and the third was "Sheewaubeketoan."[29] Unfortunately, no community identifications are given for any of the Ojibwe leaders signing this treaty, but we know the first signer was the powerful chief from Sault Ste. Marie, and most likely the second and third were also from that location. This latter conclusion is based upon the fact that the previous year at Fond du Lac, the first three Ojibwe signatures on the treaty are Shingauba Wassin, Shewaubeketoan, and Wayishkee, all identified as being from "St. Mary's," and thus, we might conclude that the "Wayishkee" who signed the Fond du Lac treaty is the same person who signed one year later with the prominent leader from Sault Ste. Marie.

At first notice, it does not appear that any leaders from La Pointe were present at the negotiations for the Butte des Morts treaty, but two years earlier, at the signing of the Prairie du Chien treaty, Shingauba Wassin, the elderly Sault Ste. Marie leader was identified as the "1st chief of the Chippewa nation,"[30] and his presence at Butte des Morts may have indicated that the Lake Superior Ojibwe bands were adequately represented, making it unnecessary for any La Pointe leaders to be present.[31]

The Butte des Morts treaty is usually given little thought in discussions on the history of the La Pointe bands, but its importance should not go unnoticed. As stated, this treaty marked the southernmost boundaries of the interior Lake Superior bands with their Menominee and Ho-Chunk neighbors and provided a map of regional tribal territories for the United States as it planned its movement westward through the Great Lakes region. With its peoples' acute sense of private property, the obvious importance of all three *boundary treaties* (1825, 1826, 1827) to the United States is clear, but in the case of the tribesmen, as Anton Treuer claims, "Strict boundary lines made little sense to people with a very different sense of property: Indians focused on use of land, whites focused on ownership."[32] Hence, these early nineteenth century boundary-setting treaties meant one thing to the tribesmen, and another to the Americans. The deep importance of this fact cannot be overstated. With the United States' Government's ratification of the three above treaties, a new time had officially opened for Lake Superior's Ojibwe communities.

## *Overview of Ojibwe World in Chequamegon Country by 1830*

1.

IN 1826, WHEN THE CHEQUAMEGON BAY leaders were paddling back to La Pointe after the days at Fond du Lac, and possibly in 1827, from Butte des Morts, they obviously pondered what was occurring to their world. They had been doing much traveling the last few years because of treaty meetings. We do not know if Chief Buffalo took his wife (or *wives*)—and perhaps other family members—along on all such trips but it would not have been unusual to do so. In Ojibwe culture, summer was traditionally the time for major social gatherings, and treaty sessions fit into this seasonal pattern very well. Surely Buffalo understood that by insisting on establishing geographic boundaries between tribal nations south and west of Lake Superior, the United States was planning further steps to change his world. As we have seen, Buffalo's Fond du Lac speech indicated he was growing uncomfortable with possibilities for the future at La Pointe.

In 1822, only two years after the Cass Expedition, two important events occurred that foreshadowed further changes coming to the Ojibwe people. One was that Lt. Bayfield of the British navy started making surveys of Lake Superior, an act leading to the first accurate chart of the lake, an essential task before serious military and commercial navigation could occur.[33] The other was that Henry Schoolcraft was appointed Indian agent in charge of the Lake Superior tribes with a headquarters at Sault Ste. Marie, bringing permanent official representation of the government of the United States closer to La Pointe. However, Minnesota Territory's Ojibwe bands were under the administration of Maj. Lawrence Taliaferro, in Fort Snelling, at St. Peters. This meant Minnesota's Ojibwe leaders sometimes found themselves traveling to Fort Snelling to meet with Taliaferro, and in the summer of 1827, a violent conflict between the Dakota—who also used the site—and Ojibwe led to several deaths at that site. This caused Washington officials to shift the Minnesota Ojibwe bands to the administration of Henry Schoolcraft, at distant Sault Ste. Marie. Taliaferro and Schoolcraft were not friends, and this change in administration would be a factor in later relationships between these two men.[34]

Some Minnesota bands were upset with this change, due to the exorbitant travel it caused. Partially to ease this problem, in 1826, Schoolcraft opened a sub-agency at La Pointe, appointing his brother-in-law, George Johnston, as Sub-agent, bringing the federal government into the midst of Chequamegon Bay. One of the charges assigned to agents was to work toward acculturating the Indians, and if Johnston followed this, in 1826, the La Pointe Ojibwe had a serious change agent in the heart of their community on a full time basis.

Henry Schoolcraft intended to replace George Johnston with John Tanner as Sub-agent at La Pointe in the spring of 1829, but because of financial problems in Washington's war department, the La Pointe sub-agency was suddenly closed, causing Johnston to move back to Sault Ste. Marie during the winter of 1828-29. The coming of John Tanner as a permanent resident on Madeline Island would doubtlessly have caused historical events to register this man's colorful presence. His strong character and deep familiarity with Ojibwe culture would have brought a new dynamic to the community.[35]

A few years later, in 1832, Chief Buffalo complained to Henry Schoolcraft about the recall of the La Pointe Sub-agent, but Washington authorities took no action until 1836, when Daniel P. Bushnell was appointed to the post. Bushnell, however, did not arrive at La Pointe until 1837, making it eight years that the site went without a resident Sub-agent.[36]

Buffalo's complaint is noteworthy. According to Schoolcraft, he expressed disappointment since under the treaty he signed at Fond du Lac, "he expected the care and protection of the American government, and that they would advance towards, instead of (as in the case of the sub-agency) withdrawing from them."[37] In this remark, Buffalo is not asking for more Americans to come into his land, but only for an official representative to give his determined attention to the needs of the Ojibwe, as agreed in the 1826 treaty. It is clear that Buffalo and leaders of the other Ojibwe bands in these years expected the Americans to fulfill their obligations. This sentiment was often remarked upon by United States officials of the times.[38]

The fact that America's Sub-agents were to work toward the "civilization" of Indian communities gives added meaning to Buffalo's remark about the withdrawal of George Johnston. Buffalo wanted the United States to meet its treaty obligations regarding the "care and protection" of the Ojibwe, but we must wonder about his desire for the agents to work as change agents in the heart of Chequamegon Bay. We should not think that by wanting American government agents at La Pointe that Buffalo was embracing their efforts to "civilize" the Ojibwe people. More likely, what was occurring by the 1830s, was that leaders like Buffalo were attempting to stand firm against the encroachment of the Americans while still accepting them as allies. This unfortunate situation—accepting the Americans as allies while beginning to understand their increasing presence as a negative foreboding of the future—must have been a preoccupation of Ojibwe leaders in these times. By the 1830s, it was becoming clear that the Americans were powerful and that the Ojibwes' abilities to negotiate as equals with them was rapidly eroding. In the earlier days of the fur trade the tribal nations could stand as equals to the French and British, but by 1830, with the Americans this equality was changing. Understanding that in the early 1830s, La Pointe's Buffalo was probably in his seventies, we might suspect that his comments to Schoolcraft included an unsettling lament for what the future might be like for his people.

In 1826, there were no Christian missionaries permanently stationed at La Pointe, but this would begin to change only a few years later when, because of a request by the Warrens, Frederick Ayer arrived at Madeline Island as a mission lay teacher. Then, a year later, in 1831, Sherman Hall and his wife—protestant missionaries—arrived to begin an extended stay, so by the end of the second decade of the nineteenth century the La Pointe Ojibwe were under serious pressure to make accommodations to the Americans.[39]

The written record is virtually silent regarding the Ojibwe voice in the coming of these missionaries except for the words of Mark Diedrich, who claims, "During the 1830s-1840s Buffalo welcomed Protestant missionaries to LaPointe."[40] One must wonder about the veracity of this statement since in the absence of any written documentation we find only Buffalo's silence, and in Ojibwe culture a silent response—until shown differently—may be best received as a negative response. It seems likely that the Warren family did not seek approval from the Ojibwe people before it asked to have missionaries sent to their community, and we are left uninformed of the Ojibwes' sentiment on their arrival. Given Buffalo's apparent consternation about his peoples' difficult situation in these times, it seems that if he welcomed the missionaries at all it might have been with a silent frustration.

## 2.

AT TIMES WE ARE GIVEN BITS AND PIECES of instances wherein Ojibwe male leaders spoke of the political challenges occurring in the early decades of the nineteenth century, but the Ojibwes' female voice is much less evident. We know that Ojibwe women, like Susan Johnston at Sault Ste. Marie, were not only interested in and informed about these things, and were powerful forces in their communities, but quite unfortunately, the written record gives us little from them. In 1826, Obarguwack, an elderly woman from an unidentified Ojibwe community, spoke in the opening session at Fond du Lac, but she was filling in for her ill husband rather than serving as a band representative in her own right.[41] For the first three hundred years or more of contact between Europeans (and Euro-Americans) and the Ojibwe, written history portrays tribal (and non-tribal) women as virtual non-players in matters of international relations. Although in important ways tribal women were involved in all important political decisions, it is only until the late twentieth century that this was understood by non-native writers.[42]

We look to the early years of written history on Ojibwe relationships with the Europeans and Americans and find a record of events essentially about the white man and how he came and changed things. We have virtually nothing from the discussions inside the native community until much later, but this shortcoming of the literature should not let us assume that these discussions did not exist. The series of shifting alliances between the Ojibwe, French, Dakota, and English we discussed in earlier chapters shows that a viable dynamic of political maneuvering ensued from the seventeenth century up to the nineteenth. Throughout these approximately two hundred years—the time of the fur trade—the native peoples were role players in these important international arenas.

In the 1820s, the written record showing Buffalo's leadership at La Pointe may be scant, but it hints at his deep concern about such challenges. By the time of the Prairie du Chien, Fond du Lac and Butte des Morts treaties, he likely sensed that the fur trade would soon end, and although the Ojibwe economy could still survive with its traditional round of winter hunting, spring spearing and sugar making, summer gardening, fall rice harvesting and fish netting, by the 1820s, he seemingly feared that its future was starting to look suspect. Surely, Buffalo's concerns about the future were foreshadowed by his earnest acceptance of Tecumseh's and Tenskwatawa's New Religion only several years previous to his signing of these treaties.

It is not insignificant that according to William Warren, among the western lakes Ojibwe leaders it was La Pointe's Buffalo and Leech Lake's Eshkibagikoonzh (Flat Mouth) who were the most enthusiastic in their acceptance of the Shawnee religious and political movement. The Leech Lake community, as the Ojibwe vanguard into Dakota lands, assumed the major role in military action against these western peoples, and a decade or two after the demise of the New Religion it was these western Ojibwe, as described by a recent writer, who assumed a stance of "passive defiance" against the Americans.[43] Perhaps it is reasonable to suggest this is precisely what was occurring with Buffalo with the coming of the 1820s. If Schoolcraft was speaking of La Pointe's Buffalo, passive defiance certainly fits the stance he took regarding his non-acceptance of an American medal at Fond du Lac in 1826, and also with his refusal to convert to Christianity until 1855. As we will see, after twenty or more years of what must have been intense pressure from missionaries, community leaders, and his own family members at La Pointe, it was only after being ill for a long time that just three days before his death he finally consented to baptism into the Catholic faith.

At the close of the second decade in the nineteenth century, the La Pointe Ojibwe community was at the door of experiencing ever more strident demands for accommodation. Under a prominent line of political leaders such as White Crane, Waubojiig, and Buffalo, the community was still enjoying its cherished way of life, but the signs were evident that more and more changes would need to be made. Americans were in the midst of the community and had no intention of leaving. The ancient Ojibwe institutions doubtlessly were under stress, and adding to this strain was the arrival of the first protestant Christian missionaries at La Pointe.

### *Protestant Missionaries Come to Chequamegon Bay*

1.

THE WARREN BROTHERS' 1818 ARRIVAL is marked as a significant event in the history of Chequamegon Bay. For several years after this date the Warren family played an important leadership role on Madeline Island, and throughout Chequamegon country. The 1950s writer Hamilton Ross claimed that the Warrens were not only successful businessmen, but that "they won the respect of the Indians through their fairness and honesty."[44] What historians have not emphasized is that with the coming of the Warrens came more pressure for the Ojibwe to assimilate into American society. Initially it seems the Warrens were focused on the fur trade, but soon it must have become evident to Buffalo and other resident Ojibwe that these new Americans were not simply dealing in furs but establishing a new community.

The Warren brothers' offspring soon began to appear, and in only a few years the question of providing them with a formal education arose, leading to thoughts of bringing a schoolteacher to Madeline Island. Previously, in order to provide a formal education, some parents elected to send their children to schools at Sault Ste. Marie, Mackinac, or even more distant locations. Some youngsters were sent to Europe for this purpose, and if these students came back to Chequamegon country they often were new forces for social change.

The children of Lyman and Truman Warren usually mentioned in the historical record are those borne to their wives, Marie and Charlotte Cadotte, but it appears Truman also had children by Ugwadadaysgee, another Ojibwe woman. Under Article IV of the Fond du Lac Treaty of 1826, a special allotment of land at Sault Ste. Marie was granted to "half-breeds" in order that they "shall be stimulated to exertion and improvement by the possession of permanent property and fixed residence."[45] In the lengthy schedule of persons to be granted lands under this article, these offspring of Ugwadadaysgee and Truman Warren are mentioned. However, Congress never ratified Article IV, so the proposed Sault Ste. Marie land was not set aside for these Ojibwe mixed-bloods.

It was Lyman Warren (at La Pointe) and William Aitkin (at Fond du Lac) who were behind the arrival of protestant missionaries in western Lake Superior country. The mission lay teacher, Frederick Ayer, came to La Pointe in 1830, and Sherman Hall, the first full time protestant missionary (with wife Betsy), came in 1831. Warren wrote to the American Board of Commissioners for Foreign Missions in Boston, asking that they send both teachers and missionaries to La Pointe.[46] It had been over 160 years since the Jesuits were in the community, and even though throughout these years its residents were in regular contact with Roman Catholic, Methodist and Anglican missionaries at Sault Ste. Marie and Mackinac,[47] this length of time afforded the traditional Ojibwe religion opportunity to function without the regular suppression of resident Christian missionaries. We have seen that in the 1830s, the Lake Superior Ojibwes were still openly carrying out the complex rites of the *midewiwin*, *wabeno*, and other religious institutions. It has been said that as late as 1836 in western Lake Superior, the Ojibwe "had preserved a remarkably unadulterated, persistent, and widespread culture."[48] However, at La Pointe, with the coming of the 1830s, the peoples' ability to continue enjoying this ancient way of life was given added strain.

William Whipple Warren was born to Lyman and Marie Warren on Madeline Island in 1825, and even though he spoke Ojibwe and held a strong interest in the history of native people, he devoted his short life to making a success of himself in the mainstream America of his day. He understood Ojibwe culture to be a relic of the past, destined to give way to the new American society, and his life typifies what was occurring to many mixed-bloods of his time. There certainly were those mixed-bloods who did not join the Americans, choosing instead to continue living the foraging life of their Ojibwe relatives, but we hear little of them. Instead, the written history tells of those who chose to attempt to assimilate into the non-native American society. By 1830, there were many voices telling the Ojibwe to do so, and at La Pointe one of the loudest was that of the Protestant missionary Sherman Hall.

2.

SHERMAN HALL AND HIS WIFE, BETSY, arrived at Madeline Island on 30 August 1831. He kept a journal and was a prolific writer of personal letters, mostly to a brother and sisters back in Weathersfield, Vermont. Fortunately, most of these writings are preserved, so we are afforded insight into the La Pointe of his times. Unfortunately, his letters are not as rich with details of Ojibwe culture as the Schoolcraft and McKenney manuscripts, since his immediate concern was to bring about the demise of Ojibwe ways, not, as is the case with writers like Schoolcraft and McKenney, to merely describe them, leaving the matter of change to those who came later. At least one of Hall's contemporaries saw him as an austere and cold person and felt he quickly turned the Ojibwe against him.[49] His missionary efforts centered on *preaching* to the people, and only after a lengthy period of instruction were his subjects allowed to join him in his religion. Obviously, in his several years at La Pointe he had few converts. For the twenty-four years that his school existed, its records indicate "only seven or eight mixed bloods or Indians joined the church by a confession of faith."[50] We have the above-mentioned letters to tell us what the Halls' thoughts about the Ojibwe were, but as for what the Ojibwe thought about the Halls we must infer from the evidence at hand. The peoples' reaction to this missionary as told in the lodge conversations that certainly occurred during Sherman Hall's time at La Pointe would be fascinating for us to read today, but we can only imagine what they were.

What we learn from the Hall letters is that the resident Ojibwe wanted little to do with him. Sherman Hall considered them to be "heathens"—that is, people without religion. The absurdity of this conclusion is immediately evident since we know that in Hall's day, the Ojibwe lived lives of deep religiosity. In the 1830s, their world was filled with spiritual beings, but due to his zealotry and extreme ethnocentrism, Sherman Hall was unable to see their religion as valid. In the quotations given below we witness the extremity of his bias and understand what the Ojibwe were confronted with during his tenure at La Pointe.

**Sherman Hall, a ninetheenth century protestant missionary at Madeline Island.**

The religious fervor of Sherman Hall was spawned by a movement in New England that occurred in the early 1800s, known as The Second Great Awakening. About a century earlier, Jonathan Edwards began the original Great Awakening (1735-1745)—a call for a renewed awareness of the fear of their god, and for a more personal involvement in making human society a truly religious experience.[51] In time this subsided, but with the American Revolution some colonists again felt the desire for a greater personal expression of their god. The resultant Second Great Awakening saw individuals become more directly involved in work to make the new American society a truly religious society, and some persons who felt this call to action turned to the issue of changing "savage" or "heathen" society into a Christian society.

In the late 1820s, Sherman Hall, Frederick Ayer and William Boutwell were enrolled at Andover Academy in Massachusetts, and all three committed themselves to establishing Christian missions among the Ojibwe people. This type of mission work involved much more than bringing a new religion to "the savage." From the beginning, what Christian missionaries were intent upon doing was to bring a new way of life to America's native people. Native understandings of a proper human existence were to be replaced with Euro-American assumptions of how humans should live. All facets of native life were eventually to be changed, from economic and political, to social and ideological. Rules of marriage, child-rearing and more were to be discarded and new ones taken up.[52]

This is what Frederic Ayer and Sherman Hall brought to Madeline Island and its resident Ojibwe, and this is what William Boutwell tried to bring to Leech Lake, Minnesota Territory. Given this background and context of the Hall's arrival, we can better understand the reticence of the Ojibwe people to immediately take up the missionaries' message. The Halls had no realistic understanding of Ojibwe culture, a fact readily evident in the earliest of Sherman Hall's field correspondence sent back to New England.

Even before landing at La Pointe, in a letter to his brother Aaron, written on 22 August 1831 from an encampment at Keweenaw, he had this to say about the local Ojibwe women: "In general these Indian women appear negligent in their persons and their families." The next summer, on 15 June 1832, from La Pointe he again wrote to Aaron, saying, "we stand here in this dreary desolate wilderness to persuade the heathen to turn from their idols to the living god . . . They are heathen and the abominations of heathenism cleave to them." A year later, on 15 June 1833, he wrote to his sister Lydia Hall, saying that after two years at La Pointe some of the shock had begun to lessen but that, "Heathenism is heathenism still. The eye by continually witnessing its abominations only becomes familiar with it, so that the heart is less affected. Its character is not changed."[53]

The Halls had visions of establishing and taking the lead in what they called "a Chippeway mission," which was to be a major Christian initiative in the western Lake Superior region. They labored to learn the Ojibwe language and were successful in translating the Christian New Testament, but we must be skeptical of their expertise. For an adult English speaker, the depths of the rich and complex Ojibwe language are not mastered easily and the following quotation shows, among other things, that Sherman Hall did not grasp its deep spirituality.[54]

On 22 June 1833, in a letter to his brother, he wrote:

> The heathen have no appropriate terms by which to designate religious ideas . . . Besides they are so sunk in degradation, and so ignorant, as scarcely to possess any moral sensibility. They hardly have a conscience that can be touched. They are so familiar with practices which are forbidden in the word of God, that it is extremely difficult to make them feel that they are sinful.[55]

These telling lines show the inability of Sherman Hall to stand outside his own world when attempting to understand the Ojibwe. His sermons on sin, hell, and the existence of a single overreaching god—concepts foreign to Ojibwe thought—must have become troublesome to the people. We can only imagine Sherman Hall as a member of the powerful American society, coming into a lodge and telling an Ojibwe family of sin and how unless they accepted his words, they would suffer an eternity in a place he called hell. Ojibwe people could refuse to accept these ideas but over time must have thought about them. They surely pondered whether or not the powerful Americans were right, since numerous examples exist in Ojibwe literature to show that eventually such ideas began to take a toll as individuals made accommodations to increasingly difficult situations.[56]

Although Sherman Hall was unsuccessful in winning many converts, in the years to follow, when the Ojibwe foraging life became more and more difficult to carry out, there were conversions to Christianity in western Lake Superior country.

Sherman Hall's tenure at Madeline Island was a lengthy one and we will return to his later letters to track his activities regarding the Ojibwe, but first we must explore the next two Schoolcraft expeditions into the region.

*Notes*

1. Chute 1998:13; Warren 1984[1885]:47.
2. Smith 1985:86; Lewis:1980[1823-28].
3. Kvasnicka and Viola, Editors 1979:1, 5-6.
4. McKenney 1959[1827]:122.
5. McKenney 1959[1827]:169.
6. McKenney 1959[1827]:165,168.
7. McKenney 1959[1827]:180-1.
8. McKenney 1959[1827]:256, 259-261.
9. Olmanson: 2007:69.
10. McKenney 1959[1827]:261-2.
11. McKenney 1959[1827]:265-6.
12. McKenney 1959[1827]:274.
13. McKenney 1959[1827]:306.
14. McKenney 1959[1827]:325; Paap 1985:174-5, 222-5; Vennum 1985: 64-72, 77.
15. McKenney 1959[1827]:295.
16. Schoolcraft 1993[1958]:11.
17. McKenney 1959[1827]:344.
18. McKenney 1959[1827]:346.
19. Diedrich 1999:69.
20. McKenney 1959[1827]:326, 469-472; Warren 1984[1885]:393.
21. McKenney 1959[1827]:462.
22. Warren 1984[1885]:394.
23. Cleland 1992:132-3.
24. Chute 1998:36-8.
25. Chute 1998:36.
26. Diedrich 1999:72.
27. Vizenor 1987:123-5.
28. Lewis 1980[1823-28].
29. Kappler: 1904:282.
30. Kappler: 1904:254.
31. Henry Schoolcraft, the Sault Ste. Marie Indian Agent, was present at the gathering and he says "Chi Waishki," as Schoolcraft spells it, is La Pointe's Buffalo. We are left to determine the relationship between the names Chi Waishki and Wayishkee.
32. Treuer 2011:235.
33. Thwaites 1896:417.
34. Treuer 2011:49-51.
35. Tanner 1994[1830]; Erdrich 1993: xi-xv in Tanner 1994[1830]; Fierst 1996:220-241, in Brown and Vibert.
36. Bushnell 1837, in WisTerrPap, Vol. 27, p. 760-1.
37. Schoolcraft 1993[1958]:118-9.
38. Bushnell 1839:230; Dodge 1837:787; 1838:1031; 1839:1187; Lyon 1839:12-3, in WisTerPap, Vol. 27.
39. Ross 1960:77.
40. Diedrich 1999:73.
41. McKenney 1959[1827]:461.
42. Child 2012; Devens 1992; Sleeper-Smith 2001; Treuer 2011:15, 25-29; Buffalohead 1983.
43. Chute 1998:4.
44. Ross 1960:73.
45. McKenney 1959[1827]:486; Ross 1960:88.
46. Ross 1960:74-5; Ely 2012:xiii.
47. Smith 1987:181.
48. Bray 1979:12, in Nicollet 1970.
49. Allen 1832, in Schoolcraft 1993[1958]:185-6; Ross 1960:87.
50. Ross 1960:86.
51. Bourne 2002:10-13, 167-171.
52. Plane 2000.
53. Hall, Sherman, personal letters of 1831-1833, at NGLVC, Ashland, WI.
54. Ross 1960:84.
55. Hall, Sherman, personal letters of 1833, at NGLVC, Ashland, WI.
56. Peyer 1979; Smith(Jones):73-4.

# 14

# The Schoolcraft Expeditions of 1831 and 1832

### *The Expedition Journals and the Ojibwe*

1.

THE SAME YEAR THE HALLS CAME to Madeline Island, Henry Schoolcraft undertook another expedition into the western lakes region. This time he was sent by Washington authorities to try to bring a halt to the sporadic conflicts between the Dakota and Ojibwe. America's national political leaders were anxious to push the country's boundary westward through the northern lakes territory the Ojibwe and others still held. Following up on their successes in getting peace treaties signed at Prairie du Chien, Fond du Lac, and Butte des Morts, they were anticipating land acquisitions in these regions but first needed to end the warfare.

Included in Schoolcraft's 1831 party were his brother-in-law, George Johnston, who acted as interpreter; Douglass Houghton, the physician; a small group of soldiers from Fort Brady at Sault Ste. Marie; a provisions keeper; and a group of unnamed Ojibwe paddlers. He intended to visit the communities at the Mississippi's headwaters but at Fond du Lac learned that unusually low water restricted his passage and would have made travel extremely difficult. So he decided to return to Chequamegon Bay, to move down the Bad River to the Namakagon and on to the west-central region of what is now the state of Wisconsin. What is important for our interests is his stay at LaPointe where he met with tribal leaders.[1]

Schoolcraft claimed the Ojibwe bands along Lake Superior's southern shores were not seriously alarmed by the recent hostilities with the Dakota. Just one year earlier they sent a number of war parties south into the disputed territories, but in 1831, their concern was less with the Dakota and more with hunger and disease. Smallpox was in the area, and a wild rice crop failure south of Lake Superior was troubling them. According to Schoolcraft, "Whatever other gifts they asked for, they never omitted the gift of food. They made it their first, their second, and their third request."[2]

At La Pointe, Buffalo was the spokesperson for the community but unfortunately we are not given his words, only Schoolcraft's summary of them. About Buffalo, he wrote, "He lamented the war, and admitted the folly of keeping it up; but it was carried on by the Chippewas in self defense, and by volunteer parties of young men, acting without the sanction of the old chiefs." According to Schoolcraft, Buffalo claimed that when allied with the British he was kept informed of the wishes of the Redcoats, but with the recent switch to the alliance with the Americans he was left uninformed of such concerns. Schoolcraft wrote that, "He was rather at a loss for our views respecting the Chippewas, and he wished much for my advice in their affairs."[3]

This is significant since Buffalo was present at both the 1825 and 1826 treaty meetings—and possibly those in 1827—in which American officials spelled out the intentions of the nation's leaders regarding the native peoples. The Subagent, George Johnston, was in Chequamegon Bay from 1826 to 1828 to serve as a local voice for American leaders, but by 1831, it had been three years since his recall. It appears by this time Buffalo was troubled about what was occurring in his region and just what the new alliance with the Americans meant. Many years earlier numerous bands had moved south and west, leaving him and his La Pointe people alone in the tribe's ancient homeland. Buffalo's 1831 statements about what was taking place in his area can be taken as a measure of his mounting concern for the immediate and long-term future of his people.

Henry Schoolcraft used this opportunity to review what he said were the sincere efforts of the American government to help the Ojibwe establish peace in their lands. He claims he summarized the recent activities of the United States—efforts on behalf of the Ojibwe communities—to include the 1825 treaty meeting at Prairie du Chien, which Buffalo had attended, and the attempts to establish boundaries between the Ojibwe and their neighbors. Schoolcraft wrote:

> The chief was evidently affected by this recital. The truth appeared to strike him forcibly; and he said, in a short reply, that he was now *advised*; that he would hereafter feel himself to be advised, &c. He made some remarks on the establishment of a mission school, &c., which being irrelevant, are omitted. He presented a pipe, with an ornamental stem, as a token of his friendship, and his desire for peace.[4]

Here we see the Chief Buffalo popular historians have presented to us. He is portrayed as a prudent and wise leader who willingly accepted the Americans as allies. Very importantly, at the time of this meeting he was approximately seventy years old. He had witnessed the last many successful decades of the fur trade, the coming and going of the British, the devastation of epidemics of new diseases, and now had to deal with an influx of Christian missionaries who argued against the powerful Ojibwe religion and the peoples' way of life. These historical events carried serious challenges to the deepest personal identities of Buffalo and his people.

Buffalo was an experienced, astute and dignified politician, learned in the ways of his world, and now he was forced to meet with American representatives like Henry Schoolcraft who, no matter how much rapport they had with the Ojibwe, were still certain they were negotiating from a position of superior power.

We should ponder why Schoolcraft's words "appeared to strike [Buffalo] forcibly," and why Henry Schoolcraft used italics to stress the word "advised" in Buffalo's puzzlingly short response. Was Buffalo uttering it in sarcasm, as if to say he was not pleased to find himself in a position where he had no option but to take the advice of the Americans? Again, we yearn to hear Buffalo's voice in his own language rather than as a translation into English. What did this prominent leader really say, and how did he emphasize his points? Henry Schoolcraft's short description of this important interchange leaves us unfulfilled. Given what we know about Buffalo's continuing interest in keeping relationships with the British open, we should not conclude that in 1831, he was a mere complacent follower of the wishes of American authorities, as Schoolcraft's account might suggest. It is very likely he was expressing a deep frustration with the difficult situation he and his people were in by 1831.

Also, what was the remark of mission schools about? Was Buffalo giving his approval to the new school Sherman Hall was starting on Madeline Island, or was he speaking against it? Finally, while it is not absolutely clear, when Schoolcraft mentions a pipe we might assume he meant Buffalo gave him a pipe as a gift—that is, a gift to take with him—not that he was merely offering a pipe ceremony in his honor. A pipe ceremony, with its manipulation of cosmological non-human spiritual forces, is always a serious matter and when such a ceremony is given in honor of someone it is a major event, so if this instance was a pipe ceremony and not the *gifting* of a pipe to Schoolcraft, it was still a very important show of respect. Whatever may have been the case, this matter of a pipe can be read as a political gesture in which Buffalo was attempting to cling to his role as a major leader negotiating between equals. Such pipes, especially one with an elaborately decorated stem, are not easily come by and any act involving one—whether as a gift, or in a smoking ceremony—is very important.

The literature tells of Buffalo giving a few pipes to American officials and always these gestures are interpreted as symbols of his friendship, but gifts like these must also be taken as expressions of Buffalo's role as a political leader, and their deeper message seems lost on past writers. Today when a pipe is used in relationships between individuals it is an extremely important event, never taken lightly, and if someone is gifted with a pipe it should be received with an awareness of the great responsibility such a gift carries. Remembering that a person never owns a pipe, instead that they *carry* it, and in this way shoulder great responsibility for its care, we see the deep significance of interpersonal relationships involving pipes. Gifts are never free, and while we should recognize the extremely important meaning in the use of the pipe for Buffalo, Henry Schoolcraft tells us nothing of his thoughts about receiving this pipe, leaving us to speculate on its meaning to him.

## 2.

THE VERY NEXT YEAR, IN JUNE, Schoolcraft was back on Madeline Island, this time leading an expedition to the headwaters of the Mississippi River. As in 1820 and 1831, he had a small unit of military personnel with him, this time led by Lieutenant James Allen, who was stationed at Fort Brady in Sault Ste. Marie; a contingent of native paddlers that, significantly, Schoolcraft left unnamed; Dr. Douglass Houghton, a physician and geologist; and William Boutwell, a protestant missionary. Another member of the party, who we learn about through Boutwell's correspondence, was Buhkwujjenene,[5] a son of Shingwaukonse, the Canadian Ojibwe leader, but it seems he left the party after coming to La Pointe, where he spent time with Sherman Hall, furthering his interest in the Christian religion. At the time Buhkwujjenene was twenty-one years old, and after a few months at La Pointe returned to Sault Ste. Marie. As a younger man, this son of Shingwaukonse made many trips with his father to the Ojibwe communities at the western end of Lake Superior and he was familiar with the individuals and families along the way. A few years after his 1832 trip to La Pointe he married Marguerite Cadotte of that location, after which the couple resided at Sault Ste. Marie. Buhkwujjenene's interest in Christianity may have influenced his father's later involvement with a number of Christian denominations.[6]

These comments on a son of Shingwaukonse help us understand that in 1832, life on the south shore of Lake Superior was not one of isolated communities of Ojibwe people that came together only on very rare occasions. As was true a century or more earlier, people traversed this long stretch of shoreline between the eastern and western extremities of the lake, and of course, far beyond, by using the birch canoe. Ojibwe communities maintained a communication system for social, economic, political, and religious purposes that later included what has been labeled *the moccasin telegraph*.

Beyond the use of canoes for water travel, for interior overland communication there was a network of runners who carried messages from community to community. Because of this we would not be wrong in stating that at a certain level there existed a single *macro*-Ojibwe community all along the Lake Superior shoreline and into the interiors of Michigan, Wisconsin, Minnesota, Ontario, and beyond. Thus, expeditions like Schoolcraft's, in 1832, were moving through a land whose residents knew each other, and who were, generally speaking, in touch with each other. Their leaders, certainly, kept in regular contact as they discussed matters pertinent to the welfare of their people, and by 1832, paramount among these matters was the nature of relations with British and American authorities. Buffalo, Mesai, Black Bird, Hole-in-the-Day, Shingwaukonse, White Crow, and many others not only knew each other, but regularly met to discuss these important matters.

Another issue that shows the extent to which the Lake Superior Ojibwe and adjacent bands were kept informed of matters important to their region concerns the Black Hawk War of

1832. Although it is usually not mentioned as one of the reasons for his trip to the Mississippi headwaters of that year, Henry Schoolcraft in part made the trip to determine to what extent the resident Ojibwe were sympathetic with the Sauk leader Black Hawk and his cause, and whether or not there was the possibility they would join him in his conflict with the Americans. After returning from the headwaters, Schoolcraft told a correspondent on 15 August 1832, that although most of the Ojibwe he encountered did not express an intent to join the Sauk leader in the conflict, he felt "there were reasons to apprehend hostilities" from the Lac du Flambeau and nearby bands due to their continued anti-American sentiments. He also learned that the Ojibwe knew about Black Hawk's conflict, and in fact that they were well informed of all the war's events. Schoolcraft learned that in 1830, 1831, and 1832, Blackhawk had asked "the whole Chippewa nation," including the band of Shingwaukonse at the Canadian side of Sault Ste. Marie, to join him in his battle, but at the time (the summer of 1832) it was unknown if a reply had been made.[7]

Schoolcraft, Allen, Houghton and Boutwell all left writings that offer valuable information about the native people encountered along the way. Unfortunately, we have none of the stories from the native members of the expedition. In particular, the journals of Lt. Allen and William Boutwell have been mentioned as most noteworthy regarding their details and richness in describing the Ojibwe people. In the paragraphs below we will discuss these writings, focusing on what they tell about the Chequamegon Bay Ojibwe of the time.

3.

THE WRITINGS OF HENRY SCHOOLCRAFT we are left with from this expedition include a number of official letters to various persons and a single longer account. This latter document is not in the form of a daily journal written in the field, but is a *narrative* composed after the fact, and obviously carefully thought out and polished. By 1832, Schoolcraft was attempting to assume the role of an expert on Indian affairs, and apparently was desirous of becoming accepted as a member of America's emerging *literati*. This document was intended to serve purpose in both pursuits, and was meant for a wide audience. Going far beyond description, it offers a discussion of selected aspects of the history of the western lakes region in which Schoolcraft gives his opinions on a wide range of related topics. For example, he attempts to explain the *mind* of the northern Indian as a product of the demands of a mobile hunting and gathering life style, and concludes that the mind he found in 1832 was the same mind the French found when they arrived three hundred years earlier.[8]

Schoolcraft's discussion of the Indian mind is intriguing for a number of reasons. One is that in it we see his awareness of what later would come to be called the *culture* of hunters and gatherers, and how this concept can indeed, be a force in what Schoolcraft was labeling *the Indian mind*. However, as much as they might hint at the psychology of the Indian, such discussions are more important for their disclosure of the minds of the writers of the time, like Henry Schoolcraft's. They can help us understand *his* motives and assumptions, but their lasting contributions to our understanding of the Ojibwe are questionable.

Amid his pages of musing, we are given descriptions of Ojibwe communities visited on the long trip. A paragraph about the expedition's brief stay at La Pointe is found, where they met the Halls and where Schoolcraft was pleased to see a Christian mission station and school. He wrote: "It is interesting to observe the dawning of the gospel at a spot, which has been long noted as the scene of Indian trade, and the rallying point of Indian war parties. It is at this place, the Chegoimegon of early writers, that tradition places the ancient council fire of the Chippewa nation."[9]

Buffalo was not on the island at the time the expedition reached it, but we are told that earlier the party met him at Keweenaw, where he had come to see John Holiday, the trader at that site. Schoolcraft said Buffalo was interested in the purpose of the expedition, and that he "presented a peace pipe as the evidence of his friendship." Here again we are left with the question of whether this was another gifting of a pipe, or just the act of Buffalo holding a pipe ceremony in the agent's, and expedition's, honor. It would have been extraordinary for Buffalo to give Schoolcraft the gift of a sacred pipe in two consecutive years, but once more, whatever the case—gift or just a pipe ceremony—Buffalo was conflating a show of respect for Henry Schoolcraft with an unvoiced statement of the chief's personal position as a prominent leader of the Ojibwe. In other words, while following protocol by his deference to Schoolcraft, he was at the same time reminding this American official that Buffalo himself also was a political "official". Thus, both the 1831 and 1832 pipe incidents between Buffalo and Schoolcraft need to be taken as meetings between two powerful political leaders.[10]

Furthermore, the image of Buffalo paddling from Chequamegon Bay to Keweenaw to meet with the resident trader is an interesting one. John Holiday had a long term as the American Fur Company trader in Keweenaw Bay at L'Ance and had considerable influence with the Ojibwe people. The Warrens were the traders at Buffalo's community in Chequamegon, but for some reason in the summer of 1832, he had business at Keweenaw. Doubtless when at Keweenaw, Buffalo met with the local Ojibwe leaders if for no other reason than to make a respectful social call, but acknowledging that a site like Keweenaw served as a conduit for communications between centers of influence like La Pointe and both the eastern American and Canadian Ojibwe communities at Sault Ste. Marie, it could be possible that with this trip Buffalo had more on his mind than agent John Holiday.

Schoolcraft's narrative includes tables of statistics about this trip. For the trading post at La Pointe he said there were two licensed clerks with four persons under their employ as interpreters, boatmen, and so forth. He said a total of six white persons were engaged in the fur trade at this post. On this trip a census of the region's natives was attempted, and we are given a population chart for all villages. The Ojibwe of La Pointe were included with those at the mouth of the Montreal and Bad River, and for these three communities Schoolcraft listed thirty-two men, forty women, 113 children and twenty-eight mixed bloods, for a total of 213 persons. This number seems low and raises the question of the accuracy of these figures. The expedition was in the region in June, a time when families were supposedly congregating in Chequamegon Bay after spending several weeks at their outlying sugarbushes, but Schoolcraft's low figure suggests many were not in the region at the time of his visit. Unfortunately, we are told nothing about the method used to take this count.

4.

IN THE WRITINGS OF THE OTHER PERSONS on the trip we find important descriptive information on the Ojibwe. Lt. Allen left a lengthy and detailed journal, one that was so impressive that Lewis Cass, then Secretary of War, sent it to the House of Representatives where it was published as an official congressional document. Doubtless this journal received a wide readership in its time and had its own effect on the nation's opinions regarding western Lake Superior country and its native people. One example of the effect the journal had is seen in the memoirs of Alfred Brunson, a nineteenth century Methodist minister who, as will be discussed below, became a Sub-agent at La Pointe for a short time. Brunson read Allen's journal in 1834, "and was so impressed with the account he gave of the wretched state of the Indians in that region" that he decided to work to have a Christian mission established in their country. As it turned out, Brunson himself soon went to the Upper Mississippi region as a missionary among the Dakota.[11]

While Lt. Allen may not have been as convinced about the need for the Ojibwe to be Christianized as Cass, Schoolcraft, McKenney, Brunson, and others were, he was certain they had to turn to farming in order to save themselves. Along Lake Superior's south shore he saw what he called an "exhausted" land, soon to be bereft of its rich fur bearing animals, and he concluded that since the Ojibwe did not understand this and apparently were not able to take action to improve their situation, their future would be tragic unless something was done to help them.

Allen described the whitefish fishery at Sault Ste. Marie and told how since 1830, two white men were earning a substantial living by operating a commercial fishing business at the site and despite local Ojibwe protestations, this illegal commercial fishing continued for years. As the expedition moved along the south shore Allen described the usual Ojibwe villages, including the sturgeon weirs in streams along the way. He said the people at Grand Island were "well clothed and look healthy." However, at Keweenaw he saw a community dangerously dependent upon the provisions provided by John Holiday, the resident trader. Allen felt the surrounding lands would soon be depleted of fur bearing animals, a situation foretelling of serious problems. Over half of Holiday's annual trade was for provisions he brought from Mackinaw, an indication that the Ojibwe were no longer producing the amount of food they needed to survive.[12]

At La Pointe he found a similar situation. The expedition arrived the night of 20 June, and stayed well into the next day. He wrote:

> This island was, in former times, a place of rendezvous for the Chippewa tribe, where they held great councils on matters which concerned the whole nation. It was also the residence of a large and powerful band. But a change of national policy, by which the several bands act less in concert, and a general impoverishment of the country in their peculiar means of subsistence, has destroyed its particular band to about one hundred and eighty-four souls, who are dispersed about the bays and islands in the vicinity, and subsist almost entirely of fish, excepting at the time of their winter hunts, when their trader furnishes them with corn and flour.[13]

These comments of "a large and powerful band" that made Madeline Island its home resonate with William Warren's belief regarding the existence of a large Ojibwe village in Chequamegon Bay in distant times. In 1832, when coming along Lake Superior's southern shore, Lt. Allen saw a land being stripped of its human food resources by over-harvesting, something that supposedly "destroyed" the large Madeline Island band, and reduced it to a smaller community (he claimed only 184 individuals). According to Allen, if not for the local trader who provided grain and flour in winter, this band would have been in a threatening situation.

This is an image of Ojibwe life along the lakeshore that Lt. Allen revisits often in his journal and may have had some validity, but it also seems possible that what he was witnessing was the usual summertime adaptation of a mobile foraging society of hunters, fishers, gardeners and gatherers, not a struggling, *remnant* community, left from earlier "glory" days. It is this sort of human adaptation—the foraging band system—that the literature shows was in the region going back to the mid-seventeenth century, and which I have argued was difficult for early European and Euro-American observers not only to understand, but simply *to see*.

Allen claimed that the annual income for Lyman Warren at his La Pointe post was $2,000.00, a sum derived from a take of "250 beaver skins, 500 martens, 50 bears, 1,000 to 1,500 rats, and 20 or 30 otters, all of excellent quality." He mentioned the efforts of the Halls with their mission school, in which they were attempting to teach English to the Ojibwe as well as to read and write their own language. However, Lt. Allen did not think much of the Hall's success. He said:

> Mr. Hall's progress, however, in the accomplishment of these benevolent ends, has not hitherto been very flattering. The Indians have manifested rather an aversion for his doctrines, and a disposition not to listen to his advise. All that lived on the island left it soon after he arrived, and they have learned his motives; and a fear for their own peculiar institutions, or some other cause, still keeps them in a great measure aloof from him. They refuse to come to church, or to attend divine worship, and the only direct means now left him of operating on their minds to his purpose is to visit them at their villages and in their lodges where, by making their hospitality subserve, he is kindly received, and listened to with seeming attention, but still with little or no apparent effect; none of the Indians having as yet shown any willingness to embrace his doctrines,

excepting one older Indian man, who has been for some time laboring under a severe disease of the lungs. Mr. Hall is not however discouraged, but hopes, by means of his school, and other efforts, to effect many beneficial results. His school at present contains twelve scholars, all quite young and mostly half breeds, the Indians having shown also an unwillingness to give him their children to instruct.[14]

With little effort we can imagine Sherman Hall paddling to the mainland in search of the people, then entering their lodges and preaching to them. Traditional rules of Ojibwe hospitality would require that he be courteously received, and for a time at least, that the people submit to his preaching. During these early years of the Hall's residence in the community, there must have been many lodge conversations about the behavior of this new protestant missionary.

Lt. Allen concluded his observations about the Ojibwe of Lake Superior by saying:

These northern Indians are generally wild, untamed, and unsubdued; they have none of the arts, institutions, or manners of the whites; and their prejudices in favor of their own particular habits and institutions, which have descended to them from their forefathers, are engrafted and rooted in their very nature, insomuch that their removal, by the ordinary means of teaching, preaching, and advise, is rather a speculative theory than a result that experience teaches us to expect . . . The present condition of most of the Chippewa Indians is deplorable. They are mostly very poor. Their country is becoming every day more exhausted of the means of subsistence hitherto used, and they are making no preparations to provide for any others . . . The Indians cannot be induced to make a change in their habits and manners, unless the advantage be immediate and tangible, and is made evident to their senses.[15]

What we see in the above quote is that in 1832, Lake Superior's Ojibwe people were holding fast to their way of life and according to onlookers like Lt. Allen, were not about to give it up. Their culture was persisting but was struggling to do so. Although he saw hardship, to use Allen's term, the people were still "unsubdued."

The expedition moved as two units, one under the direction of Henry Schoolcraft, and the other led by Lt. Allen. It left Madeline Island the evening of 21 June, and Allen's unit encamped for the night at either Basswood or Wilson Island. Henry Schoolcraft most likely encamped at either Frog or Raspberry Bay on the Red Cliff shoreline. They embarked the morning of the 22nd, made the turn at the tip of the Bayfield Peninsula and headed for Fond du Lac.

## 5.

THE JOURNAL OF DR. DOUGLASS HOUGHTON is frustratingly troublesome while being rich in its accounts of the Ojibwe people. What is so disappointing for our purposes is that the notebook describing his experiences from Sault Ste. Marie to Fond du Lac has disappeared, leaving us with nothing about the in-going trip to Chequamegon Bay. We are treated to a brief passage from the return trip when, from 7 August to 12 August, Houghton stayed on Madeline Island before embarking for his paddle back to Sault Ste. Marie. In these six days he says he saw much of the island, to include the ample gardens of its residents. He remarked that very few Indians were present.[16]

In 1832, Congress passed an act authorizing the vaccination of Indian people against smallpox, and Douglass Houghton was under orders to carry this out all along the way. He left ample written material about his experiences in the lands west of Fond du Lac, but we can only assume that what he tells of vaccinating these persons is similar to what he experienced *east* of Fond du Lac. Henry Schoolcraft mentions that along the length of Lake Superior, 699 persons were vaccinated and that the expedition "experienced no difficulty in getting them to submit to the process."[17] Houghton provides a chart showing he vaccinated a total of 2,070 individuals on the trip, 224 of those from LaPointe, and most of this latter figure being under the age of forty.[18]

From Douglass Houghton's journal we learn that the Ojibwe communities west of Lake Superior were busy with their summer activities. Their many gardens are described, and the usual seasonal ceremonies and related activities mentioned. At Sandy Lake he reported that the large band of people residing at that location was "absent on their summer hunt."[19] This most likely was an excursion onto the western prairie for buffalo. He tells of some of the traditional Ojibwe methods of treating wounds and diseases and of the peoples' interest in *his* methods.

Houghton and the other writers spoke of witnessing a scalp dance at Cass Lake. To them, such dances were markers for *savagery*. A war party had just returned from an excursion against the Dakota and a few scalps were turned over to the women. After being affixed to poles, they were held high as the dancers moved around the dance ground to the beat of hand drums.

Lt. Allen, Douglass Houghton, and William Boutwell all understood the dance as a ceremony to support a family that had lost a member to the Dakota and that onlookers were expected to offer compensatory gifts to these mourners. All writers noted that it was only the women—apparently those younger ones who were eligible for marriage—who did the actual dancing while holding the scalps as other family members gathered around.

The writers saw the economic function of this dance, but its deeper symbolism was not mentioned, and apparently not understood by them. This involves the sexual division of labor in Ojibwe society and the rule that a scalp, like the product of a man's successful hunt, is to be turned over to the women, who carry out the prescribed ritual activities such important objects demand. These complexities and their connections with the economic, political and religious institutions of Ojibwe society were lost on the expedition's journalists since, to them, *savages* lived in a world essentially without design or meaning.

What is evident in the writings of the 1832 expedition members is their difficulty to make sense out of what they considered *savage* life. At times they simply dismissed the people, as Sherman Hall did, as unfortunates who were born into *heathenism*, and as such, their existence was unorganized and without rationality. However, occasionally these observers seemed at the brink of a greater awareness when contemplating the Ojibwe—at these times they *did* see patterns and seemed able to break through to new levels of understanding, if not acceptance, but ultimately they had to dismiss the Indians behaviors and institutions as faulty and undeveloped, and thus, they concluded that the tribal way of life was not only inferior, but destined to be replaced with their own.

6.

HOUGHTON'S APPROACH TO HIS TASK of vaccinating the people is poignantly shown in a letter he wrote while at Fond du Lac on 24 June 1832. He was writing to his brother Richard and said,

> I find vaccination of the Indians an irksome task, chiefly in consequence of the great numbers. Last evening after our arrival I operated upon two hundred and forty at one sitting, and I shall complete the band to-morrow. As yet I have only found a few who had never heard of vaccination. It is astonishing to learn the fearful dread they have of the smallpox. When I commence operating they crowd around me with their arms ready, and anxiously wait their turn. I keep an accurate list of the number, age and sex of those vaccinated, together with the tribe and band to which they belong.[20]

Douglass Houghton felt that there were five smallpox epidemics in Ojibwe country over a period of time from about 1750 to 1824. He thought the first incident was caused when a war party of over a hundred men from the head of the lake brought the germ back from Montreal. The second epidemic occurred about 1770, in the far northern bands in the upper Mississippi region. According to Houghton, the Ojibwe felt the germ was carried to them in some contaminated goods sent by the agent at Mackinac. This was supposedly in retaliation for the incident at Leech Lake wherein a trader's goods were stolen and he was killed. The third epidemic took place about in the year 1784, when the germ entered from the Missouri River area and affected only those bands north and west of Fond du Lac. The fourth took place in 1802 or 1803, and only at Sault Ste. Marie, when a *voyageur* returning from Montreal brought the smallpox germ with him. The last epidemic was in 1824, and was also at Sault Ste. Marie, this time the germ coming from Drummond's Island.[21]

While these epidemics are recorded in history we have practically no documentation of their toll on the Ojibwe people involved. Again, the losses these families and communities experienced must be seen as major events that were instrumental in not only reducing population levels, but in causing untold changes in Ojibwe history.[22]

7.

THE JOURNAL OF WILLIAM BOUTWELL, the missionary, offers much about his impressions of the Ojibwe people, but unfortunately his writing tells us more about the missionary than the people he attempted to describe. Philip P. Mason called Boutwell a "religious zealot" who was "harsh in his criticisms of these 'pagan' Indians and the 'irreligious' *voyageurs* who failed to observe the Sabbath. Of particular value are his observations on Indian life and customs, which are the most candid, albeit naïve, of all the diarists."[23] As is the case with the writings of Sherman Hall, and even with Cass, Schoolcraft, and McKenney, in Boutwell's journal we see the thoughts of a person who was considered to be literate and educated in his time, but nevertheless was still very limited in his ability to go beyond the assumptions of his own world. Since we are familiar with the aspects of Indian life and activity Boutwell and his expedition members met on this trip, with a few exceptions we will offer only a summary of his observations.

At the Tobacco River west of Sault Ste. Marie, he tells of meeting a canoe from Lac du Flambeau whose occupants were delivering *wampum* to Henry Schoolcraft, telling him of their preparations to go on a military excursion against the Dakota. It is noteworthy that even after the expeditions of 1820 and 1831, which included the Americans' admonitions not to go to war with the Dakota, and also after the treaty gatherings of 1825 and 1826, where these admonitions were stated again, that the Lac du Flambeau Ojibwe were ignoring them.

At La Pointe, Boutwell tells of examining the gardens of Sherman Hall and feeling they were impressive. He noted that the resident Indians were at Bad River in gardens of their own and that later in the day:

> . . . a few Indians returned to the Island among whom was Goguagani. He is the second Chief. The old Bizhiki being on a journey to the Sault. Then Mr. S. distributed some of his presents among the Indians and made some valuable presents to the Mission family and school. Goguagani in reply said he should have been under the necessity of hunting a whole year to have purchased the articles presented.[24]

It was at Fond du Lac that Boutwell offered some pointed remarks about the *voyageurs* in the expedition. He complained that as was the case with the Indians, they did not observe his "Sabbath." He went on to say: "These men are more hopeless than the Indians, even, whose example before, and influence upon them, is most pernicious. There are few exceptions, where they are not as degraded, in intellect, and as disgusting with filth, as the Indians themselves."[25]

At the lengthy and difficult portage between Fond du Lac and Sandy Lake—it has twelve *poses*, or rest stops—Boutwell was struck by the hard work of the Ojibwe men and women as well as the *voyageurs*. Several days of rain made the trail muddy, often with water up to the knees. The party rose at four in the morning to begin the difficult task and it did not take long for Boutwell to notice the efforts of the women. Some of them carried a child and other personal effects, along with sacks of flour and other expedition provisions, throughout the long portage.

He was particularly harsh and uninformed about Ojibwe women. In 1832, this missionary was just beginning his years of work with the people and with the hindsight afforded us we can anticipate the difficulties that lay ahead of him, and more importantly, for many Ojibwe women he encountered. After noting how these women labored along the portage with more than a few heavy items on their backs—in some cases with a young child atop it all—he offered these striking comments on their character and personal habits: "Selfishness is a prominent characteristic of the squaws . . . An old squaw is one of the most selfish and capricious of beings . . . The squaws are horribly filthy in their persons, as well as sluttish in their habits."[26]

On 27 June, at the end of the portage, the people who provided the labor for this difficult task were compensated with presents from Henry Schoolcraft. Boutwell said:

> The Indians seemed highly gratified with their presents, such as tobacco, a shirt, ammunition, lead, flints and steel, fish-hooks, ribbons, mirrors, &c. The women, 10 of whom aided, received a piece of calico, thread, tobacco, awls, needles, ribbons, handkerchiefs, &c. Flour and Indian meal were issued to them which they received in the usual manner, in one corner of a dirty blanket, or an old unwashed shirt.[27]

William Boutwell describes the platform burials of the Ojibwe he found at Sandy Lake. Then on the way to Cass and Leech Lakes he, like so many of the journalists we have previously discussed, spoke with admiration of the skill Ojibwe people—to include women and even children—have in handling a canoe in water.[28] Their ease and ability to make a birch canoe do what they want it to even in difficult situations impressed the Americans.

## 8.

In summary, the writings from Schoolcraft's 1832 expedition show that in these times serious change was coming to Chequamegon Bay, but also that its Ojibwe residents were holding to the core of their old way of life. All along the southern shore of Lake Superior they were still utilizing the resources of forest, water and sky. They were hunting, fishing, gardening and gathering as throughout the year they moved from one area to the next. Along with this was the annual round of religious ceremonies they used to celebrate this old way of life. By 1832, all of this was persisting. This is a point not stressed by writers of the time, who seemed only to see what they called the poverty and hardship of the native people.

Despite the persistence of the old Ojibwe culture, there was an increased need for change, and accordingly, perhaps the most important adaptation concerned traditional food sources. All the expedition's writers noted this, but especially Lt. Allen, when he spoke of what he called the "exhaustion" of the land. Historians have used Allen's remarks to support their belief that by the 1830s, the western lakes Ojibwe were in a very serious situation.[29] Allen, like McKenney, Schoolcraft and others, was repeating the earlier sentiments of Thomas Jefferson when they said that not only did the Ojibwe have to learn farming, but it was becoming evident that the Americans had the moral responsibility to aid them with this change.

A related point is what the expedition's writers had to say about their time at Leech Lake. This western Ojibwe community had a pronounced effect on all the expedition's journalists. It was here that the Americans found people who were still in regular contact with the British across the Canadian border and who were also engaged in sporadic military skirmishes with the Dakota. They did not feel the need to warmly receive the numerous officials from distant Washington, D.C., who were coming into their country with increasing frequency since the appearance of Zebulon Pike, and as was the case in the earlier days of the fur trade, in 1832, they felt confident of their ability to take care of themselves.

Schoolcraft, Allen, Houghton and Boutwell all were impressed with the Ojibwe of Leech Lake, and all for the same reason. Henry Schoolcraft's comments were more subdued than the others but that was because his narrative was a polished product meant for a wide distribution, not a hastily written field journal. In it he attempted to *analyze and explain* what he found with these Ojibwe rather than merely describe them. By presenting himself as a learned scholar, Schoolcraft was assuming a very different stance than the other writers. Interestingly, he noted that at Leech Lake the men "walked through the village with a bold and free air,"[30] and although he tried to interpret the behavior of Flat Mouth, the leader, in a reasoned, if not "scientific" manner, his awareness that this community was unlike other Ojibwe villages the expedition visited is obvious.

Schoolcraft implied that Flat Mouth was a leader who was well versed in the use of ceremony and role-playing, and as such, an onlooker had to put much of his talk and gesturing aside. Schoolcraft's written analysis of this leader's behavior was itself filled with this same sort of political and intellectual posturing. The meeting of Flat Mouth and Henry Schoolcraft needs to be understood as a coming together of two political leaders who not only were very familiar with what we have been calling frontier, or fur trade theater, but who were expert in its self-serving use.

Perhaps Lt. Allen's analysis of the community is the most clear. He intimates that Leech Lake was an example of what the more eastern Ojibwe villages had been like before the coming of the whites. Allen said:

> This was altogether the most interesting band that we had met with among all the Chippewas whom we had visited . . . From their remoteness from white settlements, they still retain much of their native character. They have not been debased or enfeebled with whiskey, from the difficulty of obtaining it in great quantities; and unlike most of their tribe, they are strong, athletic, muscular men, of large stature, and fine appearance, looking proud, haughty, and unsubdued; and carrying an independence and fearlessness with their manner, that indicates a full estimate of their own strength.[31]

Allen speaks only of the males of the community, but from his words we can conclude that here was a group of people—to include elders, women, teens and children as well—in which all the institutions of early Ojibwe society were successfully functioning. It was the *entire* community that lay before the expedition members and it caused them to pause and consider what they were witnessing.

Douglass Houghton also was impressed. He said:

> I had never before seen indians who possessed the manly & decided appearance of these . . . The indians of this band have greater resources than any I had before seen, game, (bear, deer, elk, moose &c in abundance), fish (white fish) & wild rice. Their village was upon a sandy soil (nearly the same as most of this country) but a field of corn & potatoes planted by the indians were in a flourishing state.[32]

All the expedition's writers mentioned the house of Flat Mouth and his wife. Unlike the other families of the village who had wigwams, Flat Mouth had a larger structure made of logs. Schoolcraft and the other American leaders were invited to it for breakfast, and when seated inside, studied its contents. This couple had recently lost a son in battle with the Dakota and many of the chief's personal possessions were dabbed with a smear of vermillion, a sign that he had been done harm by his enemies. During a meeting later, he brought out a handful of medals and asked Henry Schoolcraft to remove the red markings as a gesture that his government would stand by the promise it made to protect and help Flat Mouth and his people. When describing this incident, Schoolcraft said Flat Mouth merely held the medals up in the air, but Lt. Allen wrote that he threw them into the dirt at Schoolcraft's feet, a serious affront to the officious American.

William Boutwell noted that in his opening remarks, when speaking of his people, Flat Mouth addressed Schoolcraft by saying "he was sorry that Mr. S. considered them as children, and not as men."[33] With this remark Flat Mouth was cutting through the pretension of such meetings by refusing to assume the role of child. No doubt he was also attempting to display his authority to his tribesmen by standing up to the Americans, but he was also reminding Schoolcraft and his party that the Leech Lake Ojibwe were not dependent upon them.

What is significant is that the remarks of these writers show that in 1832, they compared the Leech Lake community with those to the east—like La Pointe—and found the latter wanting. Unlike these others, Leech Lake was still an independent, free, and obviously vibrant community. Surely, an awareness of this unwelcome change sweeping over their lives is what eastern leaders like La Pointe's Buffalo were struggling with in these times. While the expedition members were in agreement that at Leech Lake they witnessed a community that, albeit in their eyes was still *savage*, was nevertheless one that had not yet been altered in a decidedly negative way by contact with the Europeans and Americans. Nearly a century earlier, Alexander Henry made the same observation when traveling into lands west of Lake Superior. He remarked that native people with the least contact with Euro-Americans were "happier" than those in regular contact with whites.[34]

The writers in the Schoolcraft expedition were intimating that the eastern Ojibwe communities had undergone a deep and near debilitating transition that spoke to dependency. In other words, by the 1830s, places like La Pointe were no longer what they had been before the coming of the Americans. The Leech Lake journals of Lt. Allen and the others hint that these observers were given pause to contemplate what they and their way of life were causing. Unfortunately, we are left only with their written words. The discussions that doubtlessly occurred during the expedition's evening dinners and around its campfires were not recorded, and like related discussions around Ojibwe camp and lodge fires, these important windows into the past are lost to us.

## 9.

BEFORE LEAVING THIS DISCUSSION of the 1831 and 1832 Schoolcraft expeditions we would be remiss if we did not make one final comment. This concerns the all-pervading intent of the trips as they related to the Ojibwe people, and how this was evident in their planning, composition and execution. Both the 1831 and 1832 expeditions, as was the case in the earlier Cass trip of 1820, and the Cass and McKenney trip to Fond du Lac in 1826, were meant to serve a purpose for the American goal of eventually pushing its boundaries westward through Ojibwe territory. In all four instances, these expeditions were conceived, organized and carried out by members of a nation that was certain about its superiority to the Ojibwe people and their culture. Not only did the Americans know they were superior, they also were convinced that it was the Indians' destiny to either adopt the American way of life—to include, of course, its religion—or to cease to exist.

To this end we can appreciate the importance of a few details of the expeditions that, although mentioned in the foregoing discussion, were not stressed. These concern the interrelatedness of political power, military force, and religion, and by extension, their impact on social and economic change.

Each of the expeditions included a contingent of military personnel that was regularly put on display. At strategic times these soldiers were drilled before the watching Ojibwe, and as part of such exhibitions, their firearms were discharged. The military uniforms, the rifles with their loud reports, and the shouted drill commands were all foreign to Ojibwe customs of war and social control. We have seen that Thomas McKenney remarked about these staged maneuvers at Sault Ste. Marie in 1826, and was struck by the crowd of tribesmen who pensively sat and watched as they quietly smoked their pipes. At Leech Lake, Douglass Houghton also noted the Ojibwe interest in the soldiers. He said, "The dread in which the indians hold soldiery is truly astonishing. They consider them as men who have sold themselves to die & are consequently afraid of nothing."[35] They were *full-time* warriors, who unlike the Ojibwe warriors, did not put their weapons down after an encounter with the enemy to resume their domestic lives.

Also, the impact of having the American flag displayed when the expedition was traveling, and prominently flown when in camp, must be noted. This banner represented The Great Father in Washington and all that he led. As a national symbol, the flag told the Ojibwe people that the expedition was part of that distant powerful nation.

The inclusion of Christian clergymen was as important as the flag and the military. We should not think that the combination of soldiers, flag and religious leaders was lost on the tribesmen. These three components of the expeditions reinforced each other. Certainly, in the minds of both the Ojibwe and the Americans, the power of the military and the government it represented was related to the spiritual power the religious leaders claimed to be bringing to western Lake Superior.

And beneath this impressive display of power was the suggestion that the Ojibwe would soon be pressed to make major changes in their culture. As we have seen, the message the Americans were bringing, finally, concerned the end of the old Ojibwe way of life.

And how was this show of force with its underlying message received by the Ojibwe? The literature from the various expeditions shows that the people were responding in their traditional manner. To a considerable extent they were still holding the course, that is, they were continuing on with their foraging adaptation, as well as responding ceremoniously. The spirit world was being turned to for direction. Throughout the writings we were shown that *midewiwin*, *wabeno*, and *jiisakaan* ceremonies were carried out from the eastern portions of Lake Superior to the western communities at the Mississippi's headwaters.

Moreover, pipe ceremonies were evident in virtually all the writings we discussed. In a previous chapter we saw the integral role of tobacco at incidents of great importance to the community. Thomas McKenney in particular spoke of what he felt was an inordinate degree of pipe smoking by Ojibwe men. For example, he noted that when coming off the water and stepping onto a beach, one of the first things done was to heat water for tea and to light the pipes.[36] The Americans missed the fact that these sessions can be interpreted as religious acts meant to placate spirits of the water. In the Ojibwe world, *nibi* (water) is a spiritual force in its own right, and when venturing out onto it humans must take ritual precautions. Just as importantly, water is the residing place of other powerful spirits who require placation, and tobacco is an acceptable item to be used for this purpose. The incidents of smoking McKenney remarked about in 1826 at Lake Superior can perhaps be understood as similar to those occurring some two hundred years earlier in eastern Massachusetts, in communities of Nantucket Indians who began attending Christian church services. Upon the completion of the services they would light pipes, and after smoking for a moment would pass them to those in attendance as they uttered thanks to their spirit forces.[37] Such acts of cultural persistence in the face of pressure to change most likely were found throughout Ojibwe communities in the western Great Lakes in the early nineteenth century.

With this in mind, we now can ponder those men at Sault Ste. Marie who, while sitting on the green observing the drilling soldiers, were quietly and we should suspect, *prayerfully*, smoking their long-stemmed pipes. The contrast of the drilling military unit with its implied message of power and the smoking men who were in touch with cosmological forces through the act of ritually using tobacco takes on new meaning. Most obviously, perhaps, is the explicit use of tobacco associated with times of treaty signing. Pipes were lit and passed at all these events in a ritual attempt to involve the *manidoog*, the greater non-human forces at the very foundation of Ojibwe existence.

These were a few of the instances wherein the Ojibwe attempted to process and understand the importance of these meetings with their new allies. On these trips to Ojibwe country, the Americans came with the trappings of their offices, with their flags and military escorts—to include their cartographers and other scientists—and with their spiritual leaders. To this show of power and authority the Ojibwe presented *their* notions of propriety and understanding, as they countered the Americans' power with their own.

**Leonard and Harriet Wood Wheeler, nineteenth century protestant missionaries at Madeline Island and Bad River, Wisconsin.**

As suggested in the discussion of Buffalo's 1826 Fond du Lac speech and in his remarks to Schoolcraft at La Pointe in 1831, it appears the tribesmen were troubled by this show of American force. By these years some of their leaders had made the trip to Washington, D.C., and witnessed the degree of power their new allies held. In the face of this power, when returning to their Lake Superior homes they had cause to ponder the future of their people.

### *Increasing Pressures for Change at Chequamegon Bay*

1.

For the new United States, by the 1830s, the concern about more military conflict with England was dissipating. A rampant nationalism was spreading through the land as America surged ahead with its efforts to grow, and the business and industrial world was laboring hard as its members competed to reap profits from what was seen as a land rich in natural resources. Opportunities for individual wealth were believed to be nearly boundless, and along the eastern seaboard, as in strategic inland locations, population centers were growing as more Europeans arrived with hopes of getting their share.

As the new nation's material desires began to be met and its resultant economic organization took form, a belief system to support this integral portion of the society's foundation emerged. An economic system is integrated with the other components of a culture, and thus, it is always intricately bound to a supporting set of rationalizing beliefs and values. The development of this ideology is complex, but in the America of the early nineteenth century, we can easily understand its relationship to tribal peoples. This belief system held that tribesmen were anachronistic and in need of change. They were to be *civilized*, i.e., to be brought into the new Euro-American way of life.

Early Euro-Americans may have *philosophically* held the myth of North America being an empty continent, but right from the beginning, the fact that the frontier never had been empty and the matter of relating to the Indian—a concern Columbus had to deal with some two hundred years earlier—was still a problem the newcomers had to face.

As America was discussing this issue, so were the native nations. Approached from the tribal view, communities like the Ojibwe also were dealing with what can be called their *frontier*. In western Lake Superior lands this has most often been understood as the southern, northern, and western edge of their world as it impinged upon that of the Ho-Chunk, Menominee, Mesquawkie, Cree, Assiniboine, and Dakota nations. By the 1830s, as military conflicts moved further west, initially the urgency of this issue was diminishing for communities like La Pointe. However, we can envision a new frontier arising to the east—a troublesome frontier with the Americans.

We have seen that tribal leaders were struggling with the challenges of this new frontier in the early decades of the nineteenth century. Flat Mouth at Leech Lake, Buffalo at La Pointe, Shingwaukonse at the Canadian community of Sault Ste. Marie, and other leaders were actively addressing this issue. Unfortunately, unlike the case of the Americans and their western frontier, the Ojibwe history of this eastern frontier is only sparingly recorded in the written literature.

2.

IN THE ABOVE DISCUSSIONS OF THE EXPEDITIONS of the 1820s and 1830s, we saw how the Americans spoke to the problem of their western frontier and what solutions were being considered. The conclusion was always one-sided: it was the Indian that had to give way. The foraging life was to be abandoned as the people *settled down* and turned to agriculture, and clearly, this material change was not enough. They needed a belief system to give meaning and credibility to their new life. Christianity had to be brought to the *savages* so their transition would be complete. Perhaps this sentiment is best stated by Henry Schoolcraft when he said, " Unless the Indian mind can be purified by gospel truth, and cleansed from the besetting sin of a belief in magic and from idolatry and spirit worship, all attempts in the way of agriculture, schooling, and the mechanic arts are liable to miscarry and produce no permanent good."[38] Schoolcraft's remarks show the unquestioned certainty that mainstream America of the times held about the need for Christianity to be brought to the tribesmen. Without this religion they would still be considered *uncivilized*. And we must note that to some Americans of the time, civilization was felt to be a characteristic of *men*.[39]

As we have noted, in the written history of Native America the concept of *civilization*, like that of *men*, too often goes undefined. It is simply offered as a given, meaning something so obvious that it needs no definition. For example, in the writings of Cass, Schoolcraft, McKenney and the others we have just discussed, it was not defined in any meaningful way. In the America of the early nineteenth century, civilization was equated with enlightenment, refinement, and similar culturally specific concepts, at the time, according to the Euro-Americans, all felt to be held by Christian American society and lacking in tribal, or *savage* society.

As in the case of the Christian missionaries' arrival in Chequamegon Bay, when the earliest American governmental agents came to Lake Superior and spoke of the need to *civilize* the tribal people they were speaking of changing the Ojibwes' entire culture. This, of course, was intended to be a wide and deep change—to include economic, political, social and religious institutions. Finally, the goal was to reach deep inside the individual Ojibwe person and change the way he, and she, saw and understood themselves. For instance, when the Halls arrived in 1831, their goal was not just to bring their religion to the Ojibwe, but to change the natives' personal, and very private, identities.[40]

Put another way, the Ojibwe were supposed to begin living and acting like *men*. Of course, this concept referred to humans who lived like Euro-Americans did, and importantly, in the 1830s, the term had racial overtones. To Caucasians there was a positive correlation between *whiteness* and *men*. This is what caused the enigma of those persons who were of mixed parentage. *Mixed-bloods* were often given special consideration in treaties since they did not neatly fit into either category of white or Indian, and because of this, they held a political stance that, in some cases, became troublesome for the Americans.[41]

From their different perspectives, both Indians and Americans felt themselves to be humans and to have exemplary lives. The Ojibwe felt *they* were enlightened and refined in comparison to the aggressive, wealth-seeking Americans. Thus, as *Anishinaabeg*, they considered themselves not only to be real humans, but they also knew they were the *civilized* ones, and therefore, as such, they were men. Surely, in 1832, as today, ethnocentrism was a characteristic of both Ojibwe and American cultures.

3.

THE NATIONAL GOAL OF CIVILIZING the Indian was seen in the words of George Washington back in 1791, when he asked Congress to authorize the expenditure of funds needed "to undertake experiments to civilize friendly Indians."[42] Consequently, the early Trade and Intercourse Acts of the late eighteenth and early nineteenth centuries contained directives to fulfill this goal, and Indian agents were obligated to carry out this charge. Their responsibility was to extinguish Indian culture, or as the historian, Francis Paul Prucha, said, they were to work "to Americanize the Indians."[43]

After Columbus, European scholars debated the nature of American Indians as they struggled to understand this relatively new—new to Europeans—example of the species. One conclusion was that they were so decidedly inferior to Europeans that they should be understood as a very early form of humanity, and perhaps, more extremely, that they may not even be humans at all. After considering this issue, Thomas Jefferson concluded that Indians had the same mental and physical characteristics of Americans, but lacked civilization. He was certain that America had the moral obligation to bring civilization to them, and of course, civilization referred to *his* way of life.

This is the problem the writers we have just considered were addressing. The difficulty, as they saw it, was how to bring civilization to the *savage*. Lt. Allen, Henry Schoolcraft,

Thomas L. McKenney and others felt a deep moral imperative to make this change, lest, as they feared, the Indian would be overrun and cease to exist, leaving the Americans with an uncomfortable awareness of their being accessories to this destruction. This is what brought missionaries to La Pointe in the 1830s. They were part of the western movement that surged into lands held by tribal nations, and they had to have an acceptable rationale for wanting to change these people.

In the United States of the early nineteenth century, the Second Great Awakening helped form the ideological component of American culture that supported not only the country's emerging economic organization, but justified the usurpation of lands occupied by humans deemed to be *savages*. The importance of this religious movement for indigenous communities like the Ojibwe was far-reaching.

4.

THERE WAS MUCH ACTIVITY in the western lakes region in the years after the return of the last Schoolcraft expedition. More Americans came to the area—some to stay—but others to move on to more distant regions. William Boutwell, for example, returned in 1832, when Henry Schoolcraft and the others passed through La Pointe on their way back to the eastern end of the lake. Boutwell stayed at La Pointe to assist the Halls in their work, but only a year later was on his way back to Leech Lake to carry out his desire to bring his religion to Flat Mouth's people.

William Boutwell, Frederick Ayer, Sherman Hall and the other missionaries were certain they were doing the right thing. As with the government Indian agents, they were working to bring an end to the way of life Buffalo, Flat Mouth and the other Ojibwe leaders were struggling to preserve. Such hopes of extinguishing the Indians' foraging cultures were not new in the western lakes region. As we have seen, back in the seventeenth century, the Jesuits were also desirous of eventually reaching this goal. Recently this was recognized as *cultural genocide* by the native Osage-Cherokee writer and theologian George E. Tinker, and was argued to have been the goal of all Christian missionaries working in Indian communities in the early years.[44]

However, in the western Great Lakes of the 1830s, it was not just the missionary field that was busy. There also was activity in the fur trade. In 1834, John Jacob Astor sold his American Fur Trade Company holdings to Ramsay Crooks (and some others), an indication that Astor saw hard times ahead. For several years, Crooks and his co-owners labored with the dying firm, only to see it slide into bankruptcy in 1842.[45]

Ramsay Crooks was forty-six years old when he became a co-owner and president of the American Fur Company. Born in Scotland, he came to Canada and took employment in the North West Company, and in 1806-07, found himself wintering-over while working with the Michilimackinac Company in Missouri Country. A few years later he traveled even further west to work with John Jacob Astor, before being assigned as his agent to the Mackinac and Sault Ste. Marie region at the eastern end of Lake Superior. Ramsay Crooks has been called "a benevolent despot, who made extraordinary profit at the expense of the Indian and the trader."[46]

Upon becoming the American Fur Company president he moved the headquarters of the firm from Mackinac to La Pointe, a move that brought more commercial activity to the region. The reason for this move was financial. Crooks planned to build a lake schooner that would operate between La Pointe and Sault Ste. Marie, to replace the more clumsy Mackinac boats that needed sixty-five boatmen to operate them. Furthermore, the smaller schooner crew could be used to catch fish, which the new ship would transport back to Sault Ste. Marie, making money for the company.[47]

Crooks, like John Johnston, the Warren brothers, Henry Schoolcraft, William Boutwell, and many other European, Canadian, and early American men in Lake Superior country, married an Ojibwe woman—in Crook's case, Emilie Pratt, the eighteen-year-old mixed-blood daughter of Bernard Pratte, a powerful partner in the trading firm of Pratte, Chouteau and Company of St. Louis. Before his marriage, Crooks fathered a daughter with an Ojibwe woman at Sault Ste. Marie. This girl, named Hester Crooks, went on to marry William Boutwell in a ceremony conducted by Sherman Hall at Fond du Lac in 1834.[48]

5.

DURING CROOKS' TENURE IN THE FUR TRADE, La Pointe was a central, and strategic, site for the short-lived American Fur Company. This is shown in the journal of the French geographer, Joseph P. Nicollet, who came to Madeline Island on 12 August 1837. Nicollet reported that at the time of his visit, "the partners" of the company met at Madeline. Company representatives present were Lyman Warren of La Pointe, William Aitken of Sandy Lake, Eustache Roussain of Keweenaw, and Gabriel Franchere and John Holiday of Sault Ste. Marie. All these men were influential fur trade figures of the time, and La Pointe was an important location to them. In 1836, it apparently was also important to distant Ojibwe leaders since, according to William Boutwell, it was reported that in October of that year, Flat Mouth, the Leech Lake leader, made the long journey to the post for several kegs of powder and a few bags of shot and ball.[49]

Flat Mouth was an influential Ojibwe leader and doubtlessly he made the long canoe trip to Madeline Island for more than gunpowder, some shot and ball. His visit shows that in 1836, the Ojibwe communities at the head of the Mississippi River kept in contact with those in western Lake Superior, and, we might presume, on this trip the Leech Lake leader spent time in political discussions with Buffalo and other La Pointe leaders.

Unfortunately, Joseph P. Nicollet wrote practically nothing of the La Pointe Ojibwe of 1837, but interestingly, he recorded thoughts about the cliffs of the northernmost point of what is today called Red Cliff. Nicollet said, "At 4:00 in the evening we passed by and visited the *Nenaboju* Rocks, one of the greatest natural curiosities one can see in America."[50] It is apparent that by 1837, these red sandstone cliffs were becoming well known to American travelers.

Nicollet made two excursions up the Mississippi and St. Croix rivers in 1836 and 1837, to do mapping work, and although he said little about the Ojibwe people in the immediate Chequamegon region, we still benefit from his words about those he encountered in the upper St. Croix river area and further to the west. Although he was one of the early nineteenth century writers who felt the Ojibwe were not men, and that they had to be Christianized and made into farmers before they could be civilized, his journal still shows an empathy and acceptance of the Ojibwe way of life practically unparalleled in his times.

Nicollet left us with a lengthy manuscript making it clear that important aspects of traditional Ojibwe culture were still functioning in western Lake Superior in the 1830s. He gives detailed accounts of *midewiwin* and other ceremonies, as well as descriptions and discussions of women's roles in food procurement, health treatment, warfare, and other aspects of Ojibwe culture. His interest in the Ojibwe language caused him to do extensive recording of vocabulary, although his manuscript on this subject has apparently disappeared. In short, the writings of Joseph P. Nicollet, like others we have already discussed, show that in the late 1830s, even though Ojibwe culture was under serious strain it was, in a significant way, still meeting the needs of its people.

Two years before Joseph Nicollet's visit to Chequamegon Bay, Frederic Baraga arrived at Madeline Island. Originally from Slovenia, this Roman Catholic priest had come to Arbre Croche in northern lower Michigan in 1832, and spent a few years at this location before moving on to several other Michigan sites, and then to La Pointe.

Frederic Baraga spent much of the next thirty-three years in communities along the south shore of Lake Superior, most of them in the general region of Michigan's upper peninsula. He spent approximately eight years headquartering at La Pointe, leaving in 1843 to go back east to Michigan where he was drawn by the arrival of numerous Catholic European immigrants. Regarding the tribal communities of Lake Superior, Baraga was a new force in the region, successfully competing with the area's Protestant missionaries. Right from the start he was at odds with Protestantism, and in a letter in 1835, complained that at La Pointe the Protestants "were deluding the poor Indians."[51]

Frederick Baraga is known today as "The Snowshoe Priest" for his mid-nineteenth century Lake Superior wintertime treks to villages and encampments where he met with his converts. His several years of work to convert tribal people to Catholicism is well known, as are his successes in learning the native language, and writing an Ojibwe dictionary and grammar. Throughout the world Christian missionaries have used a people's language as perhaps their most important tool in their work at religious conversion.

As many are today, these early missionaries were linguists who developed considerable skill in learning native languages, but unfortunately, Baraga's interest in *Ojibwemowin*—the Ojibwe language—was not matched with an interest in the Ojibwe way of life. And certainly, his deep knowledge of the Ojibwe language did not cause him to appreciate the peoples' religion. His writings show virtually no interest in studying and recording details of Ojibwe culture and especially its rich cosmology and cosmogony. Because of this, his contribution to our understanding of Ojibwe culture, to include its religion as witnessed in Baraga's time, is minor, and Bishop Baraga's role in Ojibwe history lies not in the peoples' struggle for cultural survival, except in a negative way. Cultural genocide was Baraga's goal, not the persistence of the Ojibwe language and its culture. Many other mid-nineteenth century Europeans and Americans felt Ojibwe religious beliefs were of little interest. As Michael Angel wrote:

> Many of them, like Bishop Frederic Baraga, seldom bothered to describe Ojibwe religious ideas or practices, deeming them unworthy of their attention . . . Although [Baraga's] Ojibwe dictionary and grammar were remarkable achievements, he made few efforts to understand anything about Anishinaabe cosmology because he believed it to be the work of the devil.[52]

Baraga was in western Lake Superior in the fall of 1854, when the famed treaty of that year was negotiated and signed between the Ojibwe people and the United States, but his diary makes no reference to these important events. He was in L'Ance, on Lake Superior's southern shore, from 25 September through 6 October—the spate of days of the treasty negotiations—so he easily could have gone to nearby La Pointe to be part of this major event as many other non-natives did, but he apparently chose not to do so. Instead, he was busy giving confirmation instructions, hearing confessions, administering confirmations, and so forth.[53]

We will revisit Bishop Frederic Baraga's mid-nineteenth century relationship with Chequamegon Bay's Ojibwe communities and his feelings about the peoples' religion below, and will leave this discussion by offering some comments by Louise Erdrich, the contemporary Ojibwe writer. According to Erdrich:

> The Ojibwe peoples' earliest contact with non-Natives was with the Jesuits, so there's a long history of entwinement of the cultures. But it's always up to the individual priest how much he'll allow the traditionalists into his belief system. It's anathema to the church itself to admit the truth or goodness of any other form of religion, especially a non-Christian religion. But priests are sometimes hit over the head by the fact that they're trying to teach spirituality to an entirely spiritual people, and they're trying to take their spirituality away from them in order to force another form of spirituality upon them.[54]

Four years before Baraga's arrival at La Pointe, Sherman Hall was concerned about Catholic missionaries coming into the western lakes region. In 1831, soon after Hall came to La Pointe, he began a journal in which he wrote about the potential he saw for the area. He was optimistic that in the western lakes region a busy missionary could "prevent Catholics tutoring and rearing barriers against any subsequent introduction of Christianity."[55] This bias against Catholicism was found throughout America. Hall's regular journal entries make it clear that while he initially came to convert the Indians to his religion, Hall hoped for the region to be developed into the kind of world he left behind in Vermont, and that he wanted it to be a

Protestant, not Catholic, world, and certainly not a "pagan" one. Thus, right from the beginning Sherman Hall wanted more than religious conversion. He hoped to destroy Ojibwe culture and replace it with his own.

Initially the Halls were discouraged with the poor response from the people, but by 1835, they began to feel hopeful of soon witnessing conversions to Christianity, although by this time they concluded that the seasonal mobility of the people was a serious impediment to this goal. The peoples' regular movement between Madeline Island and the mainland frustrated the Halls. In season the Ojibwe went to their gardens at Bad River and other places, and of course there were the distant sugarbushes, ricing grounds and hunting areas that pulled them away. At first in his early enthusiasm, Sherman Hall attempted to travel with them but he soon grew tired of the difficulty. It is easier for the missionary to remain stationary, as Leonard Wheeler did at Bad River, and have the "pagan" come to him (or her) rather than to move with the people.

Herein lies an aspect of Christian missionary behavior that is often unmentioned. This is that anthropologically, a religious belief system does not stand apart from other major components of the culture in which it exists. Therefore, as we have argued, Sherman Hall and his colleagues did not work to bring only a Euro-American religious ideology and the ritual and ceremonial mechanics of its expression extant in the United States at the time to Chequamegon Bay. Instead they worked to bring elements of the cultural system their religion was part of, and *sedentarism*, i.e., being stationary in one location throughout the year, was part of the Hall's notion of a proper lifestyle.

In the seventeenth century in Lake Superior country, the Jesuits were confronted with a foraging society, and in the nineteenth century the Halls were struggling with the same adaptation. Both the Jesuits and the Halls carried a deep bias against hunting and gathering peoples, since they felt their mobility was an early and undeveloped human adaptation inferior to the European and American custom of sedentarism. We have no stories from the Ojibwe about the struggles of Sherman Hall in these early years, but surely the people must have been humored at his attempts to travel with them.

To meet this problem, Hall attempted to get the Ojibwe to reside on Madeline Island the year around, and toward that purpose, in 1835, he struggled to convince two families to build houses near his own so he could, to use his word, "operate" on their minds. These presumably were log structures since he felt the native wigwam was inadequate for human habitation. In a letter dated 4 February 1835, he wrote:

> If we can get the Indian to settle and remain permanently in one place so that we can have constant access to them, we hope to operate upon them with more efficiency. So long as they move from one place to another every month and scatter in all directions for many miles around us it is difficult to do much for them . . . To think of following them from place to place to instruct them is out of the question, since they scatter so much that scarcely two families can be found together . . . To labor as we have since we have been here, while we could operate on only a few minds and that only occasionally, is truly discouraging.[56]

The ramifications of these families settling down on Madeline Island would have been far-reaching. To a great extent they would have been isolated from their extended kinship network, a relational system that was not only social, but economic and political as well. If such changes in residency persisted, the families would have had little option but to attach themselves to the economic and political system of the Halls and the other Euro-Americans on Madeline. We can easily understand that what may have been perceived as a simple change—two families living permanently near the Halls—in reality had extreme implications for the couples involved and for the local Ojibwe community.

We know little of the success of this attempt for Ojibwe resettlement by Sherman Hall, but his later letters continue to tell of his frustration with the natives' mobility, so few must have availed themselves of his offers to help in building houses for them.

We will continue to track the activities of Sherman Hall in the sections to follow since they were directly related to the La Pointe Ojibwe, and his lengthy tenure saw numerous changes come to the region. For example, after 20 April 1836, when Wisconsin Territory was established, the regional Ojibwe communities were switched from the administration of the Sault Ste. Marie and Mackinac agency to that of Wisconsin Territorial Governor Dodge.

## 6.

IN 1836, DODGE NOMINATED DANIEL P. BUSHNELL as Indian Subagent for La Pointe, the first time a government agent was assigned to the community since George Johnston's brief tenure several years previous.[57] Bushnell was soon pressed into service to travel with a large contingent of Ojibwe to St. Peters for the negotiation of a major land cession treaty. We have little to show how Buffalo and other leaders related to their new Subagent but it is clear that during his tenure of several years at La Pointe, Daniel Bushnell felt the pressure of representing the United States government on a daily basis. His budget for 1837 included three hundred dollars for an annual salary for an interpreter, five hundred dollars for "Presents to Indians," and another two hundred dollars for "Provisions for Indians visiting the Sub-agency on business," but these amounts apparently did not meet Bushnell's needs.[58] In August of 1839, two years after arriving at Madeline Island, in a letter to Commissioner of Indian Affairs Crawford, Bushnell complained of federal regulations that demanded he maintain a "constant residence" with the Indians, a rule, he felt, that worked counter to government purpose at the time, especially since he was not able "to bestow the same favors that traders are in the habit of doing."[59]

Daniel Bushnell's struggle with fur traders to win the respect and allegiance of the Ojibwe was not a new problem. It confronted American agents and Sub-agents from the late eighteenth century when they were first sent to the frontier, and continued until the end of the fur trade's power in the 1840s. In 1837, Agent Lawrence Taliaferro, at St. Peters in western Wisconsin Territory, wrote to Governor Dodge about the power of the American Fur Company in his region. The company's practice of handing out medals of John Jacob Astor to counter those of the United States was so popular that, according to Taliaferro, "The Astor Medals are in high vogue at this date." Taliaferro went on to say that traders had such control over the Indians that America's factory system of trading should be reestablished.[60] Apparently, Lawrence Taliaferro, like Daniel Bushnell, felt he had a distinct disadvantage when competing with fur traders for the allegiance of the Indians.

Bushnell argued that if an agent was to show the power of the United States government he needed to be properly funded. Of the Ojibwe, he wrote: "If the Agent does not bear the Semblance of power which they are taught to expect, they will not heed the Govt. the agent represents."[61] According to Bushnell, the Ojibwe looked to him to relieve "their extreme poverty" and when he could not meet such demands they took offense, and in numerous ways would "insult the agent."

By Daniel Bushnell's time at La Pointe, the Ojibwe had been players in several treaty negotiation sessions and had repeatedly heard United States officials speak of the "Great Father in Washington" who had the best interests of his "Ojibwe children in his heart," and how he would protect them from their enemies with his "powerful long arm" and also, in times of other difficulty, he would help them meet their needs. We have seen that American officials were quick to project this image, but the problem of financially and logistically following through was another matter. In 1839, Daniel Bushnell's voice was one of several from the frontier that asked the United States government to fulfill its promises to the Ojibwe.

Bushnell's time at La Pointe came to an abrupt halt in 1842, when he was removed from office under charges of improper behavior. It is unclear what these charges were, but agent and Sub-agent positions were political patronage appointments and were filled and cancelled at the desire of national leaders in Washington.[62]

Over the next several years, the La Pointe Ojibwe saw four different Sub-agents assigned to their community, seemingly a high number. To some Americans of the mid-nineteenth century such positions were sought after, less for their steady, although modest, salaries—Bushnell's salary for the first year was $750.00—than for the chance to enter *the Indian Trade*. For example, in the 1850s, the Minnesota Territorial agent, David Herriman, remarked that while employed as a government Indian agent he also expected to operate as a trader, and if not allowed to do so he would resign his patronage appointment. In some cases such positions provided opportunities for garnering income through the illicit handling of annual federal appropriations of goods and specie for Indian annuities, as well as for the routine operation of the sub-agency. In this manner there were a number of ways an agent could pocket illegal personal income while in the government's employ.[63]

As the local representative of the American government, an Indian agent or Sub-agent could be a powerful person—someone who could affect relationships between the Ojibwe and more distant federal officials—and La Pointe's high turnover of Sub-agents was certainly important to the resident Ojibwe, but a more pressing issue rising in the 1830s was the loss of land. Local federal Indian agents could play pivotal roles in this matter of land loss. In the sections below we consider how the Ojibwe people struggled with American desires to acquire large pieces of their lands in the western lakes region. The alliance treaties between the Americans and the Ojibwe that were signed in the decade of the 1820s were followed by several land cession treaties in each of the next three decades. As we will see, La Pointe's Buffalo was involved with all of them.

*Notes*

1. Schoolcraft 1993[1958]:114.
2. Schoolcraft 1993[1958]:117-8.
3. Schoolcraft 1993[1958]:118-9.
4. Schoolcraft 1993[1958]:119.
5. This name is obviously misspelled.
6. Chute 1998:41-2.
7. Schoolcraft 1832:148.
8. Schoolcraft 1993[1958]:51.
9. Schoolcraft 1993[1958]:11.
10. Schoolcraft 1993[1958]:12.
11. Brunson 1879:25-6.
12. Allen 1833, in Schoolcraft 1993[1958]:170; Chute 1998:157-8, 165.
13. Allen 1833, in Schoolcraft 1993[1958]:184.
14. Allen 1833, in Schoolcraft 1993[1958]:185-6.
15. Allen 1833, in Schoolcraft 1993[1958]:186.
16. Houghton 1832, in Schoolcraft 1993[1958]:242, 278.
17. Schoolcraft 1993[1958]:10
18. Houghton 1832, in Schoolcraft 1993[1958]:304.
19. Houghton 1832, in Schoolcraft 1993[1958]:248.
20. Houghton 1832, in Schoolcraft 1993[1958]:298.
21. Houghton 1832, in Schoolcraft 1993[1958]:301-2.
22. Fenn 2004[2001].
23. Mason 1958, in Schoolcraft 1993[1958]:306.
24. Boutwell 1832, in Schoolcraft 1993[1958]:314-5.
25. Boutwell 1832, in Schoolcraft 1993[1958]:317.
26. Boutwell 1832, in Schoolcraft 1993[1958]:319.
27. Boutwell 1832, in Schoolcraft 1993[1958]:319.
28. Nicollet 1970:50.
29. Danziger 1979:71.
30. Schoolcraft 1993[1958]:53.
31. Allen 1833, in Schoolcraft 1993[1958]:209.
32. Houghton 1832, in Schoolcraft 1993[1958]:259-60.
33. Boutwell 1832:334.
34. Belya 1994:246, in David Thompson-Henry Journals.
35. Houghton 1832, in Schoolcraft 1993[1958]:248.
36. McKenney 1959[1827]:269.
37. Mandrell 1996:60.
38. Schoolcraft 1993[1958]:xx.
39. Nicollet 1970[1836]:232.
40. Plane 2000.
41. Schenck 2007:viii-ix.
42. Prucha 1994[1984]:51.
43. Prucha 1994[1984]:48.
44. Tinker 1993.
45. Ross 1960:78.
46. Nute 1926:485; Ross 1960:79.
47. Nute 1926:483-502.
48. Ross 1960:80; Lavender 1998[1964]:249, 346, 357.

49. Nicollet 1970: 84, 152-3.
50. Nicollet 1970:152.
51. Danziger 1979:82. In May 2012, Bishop Baraga was declared Venerable by the pope. Among other things, a miracle is needed to advance to the next step of "Blessed," and a second miracle needed before being declared "Saint." In 1998, a reported miracle attributable to Beraga was submitted to Church authorities for their review. Baraga's cause for sainthood was initiated in 1952, by the Diocese of Marquette, Michigan. Once such a cause has begun, the title of "Servant of God" can be used to address the individual.
52. Angel 2002:106, brackets added.
53. Baraga 1990:61-2; Verwyst 1900: 280-281.
54. Erdrich 2012: "Heartbreaking Toll of Revenge" in Book Page—American Book Review (www.Bookpage.com), pp. 14-15, October 2012.
55. Hall 1831, letter at NGLVC.
56. Hall 1835, letter at NGLVC.
57. Herring 1836:63-67, in WisTerrPap, Vol.27.
58. Harris 1837:766-8, WisTerrPap, Vol. 27.
59. Bushnell 1839:29-30, WisTerPap, Vol. 28.
60. Taliaferro 1837:828-832, WisTerPap, Vol. 27.
61. Bushnell 1839:29-30, WisTerPap, Vol. 28.
62. Crawford 1842:483, WisTerPap, Vol. 27.
63. Diedrich 1999:15; Cleland 2000:97.

# 15

# Land Loss: The First Years

### *The St. Peters Land Treaty of 1837*

1.

IN 1837, THE OJIBWE SIGNED a major land cession treaty with representatives of the United States at Fort Snelling in St. Peters, in western Wisconsin Territory, now in the state of Minnesota. In this document, much of today's north-central Wisconsin along with a portion of east-central Minnesota was ceded to the United States. A few of Wisconsin's interior Ojibwe bands resided there, using the region for harvesting their traditional resources. In the decades just previous to 1837, some Americans were emigrating to regions immediately to the south and east of this vast territory, but the numbers of these newcomers were still low compared to what was to come a decade or two later, when European emigrants began to flood to the Midwest.

For several years before 1837, there were issues of timber theft from Ojibwe lands in the interior of Wisconsin Territory. Pressure for American authorities to acquire these lands was growing and lumber entrepreneurs were among those in the forefront of this effort.[1] James Lockwood, for instance, was an early fur trader at Prairie du Chien who erected a sawmill on the Chippewa River in 1830, and even though this was Ojibwe land he operated it for some years. In cases like this the American authorities deemed it best to pressure the Indians for a land cession treaty rather than forcefully remove the trespassing lumbermen.[2] Much of this vast territory held forests of mature white pine coveted by these aggressive business people. There was money to be made, since willing markets for sawn pine lumber were waiting in the numerous emerging towns just to the south, and lumbermen were eager to cash in on this opportunity.

In 1834, Henry Schoolcraft tried to quell the illegal harvesting of this Indian timber by issuing a circular declaring that any non-Indians wishing to enter the region had to seek a permit from him at Mackinac. In March of that year there were reports of timber theft as well as the sale of whiskey in the St. Croix River region which threatened to disrupt peaceful relations with the Ojibwe. Schoolcraft stated there was to be no hunting, fishing or trapping by non-Indians on Indian land, but the difficulty—or actual unwillingness—of regional American authorities to carry out this order made his gesture ineffective.[3] What his circular shows is that by 1834, the resident Ojibwe were facing an increasingly serious encroachment of Americans on their lands.

Until the treaty of 1837, lumber for settlement in southern Wisconsin was transported by water from eastern states at high cost, a fact that made the Ojibwe's white pine forests even more valuable in the eyes of business interests. Before 1837, the territory ceded in the treaty was recognized by the American government to be held by the Ojibwe people, and "the federal Trade and Intercourse Acts prohibited Americans from logging on Indian lands without special permission."[4] This problem could be resolved by negotiating a land cession treaty, but there were several other reasons put forward for the transfer of ownership of these lands.

Wisconsin Territorial Governor Dodge argued that with increased pressures for settlement, conflict between the Ojibwe and whites was certain unless the lands were ceded. Lewis Cass, then Secretary of War, argued that such a land cession would create a large barrier between the Dakota and Ojibwe that would serve to help keep the peace between these two tribes. Hence, we see that the early notion of a land barrier between adversaries was raised once again.[5]

Other concerns were that by 1837, white loggers had, in some instances, befriended or even married into some tribal communities, and received leases to set up lumber mills. White authorities were worried that this could lead to the majority of timber being controlled by a few persons, forming a monopoly over this rich resource. An incident related to this concern was the desire of a group of businessmen associated with the American Fur Company to secure permission to erect a series of saw mills on Ojibwe land in central Wisconsin Territory. In 1836, several Ojibwe chiefs and headmen petitioned the President of the United States to allow Hercules Dousman, Henry Sibley and a few others to harvest pine timber along the Chippewa River for a period of ten years.[6] Another fear was that, even as late as 1836, the Canadians along the northern border might still have an undue influence with the northernmost tribes and somehow exert pressures detrimental to American interests.[7]

It has been suggested that in the 1830s, going beyond merely leasing lands, the native people wanted *to sell* their land to the Americans. South of Ojibwe territory was a piece still held by the Ho-Chunk and they, along with the Ojibwe, reportedly felt that the land should be sold so the proceeds could be used to ease the hardships they were facing. Therefore, in 1836, "Wisconsin territorial delegate George W. Jones assured his colleagues in Congress before negotiations began that the Chippewa and Winnebago Indians themselves had asked Governor Dodge to enable them to dispose of those lands."[8] Two years later when Wisconsin Territorial business and political leaders were agitating for another land cession treaty for the remaining Ojibwe lands in Wisconsin Territory, Representative Jones suggested that the United States purchase Madeline Island and the other Indian land along Lake Superior's southern shore. According to Jones, "The Indians I understand are willing to sell."[9] This assertion is surprising, given the evidence for the Ojibwe's anger with the 1837 treaty. Understanding the efforts governmental leaders like George Jones were exerting to extinguish Indian land titles on property east of the Mississippi, we yearn for a more valid documentation of this purported Ojibwe desire to divest themselves of this Lake Superior land.[10]

Another example of American expansionistic thinking is seen in the words of the Methodist clergyman Alfred Brunson, a few years before he became a government Sub-agent at La Pointe, and one year before the 1837 treaty was negotiated. At the time he was residing in Pennslyvania, and he expressed a common Euro-American sentiment of his day when he wrote to Representative Jones about the Ojibwe living south of Lake Superior. Brunson said, "I do not believe that the Maker of the earth designed that fertile & beautiful country to be left for a few Indians to roam over in quest of game."[11]

Thus, we see that by 1837, there were several reasons put forth for a change of ownership of this large territory. Importantly, Lewis Cass, then Secretary of War, promoted the treaty as another step in fulfilling his vision of seeing the lands west of Lake Michigan opened to American settlement. To Cass and others like him, there was no doubt that the Americans were destined to push their border further and further westward. As with the lands of Michigan Territory earlier, he was certain that these adjacent regions were to be occupied by American settlers.[12]

The written history of these times tells how American officials stressed the need for the pine lumber while downplaying their desire for the land itself. Lewis Cass, for example, wrote of this need for lumber as the major reason for the treaty, but obviously always assumed that eventually the Americans would acquire the land as well. While the Treaty of 1837 has been labeled the "Pine Tree Treaty,"[13] it was, in reality, another land cession treaty. There is no doubt that early in the nineteenth century, the Americans wanted this vast region.

## 2.

On 20 April 1836, the United States Congress passed an act establishing Wisconsin Territory, and in October of that year, Governor and *ex-officio* Superintendent of Indian Affairs, Henry Dodge, issued a territorial proclamation calling for the establishment of militias in each of the new region's counties. He suggested that Congress be asked for an ample supply of arms and ammunition for citizens' use "in the event of an Indian war."[14] Most of Wisconsin's citizens were in the far southern reaches of the territory and quite probably he was referring to their security regarding bands of Ho-chunk that were still in the region, but as late as 1848, the fear of a war between the Ojibwe and the United States was clearly felt.[15] Before being appointed governor, Henry Dodge had military experience on America's western frontier and had gained a reputation for fighting Indians. In recommending his appointment to the governorship, U.S. Senator Thomas Hart Benton said "General Henry Dodge, now Colonel of Dragoons" was "accustomed to Indian character in all its phases."[16]

By 1837, several territorial militias had been formed and Dodge again spoke of the need to be on guard since, he claimed, "such is the restless disposition of all Indians that it is difficult to determine when they will commence their attacks on our frontier inhabitants."[17] Although he did not make explicit reference to Ojibwe communities in these remarks, we should expect that he meant these words be directed to all regional tribesmen, including the Ojibwe. Within two decades after 1837, militias were formed in the heart of Wisconsin's Ojibwe territory.

## 3.

Henry Dodge was appointed treaty commissioner along with General W. R. Smith of Pennsylvania, and in General Smith's absence, it was Dodge who opened the meeting for the 1837 treaty negotiations at St. Peters. Several witnesses to the gathering have left written commentary of the proceedings, and along with treaty secretary Verplanck Van Antwerp's journal, we have several documents covering what occurred. La Pointe's Chief Buffalo was present at this important gathering, and some of his words are recorded, but he was not one of the major Ojibwe speakers. Of significance are remarks Buffalo made *after* the treaty meetings were concluded. In 1837, he could have been seventy-eight years old or so, and even though he still had several years in which he showed ample energies to lead his people, nevertheless, by that date he no longer was a young man. By 1837, Buffalo had been witness to many changes in Chequamegon Bay, and at St. Peters he would learn of more to come.

Approximately 1,000 Ojibwe men, women and children gathered at Fort Snelling for the treaty negotiation session, a large portion of the Ojibwe people coming from the Wisconsin and Minnesota regions. Alfred Brunson, at the time a Methodist missionary among the Dakota along the Mississippi River, was present with three young Canadian Ojibwe men who had recently converted to Christianity. George Copway, his cousin John Johnson, and Peter Marksman came to Brunson's village before traveling further east to begin their careers as Christian missionaries. Among these three converts, George Copway would go on to some prominence as a missionary and recorder of Ojibwe history.[18] Copway and his two young friends had spent the winter of 1834-35 at the mission station in Keweenaw in Michigan, then transferred to La Pointe in the winter of 1835-36. At La Pointe, Copway and Johnson worked with Sherman Hall to translate the biblical books of Luke and the Acts into the Ojibwe language. Then, in late 1836 and early 1837, Copway, Johnson and Marksman traveled down to Lac Courte Oreilles, where they worked to begin a Methodist mission.[19] Brunson wrote that the three Canadians impressed the American crowd at St. Peters since they showed that attempts to Christianize the Indians were working, "for here were men before them who were taken wild, from the smoky wigwam, now 'clothed and in their right minds;' their skins almost as white as the whitest, and quite as white as some of dark complexions" of the Americans at St. Peters.[20]

In the written accounts of the treaty negotiation proceedings we see a problem that the Americans tried to overcome. At this gathering the United States attempted to reshape the way the different Ojibwe bands saw their overall political system. Throughout the proceedings Dodge repeatedly used the label, "the Chippewa Nation" to identify those present even though tribal leaders reminded him again and again of the impropriety of doing so. These protestations indicated that the Ojibwe saw their band system of political organization as an integral part of their identities.

Representatives from eleven Ojibwe bands eventually signed the treaty, but at the onset Dodge was concerned about the possibility of factions within and between these bands prohibiting a consensus for its acceptance. He certainly was familiar with the nature of tribal political organization and knew the problems he faced in his attempt for a quick approval of his proposals. He also was aware of two entities—the block of traders who held unpaid accounts from many Ojibwe, and the people known as "mixed-bloods"—that, for him, could have had a negative effect at the meetings. He did not want them to have an opportunity to delay, and perhaps even prohibit the land sale.

To resolve the problem of disparate bands working at cross-purposes, Dodge kept trying to change the way the Ojibwe conceptualized their overall political relationships. By using the label "Chippewa Nation" to identify all Ojibwe present, he was working with two related goals in mind. One was to overcome the matter of factions just mentioned, and the other, which in the minds of governmental leaders of the United States would be achieved several years in the future, was to ease, or facilitate, the eventual movement of all the Wisconsin, western Northern Michigan, and central Minnesota Ojibwe bands *as a single entity* to an as yet undetermined western location. This latter goal, however, was apparently not brought to words at the St. Peters meeting. Its open presentation and discussion would be reserved for a later time.

For these purposes, then, we see Governor Dodge attempting to impose new political identities onto the western Northern Michigan, Wisconsin and Minnesota Ojibwe bands. Through him, the United States devised new groupings of these people for its own purposes. "The Chippewas of Lake Superior" became the new label for the bands from L'Anse, Bad River, La Pointe, Fond du Lac, Grand Portage, and Bois Forte, as well as the smaller bands of the St. Croix Valley and the interior Wisconsin bands of Lac du Flambeau and Lac Courte Oreilles (and today's Mole Lake). "The Chippewa of the Mississippi" became the new label for the bands at Mille Lacs, Sandy Lake, Rum River, Gull Lake, and other smaller localities in Minnesota Territory.

This labeling scheme left the Pillager Ojibwe—those Minnesota bands centering near Leech Lake, Red Lake, and in that general region—in a nebulous classification exclusive of the Lake Superior and Mississippi categories.

As Charles Cleland states, the new labels—Lake Superior and Mississippi Ojibwe—had no meaning for the natives except for treaty making.[21] What is noteworthy in this persistent attempt by American authorities to re-categorize Ojibwe political identity is the unrelenting difficulty, or perhaps, *inherent inability*, of members of a *state* political system to conceptualize and accept a band system as anything but an inferior, unstructured, and ultimately invalid concept.[22]

The following words of missionary Sherman Hall tell the enormity of the problem Governor Dodge and the other Americans were facing with their attempts to change the Ojibwe political organization. Of the Ojibwe, Hall wrote:

> They are widely scattered over a vast territory. Throughout the tribe they are divided into small bands, each with its own chiefs. These bands are nearly as independent of each other as if they were independent tribes. They acknowledge no one common chief over the whole, and it would be difficult for any one person to unite the whole tribe under him. They are not likely to be concentrated or brought together into a compact body.[23]

In 1837, at St. Peters we see once again how two cultures with very different political organizations struggled to relate to each other. No doubt Dodge would have preferred to meet with a single tribal leader, or at most a small committee or council, that truly represented the different bands and had the power to make decisions on their behalf. Contrariwise, the tribesmen were put off by Dodge since he filled an unusual role—one with an inordinate degree of power. As a people the Ojibwe had met with single European and American leaders like Dodge in the past, and perhaps these encounters always held a degree of anxiety, or possibly fear. In their tribal society they were accustomed to resolving issues democratically, after what could be lengthy community-wide debate and open discussion. A single powerful man who represented a distant government and who demanded they make a quick decision on a very serious matter was an anomaly to them. We see how the Ojibwe struggled when the La Pointe contingent arrived at St. Peters and was met by Dodge's immediate request for a decision on his proposals, and again on two consecutive mornings when Buffalo asked for more time to study them. Tribal leaders were expected to take such issues before their community and allow time for a thorough deliberation before a decision was reached. Such procedures could take days or even longer, a process that worked against Henry Dodge's desire for an expeditious conclusion to the treaty proceedings.

## 4.

AT ST. PETERS, A NUMBER OF DAKOTA people were encamped nearby and the Americans feared the outbreak of hostilities, so military troops and cannon were brought to the treaty grounds and placed in strategic positions.[24] Dodge implored the Ojibwe visitors again and again not to molest the Dakota, causing Nodin, one of the leaders from the Snake River Ojibwe community, who apparently was bemused by Dodge's statements, to reply that the Dakota and Ojibwe not only wanted to be friendly, but desired to meet each other to trade and barter in peace. He seemed more concerned about the nearby soldiers and other whites, since he asked that Dodge ensure that these people stop troubling the Ojibwe. At times during their stay at St. Peters, the Dakota and Ojibwe played each other in lacrosse games. Apparently these contests, and the northern Ojibwe, in particular, were a curiosity at St. Peters.

Dodge opened the meetings on 20 July, but the La Pointe party, led by Sub-agent Bushnell and trader Lyman Warren, had not yet arrived and would not do so until 25 July. Henry Dodge was anxious to bring about a quick settlement to the sessions but Ojibwe speakers reminded him of the need to wait for the Wisconsin bands. Upon their arrival Dodge immediately attempted to get the meetings underway, but La Pointe's Buffalo asked that since he had only just arrived that he and the rest of his party be given another day to consider the proposals.

Finally, on Wednesday, 26 July, they came to the meeting grounds. However, after Dodge presented the map of the territory he hoped to purchase, Buffalo again asked for another day to consider the matter.[25]

Perhaps we can imagine the scene. Possibly a thousand or more Ojibwe people were encamped on the grounds just outside the walls of Fort Snelling during the heat of summer. Most had arrived by water—in birchbark canoes—and brought only the personal items necessary for such a trip. Makeshift shelters with their morning and evening fires dotted the parade ground adjacent to the fort. This was a large social affair for the tribal peoples, a chance to visit friends and relatives they may not have seen for some time, and rules of kin protocol were obligatory. This, along with matters of provisioning this great number of people, must have helped create a colorful, sometimes loud, and always busy, setting.

5.

GOVERNOR DODGE INSTRUCTED THE OJIBWE to select speakers for the meeting on the next day, Thursday, 27 July, and according to Van Antwerp, he told them to have only two persons speak for all eleven bands. Those chosen were Ma-ghe-ga-bo, or La-Trappe, of Leech Lake, and Bagone-giizhig, or Hole-in-the-Day, from Gull Lake, both Minnesota Ojibwes. According to the Van Antwerp journal, Hole-in-the-Day spoke to the assembled Ojibwe, but we are not told what he said. LaTrappe addressed Governor Dodge, and in what must have been a lengthy presentation, told him that the people agreed to sell the land, but that they wanted a just compensation for it, and that they reserved the right to hunt, fish and gather on it. They also insisted that mixed-blood relatives share in this compensation, and that the government cover the peoples' debts with their traders.[26]

The Ojibwe asked that the treaty only be for a period of sixty years, after which it could be renegotiated, but Governor Dodge held fast for an agreement "in perpetuity." With this, the Ojibwe leaders countered that the compensation, then, should also be in perpetuity, but Dodge insisted on a payment schedule lasting only twenty years.[27]

With an imaginative hindsight we might consider the scene at this point in the negotiations. It all could have ended if the Ojibwe had taken a stand, saying they were not going to cede the land in perpetuity, but of course this was not the case, and no doubt they felt the futility of such a stand. They knew American loggers were already moving onto the lands and that other newcomers were eminent. Any attempts to halt these trespassers most probably would have led to the American authorities' insistence that the only remaining safe recourse for the Ojibwes was to move further west. Furthermore, given the rules guiding inter-band relationships, it was only those bands actually residing on the lands the treaty spoke to that had the right to take such a stand.

Tribal leaders were being advised by their agents, traders, missionaries, and untold others, many who, it seems, were in favor of the sale. Add to this the problem of the trust—and competency—of the translators, and of course, the transcending difficulty of cultural assumptions and understandings for both the Ojibwe and English speaking Americans.[28]

What the tribesmen did insist on was their right to continue to harvest food resources from the lands, and to do this in perpetuity. Governor Dodge agreed that the people could continue to take these resources, but he inserted the phrase, "at the pleasure of the President of the United States" into the treaty document.

Then, he asked that the Ojibwe meet with their government Sub-agents to decide what would be proper compensation for the lands. This was done and the following day, Saturday, 29 July, the group met again, agreed on the amount of compensation offered, and signed the treaty.

6.

OBVIOUSLY, THE PROCEEDINGS DID NOT go as quickly and effortlessly as this brief summary may suggest. Throughout the ten days much discussion ensued and it is clear that only after the Ojibwe understood they could continue residing on the lands, and in the manner they were accustomed to—that is, that they could continue to hunt, fish, and gather in their traditional ways—did they sign the treaty paper. Regarding this important issue of removal, Charles E. Cleland writes: "The Chippewa did not understand the phrase 'during the pleasure of the President' to mean that they would have to remove from the ceded territory."[29]

After the agreement was reached, Van Antwerp makes it clear that the act of putting pen to paper was not easy. There was hesitancy to be the first to sign, until Hole-in-the-Day, the Minnesota leader from Gull Lake, rose and signed it. Only then did the others come forward. It seems obvious that this was not a treaty that the Wisconsin Ojibwe bands eagerly entered into or happily concluded. Except, perhaps, for a brief statement by La Pointe's Buffalo, the written record is very scant on the matter of just how the Ojibwe delegates really felt about the document, but there is no doubt the Americans were thrilled that it was a successful session. The Ojibwe's reaction is another matter, and in the ensuing days the long canoe trips to their homes must have been filled with contemplation.

Official documents and written eyewitness accounts of the meetings tell of the minor part played by the Wisconsin bands. Except for those living near Lake Superior, these were the bands which actually resided on the lands covered under the treaty. The chosen speakers were all from Minnesota and we know nothing about the actual process of choosing them, except that Agent Taliaferro may have been involved in this important task. The speakers made it clear that they were not presenting their own views, but merely passing on those of the Ojibwe involved, however, Hole-in-the-Day is reported to have argued strongly for the sale and supposedly worked behind the scenes to accomplish it.[30]

No doubt American government officials stood ready to influence the tribesmen at every turn. Recalling that one of the charges of Sub-agents was to acculturate the Indians to

American culture, we might conclude that the sale of this vast tract of land was something the local agents encouraged, since such a sale would lead to increased Euro-American settlement of the lands and eventually reduce the volume of hunting and gathering territories available to the Ojibwe, causing them to see the necessity of giving up "the chase." It is in this sense that Dodge's advice that the natives consult with their two Sub-agents regarding a proper monetary compensation for the lands is significant. The written record is silent, but there seems no doubt both Daniel Bushnell, the Sub-agent at La Pointe, and Miles M. Vineyard, from Minnesota's Crow Wing agency, were ready to do this service.[31]

The Van Antwerp journal is silent on the question of Maj. Lawrence Taliaferro, the government's agent at St. Peters, and his efforts to bring the sale about, but a year later, the La Pointe trader, Lyman Warren, told Henry Schoolcraft that Taliaferro was instrumental in facilitating the approval of the treaty. Taliaferro was upset with the 1827 administrative transfer of the Minnesota Ojibwe from his agency to that of Henry Schoolcraft's at Sault Ste. Marie, and a decade later this frustration may have been involved in his reputedly behind-the-scenes machinations regarding the St. Peters treaty. It was said that Taliaferro worked to assure that concerns of the Minnesota Ojibwe communities were given priority over those of the Wisconsin bands.[32] A year after the signing of the St. Peters treaty, Lyman Warren paid Henry Schoolcraft a visit at his Sault Ste. Marie office and in his memoir dated 5 October 1838, Schoolcraft had this to say about the visit:

> I took occasion to inquire into the circumstances of the cession of the treaty of the 29th of July, 1837, and asked him why it was that so little had been given for so large a cession, comprehending the very best lands of the Chippewas in the Mississippi Valley. He detailed a series of petty intrigues by the St. Peters agent, who had flattered two of the Pillager chiefs, and loaded them with new clothes and presents. One of these, Hole-in-the-Day, came down twenty days before the time. The Pillagers, in fact, made the treaty. The bands of the St. Croix and Chippewa Rivers, who really lived on the land and owned it, had, in effect, no voice. So with respect to the La Pointe Indians. He stated that Gen. Dodge really knew nothing of the fertility and value of the country purchased, having never set foot on it. Governor Dodge thought the tract chiefly valuable for its pine, and natural millpower; and there was no one to undeceive him. He had been authorized to offer $1,300; but the Chippewa managed badly—they knew nothing of thousands, or how the annuity would divide among so many, and were in fact, cowed down by the braggadocia (sic) of the flattered Pillager chief, Hole-in-the-Day.[33]

Lyman Warren's remarks are noteworthy. He was making them to Henry Schoolcraft, and it is the latter who passed them onto us. Schoolcraft, always the astute politician, was hesitant to discredit either Taliaferro or Warren. We recall that at St. Peters, Warren was one of the traders whose account books were cleared of debts incurred by the Ojibwe—in Warren's case to the amount of $25,000.00, a considerable sum in 1837—so he was not an uninterested party in the outcome of the treaty meetings. Also, Warren's self-interest can be seen in his hurry to secure a portion of the wealth to be made once the treaty was ratified. According to Ronald Satz, "Among the well-known traders who signed the 1837 treaty as witnesses and subsequently exploited the forest wealth thrown open to Americans by that agreement were Henry Hastings Sibley, Hercules L. Dousman, and Lyman M. Warren."[34]

Surely, Warren had influence with the Ojibwe, at least with those from La Pointe and the Chippewa River. Given the history of power and authority many traders had in the days of the fur trade, and given Warren's personal connection with the Ojibwe community (we recall that his father-in-law was Michel Cadotte, Jr., and thus, his wife and children were all Ojibwe), we should expect that by 1837, when the fur trade was beginning to diminish and the people were coming under increasing strain from several quarters, that his opinions would have been welcomed.

Perhaps the person of Lyman Warren can typify the important role of traders at nineteenth century treaty negotiation sessions. As Anton Treuer so candidly states, the important role of traders at St. Peters in 1837 was a major part of the session since:

> More than fifty traders made financial claims against the payments intended for the Ojibwe. Trader Lyman Warren, based at La Pointe, Wisconsin, demanded large quantities of the 1837 Ojibwe annuity payments to cover debts incurred at his post. Both Warren and William Aitkin represented the American Fur Company and had especially large claims. Warren was following an established European trader practice of inflating Indian debts, creating false claims, and using them to gouge money from Indians' government annuities. This ultimately forced Indians to buy the goods they needed with credit, not with cash, which started the vicious cycle again.
>
> At the treaty signing Warren also served as interpreter for many of the Wisconsin bands, even though his business interests were counter to those of the Ojibwe. His claims were so outrageous and forcefully stated that Indian agent Lawrence Taliaferro pulled his revolver and threatened to kill Warren if he did not sit down . . . Henry Dodge, Governor of Wisconsin Territory, intervened before events turned bloody.[35]

However, putting Lyman Warren's personal business interests aside, we should agree, as historian Satz suggests, that this prominent La Pointe trader's candid remarks about Maj. Taliaferro "lend a new perspective into the actions noted in the [treaty] proceedings."[36]

Even though removal is not explicitly mentioned in secretary Van Antwerp's journal, the remarks of several Ojibwe speakers are clearly addressing this important issue. On the morning of 28 July, for example, when speaking for the assembled Ojibwe, Flat Mouth, the prominent Leech Lake leader, said:

> My Father. Your children are willing to let you have their lands, but they wish to reserve the privilege of making sugar from the trees, and getting their living from the Lakes and Rivers, as they have done heretofore, *and of remaining in this Country* . . . There is some game on the lands yet; & for that reason also, we wish to remain on them, to get a living.[37]

The question of removing native communities to regions west of the Mississippi River had been an issue discussed by America's national leaders since the time of Thomas Jefferson, and it finally led to the Removal Act President Andrew Jackson pushed through Congress in 1830. Seven years later, by the time of the St. Peters meetings, some southern Wisconsin tribes had already been removed and for years there was talk of the eventual removal of all Wisconsin Ojibwe bands to Minnesota Territory. Such a move would give economic and political benefit to officials like Taliaferro and his associates, and this may well have been one of the primary motives behind his reported attempts to influence the sale.

Van Antwerp's journal shows that Hole-in-the-Day spoke openly and passionately of his desire to have the treaty approved, and the record shows that Taliaferro was not immune from the kind of behind-the-scenes activity Lyman Warren detailed to Henry Schoolcraft. Only a year after the signing of the St. Peters treaty, Agent Taliaferro was said to have been involved in similar activities leading to the sale of Wisconsin territorial land still held by the Dakota.[38]

In his discussion of these issues, historian Ronald Satz calls to mind the different cultural understandings and norms serving as guides for social interaction such as took place at St. Peters. The *oral* world of the Ojibwe required a demeanor that at times was opposed to mainstream American customs, as evinced by people like Henry Dodge. For example, Satz reminds us of the complex use of *silence* to transmit attitudes and feelings in Ojibwe culture. There were times in the meetings when blocks of silence must have frustrated Dodge as he hurried to conclude the deliberations in a manner favoring his interests.[39]

Satz suggests that another Ojibwe guideline for interpersonal relations is *the ethic of non-interference*. As non-approval was often exhibited by a silent response, so too, it was a firm taboo to interfere with the behavior of another. Then there was the more obvious problem of translation, wherein some English words used by Dodge were simply mistranslated, or misunderstood (or not understood at all) by the Ojibwe.

Of course, these problems of translation went both ways. The written record usually does not allow us to witness the language the Ojibwe speakers used and how the translators doubtless, at times, struggled to put it into English, especially a form of English officials like Dodge could understand. While there are some instances of tribal leaders' frustrations regarding this important aspect of the meetings, it is typically absent from the written record. This important matter of translators and their abilities to properly use native languages, to say nothing of their personal political allegiances, was said to have been an issue at St. Peters.

To the Ojibwe, the *spoken* word took precedence over the written word, and promises, agreements and assurances that may have been made in the ten days of discussions at St. Peters and were carried home in the hearts and minds of the tribesmen had little meaning to the Americans unless they were put into writing. In this regard, we see that the Ojibwe were at a distinct disadvantage.[40]

Perhaps these problems were most cryptically stated by the missionary William Boutwell (who was present at St. Peters), when he referred to the clause about the length of time the tribesmen could harvest the land's resources that Henry Dodge inserted into the treaty. Writing a month after the conclusion of the negotiations Boutwell said, referring to the Ojibwe: "they know nothing of the duration of a mans (sic) pleasure."[41]

## 7.

It seems that in some ways the few years immediately following the meeting at St. Peters were a relatively quiet time for the Ojibwe and also for the American officials. The tribesmen returned to their home regions and resumed their lives of hunting, fishing, gardening and gathering. The American officials also went home and, we should expect, went back to business as usual. Quite possibly, both parties were a bit numbed by what had transpired at St. Peters. Apparently not understanding the land sale as the Americans did, and doubtlessly anticipating the annual payments of goods and cash for the sale, the Ojibwe had, nevertheless, divested themselves of a huge portion of land and the Americans had just made a purchase of a large piece of real estate at a very reasonable price.

There is evidence to suggest that La Pointe's Buffalo was not only numbed, but also frustrated and doubtless angry at the outcome of the St. Peters meeting. On 10 December, approximately four months after the signing of the treaty, he told Sub-agent, Daniel Bushnell, the following:

> I have nothing to say about the Treaty, good, or bad, because the country was not mine; but when it comes my turn I shall know how to act. If the Americans want my land, I shall know what to say. I did not like to stand in the road of the Indians at St. Peters. I listened to our Great Father's words, & laid them in my heart. I have not forgotten them. The Indians acted like children; they tried to cheat each other and got cheated themselves. When it comes my turn to sell my land, I do not think I shall give it up as they did . . . Father, I speak for my people, not for myself. I am an old man. My fire is almost out—there is but little smoke. When I set in my wigwam & smoke my pipe, I think of what has past and what is to come, and it makes my heart shake. When business comes before us we will try and act like Chiefs. If any thing is to be done, it had better be done straight.[42]

This quotation of Buffalo's is noteworthy for the anger it expresses. If, as has been stated, he really was ninety-six years old when he died in 1855, by late 1837, Buffalo could have been in his early eighties, and doubtless was growing tired. As a child and youth he witnessed the years of French and English political struggles in his homeland, followed by the arrival of the aggressive Americans. Surely, he was familiar with the ways of these people. It seems that by the last few decades of his life he was at least minimally proficient in their language and by that time was quite familiar with their religions, politics, and other social ways. It seems clear that Buffalo knew what Governor Dodge was up to at St. Peters. Writers have stated again and again that La Pointe's Buffalo stood out among his people, and that he was not only a respected leader, but was a competent and intelligent individual.

When he said the land sold in the Treaty of 1837 was not his, and therefore, he had no right to argue against its sale, we see another instance of the workings of the Ojibwe band political system. The land belonged to the inland bands occupying it, not to the lakeshore bands further to the north. Throughout the St. Peters treaty meetings Governor Dodge tried again and again to get these disparate communities to set aside their separate political identities and to act as one, but leaders like Buffalo resisted his attempts. If the leaders of those bands not living on the actual lands involved in the negotiations had openly argued against the land cession, they would have had to go against strong Ojibwe norms about interfering in someone else's business. Thus, Buffalo could not have easily spoken openly against the sale. This, apparently, is what occurred, since the written accounts of the treaty meetings show no public disagreement with it.

Interestingly, the remarks by Lyman Warren made to Henry Schoolcraft several years later suggest that the Ojibwe leaders who spoke in favor of the sale were from the Pillager community in northern Minnesota Territory, far distant from the ceded land. Unlike the bands closer to Lake Superior, the ties between these western people and those living on the ceded lands had grown weaker over the many years since their exodus from Chequamegon Bay. This along with the strong personal characters of Pillager leaders like Flat Mouth makes it likely that these northern peoples could have more freely spoken openly in favor of the land sale.

What the written record does show is a lively interest in the manner payment for the lands was to be disbursed. When Buffalo told Daniel Bushnell that the people acted like children trying to cheat each other he was referring to the annuities and how they were to be distributed. An issue raised for some time after 1837 was whether the payments should have gone only to those who resided on the ceded lands or if they should have gone to all those who signed the treaty.

In Buffalo's remarks about how at St. Peters he listened to the words of the "Great Father" and "laid them in his heart," and that he "has not forgotten them," we see the importance of the spoken word in Ojibwe culture. Dodge told the tribal leaders they could continue residing on the ceded territory and harvest the land's resources, and that their "Great Father" was not only concerned about the welfare of their women and children, but that he had the best interests of all the Ojibwe in his heart. The poignancy of Buffalo wanting to believe this imagery is compelling, but when he went on to tell Bushnell that "When it comes my turn to sell my land I do not think I shall give it up as they did," followed by "When business comes before us [the La Pointe people] we will try to act like Chiefs. If any thing is to be done, it had better be done straight," we must wonder just what he meant.

Was Buffalo saying that, unlike the interior leaders, he would not sell his lakeshore land for any price? Or was he saying only that he would demand a much larger compensation? Or perhaps more likely, was he intimating that he knew someday soon "business" would come to him, i.e., the treaty negotiators would be at his lodge door and his La Pointe community would be confronted with the reality of what was occurring to the Ojibwe? In other words, was his remark a prescient statement about the inevitable future for he and his people? We can imagine Buffalo, an elderly man, with, as he stated, his heart "shaking" as he sits, pensively (and we might add, *prayerfully*) smoking his pipe in his wigwam at La Pointe in the winter of 1837-38. Surely he contemplated what was yet to come.

## 8.

BUFFALO WAS DEEPLY TROUBLED by the huge land sale in the Treaty of 1837. It is claimed he refused to sign the document until a number of his young men stepped forward to touch the pen, causing him to finally rise and do the same.[43] The frustration brought by this first land sale treaty for the Ojibwe people of Wisconsin Territory must have caused Buffalo to contemplate his relationship with the British, and especially with his friend at Garden River, a site just east of Sault St. Marie in Ontario, Canada. In the years just previous to the Treaty of 1837 this person, Shingwaukonse (Little Pine), had been telling the western Ojibwe leaders to maintain their positive standing with the Crown and not to give up any land to the Americans, for it would weaken their political and economic autonomy. Shingwaukonse was a visionary who had a plan for the formation of a large Ojibwe community at Garden River that would have included people from the American western Lake Superior region. At this site there was a potential to harvest timber as well as engage in mining without the interference of Canadian authorities, and Shingwaukonse stressed this economic benefit during his attempts to convince American Ojibwe communities to move to Canada.

In 1838, the first year of annuity payments from the treaty, when no American Ojibwe came to Manitoulin Island for the annual distribution of British presents, Shingwaukonse was concerned and sent a letter to Buffalo at La Pointe "upbraiding" him "for surrendering his political autonomy for a pittance in money and goods."[44] Shingwaukonse needed these western Ojibwe friends to support his own political standing with the British and he continued to work to have them move to Ontario.

In late 1838, or possibly early 1839, Buffalo replied with a long letter in which he spoke of his continuing friendship with the Canadian leader. This important document reveals much about the relationship between the western Ojibwe people and the British, and since it is usually omitted from historical writings about the Chequamegon Bay Ojibwe, here it will be given in its entirety:

My dear Friend Shingwauk I received your letter that you forwarded to me by Capn Wood, I am very satisfied to hear that your family is well as also yourself. My dear Chief I remember well what I told you last summer, I have always the same mind I don't alter it. I love too much my mouth and my heart. My pipe I sent you of my faithfulness. I also tell you my Dear Chief that nobody can + will be the master of me. I am my own Master. They tell me that our agent when he arrives to this place will intreat me to go to Prairie du Chien this summer. But I tell you that I will certainly not go but I intend to go down this summer to see our English friends for the last time as they will give us presents this summer only and then no more. I intend to go down to see the Red Coat than to receive here a little money. So I will go down. Never believe My dear Chief that any body is master of me and the Americans never shall be. The half-breeds that came to La Pointe last summer know all our chiefs, and almost all our Indians tormented me last summer—even our Traders spoke ill of me. I can tell you for my person that I will certainly go. I think altho' that the chief Ashkebuggecooshe [of Leech Lake] and his young men are very poor this winter that they are almost freezing to Death so I think he will go down to see our English friends for the last time. The Chiefs from the interior asked me to wait for them [and] that they would go along with me. I told them that I will start from here early in June, if they arrive in due season we will go down in company. Perhaps also Aiahbens will go down, he said so. For me I go down to keep my word. I honor my word very much and always wish to keep it. If I live I will see you next summer. My dear Shingwauk, we are poor. I do not know what we shall eat during the journey but still I will go. I wish you good health my Dear Friend and good health to all your family and our friends.
Your Friend Kache Whashke.[45]

In this important document, Buffalo stresses his continued friendship for Shingwaukonse, hence the gift of a pipe, and he reminds the Canadian leader that his (Buffalo's) word is good, in other words, that his mouth and heart are connected, causing him to speak from the heart. He also disclaims the notion that he is merely acceding to the will of the Americans, insisting they would never be his "master," and he tells of the poor treatment he received after returning to La Pointe from St. Peters. This is significant because it shows the mixed-bloods, traders, and even his "Indians" were angry with him for signing the treaty. This point is rarely made in the historical literature, although we should expect this negative sentiment was widespread throughout Wisconsin Territory's Ojibwe community.

The reason for his agent wanting him to go to Prairie du Chien "this summer" is unknown. We presume he was referring to the upcoming summer of 1839, and given the stature of the La Pointe leader, the rumored trip probably had to do with meeting officials of the Unites States Government. Instead, he would travel east to Manitoulin Island to meet the British since conferring with the "Red Coat" was more important than staying home for the annuity payment from the recent treaty, a payment the La Pointe people would not be allowed to take part in. We should assume, however, that given the prominence of Buffalo he probably would have been given "a little money" during the annuity distribution gathering.

Buffalo tells Shingwaukonse he will be coming to Manitoulin Island with other leaders from the Mississippi headwaters and the interior of Wisconsin Territory, and thus, there were several other bands that intended to maintain their ties with the Crown. Also, Buffalo notes that the next distribution of British presents—taking place in the summer of 1839—would be the last one made.

This letter shows that at the time of its writing, Buffalo was still preoccupied with working out relationships with his "two fathers," and that he was not holding to his commitment to the Americans in the Fond du Lac treaty of 1826 to turn away from British attempts to influence his behavior. It is obvious that by 1838, Buffalo was struggling to develop meaningful relationships with these two opposing powers.

## 9.

EVEN THOUGH IN THE ABOVE LETTER he downplayed the importance of the American annuities from the Treaty of 1837, Buffalo was concerned about the matter of who should receive them. Minnesota Territory's Pillager bands were excluded from them, a decision that upset these powerful northern communities. Also, annuities were issued on a per capita basis, and in some cases were deemed to be so small that some individuals did not bother to make the long, time-consuming trips to get them. They were disbursed at La Pointe, causing some bands to make arduous trips each fall, pulling them away from rice harvesting and early fall fishing.

Upon returning home from St. Peters and throughout the ensuing winter, Buffalo must have pondered the immediate effects of the new treaty. Charles Cleland states that "a period of confusion" followed the treaty meeting, since some Ojibwe apparently misunderstood the amount and importance of the annuities to be disbursed.[46] In the summer of 1838, the first year money and goods were to be received, Alfred Brunson claimed he met a group of Ojibwe on the St. Croix River that thought the amount of annuities it would soon be issued would sustain it for a full year, until the next annuity payment was made. According to Brunson, these Ojibwe "had neglected their usual hunting, and had few or no furs to sell to traders. They had also omitted their sugar making and planting their gardens, and had nothing to eat. Their last resort in such a strait—fishing—was impeded by high waters."[47]

However, it seems the treaty had little direct effect upon the lives of most Ojibwe, although the schedule of annuity payments conflicted with the fall rice and fish harvests. We do not know whether American officials planned it this way, but it is probable these fall payments were purposely scheduled in hopes that by coming to the annuity payment disbursements, the people might have difficulty putting enough food away for the upcoming winters and in this way become more amenable to suggestions from their Sub-agents, local missionaries, and others that they take up agriculture and other "civilized" ways. Such an assumption might seem unwarranted but, as we will see, in 1852, the scheduling of fall annuity payments at Sandy Lake, Minnesota Territory, was a tactic consciously planned and executed by United States officials in order to facilitate their attempts at the removal of Wisconsin's Ojibwe people. Also, it has been claimed that after the Treaty of 1837, the Americans timed their annuity payments to conflict with the issuance of "presents" from the Canadian government to American tribesmen.[48]

Almost immediately after returning from St. Peters, the Ojibwes became aware of more lumbermen moving into the ceded lands to set up camps for the expected large harvest of white pine. These operations had been popping up even before the ratification of the treaty by the U.S. Senate on 15 June 1838. These camps welcomed the venison, waterfowl, wild rice, maple sugar and other foods Ojibwe people brought to trade and barter for, and in some instances to sell for cash. This new economic activity may have begun to accomplish what Sherman Hall and other missionaries were unable to. In the 1830s, the incidents of this seemed largely restricted to the southern Chippewa and St. Croix River Valleys, so the Lake Superior Ojibwe communities were not immediately involved. Employment in logging camps was something the Ojibwes would pursue in earnest several decades after 1837, when these operations reached the northern portions of the state. Until then, most tribesmen continued their traditional subsistence practices.[49]

### *Carrying Out the Articles of the Treaty of 1837: Initial Struggles*

1.

AFTER CONGRESS RATIFIED THE 1837 TREATY the American officials faced the problem of how to carry out its agreements. Among other things, the treaty stipulated that the United States would send blacksmiths, farmers, and carpenters to Ojibwe country to meet the tribesmen's needs and also that the annuities would be distributed. This was no little matter, since Ojibwe bands were widely dispersed throughout the ceded territory, and they were very concerned that all those who were entitled to annuities received them and that the distribution be accomplished in a timely fashion. We do not know if they were, in truth, as enthusiastic about the government blacksmiths, farmers and carpenters coming to their territories. The transcripts from the treaty negotiations do not indicate that the Ojibwe seriously wanted blacksmiths and the other craftsmen to be sent to them, or if this is something the treaty commissioners insisted upon. While it appears likely that it would have been beneficial to have the services of a local blacksmith for his abilities to make metal tools helpful to their foraging existence—animal traps and metal parts for repairing a broken gun, for example—the Ojibwe must have understood that the coming of farmers and carpenters was intended to bring about deep changes in their lives. For example, wigwams and log or wood-framed houses were all useful for shelter, but the latter structures were immobile, and as such, represented *sedentarism*, a cultural trait with a very real potential for monumental change to the lives of foragers.

The literature discussing the times does not speak to this issue at any length. Blacksmiths, farmers and carpenters were an integral part of American life on the frontier in the mid-nineteenth century, and in American eyes were essential for changing the wilderness into a "civilized" countryside. We should expect that to the Ojibwe they were deemed helpful but also, like missionaries and teachers, were recognized as the advance units of American society and as such, foretold of a new way of life. Surely, the tribesmen felt a degree of trepidation regarding the coming of these craftsmen, yet their benefits were sometimes desired. For example, in 1843, the Lac du Flambeau leader, White Crow, and other chiefs, said their bands did not want to come north to La Pointe for annuities because of the bad influence of whites found there, but they wanted the blacksmith and farmer to remain in their communities.[50]

In his 1840 annual report to the Commissioner of Indian Affairs, La Pointe's Sub-agent, Daniel Bushnell, spoke to these issues. He said that for the three previous years the annuities were distributed too late in the season, a practice that brought hardship to the Ojibwe. He recommended they be paid "not later that the 1st of August" so the people would have ample time to return home for ricing season. Also, payments had been made as late as October, a time when the Ojibwe were "in the midst of their best hunting," and due to weather, at times may be "unable to reach their homes before the winter sets in." He wrote, "Autumn is to them the most important season; and if they fail then to make the necessary provision to meet the rigorous winters of this latitude, their sufferings are often very severe." This meant that while the annuities were very important to the people, by being distributed too late in the season, any value they had was greatly diminished.[51]

We need to remember that under the Treaty of 1837, it was the Mississippi and interior Wisconsin bands that were to be paid annuities since they were the people whose land was sold. The Pillager Band and others at the headwaters of the Mississippi, as was the case with those from the immediate southern shore of Lake Superior, did not give up land in 1837, and therefore were not to receive any annuity payments. We recall La Pointe's Buffalo remarking after the treaty's ratification that it did not pertain to his land. For years this question of who received annuities and who did not was a very divisive issue between the Mississippi, Pillager, and Lake Superior bands.

La Pointe apparently was chosen as the payment site under the 1837 Treaty for the convenience of the Americans. The annuity goods and specie were brought to the site over water, through Detroit, Mackinac and Sault Ste. Marie, and for the first years of disbursement, were transported no further. If they wanted their share of the payment, the qualifying Ojibwe bands had to come to La Pointe. Consequently, some of these bands were traveling as much as 200 miles to the disbursement site, a distance of no little length when the birch bark canoe and a person's legs were the main means of transport.

Regarding the matter of the second article of the Treaty of 1837, under which the United States agreed to provide the people with the services of a blacksmith, Bushnell told how one had been, apparently, located at La Pointe and it was agreed two others would be established at locations chosen by the interior bands. However, it was difficult to get any blacksmiths to agree to remove to such remote sites, and even if they *did* agree, it was very troublesome to transport their heavy materials by canoe. That is why the 1837 agreement to supply blacksmiths was delayed for two years.[52]

About the obligation of the Americans to bring government farmers into Ojibwe country, Bushnell noted that Jeremiah Russell, the farmer at the St. Croix station at Pokegama on the Snake River, was trying to convince the resident Ojibwe to take up farming, but that so far they showed little interest. According to Bushnell, "Little hope is entertained that the Indians will ever derive much benefit from this provision." Apparently, in 1840, the Ojibwe readily saw the value of having a blacksmith in their midst, but for some the presence of a government farmer was another matter. This indicates that at the time they were not yet willing to give up their foraging adaptation in favor of sedentary agriculture, or perhaps even to only intensify their traditional gardening practices to a degree that could be labeled a kind of "early farming."[53]

We see, then, that for the American officials the difficulty of fulfilling their agreements under the Treaty of 1837 was compounded due to the geographic distances and cultural differences involved. The problems of appropriating funds for the purchase, handling and shipping of the goods were significant, as was the matter of deciding on the actual time for disbursement. La Pointe had been chosen as the distribution site and this was of particular importance to the Ojibwe, since the numerous bands were distant from each other and some would have to expend much time and effort in traveling to the meeting.[54] This matter of where and when annuity disbursements would be made was a lingering problem for the Ojibwe, and over the next several years they repeatedly asked that sites be chosen closer to their main villages, and that the specie and provisions were distributed at times more beneficial to the people.

Indian Affairs Commissioner Carey Harris asked Governor Dodge for suggestions on how to carry out the government's obligations under the treaty, and in Dodge's reply he stressed the importance of fulfilling these obligations properly since the Ojibwe understood the annuities as something rightfully theirs. Attempting to inform Harris of the importance of understanding the Ojibwe, he said, "These remote Indians are a jealous people of their right" and that "It is fear or interest alone that govern the savage character." The disbursement of the annuities, then, was to be taken seriously and carried out expeditiously. To the Americans the matter of contracting for blacksmiths, farmers and carpenters to go to Ojibwe Country apparently did not have the priority that the annuity disbursements carried.

Dodge also told Harris that "a few flags and medals for the Principal Chiefs" should be sent to La Pointe and that "A present of a few common swords would also have a good effect." Regarding the necessity of agents and Sub-agents, like Daniel Bushnell, to give presents to the Ojibwe leaders, Dodge wrote of this gift-giving: "It is calculated to make them respected and influential with their Indians, and to counteract to a certain extent the undue influence exercised over their minds by their traders."[55] As French and British authorities did earlier, such "calculations" show that the United States government's officials consciously, and perhaps carefully, orchestrated their diplomatic relationships with tribal peoples.

2.

UNDER ARTICLES THREE AND FOUR of the Treaty of 1837, the United States agreed to disburse a portion of the annuities to persons of mixed blood and to pay their traders' debts, but American officials had postponed these disbursements over a year because of the death of Alfred Aitken, a La Pointe person of mixed Ojibwe and European descent. Aitken was killed by a group of mixed-bloods, and there was a call for revenge. The frustration of the mixed-bloods waiting for their annuities and the anticipation of a revenge killing caused unsettled times in Lake Superior country. Among other things, what this incident shows is that in the mid-nineteenth century, traditional methods of social control were still functioning in Ojibwe culture at La Pointe. We do not know what influence leaders like Buffalo—or the resident Christian missionaries and Sub-agent Bushnell—had in this matter, but it seems likely that the tribal clan system was involved.

Lucius Lyon was appointed by American authorities to dispense the annuities and pay the traders' debts, and after making a preliminary trip to La Pointe to arrange for the meeting, he informed Indian Affairs Commissioner Crawford that he feared the disturbance of the mixed-bloods could not be quelled any longer by continuing to withhold the annuity payments. About the region's mixed-bloods Lyon said, "They are a proud, sensitive people who are anxious to be recognized by the Government as citizens of the United States and to receive protection from its laws." Stating the importance of keeping "the good feelings of these Indians" he asked for a military force from Sault Ste. Marie to go to La Pointe and quiet the disturbance. To this end Colonel H. A. Lavake, who commanded a unit of mixed-bloods at Sault Ste. Marie, arrived at Madeline Island in 1839, but by that time found the matter settled. (An added note about the nature of life at Madeline Island in the 1830s, is that after Colonel Lavake and his soldiers had traveled the length of Lake Superior to get to La Pointe only to learn they were not needed, they discovered that they could not readily secure passage back to Sault Ste. Marie, causing them to spend an unexpected several weeks on the island with no immediate responsibilities.[56])

Lyon left a lengthy account of his time at La Pointe that is helpful to understand what the region's life was like in those years. Among other things, as with other observers, he felt part of the problem confronting him stemmed from the Indians' unfamiliarity with the use of *money*. He claimed it was "entirely unknown among the North Western Indians until within the last few years." Since a large portion of the annuities was to be disbursed as specie, there was the fear that much of it would quickly be in the hands of illicit whiskey dealers.[57]

Another problem Lyon encountered was that since he was disbursing annuities under authority of the Treaty of 1837, the mixed-bloods from Leech Lake, Fond du Lac and La Pointe were not eligible to receive anything because they "had ceded no portion of their country to the United States." This, of course, disappointed these individuals, some whom had traveled great distances for the meeting.[58]

In 1839, when Lucius Lyon was at La Pointe, the fur trade still was ongoing although in a state of decline. He claimed that the old "Standard of Value" that had been in use in the northwest for many years was still in effect. Thus, the medium of exchange was still the beaver skin, and the "The common Beaver skin was always counted as 1 *skin* or *plue*," but since beaver numbers were declining in some regions, trappers had turned to muskrats, causing these skins to become the exchange standard, and in those regions ten muskrat skins were equal to one beaver skin. Lyon noted that in 1839, the cash value for one *skin* was two dollars.

He remarked that at La Pointe, Michel Cadotte's account books showed the old method of accounting, that is, placing small straight marks opposite what was purchased. According to Lyon, "This was a method of marking charges that an Indian could understand; and whenever he brought furs to pay his debt, he received credit, by crossing out one of these marks, for each 'Skin' or 'Plue' that his furs might amount to."

Lyon claimed that starting in 1837, the American Fur Company was trying to abolish this old credit system, since due to the failing industry the company was increasingly unable to recover its debts. This change, he felt:

> . . . is likely to prove successful, and highly beneficial to both parties. To the Indians it will be beneficial, by teaching them to be more provident, and industrious, and to rely entirely on their own exertions, for the scanty comfort's they enjoy; and to the company and traders generally, it will be greatly beneficial, because it removes the principal cause of the losses which all have sustained, who have been engaged in the Indian trade in that region of the Country.[59]

These comments remind us of important changes underway in western Lake Superior country in the 1830s. While the Ojibwe were still relying heavily upon hunting and gathering for subsistence, they were also making important adaptations. The Americans' market economy was coming to the region, causing the people to consider a new way of acquiring and exchanging resources. Money, the all-purpose medium of exchange, was becoming part of Ojibwe culture, and would make more changes in Ojibwe lives.

We also see that by the 1830s, a new challenge was confronting the Ojibwe. This was the growing numbers of those individuals who were called *mixed-bloods* or *half-breeds*. These persons were not new to the Ojibwe, since they no doubt began appearing with the first coming of the Europeans, but by the 1830s, they were no longer just an interesting novelty. By this date they had become a political force.

3.

THE QUESTION OF HOW TO CONCEPTUALIZE these individuals, it seems, puzzled both the Ojibwe and the Euro-Americans. Persons of mixed racial descent were *betwixt and between*. They were part of both the Ojibwe and American worlds, but in some cases they had difficulty fitting into either. By the 1830s, American officials made a distinction between persons they labeled as *Indians* and those they called *mixed-bloods*, or *half-breeds*. Perhaps this was more a problem of separating culture from biology than anything else.

In American society of the time, the label *half-breed* had a pejorative connotation and was a concept that writers sometimes used in literary expressions. For instance, in the mid-nineteenth century, Walt Whitman and Herman Melville used the term in a number of their fiction pieces to show the struggles persons of mixed racial backgrounds could have at the time.[60] To officials like Wisconsin Territorial Governor Henry Dodge, *Indians* were tribesmen who lived a foraging life and seemed to desire not to change. These persons still moved with the seasons and, most often, turned their backs to government agents, teachers, and missionaries who told them to give these old customs up. Dodge saw the mixed-bloods as different from these *Indians*, and understood them as useful, but also troublesome. In 1839, when referring to the Ojibwe living in Lake Superior country, he said, "The half-breeds always exercise a great degree of influence over the minds of the Indians, and I consider them as a connecting link between the whites and the Indians; and, should they instigate the Indians to mischief on that exposed frontier, it might be attended with the most fatal consequences to our settlements on that remote border."[61]

Here we see not only that Henry Dodge classified mixed-bloods as being different from Indians, but also that he felt they were *mediatory*. To white authorities like Dodge, they could be used to influence or even control Indians. As we have already seen in the cases of William Warren, the descendents of Jean Baptiste Cadotte, and other individuals of mixed-blood, they could become important persons in regard to relations between Indians and whites.

This matter of how to conceptualize those of mixed racial parentage is graphically seen in a letter several Lake Superior "Chippewa Halfbreeds" sent to La Pointe's Sub-agent Bushnell on 24 July 1839. These persons were calling for justice in the manner of their treatment by the Americans after the death of Alfred Aitken. Regarding the killing, they said they were willing to "bury the hatchet" and give up the call for revenge, and consequently they desired their share of the 1837 annuity payments—a sum they claimed amounted to $100,000.00. They complained that at times some Americans classed them as Indians, and as such, were not covered by United States law, but at other times they were considered as "free white Citizens" and were felt to be under this law. Thus, their treatment was at the whim, and purpose, of whomever was classifying them.[62]

Hopefully with the disbursement of the annuities and the payment of traders' debts made by Lucius Lyon at La Pointe in 1839, these individuals received at least some rectification of their uncomfortable circumstances. Their situation however, would remain a problem for others in the Ojibwe community for some years to come.

## *The Close of the Decade of the 1830s at La Pointe: A Commentary*

1.

TODAY WHEN WE STUDY THE DETAILS of historical events occurring at La Pointe in the decade of the 1830s, we might see it as a time of momentous significance for the great changes it brought. The clear signs of the inevitable ending of the fur trade, the arrival of the Christian missionaries, the continuing scourge of smallpox, the visits of Henry Schoolcraft and Joseph Nicollet that reminded the people of the looming presence of the new United States, the lingering struggle with the Dakota, and the huge land sale of 1837 all are markers for obvious, if not striking change. We should remember, however, that even with these new and important events, the world of the Ojibwe people was still anchored in the age-old institutions, beliefs and practices of their foraging life. The growing numbers of the mixed-blood Ojibwe may have been orienting themselves to the increasing American presence in telling ways, but for many other Ojibwe, the foraging way of life went on despite the obviousness of change coming with the whiteman.

As we have seen, at the close of the decade smallpox revisited some of the Ojibwe bands, wrecking havoc as it had recurrently done for the last many years. Remembering the Ojibwe enthusiasm for Douglass Houghton's initial vaccinations in 1832, we see that this disease must have continued to be a lingering concern. Always threatening and sometimes devastating, it could strike suddenly and harshly. In 1839, Congress appropriated funds for vaccinating the Ojibwe and set that year's allotted amount for the La Pointe Agency at $200.00.[63] Approximately twenty years later, smallpox was still a concern when in 1854, the missionary Leonard Wheeler and his wife vaccinated the La Pointe Ojibwe after the disease suddenly erupted in the Chequamegon region.[64]

In his annual report of 15 September 1849, La Pointe's Sub-agent John Livermore said that the year had been one of little illness but the people were still "wild with apprehension" of what they called "the white man's sickness." They had heard that it was at Sault Ste. Marie and during the fall annuity disbursement they wanted to get their payment in a hurry before it came to La Pointe. Livermore claimed that "Fear of disease, but not of death, is characteristic of the Indian race." He said at that year's event the people wanted a fast distribution so they could "betake themselves to the woods."[65]

The severity of the destruction from new pathogens Europeans brought to North and South America is too easily set aside or even forgotten when we attempt to understand later historical events. This point has as much relevance for Chequamegon Bay as for anywhere in the hemisphere, and this scourge was not just a problem in the decade of the 1830s. European-introduced diseases visited the Ojibwe in the eighteenth century, as well. For example, it has been claimed that in 1783, a young chief Buffalo lost a wife and three of their sons to smallpox.[66] Unfortunately, little demographic information exists to testify to the lingering effects of these diseases, but we should not fail to include these effects in our attempts to understand why at times, as in 1837, at St. Peters, Ojibwe leaders made the decisions they did. In some cases, by the nineteenth century American governmental officials and Christian missionaries were coming amidst communities still reeling from significant losses from these diseases, and as has been suggested that reasons for some Ojibwes' acceptance of Christianity were both the threat and the actual terrible effects of the devastation these diseases wrought.[67]

As Henry Schoolcraft and the others of his 1832 expedition saw at Leech Lake, it was only in those communities distant from frequent contact with the Americans and thus, perhaps still relatively untouched by the new diseases, that a more vibrant and self-confident native existence was found. At Chequamegon Bay in the 1830s, therefore, government agents and missionaries came among a community that had witnessed what can be called the aftermath, or perhaps better, the devastation, of many years of European and Euro-American contact.

In our discussion of the earlier writings of Lewis Cass, Thomas McKenney and others, we noted the often very biased and judgmental comments about the "wretchedness" of some Ojibwe they encountered. We should understand that these tribesmen were struggling not only with matters of health and food availability, but also with the emotional trauma of the times. Surely, the hardship inflicted by diseases like smallpox was among the reasons for these struggles.

## 2.

Beginning in the 1830s, La Pointe's Protestant and Catholic missionaries engaged in what had to have been a fierce competition to gain followers, and it would not be long until, like the fur traders, they became influential intermediaries between tribal people and the American government. As difficulties in maintaining the traditional Ojibwe way of life mounted, these missionaries, in either negative or positive ways, became more important to the people. Their presence, which began in earnest with the coming of Frederick Ayer and the Halls in the early 1830s, would grow in significance.

On 20 August 1833, the Protestants formally established what they called a "Chippewa Mission" on Madeline Island, the intent being to make it the headquarters for their work throughout the entire western Lake Superior area. Two years later with the arrival of Frederick Baraga, the region's Catholic residents rallied and in only twelve days after his arrival built the priest a church. Interestingly, two of the men who helped erect the small log building were Joseph Dufault and Louis Gaudin—possible forebears of numerous Ojibwe descendents in the region today who have taken the Americanized names of DeFoe and Gordon.[68]

Baraga's coming to Madeline Island upset the Protestant missionaries, who claimed he was encroaching on their territory. A letter of protest was signed by William Boutwell, Sherman Hall, Frederick Ayer, and Edmund Ely, and sent to Henry Schoolcraft. This may have spurred the priest on, because by October of that year "Baraga had baptized one hundred forty-eight converts." For the next several years Frederick Baraga settled in and worked hard to win even more converts, and although some of the Protestant missionaries moved on to more western stations, others came to replace them. Granville T. Sproat, for instance, arrived in 1835, worked with Sherman Hall for a few years before going back east to marry, and returned in 1838. His wife eagerly assumed teaching duties in the Protestant mission school on Madeline and labored there for many years.[69]

Added to this flurry of missionary activity were the ominous signs of the pending end of the most lucrative years of the fur trade. By 1835, there were new signs that this long-time trade was struggling. American Fur Trade records show that the numbers of beaver skins shipped east that year had dropped precipitously. As had happened in the southeastern United States in previous years, deerskins were beginning to replace beaver pelts, but the foreign market for tanned deerskins would soon drop away as well.[70]

Trying to make up for the dwindling market for furs, in 1835, Ramsay Crooks attempted to enlarge the fledgling fishing industry in western Lake Superior with stations at Grand Portage, Isle Royale, La Pointe, and other sites. In 1836, over a thousand barrels of salted fish were shipped from La Pointe and the next year this had increased to two thousand, and by 1838, to five thousand. La Pointe was becoming so important that in that year many fishermen and coopers moved from the lake's northern shore to Madeline Island. This industry was deemed so promising that in 1838, when Wisconsin Territorial Delegate Jones wrote to Commissioner Harris encouraging him to push for negotiations to purchase Madeline Island from the Ojibwe, he mentioned this growing fishing industry as part of the rationale for acquiring this land.[71]

Crooks's American Fur Company was shipping the salted fish from Madeline to a warehouse in Detroit, where it was held until market demands opened up in other more easterly locations. In these times the region experienced an economic boom in this new industry but in a short time, like for the fur trade, it would be over.

Both the fur trade and this new fishing industry were tied into the American and European economy, and changes taking place in distant lands could affect places like Chequamegon Bay. In the 1830s, a sudden disinterest in beaver furs in Europe was quick to be felt in Lake Superior country, and likewise, in the eastern United States a shortage of currency affected the market for salted fish. These events and others were soon played out at La Pointe, and those Ojibwe entangled in the economy of the American Fur Company felt them. We do not know the exact number of Ojibwe involved in commercial fishing at La Pointe in these times, but from 1836 to 1840, there were "about twenty Indians" employed in the industry at Grand Portage,[72] and since La Pointe was a larger station we could expect that the number of Ojibwe involved in its fishing venture was greater. However, with the failure of this fishing operation many Ojibwe doubtless returned to their age-old subsistence economy of hunting, fishing, gathering and gardening. As we have seen, even though some of the tribesmen had begun to sell or trade goods to the region's Americans, with the failure or at least the diminishment of these activities, they could still survive by employing this older adaptation.

But by the end of the 1830s, the pressure was on. America struggled with an economic depression from 1837 to 1842, and in this larger financial context the new market of Lake Superior fish was not viable. In light of these problems, and reports of poor business practices in western Lake Superior, Crooks tried to reorganize his fishing operation. In 1838, he removed Lyman Warren as his chief trader at La Pointe, replacing him with Charles Borup. William A. Aitkin, the company's trader at Fond du Lac was also replaced.[73]

With Warren's and Aitkin's dismissals we might possibly be seeing an indication of the stern side of Ramsay Crooks—what Hamilton Ross hinted at as his "conscienceless" character and what Grace Lee Nute saw as despotism. Even though he was a long-term and apparently trusted employee for the firm, Lyman Warren's dismissal, or *firing*, is a clear indication of the difficulty of the times.[74]

Out of work, Warren took his family south to Burnet Falls, a site in north central Wisconsin Territory on the Chippewa River where he farmed, worked as a blacksmith, and eventually gained employment through the American government as an Indian Sub-agent for the local Ojibwe community. The opportunistic resourcefulness of Lyman Warren is seen once more, as it was not long before he erected a sawmill at that site. Along with this, what is important for us is that at this time Lyman and Marie Warren's son, William, returned from six years of eastern schooling to play an integral role in the life of the enterprising Warren family. There were important economic and political changes coming to the region and the Warrens would be role players in them.

During the 1830s, eastern American investors were beginning to shift their interests from the quick money available through the fur trade to what could be made from speculation in land. From the eastern end of the lake at Sault Ste. Marie, Henry Schoolcraft remarked about this when he wrote: "The rage for investment in lands was now manifest in every visitor that came from the East to the West. Everybody, more or less, yielded to it." Schoolcraft was not immune from this popular practice when he wrote on 17 August 1835 that "I embarked in a steamer for Green Bay—where I attended the first land sales, and made several purchases."[75]

The Ojibwe people in the western Lake Superior region would soon be feeling the effects of this speculation in real estate. In a literary paragraph Henry Schoolcraft entered into his memoir on 15 August of 1835, he gives us an image of what he was witnessing from his residence's strategic location immediately beside the St. Mary's River at The Sault:

> The great lakes can no longer be regarded as solitary seas, where the Indian war-whoop has alone for so many uncounted centuries startled its echoes. The Eastern World seems to be alive, and roused up to the value of the West. Every vessel, every steamboat, brings up persons of all classes, whose countenances the desire of acquisition, or some other motive, has rendered sharp, or imparted a fresh glow of hope to their eyes. More persons, of some note or distinction, natives or foreigners, have visited me, and brought me letters of introduction this season, than during years before. Sitting on my piazza, in front of which the great stream of ships and commerce passes, it is a spectacle at once novel, and calculated to inspire high anticipations of the future glory of the Mississippi Valley.[76]

A fitting way to conclude this summary commentary about the 1830s in Chequamegon Country is to note that in 1837, Michel Cadotte passed away at La Pointe. This Ojibwe-French fur trader, former British ally, and long-time local leader who was born in 1764, was the son of an Ojibwe woman and

Jean-Baptiste Cadotte—the early partner of Alexander Henry, the famous British fur trader. Perhaps we can take the passing of Michel Cadotte as a mark for the ending of an earlier way of life and the start of a new one for the mixed-bloods, the resident Americans, and all of La Pointe's Ojibwe people.

*Notes*

1. Cleland, in McClurken *et al*, 2000:26-7; Satz 1991:13-4; Bailly 1836:38-41, WisTerPap, Vol.27.
2. Nesbit 1989[1973]:94.
3. Cleland, in McClurken *et al*, 2000:26.
4. Prucha 1962a p.2, as cited in Satz 1991:14.
5. Cleland, in McClurken *et al*, 2000:27.
6. Chippewa Chiefs and Headmen 1836:53-5, Dousman 1836:645, Dodge 1836:672-74, in WisTerPap, Vol. 27.
7. Satz 1991:13-5.
8. Satz 1991:13; Jones 1836:694 in WisTerPap, Vol. 27.
9. Jones 1838:897-98 in WisTerPap, Vol. 27.
10. Brunson 1836:14 in WisTerPap, Vol. 27.
11. Brunson 1836:14-6 in WisTerPap, Vol. 27.
12. McLaughlin 1980[1899].
13. Satz 1991:13.
14. Dodge 1836:88-95 in WisTerPap, Vol. 27.
15. Rice 1848:1168 in WisTerPap, Vol. 28.
16. Benton 1836:20-1 in WisTerPap, Vol. 27.
17. Dodge 1837:137 in WisTerPap, Vol. 27.
18. Copway 1851.
19. Peyer 1997:237.
20. Brunson 1879:82-6.
21. Cleland, in McClurken *et al* 2000:20.
22. Brody 1981:273; Perry 1996.
23. Hall, Sherman, to Salah Treat, December 31, 1853, cited in Cleland as found in McClurken *et al* 2000:19.
24. Brunson 1879:84.
25. Satz 1991:140.
26. Satz 1991:141.
27. Cleland, in McClurken *et al* 2000:31.
28. Brunson 1879:85-6.
29. Cleland in McClurken *et al* 2000:32; Treuer 2011:65.
30. Satz 1991:23-4.
31. Satz 1991:18.
32. Chute 1998:151-2.
33. Schoolcraft 1978[1851]:610-612.
34. Fries 1951:11, Babcock 1924:374, Bartlett 1921:37, Citizens of the Pineries [1840], as cited in Satz 1991:30.
35. Treuer 2011:64.
36. Satz 1991:23, brackets added.
37. Van Antwerp in Satz 1991:145, italics added.
38. Babcock 1924 as cited in Satz 1991:23.
39. Satz 1991:24-31.
40. Cleland in McClurken *et al* 2000:5.
41. Boutwell 1837, as cited in Satz 1991:23.
42. Buffalo 1837 as cited in Satz 1991:31.
43. Chute 1998:125-6.
44. Chute 1998:83.
45. Chute 1998:274-5.
46. Cleland, in McClurken *et al* 2000:34.
47. Brunson 1879:113.
48. Chute 1998:78.
49. Satz 1991:30.
50. Chippewa Chiefs 1843 as cited in Satz 1991:45.
51. Bushnell 1840 in Annual Report of the Commissioner of Indian Affairs to the Secretary of the Interior, hereafter referred to as ARCIASI.
52. Bushnell 1840 in ARCIASI.
53. Bushnell 1840 in ARCIASI.
54. Schoolcraft 1839:21-2 in WisTerPap, Vol. 28.
55. Doddge 1838:102 in WisTerPap, Vol. 27.
56. Lyon 1839:91-8, in WisTerPap, Vol. 28; Chippewa Half-breeds 1839:16-8 in WisTerPap, Vol. 28.
57. Lyon 1839:96 in WisTerPap, Vol. 28.
58. Lyon 1839:91-8 in WisTerPap, Vol. 28.
59. Lyon 1839:91-8 in WisTerPap, Vol. 28.
60. Loving 1999:89.
61. Dodge 1839:1186 in WisTerPap, Vol. 27.
62. Chippewa Halfbreeds 1839:16-8 in WisTerPap, Vol. 28.
63. Dodge 1839:50 in WisTerPap, Vol. 28.
64. Bunge 2000:5 in "Redeeming the Missionary: Leonard Wheeler and the Ojibwe." In The American Transendental Quarterly, No. 14, pp. 265-75, December 2000.(http://wilsontxt.hwwilson.com/pdfhtml/04335/1P8YY/RS7.htm).
65. Livermore letter of 15 September 1849 to Orlando Brown, Commisioner of Indian Affairs, in ARCIASI.
66. Durfee in Burnham 1974 [1900]:43.
67. Gray 2007:70-5.
68. Ross 1960:83, 87, 90.
69. Ross 1960:91, 97.
70. Ross 1960:101.
71. Jones 1838 in WisTerPap, Vol. 27, pp.897-8; Ross 1960:91-99; Nute 1926.
72. Nute 1926:489.
73. Nute 1926:497; Ross 1960:98.
74. Nute 1926:497-501.
75. Schoolcraft 1978[1851]:520.
76. Schoolcraft 1978[1851]:522.

# 16

# The 1840s: Pressure Builds

### *The Start of the 1840s at Chequamegon Bay: New and Old Challenges*

1.

At La Pointe, the national and international economic problems that occurred in the 1830s carried over into the new decade. The American Fur Company's salted fish were not selling, and on 24 August 1841, Ramsay Crooks ordered Charles Borup to cease fishing activities. Surely this seriously affected the employees of the firm and those Ojibwe fishermen (and women) who were involved in supplying the La Pointe station, but the latter could turn to their traditional economy for sustenance. La Pointe's Sub-agent Daniel Bushnell discussed the possibility of just such a phenomenon.

In his 1841 annual report to Washington authorities, Bushnell remarked that because of the depletion of their traditional resources, some of the Ojibwes had "been forced to resort to fishing" for the new commercial fishing industry that the American Fur Company, and other smaller operations, began several years previous. This switch in resource procurement, he said, "had a highly favorable influence on [them], and I have no doubt contributed more than any other cause towards the improvement observable in their condition in the last few years." Even though the market for La Pointe's fish collapsed and the American Fur Company ceased its operations, Bushnell saw the possibility that the Ojibwe could continue to rely upon fish as the staple of their diets and in that way manage to stay at their present location instead of needing to move west. He felt that if they would continue to focus on lake fishing *as a subsistence activity*, "the inexhaustible fisheries of Lake Superior will afford [them] the means of a livelihood the most consonant to [their] habits and feelings; and the tendency of the change would be, judging from the experience of the past, gradually to raise [them] from [their] present degradation."[1]

This was an interesting observation on the part of Subagent Bushnell. Even though the south shore bands had always relied on fishing for a major part of their livelihood, he observed that due to the diminishing availability of food sources from hunting and fur trapping, the Ojibwes had taken up a more intense harvesting of fish as a means of subsistence, and that this was a successful change. Bushnell predicted that despite the loss of income from the sale of fish to the American market, the Ojibwes could still survive. By stepping up their subsistence fishing, presumably along with their age-old traditions of gardening, gathering and—even though possibly diminished—their hunting and trapping, they would do quite well.

This is precisely what some of the La Pointe Ojibwes did, and continue to do, up to the present day. While not providing their complete means of survival, the riches of Lake Superior and the products of some aspects of their traditional economy, along with some newer market-based activities, have played a large part in meeting their resource needs.

Perhaps we should note that while the American change agents whom Edmund Jefferson Danziger, Jr. so pointedly spoke of were hard at work to try to have the Ojibwes take up agriculture as a livelihood, those members of the Lake Superior bands were intensifying their fishing instead. However, at locations like the Chippewa River, and perhaps other inland Ojibwe communities, this was not a possibility. While inland lakes and rivers provided some fish, the available amounts never equaled the abundance offered by Lake Superior. From the perspective of the change agents, these inland bands were to take up agriculture, but according to Bushnell in 1841, "Every effort to induce these Indians, as they are now circumstanced, to cultivate for themselves, appears to be almost hopeless."[2] As Theresa Schenck noted, for these inland bands, "It fell largely to the [government] farmer to do the work for the Indians, and to deliver supplies to them in times of need and scarcity."[3]

2.

In 1841, the same year the fishing industry was halted, a few new missionaries appeared at La Pointe. The Protestant clergyman Leonard Hemenway Wheeler and his wife, Harriet Wood Wheeler, along with Miss Abigail Spooner, arrived from New England, intending to work in the new Chippewa Mission. Another missionary soon to arrive was Lucy M. Lewis.[4] The Wheelers would make their presence known as they focused on efforts to convert the local Ojibwes to their religion and way of life and Abigail Spooner also began a long career at La Pointe, teaching in the mission school. The Wheelers would stay until 1866, a period of twenty-five years, after which they moved to Beloit, Wisconsin.[5]

In late 1842, with Daniel Bushnell's dismissal from his La Pointe post, Governor Doty recommended the Methodist minister, Alfred Brunson, or as a second choice, Lyman Warren, for the La Pointe Sub-agent position.[6] Brunson accepted the offer and was appointed in October, but did not arrive at La Pointe until January 1843.[7]

In the early 1840s, it was not just the missionary and American governmental fields that were busy at La Pointe. A year after closing down its fishing operations, the American Fur Company began bankruptcy proceedings since the slumping markets for both furs and fish were too much to overcome. Historian Hamilton Ross felt major events like this bankruptcy caused "gloom" at La Pointe, and while the times must have been difficult for the Americans and those others who were directly tied into the economic system of the United States, we must wonder just how events like this affected the resident Ojibwe people.[8] In important ways, even though they were enmeshed with the greater European and American economies for centuries, they were still maintaining their own economy, and by the decade of the 1840s, it was this economic system that provided a very important component of the underpinning of their culture as well as their personal identities.

By 1840, a concern much more important to the Ojibwe than the failure of the American Fur Company, was the increasing threat of their removal to western lands. The issue of a wholesale Ojibwe removal from Lake Superior's southern shore as well as the interior of Wisconsin Territory and Upper Michigan to an undetermined western location did not disappear with the Treaty of 1837. The notion that white settlement pressure would eventually force removal and that it was morally imperative to move them to an area relatively free from the negative influence of whites on the frontier continued to be the factors American officials talked about.

Daniel Bushnell advised Dodge in 1839, and again in 1840, that any attempts at removing the Ojibwe would cause them undue hardship, and could quite possibly lead to serious conflict. About the La Pointe Ojibwe, Bushnell said: "The general policy of our Government in removing the Indians west of the Mississippi can never be carried into effect in relation to this portion of the Chippewas."[9] For a time Dodge apparently deferred to the Sub-agent's warnings, but business and other governmental leaders would not be so circumspect and only five years after signing the Treaty of 1837, Buffalo and the other Ojibwes would find themselves faced with this very serious issue.

Part of the concern was that a forced westward removal of Lake Superior Ojibwe communities would have located them closer to the Dakota, and likely would have led to bloodshed. Bushnell was aware of Dakota and Ojibwe skirmishes at Pokegama on the Snake River in St. Croix country occurring as late as August 1841 that saw some Ojibwes retreat southwards to Mille Lacs and others going northwards toward Lake Superior, and he told Washington and Wisconsin Territorial authorities that for the moment Ojibwe removal would not be appropriate. Yet, he also felt that the lakeshore bands would eventually need to move to new lands because of the worsening depletion of their traditional food resources. These he claimed, as Lt. Allen did some ten or so years previously, "are gradually failing, and must ultimately become inadequate," a turn of events that would force the people to either change their means of livelihood, or change their location.[10]

The Dakota and the Ojibwe hostilities occurring at St. Croix in the early 1840s were troublesome for all parties involved. To the Dakota, the early problem of Ojibwe bands moving into lands along their northern and eastern borders had been ongoing for a few centuries and although there had been periods of peace, by 1840, military incidents were surfacing again. To the Ojibwe it was likewise. They were being pressured to cluster around mission and government farm stations, a fact that made them particularly visible and vulnerable to attack. For the United States, this conflict needed to be resolved so the region could be "settled."

The 1830s and early 1840s were a time of unrest all through the upper St. Croix valley in Wisconsin Territory as well as in lands to its north and west. Some of this difficulty was due to the Dakota, but more was because of a sudden influx of Americans and their attempts to establish lumbering operations in the region. Central to the unrest in the area north and west of St. Croix was the unwillingness of the Ojibwes to accept *American* missionaries. Even though they signed the Treaty of 1826 at Fond du Lac wherein they agreed to refrain from being influenced by the British and to work with the Americans, these Ojibwe communities were still desirous of maintaining a degree of political and economic autonomy. This was seen in an incident in 1838, the year following the signing of the Treaty of 1837, when William Boutwell closed his mission station at Leech Lake because of his inability to win converts to his religion, yet, the very next year, 1839, a contingent of Leech Lake people journeyed to the Canadian side of Sault Ste. Marie to ask that an *Anglican* missionary be assigned to their community. This gesture shows how in the middle of the nineteenth century in the western Lake Superior region, the Ojibwes were using Christian missionaries less as purveyors of a religious ideology, and more as mediators and persons of influence with the greater national political power they represented.

At the time of Boutwell's failure at Leech Lake, Reverend Pierz at Grand Portage and teacher-missionary Edmund Ely at Fond du Lac were also having great difficulty. As early as 1836, Ely witnessed a strong sentiment against Christianity and its connection with an American desire to rid the area of Indians. He tells of a meeting at Fond du Lac on 29 May of that year, when about a dozen Ojibwe men came to his house "dressed for council—some painted—others besmeared with white clay, face & hair, & zig-zag lines drawn across their faces, giving them a most hideous appearance. All were pagans, except one." Ely goes on:

> They wanted me to tell them well why I came. They had been told that the Americans wished to do with them as they had done to other Indian nations. They would get possession of a little land, then claim much & finally drive the Indian away entirely. They (the Indians) believed me to be a forerunner of the Americans. They did not hate me. They hated those who had sent me here.

Several days later, on 6 June, Ely wrote:

> Scarce a day passes but the Indians show their hatred or opposition to us in words concerning our residence here—the land, wood, grass, fish that we use, & from all that we judge, it is evident they intend to take some oppressive course with us.[11]

Anti-American sentiment in this larger northern region was strong enough that all three missionaries closed their stations and traveled south to join Frederick Ayer at Pokegama, where together they labored to build a mission station with a farm and school.

Here, according to Daniel Bushnell, they worked "with better success," but Sherman Hall reported on 24 August 1840, that at Pokegama "The agricultural and education interests of these Indians have suffered much, the past season, from the continuance of war between the Chippewa and Sioux. They have been in a constant state of alarm."[12]

In May 1841, the Pokegama station was attacked by the Dakota, resulting in more Ojibwe leaving to move either to Mille Lacs or Lake Superior. Just previous to this, Ojibwe who beforehand had shown no interest in "becoming civilized" came to the station and while laboring under the farmers' and missionaries' guidance, began to open gardening plots. "Many new fields were fenced and broke up, and considerable quantities of corn, potatoes, and other vegetables planted," but because of the Dakota these efforts to farm were abandoned.[13]

In these years the St. Croix area was not just a region of Dakota-Ojibwe hostilities, it also was a place struggling with incoming logging operations and its associated liquor problems. For the Ojibwe, a new time had arrived bringing challenges that might have seemed insurmountable.

It was in this general region and milieu that a major battle between the Ojibwe and Dakota may have taken place. Benjamin Armstrong told of such an event at the Brule River, approximately fifteen miles from Lake Superior, that he said occurred "about October 1," in 1842, in which an aged Chief Buffalo directed a group of two hundred or so La Pointe fighters in a decisive victory over the Dakota. According to Armstrong, in the battle the Ojibwe lost thirteen persons and the Dakota lost 101. Armstrong's date for this conflict is controversial, but given the larger context of Dakota-Ojibwe skirmishes of the time, it is not improbable.[14]

Even though Buffalo would probably have been in his early eighties, it is plausible that he could have led an Ojibwe force in this confrontation. Recent scholarship by Anton Treuer adds to this plausibility when he shows that at the time, large fighting units of both Ojibwe and Dakota were raised to do battle.[15] Armstrong claims to have been an eyewitness to the skirmish and offers vivid details of the fighting. However, the numbers of the dead suggest Armstrong's memoir would not be the only place it appears in the written record. Whether or not it occurred in or near 1842 must remain uncertain but given the history of Dakota and Ojibwe conflict of the times we should concur with the possibility of this Brule River skirmish, and that it could have taken place at the time and in the manner Benjamin Armstrong claims.

In these years concerns about the Dakota must have been a preoccupation for Lake Superior's Ojibwe. We will see, below, that as late as 1849, with the incident of the Dakota captive at La Pointe, that Dakota-Ojibwe hostilities were still ongoing. When added to their other problems—American pressures for land cessions, fears of smallpox, the apparent demise of the fur trade, and missionaries' efforts at religious and social conversion—it is seen that the times were troubling, indeed. And over all this was the looming specter of removal. Although Daniel Bushnell raised questions about it, he still felt ultimately they would need to move west. His and other voices wanted another treaty with the Ojibwe, one that would open the rest of the lands in northern Wisconsin Territory and Upper Michigan, and it was not long before they had their way.[16]

## *The Treaty of 1842 and its Aftermath*

1.

THE TREATY OF 1842, BETWEEN the Lake Superior and Mississippi Ojibwe Bands and the United States, is one of the most important treaties Red Cliff's forebears ever signed. When Buffalo and the other La Pointe leaders "touched the pen," they signed away what was at the time the last of their land in what is now the State of Wisconsin. For the Ojibwe, the ramifications of this sale were both immediate and long-term. To help understand why they did this we need to examine not only the treaty meetings, but also what the Ojibwes' world was like along Lake Superior's southern shore at the time.

This treaty has been called The Copper Treaty since the purported reason the United States pushed for it was to mine the copper and other minerals known to exist near its northern boundaries. But, as was the case with the Treaty of 1837, America was ultimately after the land. By the summer of 1842, American officials stressed the need to acquire all the lands the Ojibwe bands still held south of Lake Superior.[17] Their stated motive was the minerals, but beyond this was their certainty that due to future national growth—and more abstractly, to their belief in manifest destiny—they needed to own the land itself. By 1842, the United States was experiencing economic and population growth that was pointing westward. Andrew Jackson's removal policy was surging ahead and although we usually associate it with tribal nations in the southeastern United States during the decade of the 1830s, by the 1840s, government officials were turning their eyes northward and were certain that eventually the tribes, like those in Wisconsin Territory, would need to relinquish their lands east of the Mississippi River as well.[18]

The Ojibwe themselves, and those before them, have a long history of mining Lake Superior's copper, but this mining was to be greatly intensified with the coming of the Europeans. By 1837, the Michigan legislature established a Department of Geology and appointed Douglass Houghton its director. Houghton wasted no time, and by the early 1840s, had undertaken extensive surveys of Lake Superior's mineral bearing southern shore as well as distant Isle Royale. Investors and other interested parties like Robert Stuart were eager to have Ojibwe lands opened up and they pressured authorities for a treaty. The question of what to do with the resident Ojibwe communities was troublesome but apparently there was no lack of voices ready to work to solve that problem. One such voice was Lyman Warren's, who, in 1841, wrote to Wisconsin Territorial Governor James D. Doty, offering his services to "influence the Indians to remove." Seeking political patronage, Warren seemed eager to get his share of the new mineral wealth, even if it meant moving his Ojibwe relatives from their homeland.[19]

2.

ROBERT STUART WAS APPOINTED TREATY commissioner and he called the Ojibwe together at La Pointe in August of 1842. The treaty was signed on 4 October of that year, and ratified by Congress the following year. Stuart was a stern and aggressive businessman who, along with Ramsay Crooks, was an early official of John Jacob Astor's American Fur Company.[20] He had a long history of activity in economic endeavors in the western lakes, going back at least to the 1820s, and in 1842, when asked to preside at LaPointe he was Acting Superintendent of Indian Affairs at Michigan. An associate and friend of John Jacob Astor, and active in Whig politics of the times, he is said to have applied the same "heavy-handed tactics" at La Pointe that Dodge did at St. Peters.[21]

Like Dodge had done five years previous, Stuart told the assembled Ojibwe that their "father" knew of their current problem, i.e., that they were poor since their lands were "not good" and were running out of game, and that it was becoming difficult to feed their women and children. He explained that he had been asked by their "father" to come to their aid and to help them by purchasing their lands so they could use the payment to relieve their troubled situation. This, of course, was a ruse since for some years previous to 1842, Robert Stuart was interested in the potential wealth of the land's copper deposits, and his voice was one of those clamoring for a new land treaty covering the balance of all the Ojibwes' remaining land south of Lake Superior. Also, regarding just how "poor" the land was, soon after the treaty was signed Stuart told Indian Commissioner Crawford that the Ojibwes "have considerable game, fish, and other inducements to attach them to their present homes," meaning that even though the land may not have been the best for agricultural purposes, their food sources were still adequate and would likely continue to be so for some time.[22]

Stuart's speeches at La Pointe were framed within this contrived image of concern for the Ojibwe people that he said the Washington leaders held for them, and as such were what I have labeled, in a previous chapter, as *frontier* or *fur trade theater*. However, while Stuart struck this authoritative pose it is apparent that even though the Ojibwe finally signed the treaty, they did not readily assume the role of "the child." Still carrying their anger with the 1837 treaty proceedings, they were not complacent listeners in 1842.[23]

As is the case with all such nineteenth century Ojibwe treaty negotiations, the rich discussion, and in some cases, the *repartee* that occurred within the Ojibwe community and in its interaction with Euro-American negotiators was, for the most part, unrecorded, and is often lost to us. And, as a recent writer remarks, "Unfortunately, commentary about what exactly transpired at the treaty is scarce and sometimes contradictory."[24] We do not have the benefit of a journal kept by a treaty secretary, but fortunately other observers of the negotiations wrote about them, and Stuart himself made a written record of his speeches given at the meeting. Just as importantly, in the several decades after 1842, remarks of several other witnesses to the treaty sessions have been recorded, some of them from Ojibwe leaders. Taken together, these writings provide numerous interpretations of what took place.

Similar to some other Ojibwe-American treaty negotiation gatherings, the opening formalities at La Pointe included rounds of cannon fire from shore as each new visiting party of Ojibwe arrived. Some of these groups returned the fire with muskets from the water, and perhaps not to be outdone, some members of the contingent under Chief Hole-in-the-Day from the Upper Mississippi loudly came ashore on a *bateau* specially fit with a raised dancing platform holding drummers and dancers bedecked in their special finery. There were six days of meetings, and forty-one Ojibwe headmen from Michigan, Wisconsin, and Minnesota bands were in attendance. However, the Grand Portage band, located on Lake Superior's northwestern shore, was not invited and consequently there were none of its members present.[25]

Robert Stuart opened the first day of the session with a gift of tobacco and an introductory speech before going on to present the Ojibwes with four articles he wanted included in the treaty.[26] The first was that the people could continue to hunt, fish and gather food resources over the lands. Second, a sum of $75,000.00 would be issued to the traders who held Ojibwe debts, and $15,000.00 would be provided for those persons of mixed-blood who had an interest in the land sale. Third, the Secretary of War would have a sum of $5,000.00 for an agriculture fund for the Ojibwes, and fourth, $31,200.00 in annuities would be equally divided between the Mississippi and Lake Superior bands over a period of twenty-five years.[27] The written record is silent on the Ojibwes' immediate response to these articles, but what tribal leaders soon seized upon was the length of time they would be able to reside on the lands and secure their food from them. It is obvious that the question of removal was a major concern.

3.

TO OVERCOME THE STRUGGLE WHICH Henry Dodge had at St. Peters, which was to treat the assembled bands as one political unit, right at the onset of the La Pointe sessions Stuart told the assembly that he considered them as "a nation," not independent bands, and even though they lived in their own separate locations, the United States still saw them as one people.[28]

Stuart had received instructions from T. Hartley Crawford, Commissioner of Indian Affairs, to include the Mississippi Bands in the treaty as well as in the disbursement of its annuities even though they did not reside on the lands to be treated for. He felt such a maneuver would make the unceded western lands, to include the "preserve" just to the west of Lake Superior, "common property" of both the Lake Superior and Mississippi Bands, and therefore, it would be easier to effect a future removal of the Wisconsin bands to this region. Crawford also wanted a stipulation that the Ojibwe must eventually move from the ceded lands included in the treaty, but that this move would probably not be carried out for some time.[29]

The tactic of relating to the different bands as a single political unit served two purposes: one, it allowed the Michigan and Minnesota bands "to outmaneuver the Lake Superior bands who were not interested in ceding their lands,"[30] and, two, it anticipated future attempts on the part of the United States to deal with the disparate Wisconsin Territorial bands as one entity when the time came to force the issue of removal, a removal to one, common place that they supposedly already owned.[31]

By 1842, the Michigan bands were more accommodated to Christianity and its Euro-American society than those to their west, and thus were more amenable to the sale of the Wisconsin Territorial lands than the Ojibwe who actually resided on them. The Minnesota bands, due to their distance from the lands under question, also were apparently more agreeable to the proposed sale, and consequently, Stuart was desirous of having their, and the Michigan, voices heard in the treaty discussions. This move to have "the popular white concept of majority rule" in place at the onset of the meetings was a key component in Stuart's strategy, and doubtless was not lost on the assembled Ojibwe.[32]

In 1842, the Ojibwe were keenly aware of their own political organization and how it functioned, but most likely, by that date they also were beginning to realize that native populations were facing a new time, one that involved the serious external threat of a very determined United States government. They were allies with the Americans but now this alliance was making major demands on them. Earlier, in their relationships with the French, British, Dakota, and others, whether in times of forming or breaking alliances they were able to stand firm, confident of their abilities to fulfill their community's needs. But when facing Robert Stuart at La Pointe, the Ojibwe leaders surely recognized the dilemma they were in. That is, their abilities to defend and sustain themselves were not as assured as in the past.

Furthermore, when faced with Stuart's demands, surely they felt the need to continue respecting the wishes of their separate bands, each with its concomitant rights and obligations. However, it is likely they also felt a growing necessity to overcome these differences in order to facilitate their joining together to form a larger and stronger entity to confront their very threatening situation. As a tribal system, the Ojibwe must have always recognized this paradox: at the base of their political organization was the network of disparate bands that thrived in their independence, yet knowing that they were always part of a larger system, a system that at times demanded they set these structural differences aside and come together to work as one. This tension between the freedom of separateness and the strength of unity is an inherent aspect of tribalism.

Even though the different Ojibwe bands still maintained contact by 1842—inter-band marriages continued, for instance—by this time in the western Great Lakes, the depth of this tendency toward band cohesion was strained. We recall Buffalo's remarks to Daniel Bushnell after the treaty of 1837, when he said some bands tried to cheat each other regarding treaty annuities. Some bands wanted to exclude others from sharing in the distribution of the annuities while contrariwise, those being excluded, in a self-serving argument, stressed the need for unity. Also, several years earlier, in Buffalo's remarks during the negotiations of the Treaty of 1826, when he referred to those bands that had, using Schoolcraft's translation, "deserted" the tribe's Chequamegon Bay homeland to take up residence in distant lands, we saw a lament for this inherent cohesiveness of the greater Ojibwe society. In 1826 at Fond du Lac, Buffalo was saying that he sought the support of these distant bands in his new time of need.

This adds a deeper dimension of political interest to the Treaty of 1842. The very nature of a tribal system with its separate localized bands that tended to pull away from each other (even though they recognized the need to come together when necessary) was countered by Stuart's insistence to treat the bands as one political unit. And his intimation—or perhaps it should be seen as a threat—that eventually they would have to come together and move to the "common ground" north of the St. Louis River in Minnesota Territory hints at his awareness of the structural ability of the bands to join together when necessary. Culturally the Ojibwe were still one people, i.e., they shared a common language and held similar customs, and this created the underlying cohesion between them. Thus, at the onset, when Stuart said his government was going to treat them as "a Nation," he was playing upon this deep tendency of theirs to view themselves as *one people* even though structurally they were a people composed of disparate, independent communities.[33] This tension between the local unit and the overall larger community was an inherent aspect of the Ojibwe world, and likely, Robert Stuart hoped to use it to his advantage.

This point speaks to a problem we have mentioned before, i.e., the structural differences between states and tribes. These differences are not always given consideration in past histories of the Ojibwe, whether popular or scholarly in nature. As anthropologist Richard Perry has shown, throughout the world the history of relationships between indigenous societies and state societies has been one of an imbalance of power. This has led to genocide, or in less extreme instances, a history of invasion, displacement and assimilation, all processes of societal interaction detrimental to native socio-cultural systems. In some cases, after centuries in which these relational processes were let run, it is only recently that we are witnessing a worldwide resurgence of attempts by indigenous populations at self-determination.[34] We should recognize that the history of the Ojibwe in western Lake Superior country supports Perry's argument. In 1842, the Ojibwe were dealing with an American invasion and its attempts to displace the tribesmen. Because of this, at least for some of the mixed-bloods of the time, movement toward assimilation was occurring, but for other Ojibwe, self-determination and cultural persistence was the response to the aggressive and powerful Americans.

It is in this sense that the rhetoric in the written record about the friendship Ojibwe leaders like Buffalo said they felt for the Americans must be weighed carefully. We know their relationship with this new ally was not simply an amiable one. By 1842, the tribesmen must have known that any balance of power that existed in the past between them and the Americans was shifting to the Americans' side.

4.

REGARDING REMOVAL, STUART WENT ON to emphasize that there were many whites, that other native tribes had already moved west in order to make room for them, and in time the Ojibwe would also be required to move. Finally, he told the people since their "father" did not want them to be left without a place to live, after purchasing their land he would find "a home in common for you all" in Minnesota Territory.[35]

The "home in common" Stuart mentioned was the land at the far west end of Lake Superior, north of the St. Louis River, as far west as Sandy Lake, and as far north as the Canadian border. Except for its early years as an important region for harvesting furs, this area received little attention from Europeans, and until the 1840s, from the Americans. It has been called "a preserve," i.e., a territory held in waiting for the time when eastern tribes would be moved into it.[36]

At this point we must pause to consider the Ojibwes' response to Stuart's statement that they eventually would have to move to make room for the increasing number of whites. In today's world, Stuart's remark, with its assumption of white racial and cultural superiority, is striking in its arrogance, but in Robert Stuart's world it was an assumption that the Americans did not question. The written record of the treaty proceedings, however, shows that the Ojibwe challenged it from the start.

In 1842, the Ojibwe still enjoyed clear ownership of the land Stuart offered to purchase, a total of some several million acres, but their ability to hold the land was another matter. By this date they certainly saw the difficulty of taking any political stand against the Americans, yet, as Buffalo made clear in his letter to Shingwaukonse, they did not desire to merely acquiesce to the Americans' wishes. To do so would have compromised any remnant of political autonomy they still held. Therefore, perhaps it was to their advantage to ally with the Americans and to negotiate for the best possible settlement they could get. In previous pages we suggested this understanding of the Ojibwes' situation was foreshadowed in the comments La Pointe's Buffalo uttered to American representatives like Henry Schoolcraft, Thomas L. McKenney, Daniel Bushnell and others throughout the previous decade or more. In the 1842 negotiations they asked that reservations be established on lands ceded in 1837 as well as along Lake Superior's south shore, but Stuart stood firm, saying sooner or later they would have to move.[37]

Despite the tenuousness of the Ojibwe situation, we can still ponder how they felt, deep inside, when hearing Stuart's remark that they would eventually have to move to make room for whites. Recalling how earlier observers like Lt. Allen saw the Lake Superior Ojibwe as dependent and "subdued," the written record of the treaty negotiations of 1842 shows that they resisted the notion of removal, and by extension, Stuart's implication of their inferiority. This fact points to the reality of the *cultural persistence* of the Ojibwe in the western Great Lakes as late as 1842. In the eyes of the Americans they may have been "poor, hungry, and dependent," but in their own view they still held a degree of political and economic autonomy, giving them dignity and strength.

The matter of what exactly was said, and understood, at La Pointe regarding removal remains a controversy, but thanks to some recent scholarship we are beginning to have a clearer picture of what transpired between the Ojibwe and Robert Stuart during those warm summer days on Madeline Island. Writers Ronald Satz, Charles Cleland, Bruce White, and others, because of their research involving the 1979 lawsuit filed by the Mille Lacs Band of Ojibwe against the State of Minnesota, have done an exhaustive review of the written record for the Treaty of 1842.[38] Their conclusions about this literature help us gain a better understanding of what was said, or *not* said, by Stuart and the Ojibwe leaders during their negotiations. The question of just what was put to voice, and agreed upon, in the La Pointe meetings is of great importance given what we know about the oral tradition of the Ojibwe. To them, the spoken word was their "document" just as the written word was to the Americans.[39]

What is clear is that the Ojibwe leaders responded to Stuart's opening remarks with skepticism. They particularly complained about past treaty negotiations. In essence they said what they had been told at those assemblies and what was written on the treaty paper did not agree. As for removal, they let Stuart know that they were not about to sign another treaty until they were sure they would not have to move from their lands. La Pointe's Buffalo was among those who issued these initial complaints, and in his case, as happened at St. Peters, he expressed his frustration with Stuart's urgings for a quick response, and as he did before, he stalled for more time to consider the government's proposals.

After listening to these complaints, Stuart assured the Ojibwe that they would not have to move from the ceded territory for a very long time. The leaders asked just how long he meant and it is from his reply that controversy stems. Written documents recorded in the months and several years after 1842 show a range of understandings of Stuart's response. Some witnesses say Stuart told them they would not have to move as long as they did not disturb the Americans who might be coming into the land, and some said they were told, simply, that they would never have to move. For example, Buffalo claimed they were told they could stay on the land for fifty or one hundred years if they were friendly to the white settlers, while Benjamin Armstrong (who was a witness at the assembly) like Chief Martin of Lac Courte Oreilles, said they were told that if they did not disturb the Americans they would never have to move. Regarding the Ojibwes' insistence that they not be required to move, historian Satz wrote that the Ojibwe "signatures on the treaty were obtained only after assurances that they would be able to remain in Wisconsin."[40]

Showing a slightly different understanding about the negotiations, anthropologist Charles Cleland writes, "Unlike the 1837 treaty, the Chippewa negotiating in 1842 clearly understood that there was a possibility of future removal on the part of the United States."[41] This threat of removal was contingent upon how, in ensuing years, they would react to whites moving onto the ceded lands. If there were depredations upon the whites then the United States could seek removal.

The treaty they signed states that the Ojibwe could live on the lands and harvest the resources they were accustomed to "until required to remove by the President of the United States." It is apparent the Ojibwe knew this clause was in the treaty when they signed it, but that they were led to believe it either would never be put into effect, or if it was, it would be done so far into the future that by that time it would be of little or no consequence (the matter of just what constitutes "little or no consequence" remains interesting today). In the final days of negotiation as the actual signing of an agreement grew imminent, it seems apparent that Buffalo and the other leaders "had little choice, as always, to trust the government to act in good faith."[42]

Some of the colorful, and certainly important, details of the staging and *theatrically scripted* aspects of the treaty setting are noteworthy. For example, "On October 1 Buffalo appeared, wearing epaulettes on his shoulders, a hat trimmed with tinsel, and a string of bear claws about his neck."[43] Today, such attire—with its melding of traditional Ojibwe culture and that of the Euro-American—is poignantly striking. Here was the major Ojibwe leader of the Western Great Lakes, Ke-che-wash-keenh (*Great* Buffalo), wearing classical European symbols of military power juxtaposed with a bear claw necklace—a similar symbol of military (and spiritual) power in Ojibwe culture—as he prepared to sign away thousands of acres of his peoples' lands. Just previous to signing the treaty, after stating the importance of the welfare of the traders and mixed-bloods to the Ojibwe, Buffalo is reported to have addressed his people by saying, "My friends, I cannot do anymore for you, I have done all I can. I am now going to touch the pen."[44]

Eleven years after the signing of the treaty, La Pointe's federal agent, Henry Gilbert, said a contingent of Ojibwe leaders told him "that when the treaty was made, the Commissioner assured them that the clause providing for their removal was only inserted as a mere matter of form. That a compliance with it would never be urged or insisted upon by the government . . ."[45] However, in 1843, the missionary Leonard Wheeler's understanding of what Stuart told the Ojibwe was in agreement with what was actually in the treaty clause. He claimed that Stuart told the Ojibwe they could live on the ceded lands "till your great Father requires you to remove."[46]

Twenty-two years after the treaty was signed, a delegation of Ojibwe from Lac du Flambeau, Lac Courte Oreilles and La Pointe traveled to Washington—a delegation that apparently included at least three members who had signed the 1842 treaty—and told authorities that they understood they would not be asked to move from Wisconsin as long as they did not disturb Americans who came into the region. This understanding, Ronald Satz argues, is what the written record shows the Ojibwe held in 1842, when signing the treaty, and still held in 1864.[47]

Robert Stuart's correspondence in the weeks and months after the treaty does not indicate he told the Ojibwe that they would not have to move. What he did write, soon after the treaty signing, is that he did not think the Indians would have to move "for many years to come," and furthermore, in answer to voices calling for an immediate removal of all Ojibwe from Wisconsin Territory, he said such an order "would not be in conformity with the spirit of the treaty."[48]

A point of interest for us is a recent discussion about the veracity of the writings of Benjamin Armstrong about the Treaty of 1842. In 1987, anthropologist James Clifton said Armstrong's claim that the Ojibwe were told they would not have to move as long as they did not disturb Americans was questionable since it was not "independently corroborated" by other documentation. In the 1980s, this was an important criticism and one that was picked up by the Wisconsin media and given wide regional press. Furthermore, Clifton went on to charge that Armstrong was an "inconsequential figure" in historical matters like the 1842 treaty negotiations, implying that in some parts the validity of his published memoirs was questionable.[49]

Ronald Satz argues that Clifton was in error. He goes on to say that Armstrong's remarks were, indeed, corroborated "by eyewitnesses to the treaty proceedings," and offers documentation to this effect.[50] This support of Armstrong is significant, not just for our discussion about the treaty of 1842, but because it also adds a degree of credence to our references to Armstrong's remarks about other matters of Ojibwe history we have discussed in preceding pages, and to remarks we will make in future pages as well.

5.

AFTER THE TREATY WAS SIGNED it took more than four months of debate for Congress to ratify it. Today this might seem unusual given the size and value of the lands the United States stood to gain with ratification. As we might expect, the delay was due to matters of economics and politics of the times.

Treaty opponents argued: one, that the country did not yet need the land; two, that Robert Stuart had shown undue favoritism to the large claims of the American Fur Company that were in the treaty; and three, that with its prohibition of liquor in the ceded lands, the rights of the Territory of Wisconsin to set such laws over areas of its jurisdiction were neglected. Also, some opponents were political enemies of Wisconsin's Territorial Governor Doty, and thus, would not vote for a treaty he wanted so desperately.[51]

Representatives of the American Fur Company lobbied hard for ratification since the struggling firm stood to benefit significantly. Today, it is perhaps striking that none of the above arguments for or against the treaty were focused on the wishes of the Ojibwe and their desire to remain on their lands. At the time such concerns were apparently of little importance in Congressional debates. In time there would be voices in Congress that joined those of indigenous peoples, but in 1842, their time was still in the future. The country's westward growth was surging ahead and with the regular opening of new lands there was financial gain and personal notoriety to be won. This drive supplanted the wishes of tribal people.

About a month before the treaty was ratified a council of Ojibwe leaders from the Michigan, Wisconsin and Minnesota bands met at La Pointe. La Pointe's Buffalo and the other assembled leaders voiced their frustration with the treaty, as well as those of 1837 and 1826.[52] A few months previous to this council, Buffalo sent a letter through Lyman Warren to his agent, Alfred Brunson, in which he complained of the recent treaty and asked the agent to pass his displeasure on to the "Great Father" in Washington.[53]

This council and Buffalo's letter indicate the dissatisfaction with the treaty and cause us to be puzzled with Robert Stuart's letter to Commissioner Crawford of 19 November 1842, written only a few months after the conclusion of the treaty negotiations. Regarding the Ojibwes' reaction to the recent La Pointe treaty sessions, Stuart told Crawford: "These Indians are through our late efforts, entirely reconciled among themselves, and highly delighted with the Kind and generous dealing of the Government toward them."[54] What was Stuart's purpose in this remark when he certainly must have known the Ojibwe were deeply troubled with the treaty and surely not "delighted" at all?

The Ojibwes were not alone with their discontent. Some seven weeks after Stuart sent the above letter to Crawford, La Pointe's new Sub-agent, Alfred Brunson, told Territorial

Governor Doty that the treaty was an injustice to the Ojibwe since they did not get enough for their land. He said that the seven cents an acre they received did not nearly compensate for the land's real worth. His remarks soon reached Commissioner Crawford as well as Robert Stuart, and as might be expected, the latter responded with anger. Over the ensuing year Sub-agent Brunson and Robert Stuart expressed frustration with the ideas and methods of each other and finally, at Stuart's urging, Commissioner Crawford recommended to the War Department that Brunson not only be chastised, but removed from his La Pointe position. In fall of 1843, Alfred Brunson had had enough of Robert Stuart and informed Commissioner Crawford that he would be resigning after completing his written reports, but before he could do that, on 30 November, he received notice that he had been dismissed.[55] This mid-nineteenth century confrontation between Alfred Brunson and Robert Stuart over the proper way to understand and relate to Native Americans is indicative of the national debate which was being carried on by many others at the time.

## 6.

ALFRED BRUNSON WAS AN ORDAINED clergyman who rode circuits in Ohio and Pennsylvania for about twenty years before moving his family to Prairie du Chien. Among other things, he was a lawyer, a territorial legislator, Dakota missionary, and a writer. His memoirs offer vivid details of what life was like in northern Wisconsin Territory during his short tenure at La Pointe. For example, in December of 1842, soon after his appointment, he and a few companions departed Prairie du Chien, heading north to Lake Superior. The party made it to Lyman Warren's home on the Chippewa River where Brunson stayed for three weeks, "waiting for ice to form for easier travel."[56] Finally, the party departed with Lyman Warren accompanying them as their guide, and an unnamed Ojibwe woman and her husband. The woman provided the evening meals for the fifteen days it took to reach their destination, and her husband hunted along the way. Brunson praised these hot meals of cooked fresh vegetables and venison.

While at the falls, Brunson hired young William Warren as his interpreter and William became a member of the traveling party. Brunson tells us that for the fifteen days Lyman Warren led a horse pulling an oak plank sled, while a team of dogs pulled another, as he guided the party through the winter forest and over frozen rivers and streams, before arriving at Lake Superior. Then, even though it was after sundown, the party pushed on, venturing out onto the uncertain ice, leading the horse across open cracks until it was deemed that such a trek was too treacherous. After returning to shore and camping for the duration of the night, the trip was completed with the coming of daylight, but not before experiencing more worrisome challenges as the horse was led across the broken ice in the bay.

The party arrived at Madeline Island on 3 January 1843, and soon thereafter Chief Buffalo and a contingent of his co-leaders called on the new Sub-agent. Brunson says,

> I had a long talk with them; heard all their wants and wishes, and in turn urged upon them the necessity of their adopting civilized habits. This address so satisfied Buffalo, though now fifty years of age, that he soon after took a contract to cut cordwood for the fur company. This he did not only for the profit to himself, but to encourage his men to go and do likewise.

Brunson goes on to say:

> I soon learned that the eldest son of this chief, who was heir apparent to the chiefship, had, previous to this, adopted civilized habits; had built himself a comfortable cabin house, both he and his wife dressing and living like whites, and perhaps half of the band had done the same. And before a year rolled around, by and with the consent of all the chiefs in council, a new band was organized of this class with this young chief at their head, and was called the "Pantaloon Band," all of whom, men and women, dressed and worked like whites.[57]

These quotations show the extent of the pressure the Ojibwe people at La Pointe were experiencing in the 1840s. It is unfortunate Alfred Brunson did not record the complete detail's of Buffalo's "long talk" since it would have afforded insight into his life at the time, but the Sub-agent did mention numerous of Buffalo's concerns in a later series of letters he wrote to Governor Doty. According to Brunson, Buffalo complained about the 1842 "treaty and its failure to provide for the mixed bloods, as well as the quality of treaty goods and the time and place of payment."[58] It is clear this treaty was a sore point for Buffalo and other Ojibwe leaders long after its signing.

The image of Chief Buffalo cutting firewood for the American Fur Company is telling. Alfred Brunson's memoir, like his letters written at La Pointe, show him to have been an empathic and strong voice for the resident Ojibwe, one that was not at a loss to offer criticism of American officials and policy, but he errors in estimating Buffalo's age to have been only fifty years. If as is claimed, Buffalo was ninety-six when he died in 1855, he should have been eighty-three when taking the contract to cut cordwood, not fifty.

However old he might have been, the image of the powerful, famous and dignified tribal leader taking a contract to cut this wood demands contemplation. Here he was, attempting to lead by example, and the message he was giving his people was to work like the whites as the Ojibwe took another step toward adjusting to American society. When we realize that in the years of this incident, Chief Buffalo was also said to have been telling his people to hold onto the old ways—witness his refusal to convert to Christianity until he was certain of his imminent death—we see the uncertainty of the times. Clearly the early 1840s were pivotal years for the Ojibwe.[59]

Some of what the Ojibwe were dealing with at this time is seen in a letter Sub-agent Brunson wrote to Wisconsin Territorial Governor Doty on 1 August 1843.[60] He tells Doty that within his sub-agency those Ojibwe who had been attempting to enlarge their gardens were having great difficulty in acquiring seed to plant their new plots. Corn seed in particular was at a premium and Brunson implored Doty to have more corn seed shipped to the agency. Also, a late frost had been hard on their new potato crops. Along with requests for seed, these Ojibwe were asking for more laborsaving farm tools, something that seemed to be in short supply at La Pointe. And they were asking for American clothing—pants, shirts, and the like—all indications that in 1843, Ojibwe lifestyles were changing. The aforementioned comments on Chief Buffalo's son, his wife, and their family and friends who became the "Pantaloon Band" is an example of this change.

But at the same time, Sub-agent Brunson made it clear that while some Ojibwe families were beginning to try agriculture as a means of supplying sustenance and bringing needed security to their lives, they still were struggling with problems of liquor consumption and fear from Dakota attacks. The Dakota had been threatening Ojibwe sites in the lower Chippewa River region and Brunson felt the combination of these hostilities along with the illicit whiskey trade raised the specter of an Indian war in the region. Brunson said dealers were producing a particularly foul concoction made from whiskey laced with tobacco, then cut with water, a commodity that particularly seemed to upset this Methodist clergyman-turned-Indian agent.

Whites were saying they could legally bring liquor to La Pointe since the federal Indian Trade and Intercourse Acts applied only to unceded lands, and after the treaty of 1842, all Ojibwe lands in Wisconsin had been ceded. This old issue was troublesome but Brunson told how when he discovered contraband barrels of whiskey he smashed them, possibly risking a lawsuit for destroying private property. This issue of how to stop the whiskey trade around Ojibwe communities was a lingering one that missionaries and Indian agents spoke to repeatedly in the 1840s.

Even though some Ojibwe were beginning to show more and more accommodations to American culture, Alfred Brunson still told Governor Doty that they needed to be moved further west in order to keep them from the ill effects of contact with Americans. Whites were beginning to appear on most major waterways within the limits of his sub-agency, and this meant trouble for the Ojibwe. The only solution, he felt, was to remove the Indians.

Alfred Brunson's remarks to Governor Doty show what seem to be serious thoughts of an Indian agent who wanted to do what was right for the Ojibwe, yet his concerns were all framed within the perception of a "savage" people who had no option but to accept the changes the Americans were trying to force upon them. His focus was Ojibwe accommodation and little else. In the documents from that time there is nothing to show that any Americans were working to help Ojibwe traditionalists maintain their way of life. All effort was addressed at what was necessary to extinguish traditional Ojibwe culture, and in the quickest and most cost effective manner.

7.

PERHAPS BRUNSON'S SENTIMENTS about the treaty of 1842 can be taken as an early example of public concern for the rights of indigenous people, but, more certainly, the bureaucratic response to the Sub-agent's opinions can be understood as an example of the Americans' determination not to let tribal nations stand in the way of their desire to develop the western Great Lakes region. Robert Stuart, Commissioner Crawford, Governors Dodge and Doty, and other officials were certain that ultimately the Ojibwe would not only have to move, but that they also would have to become "civilized." Far to the south, the numbers of white Americans were increasing as more and more people spread from the eastern seaboard over the Appalachian range, through the Ohio Valley and towards the Mississippi River and the lands beyond. Some were looking northward to what would soon become the states of Wisconsin and Minnesota.

By the 1840s, missionary Sherman Hall seems to have caught the excitement of the times. He was present at the signing of the treaty of 1842, by that date having been at La Pointe for ten years. On 2 February 1843, some six months after the signing of the treaty, in a letter to his brother Aaron, who lived back in Vermont, he shared some of his thoughts about his enthusiasm for his work:

> I think there never was more encouragement to labor for the conversion of these Indians than there is at present. Much impression seems to have been made upon them by the missionary efforts among them, though not a great many have yet given evidence of a radical change of heart. Their prejudices against missionary efforts . . . are much weakened since we first came among them. There would now be no objection to missionaries residing in any part of the Country. They are very much scattered, very ignorant and superstitious, and much given to sensuality, as in the case with all pagans. It is difficult to reach their hearts, or even their understandings with the truth. They seem almost as stupid as blacks, yet they are far enough from being destitute of natural endowments. Most of them have superior minds by nature; but they are minds in ruins. As a people they are given to indolence. Their vice is so deeply rooted, that it is one of the greatest hindrances to their improvement. Their wants are few, and these they do not always take pains to supply. Some of them would about as soon starve, as to work. There has been a very marked improvement in this respect as well as in many others, with the Indians of this place since I first knew them. A considerable number have made advance toward civilized life. As soon as they become Christian, they begin to improve in their external condition. The idea which has been prevalent, that it does no good to try to civilize and Christianize the Indians, is erroneous. I believe much good may be done by giving them the gospel. Paganism is degrading and cruel wherever it exits and in whatever shape; Christianity is definitely better, even in its worst forms.[61]

This long quotation gives us a glimpse into life at La Pointe in 1843, as seen through the predisposed eyes of missionary Sherman Hall. We can only wonder what changes those Ojibwe made who "improved in their external condition" after accepting Christianity. Recalling the small number of persons that converted to his religion during his long tenure on Madeline Island, there apparently were few of these changes. Sherman Hall's persistent inability to set aside his assumptions about what being human means whenever he had to interact with people racially and culturally different from himself is witnessed in his ongoing difficulty to accept Indian people as his equals. His negative remarks about the Ojibwe as well as those about Afro-Americans reminds us what life must have been like for people of color in Chequamegon Bay in the 1840s. Surely, local Ojibwe leaders like Buffalo, Oshaga, and Black Bird struggled with this as they labored to negotiate political agreements with American authorities. The above quotation may indicate an upswing in Sherman Hall's optimism about changing the Ojibwe, but it also shows that his pronounced ethnocentrism had not diminished during his busy first decade at La Pointe.

In the same year that Sherman Hall wrote the above letter, La Pointe had a visitor from the distant eastern seaboard who, like Hall, was not hesitant to offer candid statements about native people. The Methodist clergyman Charles H. Titus, of Maine, was a young twenty-four years of age when he embarked on a circuitous excursion that took him to western Lake Superior and beyond. His assumptions about the Ojibwe—and the entire Lake Superior country—are striking in their pointed negativity. They tell us much about what indigenous peoples of the western lakes dealt with in their contacts with white America in the mid-nineteenth century.

As is the case with the personal correspondence of missionary Hall, Reverend Titus, himself, gives us a glimpse of his biases and ethnocentric assumptions when he writes:

> La Pointe . . . possesses but little interest, nothing to induce one to visit it a second time. The Indians are a poor, miserable set of beings; filthy, ignorant, barbarous & deeply degraded; worthy of no confidence, seldom, even in their professions of religion. The half-breeds are but little better, except a few that have been educated. Even these, however, are not to be relied on. The French, of whom there are quite a number on the island, are often termed the A.F. Co.'s mules, or beasts of burden, & this is the most appropriate description that I can think of. They know how to paddle a canoe and carry a pack & this is generally the extent of their knowledge. A person that wishes to see the most degraded specimens of humanity would do well to visit La Pointe. Still, a love of money impels persons that are educated & have been associated with genteel & polished society, to forego all its pleasure & comforts; & spent [spend] years with these miserable wretches, for the sake of gain. Nay, more, they not only content themselves to live among them, but even unite in marriage with the filthy squaws, not because they love them, or can find any satisfaction in such a connection, but simply because they can then be more successful in obtaining the *trade* of the Indians.[62]

These comments made by a Christian clergyman are extreme, but they, along with those of Sherman Hall, nevertheless offer insight into the worldview held by at least a portion of the educated strata of American society of the times. And importantly, by the 1840s, it was this society that was extending itself westward across the continent, and the Ojibwe people, like all tribesmen, had to adapt to it. There was no choice. An example of the Ojibwes' struggle to make this adaptation is seen in the 1843 remarks of the missionary Lucy M. Lewis, when she wrote of attempts to have Chief Buffalo convert to Christianity:

> The old chief Buffalo for whom many prayers have been offered says he is too foolish to learn. He was induced to attend [a] meeting a few Sabbaths since, but appeared to spend most of the time examining the pew door . . . [However] the wife of the chief . . . was lately persuaded to attend sabbath school.[63]

The image of the aged Chief Buffalo sitting in a Christian church pew on Madeline Island with eyes cast down onto the pew door while the preacher stood before the group pontificating on the benefits of believing in the Christian god is compelling. This incident occurred in 1843, and as suggested above, it, as well as others given in previous paragraphs, shows that it was a contemplative Buffalo who struggled with the many changes his people were confronting in the early decades of the nineteenth century. Recently it has been claimed, "During the 1830-40s Buffalo welcomed Protestant missionaries to La-Pointe,"[64] but we should wonder about the ultimate purpose, and deep sincerity, of this "welcome."

Chief Buffalo had a lot on his mind in 1843. We have seen that he was a contemplative man, as witnessed by his thoughtful speech given at the 1826 Fond du Lac treaty meeting. And if, as Mark Diedrich suggests, as a much younger leader he had been present at the signing of the Treaty of Greenville in 1795, when the United States claimed the native peoples had "the right to their lands forever," providing he took those words seriously, he must have been dismayed by what was occurring to his peoples' lands nearly fifty years later. By that time he had been part of two major land cessions, and in that year he and other Ojibwe leaders were discussing their surprise about American claims for even more Ojibwe land, including the claim that the Ojibwe had sold Isle Royale, the large island in western Lake Superior northwest of the Apostle Islands.

As part of the American rush to mine copper, in spring of 1843, the United States opened a federal Mineral Land Agency Office at Copper Harbor, Michigan, and assigned General Walter Cunningham to that station. Like other government officials Cunningham was eager to issue mining leases, including those for Isle Royale. But the Ojibwe complained, saying the large island had not been included in the treaty, and the resultant frustration among American governmental and mining officials was severe.[65]

Some months after Alfred Brunson assumed his duties at La Pointe, he learned of the Isle Royale issue and was not hesitant to forward his assessment of the matter to American officials, the first being General Cunningham.[66]

Brunson told Cunningham it was the consensus at La Pointe that Isle Royale was still owned by the Grand Portage Ojibwe, and he claimed the 1842 treaty needed to be corrected so these people could be treated justly. General Cunningham's surprise that the new Sub-agent at La Pointe should say the recently ratified treaty was flawed, and also that the Ojibwe had not been treated fairly, led to some heated remarks in correspondence he immediately sent to Washington D.C. In a letter to the American secretary of war, Cunningham accused Alfred Brunson of being "insane." But he was not just upset with Alfred Brunson, he also was angry that the Ojibwe complaints about Isle Royale were inhibiting the government's desire to go ahead with the start of copper mining on the island. In the spring of 1843, the Ojibwe insistence that they had not sold the island was clouding the legitimacy of mining leases, and government officials as well as financial investors wanted this problem resolved quickly. Cunningham's condescending perception of the political standing of the Ojibwe when interacting with the Americans is seen in a remark he made regarding their assumed reliance upon treaty annuities. In a 6 October 1843 letter to James Madison Porter, the secretary of war, he boasted: "One day [of withholding payments] would have brought them to their knees."[67] Perhaps by 1843, this sort of arrogant boasting directed to those perceived as poor and powerless, like the belittling remarks of clergymen Hall and Titus given above, were commonplace and had become a regular part of Ojibwe life.

Robert Stuart was another American official upset with Alfred Brunson's accusations and tried to calm the unrest by having personal gifts requisitioned and given to appropriate Ojibwe leaders. To this end he had the government send thirty long guns of superior quality to the relevant chiefs, with "a silver plate on each stock with the chief's name engraved thereon," but the unrest continued and the very next year, 1844, he was requesting more gifts be sent to quiet the Ojibwe.[68]

Meanwhile, the Grand Portage Ojibwe band insisted it had not sold Isle Royale, but, according to a recent writer, "realizing it was unlikely they would be able to maintain possession of it" they offered to sell the island to the United States.[69] Finally, Stuart spent thirteen days at La Pointe in the fall of 1844 during the distribution of treaty annuities and was supposedly successful in settling the Isle Royale issue by managing to get the Ojibwe leaders to sign a compact in which they agreed to the cession of the island. The Grand Portage leaders signed the document, as did Buffalo, Tugwugaune, Misia, and Mukudabenase (Black Bird) of the La Pointe bands.[70] However, five years later in his annual report of 1849, La Pointe's new Sub-agent, John Livermore, told how Ojibwe leaders were still asking him to correct the Isle Royale problem, saying they never relinquished their ownership rights to that important island, and this claim as to "whether their title to Isle Royale had ever been truly extinguished " was raised repeatedly over the ensuing years."[71] Considered part of the 1842 treaty, government officials did not bother to have the Compact of 1844 ratified by the Senate and President, and without this ratification the question of the final legality of the document remains at issue.[72]

At the middle of the nineteenth century this Isle Royale issue was part of an increasing American interest in Wisconsin Territory and the western Great Lakes after the signing of the Treaties of 1837 and 1842. The latter treaty caused an almost immediate increase in newcomers to the south shore of Lake Superior, since after its ratification a copper boom occurred. The Upper Michigan Ojibwe bands needed to make immediate accommodations to this influx of Europeans and Americans, and although La Pointe's bands, like those in the interior of Wisconsin Territory, were to some extent outside the most severe influence of this mining, in diverse ways they were still affected by it. In time there were mining operations in northern Wisconsin Territory only thirty or so miles distant from Ojibwe villages at La Pointe, and importantly, the small port at Madeline Island served as a center for commerce for these interior industries. Among other problems, mining sites and lumber camps and mills attracted whiskey peddlers who dispensed their wares to the industries' workers, but also were not averse to selling their product to Ojibwe buyers.

For the Ojibwe, the mining industry presented a new opportunity to trade foods like fish, venison, rice, maple sugar and other native products for currency and manufactured items, and these trading relationships developed new social and economic bonds between the tribesmen and the Americans.[73] Although by the 1840s the fur trade and Ramsay Crooks' recent commercial fishing industry had begun their downward slide, due to the new logging and mining industries the Ojibwe were still involved in the American economic system. For most, their aboriginal economic system was ongoing, but the importance of that of the United States would only increase.

We should not think, however, that with the major land cessions witnessed by the treaties of 1837 and 1842, and with the mining and logging industries resulting from them, that the Ojibwe were welcoming a new and widespread exposure to American society and culture. There is evidence to show that soon after the 1842 treaty sessions "some may have tried to avoid contact with whites whenever possible."[74] As mentioned above, some Ojibwe were having unfortunate experiences with some white men, and in 1843, a few of Wisconsin Territory's interior Ojibwe band leaders said, "We do not wish to be near them. Whenever we are near white men we are sure to have trouble."[75] Consequently, attempting to minimize contact with whites, these leaders asked that their annuity payments be made on the St. Croix River instead of at La Pointe so they would not have to travel to the latter site, where whites were becoming more numerous.

A more extreme solution to the problem of contacts with whites after the Treaty of 1842 is seen in the case of La Pointe's Muckedaypenasse (Black Bird). This La Pointe leader was one of the many Ojibwe who were upset with the Treaty of 1842, and he disagreed with attempts to accommodate the Americans, opting instead to investigate the possibility of migrating to Canada to escape them. According to Janet E. Chute, after the signing of the Treaty of 1842:

> Some leaders thought that migration to Canada, in accordance with Shingwaukonse's plan, offered a more secure future for their families than remaining crowded onto American reserve lands. Leaders who had been forceful in opposing the surrenders [of land] at La Pointe, moreover, found themselves hounded by both American authorities and members of their own bands. As a result of internal band strife, breakaway family groups joined together in

> making a representation to the Crown through the collector of customs at the Canadian Sault in June 1845.[76]

Muckedaypenasse and Neokema, two leaders from La Pointe, traveled to Canada in June of that year to request they be allowed to bring "A number of closely related families, totaling five hundred individuals" across the border to reside at Garden River at the planned new community of Shingwaukonse.[77] Black Bird's and Neokema's 1845 request seems to have gone nowhere, but this desire to leave the La Pointe region and migrate east to the Canadian side of the St. Mary's River indicates all was not well within Buffalo's regional community. By 1842, the venerable Ojibwe leader had his dissenters, and their apparent willingness to "vote with their feet" by leaving his community and migrating to Canada shows us that by that time it was not just the split between the Mississippi and Lake bands that was troublesome to the overall Ojibwe community at the western end of Lake Superior. Buffalo was faced with a significant number of persons within his home region of La Pointe who were disenchanted enough with how things were going that they were willing to take the extreme step of migrating out of the community.

A major reason for some tribal leaders' dismay regarding contacts with whites was that since the mining and logging industries began to come into Lake Superior country, alcohol was more readily available. In 1843, Ramsay Crooks boasted about how his American Fur Company worked for years to keep liquor out of the region. He claimed that the firm had "kept these large bands of Chippewas perfectly sober" and that "It has been our constant aim, to keep intoxicating liquors out of the country, and our success we fearlessly assert has raised the Natives from poverty and distress, to comfort and comparative affluence." However, Crooks complained that by 1843, at La Pointe there was "liquor on all sides" and that he feared the "trade will be ruined."[78]

Ramsay Crooks was not alone in sounding this alarm. At the time, liquor was being smuggled into La Pointe and the rest of Ojibwe Country by water and by land. Along with incidents at La Pointe, accounts tell of problems it was creating at the St. Croix River, Sandy Lake and west to Crow Wing.[79]

Like others in the fur trade, Ramsay Crooks was concerned about the harm liquor did to tribal people, but his greater concern was with what it was doing to his business profits. In 1831-32, when the American Fur Company was associated with the St. Louis Chouteau trading firm, he lobbied Washington leaders to allow liquor into the fur trade so his agents could compete with British traders who dispensed the drug. At the time Lewis Cass was Secretary of War, and was taking a strong public stand against the use of liquor in the fur trade, even if it meant a loss of trade to the British.[80]

Fur trade literature of the times is replete with negative remarks about this problem of liquor and Indians, but some of the most balanced and empathic writing about the problem comes from James Hayes, who was appointed Sub-agent at La Pointe after Alfred Brunson's departure. Hayes was the second Sub-agent appointed after Brunson—the first being John Hulbert of Sault Ste. Marie who was appointed on 24 October 1843, but was soon transferred to Saginaw, Michigan, "without ever assuming his post at La Pointe."[81]

James Hayes assumed his position in 1844, and as was the case with Brunson, apparently took his work's responsibilities to heart. For example, in a letter of 16 August of that year he told Commissioner Crawford that the government farmer who earlier had been assigned to the Sandy Lake station "was not a practical farmer" and was causing much unrest in the local Ojibwe community, so Hayes fired the man. Like many others in government service, Indian agency farmer positions were political appointments, and in this case the appointee's qualifications appear to have been woefully lacking.[82]

The sudden presence of Sub-agent Hayes at La Pointe must have presented an interesting mix of attitudes to the community. While missionary Sherman Hall continued to see the local Ojibwe as "degraded Indians" who were "idle and lazy," and claimed that "Their minds are dark and their hearts depraved," the new Sub-agent offered a contrasting image.[83]

For example, in 1847, in response to complaints of Ojibwe depredations against whites, Hayes wrote to Territorial Governor Dodge saying:

> The Chippewas as individuals, and as a nation, are well disposed, and will continue to be so as long as the cupidity and heartlessness of the whiskey dealer will permit. I fear that in our accounts of outrages and crime, we have done to Chippewas, if no other tribe, injustice in many cases for I find on comparing them with almost any civilized community of the same size, for four years, there will be found the smaller aggregate of crime on the part of the savage; and every crime of any magnitude which has been committed may be traced to the influence of the white man.[84]

These surprisingly positive statements by La Pointe's Sub-agent stand out in the literature of the times. And there is more. His annual report of 1847 to Governor Dodge, in which these remarks are found, shows the voice of a writer who although like his American contemporaries was espousing the familiar notion of the nation's moral need to "civilize the savage," was nevertheless one of the most tolerant voices writing about the Ojibwe at that time. James Hayes was aware that the American public was receiving improper "truths" about Indian people from the letters and published articles of travelers who came to Indian Country, who after a brief exposure would write about the tribal people. Of this problem, Hayes said "Much error is scattered respecting the character, condition, &c., of the Indians, by the remarks of those who visit their country for the first time and obtain, at most, but a glimpse of their state and manner of life."[85]

However, along with his apparent empathic view of Ojibwe people, Sub-agent Hayes seemingly struggled with liquor consumption. Even though an incident at La Pointe between William Warren and Hayes led to the firing of Warren as interpreter, Warren later claimed that Hayes "was the best and most *disinterested* Agent the Chippewas ever had. During his whole career as Agent, the Fur Company agents at La

Pointe, persecuted him, because they could neither buy nor corrupt him! But liquor, the bane of many a noble and good man, laid him in the dust."[86]

The following quote of Hayes' can serve not only to summarize this man's conclusions of the Ojibwe in 1847, but also provides us with a window into what was, according to their Sub-agent, the nature of the lives of some of these tribal people at the middle of the nineteenth century.

About the Ojibwe, Hayes wrote:

> They plant to thrice the extent, and are yearly increasing the amount; and men who, four years ago, would have considered it a lasting disgrace to perform any kind of agricultural labor, now lay hold manfully and consider it highly honorable. They are fast abandoning the principal of a community of property, and each man begins to feel that his business is to provide for his own family, and to make provision in time. They have abandoned, to a considerable extent, the ceremonies and practice of their heathen worship and heathen creed; and, although they may practice it, acknowledge the truth and superiority of the white man's religion; many of them have adopted, in whole or in part, the dress of civilized men, and live, so far as their circumstances will admit, in a civilized manner.[87]

Although we should, perhaps, be careful in accepting the complete veracity of this paragraph written by a government employee who may have been concerned with making public his success in changing the Ojibwes' behavior, it might also be evident that from these remarks, more so than from any other observers we have seen, we can envision the cultural changes underway at La Pointe by 1847.

Although not as empathic as the remarks of James Hayes, other La Pointe writers of the time were saying similar things about the changes being witnessed in the Ojibwe community. The seasonal round of resource procurement through the maple sugar harvest, wild rice gathering, and so forth was still going on, but this was being supplemented by efforts to provide sustenance through what we might agree was an early attempt at farming. Also, increasingly, more and more log houses were being erected, perhaps not yet to be used as permanent year-round abodes, but simply as bases to which Ojibwe families could return upon the completion of their seasonal subsistence activities. And customs of personal attire and adornment were beginning to be altered, and very importantly, changes in religion were occurring. In these different ways the Ojibwe were adapting to the permanent presence of the Americans. Clearly, by this time serious Ojibwe cultural accommodations were underway.[88]

## 7.

BY THE LATE 1840S, LUMBERING OPERATIONS in ceded territories were drawing an increasing number of whites to the region, and more troubling incidents between them and the Ojibwe occurred. One took place in 1847, at St. Croix, when Nodin, a local Ojibwe leader, was accused of killing Henry Rust. Rust was a white man involved in the sale of liquor and amidst reports of "great excitement" at that station, Nodin was placed under arrest and went to court in Stillwater, Minnesota Territory, where he was found not guilty on evidence indicating the incident was provoked by Rust. Sub-agent Hayes of La Pointe was at the scene soon after the killing and worked to bring calm to the region.[89] This conflict prompted cries that a war with the Ojibwe was imminent, and ninety residents of St. Croix County signed a petition demanding their removal.[90]

Tension remained in the region, and the next year, white citizens at St. Croix Falls lynched an Ojibwe man for killing two white men. Captain Seth Eastman, at St. Peters, was ordered to send troops up to St. Croix Falls, as well as to ship guns and ammunition to arm the local citizenry. Henry Rice, in St. Peters at the time, wrote to Commissioner Medill, saying, "From present appearances, a war may be expected." Rice, who was working with Medill for Ojibwe removal, and was lobbying other federal leaders for that cause, went on to say, "The anticipated war between the whites + Chippewas will I fear operate against us in removal + *we* may have bloodshed."[91]

Another such incident occurred in 1849, in Chippewa Falls in the new state of Wisconsin, when after an evening of consuming alcohol, a group of white loggers went to an Ojibwe household intending to sexually molest a woman. In a response to this outrage, the woman's husband attacked one of the men, was restrained and "a mob of whites hanged the Indian to the limb of a pine tree." This lynching of an Ojibwe man supposedly was followed by a call for revenge from the Indian community and there was fear of a greater confrontation. While we cannot be certain of the details, it appears the white men were arrested, and after Ojibwe leaders agreed to let them be punished in the white court system, they "escaped" custody.92

Incidents such as these, and many less severe that doubtlessly do not show in the written record must have been widespread in the 1840s. To some whites, the resolution of these cases of what can be called *frontier justice* might have been seen as appropriate, but to the Ojibwe they most certainly were viewed differently. The growing numbers of whites in the region and their willingness and ability to use force was threatening the very existence of the Ojibwe world.

*Notes*

1.Bushnell annual report of 30 September 1941, in ARCIASI.
2. Bushnell 1841, as cited in Schenck 2007:20.
3. Schenck 2007:20, brackets added.
4. Diedrich 1999:74.
5. Ross 1960:101-2.
6. Doty 1842 in WisTerPap, Vol. 28, p. 4.
7. Brunson 1879:147.
8. Ross 1960:101.
9. Bushnell 1839 in WisTerPap, Vol. 27, pp. 1196-7.
10. Bushnell 1840 in WisTerPap, Vol. 27.
11. Ely 2012: 211-12, 292; Chute 1998:85.
12. Hall, report of 24 August 1841 in ARCIASI; Bushnell, report of 30 September 1841 to ARCIASI.

13. Bushnell, report of 30 September 1841 in ARCIASI.
14. Armstrong 1892:92-7.
15. Treuer 2011:71-4.
16. Bushnell, report of 30 September 1841 to ARCIASI; Dodge, annual report dated 22 September 1840 in ARCIASI.
17. Crawford, cited in Satz 1991:33; Stuart, cited in Cleland in McClurken *et al* 2000:18-9, 36.
18. Satz 1991:10.
19. Warren 1841, cited in Satz 1991:33.
20. Christian 2004:187-8.
21. Satz 1991:37; Cochrane 2009:119.
22. Stuart 1843 as cited in Satz 1991:39.
23.Cleland in McClurken *et al* 2000:38; Satz 1991:38; Clifton 1978:14,
24. Cochrane 2009:120.
25. Cochrane 2009:120; Treuer 2011:74-5.
26. Cochrane 2009:121.
27. Satz 1991:34.
28. Satz 1991:37.
29. Cleland in McClurken *et al* 2000:36.
30. Satz 1991:37.
31. Cleland in McClurken *et al*, 20; Cochrane 2009:123.
32. Clifton 1978:15.
33. Barnouw 1963; Clifton 1978:15.
34. Perry 1996.
35. Satz 1991:37-8.
36. Ross 1960:88.
37. Clifton 1987:15.
38. McClurken *et al*, 2000; Satz 1991.
39. White in McClurken *et al*, 2000:149.
40. Satz 1991:41.
41. Cleland in McClurken *et al*, 2000:38.
42. Diedrich 1999:73.
43. Diedrich 1999:73.
44. Wheeler 1843 as given in Diedrich 1999: 73.
45. Gilbert letter of 10 December 1853 to Manypenny, in Letters Received, Mackinac Agency, Bureau of Indian Affiars Records, microfilm copy at MHS: St. Paul, also cited in Danziger 1979:88, 229.
46. Wheeler 1843 as cited in Cleland in McClurken *et al*, 2000:38.
47. Satz 1991:41.
48. Stuart 1843:551-554 in WisTerPap Vol. 28.
49. Clifton 1987:36.
50. Satz 1991:40.
51. Satz 1991:41
52. Brunson 1843 cited in Satz 1991:39-40.
53. Buffalo 1842 as cited in Satz 1991.
54. Stuart 1842 in WisTerPap Vol. 28, pp. 489-491.
55. Brunson 1879:206; Satz 1991:44; Schenck 2007:28-9.
56. Schenck 2007:23.
57. Brunson 1879:158.
58. Schenck 2007:24.
59. Olmanson 2007.
60. Brunson letter of 1 August 1843 to Doty in ARCIASI.
61. Sherman Hall letter of 2 February 1842 to Aaron Hall found in Hall letters and papers at Minnesota Historical Society, St. Paul, MN, hereafter given as MHS.
62. Titus 1843:112-3.
63. Lewis, Lucy M. quoted in Diedrich 1999:73.
64. Diedrich 1999:73.
65. Crawford 1843 in WisTerPap, Vol. 28, pp. 599-601; Schenck 2007:27-9.
66. Cochrane 2009:124.
67. Cunningham 1843 as quoted in Cochrane 2009, p. 127.
68. Stuart 1843 in WisTerPap, Vol. 28 p. 608; Stuart 1844 in WisTerPap, Vol. 28 p. 675-6.
69. Cochrane 2009:125-7.
70. Stuart 1844 in WisTerPap, Vol. 28, p. 727.
71. Livermore, report of 15 September 1849 in ARCIASI; Cochrane 2009:131.
72. Cochrane 2009:131.
73. Cleland 1985 as cited in Satz 1991, p. 40.
74. Satz 1991:45.
75. Chippewa Chiefs 1843 as cited in Satz 1991, p. 45.
76. Chute 1998:101, brackets added.
77. Chute 1998:101-2.
78. Crooks 1843 in WisTerPap, Vol. 28, p. 598-9.
79. Doty 1843 in WisTerPap, Vol. 28 p. 611-2; Doty 1844 in WisTerPap, Vol. 28 p. 648-650; Crawford 1844 in WisTerPap, Vol. 28 p. 689-692; Borup 1844 in WisTerPap, Vol. 28 p. 705-8.
80. Christian 2004:282-3, 294-5.
81. Schenck 2007:28-9.
82. Hayes 1844 in WisTerPap, Vol. 28, p. 721.
83. Hall reports of 1843, 1844-1849 in ARCIASI.
84. Hayes report of 1847 in ARCIASI.
85. Hayes report of 1847 in ARCIASI.
86. Warren 1852 as cited in Schenck 2007 p. 153.
87. Hayes report of 1847 in ARCIASI.
88. Wheeler letter o 9 September 1847 in ARCIASI; Hall report of 14 September 1847 in ARCIASI.
89. Hayes 1847 in WisTerPap, Vol. 28 p. 1053-4; White in McClurken *et al* 2000:165; Dodge report of 1847 in ARCIASI.
90. Bowron 1847 in WisTerPap, Vol. 28, p. 1066-8.
91. Rice 1848 in WisTerPap, Vol. 28, pp. 1167-8.
92. Current 1976:154; Schenck 2007:71; White 2000.

# 17

# 1847: The Year of the Forgotton Treaties

### *Prelude to the Ojibwe Removal Order of 1850*

1.

ALMOST IMMEDIATELY AFTER THE RATIFICATION of the Treaty of 1842, the question of removing the Ojibwe communities from Wisconsin Territory surfaced in a new and more serious manner. Some government officials, like Wisconsin Territorial Governor Doty, were adamant about the need for Ojibwe removal, and as we noted, this issue had been raised by numerous voices for some years. There were other voices, however, against removal. In late 1845, under pressures to begin mining in the northern area, the United States Senate asked the president if the removal of the Ojibwe that was mentioned in the 1842 treaty had been implemented, and Commissioner of Indian Affairs Crawford responded in the negative. He went on to suggest that he saw no reason to move the tribesmen since their presence would not hamper mining operations. Three years later Sherman Hall wrote that he did not favor removal since the land ceded in the 1842 treaty was not needed for agriculture, and mining activities in the region had not yet reached the extent it was earlier thought they would. Two years after Hall's letter, apparently in response to a growing clamor for Ojibwe removal, a group of American citizens involved with mining operations along the south shore sent a petition to the president saying they saw no reason for a removal.[1] However, despite these anti-removal voices, an initiative for Ojibwe removal went forward.

As we will see, the complexities of how this finally played out over the following ten years or so involve authorities at the territorial, state, and federal levels, as well as regional non-tribal individuals, the Menominee and Ho-Chunk residents of Wisconsin and the Territory of Minnesota, and most importantly of course, the Ojibwe people themselves.

The assumption that native communities would give way as Euro-Americans "settled" the land was part of the notion of manifest destiny from the beginning. American demographers suggest that in the history of the United States, settlement is felt to have occurred when the non-Indian population reached two persons per square mile, and for much of the eastern United States this was not generally achieved until about 1890. In the 1840s, northern Wisconsin territory was heavily forested, and even though some regions to the south were witnessing population growth, the north was still relatively un-populated. Given this, Charles Cleland concluded that an increasing American settlement of lands just south of Lake Superior was not a factor for the clamor for Ojibwe removal in the 1840s.[2]

In the instance of western Lake Superior country the story of removal is complicated and, until recently, has not been studied with any degree of depth. Early published histories of the western Great Lakes seldom mentioned it, if at all. Ultimately, for the non-natives, Ojibwe removal was always perceived as a matter of tribal people standing in the way of "progress," and as such it was a *given*, that is, something so obvious that it was never questioned. For the Ojibwe it seemed to have been something dreaded, and therefore, to resist. Unfortunately, we have very little knowledge of exactly what discussions occurred within the Ojibwe community for the years removal was an issue. On the part of the regional Euro-American leaders of the time, the written record shows that finally, Ojibwe removal was about political maneuvering involving a desire for money and power, and at least one writer feels that in all this scheming the indigenous peoples were the pawns.[3]

Charles Cleland states that two causes were behind the call for removal. The least important stemmed from instances of social contact and trade between the Indians and non-Indians—issues that were inflated by the non-Indians in order to justify removal. Essentially Cleland feels that this problem originated in the non-Indian community and was due to "unlicensed trade, unapproved timber contracts and whiskey." Cleland concludes that the second and really the only valid issue behind the push for removal was "the conspiracy of a small number of Whig politicians in Washington and in the Minnesota Territory who were anxious to draw Indian patronage jobs and annuity money to the Minnesota Indian jurisdiction." In other words, there was money to be made on Indians, and governmental leaders and entrepreneurs like Alexander Ramsey and Henry Rice were eager to capitalize on this opportunity.[4]

Remembering that in the early years of the formation of the United States, territorial governors were also regional *ex officio* Superintendents of Indian Affairs, we find that in these roles, the governors of Wisconsin and Minnesota Territories were important players in the matter of the removal of tribal peoples. In Wisconsin Territory the Ho-Chunk, Menominee, Potawattomi, Sac and Fox, and others all faced removal issues. In the case of the 1850 order, it was Minnesota's Territorial Governor Alexander Ramsey who played the major role. However, before discussing the paper trail between American officials that is integral to the history of Ojibwe removal, we must mention numerous pertinent national and regional events of the times.

2.

WITH THE RATIFICATION OF THE TREATIES of 1837 and 1842, Lake Superior's southern shore, the northern interior of Wisconsin Territory, and Upper Michigan were opened to whites. It is sometimes said that in northern Wisconsin, the Treaty of 1854 opened the way for land acquisition by non-Indians, but as we will see below, the land sold to the United States in that treaty was in the northeastern portion of the Territory of Minnesota, not in the state of Wisconsin, and was quite distant from Chequamegon Bay.[5] As we will see below, the land sold to the United States in the Treaty of 1854 was in the northeastern portion of the Territory of Minnesota, not in the State of Wisconsin, and was quite distant from Chequamegon Bay.

The new lumbering and mining industries were catalysts that triggered movement into the lands ceded in the treaties of 1837 and 1842, and caused smaller internal migrations. For example, after 1842, a large number of La Pointe's residents left Madeline Island and the immediate region for the Keweenaw Peninsula, and in a lesser fashion, for the Montreal Range in Wisconsin Territory to take part in the new mining industry.[6] Although this migration caused a brief downturn in commercial activity at La Pointe, its effect on Chequamegon Bay's Ojibwe community was probably minimal.

In the early nineteenth century most of the European and American immigration into Wisconsin Territory occurred in the far southeastern portion of the region, with much smaller pockets of settlement at Green Bay, Stevens Point, and at Hudson, the western Wisconsin site along the St. Croix River across from what is now Stillwater, Minnesota.[7] By mid-century however, the stream of immigration was growing. In 1842, the number of Euro-Americans in the southern portion of the territory was "fewer than 45,000" but by 1848, it had grown to nearly 250,000.[8] At this latter date railroads were making their way to the southeastern city of Milwaukee and soon they would start reaching across the region, bringing even more immigrants in their wake.

Initially these population increases had little direct effect on the Chequamegon Bay region, but in only a few years when more whites came north, it surely was apparent to the Ojibwe that times were changing. As the numbers of these newcomers increased and the effects of their market economy multiplied, the pace of life quickened. For instance, as already noted, mines in northern Wisconsin Territory were only twenty-five miles or so inland from La Pointe, and during their construction and early years of operation incoming materials were shipped on lake vessels to Madeline Island, where their bulk was broken for delivery to their ultimate destinations. A few years later, this occurred again, with the founding of settlements at Duluth and Superior in the years before the harbors in those locales were established. Such activity brought more whites to the area and afforded opportunities for tribesmen to supplement their seasonal round of economic activity with periodic wage labor. Since 1837, part of treaty annuities had been paid in specie and the Ojibwe were quickly learning the value of these gold and silver coins.[9]

Charles Cleland offers a discussion of the challenges these events, and others, presented to northern Wisconsin's Ojibwe people. In many ways the contrasts between Ojibwe and Euro-American cultures were extreme and these cultural differences exacerbated the difficulty of adjusting to the rapidly increasing new challenges. Cleland argues that the Ojibwe showed considerable restraint throughout the two decades when this "cultural clash" was most severe. Differences ran through the entire spectrum of both cultural systems, to include their economic, political, social and religious components. For example, the strong communal ethic of sharing found in Ojibwe culture stood in stark contrast to the American value of private property. Notions of private ownership were practically unknown in the tribal world, but according to Cleland, for the whites, "In early nineteenth-century America, one's possessions and property were close to sacred, protected by law to the extent that in many circumstances human life could be taken to protect them." The Ojibwe hunter who came upon a few grazing farm animals in a forest clearing might not have hesitated to "harvest" one of them. Likewise, the same hunter might have freely "borrowed" tools and other possessions of the early "settlers" who came to Chequamegon Country. In some cases it would not be long before such cultural misunderstandings led to charges of "Indian depredations" and calls for removal.[10]

As seen above, the American practice of distributing treaty annuities at only one location, and at the government's convenience, was troublesome to the tribesmen. This was still a problem in 1843, when Alfred Brunson wrote to Governor Doty asking that annuities be dispensed at three locations—Chippewa Falls, Pokegama and La Pointe—instead of just the latter site. He explained in some detail the seasonal round of the Ojibwe, and how during the economically important months of August through October they needed to spend time in three different locales before breaking up into small groups for the important winter hunting season. Brunson's letter shows that at this date Ojibwe culture was still a mobile one, moving seasonally to different resource regions.[11]

The government's decisions regarding the location and timing of annual annuity payments to the Ojibwe were particularly egregious in the late 1840s. Missionaries Sherman Hall and Leonard Wheeler as well as La Pointe's new Sub-agent John Livermore, who replaced James Hayes in 1848, complained about them in their annual reports, saying that interior Ojibwe bands risked losing their fall rice crop if they took the few weeks of time needed to come to La Pointe for the annuity disbursements. Their important fall fishing activities followed the rice harvest and that, too, could be threatened by a late annuity gathering. This was such a problem that a few of the most distant bands did not bother to come to La Pointe for the payments. However, despite these serious complaints, annuity payment times continued to be set by the Americans and generally continued to be made in late fall. Part of the problem was the Americans' refusal, or inability, to give validity to the Ojibwes' traditional way of life, except to see it as something that badly needed to be set aside.[12]

Less importantly, other cultural misunderstandings were evident in white assumptions about the tribesmen. A poignant instance occurred in 1840, when Washington authorities shipped fifty leather saddles to La Pointe for use by the Ojibwe. Apparently feeling all Indians rode horses, it took an exchange of letters before this misunderstanding was corrected. Regarding these saddles, Hamilton Ross claims that at La Pointe:

> The local agency . . . did its best to dispose of the equipment. It persuaded several Indians to try horseback transportation, but in riding through the woods, they suffered Absalom's experience, and gave up in disgust. There was a rumor that others were induced to mount saddles in their canoes, but lifelong habit was too strong. The shipment was eventually returned to Detroit where, after moldering for several years in some warehouse, it was sent on to the Sioux.[13]

It seems true that the saddles were shipped to La Pointe in 1840, but the rest of Hamilton Ross's story might best be understood as an unsuccessful attempt at humor. It must be left unvalidated since Ross did not provide us with a source for this information. Perhaps the image of La Pointe's Ojibwe attempting to install leather saddles into their birch bark canoes might have been perceived by Ross—he was writing in the 1950s—as comedic, but today it can be seen as a comment on non-Indian perceptions of their tribal neighbors rather than a humorous remark depicting unlearned Indians back in the 1840s.

The problem of cultural misunderstandings is also seen in one of Sub-agent Brunson's long letters, this time written to Governor Doty. Writing from La Pointe on 10 January 1843, Brunson was complaining of the government's practice of shipping not only improper goods to the Ojibwe, but goods of inferior quality as well. Referring to the Ojibwe, Brunson said:

> They want no Saddles, bridles, or other trappings for horses, for the very good reason that they have no horses. They want no more frying pans, pewter plates, Yankee axes, half axes, or lathing hatchets. The axes their Smiths make suits them better than any that might be bought. They want no more table knives & forks, carving knives, or butcher knives *made for sale*. They want the regular scalping knife *such as the traders* sell them. They want no more Pins, thimbles, *fine* needles, silk or cotton threads . . .

Brunson also complained of the poor quality guns that had been shipped to La Pointe. He said:

> The guns heretofore sent them are of the poorest quality & often burst the barrel or break the lock in a weak (sic) after being in use . . . Hundreds of them are now lying useless, or being wrought up by the Smiths into some other article. The old North West English guns are the only kind that can stand them. If Americans cannot or will not make their goods as good as the English, let them keep them, & not impose them upon the Indians.[14]

Perhaps Alfred Brunson's remarks show that the persons responsible for selecting the kinds of annuity goods to be sent to the western Great Lakes were unaware of what items the Ojibwe preferred and could actually put to use. Contrariwise, items like knives and forks, fine needles and silk and cotton threads may have been purposely sent in hopes of causing the tribesmen to begin using these "civilized" tools. In this way the thoughtful selection of annuity goods was perceived as another means of "civilizing the savages," something American authorities were certain they had a responsibility to do. Of course, the possibility exists that neither of these suggestions is correct and these mismatched annuity items were due to opportunities for padding government contracts with improper annuity goods, an act bringing considerable financial benefit to those involved.

Treaty annuities, however, were not just important to both the Ojibwe and the Americans for their utilitarian or economic benefits and as instruments of cultural change. They were also important because the occasions of their disbursement drew interested travelers who recorded observations of these colorful events. As we have already mentioned, these frontier, or travel writings, fueled early images of the growing country's western "savages" and the continuing need to "civilize" them.[15] An example of such writing is that of a visitor to La Pointe known only as Professor I.I. Ducatel.[16] There is confusion as to just when Ducatel came to La Pointe, but it is likely he was there in 1845, not in 1835, as the literature claims. His article was first published in 1846, making 1845 an appropriate date for his La Pointe visit, and more importantly, he prefaces his discussion of selected aspects of Ojibwe culture with remarks about the people ceding a large portion of northern Wisconsin Territory as well as many acres in Upper Michigan to the United States, so his visit had to have occurred after the treaty of 1842 was ratified. Interestingly, some twenty-five years ago the article was described as an "unusual eyewitness description of the Ojibway Indians who dwelt along southern Lake Superior."[17]

Ducatel offered a candid, and quite detailed, account of the character and behavior of those Ojibwe at La Pointe, and from today's perspective, his remarks may appear, as historian Alan Woolworth says, "unusual." For example, Ducatel claimed the Ojibwe were "inveterate gamblers" who had several types of games involving wagering, and when coming together at any sizable gathering, it was not long before such games were underway. He also said they were "essentially a sluggish race," since unlike the white man, "it is a peculiarity of the Indian character to remain as long as possible in a state of quiescence." Professor Ducatel went on to remark about what he perceived as the Ojibwes' lack of musicality, and their penchant for having many feasts, at which they did nothing but eat and smoke. The Ojibwe also, he wrote, "have a peculiar relish for the meat of dogs."

These colorful observations aside, what is of value to us is the speech Ducatel says Chief Buffalo made at the disbursement of the annuities. In the 1840s, the La Pointe Ojibwe were accused of making depredations upon the property of whites and Buffalo responded by saying such acts *might* have been committed by some of his "thoughtless young men" and if so, when he determined who committed them he would issue reprimands. More importantly, he felt any such alleged depredations were of "a very trifling nature, and more intended as a retaliation for much greater aggressions on the part of the white men."

According to Ducatel, Buffalo said,

> . . . he had advised his people himself, as the agent had last year asked him to do, to turn their attention, more than they had previously done to the cultivation of the soil, to the planting of corn and of potatoes; but that the wide woods were still full of game, and the deep waters full of fish, and that it was difficult to prevail upon the young men to abandon these resources, to go about turning up the ground. They preferred to leave that to the care of the women, who seemed to be better fitted for such drudgery. He would, however, continue to advise them gradually to break themselves into this new system, if it were only to keep them from the temptation, when they were pinched by want, to trespass upon the potato patches of the white men. Yet he was of the opinion that if the agent looked carefully into the matter, he would find that the aggressions came most frequently from the whites upon the Indians.[18]

This quotation shows the dilemma the Ojibwe were facing in the years immediately following the signing of the treaty of 1842, and also shows the different cultural assumptions held by the tribesmen and the whites regarding the sharing of necessary commodities in times of need. Buffalo was attempting to walk the line between the demands of the missionaries, school teachers and other American authorities to turn to agriculture, and the wishes of younger Ojibwe who desired to continue their hunting, fishing and gathering ways. When hunting and fishing failed, a white neighbor's potato patch must have appeared very inviting. Furthermore, if indeed, in the 1840s, "the wide woods were still full of game, and the deep waters full of fish," it must have been very difficult for leaders to convince their people to turn to farming since in Ojibwe culture the practice of tilling the soil was considered women's work. As we have suggested above in the remarks of Daniel Bushnell, this advice about taking up agriculture (which to the whites seemed only logical), and that the Ojibwe people had been hearing for a decade or two, must have had little appeal.

This struggle of Buffalo's to accommodate the powerful Americans and still be true to his traditional way of life appears to have been ongoing in the decades of the 1830s and 1840s. Ducatel's phrase telling of Buffalo admonishing his young men to work to "gradually break themselves into this new system" might be taken as the underlying teaching the Ojibwe leader was offering his people near the end of his long life. We do not know if the exact words Ducatel used were his or Buffalo's, but we can be certain that in those times the Ojibwe were struggling to bring about a workable fit between their world and that of the Euro-Americans. Indeed, it was "a new system" that was being brought to the Ojibwe. In the 1840s, they were confronted with demands to set aside virtually all of their past beliefs and customs and take up the "system" that was American culture of the time. The ramifications of this for their deep, personal identities must have been, at times, excruciatingly profound.

3.

Other glimpses into what life in Lake Superior country was like for its resident Ojibwe people in the later 1840s appear in written reports of farmers and teachers from the La Pointe Agency for 1847. That year the government farmer at Bad River was Truman Warren, a son of Lyman and brother of William. From Bad River, Warren wrote of breaking several acres of new land, but he seemed not to have been excited about his prospects of having the people take up farming in a big way. He said that:

> The Indians have not planted anything more than Corn and potatoes, with the exception of a few hills of pumpkins. Last year, I gave them some Ruttabaga seed which they sowed, but they stole from each other before the Ruttabagas were the size of a man's finger, on which account they have not sowed any on the Farm this year, but most of them have sowed small patches at their sugar bushes some few miles up the river. I also gave them some peas for seed, but as I have seen no signs of them on the Farm, I think likely they came to the conclusion that they were better eating than sowing.[19]

Perhaps the extent of physical labor a government farmer could expend in trying to bring the new way of life to the Ojibwe is best seen in the report of Smith Mooers, the farmer at Fond du Lac in 1847. Although he said the Ojibwe helped him, it still appears that Mooers himself did much of the work he describes. He wrote:

> With the assistance of the Indians I broke up ten acres of Land, and made ½ Mile of fence—I made myself 700 rails and 50 pair of Stakes, have drawn out 2000 rails, 100 Stakes 200 House Logs–and 300 poles for House Coverings. I have made one ox sled, 3 ox yokes, dug one well 16 ft in depth—worked One month in finishing House, assisted in building three Houses, one log barn, and 2 log stables. Made 25 tons of hay. Cleared off 2 acres of ground for Meadow, &c. Our Crops of Last year Came in well, but, for which the Indians must have suffered. They were all driven in by the deep Snow, and Subsisted on potatoes and Corn, from the first days in Feb until the first of April. We raise some 400 bushels of potatoes, 100 of Corn, besides a Considerable quantity of Squashes, Ruta Bagas, Peas, Beans &c.[20]

In his 1847 report, Sherman Hall told of the return of E.F. Ely to La Pointe, to assume the role of teacher along with Miss Abby Spooner. Hall noted that there were sixty-five students enrolled in the school and that "Early in winter, several of the scholars were taken out of the school to attend a course of instruction from the Rev. Mr. Scolla, Catholic Priest at this place, and but few of them have yet returned." Here we see evidence for the split developing in the Ojibwe community at La Pointe between those preferring the Catholic version of Christianity over that of the Protestants.[21]

Leonard Wheeler also filed a report for 1847, and claimed that the Ojibwe were spending more time at the Bad River station than any year in the past and that, despite Truman Warren's less than optimistic outlook, they "give some indications of an increased desire to adopt a settled mode of life." However, he felt "the desire of the people for schools and religious instruction is not as great as it is for improvement in other respects." Wheeler also claimed the Ojibwe were "being harassed with constant fears of a removal" and if this could be curtailed along with their supply of liquor, the missionaries would "feel more encouraged to continue our labors among them than at any former period." He also remarked that with the year's successes in their work with the Indians, the missionaries might have greater determination to "break up their roving, indolent habits."[22]

In these reports we see that by 1847, the Ojibwe were beginning to accept some aspects of the new life offered them, but it also shows that they were still solidly entrenched in their old foraging way of life. However, as more Americans came to western Lake Superior country, their ability to maintain this life was coming under increased strain.

4.

IN THE 1840S, THE INCREASE in maritime activity at Madeline Island's docks brought by the nearby mining and logging industries was not all that was new at La Pointe. American business people were focusing their interest not just on these new industries, but on the profits to be made in land speculation and the related financial opportunities that would come with the expected American "settlement" of the south shore of Lake Superior and on into Minnesota Territory. Real estate investors were eager to win title to blocks of land situated at strategic locations for future town-site development. Also, there was considerable money to be made in the matter of treaty annuities. By 1842, the specie and merchandise disbursements for the 1837 treaty had been distributed at La Pointe for five years, which resulted in considerable cargo being shipped through Detroit and up to Sault Ste. Marie before arriving in Chequamegon Bay. Ever since 1837, annuity disbursements had been a point of concern for white traders and other business people, resulting in fierce competition to win government contracts to supply, ship, and handle the goods.[23]

This and other commercial activity lasted through the 1840s, but it was not long before lands further west beckoned. Minnesota Territory was beginning to interest Americans and the port of St. Paul soon became a focus for even greater financial investments. The powerful trading firm of the brothers George W. and W.G. Ewing of Indiana, and that of the Pierre Chouteau, Jr. family of St. Louis, desired to increase their northern operations. With eyes toward expected development along the Mississippi River, they anticipated gaining control of government contracts for handling Indian annuities in this undeveloped region. It would not be long before authorities were lobbied to move more tribal communities to the new Minnesota Territory so government disbursements would be routed through St. Paul instead of Detroit. At La Pointe, earlier American businessmen like Charles Borup and Charles Oakes were not turning a deaf ear to these speculative activities. They were among early investors in the St. Paul area, attempting to reap profits from the growth of this new region.[24]

In these years the La Pointe missionaries also were busy. By 1850, Frederic Baraga had left the area to reside permanently at Keweenaw, where he settled-in at L'Anse to minister to the growing numbers of Europeans drawn to the region. Baraga's replacement at La Pointe was Father John Skolla, mentioned above, who arrived in 1845, and was interested enough in the resident Ojibwe to leave several writings about them.[25]

The Protestants were also caught up in the new activity. Sherman Hall and his colleagues had, for some years, been eyeing Minnesota Ojibwe communities as future sites for missionary efforts. By the 1840s, a few of Hall's New England friends had gone on ahead to begin establishing missions in these lands. Also, Leonard Wheeler, after studying the situation on Madeline Island for a few years and agreeing with earlier opinions that the quickest way "to civilize" the Ojibwe was to train them in the domestic art of agriculture, decided to attempt to persuade the tribesmen to "settle down" in the area of their gardens at nearby Bad River, where he and Mrs. Wheeler could teach them to farm. As already mentioned, he erected a mission house at that site and worked to convince the Protestant Ojibwe to join the Wheelers at that location. Clearly, the 1840s were a busy decade at La Pointe, with people coming and going. In 1845, one of the newcomers was Vincent Roy, Jr., who arrived from the distant Canadian Red River Valley, bringing a family name that would go on to be prominent in the Red Cliff community to the present day.[26]

In 1843, William Warren and Matilda Aitken, the mixed-blood daughter of trader William Aitken, were married, and they resided at La Pointe until 1847, when they moved to Crow Wing, near the Mississippi River in western Minnesota Territory. Meanwhile, William Warren's father, Lyman, who had been suffering from ill health, was traveling from his home on the Chippewa River to Detroit for medical treatment when he died upon arriving at La Pointe in October 1847. His wife, Marie Cadotte Warren, died in 1843, and today the remains of both of William's parents rest in the mission graveyard on Madeline Island.[27]

The mining industry created a new trading opportunity for the Ojibwe. As stated above, they were able to exchange forest and lake products at mining sites for manufactured goods and cash. Because of the mining, in the late 1840s, the commercial fishing industry was revived at La Pointe, bringing another opportunity for tribesmen to establish economic relations with the Euro-Americans.[28] All of this activity, with its concomitant growth in white population, saw the new residents work toward establishing a network of local governmental organization beyond the territorial level.

Thus in 1848, Wisconsin Territory became the State of Wisconsin, and in 1849, Minnesota Territory was officially established, with Alexander Ramsey as its first governor. Unfamiliar with Minnesota Territory until this appointment, Ramsey was born in Pennsylvania, studied law and served two terms in Congress, and in 1848, as a Whig, campaigned for Zachary Taylor in his bid for the presidency. Involved with this political activity was a concerted effort on the part of whites to bring more western commerce to the Minnesota region, and of course, all of this put pressure on the Ojibwe. The early image of tribal communities being overwhelmed with the culture of the Americans that Secretary of War Knox offered back in 1791, was coming to pass, some fifty years later, for Chequamegon's Ojibwe.[29]

Perhaps we can imagine the pressure for the tribesmen to alter their traditional way of life in these times. More and more whites were appearing, bringing new ways and labor-saving metal tools, and just as importantly, the missionaries were growing more confident as the Ojibwe adapted to their intrusive presence. Traditional Ojibwe religion was under attack, but it was not just their religion that the people were being admonished to abandon. In the mid-nineteenth century Christian missionaries told them of "the superiority of Ojibwe who used cabins versus lodges, tables and chairs versus sitting on the ground, and table salt when cooking."[30] Their religion, domestic customs, dress and personal identities were all under attack, and the people struggled to adapt to this deep and personal confrontation. An example of how some individuals responded is seen in the remarks of Alfred Brunson about a visit he made to Sandy Lake's Methodist Episcopal Church's mission station in the fall of 1843. About the area's Ojibwe, Brunson wrote:

> These children of the forest, as soon as Christianized, adopt habits of civilization. One man and his wife, of such, were preparing for their winter's hunt, the last usage of savage life that they observed, and this he said he should give up as soon as he got a field large enough to raise their food. They had secured the produce of their garden for Spring and Summer use, while cultivating their garden the ensuing year and should return home after sugar making. He assured me he would not hunt or fish on the Sabbath.[31]

As was true for the reports discussed above from the La Pointe Agency employees for 1847, this is a good example of what was occurring to some Ojibwe families of those times. They had been under missionary pressure to change for at least ten years, and some were beginning to make these changes. The far-reaching effects of such a change as described in this quotation are profound. Although apparently not giving up its spring sugar-making activity, by ceasing the annual winter hunt, and presumably the other seasonal hunting and gathering trips, and staying at the site of their garden and expected larger field, this family was stepping outside of important parameters of the traditional Ojibwe social and economic world. The long-term implications of such a move could be paramount for both the couple Brunson mentioned and the rest of the Sandy Lake Ojibwe.

Yet some tribesmen were standing firm, and perhaps, as occurred at Lac du Flambeau in 1843, were expressing concern about what they were losing. They began speaking of the need to minimize contacts with the whites. It probably was in these years that Ojibwe religious leaders started to exhort their people to close important religious ceremonies to outsiders. We recall that Henry Schoolcraft and Thomas McKenney told of attending open *midewiwin* and *wabeno* ceremonies in the 1820s and early 1830s, but by the late 1840s, these sacred rites began to "go underground," that is, to be closed to non-native onlookers. By the middle of the nineteenth century, these ancient religious institutions with their complex ceremonies were becoming what are now called "secret societies," and it would take over 150 years before they would again be practiced somewhat publicly, although still with major aspects of isolation and seclusion.

Whenever a cultural system is confronted with demands for sudden and intense change, one of the first responses is a resurgence of traditional beliefs and practices. In the mid-nineteenth century at Madeline Island, Sherman Hall may have been witnessing this phenomenon. In a letter he penned to his sister in Vermont on 30 March 1847, he wrote of the reticence of some Ojibwe to give up aspects of their culture:

> Many of the Indians are wedded to their former customs of life and seem determined not to abandon it. They are under the influence of the most degrading customs and influences, and given up to almost the unrestrained indulgences of the worst passions of human nature. Their hearts are so wedded to them, that the arguments and motives of the Christian religion seem to have scarcely any influence upon them.[32]

Amidst all this, rumors of removal were circulating, and the Ojibwe were growing more concerned about this new threat. Their fears were not unfounded, for William Medill, the new Commissioner of Indian Affairs who took office in 1845, was making plans to bring this removal about. However, before he could officially raise the question of moving the Ojibwe people from Wisconsin Territory, he would present them with another request for a land cession treaty.

### *The Treaties of 1847 and the Popular View of Ojibwe Culture at the Time*

1.

IN HIS ROLE AS COMMISSIONER OF INDIAN AFFAIRS, William Medill apparently saw himself as a man with a mission. He set out "to reduce government spending, reform the much abused Indian trade, promote civilization, and deal with the problems created by the sudden expansion of the nation," all the while feeling that Indians were "ignorant, degraded, lazy, and possessed of no worthwhile cultural traits." Like many other Americans he was certain that government programs had to focus on "civilizing" them so they could be assimilated into American society.[33] To Medill, their present status—in the 1840s—was nothing more than an impediment to the expansion of the United States, a problem that was to be expeditiously remedied.

Medill's extremely arrogant and ethnocentric, if not outright racist, attitudes about native people and their cultures were not new and had been held throughout America for some time. All this aside, what is important is that by the 1840s, the nation was beginning to form a determined and focused program for administering Indian affairs, and William Medill was, perhaps, the first commissioner to lead a concerted national effort to carry this program out. The problem this brought to native people like the Ojibwe was enormous.

To Medill, Indian removal from lands east of the Mississippi River had to be completed, and in a thoughtful, planned way. Ironically for American expansionists, past removals formed a western barrier stretching from Canada to Texas that served to restrict national growth, and Thomas H. Crawford, Medill's predecessor in the Commissioner's office, had proposed to break this by concentrating Indian communities in two locations, one to the south in a region just west of Kansas and Missouri, and the other northward in Minnesota Territory at the headwaters of the Mississippi. Medill planned to put Crawford's proposal into effect, and the removal of the Ojibwes and other smaller groups in the north-central region was integral to this. Such action would leave a wide corridor through which white immigrants could easily move westward, after which the corridor itself would be filled with white settlement, while the concentration of tribes would allow for their more expeditious "civilization" and a badly needed administrative efficiency that would reduce governmental expenditures.[34]

Central to the Americans' attempts to concentrate the tribes in the northern sector were the Fond du Lac and Leech Lake Treaties of 1847. In the usual written account of Ojibwe history, these two treaties receive relatively minor attention, the implication being that for the Lake Superior Ojibwe bands, they were of little importance. Here we suggest that an understanding of the Ojibwe motives for negotiating these treaties can help us appreciate the serious situation the Ojibwe were in by the middle of the nineteenth century, and therefore, the underlying importance of the two treaties. The Wisconsin bands had not only ceded away all their lands in that territory, but were regularly threatened with removal. Therefore, by the late 1840s, the western Great Lakes Ojibwe were experiencing much pressure to make major accommodations to the increasing presence of the Americans, and the following discussion of the Fond du Lac treaty can serve to help understand what they were facing at this time.

## 2.

BY 1847, THE WESTERN GREAT LAKES Ojibwe had negotiated numerous "peace" treaties and two land cession treaties with the United States. The latter two—the treaties of 1837 and 1842—left them upset and frustrated, but also brought compensation in the form of land cession annuities that were not unimportant to them. As we have seen, popular history states that the Ojibwe had become dependent upon the fur trade as their source of livelihood, and by the 1840s, with the trade's serious downturn they were severely hampered, so by that time the tribesmen were turning to land sales for the annuity payments they would provide. This is the argument, for example, of Edmund Jefferson Danziger, Jr., who states that for the Ojibwe these annual disbursements served to replace the economic dividends offered through the failing fur trade.[35]

This conclusion leaves us with the image of the Ojibwe as a people who, up to approximately the 1840s, made two major cultural shifts in their adaptations for survival. The first occurred sometime in the early seventeenth century and was the change from a pristine foraging and gardening adaptation without significant fur trapping to a post-European contact adaptation of foraging and gardening along with the intensive trapping of fur-bearing animals for trade purposes. In time, so the story goes—perhaps by the mid-eighteenth century when Alexander Henry came among them—the Ojibwe were focusing on fur trapping to such an extent that they had become dependent upon this specialized adaptation. This way of subsistence, essentially one of market-based intense fur trapping, supposedly continued to approximately the mid-nineteenth century, a period of at least 100 years, when the international fur market collapsed. The second shift came at the time of this collapse, during the years of the major land cession treaties, when the Lake Superior bands ceded away their lands, leaving them with little but their annual treaty annuity payments. In other words, by approximately the 1840s, the one-hundred-year-long dependency shifted from the fur trade to treaty annuities.

In summary, on a first reading, the historical literature on the western Great Lakes Ojibwe might be said to show that indeed, by the 1840s, the tribesmen no longer had a source of sustenance. The most lucrative period of the fur trade had eclipsed, and given the emotional and otherwise troubling effects of missionaries, government officials and those others who for several decades had been insisting that the tribesmen switch from a foraging to an agricultural way of life, it could seem that by 1847, the Ojibwe were a people in serious distress. Furthermore, they were being told to become "civilized," in other words, to change everything. However, the change agents bombarding them with this message did not understand that such a *macro*-change was not easily accomplished.

When these negative factors are coupled with the devastating population loss and emotional stress of new diseases like smallpox that as late as the 1840s were still a lingering threat, as well as the continuing military conflicts with the Dakota,[36] it might be claimed that by 1847, the native communities were seriously struggling for survival. Seen this way, past writers have assumed the tribes were ready to submit to huge land sales and eager to receive annual annuity payments as compensation because without the annuities they were left with no source of income. Herein lies their motive for agreeing to the treaties of 1847, since as the written history claims, they had put aside, or in extreme cases, probably forgotten their traditional subsistence practices to become part of the fur trade, and now with the end of this trade, they needed something new to provide a livelihood. Thus, by 1847, the final effects of participation in the fur trade, along with a widespread population loss from new diseases, had worked to reduce the once large and strong Ojibwe nation to a mere dependent remnant of what the early French first encountered. Put more cryptically, this view suggests that by approximately the middle of the nineteenth century the aboriginal Ojibwe cultural system had all but collapsed.

## 3.

WHILE THE POPULAR WRITTEN HISTORY draws this conclusion, it also, in a contradictory fashion, tells us something else about the persistence and long-term tenacity of key elements of

Ojibwe culture. For instance, in 1832, Henry Schoolcraft and Lt. James Allen observed that at La Pointe, even after over a century of involvement in the fur trade, the aboriginal Ojibwe cultural system continued to function.[37] Eleven years later Alfred Brunson reported the same,[38] and according to historian Danziger, in 1854, some twenty years after the observations of these three writers, this system was still intact. In Danziger's words (paraphrasing Schoolcraft), the "Chippewas participation in the fur trade only somewhat modified their mode of living," and, "[In 1854] their south shore wilderness homeland and the heart of their semi-nomadic traditional culture . . . remained unchanged [from what it had been for centuries]."[39]

Thus, the written historical record appears to contradict itself. On the one hand we are told of the extreme dependency of the Ojibwe on the fur trade, and by the mid-nineteenth century, on the treaty annuities, a dependency that all but destroyed the aboriginal culture. But at the same time, it tells us that through all these years along Lake Superior's south shore the aboriginal cultural system continued to function with only minor modifications. At this point we must ask for clarification. Did the Ojibwes' involvement in the fur trade and land cession treaties cause their reputed dependency and the resultant breakdown of their old way of life? And if not, as we have already suggested, might the truism of Ojibwe dependency on the fur trade and annuities have been overstated?

To attempt to answer these questions we need to recall what John Jacob Astor understood back in 1803, when he entered the fur trade. Astor was aware, as were the French and British before him, that a successful trade required an ongoing native foraging culture. With this in mind he worked hard at lobbying American governmental officials to establish a *preserve* in which Americans would not be allowed to enter to set up farming settlements. Such a wilderness area would have allowed the aboriginal tribal cultures of the northern forests to continue living as they had done before Astor's entrance into the fur trading industry.[40]

John Jacob Astor certainly wanted the tribal communities to trap many fur-bearing animals and trade the pelts with his field agents, and in the process to become "dependent" upon them, but such a dependency, obviously, was not to entail the destruction of the old Ojibwe foraging adaptation. As we have implied, it meant just the opposite. John Jacob Astor knew his success was dependent upon at least three factors: first, the viability of the world's fur trading market, secondly, the long-term availability of the communities of the different species of furbearing animals—primarily genus *Castor*—and third, the ongoing existence of tribal foraging communities to serve as trappers. In this very real sense, we can understand that in an interesting turn, it was not the Ojibwe who were dependent upon John Jacob Astor, but it was John Jacob Astor who was dependent upon people like the Ojibwe.

This conclusion does not deny the difficult situation the western Great Lakes Ojibwe communities like that at La Pointe found themselves in during the two or three decades immediately preceding the middle of the nineteenth century, but it suggests that during these times the relationship between the Ojibwe, their habitat, and the Euro-Americans was complex, and thus, not easily characterized as one of dependency or self-sufficiency. We recall that in 1832, Lieutenant James Allen reported finding some Ojibwe communities along Lake Superior's southern shore filled with healthy, successful people, but also noted that at the Keweenaw station at L'Ance, about fifty percent of the annual account items in trader John Holliday's ledgers were for food provisions. Allen's latter observation has been noted by writers who use it to conclude that in his day, the western Lake Superior Ojibwe were becoming dangerously dependent upon food provided by their traders instead of foraging for their own. As we have noted, Lt. Allen warned that the Ojibwe lands in that region were becoming depleted of furbearing animals and soon the people would have no pelts to trade for food.

This dilemma will be addressed below, but before moving on we need to speak to one more point about the attempts of Astor's American Fur Company to allow the traditional Ojibwe culture to persist through the many decades of the fur trade. This concerns remarks Walt Harris, the Ashland, Wisconsin, writer made in 1976. Harris chastised the American Fur Company for desiring to prolong the "primitive" existence of the tribesmen so the fur trade could go on, and for using alcohol to achieve this purpose. According to Harris:

> With an unlimited supply of rum, augmented by trinkets and a wide variety of cheap goods, the giant fur company was able to promote Indian drunkenness and debauchery on a scale broad enough to ruin the Indians' old way of life . . . Agriculture, if known and adopted, could have opened the way of cultural Indian progress, but things generally had to stay primitive hereabouts, with the fur trade finally making rum the drunken Indian's staff of life.[41]

Here we see an overwrought, harsh, and simplistic rendering of the popular history notion that the fur trade not only made the Indian dependent, but destroyed traditional Ojibwe culture. And, quite interestingly, according to Harris, what should have been done instead was to bring agriculture to the Ojibwe at a very early date. Apparently Harris did not consider the attempts of missionaries and others we have mentioned to have the Ojibwe take up farming as significant.

It is noteworthy that as late as 1976, this writer was still using the notion of a natural "progression" of cultural evolution from a foraging adaptation to agriculture, a notion that culture change theorists had put to rest long ago. However, in an obvious attempt to speak approvingly of tribal leaders from his own personal home region, Harris says there were exceptions to the destruction wrought by the fur traders' rum: "One was La Pointe's Chief Mongozid, or Mamongazida, a descendant of Mudjikiwis, or Waishki, whose philosophy was built around standards that were uplifting and safe. Because of him, many Chippewas were leading a very clean and highly intelligent life. The Great Chief Buffalo was one of them."[42]

While certainly there is some truth in the accusations Harris levels at the fur traders and their willingness to use rum when trading, he errs in saying the trade ended traditional Ojibwe culture. Contrariwise, we have seen—as the remarks of

Lt. Allen, Henry Schoolcraft and others attest to—that all through the years of the fur trade the underpinnings of the culture remained in place. The fur trade did not serve to radically change this ancient infrastructure of the Ojibwe way of life because along with the goal of securing market-ready furs, the trade also needed to work to maintain the early Ojibwe hunting and gathering adaptation. There would have been no fur trade, at least as we know it, without this ancient tribal cultural system.

4.

EVEN THOUGH THE OJIBWE had been active fur trappers and traders for two centuries, by the time of Lt. Allen's visit what had finally become troublesome—even more than Astor's rum—were the persistent efforts by the Americans to "civilize" them. The long tenure in the fur trade surely brought changes to the Ojibwe way of life, but what was more important was the inexorable pressure from those change-agents who were peripheral to the fur trade. As Edmund Jefferson Danziger, Jr. put it: "Far more significant changes were wrought by the agents of civilization: white Indian agents, missionaries, copper miners, farmers, lumbermen, and townbuilders. These men and women waged war on Chippewa culture and seized nearly all of Kitchigami land for white exploitation."[43]

The goal of cultural genocide held by the Jesuits who came to Chequamegon Bay in the seventeenth century was brought again two hundred years later by the change-agents to which Danziger refers. They worked to bring about the assimilation of Ojibwe people into their (the change-agents') way of life, and to achieve this they wanted to end all aspects of tribal life. The Ojibwe political organization, kinship system, economic organization, clothing and hair-styles, transportation, foods, language, religious beliefs and institutions, and more—virtually the entire list of cultural traits—were to be cast aside and the Euro-American forms taken up. By the 1830s, it was these activities, what Danziger referred to as a "war on Ojibwe culture", that were taking a heavy toll.

Importantly, this "war" had the overtones of a *moral* war since the Euro-Americans felt they had an obligation to "fight" it. Thus, it was deemed a moral imperative that the difficult process of *civilizing the savage* be undertaken and ultimately accomplished.

5.

THE EURO-AMERICAN STORY of the post-European contact history of the Ojibwe people is an unfolding of this "battle" to bring the tribesmen into the American way of life. In the early years it is told without the benefit of the understanding of the complex processes of social and cultural change, an understanding that came only in the late nineteenth and early twentieth centuries. Early observers and writers were viewing and analyzing Ojibwe behavior without the benefit of the *culture concept* these later thinkers provided, so they struggled to make sense of what they saw. However, Henry Schoolcraft seems to have anticipated the direction in which later thinkers would move to construct these theories of change, when in 1832, he tells what he thought was the reason so many northern Native American societies were similar in their array of customs. Of the Ojibwe he writes: "The necessity of changing their camps often, to procure game or fish, the want of domesticated animals, the general dependence on wild rice, and the custom of journeying in canoes, has produced a general uniformity of life."[44]

One can see in this short quote the hint of his sense that *economic* practices were the underlying factor driving the rest of the Ojibwe cultural system and that this old way of life had been experiencing a uniform existence for a very long time. However, Schoolcraft goes on to say that:

> . . . the only marked alteration, which their state of society has undergone appears to be referable to the era of the introduction of the fur trade, when they were made acquainted with, and adopted the use of, iron, gunpowder, and woollens (sic). This implied a considerable change of habits, and of the mode of subsistence; and may be considered as having paved the way for the further changes in the mode of living and dress. But it brought with it the onorous (sic) evil of intemperance, and it left the mental habits essentially unchanged . . . [T]he people themselves are, to so great a degree *mentally* the same in 1832 as they were on the arrival of the French in the St. Lawrence in 1532.[45]

The certainty that the fur trade changed, in Schoolcraft's words, the Ojibwe "mode of subsistence" as well as causing a "considerable change in their habits" has been challenged throughout this book. His use of the notion of "mental habits" is also troublesome, since we cannot be sure just what is meant by this concept. One should think that if they were "mentally" the same for over two hundred years, that in order for such psychological stability to persist, the cultural system these "habits" emerged from and functioned in must not have witnessed the extent of change Schoolcraft suggests the fur trade brought. Like other observers of his time, Henry Schoolcraft can leave us with a rich and colorful account of Ojibwe culture, but at the same time cause us to yearn for a more adequate explanation of the causal factors underlying this way of life.

Writing as recently as thirty years ago, thinkers like historian Danziger still did not make the precise connection hoped for between the numerous, and complex behavioral aspects of a human society and the causal factors that underlay a system like that of the Ojibwe in the early nineteenth century. What Danziger claims were the components of traditional Ojibwe culture still extant in the Lake Superior region as late as 1854 are: "family-centered social ties; child rearing, marriage, death, and burial customs; religious thought and practice; art; music; loose political ties; transportation; cooperative economic spirit; seasonal rovings to sugarbush, fishing grounds, wild rice fields, garden and berry patches; and attitudes toward land ownership"[46]

Interestingly, Danziger fails to include the seasonal fragmentation of the summer villages into family-centered winter hunting camps for the taking of large animals for food purposes, an adaptation that—although as Alfred Brunson showed us was being given up by at least one family at Sandy Lake in 1843—was certainly continuing for most Ojibwe families. Also,

Danziger's word choice of "rovings" is unfortunate, for, as we have stated in an earlier chapter, its inappropriate image of how tribal foraging systems actually solved the matter of resource procurement. The Ojibwe, like other tribal foragers, did not wander, roam or "rove" through the countryside in search of food, but instead, strategically planned their seasonal movements in order to be present at particular resource harvesting sites when the time was appropriate. These movements were part of their traditional economic *organization*, a patterned system that, if anything, was not unplanned or unorganized. Furthermore, all of the cultural traits Danziger gives us are not only related to each other, but in a deeper causal manner are *functionally integrated* with subsistence, or *economic*, traits like his "seasonal rovings to sugarbush, fishing grounds, wild rice fields, garden and berry patches."

Finally, the problem is that the literature on the Ojibwe tells us that the people's dependency upon the fur trade had seriously changed their culture. Yet contrariwise, in the 1830s, they still retained that culture and according to Edmund Jefferson Danziger, Jr., they continued to hold it as late as 1854. We can only conclude that despite their reputed "dependency" on the fur trade and later on treaty annuities, at the middle of the nineteenth century the La Pointe Ojibwe were still essentially relying on their ancient foraging adaptation as the prime underpinning of their way of life. As the literature attests, for an apparently significant portion of their community, despite the effects of the fur trade and treaty annuities, the ancient seasonal round of movement to the different resource harvesting sites was still ongoing and doubtless serving to affect or give rise to the social and ideological components of the system. We should conclude, then, that despite their emphasis given in the literature, the fur trade and later the treaty annuity payments were actually *complements* to this aboriginal Ojibwe way of life, and any "dependency" on them should be understood as secondary to the age-old "dependency" on the seasonal round of customs used for harvesting their traditional food resources.

## 6.

DANZIGER'S CONCLUSION THAT THE OJIBWE shifted their dependency from the fur trade to the land sale treaty annuities would have us believe that in 1847, at Fond du Lac the tribesmen welcomed the new treaty for any annuities it would provide. Also, the land ceded away was not basic to the survival of the Lake Superior bands since the parcel was on their far western boundary and not essential for resource procurement. Another factor that doubtless motivated them was the insistence of some leaders that they had sold only the pine and mineral resources in the treaties of 1837 and 1842, not the land itself, and that they still held occupancy rights to these lands and retained hunting and gathering privileges over them. This understanding, coupled with their certainty—as popular history would have us believe—that their "Great Father in Washington" acted in the best interests of "his children," seems to have led to their signing of the 1847 treaty.

However, even though it appears that as the mid-point of the century approached the underpinnings of their traditional culture were still in place, it is clear that the winds of change were forcing more and more Ojibwe accommodations to the powerful Americans. The foreshadowing of hard times that La Pointe's Buffalo alluded to as far back as 1826, at Fond du Lac, must have been weighing heavily on the minds of tribal leaders who certainly were cognizant of their diminishing options. Therefore, the signers of the 1847 Fond du Lac Treaty could have agreed to the treaty because they really had few options but to sell those distant lands.

As the decade of the 1840s drew to a close, doubtless there were more and more voices in the La Pointe Ojibwe community telling leaders like Buffalo to sell that land. We recall the "Pantaloon Band" of one of Buffalo's sons as a possible source of such sentiment, and how Alfred Brunson claimed that by 1843, this group of tribesmen had given up their wigwams for log houses and were dressing and working like whites. We do not know if they had taken up Christianity, but it is likely they saw little purpose in turning down the annuity payments from this proposed land sale.

The demographic realities of the La Pointe bands are also important when attempting to understand motives for signing more treaties in the late 1840s. For instance, Douglass Houghton said he vaccinated 224 persons in the area back in 1832, and that year Lt. Allen remarked that the community held "about 184 souls," but we do not know with certainty what the region's Ojibwe population actually was. In a census Alfred Brunson took in 1843, he listed 608 persons making up the three bands that were in the La Pointe community that year.[47] Obviously, we cannot make much of these numbers, but we can put them into the context of what we know about the early history of La Pointe. As William Warren told, for many years La Pointe's population fluctuated since it was a major center that western Great Lakes Ojibwe people seasonally returned to for ceremonial and economic reasons. Then, for a number of generations, it was a region that transients passed through on their migrations to areas along the Mississippi, as well as the lands at its headwaters and even beyond. Therefore, we should conclude that by the early decades of the nineteenth century we are not dealing with a few thousand individuals who were still practicing their traditional culture at La Pointe. At most, it seems only several hundred Ojibwe persons were regularly in the area at that time. In a community of that size the act of several families taking up the white man's way could make a difference, especially since Ojibwe families most usually function within a much larger extended family context, so when a family began "living and working like whites" it surely affected a larger network of kin.

We also need to remember the Protestant missionaries who were working hard in the community in the decades from 1830 to 1850, and the effect they began to have on traditional Ojibwe culture. For instance, on 1 May 1845, the missionary Leonard Wheeler, his wife and several Ojibwe left Madeline Island to establish a permanent mission station at the Bad River on the mainland just south of the lake, "thereby forming a nucleus for the Bad River band, as it came to be called." According to Wheeler, at this site some Ojibwe "engaged in farming, sent their children to the mission school, attended church services, abstained from their native dances, and greatly reduced their addiction to alcohol." In 1854, at Bad River, Wheeler said, "a number of Indians, including three chiefs, joined the

Christians and called themselves 'Praying Indians.'"[48] These sorts of changes, coupled with the work of the Catholic priests Baraga and Skolla, presented an increasing challenge to traditional tribal leadership and must be included in the setting that saw Buffalo and others decide to sign the treaty of 1847.

7.

IN THAT YEAR A LACK OF OPTIONS could have been apparent to those tribesmen who signed the Fond du Lac treaty, but it may have been less important for the Pillagers of Leech Lake when asked to sign the second 1847 treaty. In 1847, these western Ojibwe were still comfortably distant from the encroachment of the Americans, and the written record shows that after a relatively effortless negotiation session at Fond du Lac, the American treaty commissioners were not at all confident they would have similar success at the northern Ojibwe community.

For the American authorities, the purpose of these treaties was to secure parcels of land in western Minnesota Territory for the placement of Wisconsin Territory's Ho-chunk and Menominee peoples. Advocates of statehood for Wisconsin Territory had been promoting their removals and in time both tribes agreed to move west, although the Menominee never did effect the move, and the Ho-chunk did so only partially and never permanently. (This story of Menominee and Ho-chunk removal is not central to our narrative so we will not pursue it here.[49]) What is of importance is William Medill's second motive for negotiating these treaties with the Ojibwe.

This initially hidden motive—hidden to the Ojibwe—was to have the various Ojibwe bands recognize their *common* ownership of *all* unceded lands at the Mississippi headwaters just west of Lake Superior, including the large piece known as the *preserve*, so hopefully the eventual removal of all Ojibwe bands in Minnesota and Wisconsin Territories (and those in northern Michigan) to this "preserve" could more easily be facilitated. Therefore, while the treaties of 1847 were ostensibly meant to secure lands from the Ojibwe for the removal of the Ho-chunk and Menominee, they ultimately were also meant to facilitate the removal of the Ojibwe themselves.

Charles Cleland claims that the Fond du Lac Treaty "was poorly conceived and poorly executed and created antagonism among the various bands of Chippewa and between the Chippewa and the United States."[50] The two American negotiators were Isaac Verplank and Henry Mower Rice, the latter name going on to become prominent in the La Pointe area in years immediately subsequent to 1847. Rice's wealth and notoriety were acquired in the western Great Lakes region and were accomplished due to his involvement in native affairs of the times. It goes without saying that today his actions are not without negative criticism.[51]

8.

WHEN AGREEING TO WORK WITH treaty commissioner General Isaac Verplanck, among Henry Rice's numerous business interests was his trading establishment at Crow Wing in Minnesota Territory, and thus he was in competition with traders of the American Fur Company. Importantly, Rice and both the Chocteau and American Fur firms would benefit if the 1847 treaties could be negotiated since these agreements ostensibly would have seen more tribal people moved into the western lands. The intended site for the treaty negotiation meetings was La Pointe, but due to difficulty from its many whiskey traders, Verplanck decided to meet at Fond du Lac, a location still in unceded lands and thus where liquor traders were prohibited from entering.[52]

Until late 1847, William Warren and his wife and children were residing at La Pointe where along with being hired to do occasional language work for the Ojibwe community, he was employed as a government interpreter, first by Alfred Brunson then by James Hayes. It was at this time that due to the apparent intemperance of Sub-agent Hayes, Warren and the Sub-agent were feuding, a problem that led to Warren's dismissal from his government employment. However, he was asked by Henry Rice to interpret during the 1847 treaty negotiations, and it seems he readily agreed.[53] Rice knew of Warren's abilities with the Ojibwe language, that he was a trusted confidante of the Wisconsin Ojibwe, and that he was not unfamiliar with the far western lands the Americans were after. Warren had been to the lands in early1847, when he accompanied Hayes on a trip to the Ojibwe communities at the headwaters of the Mississippi in order to ascertain their willingness to sell the two parcels. (Even though he was only twenty-two years old, it was on this long and apparently arduous trip that Warren seemingly started experiencing health problems that ultimately led to his early death.)

When the Fond du Lac treaty was signed, Rice and his party were faced with the problem of negotiating a similar treaty with the Ojibwe at Leech Lake. No leaders from that community were present at Fond du Lac, and since the Leech Lake band also had interests in the western parcel their agreement to the sale was required. Fearing a party of American Fur Company traders would arrive at the northern site before him and turn the Pillagers against the treaty, making its signing impossible, Rice used subterfuge to arrive at Leech Lake first. To this end he announced to those at Fond du Lac that since the season was growing short and foul weather would soon arrive, he would unload some of his party's provisions and return to St. Paul, putting off the trip to Leech Lake until spring. Instead, he paddled down to Crow Wing where, after his party was replenished, he led it up to Leech Lake and was successful in negotiating the treaty.[54] An interesting side note to this incident is a personal connection a long-time Red Cliff family has with this trip.

This connection is informative since it shows a direct involvement of the La Pointe Ojibwe community in distant matters of the times. Paul Soulier, an Ojibwe-French man from La Pointe, who later resided at Red Cliff until his death, was with Henry Rice on the quick trip from Fond du Lac to Crow Wing and up to Leech Lake. Soulier was employed as a paddler and transporter, and later was referred to by Rice as "my old voyageur friend." Of Paul Soulier, Henry Rice said, "Though he had no book learning he was brave, kind and courteous, a man of the woods and lakes, but a gentleman and one of the last of the old school."[55]

During the negotiations at Fond du Lac, Hole-in-the-Day argued that no Lake Superior bands should receive any money from the treaty because they did not own the land being sold. However, the Lake Superior leaders insisted they did indeed own the land parcels, and after much acrimony, they were to receive a sum of $17,000.00, but the Mississippi Bands were to receive a total of $63,000. As noted above, this issue with its payment disparity caused a lengthy dispute between these two communities, and also hampered future relationships between the lake bands and the United States.[56]

One important matter the Fond du Lac treaty shows is that individual Ojibwe bands recognized notions of ownership over lands they occupied in the upper Mississippi region, and that attempts by American officials to have *all* Ojibwe bands acknowledge their *common* ownership over this large region were unsuccessful. This is the same problem Henry Dodge and Robert Stuart faced in earlier treaty negotiations. Once again we see the tenacious persistence of the aboriginal Ojibwe band political system, and how this ancient structure held firm even after decades of determined attempts by American authorities to overlay it with an imposed concept of *Ojibwe nationhood.* As was the case with the European states allied with the Ojibwe peoples before them, representatives of the United States struggled to understand and accept the nature and functioning of the tribal system of political organization. It was only in the early decades of the twentieth century that political theorists were able to comprehend the complexity of a tribal system with its constituent bands. Perhaps even today the *legitimacy* of this type of political system still has not been accepted by governmental authorities from state systems.

Along with heightening negative political sentiment between the Mississippi and Lake Superior bands, another important aspect of the Treaty of 1847 is its language regarding mixed-bloods. As we have already noted, Americans were ill-equipped to understand and accept the enigma of a person of mixed racial and cultural ancestry. Ojibwe communities however, readily accepted persons of mixed blood in the early nineteenth century and certainly continue to do so today.

Until 1847, persons of mixed blood could not share in treaty annuities unless expressly stipulated in treaty language, but the new treaty decreed that if they resided in the Ojibwe community, they thereafter were to share in all annuities. At Fond du Lac, the insertion of this article was a major accomplishment for people like William Warren, and he, along with others of mixed blood, signed the Treaty of 1847 as either a "first chief" or as a "warrior." The role Warren played in having this language included seems obvious, and perhaps we should expect that his efforts at having it inserted were major. William Warren "was not considered Indian, for he lived the life of a white man,"[57] yet at Fond du Lac he became an Indian for purposes of the treaty. In the middle of the nineteenth century this *betwixt and between* character of the lives of persons of mixed blood was a prominent point when considering relationships between the Indian and American communities, although its importance has faded today.

Along with being instrumental in inserting the mixed-blood article at Fond du Lac, we also know that at the negotiations Warren vehemently argued against any undue benefits going to the representatives of the American Fur Company. He was certain his father had been irreparably harmed by accusations the company leveled against him and for the rest of his short life William "waged a personal war against the power and influence of the American Fur Company."[58] Over the next few years, when Indian removal was the major issue of the day, this fact becomes part of the mix of relationships and influences that were at play in western Lake Superior country.

## 9.

THE FOND DU LAC TREATY OF 1847, with its paper trail between Commissioner Medill and his field agents, shows that La Pointe's rumors of Ojibwe removal were substantiated. In fact, a few years previous to that date American authorities were laying plans to effect just such a removal. Medill was determined to break the western barrier caused by earlier removals, and in the summer of 1847, he attempted to do just that. His hope was that in the negotiations of that year at La Pointe, the Ojibwe bands would agree to sell their land in northeast Minnesota Territory immediately west of Lake Superior. He also intended that this new treaty would include a clause for removing the last of the Ojibwe from western Upper Michigan and Wisconsin Territory.[59] Charles E. Mix, an Indian Affairs administrator in Washington, D.C., was dispatched to join Verplanck at La Pointe, but before reaching that destination, Mix returned to Washington due to illness and was eventually replaced by Henry M. Rice. In meetings with tribal leaders at La Pointe before moving negotiations to Fond du Lac, Verplanck attempted to interest the Ojibwe in removing themselves from the land but was unsuccessful, as was his attempt to purchase the preserve, the large tract of unceded Ojibwe land in northeastern Minnesota Territory along Lake Superior's west shore.[60]

In his argument for the removal of the Ojibwe, Commissioner Medill stressed the problem of whiskey traffickers and how they were able to reach the dispersed bands with ease. Concentration of the bands would allow for better control of this problem, and also for greater ease in teaching agriculture and other benefits of "the settled life" to the tribesmen. Historian Satz suggests that Medill's emphasis on the problem of Indian drinking might have been overdone since documents of the time show it was the whites, who brought liquor to mining and logging installations, that were behind the problem, not the Indians themselves. In 1847, this was testified to by La Pointe's government Sub-agent, James P. Hayes.[61]

Pro-removal advocates, nevertheless, cited the issue of the Ojibwe misuse of alcohol as a rationale for removal. Supposedly, this abuse led to Indian depredations on whites and their property, and to these advocates the best recourse was removal of the Indians, something Wisconsin's Governor Dodge and Minnesota Territorial Governor Ramsey both strongly supported.

## 10.

AS THE ABOVE DISCUSSION SHOWS, in the western Great Lakes region the 1840s were a time of much activity in Indian affairs and the community of La Pointe was in the midst of this. An example of initiatives coming from Washington, D.C., in these years is the Indian Intercourse Act of March 3, 1847, which was partially written and soundly supported by William Medill. Through this act, he and former Commissioner Crawford tried to combat what American governmental authorities felt was the undue influence frontier traders had with Indian communities. The power trading company leaders exerted by lobbying in

Washington, D.C., is well known—the activities of Henry Mower Rice are an example of this—but on the frontier the influence of field representatives of these firms could at times overshadow that of the government's Indian agents, becoming troublesome to what Washington authorities considered good relationships between the tribes and the federal government. Central to the problems the act addressed was the negative influence of independent whiskey peddlers in Indian Country. From the days of George Washington up to the 1840s, the federal government attempted to remedy this problem, but with little success. The trouble and general unrest occurring at annuity payment times due to the availability of liquor plagued relationships between the natives and the Americans for years.

The story of the early influence some fur traders had with tribal communities is legendary in North America, and with the advent of annuity payments in the mid-nineteenth century in Lake Superior country it was felt that large portions of this money went directly from chiefs to unscrupulous traders instead of to the people, a situation causing unrest in Indian communities and something the whites deemed detrimental to sound relations between the tribes and the United States. Initially, annuities were paid to tribal leaders, who in turn distributed them to band members, but with the growing influence of the traders such payments began going directly to the traders for the settlement of accounts. Over the years of the fur trade it was customary for traders to advance credit and to have their accounts balanced at the spring rendezvous, but after the coming of treaties, this was also done at annuity payment time. Since chiefs received the annuities, the traders were usually confident that their debts would be cleared.[62] Medill's act of 1847 attempted to change this with its provision that annuities were to be dispensed directly to heads of families instead of chiefs. Both the Ewing and the Chouteau trading companies, the two firms that by the 1840s had risen to prominence in the industry, loudly protested the act.[63]

With the new regulation that annuities be dispensed directly to family heads, individual Ojibwe families probably benefited, and at La Pointe, leaders like Buffalo might have lost a degree of power. In this way, although the intent of the act was to reduce the corruption due to the influence of traders, it also reduced the influence of tribal leaders and diminished the communal aspect of tribal life by circumventing chiefs as it individualized annuity disbursements. Surely, local missionaries like Sherman Hall, Leonard Wheeler, and Father Skolla, as well as the Indian agents favored this act since it reduced tribal communalism by bringing another degree of individualism to Ojibwe life.

Frances Densmore, writing in 1929, and who interviewed Ojibwe elders who had witnessed earlier annuity payment gatherings in northern Wisconsin, gives us the colorful details of how the goods were dispensed at LaPointe after the implementation of Medill's 1847 act. It is not clear exactly what time she is speaking to although she says this is the way it was done before 1854. The usual provisions were broadcloth, calico, flannel, woolen blankets, knives, flintlock guns, combs, lead for making bullets, sewing supplies and tin dishes. Foods distributed usually included wheat flour, salt pork, and a form of baking powder or soda. Densmore claimed that:

> A few days before the payment the chief of each band with his leading warrior went to the issue clerk and reported the number of families in that band, the persons comprising the families, and any special needs they might have . . . Each chief personally received a little more than the Indians, this being called the 'surplus.' As a matter of fact, the quantity of goods required for the chiefs was taken out first, each receiving according to the size of his band, and the remainder was divided pro rata among the Indians . . . . The issuing was done expeditiously. The agent's interpreter usually acted as roll keeper. He called the name of a chief, and the chief stepped forward and stood beside him. The interpreter then called the names of the members of that band and the number of shares to which each was entitled. The chief was ready to identify the men if necessary, and to see that each was given his share. The man spread his blanket on the floor, put the articles in it, tied the corners together and threw the pack over his shoulder, giving place to the next man.[64]

Of course, there was little to keep individuals who had just received such goods from taking them to a whiskey trader and exchanging them for liquor, an act not uncommon at La Pointe in the times. As Theresa Schenck states, sometimes a family might make long and arduous journeys to an annuity payment site only to "arrive home poorer than when they set out."[65] In this regard, Medill's act likely had little effect.

Annuity payments at La Pointe were held in fall, and became festive events that—like the earlier fur trade jamborees in spring—drew hundreds, if not thousands, of individuals for what could be weeks of social activities. These activities are candidly seen in an eyewitness account of the La Pointe annuity payment for 1847, as given by Julia Spears, a sister of William Warren:

> The Chippewa were arriving every day from all parts of Wisconsin Territory, and the island was very crowded when they all arrived. Their agent was James P. Hayes; he was a good man. My brother, William Warren, was the interpreter. They were both well liked by the Indians. That year the Indians received $10 a head, and each family got a very large bundle of goods . . . They had rations issued out to them during payment . . . The day before they would start for their homes they had a custom of going to all the stores and houses and dancing for about one hour expecting food to be given them. The day before we had cooked a lot of 'Legolet bread,' a lot of boiled salt pork, and cookies to give them. They came dancing and hooting. They were naked, with breechcloths, their bodies painted with black, red, yellow, vermillion, with all kinds of stripes and figures. They were a fierce-looking crowd. They were all good dancers. After they were through they sat down on the grass and

smoked. We gave them food and they were pleased. They thanked us and shook hands with us all as they left.[66]

Julia Spears claims that the 1847 La Pointe payment was made in August so doubtless upon leaving Madeline Island the Ojibwe would soon have traveled to their ricing areas, unless they somehow had managed to complete the harvest before coming to the site. Her description of the dancers' dress and bodily decoration, as well as how after the event they spent time sitting on the grass to smoke, brings to mind similar accounts mentioned in previous pages. One such description of the Ojibwe custom regarding dancing for gifts of food was reported by Thomas McKenney back in 1826, at the Fond du Lac treaty negotiations.[67] Another such account is given by Richard Morse, who witnessed the dance in 1855, at Madeline Island.[68] The fact that this custom was still carried by the people as late as 1855 tells something about what writers like Schoolcraft and Danziger were speaking to regarding the persistence of Ojibwe culture at the middle of the nineteenth century.

William Medill's act of 1847 held a provision calling for the jailing of whiskey peddlers who came into Indian lands, but for more than a decade after the ratification of the Treaty of 1842, there were no more Indian lands in northern Wisconsin Territory. Even though territorial laws prohibited the sale of liquor, the issue of Wisconsin Territory's legal rights emerged and a debate about the legality of federal authorities to prohibit liquor traders from entering Wisconsin Territorial lands occurred. History shows, however, that while this debate went on, liquor seemed always to be available at treaty annuity payment times.[69]

The official rationale for Ojibwe removal was the reputed depredations they made upon white settlers, and since it was felt these incidents were often fueled by excessive alcohol consumption, the call for removal was not unconnected to the question of liquor on the frontier. One of the many voices speaking to this problem was that of William Warren, who argued for the prohibition of liquor in Minnesota Territory, and this stance certainly helped place his voice before a wide regional audience. He played an important role in the events preceding and pursuant to the issuance of the Ojibwe removal order and therefore, before we enter a discussion of the order we need to consider Warren's significance at the close of the 1840s.

## 11.

TODAY WE MIGHT UNDERSTAND William Warren primarily as the author of the classic book on early Ojibwe history, but one writer feels this role as historian is eclipsed by Warren's work as an interpreter for both the Ojibwe and the Americans. While his book enjoyed a welcome reception by the reading public in the late nineteenth century and is invaluable to present day students of Ojibwe history, his efforts as an interpreter were of major importance in the middle years of the century to both the native and non-native populations in western Lake Superior lands. During his adult life, Warren was an *intermediary* between Ojibwe culture and its outside world,[70] and it was in this manner that he performed an important function. At the time in the western Lake Superior area, the presence of the Ojibwe people was a controversial issue to segments of the growing immigrant American population, and of course, conversely, this new population was a concern to the resident Ojibwe. William Warren was important to both these communities.

Warren was not hesitant to present his views, and there must have been a multitude of informal occasions when he did so in the homes of relatives and friends, whether Ojibwe or non-Indian. His literary skills saw him writing many letters to relatives and American authorities in which he spoke to the current events of his day. More publicly, he wrote a series of letters to editors of regional presses, and he authored several newspaper articles signed with the *nom de plume* "O-jib-way." In these instances he spoke directly to Ojibwe matters, and there is no doubt that during the several years of his writing the name William Warren was known throughout western Lake Superior country.

Even though "he did not consider himself an Indian," and although, as has been said, "he lived the life of a white man," and despite the fact that throughout his life he "remained an observer rather than a practitioner" of Indian belief and traditions, we are still told he related well to the Ojibwe people and that they often turned to him for help during the difficult years of these times.[71] It is also noteworthy that the non-Indian population in Minnesota Territory admired him enough to elect him to the Minnesota Territorial Legislature as a representative "from the Sixth District, which then included the Crow Wing and Sauk Rapids precincts."[72] Considering all this, William Warren is a very important figure in Ojibwe history. We might lament that his wife Matilda Aitken-Warren apparently left little or no written accounts of her take on the role of her husband in these matters, but we do have some writings about him from his siblings.

When residing at La Pointe, Warren easily interacted socially with the resident Ojibwe, and Mary Warren English, William's sister, relates how at that time "he was full of life, cheerfulness and sociability, giving bold descriptions, telling heroic incidents, wonderful fairy tales from Arabian Nights, Robinson Crusoe, &c. to crowds of eager listeners, Indians of all classes, both old and young, and they in return would relate the oft told stories and traditions of the tribe."[73] Perhaps we have no difficulty imagining Warren in these years, moving freely between the Ojibwe and white communities and eagerly bringing examples of Euro-American literature to the "unlettered" Ojibwe.

By this time there was a growing belief on the part of some Americans that the oral traditions of the Indian be recorded in writing before they fell out of use and were gone. It was this sentiment that was behind the agreement of Congress in March 1847 to have the Indian Department undertake an ethnological survey of the tribes, and it was not long before William Warren was involved in this work. At this time he was struggling to meet the expenses of supporting his family, and during 1848 and into the following year, he labored to seriously record information gleaned from interviews with Ojibwe informants, information that eventually was included in this survey. This soon led Warren to begin working on a manuscript that would evolve into his history of the Ojibwe.

After his father's death, William assumed responsibility for raising his younger siblings, a task which brought financial hardship. His interpreter appointments for La Pointe Subagents Brunson and Hayes provided income but after being dismissed by the latter agent he faced a financial struggle that plagued him the rest of his life. It was during these years he began to think that his writing might provide a source of income, and by the late 1840s, he was spending much time with this pursuit.

Henry Rice understood the value of someone with Warren's language abilities and in 1847, offered him a position at his trading establishment at Crow Wing in western Minnesota Territory. But even with income from this employment the Warrens still struggled financially, so soon after settling in at Crow Wing, they rented rooms in their home to Rice's other employees as well as to travelers. Through this manner the family's monetary difficulties began to lessen. At Crow Wing the Ojibwe community asked Warren to do periodic interpreting work, and by 1849, as a mixed-blood, he was also involved in Indian lumbering activity in western Minnesota Territory. Thus, by the end of the decade of the 1840s, we see that William Warren was receiving income from a few different sources. It seems he was walking a line between working for the Ojibwe people while at the same time working for Henry Rice, and just as importantly, for himself.[74]

In July 1849, Warren was appointed to the position of government farmer at Sandy Lake. Before he could move his family, it was decided to establish a new farm site at Gull Lake, a location just on the west side of the Mississippi River where the government hoped to relocate most of the Ojibwe bands. Upon receiving this appointment Warren left the employ of Henry Rice and during the winter of 1849-1850, while at Gull Lake he focused on his growing manuscript of Ojibwe historical material.[75]

By this time Warren had spoken out against liquor on the frontier and those traders who continued to bring it to the Ojibwe, the result being that the major trading firms were viewing him with concern. At that time he was upset over his father's recent death—a death he was certain was caused by several years of harsh treatment from the American Fur Company. Also, traders were particularly upset that Warren spoke against them during the treaty negotiations at Fond du Lac in 1847. As a result, by 1849, in a private letter to his cousin George, Warren said that traders Dr. Charles Borup and Clement Beaulieu were his enemies and that "they will pursue me to my grave with their enmity."[76]

Borup was, among other business activities, the longtime representative for the American Fur Company at La Pointe who, in 1848, joined Henry Rice in his western Minnesota Territory business ventures. Clement Beaulieu, an influential mixed-blood, was a brother-in-law of La Pointe's early powerful trader, Charles H. Oakes. Clearly, it was no little matter for the still-young William Warren to offend these major economic and political figures.

However, by early 1850, Warren seems to have been emerging as a power in his own right when in a letter written in March he told his cousin George:

> I have gained many strong friends and popularity among the whites and the Indians . . . . Borup & Oakes & Beaulieu have been unable to hurt me, and they have thought me and found me of sufficient consequence to try and make a friend of me . . . . Of course they have an object in view, but rest assured that they nor other men will be able to throw dust in my eyes. I will not be a tool, and on the contrary they must be wide awake or I will make a tool of them.[77]

In western Lake Superior country the close of the 1840s was a time of opportunity for business ventures and William Warren was fully aware of what was occurring. He knew what businessmen like Henry Rice, Charles Borup, Charles Oakes and others were doing but it seems he held a degree of business acumen himself. In a revealing letter to his cousin George dated 27 March 1850, he said:

> The present prospects in this country are at present flattering for us, in two lines of business. 1st There is a company who have built a mill at Little Falls on this river. They depend altogether on the pine in the Chippeway country for a supply, for two years past this mill and the Mill at Falls of St. Anthony have paid large sums for privilege of cutting logs. This spring on acct of certain difficulties on Sioux lands an order has been sent on to the Agts of Govt to stop all Whites fromcutting or buying timber on Indian lands and a law passed denying a chief or set of chiefs the right of sale of standing timber to Whites.
>
> This has knocked the mills here in the head who will be obliged to wait for a Treaty in order to commence operations, which certainly will not be made for two or three years.
>
> Now all this operates to our benefit. By the Treaty of Fond du Lac Half Breeds are allowed the same right & privileges to the soil and annuities as Indians, and no law can prevent us from cutting our own logs and selling them to Whites. We can monopolise the business and make money like dirt. The bands that live on the Pine lands I hold in my hand.[78]

In the Upper Mississippi region in the late 1840s, William Warren was as interested in turning a dollar as many others—perhaps to include tribesmen, mixed-bloods, and nonnatives—but we know little about his actual activities in early lumbering operations in these years. Recalling that his father, Lyman, was involved in the industry on Wisconsin Territory's Chippewa River a few years earlier, we know the lumbering industry was not unfamiliar to him, and given William's understanding of the origin and supposed destiny of the Ojibwe people as written in his classic book, we might understand that in those times he viewed the clearing of the forest as part of the natural evolution of human events and, hence, an acceptable source of ready income.

The lumbering industry was part of the complex of changes coming to the Upper Midwest, and like others, Warren felt that unless something was done, the increasing numbers of Euro-Americans and the scourge of alcohol that came with them would quickly destroy native peoples. Thus, he felt Ojibwe removal was inevitable, and the quicker the better. To this end he wanted the different bands to journey to the western lands in the summer of 1850, to look them over before committing to a move. However, in a letter written that spring to his cousin George, he said the lands they were being asked to move to would not fit their needs and, "I apprehend difficulty unless a first Rate Treaty is made with them, a perpetual annuity &c The Govt will not do this unless they are forced to it by resistance &c on the part of the Indians. Rest assured that I am not sleeping but at work to carry the measure through."[79]

Today, we might agree that in 1850, the chance of the United States government agreeing to a perpetual annuity for Ojibwe people would have been infinitesimal, if not unthinkable, and we should wonder about Warren's reasoning when uttering this remark. Surely he and his family would have been among the recipients of such an unending annuity, and perhaps this was behind his assurance to his cousin that he was already at work to ensure the people presented a strong front against removal so that when the inevitable came they would receive just compensation.

Whatever Warren's reasoning, we see that by 1850, William Warren was contemplating his role in the anticipated Ojibwe resistance to the government's attempt to force a removal.

*Notes*

1. Cleland in McClurken *et al* 2000:54-5.
2. Cleland in McClurken *et al* 2000:55-6.
3. White in McClurken *et al* 2000:144.
4. Cleland in McClurken *et al* 2000:60-1.
5. It is sometimes said that northern Wisconsin land sales began almost immediately after the Treaty of 1854 was ratified, because, it is mistakenly thought, this was when these lands were surveyed and opened for public purchase, but except for the six sites specifically designated for Ojibwe reservations, the 1854 treaty spoke only to lands in the "Preserve" in northeastern Minnesota Territory, not those south of Lake Superior.
6. Ross 1960:108.
7. Cleland in McClurken *et al* 2000:54-60; White in McClurken *et al* 2000:152-3.
8. Currant 1976:3.
9. Ross 1960:111-2, 115.
10. Cleland in McClurken *et al* 2000:45-50.
11. Brunson 1843 in WisTerPap, Vol.28, p. 496.
12. Wheeler report of 14 September 1847 in ARCIASI; Livermore reports of 1848 and 1849 in ARCIASI; Hall report of 9 October 1849 in ARCIASI.
13. Ross 1960:106.
14. Brunson 1843 in WisTerPap, Vol. 28, pp. 496-7.
15. Higham 2000:2.
16. Ducatel 1977[1846]:161-172.
17. Woolworth 1977:161.
18. Ducatel 1977[1846]:163-4.
19. Warren, Truman 1847 in WisTerPap, Vol. 28, p. 1108.
20. Mooers 1847 in WisTerPap, Vol. 28, p. 1106.
21. Hall 1847 in WisTerPap, Vol. 28, p. 1109.
22. Wheeler 1847 in WisTerPap, Vol. 28, pp. 1111-1112.
23. Schenck 2007:39.
24. Kvasnicka and Viola 1979:32; Christian 2004.
25. Skolla 1936:232-34.
26. Ross 1960:111.
27. Ross 1960:112, 114; Antell 1973:36; Schenck 2007:27, 30.
28. Ross 1960:113.
29. Prucha 1986:31-49.
30. Cochrane 2009:142.
31. Brunson 1879:201.
32. Hall letter of 30 March 1847 at MHS: St. Paul.
33. Trennert 1979:29-30.
34. Satz 1979: 25, 45-9.
35. Danziger 1979:95.
36. Treuer 2011:74-81. These resurgent military conflicts with the Dakota largely occurred in the region of the Mississippi River, not in the more eastern areas of the Ojibwe in Chequamegon Bay and the central Wisconsin communities. Likewise for the north shore of Lake Superior, where Dakota attacks had ended by 1800. See Timothy Cochrane's discussion in *Minong—The Good Place (Ojibwe and Isle Royale)*, p. 115.
37. Allen 1993[1958]:163-231; Schoolcraft 1993[1958]:51.
38. Brunson 1843 in WisTerPap, Vol. 28 p. 468.
39. Danziger 1979:39, brackets added.
40. Smith 1973:95-6.
41. Harris 1976:62.
42. Harris 1976:62.
43. Danziger 1979:89.
44. Schoolcraft 1993[1958]:51.
45. Schoolcraft 1993[1958]:51, brackets added.
46. Danziger 1979:89.
47. See the Allan journal in Schoolcraft 1993[1958]:184.
48. Wheeler as quoted in Danziger 1979:85.
49. For a discussion of the proposed move of the Menominee people to western Minnesota Territory see Beck 2002:174-178.
50. Cleland in McClurken *et al* 2000:51.
51. White in McClurken *et al* 2000:157; McClurken in McClurken *et al* 2000: 394-5, 409; Paap 2006; Folwell 1956:313-318.
52. Schenck 2007:30-1.
53. Schenck 2007:30-1.
54. White in McClurken et al 2000:157.
55. Bayfield Press, 28 June 1956.
56. Cleland in McClurken *et al* 2000:51-3; Schenck 2007:37-8; Treuer 2011:87-91.
57. Schenck 2007:38,26.
58. Schenck 2007:ix.
59. Medill 1846 in WisTerPap, Vol. 28, pp. 1015-6.
60. Cleland in McClurken *et al* 2000:64; Clifton 1987:15.
61. Satz 1991:47.
62. Diedrich 1999:17-8.
63. Trennert 1979:32;Christian 2004.
64. Densmore 1929:138-9.
65. Schenck 2007:39-40.
66. Spears as quoted in Densmore 1929:140.
67. McKenney 1959[1827]:284-289.
68. Morse 1904[1857]:351.
69. Doty 1844 in WisTerPap, Vol. 28, p. 649; Ducatel 1977[1846]:170; White in McClurken *et al* 2000:161.
70. Schenck 2007:xi.
71. Schenck 2007:vii-xi, 26.
72. Schenck 2007:98.
73. English as told in Schenck 2007:30.
74. Schenck 2007:46-9.
75. Schenck 2007:51.
76. Warren 1849 as quoted in Schenck 2007:53.
77. Warren 1850 as quoted in Schenck 2007:64.
78. Warren 1850 as quoted in Schenck 2007:61.
79. Warren 1850 as quoted in Schenck 2007:62-5.

# 18

# Ojibwe Removal

### *The 1850 Ojibwe Removal Order*

1.

THE STORY OF THE ATTEMPTED REMOVAL of the Ojibwe from Wisconsin and Upper Michigan has become part of the popular history of the Chequamegon Bay region.[1] There is considerable literature on the removal attempt, but it was not until nearly 150 years after the event that it received an in-depth study. This unsuccessful attempt to move the westernmost northern Michigan and Wisconsin Ojibwe to Minnesota Territory remains one of the most important chapters in the history of not just the La Pointe Ojibwe but for all the Ojibwe people, since it shows how a large portion of this tribe overcame extreme adversity and was successful in maintaining its cultural identity. In the following sections we will outline the major events and issues of Ojibwe removal and offer a discussion of them.

2.

IN 1849, A NEW WHIG ADMINISTRATION took control in Washington, D. C., as Zachary Taylor became president. Soon after Taylor was sworn in, the Office of Indian Affairs was moved from the War Department to the newly formed Department of the Interior. Thomas Ewing, a distant relative to the powerful Indiana Ewings of the Indian trade, became Secretary of Interior, and Orlando Brown assumed the position of Commissioner of the Bureau of Indian Affairs. These were political patronage appointments that brought persons into office with little or no experience in Indian matters.[2] Thomas Ewing was "an aggressive advocate of the spoils system and set out to control the immense patronage his position afforded." He disliked Orlando Brown and within only one year, Luke Lea was appointed to replace him. Soon after assuming office the new Taylor administration was approached by numerous lobbyists, one of them being Henry Mower Rice.[3]

Henry Rice was born in Vermont, studied law for a brief time, and at age eighteen came to the western Great Lakes. In Michigan, he found employment with the survey work for the canal at Sault Ste. Marie, and later in the mercantile area at Kalamazoo. Like many other business-oriented persons of his day he decided to enter the lucrative "Indian trade," finding employment at St. Louis before moving on to other locations. In 1839, he was in St. Paul where he worked to find a way to supply upper Mississippi River posts from the south, instead of through the earlier northern route from Detroit and Lake Superior. He devised a way of using horse-drawn boats to get through St. Anthony Falls, a feat connected to the skills used in Rice's earlier days when employed at Sault Ste. Marie. The St. Anthony Falls accomplishment brought a considerable financial opportunity to the business community of St. Paul and allowed Rice to successfully compete with trading companies using the older northern route.[4]

Rice also worked as the sutler at Fort Snelling in St. Peters, in Minnesota Territory, and later at Ft. Atkinson in Iowa, where he was employed by Hercules L. Dousman and Henry H. Sibley—two names that would soon be prominent in regional politics—to oversee their trading operations with the Ho-Chunk Indians.

The exact nature of Henry Rice's involvement with the Ho-Chunk people remains unclear but it seems certain that his connection with them became more than simply a matter of a formal business relationship. A recent writer remarks that by 1846, when working as a trader at Prairie du Chien, Rice had "established kinship ties with the Winnebago."[5] Whether he was formally or informally adopted into the community, and in that way became "kin," or if he established a familial relationship through marriage or cohabitation is unclear, but another writer intimates that Henry Rice's relations with the Ho-Chunk were based on more than friendship and the economics of trade.[6] We know that in the days of the eighteenth and nineteenth centuries it was customary for both tribal leaders and Euro-American traders to welcome familial relationships established by various forms of marriage for sexual, political and economic reasons.[7] Other prominent traders and missionaries of the times entered marital relationships with tribal partners—Henry Schoolcraft, Alexander Ramsey, William Boutwell, and several of the Chouteau men for example, so we should expect that Henry Rice may have done likewise.

In 1846, under much pressure, the Ho-Chunk agreed to remove to Minnesota Territory, and Henry Rice was eager to help bring this move about. In the fall of that year he was in Washington, D.C., pressuring officials to appoint treaty commissioners to negotiate with the Ojibwe to purchase parcels of their western land for the Ho-Chunks' and Menominees' new home sites. At the time Rice was involved in land speculation and related activities throughout the entire western Lake Superior and upper Mississippi regions and he lobbied Commissioner Medill for the job to select the new Ho-Chunk and Menominee sites, but first the matter of which Ojibwe bands held ownership of these western parcels needed to be clarified. For this reason Medill postponed the Ho-Chunk move until the spring of 1847.[8]

In 1846, there was still concern about Ojibwe and Dakota conflict, so Rice argued for a piece of Ojibwe land in west-central Minnesota Territory that would position the Ho-Chunk and Menominee as buffers between these two tribes. Henry Rice was an aggressive businessman and politician who quickly rose to a position of some prominence in the 1840s, and he is said to have "had the reputation for canny dealings with traders, whether while he himself was trading, or in his government diplomacy."[9] In the late 1840s, the matter of Ho-Chunk, Menominee and Ojibwe removals offered the potential for considerable financial gain for businessmen like Rice, and consequently, he was very busy in the few years leading up to Zachary Taylor's Removal Order.

Rice eventually received the government contract to move the Ho-Chunk to Minnesota Territory, at a fee of seventy-five dollars for each tribesman removed, but interestingly, he asked Washington authorities to keep this contract secret during the time it was in effect. Later critics, however, felt seventy-five dollars a head was an exorbitant amount of money that allowed Henry Rice to see profits in excess of $100,000.00—a huge amount of money for the time. Consequently, on 6 May 1849, the House of Representatives passed a resolution to investigate this. On 17 September 1849, after the completed report was submitted, Rice escaped censoring and the matter was closed.[10]

In 1847, in the midst of the times of the Ho-Chunks' move, Rice joined Henry Sibley and others who were working with the Pierre Chouteau, Jr. Company in its trading operations on the Missouri River and in the Upper Mississippi region, and for a time he was overseeing trading posts in northern Minnesota Territory and at La Pointe. This put him in a good position for considerable financial gain when the Ho-Chunk people finally moved to western Minnesota, and he attempted to receive even more money with the anticipated removal of the Ojibwe.[11]

However, in October of 1849, Rice left the Chouteau Company and was replaced by Dr. Charles Borup, who earlier was involved in the Indian trade at La Pointe. The termination of Rice's relationship with the Chouteau firm was an acrimonious one that included threats of lawsuits. Interestingly, immediately upon his severance, he was working with a long-term Chouteau rival, the powerful Ewing family of traders. With the Ewings, Rice was put in charge of the Dakota and Ojibwe trade. At St. Paul in the fall of the same year, he had meetings with Henry Sibley and new Territorial Governor Ramsey in which matters of Ojibwe removal were surely discussed. At this time it seems Henry Rice was establishing a genuine friendship with Alexander Ramsey while his relationship with Henry Sibley was taking a turn for the worse. Soon after these St. Paul meetings Rice went to Washington, D.C., where he spent part of the winter lobbying Secretary Ewing and Commissioner Brown for the Ojibwes' removal. He was hopeful of receiving the government contract for organizing and implementing this removal and it seems Henry Sibley, who was a Minnesota Territorial delegate to Congress at the time, had the same goal.[12]

In the latter months of 1849, rumors of removal were rampant in the Lake Superior Ojibwe community and were having a negative effect at La Pointe. While Henry Rice was busy in Washington, Leonard and Harriet Wheeler were writing to relatives back in Vermont about the unsettled times they were experiencing. The Ojibwe people were showing little interest in the Wheelers's religion and Leonard was beginning to question the success of his missionary efforts. By the fall of 1849, the Ojibwe were still moving through their lands from season to season and Wheeler was troubled by their long absences from the mission station at Bad River. In moments of doubt he pondered whether instead of working with the Ojibwe, he should minister to the nearby growing white mining community at Ontonagon, Michigan, where amidst his own people he might have more success. In a 10 November 1849, letter to his father back in Vermont, in which he complained of the situation he said:

> The Indians are mostly absent from Bad River now making their fall fishing . . . [but they will] probably return home, when [they] return to their sugar camps the first of March . . . Should the condition of the Indians be such that we should not be justified in continuing our labors in that direction, there are promising fields of labor among our own people. We do not feel however as yet discouraged, in regard to the Indian department of our work. We believe the Mission exerts an important influence upon all classes. Though we do not yet see many of the pagan Indians converted we are yet living in hope that the seed sown will spring up and bear fruit. But we cannot tell what a day will bring forth. Everything here seems to be in an unsettled state; we know not what to expect, in the line of changes. This unsettled state of things was quite a trial to me when I first came to this country; but I have now become quite reconciled to it. It is peculiar to the whole western country.[13]

In December of 1849, Henry Rice was in Richmond, Virginia, where he wrote a confidential letter to Governor Ramsey disclosing his current thoughts about Ojibwe removal. Historian Bruce White feels this letter "is remarkable in revealing the naked calculation in Rice's political activity at the time, though it may very well be typical of many early Minnesota politicians and businessmen."[14] In this letter Rice speaks of his fears that a proposed new Dakota treaty for a land cession on the west side of the Mississippi could potentially cause new settlers and the business opportunities they would bring to bypass the area on the east side of the river, where his, and Alexander Ramsey's, major business interests were located. Therefore, Rice felt efforts needed to be made to delay the new Dakota treaty until after the east side of the river was settled.[15]

This letter is of particular interest for our purposes since it goes on to speak directly of the Ojibwe communities at La Pointe. Rice told Ramsey that the Ojibwe of Lake Superior should be removed from the lands ceded in the Treaty of 1842, because with their removal, "Minnesota would reap the benefit whereas now their annuities pass via Detroit and not one dollar do our inhabitants get altho' we are subject to all the annoyance given by those Indians."[16] Charles Cleland feels this letter shows "[Henry Rice's] interest was not with the fate of the Chippewa but with the white merchants of Minnesota."[17] Also, we might ponder "all the annoyance given by those Indians" Rice complained of. Apparently, by 1849, Ojibwe Indians were deemed to be troublesome and had become an "annoyance" to Henry Rice.

3.

SOME MONTHS BEFORE THESE MACHINATIONS were going on by the business and political leaders of Minnesota Territory, the La Pointe and other western Ojibwe leaders were busy as well. In 1848, they were discussing action to be taken regarding the rumors circulating about their imminent removal and in late fall of that year a group of leaders from sixteen bands, along with Benjamin Armstrong, departed for Washington, D.C., where in early 1849, they spoke before Congress, "visited President Polk, his Secretary of War William L. Marcy, and Commissioner of Indian Affairs William Medill." The delegation's intent was to put an end to the rumors about removal.[18]

This long trip, with its resultant meetings, was felt by Henry Schoolcraft to have been nothing more than "a party organized by [Armstrong] to exhibit Native individuals in the metropolis for profit,"[19] but while the chance to turn a dollar may have been one of Armstrong's reasons for the trip, it nevertheless is still an important event in the history of the Ojibwe people and doubtlessly affected its members. All the Ojibwe men who made this journey were political leaders and what they experienced and learned on the trip surely influenced their future decisions regarding the Americans' demand for removal.

Unfortunately, except for the writing of historian Ronald Satz, there has been little discussion of the trip in the literature, and some that is offered is confusing and inaccurate. For example, Mark Dietrich says the delegation went to speak with President Taylor, but it was really President Polk. Charles Cleland says the purpose of the trip was to ask that "24 reservations" be established on ceded lands for the Ojibwe bands, when it was twenty-four sections of land in the seven village locations of the bands extant at the time. These sections were to compose the *seven reservations* the Ojibwe hoped for. Cleland also erroneously indicated the trip occurred in 1846, instead of 1849,[20] and in his memoir, Benjamin Armstrong says nothing at all about it, although he offers considerable commentary on the trip of 1852.[21] By late 1848, removal rumors were prevalent in Ojibwe communities and certainly must have been given much discussion, although as usual, we have little or no record of it. Surely this delegation was the result of these conversations in the months just previous to the fall of 1848, when the trip was undertaken.

The fact that this large delegation departed from Lake Superior country when the coming of winter was imminent indicates the urgency with which the trip was taken. We remain uncertain about just what route the group took to get to Washington, but a Detroit newspaper claims it went through St. Louis, Missouri, on the way. The newspaper says:

> It took six weeks to make the trip from La Pointe, Lake Superior, to St Louis. They embarked in canoes and traversed the great inland sea to San Marie. They then disembarked, packed their canoes, war and hunting implements, entire wardrobe and provisions, on their backs, across country several hundred miles, to the head waters of the St. Croix, where they again embarked in their canoes, and glided smoothly down that stream to the great Father of Waters.[22]

This account fails to explain why the delegation first paddled to Sault Ste. Marie from La Pointe in November, only to disembark and carry its gear back west to the headwaters of the St. Croix River, where it embarked for the Mississippi. We are left to conclude that the tardiness of the original departure must have caused the party to be confronted with frozen waterways or other unforeseen problems. All this points to the extreme stress due to removal threats the Ojibwe people were under at the time, and their determination to remedy the situation by going to Washington to confront the president himself.

In Washington the group's leaders presented a petition to Congress stating: "Our people desire a donation of twenty-four sections of land, covering the graves of our fathers, our sugar orchards, and our rice lakes and rivers, at seven different places now occupied by us as villages."[23] Along with asking for sacred sites, this request points to the continuing importance of maple sugar, wild rice, fish and other traditional food sources to the Ojibwe bands, and shows that they felt threatened by the Americans and desired to safeguard their economic resources from the growing encroachment of these newcomers. Their request does not say they intended to take up agriculture, but quite interestingly, the Detroit newspaper's account of the delegation's journey claims: "They desire to permanently settle, build houses, cultivate the soil, and become settled, industrious citizens of the United States, instead of roaming hunters of the forest."[24] We can only wonder if the journalist who wrote this copy was responding to the delegation's purpose with his (or her) own notions of the culture of the Ojibwe people at the time and their supposed eagerness to give that up in favor of a more "civilized" and agricultural way of life. If this is correct, we can see herein another example of the inability of Americans to understand and accept the legitimacy of a foraging lifestyle, such as many western Lake Superior Ojibwe people still had and intended to carry on in some way in 1848.

Unfortunately, the delegation's timing was poor since it was in Washington only weeks before a new administration was to take office, so the meetings brought no immediate action. The contacts with congressional representatives however, went well, and may have had a positive effect that carried over into subsequent times.[25] In this regard the *Green Bay Gazette* had this to say about the journey:

> The Chippewa Delegation, who have been on a visit to see their "great fathers" in Washington, passed through this place on Saturday last, on their way to their homes near Lake Superior. From the accounts of the newspapers, they have been lionized during their whole journey, and particularly in Washington, where many presents were made them, among

> the most substantial of which was six boxes of silver, ($6,000) to pay their expenses. They were loaded with presents, and we noticed one with a modern style trunk strapped to his back. They all looked well and in good spirits.[26]

The late 1840s were difficult years for these Ojibwe bands. As discussed above, major land sales, the demise of the fur trade, the devastations of smallpox epidemics, recurring problems with liquor, and an unrelenting pressure to adopt the new American culture and its religion all were seriously challenging the people. As if these problems were not enough, rumors of removal certainly exacerbated them. It must have been evident that major steps had to be taken if removal to distant western lands was to be avoided. Something had to be done, and the 1848-1849 Washington trip shows that the people were working to resolve their dilemma. To this purpose we see the importance of the request of the Canadian, Shingwaukonse, that the western American bands come east and join him at the Garden River site. Such a move would have been drastic and we do not know how the majority of the American Ojibwe people actually felt about it, but the severity of removal pressures from the Americans surely meant that Shingwaukonse's request was a point of ongoing discussion. An example of the interest western Ojibwe band leaders had in maintaining their ties with the Canadian chief and his British allies is seen in the forty canoes that set out from western Lake Superior for Manitoulin Island in the fall of 1849, to be on hand when a new treaty between the Crown and the Canadian Ojibwe was to be negotiated.[27]

It is possible the Ojibwe may have been contemplating another strategy that, if successful, could have allowed them to stay in their Michigan and Wisconsin homelands. To this end it has been suggested the Lake Superior bands planned to use the sale of their interests in the *preserve*, the large tract of unceded land located along the western shore of the lake, as a "bargaining token" to gain the Americans' acquiescence to their request for reservations, and in that way end the threat of removal. As early as 1846, it was rumored that the La Pointe bands might be interested in selling this parcel.[28] It was known the preserve held minerals and that the Americans wanted them, a desire made obvious by General Verplanck's offer to purchase the land in 1847. Thus, the south shore and adjacent bands may have been contemplating the "trade" of their interest in the preserve for the right to remain on the Michigan and Wisconsin ceded lands.[29]

The members of the 1849 delegation had much to think about. They had the responsibility to make decisions that obviously could have great and lasting effects on their people, and as always, political matters were not isolated from religious protocol. Therefore, we should expect that the delegation carried out the typical ceremonial obligations demanded for their long trip. Gifts to the *manidoog* must have been proffered as these spirits were consulted for guidance in carrying out this long journey, so we should conclude that at the time, Ojibwe spiritual and political protocol was functioning as it had been for centuries whenever important contacts with allies were made. This trip shows that in 1848 and early 1849, underlying institutions of Ojibwe culture were still operative, and more important, even though they were under attack by missionaries and government officials, through these ceremonies the peoples' identities as Ojibwe were being fortified.

In response to increasing rumors of removal and of persons telling them that in the 1842 treaty they had signed away *all* their lands in Wisconsin Territory (and Upper Michigan), this delegation asked that land in this region be set aside for the villages of the several Ojibwe bands that resided there.[30] This request was not new since seven years earlier it had been made to Commissioner Stuart, during the 1842 La Pointe treaty negotiations.[31]

Another important aspect of this Washington, D.C., trip was the effect it must have had on the persons who made it. Perhaps surprisingly, La Pointe's Buffalo was a member of this delegation, even though he could have been eighty-nine years old at the time. When on this journey, he and his companions must have been given pause to consider the nature of the society they were witnessing and what such a powerful neighbor foretold for their future. Another member of this trip was Kenisteno, a leader from the Ojibwe band at Trout Lake, near Lac du Flambeau, Wisconsin, and a person who was very concerned about the removal threat. Images of the 1849 trip may still have been with Kenisteno when, after receiving the 1850 circular from Sub-agent John Livermore about the pending removal, he responded by appealing to the Canadian Ojibwe for assistance.[32]

Even though no apparent resolution to their problem was achieved by making the 1849 trip, its overall effect on the Ojibwe leaders must have been considerable. Other than the immediate political and economic matters of removal, Ojibwe leaders were given pause to consider how different the Americans' culture was from theirs. For example, Mark Diedrich claims that the delegation passed through Pittsburgh, Pennsylvania, and later when asked for his impression of the industrial city, La Pointe's Chief Buffalo reportedly remarked of his displeasure by expressing distaste with its heavy emissions of factory smoke.[33]

## 4.

In 1849, when Alexander Ramsey became the first governor for Minnesota Territory, he was immediately faced with a problem that demanded most of his attention for some time. It involved the Ho-Chunk and their displeasure with their new western home. Never happy with their need to move, many soon left western Minnesota Territory, intending to make their way back to the regions of their former Wisconsin and Iowa homes. This Ho-Chunk exodus meant their federal annuities and the income from trade they brought to Minnesota Territory was threatened. In the fall of 1849, this problem was a pressing preoccupation for the new governor.[34]

What historian Bruce White suggests is that at the same time Ramsey was struggling with this Ho-Chunk matter, he, Rice and Henry Sibley were discussing what needed to be done to move the Ojibwe. If a removal was accomplished those residing on ceded lands in Michigan and Wisconsin would be moved to Minnesota Territory, and their annuity payments would come with them. Interestingly, among others, one thing that came out of these Ramsey, Rice and Sibley meetings was that on 9 January 1850, Ramsey and Sibley chose an official seal for Minnesota Territory showing a farmer plowing the virgin soil while in the background an Indian on horseback is seen riding off to the west.[35] This symbolism of an American farming community replacing the earlier Native American tribal communities was well-known at the time.

Annuity payments were at the center of the Indian trade, and their regular occurrence was very important to regional economies. As we have already noted, the financial inflow from Ojibwe removal would affect the many business interests of individuals like Ramsey, Rice, Sibley, and others who were pushing for removal.[36]

5.

AS THE MONTHS OF 1849 PASSED, there was heightened public talk in the new Minnesota Territory of the need for Indian removal. White settlers were coming to the southeastern portion of the region, the same place where bands of Potawatomi, Sac and Fox, Ho-Chunk, Kickapoo and other Indians foraged for sustenance. Conflict between whites and these people occurred and calls of concern were heard.[37] Certainly with an eye toward eventual statehood, some of these voices anticipated a future in which the region would be completely "settled" and Indians would be a thing of the past, or at most, located somewhere out of sight, perhaps far to the west. To these voices, Indian removal was less a matter of *if* and more a matter of *when*. However, in 1849, Indians were a major part of life along the upper Mississippi River and for a time at least, for many whites their presence was deemed fortunate because of the financial gains it brought through the Indian trade. In fact, in the late 1840s, the immediate success of economic growth in regions like St. Paul was linked to this financial relationship between Indians and whites.[38]

This importance of Indian annuity payments—and the federal expenditures for maintaining military posts in Indian Country—is seen in an 1849 article in the *Green Bay (Wisconsin) Gazette* that reviewed a report on a recent geological survey of Minnesota Territory. Written in a booster style meant to encourage immigration to the region it tells of the ready opportunity for agriculture in the new area due to its rich soils. This is followed by the claim that:

> . . . nearly half a million dollars were paid out annually to the Indian tribes and for the support of the military establishment above the Falls of St. Anthony—this amount is paid in specie by the agents of the Government, and a large portion finds its way into the pockets of the farmer and mechanics in exchange for their produce and labor.[39]

Once again we are reminded that at the middle of the nineteenth century in the western Lake Superior regions, the Native American community was an important part of the overall regional culture and, of course, its economy, something Alexander Ramsey, John Watrous and others were well aware of.

There was also the matter of those Indians and whites who were joined through marriage and blood. As we have seen, by 1849, for perhaps over a century-and-a-half mating and marriage had gone on between the peoples, leaving individuals and families who were part of both Indian and white communities. Importantly, this blending was found in all levels of the region's native and non-native society.[40] The presence of these mixed family lines running throughout Michigan, Wisconsin and Minnesota Territory added an interesting degree of social complexity to the region that surely was not lost on leaders in both tribal and non-tribal worlds.

6.

THIS WAS THE CONTEXT IN THE FALL of 1849, when Governor Ramsey began drafting a proposal for Ojibwe removal. He was not raising a new issue since the sentiment for removal had been widespread for some time. This stemmed from the unquestioned belief that Indians were destined to give way to whites, but in Minnesota Territory by the fall of 1849, it more explicitly came from claims of alleged Ojibwe depredations upon whites and their property. Although the media carried news of these claims, most appear to have been fraudulent. Furthermore, the written record shows that in 1849, Governor Ramsey was busy with Ho-Chunk, not Ojibwe problems. Claims of Ho-Chunk harassments were made but it appears such allegations may have had more to do with white fears of Indians moving through the territory, and ultimately with the possible loss of annuity payments and trade revenues, than with actual depredations.

Historian Bruce White suggests that Ramsey and people like Rice and Sibley knew that to carry out an Ojibwe removal they would need to make the case for Ojibwe depredations, since under the treaty of 1837, the condition laid down for the Ojibwe to remain on ceded lands was that they not molest the region's white residents. What Alexander Ramsey did was to link the fears of Ho-Chunk depredations with the Ojibwe, and to make this reputed connection the basis for his appeal to the Territorial Legislature on 4 September. This subterfuge is strongly suggested by the record of Ramsey's activities in the latter months of 1848, the first few months he was in office. As Bruce White writes, Ramsey publicly spoke of the need to keep Minnesota Territory a safe region, but his "actions suggest that the safety of the small numbers of whites living in the ceded territory was of less importance than the economic development of Minnesota."[41]

In the months leading up to September 1849, there were complaints of Indian depredations but these were not coming from the lands ceded under the 1837 treaty, nor were they about the Ojibwe. Specifically, Ramsey's petition to the assembly referred only to complaints by settlers in the Sauk Rapids and Swan River areas, both regions in western Minnesota Territory, but that were not included in ceded lands under the 1837 treaty. It seems very likely that the depredations in the several months leading up to September 1849 which Ramsey referred to stemmed from the Ho-Chunk, not the Ojibwe. In the summer of 1849, Governor Ramsey was kept well-informed of complaints against Indians—and doubtless, as indicated above, he was very busy with such matters—so it is apparent "he knew that the so-called Indian problems were not with the Chippewa of the 1837 cession."[42]

Nevertheless, on 4 September 1849, Alexander Ramsey petitioned the legislative assembly of the Territory of Minnesota to ask the president to revoke the Ojibwe hunting and fishing rights under the Treaty of 1837, and to remove the tribesmen from ceded lands. Revocation of their resource harvesting rights would have left the Ojibwe without their means of earning a livelihood, and thus, Ramsey concluded they would have had to move onto the preserve in northern Minnesota Territory. This point is noteworthy because, as we have been arguing, it shows that as late as 1849, the Ojibwe communities in western Lake Superior were still essentially carrying out a foraging adaptation, and Governor Ramsey, with his political colleagues, knew this. In fact, in the times, everyone in the region knew it. The legislature responded to Ramsey's petition by drafting the resolution, but the legislators included the lands ceded under the treaty of 1842, as well.

The reason why the Minnesota Territorial Assembly altered the Ramsey petition can only have been to include the Michigan and Lake Superior Ojibwe bands in the removal, since none of these bands lived in Minnesota nor were residing on lands ceded under the 1837 treaty.[43] This inclusion meant that if the president approved the resolution, the Ojibwe in Wisconsin's interior as well as the northern bands living along Lake Superior's south shore, to include those in western Michigan, would have to move. What remains striking about this resolution is that a territorial governor was not asking that Indians be removed *from* his territory's boundaries, but *into* its boundaries. Surely, in the United States of 1849, when a national sentiment for the westward removal of Indian communities was generally a *given*, this was an unusual request.

Unusual or not, the resolution was taken to Washington, D.C., where it was passed by Congress and sent on to the White House. As a result, on 6 February, President Zachary Taylor signed the resolution and issued the Ojibwe Removal Order of 1850.[44]

## *Governmental Attempts to Implement the Removal Order: Ojibwe Resistance and The Sandy Lake Tragedy*

### 1.

AN EXCHANGE OF COMMUNIQUÉS FOLLOWED the issuance of Taylor's order, and it is necessary to work through them in order to understand this important time in Ojibwe history. Just as important is how the order and the machinations that created it speak to the reality of Ojibwe cultural persistence as late as the middle of the nineteenth century. President Taylor's order, of course, was issued from the White House, but it was really originated by Governor Ramsey and his territory's legislative assembly. Ostensibly, it was intended to cancel the Ojibwes' right to hunt, fish and gather on ceded lands. Ramsey and the rest of the officials knew that such a cancellation would force the Ojibwe to move to their unceded lands in Minnesota Territory. These United States governmental officials and bodies—a territorial governor, a territorial legislative assembly, the United States Congress and the executive—all knew that at the time, the Ojibwe subsisted primarily by hunting, fishing, gardening and gathering. This clearly indicates that the Ojibwe cultural foraging system was still essentially what the people were using to survive in those times. All claims of dependency on the fur trade and treaty annuities aside, as late as 1849 and 1850, this foraging adaptation was still the economic basis of their world.

### 2.

INDIAN REMOVAL HAD BEEN A TOPIC of discussion throughout much of the new United States for some time. Many voices were arguing that it was something that was meant to occur, and one of the most persistent such voices was that of Thomas L. McKenney. The writer Herman J. Viola has written that McKenney was "the major architect" of the removal program, and like many thinkers of his time, McKenney was convinced it was the Indians' destiny to convert to Christianity and in the process become "civilized." He was certain it was the moral obligation of the Euro-Americans to work to bring this change about.[45]

The four years between the issuance of Zachary Taylor's order and the signing of the Treaty of 1854 between the Ojibwe and the United States were, on the part of the Ojibwe, filled with frustration and a determined struggle to resist removal, and on the part of the United States, filled with subterfuge and political intrigue in attempts to bring the removal about. The Michigan anthropologist Charles E. Cleland feels that Alexander Ramsey and Agent John Watrous "developed a secret plan to effect removal", and that "[t]he collusion of private interest" and government authorities in this venture was well known at the time. Cleland goes on to say that "[s]ome American officials feared that Chippewa opposition to removal was so strong that troops would be required to both accomplish removal and to keep them in the west."[46] After years of struggle, removal efforts culminated with the Treaty of 1854—a date marking the beginning of a new time for the tribesmen.[47]

LIKE OTHER WASHINGTON OFFICIALS, Orlando Brown, the Commissioner of Indian Affairs, had been contemplating the removal of the Wisconsin and Michigan Ojibwe bands from ceded territory, and on 5 December 1849, he wrote to Sub-agent Livermore at La Pointe telling him plans were in the offing for moving the sub-agency to an area near or on the Mississippi.[48] This, of course, was intended to be a way of getting the resident Ojibwe bands to move without physically forcing them to do so. If they wanted to readily receive their annuities they would need to travel hundreds of miles west to the new sub-agency to get them, and Brown, like others, felt they would eventually stay at the new western location.

This presumption that over time the tribesmen would stay at the new western site is interesting in that it exposes two underlying certainties Americans held about Ojibwe life in the mid-1800s. One is that the annuities were of prime importance to the people. In fact, the payments were deemed to be so important that they were held to be essential to Ojibwe existence. The other underlying certainty has to do with the Euro-American understanding that Indians "roamed" over a countryside—a "truth" discussed above—and hence, the Americans felt the Michigan and Wisconsin bands could, more or less, make an expeditious adjustment to a new, distant, western location. The assumption of such an easy adjustment denies the importance of a metaphysical notion of *place* in Ojibwe life at the time, and it belies the reality of how a community of people with a foraging adaptation integrates its behavioral traits with the specificity of a particular ecosystem. The complexities of the details of how such a culture relates to its habitat were essentially unnoticed by American governmental authorities of the time.

Sub-agent Livermore did not receive Brown's letter until 7 February 1850, and soon thereafter read it at a council with Ojibwe leaders on Madeline Island. We should wonder just which leaders were present, since surely the bulk of the community was dispersed in its numerous winter hunting territories at that time. Nevertheless, upon hearing the message the Ojibwe were not only upset with the news but apparently openly expressed their intent to refuse to move with the sub-agency station. According to Livermore they "were considerably excited" and he claims he "exhorted them to submit to whatever their Great Father should in his wisdom think best to do in the matter, and alluded to the extreme folly of their setting up an opposition to the design of the government."[49]

Along with the dreaded news of a pending removal, it is likely that by the early 1850s, Livermore's use of the honorific title "Great Father" was ill received by the people. By this time this title was used not just for the American president but also his close representatives, like territorial governors who carried out his wishes on the frontier and even the local agents and Sub-agents. As we have already noted, as late as 1842, in the treaty negotiations with Robert Stuart the title "Great Father" was often invoked as Stuart attempted to imbue the treaty meetings with the solemnity of Washington's authority. But by 1842, the Ojibwe were responding to American officials' overtures for more accommodations in a less than enthusiastic manner. Another example is seen in Harriet Hall's letter in 1850 (given below), in which this change in sentiment is apparent. The reputed awe and respect for Washington's "Great Father" we are told the Ojibwe evinced in earlier years was giving way to a decided disenchantment and skepticism. Stated differently, the use of metaphoric titles we saw during earlier times when fur trade theater was the protocol in official meetings of European, American and tribal leaders was losing its appropriateness by the 1840s. Although in some cases these honorific titles were used for several years after 1840, by that date no longer were the Ojibwe readily assuming the stance of the "child," nor were they standing alone with this change of attitude toward officials of the United States government. By 1850, they had supporters in the non-Indian populace of western Lake Superior as well as in a much larger region.[50]

Richard Morse witnessed this change at La Pointe five years later in colorful incidents at the annual treaty payment. He claims that one of the Ojibwe speakers loudly admonished Washington officials for not delivering annuities when and as promised, and in another incident at that gathering he observed how when some Ojibwe were stranded on the mainland with no way to get to Madeline Island, others—already on the island—joked deridingly about the chances of their "Great Father" having a boat sent over to get them.[51] This change of heart in using fur trade theater with its unequal terms of address is overtly made clear in a speech given by Flat Mouth, the well-known Leech Lake leader. In December 1850, at Sandy Lake on the final day of the annuity payment—first making certain his words were being written down so they could be delivered later—this articulate orator addressed Governor Ramsey in an angry speech in which he reacted to the many Ojibwe deaths that occurred at that site:

> I speak to our Great Father at a distance: the words that you now hear will be carried to him. When I saw him he spoke to us about farms and other matters of interest to us. I believed his words would be verified in this respect, but instead of this they have been falsified. And I blame him for this. My friend, it makes our hearts sore to look at the losses we have sustained while at Sandy Lake. You call us children, but I do not think we are your children. If we were we should be white. You are not our Father and I think you call us your children only in mockery.[52]

Perhaps these words of the well-known Pillager leader sum up the sentiment Ojibwe people held about the use of the honorific title "Great Father" by 1850. Flat Mouth was speaking to the tragedy of Sandy Lake and understandably was expressing his deep anger and sorrow with what had just occurred there, but we might conclude he was summing up a wide sentiment held by the Ojibwe people about their relationship with whites in general, and governmental leaders in particular.

Soon after informing Sub-agent Livermore of plans for removal, on 6 February 1850—the same date President Taylor signed the removal order—Orlando Brown wrote to Governor Ramsey telling him to begin preparations for removal.[53] For the next twelve months, considerable letter writing ensued between persons at La Pointe, St. Paul, Washington, D.C., and a few other places. These now give us a clear picture of the exchange of ideas and the progression of events over these important months. In the following paragraphs we will discuss these communiqués as we try to understand what the Ojibwe people faced in these difficult times and how they soon took the initiative to forestall and finally end these removal attempts.

3.

ONE SUCH LETTER IS DATED 12 MARCH 1850, but instead of being from a government official it is from Harriet Hall, the now-teenaged daughter of Sherman and Mrs. Hall, who was writing to relatives living back east. Harriet had been sent east for several years of schooling and she wrote the letter after returning to Madeline Island. It offers a rare and important glimpse of Ojibwe life at La Pointe at the time:

> The Indians have now left us for their sugarbushes and the school is for the present discontinued . . . Our Indian Agent at this place has just received letters intimating the removal of the Indians this next summer. The Agent called a council and read to the Indians his letters from Washington. One of the chiefs said to him 'if I was as near the great Father as I am to you I think I would talk back to him some.' If the Indian was removed it will probably be by force, for they love their lands too well to leave them when merely commanded to do so. How sad to think of the poor Indian whose numbers are fast dwindling away, take up his blanket and march

> to some uncultivated region beyond the Mississippi, where he recognizes not in those dreary wastes, the delightful scenery of his once happy home . . . Should the Indian be removed, as they doubtless will, there would of course be nothing left for the missionary to do here.[54]

Among other things, these words from the teenaged daughter of La Pointe missionaries show that in 1850, maple sugarbushes were still an integral part of Ojibwe life, but also, just as importantly, Ms. Hall understood that the people had an attachment to the Chequamegon region that went far beyond economics. This was their homeland and they had no intention of leaving it. The quotation also touches on a point that was a concern of missionary Leonard Wheeler. This is, that after so many years of labor at La Pointe the missionaries were not eager to leave the region for a new western locale, where they would need to spend months, if not years of hard work to change a wilderness setting into a successful mission station.

4.

THE RESPONSIBILITY FOR THE MECHANICS of removal fell first of all to Commissioner of Indian Affairs Orlando Brown and he wasted little time in initiating action. In his letter of 6 February to Governor Ramsey, he set forth the immediate steps for getting removal underway. Ramsey was to take charge and use La Pointe's Sub-agent Livermore as his man in the field and all future annuity payments were to be made on unceded land, so a new agency site needed to be selected since the La Pointe subagency would be closed. If the Ojibwe wanted their payments they would have to move west to get them, and the government would work to have them stay permanently at the new distant site. Clearly, "the tool used to encourage the Ojibwe to move out of the ceded territory was a threat to cut off their annuities."[55]

Upon receiving the 6 February letter, Ramsey wrote to Livermore telling him the agency would be moved to Sandy Lake in Minnesota Territory, and that he was to tell the Ojibwe no more payments would be made at La Pointe. Ramsey then wrote to Commissioner Brown for further clarification on the timing and details of removal and Brown replied, saying the removal could only occur after Congress had appropriated funds to finance it, and that would take time, but that it should take place before the end of the 1850 open water season. Brown indicated that it could be completed in fall at the time of the annuity payment at the new western agency site and that the people "should be told that they would not be paid unless they took their families with them, and that they should be prepared to remain permanently."[56] It appears that even though these numerous letters were being exchanged with some rapidity, the administrative and budgetary gears of government were turning slowly, a fact that pushed removal further and further into the latter months of the year.

There was considerable action in the western Lake Superior country in the spring and summer of 1850 as preparations for removal unfolded. This was the opportunity persons in the American business community had been hoping for and good business practice called for them to be prepared when the removal began. Regional as well as eastern newspapers carried articles about it, and missionaries and private citizens were writing letters, often with strong opinions. Reporters for Ohio and New York newspapers, for instance, were writing that at the 1848 La Pointe annuity payment, the Ojibwe were "swindled" by traders charging exorbitant prices for provisions the Indians relied on, and one reason for the removal was that at a distant and more isolated western site traders would be able to operate more freely and "rake" even more profits from the annuity payment table.[57]

On 25 February at La Pointe, Sherman Hall wrote to his superior in New England saying the local non-Ojibwe community did not support Ojibwe removal. Later, on 22 May, the Lake Superior Journal echoed this sentiment in an article claiming the efforts of Henry Sibley, Henry Rice and Charles Borup to bring about the removal was nothing more than a scheme to make St. Paul and Minnesota Territory the center of the Indian trade so their financial investments would benefit.[58] What goes unstated in this article is that the *Lake Superior Journal* writer may have been concerned about the loss of the Indian trade to the economy in the region of the lake as opposed to that of the distant St. Paul.

Perhaps having an even greater impact on public and government sentiment were the anti-removal efforts of Cyrus Mendenhall. This "mining entrepreneur associated with the Methodist Episcopal Mission Society" was on the south shore in June 1850, where he "circulated a memorial among Americans calling for the recall of the removal order." Mendenhall's petition reached Congress where it apparently had a significant effect, and he continued to lobby for the withdrawal of the removal order for the next two years.[59] Because of these and other activities, anthropologist James Clifton concluded that "Indeed, from the start there was no evidence of local support for the Chippewa's removal."[60]

There is no doubt that by the mid-nineteenth century relations between the United States government and the Ojibwe people were not going unnoticed by the greater American public. By that time more newspapers were being printed than ever before, and as means of transportation improved it became easier for eastern travelers to attend important meetings between the tribesmen and American government officials. This worked to make the pro-Ojibwe sentiment in the American populace a growing factor in the relationships between Washington and Ojibwe leaders.

Along with government officials and persons in the Indian trade, the Ojibwe were taking action as well. An external threat such as President Taylor's Removal Order was a catalyst that served to unite some of the otherwise disparate bands into a more solid political body. Usually, when things are going well the separate bands tend to disperse and enjoy an independent existence, but under stress they may turn to each other to form a larger and more effective body. Such a political coalescence occurred with the announcement of the removal order. We should expect that in the late 1840s, there were many runners delivering messages between Ojibwe villages and that inter- and intra-band councils were commonplace.[61]

Perhaps we can understand the incident of 15 February 1850, wherein Chief Buffalo sent a Dakota captive with a contingent of persons, which included La Pointe's Black Bird, to Governor Ramsey in St. Paul as an attempt to defuse, or at least forestall, some of the government's removal activities. After the young Dakota had been taken prisoner in 1849 by some Ojibwe he reportedly was sheltered by Buffalo for some months until he was safely returned to his Minnesota home. Such an act may have been meant to show good faith to the Americans regarding the Ojibwe commitments made in the earlier meetings and treaties where they agreed to end their hostilities with the Dakota.[62]

Ten days after he met with Black Bird, Ramsey conferred with Dr. Charles Borup, earlier of La Pointe, who had recently replaced Henry Rice as the overseer of the Minnesota outfit for the Chouteau trading company, about proceeding with removal plans. Borup wanted the upcoming annuity payment to be made on unceded land at Fond du Lac on the St. Louis River, with the following year's payment to be moved to Sandy Lake. Along with the possibility of benefiting Borup's entrepreneurial efforts in lands west of La Pointe, it was felt this would more readily acclimate the Lake Superior bands to the change and make the switch to Sandy Lake much easier to accomplish.[63]

Sub-agent Livermore set to work with the removal but not before he sent a letter, dated 25 March 1850, to Governor Ramsey expressing his concerns about the matter. Livermore knew the removal could not be carried out without much difficulty and reminded Ramsey that the many canoes needed could not be built before June, when birchbark loosened enough to be taken from the trees. This fact would delay operations for two months or more. He also mentioned the problem of supplying enough food for the large amount of persons involved while en route, and that it would be very important to have enough provisions on hand at the new site before the people arrived. And he thought Charles Oakes—a prominent name at La Pointe, and someone acceptably familiar to the Ojibwe—should be hired to assist with the removal in the field.[64]

It is in the few letters of persons like John Livermore that we can gain a more genuine understanding of Ojibwe life at La Pointe in early 1850 than what is usually afforded us in the official documentation of the times. These rich and colorful bits of descriptive commentary are windows through which we might glimpse the way things were done in Ojibwe communities. For example, in the days after Livermore gave the removal message to the people, he told Ramsey, "they are often smoking the subject over, some showing a disposition to oppose the wishes of the government, relative to removal, saying they will never go." He went on to say that because of the time of year and their scattered distribution over a wide region "they would want time to market their sugar and furs, and do up their dancing."[65]

We can envision the numerous councils in which pipe ceremonies were held to invoke the *manidoog* in order to consult them about the proper way to deal with this latest problem. "Smoking the subject over" was akin to the many meetings going on in Washington and St. Paul but in a very different setting and with very different assumptions and sources of knowledge. Likewise their need to "do up their dancing" was also a required act, and was really a religious ceremony. The dancing Livermore was referring to most likely was part of the annual early spring *midewiwin* ceremonies, as well as dancing in conjunction with *jiisakaan* rites, called specifically for addressing the removal issue.

In any event, smoking and dancing involve the use of tobacco and the drum, both powerful elements used ritually to consult the spiritual world, and this would have been part of the way Ojibwe people dealt with the problem of removal. Livermore's mention of these customs shows that in early 1850, these key elements of Ojibwe culture were still used when making important political decisions.

On 2 April 1850, Sub-agent Livermore drafted a circular that was carried to the different Ojibwe bands telling of the removal order, and in time he began to receive responses. Even though he had stated Sandy Lake would be the new agency site, Ramsey was struggling with this decision and on 17 April 1850, he wrote to Livermore saying he had chosen Leech Lake as the new site. A month later Livermore wrote to say he had recently hired twelve men to work directly with the several Michigan and Wisconsin Ojibwe bands and that they would be led by Charles Oakes. Interestingly, one of the men was George Warren, William's first cousin and a close confidante, as shown in the many letters exchanged between the two.[66]

However, the role of John S. Livermore as Sub-agent at La Pointe came to a sudden end on 19 April 1850, when Washington officials replaced him with John S. Watrous, a move clearly brought about by political patronage and partisan politics. Livermore was a Democrat who had worked against Zachary Taylor in his bid for the presidency, and in 1849, the Whig, John Watrous, was among others attempting to have him removed from the sub-agency position. Furthermore, a group of Michigan citizens had also complained to Washington of Livermore's political partisanship. What may have helped in Livermore's departure was that Chief Buffalo and other Ojibwe leaders sent a petition to Washington complaining of Livermore's conduct concerning a shortage of provisions needed for the winter of 1849-50.[67]

John Watrous was from Ohio and had served in the Wisconsin Territorial legislature. He apparently entered the Lake Superior Indian trade in 1846, at La Pointe, and in 1848, was granted a license to trade at Fond du Lac, Grand Portage, and Crow Wing, but in 1849, he experienced financial difficulties and sold his trading interest to George Nettleton. Two financial supporters of Watrous when at La Pointe were John W. Bell and Charles Borup—both prominent members of the La Pointe business community who were developing new business interests in St. Paul. Both Bell and Borup were involved in attempts to move the Ojibwe west. John Watrous and George Nettleton, if not friends, were certainly business colleagues and they would go on to work together with removal issues in the following year.

Even though Governor Ramsey had announced Leech Lake as the site for the new agency he still was concerned about the appropriateness of the location. On 17 June 1850, he left St. Paul to travel to Sauk Rapids where he would join John Watrous, La Pointe missionary Sherman Hall and interpreter William Warren, to travel to Leech Lake and a number of other northern Minnesota sites to gather information that would allow him to decide on the final location. In his annual report written in October 1850, Ramsey extolled the merits of Leech Lake for the site of the new Ojibwe agency saying, "Leech Lake is *the* place."[68]

Regarding removal, he said since the congressional appropriation for its expenses "was not made at a day sufficiently early to warrant a removal this fall . . . the probability is that active measures will have to be suspended until next spring." He went on to say that some Wisconsin Ojibwe bands were already moving to La Pointe in anticipation of the move to western lands even though as late as October, "a formal order to remove has at no time been communicated to the Chippewas." However, he said, in spring "they were informed that during the year they would be called upon to do so."[69] Despite his praise for Leech Lake it was finally decided that the site was too distant to allow an expedient removal, and ultimately, Sandy Lake was chosen as the new agency site.

An important aspect of the events of 1850 is what occurred, and what did not occur, in Washington, D.C., that summer. Both Congress and the Executive were preoccupied with the question of slavery and its possible extension to new states and territories, and this took priority over any efforts for Ojibwe removal. Then, Orlando Brown resigned in May, to be effective on 1 July. Luke Lea assumed the Commissioner of Indian Affairs position and seemed to think all pressing removal efforts were being carried out in St. Paul, hence, he took no new action on removal that summer. Furthermore, after assuming office on 1 July, Lea was out of the office from late August to late October with matters of new treaty negotiations with the Dakota, leaving administrative duties to his Acting Commissioner. Meanwhile, Ramsey and Watrous were in Minnesota Territory waiting for further direction from their superiors in Washington. To complicate matters, President Taylor died in July, and soon after Millard Fillmore came to the White House. Also, Interior Secretary Thomas Ewing resigned.[70]

Typical of the complications involved is an undated petition, apparently written sometime in early 1850, from copper miners along Lake Superior's south shore who were strongly against Ojibwe removal. Perhaps it has become conventional to interpret these "citizen" petitions—including the one from mining entrepreneur and missionary enthusiast Cyrus Mendenhall mentioned above—as expressions of genuine friendship and community concern on the part of the non-Ojibwe residents of Lake Superior country, but it is likely the desire for financial return was as strong for some of these persons as it was for Ramsey, Rice, Watrous, Bell, Borup, Oakes and others whose interests lay far to the west and would have benefited if removal was effected. An example of the latter is seen in a letter of 14 June 1850, from Madeline Island's Charles Oakes (who was at the time a business associate of Henry Sibley and Charles Borup) to Henry Sibley in St. Paul. In this letter, Oakes made clear his desire to make money through Ojibwe removal. In Oakes' case he hoped to make sizable monetary profits not just from his involvement in the actual physical removal of the Ojibwe, but also from business ventures in the western region they were to be moved into.[71] The literature of the time is replete with references to frontier traders who depended upon sales of durable goods—as well as of whiskey—for their main source of income, and a good portion, if not all of these sales were directly tied to Ojibwe annuity payments.[72]

Surely the emerging business community of Lake Superior's south shore would have missed the annual influx of governmental annuity monies and related financial activity garnered through the regular treaty payments, while those businesspersons in Minnesota Territory would have welcomed them. It is in this sense that the so-called support expressed by the non-Ojibwe community in Michigan and Wisconsin at the time the resident Ojibwe bands were threatened with removal must be carefully evaluated. We are told numerous citizens were against Ojibwe removal, but not the reasons behind this positive sentiment. One should think that those business interests in Wisconsin and Michigan benefiting from the annuity payments and other governmental expenditures regarding the Ojibwe would have resisted the loss of this important revenue, and perhaps this is the motive behind at least a portion of the so-called citizen petitions to keep the Ojibwe from moving. Yet the literature is puzzlingly silent in this regard. While it stresses the attempts of the business community of Minnesota Territory to effect the removal it does not explicitly speak to Wisconsin and Michigan's similar community, with its own financial self-interest, that would have lost income if the Ojibwe communities had moved westward. Later in this book we will see how this point—the possibility of financial benefits from being located near an Indian reserve—is relevant to relations between Ojibwe and neighboring non-Ojibwe communities in northern Wisconsin in more recent times.

In the case of the undated south shore petition, it was dispatched to a congressman who sent it on to new President Fillmore, who forwarded it to Luke Lea for a report, but Commissioner Lea did not respond until June of 1851, a full year later.[73] These incidents remind us that from the perspective of the Americans, the matter of Ojibwe removal was played out within a much larger arena of political and financial concerns often far distant from Lake Superior and Minnesota Territory. Because of this there was no important activity regarding Ojibwe removal coming from Washington throughout the summer of 1850.

## 5.

IN THE ABSENCE OF FURTHER DIRECTION from Washington as the year moved along, John Watrous and Alexander Ramsey were growing anxious. Ramsey was particularly concerned about the continuing warfare between the Dakota and the Ojibwe that spring, and doubtless the negative effect it could have on removal attempts later that year. To alleviate this he convened a meeting in June 1850 at Fort Snelling between tribal leaders. (While La Pointe representatives might have been present we do not know who they may have been.) Of interest is how at this meeting Ramsey attempted to reinforce the connection between the might and power of the American government and that of spiritual forces when he told the assembled tribesmen that the military skirmishes were bothersome to him, and that, "As the Great Spirit has placed the Great Father to preside over you, if he endured this state of things any longer the Great Spirit would cease to smile on him."[74] This claim that the Great Spirit granted the American president the responsibility to rule over the Ojibwe and Dakota was of course not new, and by 1850, must have lost some of its plausibility. Going further, the deeper implication that the Great Spirit, by acting through the Great Father, wanted the Ojibwe to remove may also have been accepted with measured skepticism.

In August, while at Sandy Lake, John Watrous wrote to Governor Ramsey saying he thought the removal could not be accomplished that season due to the late date. No word of the government appropriation was forthcoming and since the navigation season ended about mid-November, there would not be enough time for the Ojibwe to make the journey without severe hardship. Watrous was fearful that in the absence of the appropriation he would be unable to supply the needed food for the few thousand Ojibwe expected at Sandy Lake. This lack of provisions, he wrote, "would be fatal."[75]

Puzzlingly, despite all this uncertainty, Watrous still dispatched a messenger to La Pointe telling the Lake Superior bands to come to Sandy Lake by 25 October 1850, for their annuity payment. We might question why he sent this notice when he was concerned about the possible lack of provisions. In this regard, perhaps it is important to understand that nominally, this was only a call to come for the annuity payment, not an order for removal, and that Watrous might actually have assumed that while the people might make the trip, they likely would return to their home areas.[76]

Theresa Schenck attempts to shed new light on this matter by offering comment on how an interpreter might have relayed the Watrous message to the people. Accordingly, she says:

> From the Indians' perspective, removal did not have to be permanent, although the authorities had tried to emphasize it as such. The Ojibwe word *gosiwin*, the word probably used by the interpreters, signified removal, encampment, one during which the government would sustain them, and after which they were free to return to their spring grounds.[77]

We are left with uncertainty as to just what the Ojibwe were actually told about the Sandy Lake annuity payment and how they understood the message. As shown below, Governor Ramsey felt at the time that no formal notice of removal had been issued to the Ojibwe, and the writer Theresa Schenck feels that he did not understand whether the removal would actually be made that fall or if the planned gathering at Sandy Lake was merely for the annual annuity payment.[78] As noted above, Charles Cleland feels Ramsey and Watrous had a "secret plan" that involved delaying the annuity payment until late in the navigation season so that after coming to Sandy Lake, the people would not be able to return home until spring. By then, they felt, many of the Ojibwe would decide to stay.

It was about this time—fall 1850—that Governor Ramsey wrote his annual report on Indian affairs to his superior in Washington, Commissioner Luke Lea. In these reports it was routine for *ex officio* Indian commissioners, like Minnesota Territory's Ramsey, to summarize the year's activities and issue recommendations for future governmental action. In this vein Ramsey reminded Lea that he had asked the Commissioner back in April to work toward having the federal Trade and Intercourse Act, which restricted the importation of liquor to Indian lands, extended to those lands recently ceded to the government. In 1850, the Wisconsin Ojibwe communities were all on ceded land and the liquor trade was a recurring problem, but Ramsey, as did others, felt such an extension would serve to help keep the illicit whiskey trade out of these communities.

Ramsey also asked that the government change its policy regarding the support of missionary schools to include the use of what were then called *manual training schools*, where students could be trained to "work" like the Euro-Americans. In the mid-nineteenth century the call for manual training schools—and/or farms—was raised by others concerned about the slow progress being made toward the government's goal of "civilizing the savages." Ramsey and others were certain that Indians would not make "progress" toward becoming "civilized" until they learned to appreciate the value of "working like whites," and manual training was one way to expedite such change. Although he seems not to have mentioned it, Ramsey probably concluded that the presence of such a school at Crow Wing would be an attraction for Wisconsin and Michigan Ojibwe to stay in the west after their removal.

Also included in Ramsey's report is demographic data on the Ojibwe residing in his area. He listed 400 persons living in Michigan, 3,000 in Wisconsin, and 4,500 in Minnesota Territory, noting that of these, 5,000 received annuities under the 1837, 1842, and the two more recent 1847 treaties. Ramsey noted that there were 2,000 Ojibwe in Minnesota who did not get any annuities.

More specific to the Chequamegon Bay area was what he said for the La Pointe bands. He claimed there were only 400 persons in these communities and although they were converted to the Catholic and Protestant versions of Christianity, the older chiefs and headmen were often "still attached to primitive customs." He stated that at Bad River, the farm under the direction of Rev. Wheeler was offering an ample return of produce, enough so there was an annual surplus, which was sold, and that the La Pointe band members were "manufacturing large quantities" of maple sugar, some of which was sold to traders. They also caught and salted large quantities of fish, which were sold. These comments indicate that by 1850, even though their traditional foraging adaptation was still the basis of their economic organization, the American market system was being utilized to a good degree by the La Pointe Ojibwe.

Finally, as stated above, Governor Ramsey told Lea that "a formal order to remove has at no time been communicated to the Chippewas" but, "they were informed that during the year they would be called upon to do so" and that by the time of writing his report many of the interior bands had voluntarily moved to La Pointe, anticipating their coming to Sandy Lake for annuities. He said when the Wisconsin and Michigan Ojibwe were removed they should be placed in a particular area west and inland from Lake Superior. He stated this was a land which held no valuable minerals, and after its white pine timber was taken (presumably by whites), the region should be given to the Ojibwe "for ever." The implication was that here was a land in which the tribesmen could dwell in peace, distant from troubling American contact. Ramsey apparently had a disdain for the region saying it held "interminable swamps" and that "It is a country no American would ever occupy."[79]

Meanwhile, John Watrous was worried about the tardiness of the shipment of specie from Washington necessary for the annuity distribution, and on 6 October 1850, he departed from Sandy Lake for St. Paul where he hoped to locate the money. Importantly, at this time—actually on 19 October—Hole-in-the-Day, the Minnesota Ojibwe leader, made a trip to St. Paul to see Governor Ramsey and speak with him about having provisions sent to Sandy Lake for the Ojibwe who were gathering there.[80] Sometime just previous to this when he concluded the federal specie was not in the city, John Watrous traveled down to St. Louis, arriving there on 21 October, where, after waiting until 26 October, he went back north to St. Paul, where he arrived on 13 November. By that late date early winter was upon the Upper Midwest and Governor Ramsey knew of the shortage of provisions at Sandy Lake.

When in St. Paul Watrous met with Ramsey, and in a letter written after that meeting, he told the governor that unless the federal monies arrived soon, "winter might close on us without a supply of provisions." Still without the federal money on 14 November, he left St. Paul to return to Sandy Lake, where he arrived ten days later. By that time, he estimated nearly 4,000 Ojibwe men, women and children had appeared at the agency.[81]

Watrous told Ramsey, "On my arrival I found that all the provisions furnished under treaty stipulations . . . had all been consumed someday previous and, this notwithstanding they [the Ojibwe] had been put upon the small ration of a pound of flour and a half a pound of pork."[82] To alleviate the situation he was able to purchase some provisions from local traders, and these were given to the people.

By this time it was late November. Some of the Ojibwe had journeyed for a few hundred miles to get to Sandy Lake only to find a scarcity—and soon an absence—of food at the agency. We do not know about provisions they may have packed for their trips and whether or not they were able to secure any through hunting or fishing along the way, although in his annual report to Washington, Governor Ramsey said provisions for the move had been stashed along the route some of the Ojibwe would be taking.[83] Given the rather sudden presence of a few thousand people at the Sandy Lake station, it is unlikely that any attempt to hunt in the region was particularly successful.

Some of the Ojibwe were suffering with dysentery and measles and many were in need of food. Deaths occurred as the weeks ground by while the people waited for the return of Subagent John Watrous. Months later newspapers covered the story, saying starvation caused the deaths.

A few days after he returned, John Watrous began distributing the annuity goods even though he still had not received the specie. The Leech Lake, Lake Superior, and St. Croix bands received their portions on 28 November, and all distribution was completed by 2 December. By this time many Ojibwe had been encamped at Sandy Lake for five to six weeks and although they received the material goods portion of the annuity payment, they did not get the specie that the government had said would also be given them.

After completing the distribution of the annuity goods on 2 December, Watrous called a council with the Wisconsin Ojibwe and informed them they would have to move to Sandy Lake the next year, since that site would be their new agency. We do not have documentation showing what La Pointe's Buffalo stated in reply but according to Julia Spears, who was present, Kichi-mah-in-gun (Big Wolf), a leader from Lac du Flambeau and Chippewa River told Watrous, "We are all of one mind. We will not remove. We cannot leave our part of the country, where we have always lived, where our forefathers lived and died. We do not like Sandy Lake, nor this part of the country. We will never come to Sandy Lake for our annuities."[84]

John Watrous estimated that approximately 4,000 persons came to the site for the payment, and the annuity roll, dated 28 November 1820, provided by Watrous shows 246 heads of families from the La Pointe bands with a grand total of 800 persons. In this amount were 198 men, 240 women and 362 children, but recalling that proxies could be used, we really do not know if this is the sum of persons who traveled from La Pointe to Sandy Lake. It was not unusual for complete families to take part in such trips, but given the tardiness of the scheduling and the resulting oncoming of the cold season it is not unlikely, as has been claimed, that some communities sent only their able-bodied men. The literature shows that about 150-170 people died in t weeks at Sandy Lake, and estimates are that on the journey home another 230-250 perished, for an approximate grand total of 400 deaths.[85]

Later, the media picked up the issue of the hundreds of Ojibwe who perished. A number of newspapers still claimed starvation caused the deaths, pointing a finger at American officials for not handling the annuity payment properly. Charles Oakes claimed the deaths were due to disease, something that could not be controlled by the government. In his report to Governor Ramsey after the completion of the payment John Watrous concurred with Oakes, saying the deaths were due to measles and dysentery. In January 1851, only a few weeks after the incident, William Warren and the Minnesota Ojibwe leader Hole-in-the-Day spoke at an evening gathering at the Presbyterian Church in St. Paul. Hole-in-the-Day stated that the government officials were at fault, partially because some of the scanty provisions disbursed were spoiled due to being soaked by water. Warren agreed but did not blame Watrous, instead saying the fault was with the late Congressional appropriation.[86] Writer Theresa Schenck feels Governor Ramsey, "whose failure to make decisions was most to blame for the disaster at Sandy Lake."[87] In late December, Ramsey traveled north to meet both Charles Borup and Charles Oakes, who assured him the Sandy Lake deaths had not occurred from starvation caused by government negligence, but from disease. A day or so later Ramsey met more friends who had been at Sandy Lake, including John Watrous, and they all journeyed back down to St. Paul where they met with their families "in time to enjoy the Christmas festivities."[88]

At the same time these men were traveling to St. Paul for their holiday celebrations, we might have little difficulty assuming what the members of the many Ojibwe communities who had come to Sandy Lake were experiencing. In the waning days of December 1850 and the early days of January 1851, they were slowly making their ways through the winter forest of Minnesota Territory and the state of Wisconsin as they returned home. For them the deaths caused by the Sandy Lake incident had not yet ended, for as Chief Buffalo estimated, approximately 250 more persons perished on this difficult, anything but joyous, journey home.[89]

6.

A QUESTION THAT PRESENTS ITSELF for the 1850 Sandy Lake tragedy concerns whether or not the Ojibwe bands sent mostly their adult males to collect the annuities. We recall that American authorities insisted the Ojibwe be told they were to bring their complete families, but the question remains whether or not band leaders chose to defy this order. In this regard historian Bruce White says the Sandy Lake annuity rolls "only record heads of families,"[90] but in actuality, the rolls show heads of families, followed by numbers of men, women and children making up these families. Some writers claim the Ojibwe saw that the intent of the Americans was to use the payment as a means of getting entire Ojibwe bands to move west, then, due to the tardiness of the season, being forced to stay. These writers stress that while some complete families seem to have made the trip, it was really mostly the adult males who came.[91] Their plan was to travel lightly and quickly. However, it appears that in many cases complete families did, indeed, make the trip.[92] James Clifton suggests that those bands that did send complete families were from the Mississippi River region that resided close to Sandy Lake, but such a conclusion ignores the large numbers of women and children listed for all of the Ojibwe bands who came.[93]

We do not have information on the age and gender of those who died from this incident, but Clifton makes an interesting point regarding these deaths. That is, if it was indeed mostly adult men who came to Sandy Lake and if the total number of those who came is about 4,000 (using the estimate of John Watrous), and assuming it was mostly males who died, it would mean that about twelve percent of this total perished. Considering these were able-bodied men—and integral to community resource procurement—then the Sandy Lake tragedy was a very serious blow to the entire Western Lake Superior Ojibwe community.[94]

Although news of the Sandy Lake deaths spread rapidly through the western Lake Superior region, it was slow to reach Washington. Sherman Hall, who was present during the payments, sent a letter about the deaths, dated 30 December 1850, to Selah Treat, his superior at the American Board of Commissioners for Foreign Missions, and Treat sent at least a portion of it on to Luke Lea. On the same date as Hall's letter, Governor Ramsey sent a report to Washington in which he included a copy of the December letter from John Watrous telling of the payment. Ramsey mentioned the financial costs of the annuity distribution, and he claimed the rumors of the Sandy Lake deaths were "highly exaggerated." These letters and the media coverage show, as historian Bruce White claims, "By February 1851, government officials in Washington had a detailed knowledge of the deaths at Sandy Lake."[95]

7.

WE MIGHT ASK WHAT WILLIAM WARREN'S role was in the events that unfolded in 1850 that culminated in the tragedy at Sandy Lake. Remembering that Warren was born on Madeline Island and through his mother was a member of the La Pointe Band of Ojibwe, it is important to track his activities as they related to his homeland. We have seen that early in the year, Warren was certain removal would occur and he intended to play a role in it. Initially he and his immediate family were residing at Gull Lake where he was employed as the government farmer while working on his history manuscript, but soon he would be enlisted in removal efforts.

An incident occurred early in the year that shows the evolution of Warren's stand on removal. This was his attempt to have Hole-in-the-Day (The Younger), an influential Minnesota Ojibwe leader, make a trip to Washington—with Warren as his interpreter—to confer with the president and also to witness the numbers and might of the Americans as seen in their numerous cities in the east. Warren felt that once Hole-in-the-Day made this trip, he would be persuaded it was folly to resist removal and could be used to facilitate removal. However, after some effort, governmental permission for the trip was denied.

In the process of attempting to have the trip approved, Warren posted a number of letters, one of which angered Henry Sibley since he felt it slighted Governor Ramsey. For some time Sibley had been a powerful influence on removal attempts and he wrote Ramsey saying: "I have told Lea that Warren is a blatherskite with just enough education to make him mischievously disposed, and that no confidence can be placed in his statements."[96]

These remarks from a prominent person like Henry Sibley are indicative of what someone like William Warren was confronted with in the middle of the nineteenth century. Sibley's image of Warren as a semi-educated mixed-blood who was "mischievously disposed" is not only interesting, but may have been a common sentiment directed to other mixed-bloods of the time who, like William Warren, were competent in both the Ojibwe language and American English. In the mid-nineteenth century in northern Wisconsin, for a mixed-blood person to have as much formal American education as Warren did was to present something new to non-Ojibwe society. Doubtless, Warren had more formal education than many non-Ojibwe on the frontier, and his ability to understand both Ojibwe and English caused both his Ojibwe and non-Ojibwe contemporaries to take pause and consider his words. Because of this, persons like William Warren enjoyed insights into both Ojibwe and mainstream American culture that could have been troubling, if not actually threatening, to those who did not hold them. This was part of the enigma of those individuals of mixed blood parentage on the frontier we have spoken to above.

In the summer of 1850, Warren was asked by the Lake Superior and Chippewa River bands to meet with them about removal, and after weeks of waiting for Governor Ramsey to approve his leaving the Gull Lake post to journey to Wisconsin, he finally received permission and departed on 17 October.[97] At the Chippewa River he encountered his sister Julia, who was residing at their aunt's home. Due to William's poor health she decided to accompany him and a large group of Ojibwe on their long trek to Sandy Lake. Thanks to Julia, we have a lengthy, detailed, and interesting written account of this trip.

Warren, his sister, and a party of leaders and others from the Chippewa River bands traveled up to Lac Courte Oreilles, where people from that band and others from Lac du Flambeau met them before moving on to the St. Croix River region, where they connected with the St. Croix and Pokegema bands before traveling down the Iron River to Lake Superior. Here they met Buffalo with his La Pointe contingent. This large group was soon traversing to Fond du Lac and on to Sandy Lake. Julia Warren felt this party was made up of seven hundred persons, although her brother felt it was only four hundred.

Julia Warren's account of this trip is revealing in how it shows this large group of people traveling through the forest, following its rivers and lakes as they relied upon a well-developed body of woodcraft and related skills. Here was a people who felt at home in this environment, and thus were confident of their ability to reach their destination without undue hardship, but they still had to be concerned. The tally of individuals made at Sandy Lake shows that young and old made this journey, and a good degree of caution had to be taken in order to prevent mishaps. Although traveling through the forest and along its waterways was part of the Ojibwe way of life in 1850, this was still a very long excursion. One can imagine this large body of people moving along, day after day, night after night, mostly in canoe and on foot. It was getting late in the season and they had to have been concerned about what they would be met with at Sandy Lake, as well as how they would make the return trip. Hunting and fishing were done along the way and nightly encampments with cooking stations were set up. These were a people with no little degree of self-reliance, but no doubt they were preoccupied with the underlying reason for their long journey. As they moved along, the threat of removal must always have been on their minds.

The party arrived at Sandy Lake in early November, where William found Matilda and the children camping in a tent. By that time measles and dysentery had broken out, and concerned about the health of his family, he decided to take it back to Gull Lake. After that task was carried out he returned to Sandy Lake to work as interpreter during the annuity distribution.

Thus, William Warren aided in having several hundred Ojibwe from the Wisconsin interior and Lake Superior, along with the St. Croix groups, journey to Sandy Lake in the fall of 1850. He was not doing so as an employee of the American government, and we do not know if the Wisconsin bands paid him for this effort. What is certain is that he made this trip as an advocate for removal.

*Notes*

1. Armstrong 1892:9-53; Burnham 1974:128;Harris 1976:121-131.
2. Trennert 1979:41-2.
3. Cleland in McClurken *et al* 2000: 61.
4. Folwell 1956 [1921]:239-241; Ross 1960:120.
5. Tanner in McClurken *et al* 2000:472.
6. Folwell 1956[1921]:310-317.
7. Christian 2004:50-2, 86-7, 307, 312, 422, 433-4.
8. Medill 1846 in WisTerPap, Vol. 28, pp. 1015-6.
9. White in McClurken *et al* 2000:157.
10. Folwell 1956[1921]:310-316.
11. White in McClurken *et al* 2000:158.
12. Cleland in McClurken *et al* 2000:61.
13. Wheeler, Leonard H., letter of 10 November 1849 to his father )brackets added). Copy in Wheeler Family Papers at NCLVC, Ashland, Wisconsin.
14. White in McClurken *et al* 2000:169.
15. Cleland in McClurken *et al* 2000:61; White in McClurken *et al* 2000:170.
16. Rice as quoted in White in McClurken *et al* 2000:170.
17. Cleland in McClurken *et al* 2000:61.
18. Satz 1991:51.
19. Chute 1998:152, brackets added.
20. Diedrich 1999:75; Cleland in McClurken *et al* 2000:64, 205.
21. Armstrong 1892.
22. *Detroit Daily Free Press*, Tuesday, 28 November 1848, p. 2.
23. Head Chiefs 1849: 1-2, as given in Satz 1991:51.
24. *Detroit Daily Free Press*, 28 November 1848, p.2.
25. Satz 1991:51-2.
26. *Green Bay Gazette* 5 April 1849, p.2.
27. Chute 1998:124.
28. Richmond 1848 in WisTerPap, Vol. 28, pp. 989-90.
29. Cleland in McClurken *et al* 2000:64; Clifton 1987:17.
30. Danziger 1979:88.
31. Clifton 1987:15.
32. Chute 1998:152.
33. Diedrich 1999:75.
34. White in McClurken *et al* 2000:160-163; Satz 1991:53-9; Cleland in McClurken *et al* 2000:60-3.
35. White in McClurken *et al* 2000:168.
36. Satz 1991:52-3.
37. White in McClurken *et al* 2000:181.
38. White quoting Fletcher in McClurken *et al* 2000:166.
39. *Green Bay Gazette*, 24 May 1849, p.1.
40. Christian 2004:50-2,432-434.
41. White in McClurken *et al* 2000:160-166.
42. Cleland in McClurken *et al* 2000:61-2.
43. Cleland in McClurken *et al* 2000:63.
44. White in McClurken *et al* 2000:160-171.
45. Viola 1973:vii.
46. Cleland in McClurken *et al* 2000:64-5.
47. Danziger 1979:89.
48. Kvasnicka and Viola 1979:41-7.
49. Livermore as quoted in White in McClurken *et al* 2000:175-176.
50. Vennum 1988:259; Satz 1991:56-7.
51. Morse 1855:339.
52. Schenck 2007:96-7.
53. White in McClurken *et al* 2000:172.
54. Hall, Harriet, letter of 12 March 1850 to eastern relatives, copy at MHC, St. Paul.
55. White in McClurken *et al* 2000:173.
56. White in McClurken *et al* 2000:177.
57. Satz 1991:53.
58. Hall, Sherman, letter of 25 February 1850, copy at MHC; Lake Superior Journal of 22 May 1850.
59. Mendenhall as given in Clifton 1987:21.
60. Clifton 1987:21.
61. Clifton 1978:17, 21.
62. Morse 1904[1857]:367; White in McClurken *et al* 2000:173.
63. White in McClurken *et al* 2000: 173-4.
64. White in McClurken *et al* 2000: 176.
65. Livermore 1850 as given in Schenck 2007:83-4.
66. White in McClurken *et al* 2000:177-8; Schenck 2007:85.
67. White in McClurken *et al* 2000:179.
68. Ramsey, Alexander, annual report of 1850 in ARCIASI; White in McClurken *et al* 2000:185.
69. Ramsey, Alexander, annual report of 1850 in ARCIASI.
70. Clifton 1987:22; White in McClurken *et al* 2000:187.
71. Oakes 1850 as given by White in McClurken *et al* 2000:179.
72. Boutwell as given in White in McClurken *et al* 2000:238.

73. White in McClurken *et al* 2000:188.
74. White in McClurken *et al* 2000:183-4.
75. Watrous as given in White in McClurken *et al* 2000:189.
76. White in McClurken *et al* 2000:190.
77. Schenck 2007:88.
78. Schenck 2007:87-8.
79. Ramsey, Alexander, annual report of 1850 in ARCIASI.
80. Schenck 2007:95.
81. Watrous letter of 10 December 1850 to Alexander Ramsey, included with Sandy Lake Annuity Roll dated 28 November 1850 (copy in author's possession).
82. Watrous letter of 10 December 1850 to Alexander Ramsey (brackets added), included with Sandy Lake Annuity Roll dated 28 November 1850 (copy in author's possession).
83. Ramsey, Alexander, annual report of 1850 in ARCIASI.
84. Spears as given in Schenck 2007:92-3.
85. Rasmussen 2003:18-9; White in McClurken *et al* 2000:194; Clifton 1987:25; Satz 1991:58; Watrous letter of 10 December 1850 to Alexander Ramsey, included with Sandy Lake Annuity Roll dated 28 November 1850 (copy in author's possession).
86. Watrous letter of 10 December 1850 to Alexander Ramsey, included with Sandy Lake Annuity Roll dated 28 November 1850 (copy in author's possession); White in McClurken *et al* 2000:195-6.
87. Schenck 2007:95.
88. Schenck 2007:95.
89. Clifton 1987:25
90. White in McClurken *et al* 2000:194.
91. Cleland in McClurken *et al* 2000:65.
92. Rasmussen 2003:17-9, 25.
93. Cleland in McClurken *et al* 2000:65; Rasmussen 2003:25; Clifton 1987:23; Sandy Lake Annuity Roll, 28 November 1850 (copy in author's possession).
94. Clifton 1987:25.
95. White in McClurken *et al* 2000:196-8.
96. Sibley 1850 as given in Schenck 2007:87.
97. Warren 1850 in Schenck 2007:113.

# 19

# 1851: A Year of Great Difficulty

### *William Warren, Chief Buffalo, and the Renewed Attempts of Ramsey and Watrous for Ojibwe Removal*

1.

ON NEW YEAR'S DAY, WILLIAM WARREN and the other eighteen members of the Minnesota Territorial Legislature met in St. Paul to begin the new session. Warren had resigned his position as government farmer at Gull Lake a month earlier, to be effective 31 March 1851. His brother Truman would take over his responsibilities at Gull Lake until the end of March, and William moved his family into a St. Paul house owned by Henry Rice where they would reside through the legislative session.[1]

By that time William Warren was known as a literate young man, and according to Theresa Schenck he "presented himself to the assembly as an intelligent, capable, well-spoken legislator." Be that as it may, his legislative career was short-lived.

Near the end of the three-month session he and six other members resigned from the House over a dispute regarding the reapportionment of a few northwestern districts. Later in the year, during the election for the next session, Warren was busy with Ojibwe removal efforts, which apparently did not allow him to seriously campaign for reelection, and the final election results saw him defeated by six votes. He appealed this outcome but after consideration by a select committee of the legislature his appeal was denied. Shouldering this disappointment, Warren and his family returned to Gull Lake before moving to his wife's father's home and trading establishment at Two Rivers, on the Mississippi River in north central Minnesota Territory. At this time he was a young twenty-five, with a wife and children, out of work, and struggling with his health. Once again he was preoccupied with financial problems and turned back to his Ojibwe research materials, hoping they might be a source of family income.[2]

The early months of 1851 were an important time for both Warren and the Ojibwe people. No doubt the different bands were registering the unfortunate impact of Sandy Lake and were holding ceremonies and councils to determine what recourse they had to alleviate their serious situation. During these months a momentum was building to resist the government's increasing pressure to move, and in complex ways William Warren would be part of it.

An incident occurred early in the year that elucidates the seriousness of the issue, and as we view the chronology of events played out over the ensuing months we see the challenges Warren confronted during the last two years of his short life. As we noted, the relevancy of his life to our interest in Ojibwe history for the Chequamegon Bay region is obvious. His thoughts and actions as shown in his personal letters and the other literature of the times speak directly to problems found not only at La Pointe but in all the western Michigan, Lake Superior, and interior Wisconsin bands. For this reason we will discuss several letters Warren wrote in the early months of 1851.

2.

IN LATE 1850 AND EARLY 1851, articles appeared in the Minnesota press that raised questions about the Sandy Lake tragedy, serving to keep the issue of Ojibwe removal before the public. Someone—we do not know who, but Warren intimated it was a few influential members of the fur trading community—invited Hole-in-the-Day to speak to this matter at the St. Paul Presbyterian Church the evening of 8 January 1851. The Minnesota Territorial Legislature had just convened and was invited to attend, and one of its newest members, William Warren, was to serve as interpreter.[3]

Hole-in-the-Day (The Elder) was an influential Ojibwe leader in Minnesota Territory up to his death in 1847, and by 1851, his son Hole-in-the-Day (The Younger) had pretensions of being accepted as the chief spokesperson for all the region's Ojibwe bands, something Warren could not approve of although he and the young Gull Lake chief apparently still respected each other and were able to maintain a degree of friendship. After the St. Paul speech however, this relationship took a turn for the worse.[4]

In his presentation on 8 January, Hole-in-the-Day argued that the government and its territorial representatives were at fault for what occurred at Sandy Lake. Furthermore, he suggested that due to the incident, relations between the Ojibwe and whites were in an ominous state, the implication being that physical conflict could erupt. Immediately after Hole-in-the-Day's presentation, William Warren rose to say that while the young chief suggested it was the local authorities who were at fault, the cause of the tragedy emanated from a more distant source, that being the United States Congress for its late appropriation of funds needed for provisions.

Hole-in-the-Day took offense to Warren's remarks, and in an open letter dated 16 January 1851 that appeared in a St. Paul newspaper, he reiterated his accusations regarding the cause of the tragedy and accused Warren of "duplicity and opportunism" in his support of local authorities.[5] Warren, he implied, was afraid of alienating local white officials since they were his source of income. Despite these flare-ups, William Warren and Hole-in-the-Day (The Younger) reconciled their differences over the Sandy Lake tragedy, and genuinely renewed their friendship in 1852, just one year before Warren's early death.[6]

Warren replied to Hole-in-the-Day's January 1851 negative letter with a long letter to the Minnesota press in which he suggested Hole-in-the-Day's letter was written by someone else, most probably a person connected with the community of traders, a contingent of persons Warren had alienated as far back as 1847 with his speeches during the Fond du Lac treaty negotiations. Shortly thereafter he wrote his cousin George stating that it possibly was Julia Oakes (Mrs. Charles Oakes) who actually wrote the letter. Interestingly, Julia Oakes was a sister to Clement Beaulieu and to Elizabeth Borup, who was married to Dr. Charles Borup. As stated above, such sibling and marital connections show that in the mid-nineteenth century in Ojibwe Country, a network of influential mixed-blood persons was central to the power structure. Certainly such relationships added to the complexity of the social and economic networks Ojibwe leaders like La Pointe's Buffalo had to maneuver in as they led their people.[7]

That January, Warren wrote three more letters that help us understand what was occurring at this critical time. On 15 January, he told his cousin George that Governor Ramsey no longer accepted Hole-in-the-Day as a credible spokesperson for all the Ojibwe, and would likely approve a proposal from the Wisconsin Ojibwe that they—with Warren as interpreter—go to Washington to meet with the president. The idea for this trip predated the Sandy Lake meeting. In fact, Warren claimed the reason so many Wisconsin Ojibwe leaders went to Sandy Lake in late 1850 was to solicit the other bands for financial contributions from their annuity payments to fund this hoped-for Washington trip. In Washington, they could present their case for non-removal to the president, after which they expected he would cancel the removal order.

The people felt removal was the idea of John Watrous and other local officials for self-serving ends. If the order was genuine they wanted to hear it from the mouth of the "Great Father" himself. Only then would they consider it.[8]

However, they felt the president would not renew the order. Instead, he would revoke it. Contrarily, Warren was sure the order would not be revoked, and he felt only after the people heard this from the president himself could removal be carried out. To this end he told his cousin: "*They have got to remove*—and our only course is to get it done as well as we can in [a] manner which will conduce best for to the interests of the Indians as well as our own."[9]

Warren wrote a second letter to his cousin on the same day he wrote the above. Here he urged George—who was in Wisconsin—to prepare the people for a trip to Washington, then said, "If we manage *together* and *rightly* we can making (sic) something out of the removal—and you know well that the Govt will have to use us in this business." Once again, we see that William Warren felt strongly that removal was not only inevitable, but that it was the best recourse for the people, and that through all this both he and his cousin could benefit financially. An added bit of interest found in this letter, as is seen in other correspondence William sent his cousin in these times, is that he was urging George to come to Minnesota Territory and accept a position working for Henry Mower Rice. He told George how Rice was expanding his investments westward into the Red River Valley and that "Mr. Rice is anxious to see you. He is going in heavy at Red River this spring and says you are just the person he wants to take charge of his business there."[10]

A week after writing these letters Warren wrote a third, this time to Governor Ramsey, in which he laid out his thoughts on removal and the pressing need that it occur soon. He told Ramsey the Ojibwe were firmly against removal for three reasons: first was their love for their present homeland, a place where their forebears were buried; secondly, their understanding of the Treaty of 1842 was that they would not have to move, at least for a very long time. Furthermore, they insisted they did not sell the land in that treaty, just the right to mine the copper; thirdly, they felt the lands they were being asked to move to in Minnesota Territory would not fit their needs.

Warren stressed to Ramsey that after the 1842 treaty the people thought they would never have to move, and on this understanding some began to make major changes in their lives. He claimed that at least 400 persons "have become partially civilized, living by agriculture, owning farms, and stock, living in houses and professing the religion of the whites." These people, he said, would be unnecessarily hurt by removal. Moving them would be "like throwing them back into the darkness, poverty and degradation from which the untiring efforts of their missionaries and natural advantages of their villages have gradually lifted them." As Theresa Schenck notes, this reference apparently was to those Ojibwe at L'Ance and Bad River who had begun taking up farming.[11]

Warren went on to say removal would be very hard on the people since by going to the western lands they would need to call forth their deepest abilities to overcome the new, undeveloped country, and since they would be closer to the Dakota the danger of igniting their old "war fever" was considerable. Approximately 4,000 people would be involved and the government would need to expend ample funds to ensure removal was done correctly. Warren intimated that as planned by Ramsey and Watrous, removal would be akin to returning the Ojibwe to "the wilderness" and they would need to steel themselves for this challenge, a process that could become a troublesome threat to neighboring frontiersmen and "eventually lead to trouble mischief and bloodshed!"

Warren did not hold back as he presented Ramsey with what he considered the serious problems removal could create. He was arguing that a sizeable financial appropriation was required to ensure the operation was carried out properly, and, of course, it was his intent that he would be compensated for his role in this undertaking. Despite the many difficulties, he stated he was still certain removal should go forward, and that with appropriate measures could be accomplished properly. The first step was for Ramsey to approve the trip to Washington, D.C., and Warren suggested such an undertaking would be even more effective if the governor himself joined Warren and the Ojibwe leaders on this journey.

In tribal meetings during 1850, the Ojibwe bands had already chosen persons to make the Washington trip, their names composing an interesting "Who's Who" of Ojibwe leaders at the time. Warren said the two overall persons chosen to lead the delegation were Buffalo of La Pointe and Ah-mous of Lac du Flambeau. Other members were Osh ka-ba wis of the Wisconsin River bands; Ke-wan-see from Lac Court Oreilles; Nuh ang abe from Long Lake; Buffalo of St. Croix; Ke noshay of the Chippewa River; Osho gay, the speaker for the La Pointe band; and Nug au nub, the speaker at Fond du Lac. Four mixed-bloods were also to be part of the delegation. According to Warren they were: "Vincent Roy of Lapointe, Edward Conner of Wisconsin, George P. Warren of Chippeway and Alex. Corbin of Lac Coutereille." He went on to tell Ramsey that since these leaders were all from the Lake Superior community (and inland Wisconsin), it would be politically wise to add representatives from the Minnesota Pillagers due to the "jealousies and ill will existing between these two divisions of the same tribe which should be immediately done away with." For this purpose he told Ramsey that Chief Flatmouth and two headmen or warriors should also be part of the delegation.[12]

Alexander Ramsey seemed impressed with Warren's long letter since he sent it on to Commissioner Luke Lea with a note of support. Despite Henry Sibley's aforementioned concern about Warren, doubtlessly by mid-January, 1851, it was felt by some Washington and Minnesota Territorial officials that Warren could be useful in their attempts at furthering removal efforts.[13]

In still another letter to George Warren, dated 4 February 1851, William spoke of ongoing efforts of fur trading company interests to get John Watrous removed from his position as special agent for Ojibwe removal and how "The Company have tried hard, and are still trying to have him removed, and have that old fool, Chas Oakes appointed, but they will not succeed. It is like jumping from the frying pan into the fire—and I prefer keeping in the frying pan, and have therefore thus far supported Mr Watrous." Here Warren's animosity toward the traders, and in this case especially Charles Oakes, comes through.[14]

In this February letter Warren also said that *the government was desirous of negotiating another treaty with the Ojibwe*, apparently for their remaining land immediately to the west of Lake Superior. This is one of a few indications in the literature that show the treaty of 1854 was being discussed for at least a full year and a half before Buffalo's famous 1852 trip to Washington, D.C. It also hints that the revocation of the Ojibwe removal order may have been agreed upon by Washington authorities as early as February 1851, the date of Warren's letter. In a note of self interest Warren told his cousin George that if, as Warren thought, Col. A.M. Mitchell, the Minnesota Territorial federal marshal were chosen as a treaty commissioner, "we have everything to hope for. He will make no Treaty unless he has plenty to gain and will do all he can for Half Breeds."[15]

Here Warren is speaking directly to the matter of treaty commissioners and how in some instances they functioned with personal ends in mind. Perhaps, as was the case with regional Indian agents, it was a given in American culture on the frontier that treaty commissioner appointments were patronage positions that provided opportunities to garner wealth beyond the appointee's salaries. In this sense it may be significant that on 27 February1851, Congress passed a resolution that mandated future commissioners "would be appointed from among officers and agents of the Indian office," and not from other non-official sources.[16]

Warren's certainty that both he and George would benefit from Col. Mitchell's appointment is revealing. As literate mixed-bloods, William and George Warren, and their immediate families, were in favorable positions to benefit monetarily from involvement as government employees in the removal process, and as we have already seen elsewhere, William's personal correspondence explicitly shows that he fully hoped to receive the financial gain such appointments would bring him.

## 3.

THERE WAS MUCH GOING ON in western Lake Superior country in early 1851, as the above brief discussion of William Warren's correspondence shows. Passions were heated as removal continued to be an issue. We are treated to a wealth of literature for these times, but unfortunately, it discloses little of the details occurring in Ojibwe communities. What we have, essentially, are the remarks of outsiders—at times we can clearly place those of William Warren among them—who tell us what the Ojibwe people were doing and saying in these important times, rather than the remarks of the Ojibwe themselves. That is the reality of early Ojibwe written history, and we are left to patch together what the people were thinking and saying at these times. Occasionally we are treated to a brief statement from a leader like La Pointe's Buffalo, but that is invariably presented in English, leaving us to ponder the problems of translation. To a great extent the voices of the rest of the people are practically silent and we are left to struggle in our attempts to hear them. But as we have seen, an exception to this silence is Buffalo's 1838 letter to Shingwaukonse, in which we see the open friendship between these two leaders and Buffalo's resolve to maintain his contacts with the British.

Along with this continuing effort to successfully manage relationships with both the Americans and British, another truth comes through for the bands south of Lake Superior. As Charles Cleland so adequately stated, "The Wisconsin Chippewa dug in their heels."[17] As the new year of 1851 started and fresh attempts to push removal were witnessed, the resistance of these bands grew. At times it was shown in "*sullen silence*,"[18] but at other times in loud disagreement, and this was a resistance that carried on through the entire year. Some of this resolve to resist the American efforts for removal was fueled by the relationships the Ojibwe south and west of Lake Superior were maintaining with Shingwaukonse. Puzzlingly, William Warren's writings do not indicate he was familiar with these ties so the people must have been keeping knowledge of them from him. Recalling Warren's earlier assurance that removal to a western site would leave the Ojibwe relatively free from the negative influences of Americans, we ponder what his reaction might have been to the suggestion of a removal to the *east* to join the proposed self-sufficient Ojibwe community in Ontario.

Be this as it may, almost immediately after their holiday festivities at the year's end, Governor Ramsey and John Watrous initiated what Charles Cleland has called "a more subtle approach to removal."[19] Pressure was coming from both Buffalo and the missionaries at La Pointe, and on 9 February 1851, the two men met in St. Paul to discuss their next steps, apparently among them the plan to agree to an Ojibwe trip to Washington. Ramsey stressed the need to correct the problem of adequate provisions that plagued them at Sandy Lake months earlier, and he insisted that enough food be purchased and readied. Also, he wanted more crops planted at the Minnesota farming sites so the produce would be available later in the year. In accordance with these suggestions, in a few weeks Watrous wrote to Ramsey saying he had finalized plans to not only enlarge existing government farm sites in Minnesota, but to open new ones. In this regard, on 24 March 1851, the La Pointe people were told not to do their usual spring planting since they were to remove to Fond du Lac, where provisions would be provided.

In their early February meeting, Ramsey warned Watrous to be prepared for attempts from the trading community to forestall and cause this removal to fail. Ramsey possibly was speaking about Henry Rice and others who he thought desired to derail his new removal effort in hopes of continuing to glean profits from annuity payments and to be awarded the contract for removal in the event the government's current initiative failed and it was opened to private businessmen. As the year unfolded and Ojibwe resistance solidified, this specter of Henry Rice lurking somewhere in the distance waiting for his opportunity to capitalize on a failed removal surfaced again and again.[20]

Watrous wanted the Wisconsin and Michigan bands to ultimately remove to Sandy Lake, and early in spring he intended to lure them westward with the promise of paying them their annuities. They would be given both their annuity goods and specie for 1851, as well as the specie for 1850 that was still owed them, and all payments would be made at Sandy Lake. However, unknown to the Ojibwe, the 1851 cash payment would purposely be delayed so late in the season that, hopefully, the people would be discouraged from returning to their eastern homes.[21]

To begin removal, Watrous set 10 June 1851 as the date for the Michigan and Wisconsin bands to assemble at La Pointe, where he would tell them they were to remove to Sandy Lake for their cash payments for 1850 and 1851 as well as their goods payment for the latter year. As it turned out, as 10 June approached a few hundred people did actually assemble at La Pointe, but Watrous did not arrive until 12 July, by which time many had returned home in disgust. Talk of this incident would surface repeatedly through the summer as evidence of the agent's propensity to lie to and deceive the people.

Part of the reason Watrous did not appear at La Pointe on 10 June was that he was busy attempting to get the St. Croix bands to remove. Governor Ramsey hoped to move some, if not all, of these people to Mille Lacs in Minnesota Territory. At this time the lumbering industry was growing in the St. Croix region, bringing the fear of more conflict between incoming whites and the resident Ojibwe. Persons in the Snake River and Pokegama communities began spending time in the nearby Mille Lacs area to escape the difficulties the lumbering industry could bring, and some began to stay. Soon John Watrous was working to get more to move to Mille Lacs and he recruited Sherman Hall to work with him in these efforts. In time, however, he changed plans and began to try to move the bulk of the St. Croix people to Crow Wing.[22]

It was during these several weeks of early summer 1851 that William Warren doubted John Watrous would hire him to assist in removal efforts because of the less-than-friendly relations between the two men. There were hard feelings due to Warren's perceptions of Watrous's handling of the Sandy Lake affair, so Warren sought employment as an interpreter for Governor Ramsey in his upcoming treaty negotiations with the Pembina Ojibwe in northwestern Minnesota Territory. Ramsey had intimated, or as Warren said, *promised*, he would hire Warren for this work, but as it turned out he appointed James Tanner instead.[23]

Simultaneous to Warren's attempts to secure this employment, on 24 June 1851, John Watrous wrote to him to ask that he join the new removal team as one of three "conductors" who would usher the Michigan and Wisconsin Ojibwe westward. Perhaps due to postal delays common in the times, Warren belatedly learned of the job offer, and upon its receipt he readily agreed to take it.

This appointment, however, was made with some anxiety on the part of John Watrous. Theresa Schenck claims, "Additional instructions were given to Warren that indicate a certain hesitancy, perhaps even mistrust, on the part of Watrous."[24] These instructions served to remind Warren of the importance of removal and that he was expected to wholeheartedly work with the other officials in order to bring about its successful conclusion. When acknowledging Warren's acceptance of the position, Watrous included the following revealing statement in his reply: "I need not tell you that it becomes necessary for me to lay aside all personal feelings at this time to accomplish the removal, my views are not changed or altered."[25]

Clement Beaulieu was also appointed a removal conductor, and the Reverend William Boutwell was to serve as an assistant superintendent of removal, headquartered at La Pointe. Another assistant was the aged Charles Oakes. Beaulieu would be in charge of bringing the Wisconsin River and Lac du Flambeau bands to La Pointe, and Warren was to usher those from the Chippewa River, Lac Courte Oreilles, Long Lake, Lake Chetek and Lake Pahquahwong—all from the interior of Wisconsin. Warren was given two assistants: Alexis Corbin and William's cousin, George Warren. Beaulieu and Boutwell were to receive four dollars a day, plus expenses, and Warren would receive three dollars a day, with expenses.[26]

Warren left his home at Two Rivers, Minnesota Territory, on 6 July 1851, and after a stop at his sister's home in St. Paul, arrived at Wisconsin's Chippewa River on 13 July. From there he set right to work attempting to convince the people to travel to La Pointe where they would assemble with other bands before moving on to Fond du Lac and then Sandy Lake. As he soon discovered, his task would not be easily accomplished.

4.

EVENTS OCCURRING DURING THE FEW MONTHS preceding Warren's journey to interior Wisconsin are integral to an understanding of the give and take of political relations between the Ojibwe people and local and distant American authorities. The complexities of the storyline of these events are usually not given in earlier, published accounts of Ojibwe history, and for us to gain a deeper understanding of what the people went through in 1851, we must look with some detail at the letters and other correspondence.

The earliest months of the year likely were an uneasy time for Washington authorities involved with Indian affairs in the Midwest. As we have seen, the aftermath of the Sandy Lake tragedy brought accusations of responsibility pointed at Washington. On top of that, as the year unfolded a growing resistance to Ojibwe removal was becoming troublesome, a resistance some feared could erupt into warfare. This resistance quickly led to an order to temporarily halt Ojibwe removal. The Minnesota writer Bruce White has traced the paper trail that led to the initial suspension of the presidential order[27] and shows that it started in spring 1850, with a petition from white citizens of Lake Superior's south shore. This was sent to Congress, passed to the president, then to Interior Secretary Alexander H.H. Stuart, and on 3 August, finally forwarded to Commissioner of Indian Affairs Luke Lea for a report. Lea prefaced his response by saying he received many letters "from sources of the highest consideration," all protesting Ojibwe removal, but he did not write the report until some ten months later, on 3 June 1851.[28] This report is of considerable importance since it shows that resistance coming out of La Pointe and other Ojibwe communities was causing Washington authorities to reconsider their earlier decisions concerning the Ojibwe people.

In his 3 June report, Lea recommended the removal order be modified to exclude portions of the L'Ance, Lac Vieux Desert, Ontonagon, Keweenaw, La Pointe and Bad River bands, "for the present," if they so wished. Presumably this recommendation was meant to apply to the more assimilated Ojibwe, perhaps many of them being of the mixed-blood community who were taking up farming, and who likely had incorporated aspects of Christianity into their lives. This may be the first indication in the written record that Department of Indian Affairs officials were reexamining the 1850 Removal Order. It also is significant that in his report Lea identified two communities in the immediate Chequamegon Bay area. His use of "Bad River" refers to the Ojibwe community in which Rev. and Mrs. Wheeler were active, while the "La Pointe" band must have been referring to the remaining Ojibwe community, which later became known as the Red Cliff band. Therefore, Lea's terminology indicates that by the early 1850s, the label "La Pointe band" no longer was meant to refer to all the Ojibwe persons using Madeline Island and the Chequamegon Bay region as the immediate center of their homeland. Instead, it referred to only those persons *not* settling in at the old gardening site at Bad River with the Wheelers. In fact, using Lea's 1851 terms, the label "La Pointe band" must have been referring to the Ojibwe *other than* the Bad River community. These non-Bad River people, apparently largely led by Chief Buffalo, in only a few years would be known as the Red Cliff Ojibwe band. (The importance of these labels will be revisited again below in the discussion of the Treaty of 1854.)

Seven weeks later Luke Lea must have written a second communiqué, dated 23 August, to the Interior Department because it is referred to by the Acting Secretary in his letter of 25 August, in which he told Lea: "As your request in your letter of 23 inst. you are authorized to instruct Agent Watrous to suspend the removal of the Chippeway Indians until the final determination of the President upon the subject of your letter of the 3rd June 1851 can be communicated to him." Unfortunately, it appears that this 23 August letter of Commissioner Lea has not yet surfaced. Upon receipt of the 25 August letter, Luke Lea telegrammed John Watrous on the same date he received that letter, telling him to suspend the removal. The obvious importance of this telegram will be discussed below.[29]

DURING THE SUMMER OF 1851, Commissioner Lea left Washington to come to Minnesota Territory to negotiate with the Dakota about land purchases, and Alexander Ramsey, as *ex-officio* Commissioner of Indian Affairs for Minnesota Territory, was part of these meetings. After their completion Ramsey immediately undertook negotiations with the Pembina Ojibwe in the Red River Valley, a matter that kept him out of his St. Paul office even further into the summer season.

Thus, Ramsey had little to do with Ojibwe removal during these months, a fact that meant decisions about day-to-day details were left to John Watrous, a man the Ojibwe people held a strong distaste for. To make matters even more uncertain for them, during this time Charles Oakes, a person we are told they were able to relate favorably to, resigned his position as an assistant superintendent of removal with the Watrous team.[30]

An important part of the events unfolding during these critical months concerns the long-term plan William Warren had for the Ojibwe. In his second letter written to his cousin George on 9 July 1851, marked "private," he disclosed for the first time his desire to work to reorganize the tribal structure of the Wisconsin and Michigan bands in order to improve their political power when negotiating with the American government. Apparently unknown to others before this disclosure, Warren hoped to bring the disparate Ojibwe communities together to form a single political body "which would be able to bargain with the government from a position of strength."[31] As Warren told his cousin, "My main object is a complete and full organization of the tribe and Half breeds if possible after this year. 'United action' must be our motto."[32]

This very interesting notion surely preoccupied William Warren during the trying months of 1851, as he struggled to bring the interior Wisconsin bands up to Lake Superior. When sharing this plan with his cousin, as Theresa Schenck said, he "indicated that he hoped to meet with all the Lake Superior Ojibwe at La Pointe, and there to explain to them his plan for unity."[33]

This vision of a united Ojibwe community, joined in a truly communal effort to not only survive but to do so as a powerful single political unit, has similarities to that of Shingwaukonse in Ontario, and must have been with William Warren for some time. Perhaps we can imagine his sentiments in 1850, when he and his sister made the long trek with the people from interior Wisconsin to Sandy Lake, and how poignant the outcome of that tragic effort was for him. And perhaps too, we can contemplate what some might say is the political naïveté held by Warren in his vision. We have already discussed the tenacity of the Ojibwe band system, which persisted over the hundreds of years of European and American contact, and should wonder about just how he intended to transcend this ancient political organization to bring his plan for unity to fruition. As we have seen, the very nature of a tribal system includes a network of separate bands that can coalesce temporarily when seriously threatened, or for regular ceremonial purposes, and return to their separate existences when the tension—whether negative or positive—is relieved. Given his certainty that the Ojibwe had to become "civilized," Warren was doing what the Christian missionaries were trying to do, that is, to get the people to stop "roaming" through the forests and over the waters and bring them together in a setting where missionaries and other change agents could, as Sherman Hall put it, "operate on their minds." In the process the tribesmen would become "civilized," i.e., change into sedentary Christian agriculturalists.

Thus, Warren wanted the same changes as the culture change agents, and for the same ultimate purpose, but his plan had a twist. Unlike the missionaries and others who asked the people to simply put aside one way of life and take up another, in his desire to help them form a united front he wanted them to seize some *bargaining power*. However, we might ask what it was they had left to bargain. Recalling the popular image of Ojibwe culture in 1851, as presented by historians and others, they were said to be a dependent people who resided in a land nearly bereft of the natural resources they needed to survive.

However, even given this image there may have been a number of negotiable items still held by the Ojibwe, and perhaps Warren planned to discuss them at his hoped-for La Pointe gathering. The most prominent may have been the *preserve* in northeastern Minnesota Territory, a large expanse of land known to hold an undetermined wealth of minerals. We discussed this matter above, and as just noted in his 6 February 1851 letter to George Warren, William Warren mentioned the American government's desire to acquire this land parcel through another treaty. As we will see below, by 1851, commentary about the need for such a treaty must have been a topic of discussion for American officials, land speculators and others.

A second item that might have been negotiable was the matter of a *peaceful* resolution to the issue of removal. The literature does not show that Warren intended to use fear of an Ojibwe war as a bargaining chip, but as already indicated, it does show that in the immediate decade preceding the 1854 LaPointe treaty, fear of military conflict with the Ojibwe was not non-existent. We recall Hole-in-the-Day's statement about the threat of Ojibwe physical conflict after the Sandy Lake incident, and also John Watrous's pleas for military assistance at LaPointe during the summer of 1851. That same summer, La Pointe's Sherman Hall apparently accepted the possibility of imminent Ojibwe warfare.[34] Already mentioned was Henry Rice's fear in 1848, only three years earlier, that the upper St. Croix valley could easily erupt in war between the Ojibwe and the United States. Thus, it is apparent that at the mid-century the possibility of warfare between the Ojibwe and the United States was feared in several quarters.

There is one more item William Warren might have been contemplating as a discussion topic at La Pointe. This is seen in the pathos witnessed in what was perceived by white America in the early nineteenth century as *the ending of a way of life*.[35] Even though the early literature repeatedly spoke of the unquestioned need for the "savages" to give way and accept Christianity and civilization, it also shows that there were those whites who at times took pause to ponder what was occurring in this, to some, perhaps poignant transition.

We are told that especially as a younger man, William Warren sat beside the fires of the peoples' lodges and shared in their discourse about their world. It is apparent he enjoyed this deep tribal aspect of his identity and we might expect, in a paradoxical way, perhaps known only to a mixed-blood person, that he respected—if not outright admired—such a way of life even though he felt it was "fated" to give way.[36] In this regard it is not unimportant to note that although he was raised as a Christian, attended a few missionary schools, and doubtlessly was familiar with Ojibwe traditional religious beliefs and practices, William Warren was not a crusader for religious change as many of his compatriots were. As suggested by Theresa Schenck, "He was not strongly religious,"[37] yet he still felt the Ojibwe needed to become "civilized," and in his day this meant they had to accept Christianity. Warren knew the people were at a very critical time in their history and in his eyes they had to make significant changes. Very importantly, he was aware they were being told to give something up. *That something was their age-old way of life.* In other words, he knew that *cultural loss* was part of the process of becoming "civilized." In the eyes of the change agents, when undergoing such a process something very valuable is gained. Perhaps to William Warren, something valuable is also lost.

Warren's intimation that the aggressive Americans were aware they were destroying an ancient way of life in western Lake Superior country was one of the rationales for writing his history book on the Ojibwe. Warren wrote for a white readership, and perhaps the most pressing reason for writing was the financial return he hoped it would bring, but it is also evident he was doing the hard work of constructing a valuable manuscript for a second reason. Like others in the literate world of his time, he felt the ancient Ojibwe way of life should be recorded in writing before it disappeared. The myth of the vanishing American Indian did not appear full blown in America for several more decades, but in 1852, Warren said he wanted "to snatch from oblivion what may be yet learned of the fast disappearing red race."[38] This sentiment is similar to what we noted in an earlier chapter about the remarks of some members of the 1832 Schoolcraft Expedition to the headwaters of the Mississippi River. The comments some of this expedition's members made about the Leech Lake Ojibwe community also suggested contemplative thoughts about cultural loss Ojibwe people were experiencing because of the coming of the Americans.

Attempting to grant a degree of plausibility to Warren's plan to develop a strong political unity throughout all the Ojibwe bands, we perhaps must recognize that by early 1851, the Chequamegon Bay Ojibwe, as was true for all the Michigan and Wisconsin bands, were in a very serious situation. If ever there was a time for them to transcend their age-old tribal system with its disparate bands and come together in a serious attempt at unity, it was in the early summer of 1851. In this sense, we may agree that the times were desperate, and remedial action was required.

Unfortunately, we do not know how the people would have responded to Warren's plan if he had been able to present it to their assembled group at La Pointe. The written record is silent about any reaction leaders like Buffalo might have had to it, or even to rumors of it.

5.

JOHN WATROUS FINALLY MADE IT to La Pointe on 12 July 1851, and as he expected, he found strong resistance to his plans. On the first of the month when still at Sandy Lake he had heard about these difficulties, and in a letter to Ramsey of that date he repeated his recommendation that a company of infantry be dispatched to La Pointe. He told Ramsey: "I fear, without the assistance of the military, I shall be unable to get the Indians started to Fond du Lac after their assembling at La Pointe. The place is much infested with whiskey and to suppress this traffic without some assistance from the military is impossible and equally so to control the Indians when they have access to it." Later in the month after arriving at La Pointe he again wrote to Ramsey asking for military aid. He estimated that 500 people were on hand, with many more expected when Beaulieu and Warren arrived with their groups from the interior.[39]

Perhaps we can imagine the scene on Madeline Island, in which several hundred Ojibwe were camping near the meeting grounds with their temporary shelters and cooking fires as they visited with relatives and others from distant bands, all discussing rumors of removal and anticipating the receipt of the cash and goods annuity payments. The traders, so ubiquitous at these gatherings, no doubt were nearby, ready to do business. There must have been much talk, laughter, and perhaps tribal games of one sort or another, but over this almost festive scene hung the question of removal.

In a letter of 29 July sent to Governor Ramsey, William Boutwell told how earlier in the summer a number of interior Wisconsin bands arrived only to find that Agent Watrous was not there, and that he had made no arrangements for provisions to feed their people while on Madeline. Boutwell claims that beyond their serious disappointment, they said in the future they would respond only to the call of "Chiefs and Braves on the Lake," and not to anyone else.[40] This resolute pronouncement to ignore the calls of Agent Watrous, or any other non-Ojibwe, says something about the extent of community cohesiveness developing between the Ojibwe bands in the summer of 1851. Watrous's call for the June La Pointe meeting led to a determined stand against him, and in this way William Warren's vision of a united Ojibwe front opposing removal may not have been unrealistic.

Chief Buffalo surely was in the midst of this colorful scene. This was Buffalo's home ground and he had to have been very busy with the removal threat for a year or more, holding councils, attending ceremonies and generally helping to formulate a plan of action. As the Assistant Superintendent of Removal, William Boutwell was also in the midst of this resistance, but obviously with a different perspective than Buffalo. In a letter written from La Pointe late in July, Boutwell relayed to Governor Ramsey what he was witnessing. He told how after John Watrous arrived and announced to the assemblage that they were to travel to Sandy Lake for their annuity payments, the people were "manifestly much disaffected," and that Chief Buffalo told Boutwell the Ojibwe demanded to be paid at La Pointe. As we will see below, there is documentary evidence to show that after some time, Buffalo agreed to lead his people to Fond du Lac to receive the annuities, but he refused to go any farther than that.[41]

At this time we see an image of Buffalo as a leader who, in 1851, seemed to have crossed a line in his relations with American authorities. No longer was he generally acquiescing to their wishes. Instead, by the summer of 1851, he stood firmly against them. After days of deliberation between Watrous and Buffalo, Boutwell told Ramsey how Buffalo was not relenting, and just as firmly, how Watrous refused to accept the aged leader's stance, telling Buffalo his people must go to Sandy Lake. As Boutwell put it, "The Old Buffalo stoutly insisted & the agent as firmly maintained his ground."[42]

This approximately six-week summer standoff at La Pointe is one of the most poignant images in the history of the Chequamegon Bay Ojibwe. At this time Buffalo was reputedly ninety-two years old, and he was fully aware of the power of the Americans. He had made a trip to the eastern seaboard only two years previously, where he witnessed the young nation's industrial cities with their large numbers of people. And certainly he was aware of the great size of the American military, yet he stood firm as he insisted his people would go no further than Fond du Lac.

While Buffalo was not budging at La Pointe, William Warren was encountering grave problems on the Chippewa River. Governor Ramsey had granted provisions in the amount of ten barrels of flour, three barrels of pork, fifty pounds of gunpowder and 100 pounds of shot for Warren to provide to the people as they moved up to La Pointe and on to Fond du Lac,[43] but Warren claimed in early July he had assembled five villages, comprising 850 individuals, and that these few provisions were woefully inadequate. He pleaded for permission to requisition more, but apparently to no avail. Consequently, the people were waiting until the completion of the wild rice harvest before moving north, and this could be in late August or even early September. Quite interestingly, as it turned out, Watrous was experiencing similar difficulties at St. Croix, where the people also worked to complete their wild rice harvest before moving, thus postponing the agent's arrival at La Pointe for his summer meeting.

What we note in both these instances is that the people were turning to their traditional subsistence practices while the government's officials were offering to provide them with American foodstuffs, i.e., wheat flour and pork. Once again we see an indigenous people determinedly utilizing their own traditional culture in times of stress when they were asked to turn away from it in favor of the outsiders'. It seems likely that the bands Warren was with on the Chippewa River, and perhaps some of those Watrous was with at St. Croix, were insisting on completing the rice harvest because they would need that food for the upcoming winter *at their present locations*. In other words, they might never have intended to remove, instead going about their seasonal routine as they did each year. It is possible, however, that even as they were taking the few weeks' time required to complete the rice harvest for their usual winter food supply, they also may have been using it as a delaying tactic in hopes of prolonging their departure so there was time to make the trip to Washington, after which they expected the removal order would be revoked.

This notion of viewing the rice harvest as a means of forestalling removal gains credence when we see that during the summer of 1851, the Ojibwe bands were dispatching runners with tobacco to the villages bringing the message to stand firm against removal. The message emanated from Buffalo and his cadre of assistants at La Pointe. Warren told Ramsey he suspected these runners were encouraging "an extended league throughout the whole tribe (excepting the St. Croix villages) not to remove. Pipes[,] wampum and tobacco have been sent from village to village to effect this purpose."[44] Since this tobacco came to the Ojibwe as gifts from the American government intended as encouragement for removal, the irony of how it was used at cross-purposes to its original intent is striking.

Here is another scene in Ojibwe history that calls for thought. According to Warren, these runners were dispatched with tobacco, pipes and *wampum*. Remembering that the Ojibwe pipe is a very important and sacred ritual item, we see that these runners were not merely bringing a *verbal* message. Tobacco and pipes are both ritual items pertaining to the *manidoog* world, and their presence sanctifies the setting they are in and the purposes they are put to. Just as important is Warren's mention of *wampum*. *Wampum* typically refers to a belt of beads or shells that is passed between parties, in some instances to depict a message, and in others to solemnize an agreement. In an oral culture it serves to enhance the spoken word that accompanies it, and as such, it was an important trade item on the Wisconsin frontier even though references to it are rarely found in the literature of the Ojibwe.[45] In the above instance, it doubtless was included in the runners' retinue of material objects to add deep importance to the message to resist removal.

Two major problems Warren told Ramsey he was encountering at the Chippewa River were the recurring disagreement over the Treaty of 1842 and the peoples' distrust of John Watrous. As we have already noted, the Ojibwe insisted that in 1842, during the negotiations with Robert Stuart they were led to believe they would be able to remain living on their Wisconsin and Michigan lands for a very long period of time, if not forever. This persistent argument—and it went far beyond the summer of 1851—suggests that, as often seemed to have been the case in these land treaty cessions, what the people understood was written in the treaty may have been at odds with what was actually there.

The issue of Robert Stuart and his treaty of 1842 stands out in Ojibwe history as one of the most troublesome incidents they ever encountered. Regarding John Watrous, Warren told Ramsey that even before he failed to keep his 10 June appointment at La Pointe he had lost favor with the people. It was this same agent who was rumored to have been overly extravagant with gifts of medals and provisions at St. Croix as he worked to convince those Ojibwe to move west, at the same time William Warren was laboring at the Chippewa River with a much smaller larder—and apparently with no personal gifts, like medals, to help his cause. This indictment of John Watrous would come back to seriously affect William Warren. In the end, despite the hardships at the Chippewa River that summer, Warren told Ramsey he still hoped to assemble his interior bands and lead them up to La Pointe by 1 October 1851.[46]

## 6.

AS THE MONTH OF JULY PASSED, things were not going well for John Watrous at La Pointe. Buffalo was intransigent, and there were rumors that Beaulieu was having problems at Lac du Flambeau. Even more, there was no word from Warren at Chippewa River. Watrous was to be in Crow Wing soon to begin making the annuity payments for the Mississippi River bands and he was running out of time. Through all of this William Boutwell was keeping Governor Ramsey informed of the proceedings at La Pointe and in one letter he told how distraught Watrous was becoming. In response Ramsey wrote the agent on 14 August 1851, offering what has become a familiar quote: "Be of good cheer, and try to conquer all obstacles in the way of removal."[47] On 7 August 1851, to the relief of Watrous, Clement Beaulieu and fourteen persons from Lac du Flambeau arrived, with more to follow.[48]

After Beaulieu's arrival, Watrous was feeling more optimistic about the possibility of the removal plan actually being carried out, but he was growing frustrated with William Warren. The traders did not want removal so they could continue to profit from annuities paid at La Pointe. While he must have felt Warren was a vehement opponent of the trading community and its willingness to dispense liquor to the Ojibwe, John Watrous still suspected Warren was subversively working against him by telling the Chippewa River bands not to move north. Watrous later told Ramsey the only reason he hired Warren as a removal conductor was to quiet his (Warren's) attempts to obstruct removal efforts. By assigning Warren the responsibility of supervising the removal of Wisconsin's interior bands he was situating him within a context where he (Warren) could be held accountable for his actions.[49] However, Theresa Schenck feels Warren's personal correspondence of the time shows he was not working to obstruct removal. She notes that he was telling the people to move in order to be free of the inflammatory influence of the traders. Of Warren, Schenck says these letters "belie any subversive effort on his part to convince them to remain on their lands or to return after payment."[50]

Soon after Clement Beaulieu arrived, John Watrous turned up the pressure by beginning a series of councils that ran for several days, starting on 13 August with a six hour session, and followed by five consecutive days of meetings.[51] We might wonder what transpired during these sessions. Surely they were meetings in which the agent tried repeatedly to persuade the Ojibwe to move only to be countered by Buffalo and the other leaders who spoke against it. The correspondence William Boutwell sent to Ramsey hints at the emotion of these meetings but we yearn to hear the Ojibwe voices in these councils. The image of all that was involved in these five days of open-air sessions on the council ground at Madeline Island in the summer of 1851, in which Ojibwe leaders argued for non-removal while officials of the American government responded with the contrary, is thought-provoking today. The surrounding encampments with their cooking fires, the ubiquitous community dogs amidst everything, the non-Ojibwe onlookers seated at and milling around the fringes of the grounds, the native and non-native children darting in and out of the crowd throughout the day, and all else that these meetings entailed offers a very colorful scene.

No doubt in the meetings John Watrous threatened to call in the military to effect a forced removal and although it is not clear, this may have been a factor in the eventual resolution of the dispute. The specter of a confrontation with the U.S. Army at La Pointe must not have been a pleasant image for the aged Buffalo, or for John Watrous. We have seen that for some time rumors of the Ojibwe going to war over removal circulated in the region and despite the literature's images of a community of tribesmen decimated by smallpox, seriously harmed by the Sandy Lake incident, and perpetually troubled by the traders' rum, it appears that in 1851, these rumors had a realistic aspect to them. Buffalo's summer standoff at La Pointe certainly must not have worked to relieve John Watrous's anxiety such rumors doubtlessly generated.

By mid-summer the Ojibwe had lost all confidence in Watrous, and for months Buffalo, his sub-chiefs, and other leaders had asked for permission to make the trip to Washington to meet with the president to present their case, and if the removal order was valid, to hear it from the mouth of the "Great Father" himself. The fact that these leaders asked for permission reminds us of political protocol extant in the early nineteenth century in America. The need for permission points to the underlying inequality of relations between tribal and Washington leaders. The Ojibwe also wanted their cash annuities from 1850, which were now a full year late, as well as the cash and goods payments due for 1851, and Buffalo wanted these to be paid at Fond du Lac. These were the two concerns they kept presenting to the agent. No doubt their annuities were important to them, but it is evident the proposed Washington trip was much more so, and as both Boutwell and Watrous stated, the Washington trip was their priority.[52]

Perhaps well over one thousand Ojibwe people congregated at La Pointe by early August, even though some had returned home in disgust upon hearing they would not be paid their annuities at that location.[53] A few weeks before 13 August, the western Michigan bands from L'Ance went back home, choosing to relinquish their annuities in favor of keeping their farming plots they had purchased in the Keweenaw area. Surely the exodus of these people increased the tension at La Pointe and threatened to bring the entire matter of removal to an abrupt end.

The details of exactly what transpired in mid-August at what had to have been very tense, if not emotional, meetings between John Watrous (and his assistants) and the Ojibwe on Madeline Island are unknown, but the correspondence of Watrous and William Boutwell provides a window to aid our understanding of these important events. The general outline of proceedings described in their writing is similar, but unfortunately, some of the details are not in complete agreement. An example is what transpired when a compromise was finally reached on 19 August.

As we have seen, Governor Ramsey was enforcing Orlando Brown's order to pay annuities only on ceded lands, a rule that would bring cash to the Minnesota Territory's economy. In line with this decree, at La Pointe John Watrous insisted the people would have to travel to Sandy Lake for their payments, and that those who did not go—including the mixed bloods—would not be paid. After a few weeks of the Buffalo-Watrous standoff, William Boutwell tried to persuade Watrous to relent and make the payments at Fond du Lac, a site on land the Ojibwe had not yet ceded to the United States, and as we have seen, a location they agreed to move to.

In a letter to Governor Ramsey dated 24 August, John Watrous claimed that his first council with the people was on 13 August, and after five days of not being able to compromise, late in the day on 18 August the Ojibwe finally "stated the terms upon which they would remove," this being the payment to them of the sum of $200,000.00. Watrous claims he became indignant at what apparently was for him a ludicrous proposal, and threatened to break off the meetings and leave La Pointe in the morning. This threat caused yet another council, held the following morning, 19 August, at which Watrous pledged to do three things. First, he would make the cash payments for the annuities for both 1850 and 1851 at Fond du Lac instead of Sandy Lake. (He claimed the annuity goods were shipped from St. Paul to Sandy Lake and simply were too cumbersome to be expeditiously moved to Fond du Lac, so the people would have to travel to Sandy Lake for them.) Second, Watrous would provide fishing equipment for the Ojibwe once they moved to Fond du Lac, and he would feed them for one year, as well as open fields and build houses for them at that location. Third, he would ask permission for and recommend that the Ojibwe leaders be allowed to make the trip to Washington during the upcoming winter, and he would accompany them on this journey. (Apparently the Ojibwe insisted Watrous travel to Washington with them so he would be witness to what they felt would be the president's cancellation of the removal order.)[54]

In a letter William Boutwell wrote to Governor Ramsey on 18 September 1851, we get a different reading of the events leading to the compromise. He claimed that once Watrous and the Ojibwe arrived on Madeline Island they began:

> . . . a series of counsels for 10 days. the Inds. disputing every inch of ground, absolutely refusing to remove & stoutly maintaining the right of soil, declaring they would encounter famine & death before they would relinquish their rights & go, declared the treaty of 42 a fraud, and nothing less than [$]200,000 would compensate them for what they should be compelled to leave in the event of removal.[55]

Boutwell's letter does not support the claim of Watrous that on 18 August the Ojibwe said they *would* remove if they were paid $200,000.00. He states instead that the Ojibwe told the agent that *if they were forced to remove*—supposedly by the military Watrous threatened to use—they would want at least $200,000.00 to "compensate them for what they should be compelled to leave." This latter statement is quite different from how John Watrous put the matter of the $200,000.00 to Governor Ramsey, and perhaps we would be correct in concluding the $200,000.00 was to make restitution to those Ojibwe who had opened fields, built houses and outbuildings, as well as purchasing livestock and horses at La Pointe, L'Ance, and elsewhere, when undertaking agriculture. It was on the next day—19 August—after the three pledges of Watrous, that the removal finally began.

In discussing William Boutwell's interpretation of the 19 August meeting sent to Ramsey, the writer Bruce White says that according to Boutwell:

> At one point the 'mass' rushed from the council in 'a perfect frenzy' to pack everything for a return to the interior. It may have been at this point that a compromise was reached. Boutwell suggested that Beaulieu was crucial to the compromise, apparently persuading 'the braves to come to our aid.' Watrous's pledges persuaded chiefs and braves to consent to remove. They said they would send their young men with tobacco to bring out the remaining members of the bands. Boutwell wrote that the permanence of the removal agreed to turned '*much, very much* upon the question, whether their wishes are regarded in visiting their G. Father & laying the subject of their grievances before him. Nothing short of this will satisfy them. Indeed the hope of attaining this object, weighed more with them than any other or than all other considerations in inducing them to yield the point & remove'.[56]

What are we to conclude from this? Obviously, among other things, the old Ojibwe political organization was still a factor at La Pointe in mid-August 1851. The opposition of war chiefs with their warriors, and the civil chiefs like Buffalo and their followers, was working as the resolution to the weeks-long standoff was achieved. We yearn to know what Clement Beaulieu did or said to gain the cooperation of the "braves" who, according to William Boutwell, caused the Ojibwe to agree to leave La Pointe and paddle to Fond du Lac.

And just what did Boutwell mean in his remark about "the permanence" of the removal agreed to? All through the summer of 1851, Watrous and his assistants were fearful that the Ojibwe might agree to remove but once the annuity payments were made would immediately turn around and return home. As already stated, we might conclude that the Ojibwe agreed to remove permanently to Fond du Lac but only if Watrous would work to bring approval for their Washington trip, a trip they were certain would cause the cancellation of the removal order. Therefore, if they did remove, and then the order was cancelled, they could immediately return home. It is interesting that the Ojibwe leaders might have been under the impression that Agent Watrous had the power to cause the approval of the trip. However, they could not be certain that the president would, indeed, cancel the order, and the Ojibwe must have known that. Even though they apparently felt the president *would* cancel the order, they could not finally be sure, and so, agreeing to remove was still a gamble.

We should remember the point Theresa Schenck makes about how the English verb "to remove" might have been translated. If she is correct, and *gosiwin* was the Ojibwe word translators chose to use, then, as she suggests, even though the American authorities stressed a permanent removal, to the Ojibwe "removal" might have been understood to mean a temporary move, not a permanent, final removal. This question could also help explain why Buffalo and others agreed to move to Fond du Lac.

The issue raised by these events, and one that the written literature fails to ask, is whether or not, in the summer of 1851, Buffalo really agreed to remove *permanently* to Fond du Lac. This is an important question due to its bearing on the image of Chief Buffalo as a strong leader. Today's mystique of Buffalo includes the belief that he refused to give up the ancient lands of his people—most importantly, those in the immediate La Pointe region—yet, the written literature shows us he might actually have agreed to make a permanent removal to the unceded lands at Fond du Lac during that decisive month of August in 1851. (We also are left with the enigma of the fact that back in 1842, Buffalo was one of the signatories on the treaty that saw the Ojibwe sign away what was left of all their land in what is now Wisconsin.)

Ojibwe oral traditions maintain that Buffalo stood firm and never relinquished occupancy of his homeland at La Pointe right up to his death in 1855, but the written literature of the time is not clear and could be interpreted to show that in late summer of 1851, Buffalo did indeed lead his people from Chequamegon Bay and Madeline Island when he agreed to remove to Fond du Lac. Some insight to this matter is found in William Boutwell's letter of 18 September, as discussed above, but does not answer this important question.

The dichotomy of *civil* and *war* chiefs within the structure of the Ojibwe political organization likely was integral in what occurred to bring about the compromise between John Watrous and the Ojibwe. Buffalo was a leading civil chief, meaning he spoke for negotiation, compromise and the like in matters of political relations, while contrariwise, the war chiefs—with their cadre of "braves"—stood ready to settle matters with force. This interplay of civil and war leaders suggests that in 1851, an important portion of the old Ojibwe political system was still a factor in the peoples' relationships with outside governments. It also reminds us that during the summer of 1851, the actuality of warfare occurring between the United States and the Ojibwe bands of Lake Superior was a possibility.

COMMISSIONER LUKE LEA'S TELEGRAM ordering Watrous to suspend removal, sent from Washington on 25 August, arrived at La Pointe on 3 September but was not shared with the Ojibwe. In his letter of 18 September to Ramsey, Boutwell went on to say little had occurred since the agreement of 19 August, a period of a full month. Watrous was still waiting for the arrival of William Warren and his contingent of Ojibwe bands from the interior. Boutwell noted that on 28 August, 150 people left La Pointe for Fond du Lac and the rest (500-600) would soon follow. He closed the letter with: "I would only add, on the 3rd of Sept. a telegraphic dispatch came to hand viz. 'Suspend active operations in the removal until further orders.' The purport of the order remains a secret & as the Inds. are ready to go I shall start them." Thus, as Bruce White notes, even though William Boutwell says the removal was underway in the fall of 1851, Lea's telegram "called into question the entire authority under which the removal effort operated."[57]

A bit of the spirit of these difficult days is seen in a letter Leonard Wheeler wrote from Bad River to his father on 22 September 1851. Apparently while the above acrimonious negotiations were unfolding on Madeline Island, the Wheelers were at home at their mission station a few miles south on the mainland at Bad River. In his letter Wheeler said:

> . . . most of the Indians have been absent since the middle of July. They are now about us again, and perhaps for the last time. They have been ordered to remove from here to Fon du Lac, where they will go in a few days for their payment. Our Indians are very unwilling to remove permanently and say they will come back, as they doubtless will; after they get their money. They are in a very unsettled condition, and their prospects look not a little dark. We shall remain here during the winter and perhaps permanently, but this is somewhat doubtful.[58]

7.

THE DETAILS OF THE ORIGIN of Commissioner Lea's telegram to suspend removal operations are revealing in that they show that as early as 3 June 1851, he recommended the removal order be modified to allow portions of the Lake Superior bands to remain where they were, at least "for the present." Apparently others, and the interior Wisconsin bands, would still be expected to remove. Unfortunately, Lea left Washington on 4 June, the day after he sent this recommendation to the Indian Affairs Office, and did not return until late August, when he sent a second letter to Indian Affairs inquiring about his earlier recommendation. This brought a reply, dated 25 August, from the Acting Secretary authorizing him to suspend removal until the president could make a determination on Lea's report of 3 June. On the receipt of this letter Lea immediately sent the telegram to John Watrous ordering the suspension of removal operations. It is noted that unlike in his June report, where he recommended suspension of operations for *portions* of the lake bands, in his August telegram he spoke to *all* removal operations. We might think that Ojibwe resistance to continuing removal efforts in early 1851, strong commentary about Sandy Lake in the media, and personal correspondence from what Luke Lea called "sources of the highest consideration" were the root causes for the issuance of the suspension order.

However, Bruce White raises the question of the possible involvement of Alexander Ramsey and a new factor for this decision to suspend removal. We note that Ramsey came to Washington in spring to meet with Commissioner Lea about the upcoming Dakota treaties, but doubtless to discuss other territorial concerns as well, including Ojibwe matters, and as White says, Lea wrote his suspension recommendation "shortly after the visit of Governor Ramsey." Then, the day after Lea wrote this report he left Washington to travel to Minnesota Territory to negotiate the treaties with the Dakota—a negotiation process that included Ramsey—and after the completion of these negotiations he returned to the capital where he immediately wrote the letter to the Interior Department secretary inquiring about any action taken on his recommendation to suspend Ojibwe removal. Surely during these months in Minnesota Territory when Lea and Ramsey were together they discussed Ojibwe removal. The number of incidents when Lea and Ramsey were in each other's company in the first several months of 1851 leads Bruce White to conclude "there is reason to believe that Ramsey may have been aware of the suspension order before it was given. He may actually have urged Lea to send it." White's interesting speculation on Ramsey's involvement in the suspension order raises the question of motivation. Why would Alexander Ramsey, the Governor of Minnesota Territory, have wanted to halt Ojibwe removal when he was the person who initiated the removal order a year or so previous?[59]

As noted above, Ramsey was one of the officials receiving blame for the Sandy Lake tragedy, and throughout 1850 and 1851, he was also aware of the newspaper articles, letters and petitions speaking against Ojibwe removal. Some of these pieces of correspondence were sent directly to him, and in early 1851 they had to have been on his mind. Surely these matters were a topic of discussion with federal officials when he was in Washington and when these same officials came to Minnesota Territory.

Bruce White speculates that Lea may have "obtained some new information in Minnesota during his time in the company of Alexander Ramsey." Assuming this was the case, it could be possible the "new information" concerned the emerging notion held by American authorities to allow the Wisconsin and Michigan Ojibwe to remain where they were if they agreed to sell the "Ojibwe preserve," the large land parcel just west of Lake Superior. We recall that the Americans had long coveted this last large piece of Ojibwe land in eastern Minnesota Territory, and in his 1851 annual report to Ramsey, Watrous mentioned the mineral wealth the preserve held and the need for a new treaty to acquire it.[60] As we have discussed, in his 4 February 1851 letter to cousin George, William Warren also spoke of the Americans' desire for a new Ojibwe land treaty. It appears that by 1851, this desire was a regular topic of discussion for American officials.[61]

A few weeks later, in a letter of 2 January 1852 to Watrous, Ramsey stated he expected "a change coming in the government's policy toward the Lake Superior Ojibwe," although he later told the agent this may have been a "hasty" conclusion on his part.[62] Just beginning to come into focus at this time, and hinted at by these remarks of Ramsey, may have been the still unformulated plan to let the Michigan and Wisconsin bands reside where they were if they agreed to sell the preserve.

If these presumptions are correct, American officials might have been concluding that the troublesome protestations from Buffalo and the other Ojibwe leaders as well as Luke Lea's "sources of the highest consideration" could be pacified by a tradeoff in which the Ojibwe would be allowed to remain where they were if they agreed to a new land treaty for the preserve. This trade, however, would not be possible if the Ojibwe were effectively removed, or if the presidential order for removal was cancelled. If either of these events occurred the threat of removal would be over and the Americans would have had nothing but a monetary compensation to offer for the preserve. By the end of 1851, the Ojibwes' resolve against selling any more land to the Americans may have been so firm that Ramsey and others might have felt they needed more than money to have the tribesmen come to another treaty negotiation session. Furthermore, by late 1851, all annuities were being paid on unceded lands, so Ramsey's goal of bringing these monies to Minnesota Territory was fulfilled. Thus, even though he initially wanted Ojibwe removal, sometime in 1851, Ramsey's hope for the Territorial acquisition of the mineral-rich preserve may have caused him to seek a suspension of the removal order to allow for the trade. This interesting matter will be revisited below.

8.

WILLIAM BOUTWELL DISPATCHED an Ojibwe runner named Yellow Beaver from La Pointe to carry the telegram to John Watrous at Sandy Lake. The written record shows that Yellow Beaver was paid for delivering the message, so we are assured Watrous actually received it.[63]

It is likely Lea's telegram reached him on or about 11 September at Sandy Lake, but there is nothing in the written record to show that he notified his superior—Governor Ramsey—or the Ojibwe people. However, about a week earlier Luke Lea wrote a letter dated 5 September to Selah B. Treat of the American Board of Commissioners of Foreign Missions in Boston, telling him of the order, and Treat soon sent this information to Sherman Hall at La Pointe. Also, at about this time the *Lake Superior Journal* ran an article proclaiming that the removal had been stopped, so the news of the suspension was quickly dispensed throughout the western Lake Superior region. Unfortunately, we have no knowledge of how or when it exactly came to Buffalo and his co-leaders at La Pointe, and of the reaction such news would have elicited.[64]

Some nine days after receiving Lea's telegram, Watrous wrote his annual report to Ramsey, a document striking for its method of handling the suspension order. No direct mention is made of Lea's telegram, instead, as Bruce White says: "Watrous here used the strategy of stating that the removal effort was an accomplished fact and that there was little left to do. Since all actions were completed, there was nothing to cease doing." Watrous told Ramsey the final tally would show that 3,000 people had been removed, and while some 700 remained on ceded lands in Wisconsin and Michigan, in time these were certain to move westward. He opined that even though many had removed they would probably return to their old locations, causing "depredations and plunder" on non-Ojibwe people and property along the way, and he urged that a military fort be established at the head of Lake Superior to work to prevent this.[65]

We might wonder why Watrous said so many Ojibwe would return to their eastern homes wrecking havoc on whites along the way. Except for some reputed cases of Ojibwe persons molesting the "potato patches" of whites, (mentioned above), the written record is practically silent on any "plunder and depredation" the Ojibwe ever brought to bear upon white persons and property in the western Lake Superior area, and as Bruce White tells, the record for 1851 and the immediate years is silent on this matter. Perhaps Agent Watrous, in an attempt to counter the negative criticism he was receiving from the tribal people and others in the trading community, resorted to the stereotyped image of "savages" prevalent at the time to give the public impression that his—self-proclaimed—success at moving the "thousands" of Ojibwe was a major accomplishment.

Bruce White feels Watrous was aware his report would be public information, and thus he carefully crafted the document in order to "give the public impression that the removal had been successful and to forestall any further order that he suspend the operation."[66] By precluding further action on the part of Washington authorities toward suspension, Watrous was allowing his and Ramsey's removal efforts to continue into the waning weeks of fall and early winter. Governor Ramsey wrote his annual report—to Luke Lea—shortly after receiving the Watrous report, and essentially reiterated the information Watrous sent him. Finally, in turn—and almost immediately upon receiving the Ramsey document—Lea wrote his annual report for the Secretary of the Interior, in which he also repeated the information provided by Agent Watrous. Thus, the effect of John Watrous's words about removal was far-reaching. These three reports all stated the removal was practically completed, with only minor details left to finish the job.

In his report Lea urged, as Watrous and Ramsey had already done, that a new treaty with the Ojibwe be negotiated to purchase all their remaining lands west of the Mississippi River, and to concentrate the various bands and villages in one Minnesota location. This desire to secure the Ojibwe preserve was becoming very evident at the close of 1851.[67]

During the remaining three months of the year John Watrous traveled between La Pointe, Fond du Lac and Sandy Lake to make the required specie and annuity goods payments to the Mississippi and Lake Superior bands. Despite his forced agreement to make the cash payment to the lake bands at Fond du Lac, it was still his intent to make the others at distant Sandy Lake. He agreed to be at Fond du Lac by 1 October to pay the Lake Superior bands their cash annuity, but told Ramsey he intended to stall that payment until after the close of open water "in order to throw every obstacle in the way of their returning to their old homes."[68]

He told the Ojibwe he would be at Fond du Lac on 1 October to make their cash payment for 1850 and 1851, but did not keep that appointment. After arriving on 5 October he held councils with the Ojibwe in which he tried to convince them of the need to delay the annuity payments because, as he claimed, the site was "much infested with whiskey dealers." Sometime before 17 October, William Warren finally arrived at Fond du Lac with the advance party of Ojibwe from Wisconsin's interior and said 500-600 persons were following him. By this time the relationship between Warren and Watrous was in tatters.[69]

On about 17 October, Watrous left Fond du Lac to go to Sandy Lake for the Mississippi and Pillager payments. He stayed there for the next few weeks, making the cash and goods annuity payments to the Minnesota bands, and on 3 November, the goods payments to those of the Lake Superior bands who were there. It seems apparent that few of the lake bands bothered to make the late trip to Sandy Lake for this payment. By that time the region was heading into early winter and the navigation season would soon be over. The 1850 and 1851 cash payments due to the Lake Superior bands were not made before the close of the year.

Unfortunately we do not have a detailed account of the events at Fond du Lac from 1 October, the date the cash annuity payment was to be made, through the ensuing weeks, but we do know that Agent Watrous held a series of meetings at which he attempted to have the Ojibwe accept his decision to postpone annuity payments because of the many liquor dealers at the site. Finally, since Watrous refused to make the payments, some Ojibwe felt absolved from their 19 August agreement to remove to Fond du Lac, and returned home, Chief Buffalo among them. Thus, it seems the August 1851 removal of the Ojibwe from La Pointe to Fond du Lac lasted only about two months.[70]

In the closing months of the year politically slanted articles in regional newspapers spoke to the success or failure of the government's removal efforts, and Agent Watrous was both applauded and criticized. As a response to this, when back in St. Paul on 15 December he wrote a letter to Governor Ramsey in which he summed up his removal efforts for the year. He informed Ramsey that "active operations have now ceased." Three months earlier he stated in his annual report, written in mid-September, that about 3,000 persons would be removed to Minnesota Territory, but in this December summation of removal activities he said only 1,600 to 1,700 persons would be listed on the Fond du Lac removal roll when it was completed at the end of the month. He also claimed that except for two, all chiefs had moved, and excluding the L'Ance band and some persons from Lac Vieux Desert and a few other smaller bands that were inflicted with measles, the Ojibwe people essentially were now in Minnesota Territory. He expressed certainty that because of Ramsey's rule that only those who removed would be paid their annuities, in time the remnant groups remaining in Wisconsin would surely remove. We note that the agent's scaled-down tally of persons removed was still drastically inflated. In early 1852, La Pointe's Reverend Wheeler stated that after all the pressure and activity involved with the government's removal efforts, no more than 200 persons had actually removed.[71]

9.

ALL THROUGH 1851, THE PROGRESS of the removal efforts was being watched and commented upon by the non-Ojibwe community in the western Lake Superior region. The early petitions emanating from white citizens in Michigan and Wisconsin are cases in point. At the end of the year the St. Paul newspapers' role in this discussion turned bitter as the editors and correspondents of the *Minnesota Democrat* and the *Minnesotian* squared off in an argument about whether or not removal was successful.

This commentary began on 18 November, with a brief piece in the *Minnesota Democrat* that pronounced the removal "a complete failure," promising to tell more in future articles. In a 22 November piece the *Minnesotian* refuted this charge and hinted that William Warren wrote the *Democrat* article, making it untrustworthy. A week later the *Minnesotian* explained that right from the start the trading community worked to counteract the efforts at removal, and given these hardships, concluded that Agent Watrous had been quite successful. The writer stated that Clement Beaulieu had succeeded at Lac du Flambeau, but Warren had failed at the Chippewa River. Then, in an article dated 6 December, the *Minnesotian* resumed its attack on Warren, saying his arguments were not valid since he "possessed all the duplicity of the Indian race." This article reverted to what was a common criticism of some persons of mixed-blood at the time, that is, it characterized William Warren as having a "partial education" and of associating with "the worst class of a frontier white population."[72]

On 10 December, the *Minnesota Democrat* countered with an article written by Warren in which he detailed his efforts to have the interior bands move, and he insisted it was always his intention to lead his charges to Sandy Lake, not Fond du Lac. He claimed that despite John Watrous's statement that Sandy Lake was the ultimate destination for the Ojibwe, and that it was the site where payments of both the cash and goods annuities were to be made, he (Watrous) really wanted the cash payments to be made at Fond du Lac where his trading friend, George Nettleton, and others could benefit. At the time, this must have been a startling accusation, and one Warren did not expect to go unchallenged.

In what is an interesting disclosure regarding his several motives for taking employment as a government removal "conductor," Warren said it was always his intent to lead the people to Sandy Lake so the annual annuity monies would benefit Benton County, his home region in western Minnesota Territory. As Warren explained:

> I have worked hard all summer to secure the payment of the cash annuities due the Chippewas, amounting to $44,000, all at Sandy Lake, on the Upper Mississippi; and this was one of the main motives which led me to join the Chippewa removal. I knew it would benefit Benton County and the Territory at large. The money would naturally have found its way down the Mississippi, (the natural channel) and instead of hard times, we should have had easy times, and money would have been plenty.[73]

Here we again see the importance of federal treaty annuities to local non-Ojibwe economies. On another level, also as noted above, we are reminded that as a mixed-blood, William Warren was living in two worlds. On the one hand it seems he was sincere in his beliefs that removal and the payment of annuities would benefit the Ojibwe people, but on the other hand was the reality of his self-interest in having cash annuities ultimately benefit his friends, neighbors and "constituents" in Benton County. Thus, in an interesting way, Warren was accusing Watrous of having motives not completely dissimilar from his own. That is, they both intended for the cash annuities to ultimately benefit persons other than the Ojibwe.

On 13 December, William Boutwell entered the fray with a letter in the *Minnesotian* in which he rebutted Warren's attack on John Watrous. Boutwell insisted that Sandy Lake had always been the destination Watrous sought for the payment of Ojibwe annuities and accused Warren of being "devoid either of truth or moral honesty."[74] Warren countered with a letter of 31 December in the *Minnesota Democrat* in which he expressed shock and dismay at Boutwell's personal attack, but he stood his ground regarding his insistence that the Watrous plan always was to make the annuity payments at Fond du Lac instead of Sandy Lake.[75]

Surely, as was the case with the regional press, the tribal community must have been abuzz with talk of the removal, and councils of chiefs and headmen as well as religious ceremonies likely were occurring regularly throughout these trying times at the close of the year.

10.

CLEARLY, THE OJIBWE VOICE was not silent during these last months of 1851. The written record shows that over this time at least three petitions were sent to Washington, D.C., and at least two delegations of representatives from La Pointe were dispatched to Governor Ramsey in St. Paul. Bruce White notes that some of these initiatives supported several of the newspaper charges made by William Warren.[76] For example, a 1 September petition from twenty Wisconsin and St. Croix chiefs, written at Fond du Lac and addressed to Washington authorities, complained of Agent Watrous and asked once again for Ojibwe delegates to make the trip to Washington to see the "Great Father" about canceling the removal order.

Another, from La Pointe and addressed to Luke Lea, is dated 6 November and is signed by twenty-eight chiefs. They complained about Agent Watrous much more vociferously than the earlier petitioners, an indication that as the year wore on frustration about him mounted. They also reviewed their difficulties with the Treaty of 1842 and its bearing upon the removal order, and stated their anger about the hardships and losses at Sandy Lake the previous winter. This lengthy petition was transcribed by Leonard Wheeler and witnessed by Sherman Hall, and the fact of its long list of signatories tells of a widespread frustration throughout the Ojibwe community with John Watrous and his removal efforts. Also, we might consider the type of community gathering from which a petition like this emanated. The fact that all of the twenty-eight chiefs and headmen signed this document indicates that these persons probably had input in the issues the petition presented. Traditionally, such gatherings epitomized the democratic process since they allowed for all persons present to speak their piece before final deliberations and conclusions were drawn.

A third petition, dated 8 November from Lac Courte Oreille and Wisconsin River leaders, expressed discontent with Watrous. It also supported Warren's statement that annuity payments were expected to be made at Sandy Lake, where the problem of predatory traders was less pronounced.

In December, Ojibwe representatives from La Pointe were in St. Paul, Minnesota, to deliver a letter from Chief Buffalo to Governor Ramsey. Two of Buffalo's sons and the young Chief Oshaga (who also may have been a son of Buffalo) made the journey, and Ramsey's diary shows that such a delegation met with them on 16 December and how they stressed again the importance of a trip to Washington. Along with Buffalo's letter, this delegation carried a letter of introduction from missionary Sherman Hall which reviewed the three pledges John Watrous made at La Pointe in August, and explained why the La Pointe people felt justified in leaving Fond du Lac in October.

Apparently in response to this visit, Ramsey wrote a letter to Buffalo, dated 19 December, in which he claimed to regret the La Pointe peoples' decision to abandon Fond du Lac and return home on 20 October, and he said he ordered Watrous to make the 1850 and 1851 cash annuity payments to the Lake Superior bands if they agreed to move back to Fond du Lac in spring. Ramsey also assured Buffalo that he had written a letter to Washington recommending the trip to see the president about removal. On the same date Ramsey wrote another letter to Watrous telling him to make the annuity payments, but he did not indicate where or when the agent was to do this.

On 22 December Ramsey's diary shows that he dined with four La Pointe chiefs and a trader named Jean Baptiste Roy. We know Chief Buffalo was struggling with health problems by this time—he could have been ninety-two years old—and apparently he was not involved with this delegation. The governor was presented with another letter, this one written by Roy. It told of the group's confidence in William Warren, and their hope that he would have been with them to present their wishes to Ramsey, and also, as so many Ojibwe representatives were doing at this time, it stressed the importance of a trip to Washington. This delegation visited Ramsey again on 24 December but was without an interpreter so it returned on Christmas Day just before departing the city. Apparently as a gesture of good will, at that meeting Ramsey issued the delegation provisions of pork, flour, sugar, tea, blankets, leggings and tobacco before it began its long winter journey back to Lake Superior.[77]

Just before the end of the year, on 26 December, Ramsey wrote another letter, this time a summary of removal efforts, to Commissioner Luke Lea. Interestingly, he told Lea of the "success and partial failure" of the year's removal activities. Until that date this may have been Ramsey's only written admittance that removal had not been completely successful. Using John Watrous's inflated numbers, he claimed nearly 2,000 Ojibwe had been removed from the ceded lands of Michigan and Wisconsin and any resumption of removal for the upcoming year would not be needed.

He also spoke of the government's practice of only paying annuities on unceded lands, and how this troubled the Ojibwe, but he felt it should not be changed except possibly for the La Pointe bands. However, this deviation from the rule for La Pointe was to be perceived by the people as a "connivance" of the agent, not as a real rule change. Ramsey felt the policy of paying annuities only on unceded lands was a driving force behind any success the removal efforts had achieved.

What we see at the close of the year of 1851 is that the Michigan and Wisconsin Ojibwe community was persistent in its attempts to gain approval for a trip to Washington to determine whether or not the removal order was valid. The petitions and delegations of the last two months of the year indicate that the peoples' resolve had not faltered. They were not giving in to the Americans, as they challenged Ramsey's and Watrous's insistence that they move west. The notion that they might solve the removal problem by agreeing to the call of Shingwaukonse to move east was being considered, but first they wanted to hear from the American "Great Father" to see whether removal really was what he wanted.

*Notes*

1. Schenck 2007:99.
2. Schenck 2007:100,156-7, 122.
3. Treuer 2011:102-106.
4. Schenck 2007:108.
5. Schenck 2007:104
6. Treuer 2011:106.
7. Schenck 2007:192.
8. Cleland in McClurken *et al* 2000:64.
9. Warren as given in Schenck 2007:110, brackets added.
10. Warren as given in Schenck 2007:110-112.
11. Warren in Schenck 2007:114, 192.
12. Warren in Schenck 2007:116-7.
13. Schenck 2007:118.
14. Schenck 2007:118.
15. Warren in Schenck 2007:119.
16. White in McClurken *et al* 2000:202.
17. Cleland in McClurken *et al* 2000:67.
18. White in McClurken *et al* 2000:67; Schenck 2007:132.
19. Cleland in McClurken *et al* 2000:67; White in McClurken *et al* 2000:199.
20. White in McClurken *et al* 2000:201; Schenck 2007:133.
21. Watrous as given in White in McClurken *et al* 2000:201.
22. Cleland in McClurken *et al* 2000:66; White in McClurken *et al* 2000:201.
23. Schenck 2007:126-9.
24. Schenck 2007:126.
25. Watrous as given in Schenck 2007:126.
26. Schenck 2007:126-7.
27. White in McClurken *et al* 2000:210-1.
28. Lea as quoted in Cleland in McClurken *et al* 2000:67.
29. Cleland in McClurken *et al* 2000:67; White in McClurken *et al* 2000:210.
30. White in McClurken et al 2000:202-3.
31. Schenck 2009:xiii; Schenck 2007:65,127.
32. Warren as given in Schenck 2007:128.
33. Schenck 2007:127.
34. White in McClurken *et al* 2000:217.
35. Warren 2009[1885]:10.
36. Warren 1984[1885]:23-5.
37. Schenck 2007:x.
38. Warren 1984[1885]:27.
39. Watrous as given in White in McClurken *et al* 2000:204-5.
40. Boutwell as given in White in McClurken *et al* 2000:205.
41. Boutwell as in White in McClurken *et al* 2000:205.
42. Boutwell to Ramsey as in White in McClurken *et al* 2000:205.
43. Warren in Schenck 2007:130.
44. Warren in Schenck 2007:130; Boutwell in White in McClurken *et al* 2000:205-6 brackets added.
45. J.W.B. for Supt. In WisHisColl, Vol. XX.
46. Schenck 2007:132.
47. Ramsey as given in White in McClurken *et al* 2000:206.
48. Watrous in White in McClurken *et al* 2000:207.
49. Watrous as given in White in McClurken *et al* 2000:216.
50. Schenck 2007:133.
51. White in McClurken *et al* 2000:207.
52. White in McClurken *et al* 2000:208, 215.
53. White in McClurken *et al* 2000:206-7.
54. White in McClurken *et al* 2000:207-8.
55. White in McClurken *et al* 2000:208.
56. White in McClurken *et al* 2000:208-9.
57. White in McClurken *et al* 2000:209.
58. Leonard Wheeler letter to father, dated 22 September 1851, original at NGLVC.
59. White in McClurken *et al* 2000:210-11, 251.
60. White in McClurken *et al* 2000:211-214.
61. Schenck 2007:119.
62. White in McClurken *et al* 2000:226.
63. White in McClurken *et al* 2000:211.
64. White in McClurken *et al* 2000:211, 216.
65. White in McClurken *et al* 2000:212-3.
66. White in McClurken *et al* 2000:213.
67. White in McClurken *et al* 2000:214.
68. White in McClurken *et al* 2000:215.
69. White in McClurken *et al* 2000:216.
70. White in McClurken *et al* 2000: 223-4; Schenck 2007:150, 155.
71. White in McClurken *et al* 2000:217-8, 302-4.
72. Minnesotian in Schenck 2007:141.
73. Warren as given in Schenck 2007:142.
74. White in McClurken *et al* 2000:219-20.
75. Schenck 2007:145-150.
76. White in McClurken *et al* 2000:220.
77. White in McClurken *et al* 2000:224.

# 20

# 1852 as Prelude to the Treaty of 1854

### *Lingering Removal Attempts, the Watrous Investigation, and Chief Buffalo's Trip to Washington, D.C.*

1.

BY THE START OF THE NEW YEAR OF 1852, the Lake Superior Ojibwe bands still had not received their cash annuity payments for 1850 and 1851. We know they were eager to receive these monies and in many cases their delay probably caused a hardship, but we should assume that to a great extent this was countered by the peoples' traditional efforts at securing sustenance. It was the heart of winter and even though 1851 saw disruptions by John Watrous's and Alexander Ramsey's renewed attempts at removal, at the year's close, except for those mixed-bloods who were accepting aspects of Christianity and undertaking farming, most of the people were settled-in at their winter hunting grounds. The deep backdrop of the rhythm of traditional Ojibwe seasonal movement continued for many people all through the numerous efforts by missionaries, government officials and other change agents to have them cease this old way of life and accept new self-conceptions as "settled" Christian agriculturists.

When John Watrous informed the Ojibwe bands that he wanted them to congregate at La Pointe on 10 June, he signaled the start of what became a troublesome year. Throughout the ensuing months the question of removal was constantly before the people, as runners doubtlessly carried messages between bands and leaders traveled for what must have seemed like endless parleys.[1] Rumors of removal spawned by Luke Lea's telegraphed suspension order and Leonard Wheeler's growing resistance to any forced removal meant there was much to talk about. Because of this, the entire year of 1852 was a stressful time for the Ojibwe of western Lake Superior country. On occasion it may have been only a few select leaders and their immediate auxiliaries who made the many trips for meetings, but as was the custom, at other times entire families packed up and undertook the lengthy canoe trips—strenuous journeys that could involve long, tiresome portages. All of this political activity, of course, would have drawn people away from their efforts at the usual methods of gaining a livelihood. When they should have been hunting, fishing, gardening, or going about other work to harvest resources, they might instead have been encamped at a council ground where government agents like Clement Beaulieu, William Warren, Charles Oakes, William Boutwell, John Watrous, or several others used argument and cajolery to convince them to remove.

The single hope to halt removal was the proposed trip to Washington, D.C. The desire to make this long eastern trip originated sometime during 1850, and remained a preoccupation through 1851. All this time the people held to their understanding of the Treaty of 1842, which assured them they would not have to move for a very long time, if at all, and they expected the president would agree. Meanwhile, their time of troubling uncertainty with its interruptions by removal conductors worked against the normal flow of what was Ojibwe culture, but as we saw with the fall wild rice harvest in late 1851, despite this hardship, the people still carried out their old customs for securing a livelihood. And we should expect, as always happens when a community is under extreme stress, spiritual leaders were regularly turned to for help in such unsettling times. Surely, the year 1852 saw many ceremonies in which the spirits were invoked for guidance. As was the case with political leaders, it was a time when spiritual leaders were expected to step forward and help lead the people through this great difficulty.

However, the Ojibwe were not the only ones faced with adversity. John Watrous was aware of increasing complaints about him, and his struggles with William Warren must have seemed unrelenting. And as already noted, in December 1851, Alexander Ramsey acknowledged that the yearlong activities at Ojibwe removal had not been completely successful. Both he and his chief removal officer had to have been concerned with what the next year might bring. Ramsey had some trepidation about the mounting federal expenditures he authorized for the past year's removal attempts—costs that Congress might demand an explanation for, given the incomplete outcome of the overall removal project.[2]

Despite Watrous's claim of success in having the Ojibwe move west, it had not been a good year, the problem stemming from "the discontent of the Lake Superior bands."[3] Their consternation about his hesitancy to recommend their trip to Washington, D.C., and about his refusal to issue the annuities at La Pointe had stalled removal. He knew the pledges he was forced to make regarding the new houses and fields at Fond du Lac, as well as agreeing to provision the few thousand persons for a full year at that site, would be a considerable drain on removal appropriations, and gaining Congressional approval for any new expenses might not have been easy. All of this could have caused the public and government officials to scrutinize the year's activities in ways that could have been troublesome to his and Ramsey's plans.

Furthermore, the intent to use the annuity payments as something to lure the bands westward began to unravel when Ramsey ordered Watrous to make an exception for Buffalo and to include the mixed-bloods in this payment. Perhaps this order was seen as an unvoiced foreshadowing of the ultimate failure of Ojibwe removal for both Ramsey and Watrous. Certainly Chief Buffalo and his co-leaders must have understood it as a victory of sorts for them and their people.

To compound these difficulties, back in early November 1851, the L'Ance band sent a formal complaint to their Sault Ste. Marie agent about John Watrous's refusal to pay them their annuities unless they moved west, a breach of Robert Stuart's statement back in 1842 that annuities should be paid at L'Ance.[4] Perhaps more importantly, they requested the removal of Watrous as their government agent. The L'Ance complaint was forwarded to Washington and soon Governor Ramsey was told to undertake an official investigation. This event was another indication that Ojibwe removal was not proceeding as originally planned.

The L'Ance band leveled five detailed charges against John Watrous. They were: one, he had lied to them so much that they lost all confidence in him; two, he put his self-interest before theirs, and he was in collusion with traders for financial gain; three, in the past when in the trading business at La Pointe he had sold liquor to Indians, something that was illegal; four, his practice of seducing and co-habiting with Ojibwe women was moral behavior unbecoming a high-level government official; five, he bribed tribal leaders and treated some unqualified individuals as chiefs, a practice that disrupted the Ojibwe civil polity.[5]

These were important accusations that called for a thorough investigation, and each was a remark about the peoples' concern for the well-being and maintenance of Ojibwe society. More important than the obvious comment on the inappropriateness of a government official's personal behavior was the deeper message that John Watrous was harming the community in unacceptable ways. Thus, the five L'Ance complaints were statements about threats to the viability of the Ojibwe way of life in 1851, and in their own ways each of the negative behaviors the agent was being accused of was severely harming the community. For example, after European contact, a problem for North American cultures was that these new outside officials would sometimes recognize tribal leaders of their own choosing. This was a tactic meant to undermine the traditional tribal political system and was, at times, done outwardly by *appointing* new tribal leaders, and at other times less explicitly, by bestowing gifts and marks of office upon individuals who were not recognized by the community as bona-fide leaders. Obviously this act of "making chiefs" worked to undermine the political order in Ojibwe society and could have far-reaching negative effects.[6]

Alexander Ramsey carried out what Bruce White has called "a cursory investigation" of the L'Ance charges and ultimately exonerated John Watrous of all five. Apparently he did not bother to consult the L'Ance complainants, or any other Ojibwe people about the complaints. Instead, he conferred only with persons in the non-Ojibwe community. Striking evidence of Ramsey's disdain for any validity of the L'Ance complaint is seen in the following remarks he sent to Commissioner Lea:

> *From the mental and moral constitution of Indians, their complaints are entitled to but little consideration.* They poorly appreciate the benevolent care of the Government and esteem its agents inimical to them, if their most extravagant and foolish desires are not gratified. An officer who checks their follies, and thwarts their savage purposes, incurs their dislike while the crouching creature who supplies them with whiskey secures great influence with them.[7]

This quotation harks back to the demeaning remarks, discussed above, about the Ojibwe made by Walter Cunningham and the clergymen Hall and Titus in the early 1840s, and is a stark reminder of the difficult world the Ojibwe of western Lake Superior were residing in at the start of 1852. Governor Ramsey was Minnesota Territory's *ex-officio* Commissioner of Indian Affairs and one of the most powerful local representatives of the United States government, and as such, the tribal people were obligated to work with him. He was married to an Ojibwe woman and obviously intermingled with her extended family, all the while carrying these deep negative sentiments for his in-laws, while supposedly, outwardly evincing favorable behavior. This inherent duplicity must have been evident to the Ojibwe. Apparently Chief Buffalo and the other Ojibwe leaders never learned of Ramsey's demeaning remarks, but we might ponder their significance. They suggest that any favorable outward behavior officials like Ramsey exhibited to the Ojibwe people was a façade over a deeper core of cultural and personal bias that ultimately must be considered when attempting to understand the history of Ojibwe culture in western Lake Superior lands. Remembering that generally the Euro-American community viewed itself as inherently superior to the tribal world—and acknowledging that in most cases this superiority was perceived as *god-given*—and accepting that perhaps most of the American officialdom, if not the entire community of the times carried this arrogance, then these removal years were very difficult for the Ojibwe.

In his detailed study of the paper trail for the Watrous investigation, Bruce White identified some revealing facts about Alexander Ramsey's and John Watrous's relationship—facts that might have motivated Ramsey to draw the conclusion he did. White feels Watrous and Ramsey had a relationship that "transcended their official connection." For instance, documents show that in 1852, Watrous loaned Ramsey the sum of $1,000.00, interest free, and although we do not know the purpose of this loan, we do know it came after Ramsey completed his investigation. However, White is careful to say, "It should not be supposed that this single financial transaction can explain Ramsey's entire conduct in his investigation of Watrous."[8]

White feels Ramsey's investigation was a matter of politics, with any concern for the Ojibwe of secondary importance. At issue were the recent land sale treaties Ramsey and Sibley negotiated with the Dakota and the Pembina Ojibwe.

Southern senators looked with criticism upon such a large expansion of public lands in a territory that could soon become a northern state. In this way, White argues, national politics in the halls of Congress had a direct effect on the outcome of the Watrous investigation in western Lake Superior country.[9]

Ramsey and Sibley wanted the Dakota and Pembina treaties to be approved by Congress and to assure this they needed maximum support. Any difficulties due to the L'Ance complaints about Watrous could have readily reflected on Ramsey, thereby damaging the chances for ratification of the treaties. According to Bruce White, "This more than anything explains Ramsey's conduct of the Watrous investigation."[10]

2.

JOHN WATROUS FINALLY MADE the 1850 and 1851 cash annuity payments to the Lake Superior bands during 22-24 January 1852, at Fond du Lac.[11] Events during these three days are significant for a few reasons. One is the ongoing activity of traders who preyed upon the Ojibwe during annuity payment times, and another is how they show the growing role La Pointe's protestant missionary, Leonard Wheeler, was taking regarding the resistance to removal. A third is the appearance of a few names that not only reappear in the historical literature of Chequamegon Bay, but continue to be found in the community of Red Cliff, Wisconsin, today.

Apparently by 1852, whiskey dealers were becoming as ubiquitous at Fond du Lac as they earlier were at La Pointe. Leonard Wheeler was present at the payment and claimed the availability of liquor was a serious problem, and in an attempt to glean even more of the annuity cash from the Ojibwe some traders opened gambling houses the day after the payments were completed.[12] Numerous claims of irregularities involving liquor, gambling and the methods of disbursement of annuities are found in the literature, all reflecting on Agent Watrous, who was overseeing the payment proceedings.

Interestingly, a few personal names occurring in the written record of the Fond du Lac payment go on to appear in the later history of the Chequamegon Region. One is John W. Bell, the commissary for Watrous at Fond du Lac, who later was the Justice of Peace on Madeline Island and whose family name continues to have a presence in that community. At Fond du Lac, Bell was accused of improper behavior regarding the disbursal of government goods, as well as being intoxicated at times while in the employ of Watrous. His later time as a colorful official at La Pointe is recorded in area newspapers.[13] Other names of local interest are William E. Van Tassell, the government blacksmith at Fond du Lac, and later at La Pointe, who was part of the payment team. Today a point of land on Lake Superior's shoreline just south of Bayfield is known as Van Tassell's Point. Pery Roy, a clerk for trader George Nettleton, and both Vincent Roy and Vincent Roy, Jr. were present. The former Vincent Roy was a clerk for La Pointe trader Julius Austrian. The Roy family name is found throughout numerous Ojibwe communities today, and Julius Austrian later became a powerful business figure at La Pointe.

A Peter Van de Venter also was present during the payments. Van de Venter—in a few spellings—is a well-known name in the region today. And Michael Bazinet, who was said to have nine children, was one of the Ojibwe persons who received annuities at Fond du Lac. Bazinet was an assistant of Michel Curot, the early fur trader at St. Croix, and is the French version of Basina (usually pronounced Bas-nee), a well-known family name at Red Cliff and Bad River, Wisconsin, today. In these surnames we see a direct connection between today's western Lake Superior Ojibwe communities and the troublesome removal years of the mid-1850s.

In his correspondence to Alexander Ramsey during these times, John Watrous told of his growing consternation with the La Pointe missionary Leonard Wheeler. It is at this time, the winter of 1851 and 1852, that Wheeler began taking an active role in Ojibwe removal.[14] Soon after arriving at La Pointe in 1840 he became a prominent force in the community, but until 1851 seemed to direct his energies to Christian conversion. As we have seen, he chose to accomplish this by working to have the people abandon their hunting and gathering adaptation and turn to agriculture. In 1845, he left Madeline Island to relocate on the mainland at nearby Bad River where he began this project.

In January 1852, Wheeler was asked by the La Pointe Ojibwe to accompany them on their journey to Fond du Lac. He claimed the people were hard-pressed and in need of someone to trust at this difficult time. In this act of turning to Reverend Wheeler we may be seeing something new at La Pointe. The people did not trust their agent, John Watrous, and although they related well to William Warren, at this time Warren was experiencing his own problems, not the least of which was his rapidly failing health. It is significant that Wheeler was sought out instead of Sherman Hall. Hall always had problems relating to the Ojibwe and by 1852, he had become a removal advocate, perhaps partially due to his hope for a government appointment in western Minnesota Territory.

The matter of the role of the Catholic clergy at La Pointe in the removal years is also interesting, foremost for its minimal presence in the literature of the times. We have seen that after arriving in 1835, Father Frederick Baraga worked in La Pointe for only eight years, and of those, one was spent in Europe on a fund-raising tour. He left La Pointe in 1843 to expend his energies in the European-American mining communities in the Keweenaw in Upper Michigan.[15] Two years later, in 1845, Father Otto Skolla arrived at La Pointe but stayed for a span of only five years, leaving in 1850, supposedly due to the problems of Ojibwe removal.[16] It was not until 1853 that Catholic clerics returned to La Pointe, and then over the next twenty-two years at least nine different clergymen ministered to the community.[17] Thus, in the difficult removal years, while the number of Ojibwe in the La Pointe bands who might have been receptive to Roman Catholicism may have been significant, there was no clergyman present to offer leadership. Perhaps it is noteworthy that given the emphasis on Frederic Baraga in Ojibwe history, even though he was working in the western Lake Superior region at the time, his name is virtually absent from the removal literature.

3.

IT WAS DURING THE ANNUITY PAYMENTS at Fond du Lac that Leonard Wheeler began to irritate John Watrous in new and more serious ways. In the early stages of removal efforts the protestant missionary was concerned with how he and his mission station at Bad River might be affected, and John Watrous claimed that in the summer of 1851, Wheeler was telling the Ojibwe people they did not need to remove, but apparently he was not speaking out in ways that were overly upsetting to the agent. It was in the fall of 1851, when knowledge of Luke Lea's telegram to suspend removal operations spread through the region, that Wheeler began to speak up in more troublesome ways, and later at Fond du Lac he continued to do so. At that time, according to Watrous, Wheeler became "quite to [sic] efficient" in matters of his role as advisor to the Ojibwe.[18]

Through his twenty-five year tenure of working with these people, Leonard Wheeler developed a growing empathy for them, and although he never relented in his attempt to convert them to his religion, he did grow to accept them as fellow humans and to stand beside them as an advocate during the difficult removal years. The same cannot be said about Sherman Hall. At Fond du Lac, Watrous charged that Wheeler had "gone beyond his calling as a missionary," and the agent lamented that Wheeler was not as "prudent" as his colleague, Sherman Hall.[19]

At Fond du Lac, Wheeler challenged Watrous about his pledges to open fields, build houses and feed the people for a year, and asked him when he would fulfill these promises. Perhaps facetiously, Wheeler asked Watrous how much land had been cleared and planted, and he claimed the agent told him it never was his intent to carry out the promises because he wanted the Ojibwe to be moved west of the Mississippi. This disclosure by Watrous is a good example of the agent's deceit the Ojibwe complained about.[20]

Unlike Leonard Wheeler's open stand with the people, Sherman Hall was more circumspect in matters of their defense. When Ramsey wrote to Hall asking about the L'Ance charges against John Watrous, Hall was quite supportive of the agent. He claimed not to be aware of any incidents wherein Watrous committed any of the charges leveled against him and implied the L'Ance people were in error in making them.[21]

In late 1851, Sherman Hall wrote to his superior, Selah Treat of the American Board of the Commission of Foreign Missions, about Luke Lea's telegram and in turn, Treat wrote to Ramsey inquiring about the status of removal. In the mid-nineteenth century, Selah B. Treat was an influential member of the eastern establishment and one of the voices amidst the "sources of the highest consideration" Luke Lea had talked about earlier. Ramsey wrote to Treat to explain his view of removal, and then in May 1852, the governor wrote a letter marked "confidential" to Hall telling of his decision to exempt the lake bands of La Pointe, Bad River, L'Ance and Ontonagon from the removal order "at least for a time." In discussing this letter, Charles Cleland remarks how this "new, more subtle removal approach" shows "Ramsey's considerable political acumen." According to Cleland, Ramsey was "co-opting the missionary opposition" to removal by treating the lake bands differently from those of the interior who did not have missionaries and a verbal white citizenry supporting them. This "divide and conquer approach" would still make removal mandatory for the interior bands, but those of the lake were to be excused for a while.[22]

Thus, we see that by spring 1852, the American officials were uncertain about their immediate future steps for Ojibwe removal. The firm opposition from Buffalo and the other Ojibwe leaders, with the apparent encouragement from Leonard Wheeler and the support of some influential members of the white citizenry, was having an effect on both the removal team and their Washington superiors. However, it seems that Ramsey's May letter to Hall did not mean he was wavering on his intent for the Lake Bands to remove—they still had to travel to unceded land for annuity payments, and this decision to exclude them from removal "for a while" was only a stop-gap measure meant, as Cleland notes, to appease the missionaries.

Given this, we see that while the local American officials were struggling with indecision, the Ojibwe community was clear on its course of action. It stood firm in its resistance and was busy planning its next step. By repeatedly asking both Governor Ramsey and Agent Watrous to seek approval for the trip to Washington, the Ojibwe people were following the dictates of protocol, but were growing tired of waiting for a response. Buffalo and his co-leaders were ready to act, and soon they did so.

On 13 March 1852, Buffalo was in Bad River, having a letter written for Governor Ramsey about plans to make the Washington trip. He told Ramsey:

> My Father
>
> I send you my salutations and wish to tell you how I feel, and what I want. I feel very anxious that the Lake Indians should hereafter be paid at La Pointe, Viz. the La Pointe, Grant Portage, Ontonagon, L'Ance & perhaps the Fond du Lac Indians. I say nothing of the Inland Indians.
>
> If you have not as yet received any answer to the letter you wrote to Washington, requesting permission for me to see the President, I wish you would be so good as to send me by the bearer, a letter of recommendation to him, for I wish to start on my way to make him a visit, just as soon as my canoe will float on the Lake in the Spring.
>
> This is all I have to say
> Your Friend, Buffalo
> X His Mark[23]

This short and perhaps cryptic statement by Buffalo shows that while he was still following protocol he was also taking decisive action. No longer content to wait passively for American authorities to act, the Ojibwe were taking the initiative.

Ramsey did respond to Buffalo's letter, but apparently it was too late. He wrote on 5 April, saying he had received no word from Washington, and in the old language of *frontier theater* he told Buffalo, "you know that if his red children wish to see him they should obtain his previous consent without which they would not be welcome." He claimed he would soon be in Washington and "see your 'Great Father,' and if possible, accomplish that which will be satisfactory to you all." Once again, Ramsey, like Watrous, was likely attempting to delay any action Buffalo might take that would jeopardize their removal plans.[24]

4.

WE DO NOT KNOW IF BUFFALO ever saw Ramsey's letter, but a small contingent of La Pointe leaders set out sometime in April 1852 to visit the president and have the removal order remanded. Unfortunately, we do not know all we would like about the details of this important trip, but we do know it was made, and its recurrent telling has become a significant part of Ojibwe history. Over time this trip has grown in significance and has become an important part of the *mythos* surrounding Chief Buffalo. Despite the limited nature of what we know as factual evidence for the trip's details, it continues to be retold again and again in oral and written form, and even on canvas. An example of the latter is the recent series of paintings done by Minnesota Ojibwe artist Carl Gawboy exhibited at the Madeline Island Museum at La Pointe in the summer of 2007, depicting Buffalo and his contingent in a reception with President Fillmore. One of the paintings shows Fillmore handing Buffalo what is presumably a document telling of his cancellation of the 1850 removal order.

In 1891, thirty-nine years after it took place, Benjamin Armstrong recited a first-hand account of the Washington trip to Thomas Wentworth of Ashland, Wisconsin, who wrote it up and published it as part of a memoir of Armstrong's life. At the time Armstrong was seventy-one years old, and in a disclaimer, he informs us he was not sure about the dates for the events he describes, but that in his telling they "will be essentially correct, and . . . a strict adherence to facts will be followed."[25]

As already noted, while controversial, Armstrong remains a valued participant in, and commentator on, the historical times we are attempting to understand. He was not a critical onlooker in the way most European and American writers we have been discussing were. He was a businessman and as such, apparently had profit motives as strong as most others like him in the region at the time, but his agenda was not like that of the missionaries or government agents. We do not know that Benjamin Armstrong worked to destroy traditional Ojibwe culture and bring civilization to the people, and despite the obvious errors in his memoir, his supposed fluency in the Ojibwe language and apparent level of acceptance and trust by the Ojibwe community makes it mandatory that we give his memoir careful consideration.[26]

Benjamin G. Armstrong was born in Alabama and came to western Wisconsin in about 1840. He was a trader at La Pointe, professed to be fluent in the Ojibwe language, and later went into business in Ashland. A non-Indian, he claimed to have married a daughter of Chief Buffalo and to have been adopted by the chief as a son. In the following paragraphs we will summarize Armstrong's recollections of the Washington journey.

He says it began on 5 April and:

> Chiefs Buffalo and O-sho-ga, with four braves and myself, made up the party of six men. On the day of starting, and before noon, there were gathered at the beach at old La Pointe, Indians by the score to witness the departure. We left in a new birch bark canoe which was made for the occasion and called a four fathom boat, twenty-four feet long with six paddles. The four braves did most of the paddling, assisted at times by O-sho-ga and sometimes by Buffalo. I sat at the stern and directed the course of the craft.[27]

We are not told the names of Armstrong's "four braves" and there is confusion as to the actual size of the party. Armstrong says it was composed of Buffalo, Oshaga, "four braves" and himself, a total of seven men, but in his narrative he says it was "a party of six men." A photograph in the Armstrong memoir said to be of the party shows only six men, one of them being Benjamin Armstrong.

This small group took minimal provisions, intending to rely on fish and game taken along the way. Moving along the lakeshore, on the first night they camped at the mouth of the Montreal River, the second night at the Iron River, and they spent the third and forth days at Ontonagon where they gathered signatures on a petition asking the president to remand the removal order. Armstrong claims several prominent people who knew the president signed the document, and later when the paper was presented to Fillmore he professed to recognize them.

More stops were made at Portage Lake, Houghton and Hancock, and Marquette. Reaching Sault Ste. Marie, they were stopped by officers from Fort Brady who at first refused to let them pass, but were eventually convinced by Armstrong to do so. Then it was down to Detroit where they were halted again, this time by the Indian agent, but as at Sault Ste. Marie they were allowed to proceed. From Detroit they took a steamer to Buffalo, where the men boarded a train for Albany. Armstrong claimed these were the first railroad cars any of them had ever seen but that is unlikely since Buffalo had made a similar trip to Washington in 1849.

From Albany they took another steamer to New York City where they spent "a few days." Upon reaching the city, Armstrong said, they had "only one ten-cent silver piece of money left" and had to give a " 'bus driver some Indian trinkets . . . to haul the party and baggage to the American House." Armstrong had some letters of introduction for certain persons in the city and apparently was able to receive some financial assistance from them. However, despite this assistance, he said, "The next day I put the Indians on exhibition at the hotel, and a great many people came to see them, most of whom contributed freely to the fund to carry us to our destination."

A dinner was taken at a private home with a group of men and women fascinated with these men from "the wilderness." Armstrong said that after some days of this when enough funds were raised, the "trinkets" were recovered from the driver, the hotel bills were paid, and "on the 22d day of June, 1852, we had the good fortune to arrive in Washington."

We are not told the means of conveyance from New York City to Washington, but upon arriving, Armstrong took the men to the "Metropolitan Hotel and engaged a room on the first floor near the office for the Indians, as they said they did not like to get up high in a white man's house." He claims he arranged for the men to have their meals brought to their room because he "did not wish to take them into the dining room among distinguished people." The next morning he set out to locate the office of the Commissioner of Indian Affairs to arrange for a meeting.

At this he was unsuccessful. He was not only turned away but was told to "take your Indians away on the next train west, as they have come here without permission." Greatly discouraged, he came back to the hotel to find "Buffalo surrounded by a crowd who were trying to make him understand them." When Armstrong explained that Buffalo was "the head chief of the Chippewas of the Northwest," the crowd was impressed and the party was asked to enter the dining room and take a table.

The group of diners included Senator Briggs of New York, who offered to help the party. Briggs was successful in arranging an audience with President Fillmore, and accordingly, the next day at three p.m. the party found itself in a reception with the president. The first order of the meeting was a pipe ceremony. According to Armstrong:

> When we were assembled Buffalo's first request was that all be seated, as he had the pipe of peace to present, and hoped that all who were present would partake of smoke from the peace pipe. The pipe, a new one brought for the purpose, was filled and lighted by Buffalo and passed to the President who took two or three draughts from it, and smiling said, 'Who is the next?' at which Buffalo pointed out Senator Briggs and desired he should be the next. The Senator smoked and the pipe was passed to me and others, including the Commissioner of Indian Affairs, Secretary of the Interior and several others whose names I did not learn or cannot recall. From them to Buffalo, then to O-sho-ga, and from him to the four braves in turn, which completed that part of the ceremony. The pipe was then taken from the stem and handed to me for safe keeping, never to be used again on any occasion. I have the pipe still in my possession and the instructions of Buffalo have been faithfully kept. The old chief now rose from his seat, the balance following his example and marched in single file to the President and the general hand-shaking that was began with the President was continued by the Indians with all those present. This over Buffalo said his under chief, O-Sho-ga, would state the object of our visit and he hoped the great father would give them some guarantee that would quiet the excitement in his country and keep his young men peaceable.[28]

This opening ceremony was followed by an hour-long talk by Oshaga about the peoples' understanding of the Treaties of 1837 and 1842, and how in these treaties the people did not sell their land, only the pine and minerals they held. He also stressed that in 1842, it was agreed the treaty annuities would be paid at La Pointe, not some distant western site.

Oshaga explained it was understood that the Ojibwe could remain residing on the lands as long as they did not harass or harm incoming whites, and when hearing of the removal order they were incredulous. It was decided to take an immediate survey of the entire treaty area and runners were sent out to see if any infractions of the agreement had occurred. None were found so the people were puzzled by the reason for the removal order, and Oshaga implored the president to explain why it was issued.

When Oshaga was finished, Armstrong presented the signed petitions and in closing the President said the government would pay the group's hotel bill and that it was welcome to tour the city for a week. Two days later the party had dinner with the President after which, according to Armstrong, he said he would countermand the removal order and see to it that annuities would be paid at La Pointe. These orders were stated in "a written instrument" that Armstrong claims the president then handed to Buffalo to have interpreted to his people. Finally, on 28 June 1852, the party left Washington, "going by cars to La Crosse, Wis., thence by steamboat to St. Paul, thence by Indian trail across the country to Lake Superior."[29]

## 5.

THIS SUMMARIZED VERSION OF THE 1852 TRIP as told by Benjamin Armstrong can serve as a starting point in our analysis of the journey, but we should realize that it holds many errors, and that other renderings of the trip exist. Some were passed down in the oral tradition by the Ojibwe and continue to be told to the present day, but an "oral tradition" can also be found in the non-Ojibwe community. The retelling of the 1852 journey goes on in this community and is a viable aspect of today's popular history for Chequamegon Bay.[30] Another version of the trip has been suggested by Bruce White's analysis of the government's accounting documents and other official correspondence that makes up an important portion of the journey's paper trail. Perhaps an example of the least trustworthy instances of commentary on the trip is seen in its recounting found in journalistic writings, whether from 1852 newspapers or in those of a much later time. Among the latter, and one that offers an example of the permutations such an important event can take over time, is a 2004 newspaper article claiming that during the White House meeting "A *treaty* was signed with President Filmore (sic) countermanding the order for removal of Indians from this area in 1852."[31] Similarly, some thirty years ago in a well-respected article discussing the Treaty of 1854, another writer claimed: "In 1852 during Millard Fillmore's administration, a Chippewa delegation to Washington convinced him to countermand the removal order."[32]

The written instrument Benjamin Armstrong spoke of, whether in original or copy form, has never surfaced, and while it is entirely possible such a document was given to Buffalo, there are plausible indications that it was not. If the document was given to Buffalo, most certainly official administrative procedures would have required that a copy was sent to Ramsey and, possibly even Watrous. While Ramsey and Watrous might have kept the communiqué hidden, it seems certain that the official communication channel the remanding order would have traveled through could not have done so. Supposedly, it originated in the chief executive's office, then went to the Interior Secretary, then to the Commissioner of Indian Affairs before being sent out to Minnesota Territory, where it presumably would have gone to Ramsey and finally down to John Watrous. Numerous incoming and outgoing office daybooks along this paper trail would show evidence of such an important executive order. However, these daybooks show no record of the document. Just as significantly, "the subsequent action of the field agents do[es] not indicate that they received word of any cancellation."[33] But most importantly, the actions of Buffalo and his co-chiefs immediately upon returning home attest that President Fillmore did not explicitly tell them, whether in writing or by voice, that the order was remanded and annuity payments would hereafter be made at La Pointe. In this regard, the Armstrong memoir is in error, a matter we will address below.

Recalling that Armstrong claimed the group left Washington about 28 June and that it passed through St. Paul, we might assume that when in the city Buffalo would have attempted to contact Ramsey to tell him what had been learned. It is likely the return trip took at least a week or more, so such contact could have occurred in early July. However, Armstrong's memoir is mute on the matter of Buffalo and Oshaga communicating with Governor Ramsey or John Watrous in any manner during the days immediately following their return. What he does claim is that after leaving St. Paul, the delegation encountered a number of Ojibwe persons from various bands who were told by Buffalo that "at the expiration of two moons," their leaders were to attend a "grand council at La Pointe, for there was many things he wanted to say to them about what he had seen and the nice manner in which he had been received and treated by the great father."[34] Armstrong's recollection that the group passed through St. Paul is in error, and although upon reaching Ojibwe country any people met along the way would likely have been informed about what was learned, Armstrong's statement of the group's fond memories of its treatment when in Washington is puzzling.

Contrary to Benjamin Armstrong's silence, we *do* know that Buffalo and Oshaga contacted Governor Ramsey soon after returning to La Pointe. Accordingly, in a letter sent from La Pointe to Ramsey dated 23 July 1852, they told the governor that in Washington they learned it was *he*, and not Washington officials, who had the authority to decide whether or not the Ojibwe were to move west of the Mississippi River.[35] Surely, if President Fillmore had told them they did not have to move they would have told this most important news to Ramsey. Because Buffalo's and Oshaga's letter holds several pertinent statements and disclosures we will provide it in its entirety, without any corrections in its spelling or grammar:

> Lapoint L. Superior Wisconsin
>
> July the 23 1852
>
> My father I have just returnd from Washington. I lirnd that you was the one that had to say that we had to go or stay. If that is the case do as you agrad that you would doe, las winter when I visited you, you told me that if it was left for you to sa you would do all that was in your power to have us stay at lapoint. It is left to you to say wether we will be permitted to remain or not. We had gust as leave die as to go west of the Mississippi River. I want you to rite to me and let mee noe my destiny. If we do go we will not go farther then Fodu Lac. I donot want to lose my paymenent. If I haft to give up my home I will not go farther than I can help. That is what we have concluded on. Bufalo head chief Oshoga the 2nd chief and all the head men at lapoint. My father I hope that you will pitty ower condision. If the white men don't fulfil their contract with us we have no way of making them comply. But if we do not you will soon compel us to do it, or if we don't comply with your wishis you will drive us to it in some way, either by killing us off or puting us in jail or taking ower payments from us. Now father have compasin on us. Try and benafit us instid of the traders. Tha ar all able to liv and we ar not able to liv with out ower payment so father you will try to have us partisipate in ower anewatis this fall. You will pleas rite to us if you pleas. We knoe that it is not worth while for us to ask enathing of the ajent becaus on ower return from Washington we ast him to give us a shirt to put on when we got in to New York and he would not giv us a shirt. So we will not ask him for enathing again if we can help it. But we ask these favors of you and hope that you will grant us the saime you will anser this letter as soon as you can and let us knoe what we may depend on. We want to knoe the truth and nothing else.
>
> So nothing more at present. But remain your afectnet children
>
> Buffalo
> Oshoga
> chiefs at lapoint
> to thair father at St Pauls[36]

Here we see the most powerful Ojibwe leader of the region—reputedly ninety-three years old—and La Pointe's second chief pleading with Ramsey, and although it is couched in the familiar, and by now perhaps outmoded rhetoric of the middle ground with its roles of "father" and "child," this letter is a very moving document as it cuts through these time-worn theatrics. In their winter meeting Ramsey apparently was clear in his thoughts about the La Pointe people staying where they were. This *verbal* pledge was worth just as much to Buffalo and Oshaga as a written document, and on 25 July 1852, some seven months after it was made, they were imploring Ramsey to keep his word.

6.

THE BUFFALO AND OSHAGA LETTER has been said to hold "the most compelling evidence" of what the Ojibwe delegation learned in Washington. First, as Armstrong claimed, upon their return from the east the Ojibwe leaders may have assured their people that the removal order had been cancelled and their annuities would be paid at La Pointe because they "may have assumed that the discretion . . . given Ramsey did in fact mean that the order was revoked." But there was a major contingency, which was that Ramsey would have to follow through and issue an order that the people could stay and that the annuities be paid in their homeland. In early Ojibwe culture a spoken promise was considered inviolable, so Buffalo and Oshaga likely assumed Ramsey would be true to his word, and therefore, in effect, the removal order should have been a dead issue. This assumption could explain aspects of Armstrong's recollections of the actions of Buffalo and Oshaga in the summer of 1852 upon their return from Washington.[37]

What is also stated in the letter is that Buffalo, Oshaga, and the other La Pointe leaders had decided that if they were compelled to remove, they would go only as far as Fond du Lac. In other words, the leaders were hoping Ramsey would be true to his word, but in case he was not, they would abide by his decision only to a point. Thus, the peoples' joy at hearing the news brought by the Washington delegation was at best a *guarded* joy, and their jubilation Armstrong wrote about was a *hopeful* jubilation.

Just as importantly, the Buffalo and Oshaga letter shows that in the summer of 1852, unequivocally, the La Pointe people were willing to leave Chequamegon Bay and permanently remove to a more westerly site. Fond du Lac, of course, was not west of the Mississippi River, was on unceded land, and perhaps was deemed close enough to La Pointe so that some felt it was still within the greater limits of their homeland, but it was one hundred miles or more from Madeline Island, and in a time of canoe and foot travel, not an insignificant distance. Therefore, we are left with the fact that despite what the Ojibwe oral literature might claim and contrary to what some writers have emphatically stressed, in 1852, the La Pointe Ojibwe did eventually agree to permanently leave Madeline Island and their immediate Chequamegon homeland.

We recall that several months previous, in the fall of 1851, Buffalo agreed to move to Fond du Lac and actually led some people there, but it is unclear if he meant it to be a permanent move or not. In the July 1852 letter, however, it is clear that the agreed-upon move was understood to be permanent. When Buffalo and Oshaga said, "If I have to give up my home I will not go farther than I can help. This is what we have concluded on. Bufalo head chief Oshoga the 2nd chief and all the head men at lapoint," the home they referred to was the La Pointe region. This acquiescence to a removal from this traditional homeland that centered on Madeline Island is perhaps the most noteworthy indication that in the summer of 1852, Buffalo and his people perceived their situation to be extremely difficult. There must have been a very intense discussion in La Pointe councils before this agreement to move was reached and the Ramsey letter was sent. Some dissenting voices likely held out for the option of abiding by the admonition from Shingwaukonse not to give in to American demands.

The notion that the people saw their situation to be serious is supported by the plea of Buffalo, Oshaga and the headmen that implores Ramsey to "pitty ower condision." This is classic fur trade theater, as they revert to an earlier protocol with its role of the "child" that plays upon the sympathy and responsibilities of the "father," but the tone of their letter suggests more. By using the image of the Ojibwe people as a very poor and helpless people—without power—we also see a pose analogous to persons on a spiritual fast who put themselves into a state of hunger and helplessness as they beseech the powerful figures of the *manido* world for help. In other words, the 1852 letter to Governor Ramsey is couched in the imagery of the power-control belief system of the traditional Ojibwe worldview, and as such it suggests that in the summer of 1852, Buffalo and his co-leaders were functioning within this ancient cultural framework as they struggled to meet their latest crisis.

However, when they said the Ojibwe could do nothing when white men fail to fulfill their promises, they may have gone beyond this metaphorical infrastructure of Ojibwe religious ideology. In the past, in the lucrative days of the fur trade for instance, as "children" they had some power due to the furs they procured. But if we agree that the notion of trading the Ojibwe preserve for the right to remain in their homelands might not yet have risen to the level of being an actual bargaining item by the summer of 1852, then by that time their reciprocal relationship with the Euro-Americans had atrophied to a precarious position in which the Ojibwe may have feared they no longer had anything with which to bargain. Their pose of a pitiful child may have become uncomfortably realistic. By that date perhaps Buffalo, Oshaga, and their co-leaders could no longer suspend their disbelief so even though they were still abiding by protocol, it was a near-empty imagery and they could do little but plead with Ramsey for his understanding of their situation.

The poignancy of the plea for sympathy from Alexander Ramsey takes on further meaning when recalling Buffalo's relationship with Shingwaukonse and the latter's dream of forming the large Ojibwe community at Garden River, Ontario. The difficult situation of the Ojibwe in 1852 would have caused Buffalo and the rest of the leadership to ponder Shingwaukonse's invitation to come east and be part of this community. After they returned from Washington and encountered Ramsey's reticence to act on his pledge to help them stay in their homelands, such a move, especially with the economic opportunities of lumbering and mining that could have been part of the new community, surely had a degree of appeal to Buffalo and the rest. However, moving east rather than west would still have been *moving*, and no matter the strength of its appeal, it would have been an extreme act. The ramifications of this fact, its merits and demerits and more, must have been discussed at length in the La Pointe councils.

The delegation just returning from Washington witnessed the strength of the Americans as seen in New York City, Washington, D.C., Albany, Buffalo, Detroit, and other locations, and this strength in numbers and military prowess might have been what Armstrong said Buffalo wanted to relay to the people immediately upon returning home. Certainly, what these men experienced on this trip caused them to ponder their people's dire situation. If in the summer of 1852 La Pointe's young men raised the notion of using physical force to resist removal it must have been quickly countered by the more judicious views of the returning delegation members. Yet a hint of a threat of using physical force is seen in the memorial for the president from Buffalo, dated 12 June 1852, that was dictated to George Johnston at Sault Ste. Marie and included with a petition to the president from Lake Superior's south shore, dated 4 June 1852. This memorial and petition were carried to Washington and reached the president that summer. In the memorial, Buffalo tells of his understanding of the Treaty of 1842 and his dismay with the removal order. He states that the Ojibwe had not harmed any whites in the area of ceded lands, so he asks the president "Why therefore should you thus act towards me and since two years past pushing me to rise from my peaceable position[?]"[38]

The scene of a reclining, *peaceful* Chief Buffalo, at rest in his homeland, who begins to stir and rise to meet the challenge of an unexpected presidential removal order is an example of the allegoric imagery used by tribal speakers in formal discourse during the eighteenth and nineteenth centuries. Buffalo was the acknowledged leader of the Lake Superior bands and as such was the figurehead for the few thousand people making up this overall community. His use of the phrase "rising from [a] peaceable position" may have been meant as a metaphor for the marshalling of the forces of the lake bands to prepare to meet the crisis brought by the unanticipated removal order. Such imagery with its implied threat of the use of physical force might appear outdated by the summer of 1852, and perhaps this was recognized by Buffalo, and another reason why he asked Ramsey to "pitty ower condision." It may have been that Buffalo understood that "pitty" was the most he could hope for.

7.

Benjamin Armstrong does not mention the fact that once the Buffalo delegation arrived in Washington they discovered that John Watrous was also in the city. We do not know why the agent was there but Bruce White feels a few matters could explain his presence. One was that he could have heard of the La Pointe party's departure and wanted to be on hand when it arrived in Washington in order to defend himself against any accusations Buffalo and the others might make against him.

Another reason Watrous may have been there could have been related to a letter Leonard Wheeler wrote to Selah Treat about the January Fond du Lac annuity payment. In the letter Wheeler leveled complaints against Watrous and went so far as to say the agent was unsuited for his position. Treat sent portions of Wheeler's letter to Commissioner Luke Lea and suggested Lea investigate the matter, although, in an interesting turn, Treat downplayed the missionary's accusations. We know that when Watrous was in the city, Lea shared Treat's letter with him and over a period of weeks John Watrous sent Lea a number of letters responding to Wheeler's charges. Finally, it is possible Watrous might have gone east to lobby for continued support for the stalled Ojibwe removal project.[39]

By June 1852, the annual reports for 1851 by Watrous, Ramsey, and Luke Lea's department, with their misleading conclusions of the success of removal efforts, had been processed by the requisite government offices and reported on by a few newspapers. Both the St. Paul *Minnesotian* and the *New York Sun* for instance, wrote of the success of Ojibwe removal. Contrary to this, by March 1852, both La Pointe missionaries Wheeler and Hall told Selah Treat that after the January Fond du Lac payment almost all the Ojibwe had returned home. In June, however, these negative accounts of removal efforts seem not to have come to Lea's awareness, or if he had learned of them he gave little heed.

John Watrous apparently arrived in Washington shortly before the La Pointe delegation, and he must have been pleased to learn of the president's recent approval of Ramsey's handling of the investigation into the agent's conduct. This doubtlessly buoyed his spirits as he prepared his responses to Wheeler's charges, and also as he lobbied Lea on the need for the government's continued removal efforts. He suggested that the agency be moved from Sandy Lake to a site on the Crow Wing river due to its suitability to agriculture, or if that was not possible, to the Long Prairie site, earlier meant for the Ho-Chunk. Watrous also spoke of the need for the establishment of a manual training school in western Minnesota Territory to facilitate the peoples' movement to "civilization."[40]

By June 1852, Commissioner of Indian Affairs Luke Lea was faced with deciding whether or not the government's Ojibwe removal policy should be reactivated. His information told him that although the Sandy Lake incident had been unfortunate, in the latter months of 1851, removal efforts were more successful. In fact, as Watrous insisted, they were so successful that only a small number of Ojibwe still resided on ceded lands and if the policy of making annuity payments on unceded lands was continued those people would soon remove by their own volition. Furthermore, the president could have become involved in a decision to renew removal efforts, and a special appropriation from Congress would be required—both events that could lead to a re-examination of past efforts and a rekindling of anti-removal sentiments against chief removal agent John Watrous, all problems the Indian Department would not welcome.

These difficulties could be avoided if Lea agreed to Watrous's plans, and essentially, this is what the commissioner did, but without explicitly saying so. Lea's final decision on Ojibwe removal is found in a letter he wrote to Governor Ramsey on 19 June 1852, in which he said: "The views of Agent Watrous in regard to [the question of Ojibwe removal] seem to be correct, but the whole matter is submitted to you for your consideration and if you concur with the agent you will take the necessary measures for carrying them into effect."[41] This letter is integral to an understanding of what Buffalo and Oshaga most likely learned about their dilemma when in Washington, D.C.

Wallace B. White, the personal secretary of Governor Ramsey, was also in Washington when the La Pointe delegation and John Watrous arrived. White came to the city for a number of reasons, all involving various Territorial concerns Ramsey had with a number of governmental offices. Among these matters was the Ojibwe removal question, and in a letter dated 22 June 1852, Wallace B. White told Ramsey he had learned that any possibility for a special Congressional appropriation for new removal expenses was out of the question, and regarding the continuance or termination of removal, he told Ramsey that "Any course you may advise will meet with the sanction of the Ind. Dept." Thus, the letters Luke Lea and Wallace B. White sent to Ramsey show that "by the third week in June 1852, it had been decided that the matter of the removals would be left to the discretion of Governor Ramsey. No further action would be taken by the president."[42]

*These letters were written and sent from Washington in late June 1852, and most importantly, it seems that almost immediately after their posting, the La Pointe delegation arrived in the city.* We can now understand that Benjamin Armstrong's recollection of the cold reception his party initially received by Indian Department officials may have been correct. At the Washington level the important decisions about Ojibwe removal had just been made, but the unexpected appearance of the Ojibwe leaders could have brought the whole matter to the president's attention, bringing about a decision that the department did not want to be made.[43]

In this regard, on 29 June 1852, Luke Lea, perhaps hurriedly, wrote to John Watrous, who was still in the city, telling him to oversee the Ojibwe delegation and escort it back to Northern Wisconsin. Lea allowed a sum of $400.00 to Watrous for the expenses of the journey. Ramsey's secretary, who apparently was in contact with both John Watrous and the Ojibwe delegation when in Washington, made an interesting comment in a letter he wrote to Ramsey on 1 July 1852, immediately after the group's departure. According to Wallace B. White, "Watrous left yesterday morning with Buffalo & the other Chippewa chiefs. Lea sent Watrous off with flying colors & the Indians with a flea in their ear."[44]

This puzzling remark about the delegation's departure becomes understandable when we recall that by the end of June, Luke Lea had absolved Watrous of the new complaints from Leonard Wheeler, and with this had just given the agent a mandate for continuing his approach to Ojibwe removal, so at the end of June 1852, "the colors" of John Watrous must indeed have been flying high. We can imagine the reaction of Buffalo and his companions upon learning of this turn of events, and no doubt the delegation was frustrated when it was put into the hands of the agent who over the past year had been causing the Ojibwe such great discomfort. Furthermore, Buffalo, Oshaga and their four companions had suffered a long and arduous journey to Washington only to be told the person who had the discretion to decide whether they remove or not was back in Minnesota Territory. On 30 June 1852, when the La Pointe delegation left Washington, D.C., the "flea in their ear" Wallace B. White spoke of must have been quite annoying.

Benjamin Armstrong's memories of the delegation's return trip were in error. "Government financial records" show that John Watrous and the party left Washington on 1 July for New York City, and after boarding there for a night, left on 2 July for Albany, then went by railroad to Buffalo and by steamboat to Detroit, arriving by the sixth of the month. It traveled on, again by steamboat, to Sault Ste. Marie, and on 9 July left The Sault, possibly also by steamboat, for La Pointe, where it arrived on or before 14 July. It is unknown if Watrous stayed with the group for the entire trip since he was in St. Paul by about mid-July and soon left for the agency at Sandy Lake. As we have seen, at least the start of this trip is corroborated by Buffalo and Oshaga in their 23 July letter to Ramsey where they tell of arriving in New York City on the way home.[45]

## 8.

We are left with the question of whether or not the Buffalo and Oshaga delegation really did have an audience with President Fillmore in the summer of 1852, and if so, what actually transpired during such a meeting. La Pointe's missionary, Leonard Wheeler, claimed that upon arriving in Washington, the delegation "had been sent home without a hearing,"[46] and this could be the reason Buffalo and his group left town with the "flea in their ears," but it is unknown from whence Wheeler learned his information. Despite Benjamin Armstrong's difficulties with recalling the details of this important journey almost forty years after its taking, we might agree that the group did, indeed, take part in a reception with the president and a select group of interested political leaders. A meeting of this nature would have been monumental to a person like Armstrong in the early years of the young country and it is unlikely he would soon have forgotten it. Furthermore, aspects of the richness of his details in its retelling—to include those of the chance meeting with the interested congressmen at dinner earlier—have a ring of credulity to them. Therefore, perhaps the easiest solution to the question of whether or not such a meeting ever took place is to believe Benjamin Armstrong's recollections, along with contemporary Ojibwe oral traditions about the trip, and leave it at that.

However, given the reality of the errors in Armstrong's memoir, and much more importantly, the hard evidence of the trip's paper trail as recently uncovered by Charles Cleland and Bruce White, we are confronted with a dilemma. In today's popular history the scene of Buffalo and President Fillmore standing eye to eye, as crafted in the Carl Gawboy painting wherein Fillmore is handing Buffalo a paper canceling the removal order, is compelling, but the surviving papers that document another scenario cannot be ignored.

If the paper instrument President Fillmore supposedly handed Buffalo *did* surface sometime in the future, the evidence at hand indicates it would not be an explicit order to remand removal. Instead, it would be a written statement saying Governor Ramsey had the authority to enforce or cancel the removal order as well as to decide if annuities would be paid at La Pointe or only on unceded land. In other words, the best evidence to date tells us that if the La Pointe delegation did have an audience with the president it was a meeting in which the "Great Father" neither restated Zachary Taylor's 1850 removal order nor remanded it. At most he confirmed Ramsey's authority to make the ultimate decision.[47]

As Bruce White so aptly put it, by the summer of 1852, Buffalo and the rest of the Ojibwe learned that "the removal order was no longer 'the pleasure of the president' as they had been told by Ramsey, Watrous and others throughout the removal efforts of late 1851 and early 1852. Instead, it had become 'the discretion of the governor' a situation not contemplated in the treaties of 1837 and 1842."[48]

However, the scene of Buffalo, Oshaga and their companions setting out in a birch bark canoe from western Lake Superior on a long trip to Washington, D.C., to confront the president and have him cancel the removal order is still a powerful image. The La Pointe delegation led by Chief Buffalo *did* make the long trip to Washington, and perhaps the question whether or not they saw the president becomes moot. What they *did* do is make a strong statement about the Ojibwe peoples' determination to overcome their difficult situation, and their efforts are of great importance today. No matter what actually occurred in Washington, Buffalo's 1852 trip has become iconic in Ojibwe history. As Ojibwe people struggled under the adverse conditions of the removal years, so have their descendents struggled in the times that followed, and today the image of Buffalo's 1852 trip with its folkoric character remains a treasured inspiration.

Given this, "[T]here is in fact strong evidence that the Lake Superior Ojibwe or individuals representing them were able to meet with the president sometime in late June just as Armstrong had remembered." This evidence is in the administrative notations written on the outside of the two folded paper petitions the group brought to Washington. Resting today in the National Archives in the city, these documents attest to the fact that they were delivered into the hands of the president by someone other than the secretary of the interior or the commissioner of Indian affairs. The notations show that the petitions were in the president's office and referred to the secretary of the interior and Indian Commissioner Luke Lea on 30 June 1852, and after a conversation about them between Lea and the president on that date, they were recorded in the Indian Office on 1 July 1852. Thus, these petitions show that *they* reached the president even if the members of the delegation were not successful in doing so.[49]

9.

THE YEAR 1852 IS MARKED in Ojibwe history as when the ninety-three-year-old Chief Buffalo led his delegation to Washington, D.C., to have President Zachary Taylor's removal order cancelled, but it is also the year in which another significant event in Ojibwe history occurred. This is the drafting and signing of a petition to British authorities for permission for several American Ojibwe leaders to bring their people east to join Shingwaukonse at his proposed united Ojibwe community at Garden River, Ontario. This important petition was given to George Ironside, the Canadian Indian Superintendent at Manitowaning, Manitoulin Island, Ontario, in the summer during the year's distribution of presents at that site. Surprisingly, it is not mentioned in any previous American writings on Chequamegon Bay's Ojibwe history.[50]

The exact date of the petition is unknown, but it was sent and received sometime during the summer of 1852. Just previous to its arrival Shingwaukonse received a *wampum* belt from western Ojibwe leaders with a similar message. Ogista, a son of Shingwaukonse, had been the mediator who oversaw these matters, and he was to make arrangements for the arrival of the Americans at the Canadian site once British officials gave their approval for the migration.[51]

The names of twenty American Ojibwe leaders were on the petition, the first being that of Flat Mouth of Minnesota Territory's Leech Lake. Beneath these names was the following message, under which was the signature of Muckedaypenasse (Black Bird) of the Bad River community at La Pointe. Black Bird wrote:

> On behalf of the above chiefs I have inquired of the Sault Ste. Marie and Garden River chiefs if they would be willing to allow these American Indians to come east and settle on their lands. They are willing with your consent to allow this. We now ask your leave.[52]

Two thousand persons were expected to make up this migration and British officials were both surprised and concerned. They feared such a large concentration of Ojibwe would be troublesome and work against the Crown's plans for the development of its western frontier. The British immediately announced their disapproval of the initiative and this seems to have ended the matter. The written record tells nothing more of it.[53]

Flat Mouth's involvement in this is not unexpected since he expressed an aggressive anti-American sentiment going back to at least the 1820s, when the Cass Expedition came to Leech Lake. What is significant is the representation of so many prominent Ojibwe leaders from such a wide spread of band territories. With the understandable exception of L'Ance—where the Ojibwe were involved with farming and were purchasing their acreages—the entire region of the Lake Superior Ojibwe bands is represented in this petition. Signers from Minnesota Territory were from the Red Lake, Leech Lake, Grand Portage, and Fond du Lac communities. Michigan was represented by leaders from Ontonagon, and Wisconsin by leaders from virtually every large Ojibwe band. We see that Black Bird of the Bad River band of La Pointe played a prominent role, and the involvement of both Amous, of Lac du Flambeau, and Kenisteno of nearby Trout Lake, who were part of the 1849 Ojibwe delegation to Washington, D.C., should not be surprising. Leaders from Wisconsin's remaining Ojibwe bands at Lac Courte Oreilles, Lake Chetek, St. Croix (Fol a-Voin), and Chippewa River are also included.

Significantly absent from the petition are the names of Buffalo, Oshaga, and except for Black Bird, any other chiefs at La Pointe. Just how we should read this is unclear, but it is possible these leaders were absent from their home area when Black Bird sent the petition because they were on their 1852 trip to Washington, D.C. The other possibility is that they did not support the petition, and this could mean there was a serious split in the Lake Superior bands regarding their relationships with the American and British powers. If this was the case then the timing of the petition could indicate it was purposely sent when Buffalo and his immediate co-leaders were not present to argue against it, or even prevent it. This scenario, however, may seem unlikely given Buffalo's 1838 letter to Shingwakonse in which he assured the chief of his friendship and his determination not to be controlled by the Americans.

It is possible Black Bird, Flat Mouth, Amous, Kenisteno, and the others had little faith that Buffalo and his group would have any success in having the removal order remanded, and consequently another solution to the threat of removal had to be kept open. The allure of the British and their wealth coupled with the vision of Shingwaukonse that together the American bands and those on the Canadian side of Sault Ste. Marie could utilize their own economic resources with minimal encroachment from others—to include the Crown—might have been deemed a valuable option. Such migrations north to Canada to escape the Americans were not unfamiliar to the Ojibwe in the western Great Lakes regions. Basil Johnston, the Canadian Ojibwe writer, tells of just such an event occurring for his family during the decade of the 1830s, when it left the country west of Lake Michigan to migrate to Canada.[54]

With the firm refusal of British authorities to approve the migration of Black Bird and the others to Garden River, the western Ojibwe bands were faced with the need to maintain an even more determined resistance to Ramsey's and Watrous's removal activities. And, perhaps the notion of "trading" the Ojibwe preserve for the remanding of removal became more acceptable.

10.

THE BALANCE OF THE SUMMER OF 1852 must have been an anxious time for Buffalo, Oshaga, and other leaders sympathetic to them. As they pondered the possible reaction of Governor Ramsey to their Washington trip, they also had to consider how to accommodate those local "breakaway families" who wanted to move to Canada as early as 1845, and now—in 1852—those apparently two thousand fellow Ojibwe from Minnesota Territory, Michigan, and Wisconsin bands who stood ready to do the same. In this regard the timing of the Black Bird petition to Canadian authorities and the Buffalo letter to Ramsey in the summer of 1852 is crucial. If the negative Canadian response to the petition was received before the 23 July letter was drafted by Buffalo and Oshaga to Ramsey, with its agreement to move to Fond du Lac, then the inclusion of "all the La Point chiefs" as signatories to Black Bird's petition becomes more understandable. By 23 July, Black Bird and others who argued for the migration to Canada would no longer have had that option and may have begrudgingly agreed to the Fond du Lac move. However this may have been, Buffalo and his immediate followers were left with the reality of having a sizable number of members in the Lake Superior Ojibwe bands who favored the Canadian move, and consequently, harbored troubled feelings not only about the Americans, but it would follow, also about Buffalo's leadership.

Beyond this pressing important political matter there lay the more immediate need of food procurement. In the summer of 1852, all Ojibwe were caught between going ahead with their traditional preparations for fall harvesting activities, or forestalling these due to the possibility of a forced move westward. It appears it was largely some of the mixed-bloods who were making initial overtures to take up farming in the Michigan and Chequamegon regions, and for them it must have been an especially troublesome time. Some of these individuals were expending considerable physical effort in clearing the forest, acquiring livestock, and erecting outbuildings for agricultural use. If they were forced to move west all this could be for naught. These concerns were allayed for the persons of the L'Ance Band however, when Luke Lea exempted them from removal and announced they could have their annuities paid at Keeweenaw Bay. The pressure from their leaders, some white citizens from the area, and the Michigan Legislature caused Lea to make this decision.[55]

The other Lake Bands must have been discussing John Watrous's pledge to open fields for them at Fond du Lac and his promise to provide provisions for a year as they established their farms. Given the agent's record of deceit they may not have believed he was serious in making these pledges.

In the heat of this uncertainty the missionaries were also troubled, since their future was as unclear as that of the Ojibwe. Efforts at religious conversion by the Halls and Wheelers were hampered by the unending removal attempts with their meetings, parleys, and general social disarray. The question of whether to make the tiresome treks west for annuities or forego them to stay home and garner what resources one could were ongoing. In a letter from Bad River written to his father in July 1852, Leonard Wheeler captures some of this concern:

> The people will be absent a little more than a month before they will be here again. There is not much prospect that they will receive their annuities any more on the Lake. If they remain here they will have to depend entirely upon their own resources for a livelihood. This we do not regret. They will have to exert themselves more but this will be a benefit rather than injury to them . . . The prospects ahead, in regard to the removal of the Indians, have been so unsettled we have not known what to do.[56]

Then, the letter Buffalo and Oshaga sent to Ramsey in late July asking him to follow through on his statement about his support for them to remain in their homelands was answered on 10 August. This reply must have been both puzzling and a bitter reality to the La Pointe leaders. In it Ramsey said nothing about the most important point made by the Ojibwe—that is, his commitment, if he were given the power, to help fulfill their desire to remain where they were. Instead, he said: "You learned in your late visit to Washington, that it is still the wish and purpose of your 'Great Father' that you should remove from the lands you sold him in the treaties of 1837 and 1842." This is a perplexing statement, since it appears the Ojibwe learned nothing of the sort in Washington. We can only conclude that by uttering this remark, Ramsey was deflecting the issue of his earlier pledge to let them remain where they were to the more recent agreement of Buffalo, Oshaga and the others that if they were forced to remove, they would go no further westward than Fond du Lac. Ramsey was quick to add, "I hereby promise you, and you may show this promise to your agent, that if it is, as you have indicated in your letter, your desire not to remove further west than Fond du Lac, you shall be permitted to remain undisturbed in that place." Perhaps the last thing the Ojibwe wanted to hear at this point was another promise from an American official.[57]

As Charles Cleland so succinctly puts it, "Ramsey . . . reneged on his promise to support the La Pointe or Buffalo's band in remaining on Lake Superior." By ignoring what Buffalo and Oshaga told him about what they had learned in Washington, he shifted the issue to the compromise offered by Buffalo and the others to move to Fond du Lac.

By this time Alexander Ramsey must have been feeling more comfortable with the removal matter, and in his 26 October 1852 Annual Report to Commissioner Luke Lea in which he summarizes the year's activities with the Ojibwe, he evinces a tone of assuredness that might have been masking his true feelings. These annual reports are useful to us for their summation of Ramsey's understanding of a range of topics regarding Native Americans, but we must remember that these documents were meant to impress Washington authorities with the effectiveness of patronage field officers like Ramsey who were expected to carry out directives handed down to them. In this regard, Ramsey praised the policy of forcing the Ojibwe to travel to unceded lands for their annuity payments. He claimed "a favorable influence has been secured by means of the annuity system [since those persons receiving annuities] are gradually being brought under control."

Even though many Ojibwe had not removed, he was certain most of the people would eventually do so in order to receive their distributions.[58] Although he admitted removal had not gone as well as hoped, he informed Lea that the plan to switch the procurement site for purchasing supplies for annuity payments from St. Louis to St. Paul had been a success. He claimed the goods were cheaper in St. Paul and transportation costs were less, and also that "the community in the neighborhood of the Indians is profited." He did not disclose that his and Watrous's goal of "profiting" this community through the financial benefits of the annuities was a major step toward the economic development of the Upper Mississippi region—something he, Watrous, Henry Sibley, Henry Rice, and others in the local political and business communities were working hard for.[59]

As if to remind Lea that the matter of "civilizing the savages" was a difficult task, Ramsey discussed his understanding of the motivations behind much of Ojibwe behavior—such as a penchant for holding "the passion for war"—and that although under the guidance of missionaries and others an Indian may accept American education and some of "the comforts of improved society," they may suddenly, without warning, revert to their ways of "savagery." He felt the long history of missionary activity with the Ojibwe from the early times of the French down to 1852 was "almost without success," but that the efforts of missionaries—and the government cost of helping support these labors—should continue because "The missionaries in this region have uniformly been useful auxiliaries to the government, and, in a thousand ways, of incalculable service to the Indian."

Continuing in this vein, as if to inform Lea of the true nature of the difficulty of those on the frontier who were regularly laboring to change the Ojibwe, Ramsey spoke of the continuing struggle to have the tribesmen take up Christianity. To prove the uselessness of native spiritual practices he told Lea how during certain ceremonies a person might enter "a heated pent-up lodge, and, with all the convulsions of enthusiasm, utter a confused medley of sounds as oracles," as if to show that the person was truly in touch with the Supreme Being. In other words, Ramsey was eager to have sweat lodges and shaking tent ceremonies replaced by what he considered true religious practices. Finally, Ramsey informed Lea that in 1852, the Ojibwe were still functioning within the parameters of their foraging culture and that it would take much effort on the part of America's change agents to bring them to "civilization." The Ojibwe, he said, still used "habits of craft" from the two "absorbing pur suits of their lives," these being "hunting and war," and this reality was hindering their relations with the American government. The sooner they were removed to western lands where they could be enticed to take up a settled existence based upon the practice of agriculture, the better.[60]

Ramsey's remarks in his 1852 annual report say much about the persistence of the structural underpinnings of Ojibwe culture at such a late date. After approximately thirty years of intense Christian missionary activity in their home region, the people were still utilizing their ancient belief system. And their interest in hunting and warfare were still evident.

## 11.

WHILE GOVERNOR RAMSEY was publicly expressing the importance of removal, Leonard Wheeler was not. The fall 1852 annuity payments which were to be made on Lake Superior were not done so, and due to more of Watrous's stalling, were postponed until December, a delay causing undue hardship. To compound the problem, at the agent's doing, the payment site was switched to the new agency at Crow Wing. Consequently, few lake and interior Wisconsin bands made the long journey to the new site, some choosing to rely on their traditional hunting and gathering practices for winter sustenance. For instance, in a 20 November 1852 letter to Selah Treat, Leonard Wheeler reported that the Bad River people had "given up" any hopes of receiving the annuities, deciding instead to do more hunting and trapping for the upcoming winter's food supplies. Once again the record shows that by the 1850s, even though some Ojibwe people were accepting new ways of securing sustenance, when under threat they turned to their traditional means of procuring food.

An interesting detail of the discussion occurring in Washington, D.C., regarding Ojibwe removal is found in an exchange of letters between Selah Treat of Boston, Congressman O. S. Seymour, and an Indian Department clerk, who perhaps was Charles Mix. By late summer of 1852, given the uncertainty of the matter, Treat had written to Seymour in an attempt to learn just what the government's policy regarding removal really was. Seymour contacted the Indian Department and was given a reply—possibly by Mix—stating that *the question of using force* to effect the removal of the Ojibwe from Michigan and Wisconsin had been discussed by governmental authorities, but it was decided to let Governor Ramsey make the ultimate decision on this matter as well as on the payment of annuities. As noted, Agent Watrous had written at least two letters to Washington asking for troops to help with removal at La Pointe.

Thus, as late as 1852, the possibility of the U.S. Military being called in to forcefully remove the Ojibwe people from their lakeshore and interior Wisconsin and Upper Michigan lands was entertained in Washington. Approximately ten years after 1852, the fear of physical conflict between western Lake Superior's Ojibwe people and the Euro-American community rose once more with concerns related to Minnesota's Dakota Conflict (see below). This notion of physical strife between the Ojibwe and the United States was recently voiced in a speech given on 13 May 2006 at Red Cliff by Mark Montano, who at the time was the community's Vice-Chairperson. Montano referred to the matter just discussed when he told a gathering of regional members of the Democratic Party that an "Ojibwe War" with the United States was an expressed fear of white settlers in northern Wisconsin during the removal years.[61]

While there may have been voices in the Ojibwe community who wanted to strike out against the Americans in the latter months of 1852, it is likely others who spoke for conciliation tempered these advocates. The people wanted their annuities and the concession of Buffalo and his co-leaders to move to Fond du Lac likely was made to satisfy the American authorities but also to appease those Ojibwe voices arguing for physical conflict. If the move was made the annuities would be paid and the people could have settled into their routine to prepare for the upcoming winter.

During the summer of 1852, John Watrous's suggestion that the Sandy Lake Agency be moved to nearby Crow

Wing in Minnesota Territory was carried out. The latter site was being developed for agricultural purposes and was an improvement over the lower, wetter lands at Sandy Lake, and it was hoped these more appropriate lands would improve chances of convincing the Ojibwe to move westward. To aid in this move a manual training school was to be established at the site, and Watrous offered the position of superintendent to Sherman Hall. The missionary accepted the offer, signing a contract for seven years, but did not start work at Crow Wing until March 1853.[62]

Also in the summer of 1852, Luke Lea excluded the L'Ance Band from removal and announced they would receive their annuities at Keeweenaw,[63] but the rest of the eastern bands were told to come to Crow Wing in October for their annuities. Some did, but they had to wait at least two months before the payment was made, and once again they went into debt to their traders for food. John Watrous's annuity payment roll shows that 2,704 individuals were paid at Crow Wing, but it appears few were from interior Wisconsin and Upper Michigan. Only fourteen persons (representing forty-five individuals) were listed as being from La Pointe. As was the policy of Ramsey and Watrous, only those people or their representatives who actually traveled to the site received payment. The goods and specie for those who did not come to the site (or send a representative) were withheld for a spring payment.[64]

This December payment at Crow Wing concluded removal efforts for 1852. Winter had set in and the Ojibwe went home to their usual encampments. As we will see, removal efforts would never again reach the fervor they had during the few previous years. National political changes were underway in the United States as new political leadership prepared to take control of the key positions in Washington and in Minnesota Territory.

For the Ojibwe bands in western Lake Superior there must have been political maneuvering underway as well, given the advanced age of Chief Buffalo. Assuming that he was in his early nineties, there had to have been an ongoing discussion about who would assume leadership with his eventual passing. As it turned out, despite struggling with failing health, the aged leader would go on for three more years. However, given the increasing presence of the Americans and what that fact would bode, there had to have been serious concern for what the future would hold for the people.

*Notes*

1. Armstrong 1892:16.
2. White in McClurken *et al* 2000:233, 257-8.
3. White in McClurken *et al* 2000:226-7.
4. Cleland in McClurken *et al* 2000:27.
5. White in McClurken *et al* 2000:228.
6. Warren 1984[1885]:135-6.
7. White in McClurken *et al* 2000:239, italics added.
8. White in McClurken *et al* 2000:243.
9. White in McClurken *et al* 2000:243.
10. White in McClurken *et al* 2000:243.
11. Schenck 2007:153; White in McClurken *et al* 2000:231.
12. White in McClurken *et al* 2000:233.
13. Burnham 1974:129-30.
14. Schenck 2007:155.
15. Verwyst 1900:184-5; Levi 1956:44-9; Ross 1960:110.
16. Burnham 1974:128.
17. Levi 1956:50.
18. White in McClurken *et al* 2000:231.
19. White in McClurken *et al* 2000:231.
20. White in McClurken *et al* 2000:232.
21. White in McClurken *et al* 2000:240-1.
22. Cleland in McClurken *et al* 2000:68-9.
23. Buffalo in White in McClurken *et al* 2000:245-6.
24. White in McClurken *et al* 2000:246.
25. Armstrong 1892:Preface.
26. White in McClurken *et al* 2000:245.
27. Armstrong 1892:16.
28. Armstrong 1892:28-9.
29. Armstrong 1892:31.
30. Danziger 1979:89; Levi 1956:60; Beebe 1980:111.
31. *Ashland Daily Press* of 18 November 2004, italics added.
32. Danziger 1979:175.
33. Cleland in McClurken *et al* 2000:70.
34. Armstrong 1892:31.
35. Cleland in McClurken *et al* 2000:70; White in McClurken *et al* 2000:253-4.
36. White in McClurken *et al* 2000:253-4.
37. White in McClkurken *et al* 2000:253, 255.
38. Buffalo as in White in McClurken *et al* 2000:246-7.
39. White in McClurken *et al* 2000:247-255.
40. White in McClurken *et al* 2000:249-251.
41. White in McClurken *et al* 2000:251.
42. White in McClurken *et al* 2000:251-2.
43. White in McClurken *et al* 2000:251-2.
44. White in McClurken *et al* 2000:252.
45. Buffalo and Oshaga in White in McClurken *et al* 2000:256, 253-4.
46. White in McClurken *et al* 2000:261.
47. Cleland in McClurken *et al* 2000:70; White in McClurken *et al* 2000:255.
48. White in McClurken *et al* 2000:255.
49. White in McClurken *et al* 2000:252-3.
50. Chute 1998:153.
51. Chute 1998:152-3.
52. Chute 1998:153.
53. Chute 1998:153.
54. Johnston 1999:20-5.
55. Cleland in McClurken *et al* 2000:70.
56. Leonard Wheeler's letter of July 1852 to his father, original at NGLVC.
57. Ramsey letter to Buffalo of 10 August 1852 in White in McClurken *et al* 2000:258.
58. Ramsey Annual Report of 1850 in ARCIASI.
59. Cleland in McClurken *et al* 2000:71.
60. Ramsey Annual Report of 1850 in ARCIASI.
61. Mark Montano: speech given at Red Cliff on 13 May 2006 as noted in fieldnotes of that date by Howard D. Paap.
62. Sherman Hall, Annual Report dated 8 September 1853 to D.B. Herriman, Indian Agent, in ARCIASI.
63. Cleland in McClurken *et al* 2000: 70.
64. White in McClurken *et al* 2000:262.

# 21

# 1853 and 1854: Monumental Years

### *The End of Ojibwe Removal and the Treaty of 1854*

1.

THE WESTERN LAKE SUPERIOR OJIBWE annuity payment gatherings began in 1838 with the first distribution for the ceded lands involved in the Treaty of 1837, and except for the difficulty caused by the removal attempts of Alexander Ramsey and John Watrous, continued annually for the La Pointe bands for thirty-seven years up to 1875, when the last payment for the Treaty of 1854 was made. Right from the start, these gatherings became an important part of the annual cycle of social events for those Ojibwe involved. Unfortunately, the descriptions and commentary about them found in the literature is limited, and of course biased due to their being written, largely, by non-Ojibwe participants or on-lookers. Over the years the Ojibwe versions, interpretations and understandings of these events have mostly slipped away, but for a few generations they must have been a colorful part of the community's oral history, and their recounting surely was significant for what can be called an Ojibwe oral historical literature.[1] Our understanding of the importance of these gatherings from the Ojibwe perspective therefore is limited, but at least one aspect of them is clear: the Ojibwe people were aware of the economic value of these payments to both themselves and the Americans. They knew the region's traders benefited from these distributions, and that in many cases government officials were personally financially involved with the trading business community.

In December 1852, when the few members of the Wisconsin bands who journeyed to Crow Wing returned home, they left behind that portion of the annuities belonging to their fellow tribal members who did not make the long trip nor send representatives to receive their shares. Surely there was ongoing discussion about what ultimately would happen to these undistributed provisions and specie. The government's policy of issuing payments only to those who traveled to the distribution site—or sent proxies—meant a good portion of the annual allotment was forfeited. However, in 1852, due to the payment's long delay John Watrous agreed to issue the balance of the specie and provisions in spring, when he hoped the rest of the annuitants would remove to unceded lands.[2]

As we have noted, we do not know exactly how many Ojibwe actually appeared at the new agency, but the low figures indicate there was much resistance to the manner, time and location of the 1852 payment. As always must have been the case, the Ojibwe community pondered the way in which annuities were handled and distributed by the appointed representatives of the United States government, and probably commented on the quantities of specie and provisions each annuitant actually received. Similarly, there likely were remarks regarding which headmen were given additional shares before the general distribution began,[3] and about which traders were allotted portions as payment for debts incurred by Ojibwe persons since the previous year's distribution. Whether or not the amounts given the traders were accurate certainly was a perennial topic of discussion. Chief Buffalo's and Oshaga's admonition to Governor Ramsey to "Try and benafit us instid of the traders" is an example of this concern. The writings of William Warren also show the Ojibwe perception that at annuity distribution times it was the traders who regularly received a large share of the specie, and perhaps ultimately the goods as well.

As the year 1852 drew to a close the question of the disposal of the undistributed annuities remaining at Crow Wing was not a minor matter, since that year "There was in fact over $8,040 left in annuity money at the agency."[4] In that time in western Lake Superior country the sum of eight thousand dollars and the relatively large portion of provisions still stored at the site were significant. Once again this shows that Ojibwe treaty annuities were an important part of the economy for the relatively young Minnesota Territory and the northernmost portions of the new state of Wisconsin. We are reminded of the desire of Ramsey, Watrous, and others—including William Warren—to bring these monies and provisions to Minnesota Territory. Interestingly, the written literature has stressed the assumed importance of treaty annuities to the Ojibwe economy but their similar importance to the early American economy of the region receives little mention.

In this instance, we recall the words of Edmund Jefferson Danziger, Jr., who claimed that as the fur trade declined, its economic importance for the Ojibwe was replaced by that of the treaty annuities. We discussed the veracity of this contention, particularly due to the continuing role of the traditional Ojibwe hunting and gathering economy and its persistence all through the fur trade and into the initial decades of treaty annuity times.

However, treaty annuity payment gatherings were not solely about economics. Something that has not received adequate consideration in the Ojibwe historical literature is the non-economic *social* importance of both the fur trade rendezvous and the annuity payment get-togethers. These were not unimportant social events since for the Ojibwe they allowed a coming together of individuals, kin groups, and bands that otherwise were often separated throughout most of the year. In this way, these gatherings were not unlike the earlier Feasts of the Dead and the colorful fur trading spring rendezvous we discussed in a previous chapter.

As we recall, summer was a time for the people to travel between villages and congregate for reasons of courtship, as well as political and other purposes, all being integral to the proper functioning and maintenance of overall Ojibwe society. For the Ojibwe, this is what added a degree of frustration to the way John Watrous delayed the annuity payments during the few years when he and Ramsey attempted to enforce removal. When payments were made in December, as was the case in 1852, their social functions were all but eliminated, and the people had little incentive to attend the events other than for purely economic reasons.

As we have discussed elsewhere, soon after the first annuity payment in 1838, concerned voices, like that of La Pointe's Sub-agent Alfred Brunson, pleaded with American government officials to hold annuity distribution events around the Ojibwe seasonal resource harvesting schedule. However, Ramsey and Watrous ignored these admonitions as they purposely set annuity payment times to suit their attempts at a forced removal, and after setting a date they routinely delayed payment even further.

As we will see in discussions below, for the non-Ojibwe community these yearly payment gatherings soon became prime social times for interested individuals to travel to, and mingle with persons on what was then the frontier of American society. Some valuable insights into the functioning of Ojibwe society, particularly in the La Pointe region of the immediate post-removal years, come from the written accounts of these events.[5]

2.

IN 1852, DESPITE THE EFFORTS OF BUFFALO and the other leaders who were insisting that annuities be paid at La Pointe like the 1842 treaty stipulated, Alexander Ramsey and his agent John Watrous were still holding firm to Orlando Brown's decision to ignore the stipulation and attempt to lure the Ojibwe westward with the rule that annuities must be paid only on unceded lands, and only to those individuals—or their appointed representatives—who appeared at the agency at the announced time. That summer when Buffalo and Oshaga with their co-leaders returned from Washington, D.C., Ojibwe resistance to removal was especially strong, and when the annuity distribution was delayed into December this sentiment must have been acute. What should be recognized is that while the Ojibwe people wanted their annuities, the traders and other members of the business community likely wanted the Ojibwe to have them—especially the specie—since they doubtless felt it would soon pass into non-Ojibwe hands. For this reason the refusal of the large numbers of Wisconsin persons to appear at Crow Wing for the distribution was troublesome to the Minnesota Territorial non-Ojibwe community. We should conclude that as is claimed for the Ojibwe, in some manner these non-Ojibwe persons *depended* on the annuities. In 1852, the Indian trade was still an integral part of the economy of western Lake Superior country, and this dependency of the non-Ojibwe community on these annual injections of cash was, perhaps, critical. This conclusion suggests that the complex relationship of the Ojibwe community and its neighboring non-Indian community must be seen as more of *an interplay of dependencies* rather than simply one of the tribal people becoming increasingly dependent upon the Americans. Reciprocity, in its several aspects, is always evident between Native American communities and their non-native neighbors, and surely this fact is just as relevant for today's world as it was in the nineteenth century.

Almost immediately after John Watrous closed his annuity payment roll for Crow Wing in December, the matter of the undistributed specie and provisions was in the news. In January 1853, a fire destroyed the new agency buildings. While it seems the stored provisions were reduced to ash, the fate of the undistributed specie is not so certain.[6] In his memoir, Benjamin Armstrong implies that the agent made off with the money, and that this fire was another instance of his unscrupulous behavior concerning the Ojibwe and their property.[7] Two years later, another accusation against John Watrous concerned a $20,000 cash deposit he was rumored to have made into the bank of Charles Borup, a sum that supposedly belonged to the Ojibwe. With over one-hundred-and-fifty years of hindsight we should be suspicious of the roles of John Watrous and his friends in these matters, but Bruce White notes that at least for Benjamin Armstrong's discussion of the fire, it "should probably be taken more as an indication of the extent of cynicism among the Ojibwe about Watrous than as any immediate proof of wrongdoing on his part."[8]

Armstrong writes about the search for melted coin in the Crow Wing fire's ashes, and how all that was recovered were "two fifty-cent silver pieces,"[9] but Watrous claimed "the government annuity money was not lost."[10] What perhaps is noteworthy is after the fire Watrous asked Governor Ramsey to allow for the purchase of new provisions from the mercantilist and banker, Charles Borup—a friend and business associate of Watrous—of St. Paul, for issuing to those Ojibwe who were not able to get to Crow Wing for the payment in December, but supposedly would appear in spring. Ramsey allowed Watrous "to borrow" goods from Borup for this purpose, and new provisions were sent to Crow Wing for storage. Interestingly, in the absence of any storage facilities at the destroyed agency, these goods were placed into the trader Clement Beaulieu's store—Beaulieu was another friend and associate of Watrous—to await the spring arrival of any Ojibwe. However, sometime before spring Beaulieu's store also burned, supposedly destroying the new goods. As if two fires were not enough, a third Crow Wing fire occurred in early 1854, destroying the agency warehouse and the annuity goods stored within, but this last fire appears to have been purposely set as part of the years-long dispute between the Mississippi and Lake Superior bands over the proper distribution of annuity goods.[11]

Suspicions about the first two fires continued for some time, as accusations of improper behavior on the part of John Watrous, bankers and traders went on. For example, in an ensuing investigation government agents noted that some St. Paul citizens openly remarked that "Dr. Borup is a shrewd, cunning, and designing man, and that he would not scruple to defraud the government."[12] Similarly, later in 1853, Leonard Wheeler claimed government officials were holding Watrous on corruption charges, but to date this has not been corroborated by any written documentation.[13]

Perhaps what is most noteworthy for us about the first two fires and the statements of Wheeler and others is the perception the Ojibwe likely held of these matters in 1853. The fires and accusations fit the overall pattern of fraud and deceit the people witnessed from the traders and government agents. At the start of the second half of the nineteenth century, the La Pointe and other Ojibwe bands must have felt the pressure brought by the Americans as they crowded ever closer. It was a difficult time and although it was almost six months after Buffalo's and Oshaga's return from Washington, D.C., Governor Ramsey had not yet cancelled the removal order. Recalling his puzzling letter in response to theirs, in which they implored him to follow through on his pledge to let them remain living where they were, we see that it must have been an anxious time for the Ojibwe.

3.

AS THE LATTER MONTHS OF 1852 PASSED and Ojibwe removal concerns continued, important political changes were going on in the greater United States. The Whig Party was losing control of the presidency as the Democrats gained favor near the end of the year. The result was that in March 1853, Franklin Pierce replaced President Millard Fillmore, Robert McClelland became Secretary of the Interior, replacing Alexander H.H. Stuart, and George W. Manypenny assumed the position of Commissioner of Indian Affairs, replacing Luke Lea. More locally, Willis Gorman became Governor of Minnesota Territory, David Herriman was appointed agent at Crow Wing, and Henry Gilbert became the bureau's agent at Detroit. Manypenny, Gorman, Herriman and Gilbert would soon be playing important roles in the new government's relationships with the Ojibwe people at Chequamegon Bay. Once again, Buffalo, Oshaga and the other Ojibwe leaders had to accommodate a change in American office holders, and they discovered that these officials were a "new team with new ideas and objectives" who wasted no time in putting its plans into effect.[14]

With the new administration and its many patronage appointments, a familiar name in matters of Ojibwe removal that had been relatively quiet for a few years now reappears in the removal literature. Henry Mower Rice, the one-time law student, military post sutler, river locks builder, fur trading post clerk, mercantile businessperson, and now politician, land speculator, and supposed "friend of the Indian," came back on the public stage to resume a more visible role in regional Indian affairs. After Willis Gorman replaced Alexander Ramsey as Governor of Minnesota Territory, it was quickly evident that Henry Rice and the new governor had differences of opinion about how to handle Indian affairs, and the next few years witnessed an ongoing conflict between these two influential men.[15]

However, the change of administrative personnel that brought new individuals into office, each with their own backgrounds, personalities, and assumptions, was secondary in importance to the deeper backdrop of westward expansion occurring in the United States. As we have seen, in the early 1830s, the policy of Indian removal was used to place tribal peoples far to the west, out of the way of incoming Euro-American communities. But only a decade or so later it was evident that the removal policy was causing unforeseen problems. While the issue was multi-faceted, primarily it was a matter of emigrating Indian communities coming into conflict with established western tribes, and secondly, the tribes that moved were quickly perceived as a barrier to new westward non-Indian expansion. Thus, by the mid-1840s, it became apparent that the much-heralded removal policy was not the panacea to "the Indian problem" it had been felt to be, and another solution needed to be found.

It was, therefore, that "By the early 1850s a bold, new Indian policy emerged which was based on the idea that Indians could be collected on reservations in their home territories where they would be taught the skills of civilization."[16] The rudiments of this new policy had been taking form for some time, but it was through the efforts of Charles Mix, a Bureau of Indian Affairs clerk, and incoming commissioner George Manypenny that the policy took form and was put into effect.

In 1851, Luke Lea had been successful in reorganizing the Bureau of Indian Affairs in accordance with the country's rapid westward expansion when he was able to get congressional approval to establish three administrative superintendencies for the burgeoning region east of the Rocky Mountains. Northern, Central and Southern Indian Affairs Superintendencies were set up in hopes that this new organization would help expedite the "settling" of the western frontier—a vast region in middle-America running from the Canadian border to Mexico and the Caribbean shores.

From the new country's perspective, this frontier needed to continually move westward as the assumed superior American way of life replaced that of the tribesmen. Conversely, to the tribal people, central to their perspective was the problem of how to meet this threatening challenge of geographic expansion.[17] In the case of the Ojibwe, at Chequamegon Bay Buffalo and his co-leaders struggled to marshal their people and resources to meet this challenge.

By 1853, the effects of industrialization in the eastern portion of the continent were sweeping westward and the ideological belief systems supporting these changes were important components of this movement. This is candidly seen in the words of Bureau of Indian Affairs Commissioner Luke Lea, when in late 1852, he wrote what was to become his last annual report to Secretary of the Interior Stuart. Lea used the threefold paradigm of "Savagery, Barbarism and Civilization" to describe the cultural change he was witnessing on America's western frontier. Accordingly, he concluded:

> When civilization and barbarism are brought in such relation that they cannot exist together, it is right that the superiority of the former should be asserted and the latter compelled to give way. It is, therefore, no matter of regret or reproach that so large a portion of our territory has been wrested from its aboriginal inhabitants and made the happy abode of an enlightened and Christian people.[18]

In important ways these are enlightening, if not amazing, words. They epitomize the Euro-American self-assuring cultural arrogance native peoples like the Ojibwe had to deal with in North America from the beginning of European contact, but while in earlier times it was easier to make accommodations to it, by 1853 things had changed. As we have seen in the letters and oral remarks of leaders like Buffalo and others, it was becoming more and more difficult to adjust to the wave of cultural change the Americans were bringing to western Lake Superior lands.

Entrepreneurs like Henry Rice were riding the crest of this wave. Like others in the Indian trade with its initial emphasis on furs, by 1853, Rice had diversified his focus to include land speculation and related economic ventures. As America's founding fathers and many others knew from first-hand involvement,[19] there was much money to be made in the purchase and resale of Indian land, and Henry Rice did not plan to let this opportunity pass him by. Like many business-minded persons in the years before them, Henry Rice and his associates maintained high-level contacts in Washington, D.C., and through regular lobbying attempted to affect political decisions concerning Minnesota Territory and adjacent lands. As had been the case in the 1840s, in the 1850s, Rice was called upon to take part in land cession treaty negotiations with the region's Dakota, Ho-Chunk, and Ojibwe people, and the written record of these negotiations shows he was a very busy man.

Another busy man was George W. Manypenny. Like other men of his times whose names come to us in the literature of Ojibwe removal, in the mid-nineteenth century Manypenny was caught up in the numerous opportunities for garnering personal wealth available on the western frontier. In Ohio he was a newspaper owner and editor, a builder of roads, dams and canals, and a partner in a firm organized to transport mail in the growing Old Northwest. Like other young, aggressive men, he finally gravitated to law, its practice and administration. As so often happened to those in the legal profession, he soon was involved in real estate sales and development. Perhaps we need not be surprised that by 1853, he sought a high-level political appointment. That year he ran for the position of governor of Ohio, but lost by only three votes to William Medill, the former commissioner of Indian affairs. Almost immediately he was asked to join the Pierce administration to replace Luke Lea, and although he was not familiar with the concerns of American Indians, he soon was among the many Americans who felt they understood how to address the difficulties tribal peoples were presenting to the country's westward expansion.[20]

As Commissioner of Indian Affairs, Manypenny was immediately forced to address the problem of sweeping Indian communities aside in order to allow this expansion of American society to continue, and his energies were spent on negotiating a long series of land cession treaties. In time, Manypenny streamlined the format for treaties, causing those he presided over later in his term to be very similar in wording and overall character as he rushed them to Congress for ratification. During his five years in office he negotiated a total of fifty-two treaties, more than any commissioner before or after him, and in 1856, in his final annual report, he noted that during his tenure as commissioner he oversaw the transfer of ownership of approximately 174 million acres of land from native nations to the United States.[21] Today we might struggle to comprehend the many ramifications of these figures for tribal communities like those of the Ojibwe. From his point of view, no doubt George Manypenny was proud of his work, and it is important to understand that this huge divestment of Indian land occurred during the short time span of only five years. For this reason and others, the mid-nineteenth century was a very important and tragic time for America's tribal nations. Geographically, their worlds were dramatically shrinking as their borders increasingly moved toward them.[22]

The nineteenth century plains wars were just beginning when Manypenny assumed leadership of the Office of Indian Affairs, so he was forced to address this problem. It did not take him long to conclude that the loud voices advocating for the American military to take control of Indian matters were wrong. Along with an anti-military stand he also spoke out against the government's practice of negotiating Indian treaties with articles for annuity payments. He argued that such annual payments encouraged Indians to postpone the inevitable: the destruction of tribal culture as Indians turned to a new way of life based upon agriculture and what the non-tribal society called *individual initiative*. Tribal people were to learn how to work as other Americans did. Two prominent features of Manypenny's administration became these anti-military and anti-annuity stands.

George Manypenny was one of a number of professional persons in the nineteenth century who pondered the challenge native cultures presented to the country, and several years before his passing he published an influential book detailing his ideas about how to address this national issue. For years after his death in 1892, his writing had a far-reaching influence on America's Indian policy decisions.[23]

Soon after taking office, George Manypenny argued against Indian removal. With obvious input from Charles Mix, he agreed that a more appropriate policy was to establish reservations, more or less where native communities were already located, and to protect them from encroachment while they became Christianized and agricultural. Key to Manypenny's proposal was for the American government to seriously take the charge to protect these communities as they were guided through their macro-cultural change. To facilitate this end, education as practiced in the United States at the time and Christian missionary work were to work in tandem on this important issue. Like others before him, Manypenny was certain tribal people had to give way as they assimilated into American society, but instead of removal he argued for what was, to him, a more humane manner of bringing about their change.

In 1853, when assuming office and being handed the responsibility to deal with Ojibwe removal, George Manypenny almost immediately initiated action that halted the work of Ramsey and Watrous in western Lake Superior country. At that time, as Charles Cleland said: "The attempt to remove the Wisconsin Chippewa came to an end; a failure from start to finish."[24]

## 4.

WHILE THESE HIGH-LEVEL administrative changes in American government were happening during the winter of 1852-53, the

Ojibwe of Chequamegon Bay struggled with their uncertain situation. We know few of them journeyed to Crow Wing for the annuity payment at the end of the year, and that presumably in fall the bulk of the bands had done what they needed to do with the coming of winter. That is, after putting up their wild rice harvest and the produce from their gardens they did their fall fishing before dispersing into smaller family-centered groups to settle-in at their numerous hunting areas. Although the changes occurring in Washington may have been relatively unimportant to them, there surely were rumors about what effects they might have locally. The Ojibwe knew that during the early months of 1853 at La Pointe, Sherman Hall, his wife and children were preparing for their move to Minnesota Territory, a move that must have been read as an indication that, for them, the possibility of removal was still alive. Since spring Hall had been laboring at Crow Wing in Minnesota Territory to erect the buildings for the new agency farm and school, and in July he moved his family, along with Mr. and Mrs. Pulcifer and Henry Blatchford, the La Pointe teachers and interpreter.[25]

We know the Ojibwe were aware of the Watrous investigation and perhaps they also knew of negative sentiments toward Governor Ramsey that had been expressed in the region's media for several months, which led to a congressional investigation during the summer and fall of 1853. This concerned his role in the negotiation and distribution of the cash settlement from a recent treaty with the Dakota of Minnesota Territory. Ramsey was accused of mishandling these treaty funds but was exonerated of wrongdoing by a congressional committee. (However, the Minnesota historian William Watts Folwell felt this decision did not fit with the facts of the matter.)[26]

Also, as the petitions garnered by Buffalo and Oshaga in 1852 from the non-Ojibwe citizenry along the lakeshore show, the Ojibwe were fully aware of the growing negative sentiments for removal held by the non-Ojibwe community in the Michigan and Wisconsin regions. Witness the January 1853 Michigan legislative resolution which "urged that Lake Superior Chippewas who were acculturated, voting citizens of the state not be moved to Minnesota,"[27] and although this resolution referred only to those mixed-bloods who had taken up agriculture at L'Ance, Michigan, there likely was no lack of opinion about it in the greater regional Ojibwe community.

Likewise, the matter of the people at La Pointe temporarily being excused from removal by Luke Lea and from having to travel westward for their annuity payments by Ramsey may have leaked to the tribesmen and, if so, was a topic of discussion. The people would have pondered just what these exceptions meant, and what they might have led to. Then, perhaps most importantly, there was the lingering matter of the Ojibwe preserve in northeastern Minnesota Territory. The Ojibwe knew the Americans coveted this vast region for its mineral resources, and surely they felt United States officials would soon move to try to acquire it.

As we have argued, as disruptive as removal attempts were, to a considerable extent the Ojibwe were still using their traditional resource procurement activities. Their tribal economic organization remained integral to this cultural system at the foundation of their regular routine as they moved with the seasons, traveling to strategic areas for harvesting foods. Bruce White makes it clear that in the years of removal pressure, even given significant adaptations to Euro-American culture, the Ojibwe in Wisconsin and Minnesota Territory were still utilizing a hunting, fishing, and gathering subsistence adaptation.[28] As we have referred to above, La Pointe's sub-agent John Livermore understood this in early 1850, when he stated that in March of that year the Ojibwe were "widely distributed in their sugarbushes and hunting grounds." Also, again already noted, Livermore said that immediately after closing down their sugarbushes the people needed time "to market their sugar and furs and do up their dancing."[29] We have commented upon the significance of the "dancing," i.e., that it indicated spring medicine lodge (*midewiwin*) ceremonies were still extant at the time of Livermore's writing. Interestingly, along with showing the peoples' continued reliance upon their traditional economic and religious institutions, his remark about "marketing" shows a modification the people made in their economic system, a change that did not halt earlier practices, but in a complex way sustained them by adding the new to the old. Apparently, by 1853, much of the sugar the Ojibwe produced was either bartered or sold to Euro-American buyers.

After stressing the degree of cultural persistence the Ojibwe exhibited in the early 1850s in the western Lake Superior region, we would be remiss if we did not mention that some observers of the time implied it was precisely this tenacity of the people's clinging to their traditional culture that was causing hardship. To these commentators the people were struggling due to the diminished amounts of food animals remaining in the hunting and fishing areas. As claimed by visitors like Lt. James Allen some thirty years previous, the Lake Superior area had supposedly fallen victim to over-harvesting of game and the Ojibwe people were suffering.

These mid-nineteenth century comments about Ojibwe hardships are difficult to access. They hark back to earlier commentary by the Jesuits in the seventeenth century and through ensuing years, right up to remarks from persons like the Christian missionary Sherman Hall, who complained of the "wretchedness" of the people during his tenure at La Pointe. As we have discussed above, these culturally formed perceptions from the non-native community were at least partially due to the viewers' inability to understand the validity of a way of life distant from their own Euro-American industrial adaptations. Like many Americans of the times, these commentators saw a people who needed to change their way of life, and felt the most expedient way open to them was to become Christian agriculturists.

However this may be, the point is that the Ojibwe still tried to hold to their own cultural ways, and as the reference to "dancing" shows, they included regular interaction with the "Manito World" for guidance in these endeavors. It is important to understand that Ojibwe spiritual protocol demanded this interaction continue.

Unfortunately, we do not know the actual number of persons who were living in this traditional manner in the 1850s, but we should agree that at the time not all Ojibwe in western Lake Superior country were sedentary farmers. And we know that even those at Bad River and L'Ance who were cultivating fields were still doing some hunting, trapping and snaring of animals, maple sugar manufacturing and wild rice harvesting.[30] And of course, their means of handling health matters continued, i.e., they still used their traditional *pharmacopoeia* as they harvested various plants for medicines and other, more utilitarian purposes. The Ojibwe are known for their heavy use of the plant world and surely the important role of bark, leaves, roots and fibers must have continued through the mid-nineteenth century.

Even though the people eagerly welcomed aspects of American medicine, as seen in their desire to be vaccinated against small pox by Douglass Houghton in 1832, and again in 1854 at La Pointe by Leonard and Harriet Wheeler, as late as 1862, Wheeler claimed that at La Pointe the people did not want the medical service offered by the American government. This telling comment can only mean that for some ailments the people still turned to their own methods of treating illness and disease, a fact that says much about their retention of Ojibwe culture at the time.[31]

Therefore, even though some persons were experimenting with agriculture, they did not turn away from the entirety of their earlier subsistence and accompanying adaptations. Most certainly their worldview continued to involve an intimate understanding of the importance of their relationships with both human and non-human life forms. By 1853, even after years of pressure to cast it aside, hunting and gathering remained at the base of their cultural system. Evidence for this is seen in a letter of 27 May 1854, from Henry Gilbert to George Manypenny, in which the sub-agent requests that changes be made in the sorts of goods shipped to Lake Superior for issuance to the Ojibwe. According to Bruce White, Gilbert asked for "fewer dry goods and more guns, camp kettles, traps, cooking stoves, and cooking utensils. Some of these goods were clearly designed to fit in with the seasonal hunting, fishing, and gathering activities still carried on by these Ojibwe."[32] This shows who the Ojibwe were in the early 1850s, and how they doubtless saw themselves. And it is important to note that when discussing this historical time period for the Lake Superior Ojibwe and their adjustment to important changes in aspects of their material, or technical, world, all of this change was supported by their continuing relationship with the "Manito World." In other words, their religious ideology remained integral in its role of reinforcing the ongoing functioning of their community's subsistence efforts.

We need to acknowledge that when undergoing major change a society does not set aside its complete cultural system. Instead, the process of such important change is *crescive*, that is, it builds upon itself more slowly, and does not typically suddenly occur as an all-or-nothing phenomenon.

The written record is quick to suggest that by the 1850s, the western Lake Superior Ojibwe were faced with making major cultural changes, but it does little with what such extreme pressure was causing deep within the Ojibwe community. This is the *conservative* internal reaction to outside pressures for such change. A careful reading of the literature, and a familiarity with the internal functioning of Ojibwe communities today, shows that countering these outside pressures was a call to stay the course, in other words to not be too quick to abandon old ways of understanding the world and living in it. The continuation of traditional religious ceremonialism as mentioned by Sub-agent Livermore is a case in point. Using the verb "dancing" as a metaphor, we can agree that even amidst the deep challenge of the mid-nineteenth century, the Lake Superior Ojibwe were still *dancing*, i.e., in deep ways were still living in the socio-cultural world of old.

We should recall that this ongoing existence of Ojibwe culture in the middle of the nineteenth century in western Lake Superior country is remarked about in the historical literature. The personal letters of Leonard Wheeler show this when, as late as the 1860s, he lamented that after over twenty years of effort he had little success in converting the people to his religion. However, he *had* been successful in helping them develop practical adaptations to the Americans.[33] Perhaps this ability to hold on to their own religious beliefs and practices is most candidly seen in the case of Chief Buffalo, who resisted conversion to Christianity for all but the last few days of his long life. In 1855, when he was gravely ill, only three days before he passed away he relented under great pressure and was baptized into the Catholic faith. Wheeler's lament and Buffalo's resistance will be discussed further in the next chapter.

To conclude, as invariably happens when a culture is faced with powerful forces demanding major change as the Ojibwe were in the early 1850s, the community's response to such demands includes a call to solidify its traditions and way of life as it struggles to meet this challenge. We can see that this conservative aspect of culture was functioning in the Ojibwe community, and contrary to the perceptions of some past historical writers, the Ojibwe's earlier way of life did not suddenly cease, leaving them "culture-less," or as is often assumed—witness the above quote of Edmund Jefferson Danziger, Jr.—in a state of abject poverty. Although they were under great duress as they negotiated accommodations to the powerful Americans, they still had their culture. The new Christian farming way of life they were being admonished to accept did not suddenly, *and completely*, replace this earlier *Ojibwe* way of life.

## 5.

SOON AFTER ASSUMING THEIR OFFICES in 1853, the new American officials most directly involved with Indian affairs began making changes. In September, Governor Willis Gorman wrote to Commissioner Manypenny strongly suggesting that annuity payments for the Ojibwe be made later that month, rather than deep into winter as Ramsey and Watrous had done. As Alfred Brunson and others had urged in previous years, Gorman stressed the importance of this timely distribution, emphasizing the severity of the winters in the Lake Superior region and the great danger they presented to traveling Ojibwe families.[34]

This sudden change in sentiment for the Ojibwe people was also seen in the actions of Charles Mix, the chief clerk in the Indian department who at times assumed the role of acting commissioner, and Robert McClelland, the Secretary of the Department of the Interior. We are still uncertain why he did it, but in August 1853, unknown to Governor Gorman, Mix told McClelland the annuities for the Lake Superior bands should be paid on the lake instead of an inland site well into Minnesota Territory. McClelland quickly agreed, and preparations for the distribution were soon underway. To the great joy of the Ojibwe, payment took place at La Pointe in mid-October 1853. With the completion of this act Orlando Brown's order that annuities be paid only on un-ceded land was swept aside.[35]

The La Pointe people were not aware the payment was forthcoming until Henry Gilbert arrived at Madeline Island on 9 October, and their happy reaction soon became a celebration witnessed by missionary Leonard Wheeler and told in a letter to his parents written on 20 October, the day the payment was completed. According to Wheeler: "America does not contain happier company than is congregated on this island to night. I have been out this eve to some of the lodges to rejoice with those that do rejoice . . . . Some of our people are so happy and so excited that they could not sleep at all the first night."[36] Although he had the year wrong, Benjamin Armstrong doubtless was referring to the same event when he recalled the incident several decades later. About the annuity payment gathering Armstrong claimed, "the most perfect satisfaction was apparent among all concerned."[37] Before the end of 1853, Willis Gorman officiated at another annuity payment, this time for the remaining Ojibwe bands, held at St. Croix Falls, Wisconsin, a location also on ceded lands.[38]

These two events are important for a number of reasons, but perhaps the most obvious is that after two years of contentious letter writing and meetings between Ojibwe leaders and Ramsey, Watrous and their appointees concerning the location and timing of annuity payments, this acrimonious confrontation came to a sudden, and for the Ojibwe, unanticipated happy ending. To the La Pointe bands and other Ojibwe people the payments ushered in a new time for their relationship with American authorities. Something had changed, and the following winter—that of 1853 to 1854—was decidedly less anxious than the previous two.

An indication of this feeling of relief from the dread of removal is seen in a letter Leonard Wheeler wrote to his father on 31 January 1854, only approximately three months after the annuity payment. The tone of the letter is decidedly more upbeat than those written throughout the previous year or more as it shows both the missionary and the Bad River Ojibwe people relaxing a bit and expressing optimism for the future. Wheeler claimed the people were looking forward to planting their fields in spring and that for the first time in a long time there was no liquor at Bad River. He said the mission school was full of young students, the adult church meetings were well attended and a once-a-week "singing school"—in which the singing was "mostly in Indian"—had been started and was well attended. However, this newfound optimism was immediately followed by an unsettling breakout of smallpox in the community the very next month which lasted into early spring.[39]

Another troubling incident was the receipt of letters from Wheeler's fellow missionary, Sherman Hall. At the urging of John Watrous, Hall had moved his family to Minnesota Territory where he was to oversee a new manual training school for the Ojibwe, but in early 1854, the missionary had soured on the entire initiative. He told the Wheelers he was very unhappy, that there was much liquor in the area, and that he wanted to return to La Pointe. He claimed the Crow Wing station "is no place for the Indian" and that he, Hall, "opposes removal." Harriet Wheeler told her parents that "In almost every letter [Hall] charges us to tell the indians not to come [to Crow Wing] even if they have to forfeit their annuities."[40]

As positive as the La Pointe and St. Croix payments of 1853 were for the people, the payments were not completed without their share of misunderstandings and unnecessary hardships. The complicated St. Croix payment was not finished until the very end of the year, and some of the interior Wisconsin and Minnesota Territory bands experienced great difficulty before receiving their distributions. Part of the problem involved the lingering policy of the past administration. As we saw, under this policy the Lake Superior bands were excused from traveling to unceded territory for payment, but not the interior Wisconsin bands, and until the removal policy would be clearly cancelled, this inequity remained. Charles Mix's decision to split the payment between the new Detroit and St. Louis Indian Affairs Districts also made things more difficult than they need have been. Apparently following the earlier program, it was Mix's decision that the La Pointe payment would only be distributed to the Grand Portage, Fond du Lac, La Pointe, Ontonagon and L'Anse bands. The rest were to be handled by new Agent David Herriman of the Crow Wing Agency in Minnesota Territory. Consequently, some interior Wisconsin bands traveled to La Pointe only to be refused payment, meaning if they wanted their distribution they needed to travel to Crow Wing or St. Croix Falls much later in the year. These and other related issues caused undue hardship to the smaller inland bands before receiving their payment at year's end.[41]

There is one further twist regarding the 1853 annuity payments. This is the involvement of Henry Rice in the discussions that preceded the St. Croix Falls payment. Rice had initially supported removal of the Wisconsin and Michigan Ojibwe bands, and when not given a government contract to effect the removal was later suspected of changing his mind and discouraging the removal effort in order to reap personal financial returns. By 1853, he had become a Minnesota Territorial delegate to Washington, D.C., and held differences of opinion with Willis Gorman on how to handle Indian matters. Although both were Democrats, these two men were not friends. The problem was exacerbated by Rice's displeasure with a recent treaty Gorman negotiated with the Ho-Chunk that would have—Rice felt—placed a new Ho-Chunk reservation too close to white settlers in the St. Croix region. These settlers were Rice's constituents and along with their displeasure with the possibility of having Ho-Chunk neighbors, they felt the local Ojibwe bands were also a problem. Thus, Henry Rice seems to have felt that by distributing annuities at the St. Croix site, Gorman was encouraging the Ojibwe people to stay instead of moving westward.[42]

Willis Gorman saw Henry Rice as a major player in the old matter of fraud in the Indian trade, and by 1853, felt Rice was representing these unlawful interests in Congress. About this "quarrel" between Gorman and Rice, the historian Bruce White says, "It was yet another example of the way in which Native people were the political football kicked around by early Minnesota politicians."[43]

## 6.

THE ABOVE TWO ANNUITY PAYMENTS foreshadowed the beginning of the end of the removal policy, and they were the start of more changes coming to the Ojibwe. After completing the La Pointe payment Henry Gilbert wrote his report on 31 October to Commissioner Manypenny, in which some of these changes were discussed. Gilbert initially reviewed old grievances about John Watrous told to him by the Ojibwe leaders, but most important was their great fear of removal—a fear so strong Gilbert was certain they would rather have died than be forced to move. Consequently, he suggested to Manypenny that the people be allowed to remain where they were, in Gilbert's words, so they could "acquire lands and make settlements and improvements" at these traditional locations. Gilbert was likely using his notions of what could occur to the Ojibwe if the threat of removal was ended. He does not tell us the people told him they wanted to "acquire lands" on which they would "make settlements and improvements," in other words, lands on which they would build permanent houses and outbuildings, and on which they would clear the forest for fields for crops. The phrases, "acquire lands" for "settlements and improvements," apparently came from Henry Gilbert, not the Ojibwe themselves.

We should only conclude that the people were asking, simply, to be allowed to remain where they were, doing the things they had been doing. That is, they desired to continue carrying out their present way of life, which of course included hunting and gathering, gardening, and by late 1853, likely newer pursuits like bartering or otherwise exchanging the products of their efforts with the Americans, and even periodic work as wage laborers. Gilbert did not explicitly state the matter of taking up agriculture, although we should think farming was what he was referring to. Surely agriculture was something he, Manypenny, and other change agents assumed would come to the people. Perhaps we should also expect that by the end of 1853, some of the Ojibwe who were not already dabbling in farming might also have agreed it would eventually become part of their lives.[44]

In his report, Henry Gilbert also told Manypenny the removal policy should be abandoned, and a written document stating this drawn up and presented to the people. He was certain that until this was done they would not be willing to discuss much of anything with the American authorities, and although he did not say he was afraid conflict would break out if removal were not abandoned, his report intimates he felt it was a possibility. There is no written record to show whether the document Henry Gilbert speaks of was drawn up and given to the people anytime soon after his request. As we already noted, at the end of October 1853, when Gilbert was writing his report, Washington officials might have felt that the drafting and issuance of this document was premature and would have tipped the hand of the American authorities who desired to use the end of removal as leverage when bargaining for the Ojibwe preserve. This could be part of the reason Alexander Ramsey never meaningfully responded to the Buffalo and Oshaga letter they sent upon their return from the 1852 Washington trip, and why Ramsey never issued a document terminating the removal policy.

Sub-agent Gilbert's remarks show that as of 31 October 1853, the Ojibwe people had *not yet received* such a written statement from the Americans saying their removal policy was abandoned. What Gilbert's request suggests is that the paper supposedly handed to Buffalo by President Fillmore nearly a year and a half earlier did not state that the removal order was remanded, but, as we suggested, only that the decision to cancel removal was in the hands of Governor Ramsey. *Obviously, Gilbert's request would not be understandable if a document canceling the removal order had already been given to the people.*

Before concluding his report Henry Gilbert told Manypenny, almost as an afterthought, that he felt the grievances and complaints of the people could be rectified with a new treaty, one in which the Ojibwe preserve would be transferred to the Americans. About the preserve Gilbert claimed, "*They* [the Ojibwe] *consider it valuable, as it really is, but have no desire to retain it provided they can be furnished with homes in the manner I have stated.*"[45] Here Henry Gilbert makes it clear that the Ojibwe were willing to exchange their rights to the preserve for the right to remain in their home areas, and as suggested earlier, they realized the value of the preserve and would not give it up without something valuable in return.

We have noted that even before the close of 1853, the question of the end of the removal policy was engendering discussion in Congress and western Lake Superior country. Integral to these conversations had to have been the Ojibwe determination not to remove and the resultant fear of conflict felt by the non-native community. Perhaps in the early years the fear of warfare with native peoples always was a concern for frontier regions witnessing an influx of non-natives. And to the business community, to include land speculators like Henry M. Rice, conflict—or worse yet, outright war—with a region's resident Indian population was a near anathema. Some quarters of the Ojibwe community also doubtless wanted peace. In 1853, as a civil chief, not a war chief, Buffalo was working to keep his people from readily going to war with the Americans. His determination, at age ninety-three, to undertake the arduous 1852 trip to Washington, D.C., to meet with the president and attempt to use diplomacy to end removal must be seen as part of this determination to achieve peace. It was under these conditions that the subject of one more land cession treaty between the United States and western Lake Superior's Ojibwe people began to germinate and it soon surfaced in new and more serious ways.

As seen above, as far back as 1847, and again in 1851, the non-native community was discussing the possibility of one more treaty with the Ojibwe. These conversations concerned the cession of the last large Ojibwe land parcel remaining in northeastern Minnesota Territory, but at the time the Ojibwe were firmly against selling any more land to the Americans. A reference to this treaty appears in Benjamin Armstrong's memoir where he reviews Buffalo's return from Washington. According to Armstrong, when passing through Ojibwe villages before reaching Madeline Island, Buffalo told the leaders "to send a delegation, at the expiration of two moons, to meet him in grand council at La Pointe, for there was many things he wanted to say to them about what he had seen and the nice manner in which he had been received and treated by the great father."[46] When Buffalo said he wanted to tell his people "what he had seen" in the eastern United States he must have been referring to the large population of Americans he traveled through, with its cities and military installations. Buffalo and his party likely were given cause to conclude they needed to negotiate a peaceful resolution to the peoples' differences with these strong Americans. Armstrong goes on to say that annuities were paid at La Pointe that fall—1852—but as we saw, he was in error. That year they were not paid until December, and they were distributed at Crow Wing, not La Pointe.

The La Pointe annuity payment Armstrong recalled as being made in 1852 actually occurred in 1853. What is important for our purposes is that Armstrong says after the payment was completed, Buffalo spoke to the gathering of people and told them "that there was yet one more treaty to be made with the great father and he [Buffalo] hoped in making it they would be more careful and wise than they had heretofore been and reserve a part of their land for themselves and their children."[47] Writer Mark Diedrich understands this latter statement of Armstrong's to mean that when in Washington, Buffalo "was told another treaty was to be made."[48]

The reason for Diedrich's deduction is unclear. As the delegation's interpreter, Armstrong was present throughout all of its meetings in Washington, and nowhere does he say Buffalo "was told" another treaty was necessary. Diedrich's statement suggests the initiative for one last land cession treaty came from President Fillmore or his appointees and that the Ojibwe were merely reacting to it, but there is nothing in the written record to support this conclusion. Diedrich's contention that the notion of one last treaty came only from the Americans is not supported by the written evidence. Thus, it is an unfortunate conclusion since it poses the Ojibwe as mere dependent people who were unable to affect their future. Despite the truth of Bruce White's image of the people being "political footballs kicked around by American officials," despite being in a difficult time in 1853, the Ojibwe were anything but mere dependents who bowed to the dictates of the Americans.

By the end of 1853, the Americans were very concerned about the possibility of warfare with the Ojibwe. As we have seen, the historical record shows that in the decisive years of the mid-nineteenth century, the Ojibwe were quite proactive in the matter of determining their destiny. Buffalo's and the other's contacts with the British at Sault Ste. Marie attest to this. Thus, Armstrong's remark about Buffalo telling his people one more treaty was needed could be interpreted as meaning it was Buffalo and his co-leaders who originated this idea. The possibility of physical conflict might still have lingered as an option for some quarters of the Ojibwe community, but by the start of 1854, those who supported this path likely were in the minority. With the negation of Black Bird's petition by British authorities in 1852, the tactic of bargaining the preserve for the cancellation of removal may have become the last viable solution.

A second reference to a treaty comes from the 6 February 1854 report Willis Gorman sent to Commissioner Manypenny after the completion of the 1853 annuity payment at St. Croix Falls. Gorman reiterated the grievances of the people and felt that their difficulties could be met through a treaty allowing them to remain in their home areas. He suggested such a treaty could also be the instrument through which the title to the Ojibwe preserve could be transferred to the United States.[49] This is the first clear evidence in the written record that American authorities were relating the cession of the Ojibwe preserve to the end of removal, and in uttering this remark Willis Gorman was reacting to overtures from the Ojibwe community he mentioned in his 31 October 1853 report to Manypenny. This overture was the peoples' notion of bargaining the preserve for the right to remain where they were, and this suggests they—the Ojibwe—originated the notion of trading the preserve for the end of removal.

We recall that the United States had desired to purchase the mineral rich preserve for several years and that the commissioners for the Fond du Lac Treaty of 1847 raised the matter with the Lake Superior bands, but Buffalo and the people were still angry about the Treaty of 1842 and were resolved to sell no more land to the Americans. Related to this firm stand by the La Pointe Ojibwe seems to be the ongoing communications western Lake Superior Ojibwe leaders were having with Shingwaukonse of Ontario's Sault Ste. Marie at the time. Four years later, in 1851, when mineral prospectors were penetrating the preserve and disturbing the Ojibwe, the issue of a sale surfaced again.[50] Then in the spring of 1854, a bill was introduced in the United States Congress to "extinguish" all Ojibwe rights to remaining land east of the Mississippi. It passed through the House but failed to gain Senate approval until early December of that year.[51]

The proponents of this bill assumed the Ojibwe would be removed and their lands taken over by the incoming citizenry as a matter of course, but for long months the bill struggled in the Senate. This was not due to a refusal of some congressmen to approve the large financial outlay needed to purchase the preserve, but was caused by a growing disenchantment with Andrew Jackson's removal policy. Some congressional voices felt this policy was not working as planned—that instead of expediting the "advancement" of the Indian to a civilized state, it was implicated in what whites saw as a nagging failure of indigenous peoples to leave their former way of life behind in favor of the new.[52] Commissioner Manypenny surely was involved in these senate discussions and less than a year after he received Gorman's reports, of 31 October 1853 and 6 February 1854, with their remarks relating the end of removal to the purchase of the preserve, he took action.

7.

IN AUGUST 1854, GEORGE MANYPENNY wrote a quick series of letters to Henry Gilbert and David Herriman telling them to try to negotiate for the preserve during the gathering for the annuity payment at La Pointe that fall. Gilbert was to be the main negotiator and in order to expedite negotiations, Herriman was to bring only a very few Mississippi band leaders to La Pointe. Manypenny's letters were a surprisingly abrupt notice, given the time needed for mail to move from Washington to the far western Great Lakes country, and tells us the field activities for the Treaty of 1854 were initiated and accomplished in a comparatively short span of time.

Manypenny's letters are interesting for at least two reasons. One, as noted by Bruce White, is that they suggest a degree of naiveté on the part of the Commissioner since he apparently assumed the few Ojibwe leaders coming from the Mississippi bands could readily negotiate such a large land cession treaty without first bringing the matter before their people.[53] Secondly, on the other hand, Manypenny knew from

Willis Gorman's 31 October 1853 report that the lake bands were ready to negotiate for the preserve, and thus, he was aware this proposed land cession had been discussed in Ojibwe communities for some time previously. Because of this, Manypenny's apparent sudden action to order Gilbert and Herriman to try to negotiate the treaty may not have been as unanticipated as it seems.

Even before formal negotiations were underway Manypenny told Gilbert to offer the Ojibwe $500,000.00 for the preserve—one-half of a million dollars, and a good sum of money in 1854—along with the right to keep their homes in their present regions—in other words, to put an end to the removal order. The fact that American officials made *both* the significant cash offer and agreed to end their removal attempts may be interpreted as a concession, or perhaps a counter move, to the Ojibwe's determined stand not to remove. With this early offer the Commissioner was seconding Gorman's comment of a few months previous that the government most likely would need to give up its efforts at Ojibwe removal in order to purchase the preserve. In addition, it suggests that by mid-1854, national sentiment had turned against Andrew Jackson's removal policy in favor of Manypenny and Mix's "assimilation in-place" policy.

Interestingly, both Gilbert and Herriman were ordered to keep their activities toward the land sale goal secret due to "adverse interests." This likely was a reference to elements of the Indian trade, like Henry Rice, that still desired the Ojibwe—and their regular annuity payments—be removed to western Minnesota Territory. In these communiqués Manypenny suggested the agents discuss changes in the locations of blacksmiths and other government employees that had been agreed upon in earlier treaties in order to more easily realign these services with the new locations the people might desire. These directives show the sense of detail and urgency in Manypenny's initiatives for change in the way the government handled Indian affairs. He wanted quick and sometimes quiet action, a *modus operandi* that ran counter to the more deliberate and thoughtful manner of negotiation demanded by tribal political systems.[54]

Manypenny felt the negotiations for the preserve could be "a hard sell" because he was aware of the attempts of earlier treaty commissioners to unite the disparate Ojibwe bands into a single political community with common concerns and goals and how this caused extreme animosity between the Mississippi and Lake Superior peoples.[55] To overcome this he suggested Gilbert try to split the preserve into an eastern and a western portion, with the former being the Lake bands' and the latter that of the Mississippi bands. This division would call for two negotiation meetings, the second—that with the Mississippi Bands—to take place in Washington, D.C., the following year.[56] While Manypenny seemed to be the first to suggest this division of the preserve, Benjamin Armstrong claimed it was he and Chief Buffalo who initially proposed the idea.[57] Government officials also apparently felt it would be a "hard sell" because of the Ojibwes' determination not to remove, and that physical conflict in western Lake Superior country could be a very troublesome and unfortunate outcome of a forced removal.

The 1854 La Pointe annuity payment was made on 29 September for the Lake Superior and other Wisconsin bands, and a new treaty was quickly negotiated and signed the following day, 30 September. Eighty-five chiefs—seventy from Wisconsin and fifteen from Minnesota Territory—signed the document, but notably absent from the long list of those who "touched the pen" at La Pointe that day was the name of Oshaga, Chief Buffalo's co-leader and speaker, and apparently one of his several sons. Oshaga had succumbed to smallpox in spring of that year and surely Buffalo, his large family, and the entire Ojibwe community mourned the loss of this young and respected leader.[58] We know little about Oshaga but given his years of political experience during the difficult removal times, it is certain that with his passing the Ojibwe people lost a very valuable leader, one that could have done much to guide them through the difficult years immediately after 1854.

The exchange of letters between Commissioner Manypenny and his field agent, Henry Gilbert, make it clear that the prime motive for the United States to attempt to negotiate the Treaty of 1854 was to win the purchase of the Ojibwe preserve, not to negotiate an arrangement with the Ojibwe that would allow them to remain in their homelands on parcels already ceded in earlier treaties. From the perspective of the Americans this was always clear. In other words, for them the major goal of the new treaty was land cession, and the land to be ceded was the preserve in northern Minnesota Territory. Contrarily, it seems just as clear that from the Ojibwe perspective the major goal of the treaty was to secure land parcels within the area ceded away in the treaty of 1842, and in this manner put an end to Zachary Taylor's 1852 Removal Order.

The inordinately large number of signatories on the 1854 Treaty shows the great size of the gathering and the enormity of the task to have the treaty successfully negotiated and signed in such a relatively short time. This suggests something about Henry Gilbert's skills in negotiating with so many Ojibwe people at one gathering, but also that as the American authorities were focused on their goals, so were the Ojibwe. Both parties in the treaty knew what they wanted and the Ojibwe, especially, stood their ground. The fact that eighty-five tribal leaders signed the document so quickly means there must have been a wide consensus throughout their communities on what was wanted well before 30 September. It is apparent that the trade-off of the preserve for the end of removal with the right to remain in their home areas was discussed throughout the various bands and agreed upon long before that date. Important aspects of Ojibwe culture, and its moccasin telegraph, were operating in Chequamegon country in 1854.[59]

Unfortunately, we have minimal documentation of the details of these discussions, but Benjamin Armstrong claims the Ojibwe had several days of meetings at La Pointe in the fall of 1854, before the treaty council was officially opened.[60] James Scott, an early historian at the Bad River Ojibwe community, supported this when he said in the summer of 1854, it took "thirty days of deliberation" before the treaty was signed.[61] Except for these few remarks our understanding of the proceedings of the treaty negotiations come largely from the paper trail left by Euro-Americans other than Armstrong. But we do know the Ojibwe people stood firm with their demands. Henry Gilbert told Commissioner Manypenny that he simply was unable to have the entire preserve treated for at La Pointe and that he could not bring both the Mississippi representatives and the Lake Superior band leaders to a joint council until he agreed to split the preserve into two parcels, but once that was done it seems negotiations moved along quickly.

Whether it was Armstrong and Buffalo, or Manypenny, and perhaps others who first raised the matter of splitting the preserve is unclear. Be this as it may, due to the pressures from the several special interest groups on site and the Ojibwes' resolve to win an end to removal and secure land holdings in their home areas, the Americans must have been concerned about the success of the gathering. This concern, along with the logistics of successfully carrying out such a large meeting—the commissarial obligations for the Americans must have been huge—led Charles Cleland to say because of animosity between the Mississippi and Lake Superior bands, the negotiations "were a near fiasco."[62]

It was estimated that more than 4,000 persons from the numerous Ojibwe communities, as well as interested mixed-blood persons, traders, and others who wanted to observe and influence the proceedings, all to their personal benefit, congregated on Madeline Island. It was the end of September so the rice harvest could have been completed, a fact allowing more people to attend the gathering than otherwise would have been possible. In early fall the weather was hospitable so travel to the site must have been easily accomplished, and as was the case at previous treaty negotiations the treaty commissioners made provisions available for this large crowd, so once again the gathering must have had a festive character with its large encampment, lodge fires, and all else involved.[63]

Gilbert sent the signed treaty to Commissioner Manypenny in Washington, but in an unusual move the Commissioner did not immediately rush it to Congress for ratification. George Manypenny wanted the large Ojibwe preserve with its mineral riches to come into the hands of the United States, and to facilitate this it appears he held the new treaty until the Congressional bill "to extinguish" all remaining Ojibwe land holdings east of the Mississippi River was passed by Congress. We recall this bill had been submitted to Congress in the spring of the year, was easily passed by the House, but was struggling for Senate approval in very late 1854. At issue was the growing national sentiment that although Jackson's removal policy may have been successful in physically moving Indian communities to distant regions, it was failing in its second goal of leading to the transformation of these "savages" into "civilized" persons. By 1854, after much effort and expense of removing the Indian from the path of the advancing frontier, this ultimate goal of "civilizing" the Indian was not moving forward in a rapid and effective manner.

The failure of this bill to pass through Congress might have had an adverse effect on attempts to win ratification of the new treaty with its large land purchase, so it seems Manypenny tried to ease the bill's passage by including a reference to the Ojibwe preserve in his 25 November annual report to Secretary of the Interior McClelland. In bringing the Secretary up-to-date on the matter of Ojibwe removal, he made the following observation about the Michigan and Wisconsin communities: "it might be necessary to permit them all to remain, in order to acquire a cession of a large tract of country they still own east of the Mississippi, which on account of its great mineral resources, it is an object of material importance to obtain."[64]

Here we see the Commissioner of Indian Affairs disclose the Americans' underlying reason for agreeing to the end of Ojibwe removal. In other words, in late 1854, after the treaty agreement, which included the trade-off of the end of removal for the preserve, Manypenny shows us that the United States was aware that to get the preserve, it likely would have to give up its long-valued goal of Indian removal, at least in the case of the Ojibwe.

Once the bill to extinguish all Ojibwe land holdings east of the Mississippi River was passed, Manypenny sent the treaty—on 8 December—to Secretary McClelland, who passed it on to President Pierce. Pierce gave his approval and sent it to Congress on 20 December, where it was ratified on 10 January 1855. Once put into motion by Manypenny, negotiations and final approval for the Treaty of 1854 moved quickly.

## 8.

TODAY IT MIGHT BE CONVENTIONAL to think that the reason the Lake Superior Ojibwe bands still reside at the locations they have been at for the last few hundred years is because of the persistent efforts of La Pointe's Chief Buffalo. His two trips to Washington, D.C., in the middle of the nineteenth century and his determined leadership in the peoples' resistance to removal are said to be the causes for the end of Ojibwe removal efforts. When Buffalo's supposed advanced age is added to this—along with the image of he and his small party pushing off for Washington on the shore of Lake Superior in a birch bark canoe—we have *the stuff of legend*. Consistently, in all the written documents available to us, Buffalo is described as a very impressive leader. In this regard, we are told he stood out among his people, and the oral literature is generally similar in its praise.

We have seen that Zachary Taylor's Ojibwe Removal Order seems never to have been cancelled by an official written instrument. Instead, it was put to rest by the second article in the Treaty of 1854, authorizing the establishment of reservations in land ceded in the Treaty of 1842. This article does not mention removal, but by allowing for the reserves it thereby negates any further removal attempts. It is not insignificant that the very first—and therefore, the *priority* article—in the Treaty of 1854 spoke solely to the matter of the sale of the preserve, and the second addresses reservation of land parcels in each of their home areas for the involved Ojibwe bands. Therefore, the treaty's first two articles get right to the exchange, or trade, of the preserve for the seven parcels of reservation lands, and in doing so, effectively end removal.

Buffalo's leadership doubtless was integral to Ojibwe success in stopping removal efforts but the importance of the trade-off must be weighed. While Chief Buffalo's tireless efforts at standing up to American authorities are at the very center of causes leading to the ending of removal, the role of the exchange of the preserve also was of great importance. As it turned out, in order to win the end of removal, the Ojibwe had to give something up in exchange and this was their mineral-rich western preserve.

In summary, although present-day oral traditions as well as a first reading of the literature of Ojibwe removal says it was the efforts of La Pointe's Chief Buffalo that stopped removal and led to the Ojibwe people retaining home bases on their long-held homelands, a more careful analysis of these past events shows there was more at play. Something as valuable as the end of removal and the acquisition of parcels of land for permanent communities does not come easily. Therefore, it is possible the American authorities used the offer of the cancellation of President Fillmore's removal order and establishment of permanent homes on ceded lands as leverage to acquire the large mineral-rich expanse of remaining Ojibwe land in northeastern Minnesota Territory.[65]

This suggestion, however, fails to recognize the political astuteness of the Ojibwe since it can also be argued that their leaders used the sale of their preserve—as James Clifton suggested—as a "bargaining token" for securing both the end of removal and the right to remain on their homelands. Thus, in other words, at La Pointe back in the fall of 1854, the Ojibwe successfully negotiated for their right to permanently remain in their chosen homelands.

In our final chapter we will discuss pertinent details of the Treaty of 1854 and see why the La Pointe meeting for negotiating the treaty has been called "the most important event in Chippewa history since the coming of the white man."[66] This discussion will serve to end this book's exploration of the early history of the Ojibwe people in Chequamegon Bay.

*Notes*

1. Goody 2000.
2. White in McClurken *et al* 2000:262.
3. White in McClurken *et al* 230; Densmore 1929:138-9.
4. White in McClurken *et al* 2000:262.
5. Kohl 1985[1860]:2-3; Densmore 1929:138-40.
6. White in McClurken *et al* 2000:262-5.
7. Armstrong 1892:13-4.
8. White in McClurken *et al* 2000:262-4.
9. Armstrong 1892:14.
10. White in McClurken *et al* 2000:262.
11. Leonard Wheeler, letter of 27 October 1853 to father, original at NGLVC; White in McClurken *et al* 2000:278-9.
12. Browne 1855 as given in White in McClurken *et al* 2000:263.
13. Leonard Wheeler, letter of 27 October 1853 to father, original at NGLVC.
14. Cleland in McClurken *et al* 2000:82; Leonard Wheeler, letter of 3 January 1853 to his mother, original at NGLVC.
15. White in McClurken *et al* 2000:272-3.
16. Cleland in McClurken *et al* 2000:80.
17. Brown 2001[1970].
18. As found in Kvasnicka and Viola 1979:54.
19. Taylor 2006.
20. Kvasnicka in Kvasnicka and Viola 1979:57-67.
21. Kvasnicka in Kvasnicka and Viola 1979:60, 62.
22. This phenomena is graphically depicted in the novel entitled *The Surrounded*, written by D'Arcy McNickel, the twentieth century Blackfeet/Osage writer.
23. Manypenny 1880.
24. Cleland in McClurken *et al* 2000:71.
25. Sherman Hall Annual Report of 8 November 1853, to D.B. Herriman, Indian Agent, in ARCIASI.
26. White in McClurken *et al* 2000:264-5.
27. Danziger 1973:178;1979:88.
28. White in McClurken et al 2000:293-7.
29. Livermore as given in White in McClurken *et al* 2000:295.
30. Leonard Wheeler letter of 10 November 1849 to father, original at NGLVC.
31. Bunge 2000:5; Leonard Wheeler letter of 19 September 1862 to father, original at NGLVC.
32. White in McClurken *et al* 2000:275.
33. Bunge 2000:5; Leonard Wheeler, Annual Report to Selah Treat (American Board of Commissioners for Foreign Missions), dated 1 August 1865, original at NGLVC.
34. White in McClurken *et al* 2000:266-7.
35. White in McClurken *et al* 2000:266-7.
36. Leonard Wheeler letter of 20 October 1853 to father, as in White in McClurken *et al* 2000:267.
37. Armstrong 1892:32.
38. Cleland in McClurken *et al* 2000:71.
39. Leonard Wheeler letter of 31 January 1854 to his father, original at NGLVC.
40. Harriet Wheeler letter of 6 March 1854, brackets added, original at NGLVC.
41. White in McClurken *et al* 2000:269-275.
42. White in McClurken *et al* 2000:272-4.
43. White in McClurken *et al* 2000:274.
44. Gilbert 1853 as given in Cleland in McClurken *et al* 2000:71.
45. Gilbert as quoted in White in McClurken *et al* 2000:268, italics and brackets added.
46. Armstrong 1892:31.
47. Armstrong 1892:32, brackets added.
48. Diedrich 1999:76.
49. Gorman 1854 as noted in White in McClurken *et al* 2000:268; Cleland in McClurken *et al* 2000:71.
50. Cleland in McClurken *et al* 2000:82.
51. White in McClurken *et al* 2000:275.
52. White in McClurken *et al* 2000:275.
53. White in McClurken *et al* 2000:276.
54. Cleland in McClurken *et al* 2000:83-5;White in McClurken *et al* 2000:275-8.
55. Cleland in McClurken *et al* 2000:83.
56. Cleland in McClurken *et al* 2000:84; White in McClurken *et al* 2000:276-8.
57. Armstrong 1892:35-6.
58. Bartlet 1929:68-77; Diedrich 1999:69; Morse 1857:348; Julia Wheeler, letter of 8 February 1854 to her grandparents, original at NGLVC.
59. White in McClurken *et al* 2000:276-7.
60. Armstrong 1892:33-6.
61. Munnell 1996, in *News from the Sloughs (Bad River's Monthly Newspaper)*, February 1996, Vol. 1, issue 10, p. 22.
62. Cleland in McClurken *et al* 2000:84.
63. Cleland in McClurken *et al* 2000:84.
64. Manypenny as given in Cleland in McClurken *et al* 2000:72.
65. Danziger 1979:87.
66. Danziger 1979:89.

# 22

# The Treaty of 1854

The year 1854 is recognized as one of the most important in the history of the Lake Superior Ojibwe. As we have seen, this was the year the La Pointe treaty was negotiated and signed, an act said to be a "turning point for the Lake Superior bands."[1] Something changed with the signing and following Congressional ratification and presidential approval of the La Pointe Treaty. The Ojibwe people suddenly moved from several decades of severely troubling times to a more peaceful future, but at the end of 1854, the undetermined nature of this future had to have been troubling.

Today at Red Cliff, 30 September, the day the treaty was signed, is called Treaty Day, and is usually recognized as a holiday for tribal employees. But it is not a holiday celebrated joyously with loud marching bands and patriotic speeches. Instead it is spent in a quieter, more thoughtful manner as contemporary Ojibwe people contemplate the lasting meaning of the treaty.

The oppressive problems of the 1852 Removal Order abruptly ended on 30 September, but since the future was uncertain, leaders like Buffalo and others must have discussed it at length. As we saw, the historian Edmund Jefferson Danziger, Jr. claimed that after the signing of the treaty, the American agents of civilization—both men and women—"waged war on Chippewa culture." The Ojibwe people, according to Danziger, "began a new journey down the white man's road. For nearly a century it was a road without turning, a one-way street to cultural disintegration and crushing poverty."[2] Danziger's is a particularly, and perhaps unnecessarily, harsh assessment of Ojibwe life at places like Red Cliff for the past 100 and more years, and we should question the degree and extent of "cultural disintegration and crushing poverty" he so clearly states was to be the long future of the people. By late 1854, the Ojibwe knew adversity, but they also knew the tenacity and strength of their own culture.

In 1854, another matter of some importance was Chief Buffalo's ability to continue providing leadership for his community. He was said to have been in his mid-nineties at the time of the signing of the treaty, and was experiencing health problems. According to one Chequamegon Bay historian, "Chief Buffalo was seriously ill" during the summer of 1854, when the new treaty was being negotiated.[3] Although there are indications in the literature that he was still an active leader almost up to the time of his death in the fall of 1855, in 1854, the combination of his illness and advanced age pointed to an imminent change in leadership. It seems that over the two years following his 1852 trip to Washington he continued to provide active leadership for his people, but through this time, due to his deteriorating health, his role as *the* political leader for the western Lake Superior Ojibwe began to change. Ojibwe tradition mandated that the next in line would have been his oldest capable son, but the question of who the community would accept as the person to eventually replace him likely was a topic of some concern.

We recall the question of mid-nineteenth century political leadership among the western Lake Superior Ojibwe bands raised by both the 1845 attempt of Black Bird and Neokema, both La Pointe leaders, to move their communities to a residential site north of the American border at Sault Ste. Marie. And we also remember the following 1852 petition, signed by Minnesota's Flat Mouth, La Pointe's Black Bird—and virtually all other major western Michigan, Wisconsin, and Minnesota Ojibwe band leaders—to Canadian authorities for permission for these bands to move to Canada, and how this petition pointed to differences of opinion—especially at La Pointe—regarding the Ojibwe political relationship with the Americans. This issue is important since it points to complexities of political leadership that are integral to an understanding of Ojibwe culture and history in western Lake Superior, not just in the mid-nineteenth century, but in today's world as well.

The Treaty of 1854 is considered a marker for the coming of major change for the Lake Superior Ojibwe people, and so it is a document that helps us understand what this community's pressing concerns were at the time. A serious study of the articles of the treaty helps us grasp what was occurring in the western Lake Superior region in the middle of the nineteenth century, and particularly, how the population of the new United States was moving in on the Ojibwe community. The Americans, with their culture of industrial capitalism, Christianity, and its singular worldview had a rapidly growing presence. By 1854, it must have been obvious that the foraging life of the Ojibwe's was at a crucial point in its long existence.

The LaPointe Treaty of 1854 addresses this matter of deep and pervasive cultural change facing the people, and to allow the reader to better understand the treaty's importance, in the next few pages we will conclude this book by presenting and discussing most of the details of its thirteen articles as we offer commentary about their long-term ramifications for the Ojibwe people.

### *The Articles of the Treaty of 1854*[4]

1.

Article One

THE CHIPPEWAS OF LAKE SUPERIOR hereby cede to the United States all the lands heretofore owned by them in common with the Chippewas of the Mississippi, lying east of the following boundary-line, to wit: Beginning at a point, where the east branch of the Snake River crosses the southern boundary-line of the Chippewa country, running thence up the said branch to its source, thence nearly north, in a straight line, to the mouth of East Savannah River, thence up the St. Louis River to the mouth of East Swan River to its source, thence in a straight line to the most westerly bend of Vermillion River, and thence down the Vermillion River to its mouth.

The Chippewas of the Mississippi hereby assent and agree to the foregoing cession, and consent that the whole amount of the consideration money for the country ceded above, shall be paid to the Chippewas of Lake Superior, and in consideration thereof the Chippewas of Lake Superior hereby relinquish to the Chippewas of the Mississippi, all their interest in and claim to the lands heretofore owned by them in common, lying west of the above boundary-line.

For the Americans the main reason for the treaty was to win the cession of the Ojibwe preserve, and the priority of this goal is seen by the placement of the sale of the easternmost portion of this large parcel of land into the treaty's very first article. Given this priority, it might seem that all other articles are afterthoughts. As we have mentioned, there was a strong, and growing, sentiment in the United States to bring about the relinquishment of ownership of all Ojibwe lands west of the Mississippi River. Since this large expanse of land in northern Minnesota Territory held vast reserves of minerals, by 1854, the hope was to expedite its purchase. To help facilitate this end, the Americans divided the large parcel into an eastern and a western portion, the former being in the possession of the Lake Superior bands and the latter in that of the Mississippi River bands. Once decided upon, the Americans quickly applied this divide and conquer tactic—witness the haste with which Agent Henry Gilbert was informed of and ordered to carry out the cession of this vast parcel to the Americans. When Gilbert was unable to accomplish the transfer of ownership of the complete parcel, he proceeded to treat for its eastern portion. With the success of this venture, the very next year Agent Harriman brought a small contingent of Mississippi leaders to Washington, D.C., to treat for the remaining western portion. Harriman brought some of the Mississippi leaders to La Pointe in 1854, but they did not cede their portion until 1855, with the quickly but carefully orchestrated treaty meeting of that year. With the signing of this second treaty the Americans achieved their goal of acquiring the balance of the Ojibwe preserve.

Article Two

The United States agree to set apart and withhold from sale, for the use of the Chippewas of Lake Superior, the following described tracts of land, viz:

1st. For the L'Anse and Vieux De Sert bands, all the unsold lands in the following townships in the State of Michigan: Township fifty-one north range thirty-three west; township fifty-one north range thirty-two west; the east half of township fifty north range thirty-three west; the west half of township fifty north range thirty-two west, and all of township fifty-one north range thirty-one west, lying west of Huron Bay.

2nd. For the La Pointe band, and such other Indians as may see fit to settle with them, a tract of land bounded as follows: Beginning on the south shore of Lake Superior, a few miles west of Montreal River, at the mouth of a creek called by the Indians Ke-che-se-be-we-she, running thence south to a line drawn east and west through the centre of township forty-seven north, thence west to the west line of said township, thence south to the southeast corner of township forty-six north, range thirty-two west, thence west the width of two townships, thence north the width of two townships, thence west one mile, thence north to the lake shore, and thence along the lake shore, crossing Shag-waw-me-quon Point, to the place of beginning. Also two hundred acres on the northern extremity of Madeline Island, for a fishing ground.

3rd. For the other Wisconsin bands, a tract of land lying about Lac Du Flambeau, and another tract on Lac Court Orielles, each equal in extent to three townships, the boundaries of which shall be hereafter agreed upon or fixed under the direction of the President.

4th. For the Fond Du Lac bands, a tract of land bounded as follows: Beginning at an island in the St. Louis River, above Knife Portage, called by the Indians Paw-paw-sco-me-me-tig, running thence west to the boundary-line heretofore described, thence north along said boundary-line to the mouth of Savannah River, thence down the St. Louis River to the place of beginning. And if said tract shall contain less than one hundred thousand acres, a strip of land shall be added on the south side thereof, large enough to equal such deficiency.

5th. For the Grand Portage band, a tract of land bounded as follows: Beginning at a rock a little east of the eastern extremity of Grand Portage Bay, running thence along the lake shore to the mouth of a small stream called by the Indians Maw-ske-gwaw-caw-maw-se-be, or Cranberry Marsh River, thence up said stream across the point to Pigeon River, thence down Pigeon River to a point opposite the starting-point, and thence across to the place of beginning.

6th. The Ontonagon band and that subdivision of the La Pointe band of which Buffalo is chief, may each

> select, on or near the lake shore, four sections of land, under the direction of the President, the boundaries of which shall be defined hereafter. And being desirous to provide for some of his connections who have rendered his people important services, it is agreed that the chief Buffalo may select one section of land, at such place in the ceded territory as he may see fit, which shall be reserved for that purpose, and conveyed by the United States to such person or persons he may direct.
> 7th. Each head of a family, or single person over twenty-one years of age at the present time of the mixed bloods, belonging to the Chippewas of Lake Superior, shall be entitled to eighty acres of land, to be selected by them under the direction of the President, and which shall be secured to them by patent in the usual form.

This is the longest article in the treaty since it speaks to the designation of each of six pieces of land, or *reservations*, within ceded lands for the Lake Superior bands, and perhaps just as importantly, it allows for persons of the Ojibwes of Lake Superior of *mixed blood* to select eighty-acre parcels for their own use.

It is important that we remember that the Ojibwe raised the issue of securing sites for their six communities' home bases again and again in the years immediately preceding 1854. They did so during the negotiations for the Treaty of 1842, only to be quickly rebuffed by Robert Stuart.[5] Then, almost immediately after that treaty was ratified, when early rumors of removal circulated and the people realized the Americans were insisting the Ojibwe had signed away all their remaining land in Wisconsin and Michigan, they again asked for reserves in their homeland *and kept raising the issue over the ensuing years*. The goal of ending removal and securing these reserves were the purposes of the 1849 and 1852 Ojibwe delegations to Washington, D.C. In 1854, twelve years after the Treaty of 1842—a time during which the people kept asking for these reserves—agreement was finally reached on their establishment, and this act decisively ended any threats of removal.[6]

We note how this article allows the Ontonagon leader and La Pointe's Buffalo to each select four sections of land, at a later time, on the shore of Lake Superior for their peoples' communities. The reason for this specific amount and the delay is unclear, except that it might have been deemed these two communities were too small to warrant larger tracts, and given the haste with which this treaty was organized and negotiated, that the two leaders desired more time to make their selections. We also note that Buffalo asked for the right to select one more parcel in the newly ceded territory for a gratuity for Benjamin Armstrong, who, as Armstrong claimed in his memoir, Buffalo wished to compensate for the important assistance he had provided Buffalo and his people over the preceding difficult years.[7] The parcel Buffalo chose for Armstrong was a tract of land where the city of Duluth, Minnesota, now stands.

In this article we see that when addressing the tract of land set aside for the La Pointe band, a parcel of two hundred acres at the northern tip of Madeline Island was reserved as "a fishing ground." The literature does not readily speak to the details of this action—how and why it was done—but since the La Pointe band traditionally used this site as a base of operations for fishing several nearby and more distant sites amongst the other islands, we see that this is a particularly important site to the La Pointe Ojibwes.

In 1854, the label "The La Pointe Band" included those members who had begun clustering their home base in the area of the gardening sites on the mainland at *Mashkii ziibiing*, or Bad River, south of Madeline Island, as well as Buffalo's family of followers who identified more with a site on the mainland to the west of Madeline Island, recognized as *Miskwaabikaang*, or Red Cliff. At that time the La Pointe Band included both these sub-bands, and their recognition in the treaty of 1854 resonates with political differences evinced by the attempts of significant numbers of Lake Superior Ojibwe leaders to relocate to Canada only a few years previous.

We recall that in 1845, Leonard and Harriet Wheeler, the protestant missionaries on Madeline Island, moved their base of operations to the mainland at the ancient gardening site on the Bad River, a move prompting a later historian to remark that this move was significant since it led to "forming a nucleus for the Bad River band, as it came to be called." In a similar manner, when the Treaty of 1854 identifies "that subdivision of the La Pointe band of which Buffalo is chief," we see that by that time there were at least two subdivisions in what was still known as The La Pointe Band, and this suggests that in 1854, Buffalo's authority was not reaching all quarters of this overall La Pointe Band of Ojibwes.

The last section of Article Two allowing for any Ojibwe person of mixed-blood who is part of the Lake Superior Chippewa, a head of a family, or over twenty-one years of age at the time of the signing of the treaty to select eighty acres of land is informative. These persons, it was anticipated, would (or perhaps, it was assumed, *should*) take up farming as a way of life. The treaty is not clear on just where in the ceded territory these selections could be made. This article shows the perhaps generally accepted sentiment that agriculture would be something Ojibwe people eventually would accept as their future way of life.

Regarding these mixed-blood persons, what is apparent is that at La Pointe, the leadership once again acted in an inclusive manner when it insisted the treaty speak directly to the assumed needs of mixed-blood Ojibwe persons.

> Article Three
> The United States will define the boundaries of the reserved tracts, whenever it may be necessary, by actual survey, and the President may, from time to time, at his discretion, cause the whole to be surveyed, and may assign to each head of a family or single person over twenty-one years of age, eighty acres of land for his or their separate use; and he may, at his discretion, as fast as the occupants become capable of transacting their own affairs, issue patents therefore to such occupants, with such restrictions of the power of alienation as he may see fit to impose. And he may also, at his discretion,

make rules and regulations, respecting the disposition of the lands in his discretion, make rules and regulations, respecting the disposition of the lands in case of the death of the head of a family, or single person occupying the same, or in case of its abandonment by them. And he may also assign other lands in exchange for mineral lands, if any such are found in the tracts herein set apart. And he may also make such changes in the boundaries of such reserved tracts or otherwise, as shall be necessary to prevent interference with any vested rights. All necessary roads, highways, and railroads, the lines of which may run through any of the reserved tracts, shall have the right of way through the same, compensation being made therefore as in other cases.

This article allows for the American government to determine the boundaries of the new reservations by survey, and also enables the government to divide each reservation into parcels that could be assigned to individual Ojibwe persons. This is the beginning of what in 1887 became the federal program to divide reservations into farm-sized allotments, and by inserting this article it is clear the intent of the United States representatives was that the Ojibwe people would settle into these reservation parcels and become farmers. Going deeper, we might agree that the mere idea of an unchanging boundary marking off a portion of the land that almost suddenly has become the private property of an individual must have had the potential for causing a profound change on most Ojibwe people. The concept of *real estate*, to say nothing of its boundaries, speaks to the notion of private ownership of *property*, something integral to the new American way of life coming to the western Lake Superior Ojibwe in 1854.

The intent of this cumbersome treaty article with its series of qualifiers was also to allow the Americans to regulate the disposition of these farming parcels in cases where owners become deceased or gave up ownership, if it was determined that marketable minerals were found on the lands, or if yet-undetermined matters would rise to "compromise" ownership. The proviso that roads, railroads, and highways would have preferred right-of-way status on any of the parcels also shows the American government's assumption that these important aspects of American society would eventually come to these reservation lands.

Finally, what this article shows is the intent of the Americans to continue working toward the assimilation of the Ojibwe into the greater nineteenth century society and culture of the United States, or as some writers put it: the *destruction* of the Ojibwe way of life.

Article Four
In consideration of and payment for the country hereby ceded, the United States agree to pay to the Chippewas of Lake Superior, annually, for the term of twenty years, the following sums, to wit: five thousand dollars in coin; eight thousand dollars in goods, household furniture and cooking utensils; three thousand dollars in agricultural implements and cattle, carpenter's and other tools and building materials, and three thousand dollars for moral and educational purposes, of which last sum, three hundred dollars per annum shall be paid to the Grand Portage band, to enable them to maintain a school at their village. The United States will also pay the further sum of ninety thousand dollars, as the chiefs in open council may direct, to enable them to meet their present just engagements. Also the further sum of six thousand dollars, in agricultural implements, household furniture, and cooking utensils to be distributed at the next annuity payment, among the mixed bloods of said nation. The United States will also furnish two hundred guns, one hundred rifles, five hundred beaver-traps, three hundred dollars' worth of ammunition, and one thousand dollars' worth of ready-made clothing, to be distributed among the young men of the nation, at the next annuity payment.

This article sets the monetary and goods payment agreed to as partial compensation for the land cession, and the nature of this payment—especially of the kind of goods involved—shows the intent that the Ojibwe would be giving up their foraging form of culture for that of a settled agrarian way of life.

The United States also agreed to pay the Ojibwe chiefs a sum of $90,000.00, and it was the chiefs, in open council, who could decide upon the ultimate nature of the distribution of this cash and merchandise. It was not unusual for tribal leaders to receive personal compensation for their efforts to win a community's approval of a treaty, and given that there were seventy Michigan and Wisconsin leaders who signed the La Pointe document, this sum does not seem inordinately large. Perhaps the bulk of these monies went to traders the chiefs were indebted to, but also remembering that Ojibwe chiefs ideally did not hold large sums of personal wealth, serving instead as conduits through which material wealth flowed to their community, we might assume that, ideally at least, the greater portion of this sum of $90,000.00 quickly moved outward to the Ojibwe people.

A sum of $6,000.00 in farming implements, household furniture and cooking utensils was to be distributed to Ojibwe mixed-bloods at next year's annuity payment. Here again we see the deference shown to persons of mixed-blood.

A second distribution to be made at the 1855 annuity payment was for "the young men of the nation." Here the United States agreed to provide "two hundred guns, one hundred rifles, five hundred beaver traps, three hundred dollars' worth of ammunition, and one thousand dollars' worth of ready-made clothing." This distribution shows that hunting and the trapping of beaver was still an important aspect of the Lake Superior Ojibwe economy in 1854, and that the community's young men were doing this work. The "ready-made clothing" indicates that manufactured shirts, trousers, and perhaps outerwear, shoes, and so forth, were becoming accepted by these young men. However, it might also have been the case that American officials were being counseled by missionaries and other change agents that these articles should be distributed in hopes that the men would use such "civilized" items of clothing to replace their traditional leather, and therefore, "less acceptable" mode of dress.

Once again, the allotment of guns, ammunition and traps shows the continuation of the Ojibwe foraging adaptation, but it also tells us that the "young men" of the Ojibwe community were a concern of the Americans as well as the Ojibwe chiefs. These were the "fighting men" who would have been expected to confront the Americans in situations of physical conflict if it should ever occur, and both the chiefs and American officials may have agreed it was necessary to appease them with these provisions. In tribal societies like that of the Ojibwe, the young men were a political force that needed to be recognized and accommodated, lest they act in ways contrary to the wishes of the leadership.

In a related matter, concern about the young Ojibwe women and their ability to affect political matters regarding the peoples' relationship with the new American government seemed to be a lesser concern. Perhaps it was felt the matter of appeasing these persons was met in the distribution of household goods and the specie for use with "moral and educational purposes."

> Article Five
> The United States will also furnish a blacksmith and assistant, with the usual amount of stock, during the continuance of the annuity payments, and as much longer as the President may think proper, at each of the points herein set apart for the residence of the Indians, the same to be in lieu of all the employees to which the Chippewas of Lake Superior may be entitled under previous existing treaties.

The Iron Age had clearly come to the Ojibwe, and history shows that in the mid-nineteenth century, a blacksmith was a valuable adjunct to a viable Ojibwe community. Presumably, blacksmiths were needed for their ability to fashion and repair farming implements and household items, but as Agent Brunson noted earlier at La Pointe, they were essential for the repair and maintenance of firearms and trapping equipment. Brunson's remarks, and others in the literature of the time, show that while the change agents Danziger speaks of intended the blacksmiths would serve to make and repair metal implements that were integral to the agrarian "civilization" the Ojibwe were to take up, in reality these blacksmiths were more important for their ability to make and repair implements the tribesmen needed to successfully maintain their hunting, fishing and trapping—in other words, their earlier *foraging* adaptation. Perhaps, in an interesting twist, while blacksmithing was acknowledged to be necessary for farming, at the same time it was also needed for an ongoing hunting, fishing, gardening, and gathering way of life.

Unfortunately, an in-depth study of the history of blacksmithing in western Lake Superior Ojibwe communities and its role in tribal culture at the time has not yet been undertaken. Such a study, with its details of the technology of the craft, could speak to the relationship of blacksmithing to both the changes and persistence of Ojibwe culture occurring in the nineteenth century. Also, it could help elucidate the peoples' understandings of and relationship with *iron* and the requisite tribal concerns regarding its spirituality. As was true with copper, iron was perceived as something with special concerns, and the almost sudden introduction of this metal and tools made from it, followed by their rapid pervasiveness throughout the Ojibwe world, must have had many important ramifications.

> Article Six
> The annuities of the Indians shall not be taken to pay the debts of individuals, but satisfaction for depredations committed by them shall be made by them in such manner as the President may direct.

This article directed that government officials could not withhold an individual's annuity payment in order to liquidate any debts they had with individuals, but the article's main purpose was to speak to traders claiming outstanding debts of individual Ojibwe persons. However, these annuities could be used to rectify any depredations brought upon non-Indians. Apparently the matter of "Indian depredations" was still a concern of the Americans in 1854, but the Ojibwe were adamant about not having their money withheld in order to pay trading debts. Profit-taking opportunities of the Indian trade, particularly traders presenting irregular past-due accounts to treaty commissioners and annuity officials, was still evident as late at 1854.[8]

> Article Seven
> No spirituous liquors shall be made, sold, or used on any of the lands set apart for the residence of the Indians, and the sale of the same shall be prohibited in the Territory hereby ceded, until otherwise ordered by the President.

The scourge of alcohol continued in Ojibwe country in 1854, and numerous sources in the literature tell of this.[9] This article speaks to both the new parcels reserved for the numerous Ojibwe communities as sites of residence, and also to the entire larger parcel ceded to the Americans. This decree prohibiting the sale of liquor was later lifted, but it remains a contentious issue today.

> Article Eight
> It is agreed, between the Chippewas of Lake Superior and the Chippewas of the Mississippi, that the former shall be entitled to two-thirds, and the latter to one-third, of all benefits to be derived from former treaties existing prior to the year 1847.

This article speaks to the lingering matter of a just distribution of payments from the treaties of 1837 and 1842. Most of the land ceded in these earlier treaties had been held by the Lake Superior bands, yet a good portion of the payments went to the Mississippi bands. This problem festered for years and in 1854, an attempt was made to put it to rest.

Article Nine
The Untied States agree that an examination shall be made, and all sums that may be found equitably due to the Indians, for arrearages of annuity or other thing, under the provisions of former treaties, shall be paid as the chiefs may direct.

After years of difficulties, here the United States agreed to investigate the Ojibwe complaint that some annuities, and other payments from treaties prior to 1847, had not yet been paid. Any arrearages were to be cleared and paid under the direction of the chiefs. Here the lingering legacy of Alexander Ramsey and John Watrous was finally addressed, but not yet resolved.

Article Ten
All missionaries, and teachers, and other persons of full age, residing in the territory hereby ceded, or upon any of the reservations hereby made by authority of law, shall be allowed to enter the land occupied by them at the minimum price whenever the surveys shall be completed to the amount of one quarter-section each.

Here we see the intent of the Americans to cause change agents like missionaries and teachers to gain a "permanent" land holding in both the land ceded (the preserve) and on the parcels designated for the new Ojibwe reservations. The literature is unclear about what was behind this article, other than the assumed pressure from these persons, i.e., the missionaries, teachers, and "other persons of full age," at the time of the treaty gathering. The issue of the Ojibwe communities desiring the granting of these persons full ownership to a quarter-section of land within the surveyed boundaries of the new reservation communities is also an important question. It is likely today, given the interest Ojibwe communities have in reclaiming lands within the outer parameters of their reservations, that the legal ownership of such designated parcels is under investigation.[10]

Article Eleven
All annuity payments to the Chippewas of Lake Superior, shall hereafter be made at L'Anse, La Pointe, Grand Portage, and on the St. Louis River; and the Indians shall not be required to remove from the homes hereby set apart for them. And such of them as reside in the territory hereby ceded, shall have the right to hunt and fish therein, until otherwise ordered by the President.

This article was one the Ojibwe were greatly concerned about. It held agreements that effectively ended the policy of removal, and as argued by Charles Mix, declared that annuities would hereafter be paid at L'Ance, La Pointe, Grand Portage and Fond du Lac. Also, as was done in both the 1837 and 1842 land cession treaties, it allowed the people living on the newly ceded lands to continue harvesting resources within this territory "unless otherwise ordered by the President." Thus, the long, contentious battle over removal and the sites where treaty annuities would be paid came to an end. And, importantly, as noted by Charles Cleland, the provision allowing the continuance of hunting, fishing and gathering indicated that in 1854, there still were Ojibwe relying on this practice as a significant part of their livelihood.[11]

Article Twelve
In consideration of the poverty of the Bois Forte Indians who are parties to this treaty, they having never received any treaty annuity payments, and of the great extent of that part of the ceded country owned exclusively by them, the following additional stipulations are made for their benefit. The United States will pay the sum of ten thousand dollars, as their chiefs in open council may direct, to enable them to meet their present just engagement. Also the further sum of ten thousand dollars, in five equal annual payments, in blankets, cloth, nets, guns, ammunitions, and such other articles of necessity as they may require. They shall have the right to select their reservation at any time hereafter, under the direction of the President; and the same may be equal in extent, in proportion to their numbers, to those allowed the other bands, and be subject to the same provisions.
They shall be allowed a blacksmith, and the usual smithshop supplies, and also two persons to instruct them in farming, whenever in the opinion of the President it shall be proper, and for such length of time as he may direct. It is understood that all Indians who are parties to this treaty, except the Chippewas of the Mississippi, shall hereafter be known as the Chippewas of Lake Superior. *Provided*, that the stipulation by which the Chippewas of Lake Superior relinquishing their right to land west of the boundary-line shall not apply to the Bois Forte band who are parties to this treaty.

Here the Bois Forte Band of Ojibwe in northeastern Minnesota Territory was given special recognition since the bulk of the newly ceded lands were in this community's region, and also because this band had not been the recipients of annuities from any previous treaty and were felt to be in particular need of assistance.

The second item in this article stipulating that the bands who signed the treaty and relinquished their right to that part of the preserve lying west of the new boundary line would hereafter be called the Chippewas of Lake Superior remains controversial today. This method of categorizing the western Lake Superior Ojibwe communities is meaningful only for the purposes of the La Pointe Treaty of 1854. Such a classification of Ojibwe bands has no other meaning. As noted in a previous chapter, this was part of the tactic of Commissioner Manypenny and other American officials to divide the Ojibwe bands in order to facilitate the government's purchase of the preserve.

Article Thirteen
This treaty shall be obligatory on the contracting parties, as soon as the same shall be ratified by the

President and Senate of the United States.
In testimony whereof, the said Henry C. Gilbert, and the said David B. Herriman, commissioners as aforesaid, and the undersigned chiefs and headman of the Chippewas of Lake Superior and the Mississippi, have hereunto set their hands and seals, at the place aforesaid, this thirtieth day of September, one thousand eight hundred and fifty-four.

Henry C. Gilbert and David B. Herriman signed the treaty as its Commissioners, and Richard M. Smith signed as the Secretary. A total of eighty-six Ojibwe leaders signed it, including fourteen from the La Pointe Band (Buffalo's was the first La Pointe signature, Black Bird's being the fifth), three from Ontonagon, five from L'Anse, two from Vieux De Sert, four from Grand Portage, forty-two from Fond du Lac, fourteen from Lac Courte Oreilles, eleven from Lac du Flambeau, three from Bois Forte, and fifteen from the Mississippi bands. Seven interpreters signed it, and the treaty's writer(s) concluded by claiming the document's execution was witnessed by eleven men, the first such signature being that of Henry M. Rice, and the last that of the La Pointe missionary, Leonard H. Wheeler. The primacy of the signature of Henry R. Rice as a witness to this very important land cession treaty speaks to the probable enormity of his involvement in the details of the negotiations. And as the last witnessing signature, the name of the long-time protestant Christian missionary at La Pointe, Leonard H. Wheeler, is also significant. By 1854, Wheeler had come out as a serious critic of Ramsey's attempts at a forced Ojibwe removal and likely he was pleased that the treaty ended this policy.

Again, the long list of Ojibwe leaders who signed this treaty is striking. It shows the importance of the matter being negotiated, and as mentioned, suggests the Ojibwe people had spent much time discussing the issues the treaty addressed. Such quick overall consensus seems rare with a band system of governance.

The necessity of having a distant body of officials (Washington, D.C.) holding the last word on the approval or disapproval of a treaty that had sometimes gone through a long and arduous negotiating process must have troubled the Ojibwe. They of course did not have a distant "congress" or overall leader—*tribal* Great Father—who could approve or disapprove what their leaders and the American government's treaty commissioners had struggled to agree on in the field. The members of Congress and the president were obviously not present at the negotiation meetings, and thus, did not receive the peoples' speeches and discussions first hand. They received them *ex post facto*, doubtless verbally by persons who later told them of the La Pointe gathering, and of course, in summary written form. They received them through the secondhand view of the Americans, a form of transmission that could not include the entirety of the drama, color, and important overall affect of the negotiation setting, acquired only by those who witnessed them firsthand.

Regarding the matter of a distant Congressional authority having the final say about the treaty's approval, the Ojibwe people knew this, and perhaps they looked upon the treaty commissioners as somewhat deficient, or inadequate, since even by giving their word and signing the treaty they had not assured its legitimacy and legality. Such findings had to wait for the deliberations of a greater, distant authority. Today for the Lake Superior Ojibwe communities, this problem of relating to an American authority in distant Washington, D.C. continues, and this helps to show, once again, the contrasting nature of the two societies involved. The United States, as a complex *state system*, was obviously structurally different from the Ojibwe *tribal system*, and this difference would continue to impede attempts at diplomatic relations between these two very different communities.

Lastly, much discussion during treaty negotiations at La Pointe was initially offered in *Ojibwemowin*, the Ojibwe language, then it was translated into a mid-nineteenth century American-English—although there probably still was a good degree of French spoken at the 1854 La Pointe negotiations. The old issue of an accurate translation must have been a constant problem.

*Notes*

1. Danziger 1979:89.
2. Danziger 1979:90.
3. Harris 1976:129.
4. http://digital.library.okstate.edu/kappler/vol2/treaties/ch0648.htm.
5. Clifton 1978:15.
6. Cleland in McClurken *et al* 2000:72.
7. Armstrong 1892:37-9.
8. Kohl 1985[1860]:53-7.
9. Ely 2012:xxvii.
10. Witness the recent ongoing work of the Red Cliff community in investigating county land records regarding the transfer of tribal lands to taxable status. See the newsletter of the "Treaty Natural Resources Division, Red Cliff Lake Superior Chippewa," Volume 1, Issue 3, Fall 2012, page 15.
11. Cleland in McClurken *et al*, 2000:85.

# Epilogue

DURING THE COLD DAYS OF THE WINTER of early 1855, when the La Pointe Ojibwe people learned of the president's signing the treaty, they must have uttered sighs of relief. The aged and ill Chief Buffalo was still with them, and for many his presence likely lent an air of rectitude regarding this resolution to the peoples' long struggle to remain living in their homeland.

The people were free to remain in Chequamegon Bay, but they would soon witness the arrival of many more non-Ojibwe Americans and European immigrants, some of whom were determined to claim homes in Lake Superior country. And as Edmund Jefferson Danziger, Jr. told, these "agents of change" would be relentless in their efforts to "civilize" the tribal people.

The Ojibwe had been in Chequamegon Bay for hundreds of years, had met the French, then the English, and now the Americans. All these newcomers had assumed a self-appointed superiority over what they called the savage. The Ojibwe had watched, listened, and as we saw, persisted. At the start of the new year of 1855, the people settled in for what was to come.

# Bibliography


Adams, Arthur T. (Editor)
1961 [1885]. The Explorations of Pierre Esprit Radisson. Minneapolis: Ross and Haines.

Anderson, Gary Clayton
1984. Kinsmen of Another Kind: Dakota White Relations in Upper Mississippi Valley 1650-1862. Lincoln: University of Nebraska Press.

Angel, Michael
2002. Preserving The Sacred (Historical Perspectives on the Ojibwe Midewiwin.) Manitoba: The University of Manitoba Press.

Antell, Will
1973. William Warren. Minneapolis: Dillon Press, Inc.

Armstrong, Benjamin G.
1892. Early Life Among The Indians—Reminiscences from the life of Benj. G. Armstrong—Treaties of 1835, 1837, 1842 and 1854. Habits and Customs of the Red Men of the Forest. Incidents, Biographical Sketches, Battles, Etc. Dictated to and written by Thomas P. Wentworth, Ashland, Wisconsin: Press of A. W, Bowron.

Armour, David A., and Keith R. Widder.
1986. At The Crossroads (Michilimackinac During The American Revolution.) Michigan: Mackinac State Historic Parks.

Axtell, James
1981. The European and the Indian. (Essays in the Ethnohistory of Colonial America.) New York: Oxford University Press.
1992. Beyond 1492 (Encounters in Colonial North America.) New York: Oxford University Press.

Baraga, Frederic
1847. Chippewa Indians as Recorded by Rev. Frederick Baraga in 1848. Vol. 10 Studia Slovenica, League of Slovenian Americans. New York and Washington, 1976.
2001 (1990). The Diary of Bishop Frederic Baraga. Detroit: Wayne State University Press.

Barnouw, Victor
1963. Culture and Personality. Homewood: The Dorsey Press, Inc.

Bartlett, William
1929. History, Tradition, and Adventures in the Chippewa Valley. Chippewa Falls, Wisconsin

Beck, David R. M.
2002. Siege & Survival (History of the Menominee Indians, 1634—1856.) Lincoln: University of Nebraska Press.

Beebe, Evedene Ruth
1980. Sunrise at Morning Hill. Self Published.

Bellin, Joshua D.
2000. The Demon of the Continent (Indians and the Shaping of American Literature.) Philadelphia: University of Pennsylvania Press.

Benton, Marjorie F. (Editor)
1988 (1972, 1986). The Golden Days of LaPointe, Bayfield, Ashland, Washburn. (Historical Study of Chequamegon Bay Area.) Ashland: American Association of University Women.

Benton-Banai, Edward
1987. The Mishomis Book (Voice of the Ojibway.) St. Paul: The Red Schoolhouse

Berkhofer, Robert F.
1979. Images of the American Indian from Columbus to the Present. New York: Vintage.

Bewer, Tim
1999. Acorn Guide to Northwest Wisconsin. Madison: Prairie Oak Press.

Bieder, Robert
1995. Native American Communities in Wisconsin, 1600—1960. Madison: University of Wisconsin Press.

Birk, Douglas
1989. John Sayer's Snake River Journal, 1804-05. Institute for Minnesota Archeology, Inc.

Black-Rogers, Mary
1986. "Varieties of 'Starving': Semantics and Survival in the Subarctic Fur Trade, 1750-1850," in Ethnohistory 33 (4), pp. 353-383.

Blair, Emma Helen (Translator and Editor)
1996 [1911]. The Indian Tribes of the Upper Mississippi Valley and Region of the Great Lakes as Described by Nicolas Perrot, French commandant in the Northwest; Bacqueville de la Potherie, French royal commissioner to Canada; Morrell Marston, American Army officer; and Thomas Forsyth, United States agent at Fort Armstrong. Volume 1 and 2. Lincoln: University of Nebraska Press.

Borneman, Walter R.
2005 [2004]. 1812—The War that Forged a Nation. New York: HarperCollins Publishers.
2007 [2006]. The French and Indian War. New York: HarperCollins Publishers.

Bourne, Russell
2002. Gods of War, Gods of Peace. (How the Meeting of Native and Colonial Religions Shaped Early America.) New York: Harcourt, Inc.

Bray, Martha Coleman (Editor)
1970. The Journals of Joseph N. Nicollet. (A Scientist on the Mississippi Headwater, with notes on Indian Life, 1836-37.) (Translated from the French by Andre Fertey.) St. Paul: Minnesota Historical Society.

Brody, Hugh
1998 [1981]. Maps and Dreams. Prospect Heights: Waveland Press, Inc.
2000. The Other Side of Eden. New York: North Point Press.

Broker, Ignatia
1983. Flying Night Woman—An Ojibway Narrative. St. Paul: Minnesota Historical Society Press.

Brown, Dee
2001 [1970]. Bury My Heart at Wounded Knee—An Indian History of the American West. New York: Henry Holt and Company.
Brown, Jennifer S. H. and Laura L. Peers
1988 [1970]. The Chippewa and Their Neighbors: A Critical Review, In Hickerson, Harold, 1987 (1970), pp. 135-146.
Brown, Jennifer S. H., and Elizabeth Vibert, (Editors)
1988. Reading Beyond Words. (Contexts for Native History.) Peterborough: Broadview Press.
Buffalohead, Priscilla K.
1983. A Fresh Look at Ojibway Women (Farmers, Warriors, Traders) in Minnesota History (The Quarterly of the Minnesota Historical Society), Vol. 48, No. 6, Summer.
Bunge, Nancy
2000. "Redeeming the Missionary: Leonard Wheeler and the Ojibwe," In The American Transendental Quarterly, N-14, No. 4, December 2000, pp.265-275. (http://wilson-txt.hwwilson.com/pdfhtml/04335/1P8YY/RS7.htm).
Brunson, Alfred, A.M, D.D.
1879. A Western Pioneer: or, Incidents of the Life and Times of Rev. Alfred Brunson, A.M, D.D, Embracing a Period of over Seventy Years. Vol. II. Cincinnati: Hitchcock and Walden.
Burnham, Guy M.
1974 [1929]. The Lake Superior Country in History and in Story. Ann Arbor: Published by Browzer Books, set up and printed by Edwards Brothers, Ann Arbor, Michigan.
Busch, Jane C.
2008. People and Places: A Human History of the Apostle Islands (Historic Resource Study of Apostle Islands National Lakeshore.) Omaha: Prepared under contract to the Midwest Regional Office, National Park Service, United States Department of the Interior.
Calloway, Colin G.
2006. The Scratch of a Pen (1763 and the Transformation of North America.) New York: Oxford University Press.
Carter, Harvey Lewis
1987. The Life and Times of Little Turtle. Urbana: University of Illinois Press.
Child, Brenda J.
2012. Holding Our World Together (Ojibwe Women and the Survival of Community.) New York: Viking Press.
Christian, Shirley
2003. Before Lewis and Clark. New York: Farrar, Straus and Giroux.
Chute, Janet E.
1984. The Legacy of Shingwaukonse (A Century of Native Leadership.) Toronto: University of Toronto Press.
Cleland, Charles E.
1982. "The Inland Shore Fishery of the Northern Great Lakes; Its Development and Importance in Prehistory," *in* American Antiquity, Vol. 47, No. 4 (October 1982), pp. 761-784.
1992. Rites of Conquest (The History and Culture of Michigan's Native Americans.) Ann Arbor: The University of Michigan Press.
Clifton, James A.
1987. "Wisconsin Death March: Explaining the Extremes in Old Northwest Indian Removal," *in* Transactions of the Wisconsin Academy of Sciences, Arts and Letters. Madison, WI.
Cochrane, Timothy
2009. Minong—The Good Place. (Ojibwe and Isle Royale.) East Lansing: Michigan State University Press.
Copway, George
1851. Reflections of a Forest Life. London: C. Gilpin.
Curot, Michel
1911. A Wisconsin Fur-Trader's Journal, 1803-04, *in* Collections of the State Historical Society of Wisconsin. Vol. 20, pp. 396-471.
Crouse, Nellis M.
1956. La Verendrye, Fur Trader and Explorer. Ithaca: Cornell University Press.
Currant, Richard N.
1976. The History of Wisconsin. Vol. II: The Civil War Era, 1848-1873. (William Fletcher Thompson, General Editor.) Madison: The State Historical Society of Wisconsin.
Danziger, Edmund Jefferson, Jr.
1973. "They Would Not Be Moved," *in* Minnesota History, Vol. 43, Spring 1973, pp.175-185.
1979. The Chippewas of Lake Superior. Norman: University of Oklahoma Press.
Davidson, John N., A.M.
1895. In Unnamed Wisconsin. (Studies in the History of the Region Between Lake Michigan and the Mississippi. To which is appended a memoir of Mrs. Harriet Wood Wheeler.) Milwaukee: Silas Chapman, Publisher.
Dean, Bradley
2003. "Annotating the Jesuit Relations, Parts I, II, III." In The Thoreau Society Bulletin, No. 242-244, Winter-Summer. Concord: Massachusetts.
Demos, John
1995. The Unredeemed Captive. New York: Vintage Books.
Densmore, Frances
1973 [1910, 1913]. Chippewa Music, Volumes I and II. Smithsonian Institution, Bureau of American Ethnology. Bulletins 14 and 53. Minneapolis: Ross & Haines, Inc.
1970 [1929]. Chippewa Customs. Minneapolis: Ross & Haines, Inc.
Devens, Carol
1992. Countering Colonization (Native American Women and Great Lakes Missions, 1630-1900.) Berkeley: University of California Press.
Diedrich, Mark
1992. Ojibway Chiefs—Portraits of Anishinaabe Leadership. Rochester: Coyote Books.
Donnelly, Joseph P., S.J.
1993. Jacques Marquette, S. J. (1637-1675). Chicago: Loyola University Press.
Dowd, Gregory Evans
1992. A Spirited Resistence. (The North American Struggle For Unity, 1745-1815.) Baltimore: John Hopkins University Press.
Ducatel, I. I. (Prof.)
1977 [1846]. "A Fortnight Among the Chippewas of Lake Superior," in The Minnesota Archaeologist, December, Vol. 36, No. 4, pp. 161-172.
Dunbar, Willis E.
1970. Lewis Cass. Grand Rapids: Wm. B. Eerdmans Publishing.
Edmunds, R. David
1994. The Shawnee Prophet. Lincoln: University of Nebraska Press.

Ely, Edmund F.
2012. The Ojibwe Journals of Edmund F. Ely, 1833—1849. (Edited by Theresa M. Schenck.) Lincoln: University of Nebraska Press.
Erdrich, Louise
1999. The Birchbark House. New York: Hyerion Books.
2012. "Interview by Alden Mudge, about The Heartbreaking Toll of Revenge," pp. 14-15. In "Book Page," of American Book Review, October 2012. (www. Bookpage.com).
Feldman, George Franklin
2007. Cannibalism, Headhunting and Human Sacrifice in North America. Chambersburg: Allan C. Hood & Co.
Fenn, Elizabeth A.
2004 [2001]. POX Americana (The Great SMALLPOX Epidemic of 1775-82.) Phoenix Mill: Sutton Publishing.
Folwell, William Watts
1956. A History of Minnesota. (Four Volumes.) St. Paul: Minnesota Historical Society Press.
Fournier, Martin
2002 [2001]. Pierre-Espirit Radisson 1636-1710. Quebec: McGill-Queen's University Press.
Gallay, Alan
2002. The Indian Slave Trade. New Haven: Yale University Press.
Gara, Larry
1962. A Short History of Wisconsin. Madison: State Historical Society of Wisconsin.
Gilfillan, Joseph
1904. The Ojibway (A Novel of Indian Life of the Period of the Early Advance of Civilization in the Great Northwest.) New York: The Neale Publishing Company.
Gilman, Carolyn
1992. The Grand Portage Story. St. Paul: Minnesota Historical Society Press.
1995. Where Two Worlds Meet—The Great Lakes Fur Trade. St. Paul: Minnesota Historical Society Press.
Godfrey, Anthony
1998. Traditional Cultural Property (TCP) Study, Red Cliff Reservation Shoreline, Wisconsin. (DRAFT prepared for the Superior Water-logged Lumber Co.) Salt Lake City: U.S. West Research, Inc.
Goggin, John M.
1951. The Mexican Kickapoo Indians. Albuquerque: University of New Mexico Press.
Goody, Jack
1996. The Power of the Written Tradition. Washington, D.C. Washington, D.C.: Smithsonian Institution Press.
Graham, Loren R.,
1995. A Face in the Rock (The Tale of a Grand Island Chippewa.) Washington, D.C.: Island Press.
Gray, Susan Elaine
2006. "I Will Fear No Evil." (Ojibwa Missionary Encounters Along the Berens River, 1875-1940.) Calgary: University of Calgary Press.
Grim, John A.
1999. The Shaman. Norman: University of Oklahoma Press.
Hall, Robert L.
1996. An Archeology of the Soul—North American Indian Belief and Ritual. Urbana: University of Illinois Press.
Hall, Sherman
1831-1875. Personal Letters and Papers. St. Paul: Minnesota Historical Society.
Hallowell, A. Irving
1964. Ojibwa Ontology, Behavior, and World View, *in* Primitive Views of the World, Stanley Diamond, Editor, pp. 49-82. New York: Columbia University Press.
1974 [1955]. Culture & Experience. Philadelphia: University of Pennslyvania Press.
1992. The Ojibwa of Berens River, Manitoba. (Ethnography Into History.) (Jennifer S. H. Brown, Editor.) New York: Harcourt Brace Jovanovich College Publishers.
Hamilton, R. N., S. J.
1970. Father Marquette. Milwaukee: William B. Eerdmans Publishing.
Harris, Walt
1976. The Chequamegon Country, 1659-1976. (Around Which is Built the Highlights of Lake Superior Regional History for 300 Years.) Fayetteville: Walter J. Harris.
Hickerson, Harold
1970. The Chippewa and Their Neighbors: A Study in Ethnohistory. New York: Holt, Rhinehart and Winston, Inc.
1971. "The Chippewa of the Upper Great Lakes: A Study in Sociopolitical Change." In North American Indians in Historical Perspective, Eleanor Burke Leacock and Nancy Oestrich Lurie, Editors. New York: Random House.
1974. Ethnohistory of Chippewa in Central Minnesota. New York: Garland Series in North American Indian Ethnohistory.
1988 [1970]. The Chippewa and Their Neighbors. (A Study in Ethnohistory.) Revised and Expanded Edition – with review essay and bibliographical supplement by Jennifer S. H. Brown and Laura L. Peters. Prospect Heights: Waveland Press, Inc.
Hickey, Donald R.
1997. The War of 1812. (A Forgotten Conflict.) Urbana: University of Illinois Press.
Higham, C. L.
1998. Noble, Wretched, & Redeemable. (Protestant Missionaries to the Indians in Canada and the United States, 1820-1900.) Albuquerque: University of New Mexico Press.
Holzhueter, John O.
1974. Madeline Island & The Chequamegon Region. Madison: The State Historical Society of Wisconsin.
Jenkins, Phillip
2003. Dream Catchers. (How Mainstream America Discovered Native Spirituality.) New York: Oxford University Press.
Jesuit Relations and Allied Documents (Edited by Rueben Gold Twaites, 1896-1901.)
1610.1791. Travels and Explorations of the Jesuit Missionaries in New France. 73 Volumes. Cleveland: The Burrows Brothers Company, Publishers.
Johnston, Basil
1999. Crazy Dave. St. Paul: Minnesota Historical Society Press.
Jordahl, Harold C., Jr., with Annie L. Booth
2000. Environmental Politics and the Creation of a Dream. (Establishing The Apostle Islands National Lakeshore.) Madison: The University of Wisconsin Press.
Kappler, Charles J.
1904. Indian Affairs: Laws and Treaties. Vol. II, Treaties. Compiled and edited by Charles J. Kappler. Washington: Government Printing Office.

Kellogg, Louise P., (Editor.)
1917. Early Narratives of the Northwest, 1634-1699. New York: Charles Scribner's Sons. Online facsimile at http://www.americanjourneys.org/aj-047/.
1968 (1925). French Regime in Wisconsin and the Northwest. Madison: State Historical Society of Wisconsin.
1935. The British Regime in Wisconsin and the Northwest. Madison: State Historical Society of Wisconsin.

Knobloch, Frieda
1996. The Culture of Wilderness. Chapel Hill: The University of North Carolina Press.

Kohl, Johann Georg
1985 [1860]. Kitchi-Gami (Life Among the Lake Superior Ojibway.) Translated by Lascelles Wraxall. New introduction by Robert Bieder. St. Paul: Minnesota Historical Society Press.

Kugel, Rebecca
1965. To Be The Main Leaders Of Our People. (A History of Minnesota Ojibwe Politics, 1825-1898.) East Lansing: Michigan State University Press.

Kvasnicka, Robert N., and Herman J. Viola, (Editors)
1979. The Commissioners of Indian Affairs, 1824-1977. Lincoln: University of Nebraska Press.

LaDuke, Winona
1999. Last Standing Woman. Minneapolis: Voyageur Press.

Languth, A.J.
2006. Union, 1812. (The Americans Who Fought The Second War of Independence.) New York: Simon and Schuster.

Larson, Lars, Ph.D.
2004. Chequamegon Bay and its Communities, I—Ashland, Bayfield, LaPointe. A Brief History—1659-1883. Self-Published.

Larson, Norman W.
1997. "Historical journal recalls fur trader's Cornucopia visit in 1804," *in* The Bayfield County Journal, Thursday, September 28, 1989, p. 12.

Lavender, David
1998 [1964]. The Fist in the Wilderness. Lincoln: University of Nebraska Press.

Levi, Carolissa M., F.S.P.A.
1956. Chippewa Indians of Yesterday and Today. New York: Pageant Press, Inc.

Levi-Straus, Claude
1980. Naked Man (Introduction to a Science of Mythology, Vol. 4, Translated.) New York: Harper-Colophon Books.

Lewis, James Otto
1981. American Indian Portfolio (An Eyewitness History)—1823-1828. (Introduction by Phillip R. St. Clair–1980.) Kent: Volair Limited.

Lewis, Norman
1988. The Missionaries. (God Against the Indians.) London: Picador.

Lockwood, James H.
1903 [1856]. "Early Times and Events in Wisconsin," in Collections of State Historical Society of Wisconsin, Vol. II.

Loew, Patty
2001. Indian Nations of Wisconsin. (Histories of Endurance and Renewal.) Madison: Wisconsin Historical Society Press.

Lund, Duane L.
1977. Tales of Four Lakes. (Leech Lake, Gull Lake, Mille Lacs Lake, the Red Lakes & the Crow Wing River.) Staples: Dr. Duane R. Lund.
2000. Lake of the Woods—Featuring Translations of Pierre La Ver'endrye's Diaries and Father Alneau's Letters. Staples: Dr. Duane R. Lund.
1995. The Indian Wars. Staples: Dr. Duane R. Lund.

Malhiot, Francois Victor
1910. A Wisconsin Fur-Trader's Journal, 1804-05, *in* Collections of the State Historical Society of Wisconsin, Vol. 19, pp. 163-233.

Mandrell, Daniel R.
1996. Behind the Frontier. Lincoln: University of Nebraska Press.

Manypenny, George
1880. Our Indian Wards. Cincinnati: Robert Clarke, Co.

Marshall, Albert M.
1954. Brule Country. St. Paul: The North Central Publishing Co.

Mason, Phillip, (Editor.)
1993 [1958]. Schoolcraft's Expedition to Lake Itasca (The Discovery of the Source of the Mississippi.) East Lansing: Michigan State University Press. Means, Philip Ainsworth
1917. Preliminary Survey of the Remains of the Chippewa Settlements on La Pointe Island, Wisconsin. Smithsonian Miscellaneous Collections, Vol. 66, No. 14, January 1917.

McClurken, James M., *et al.*
1998. Fish in the Lakes, Wild Rice *and* Game in Abundance. (Testimony on Behalf of Mille Lacs Ojibwe Hunting and Fishing Rights.) East Lansing: Michigan State University Press.

McKenney, Thomas L.
1959. Sketches of a Tour to the Lakes, of the Character and Customs of the Chippeway Indians and of Incidents Connected with the Treaty of Fond Du Lac. Minneapolis: Ross & Haines, Inc.

McLaughlin, Andrew C.
1980 [1899]. Lewis Cass. New York: Chelsea House Publishers.

McNally, Michael D.
2008. Honoring Elders. (Aging, Authority, and Ojibwe Religion.) New York: Columbia University Press.

Merriam, G. & C.
1959. Webster's New Collegiate Dictionary. (Second Edition.) Springfield: G.C. Merriam Co. Publishers.

Meyer, Melissa L.
1993. The White Earth Tragedy. (Ethnicity and Dispossession at a Minnesota Anishinaabe Reservation.) Lincoln: University of Nebraska Press.

Moffitt, John F. and Santiago Sebastian.
1997. O Brave New People. (The European Invention of the American Indian.) Albuquerque: University of New Mexico Press.

Morse, Richard F.
1904 [1857]. The Chippewas of Lake Superior. In Collections of the State Historical Society of Wisconsin, Vol. III, pp. 338-369.

Munnell, Michael D.
1996. "The Act that changed a nation," *in* News from the Sloughs (Bad River's Monthly Newspaper), February 1996, Vol. 1, Issue 10.

Neill, Edward D., A.B.
1885. "History of the Ojibways, and Their Connection with Fur Traders, Based Upon Official and Other Records," *in* Collections of the Minnesota Historical Society, Vol. V, pp. 408-409. Facsimile online at http://books.google.com/?id=eWFKAAAAYAAj+pg=PAS=lpg=PAS+dg=Edward+Neill,=Ojibwe.
Nelson, George
2002. My First Years in the Fur Trade (The Journals of 1802—1804). Edited by Laura Peers and Theresa Schenck. St. Paul: Minnesota Historical Society Press.
Nesbit, Robert C.
1989 (1973). Wisconsin: A History. Madison: University of Wisconsin Press.
Nute, Grace Lee
1926. "The American Fur Company's Fishing Enterprizes on Lake Superior," *in* Mississippi Valley Historical Review, Vol. 12, No. 4, (March), pp. 483-502.
1969 [1941]. The Voyageur's Highway. St. Paul: Minnesota Historical Society Press.
2000 [1944]. Lake Superior. St. Paul: Minnesota Historical Society Press.
O'Brien, Jean M.
1998. Dispossession by Degrees. (Indian Land and Identity in Natick, Massachusetts, 1650-1790.) New York: Cambridge University Press.
Olmanson, Eric D.
2007. The Future City on the Inland Sea. (A History of Imagination Geographies of Lake Superior.) Athens: Ohio University Press.
Paap, Howard D.
1985. Ojibwe Midewiwin: A Structural Analysis. (Ph.D. Dissertation, The University of Minnesota.)
1996-2012. Field Notes in possession of the author.
1998. A Review of the Traditional Cultural Property (TCP) Study—Red Cliff Reservation Shoreline, Wisconsin, prepared by Anthony Godfrey, PH.D., principal investigator for U.S. West Research, Inc., October 31, 1998. (Copy at Great Lakes Indian Fish and Wildlife Commission Archives, Odanah, WI.)
2001. A Northern Land (Life with the Ojibwe). Oregon: Badger Books, Inc.
2008. Raspberry River. St. Cloud: North Star Press, Inc.
2009. "Gitchigami" *in* Pure Superior, by Jeff Richter, pp. 31-34.
2011. The View from the Creek (Notes from Lake Superior's Ojibwe Country). St. Cloud: North Star Press, Inc.
Paap, Howard D. (with Haijo Westra and Mary Eggermont-Molenaar)
2007 "J.P.B. De Josselin de Jong, the Return of Wenebozho, and an Ojibwe Myth in Latin," *in* European Review of Native American Studies, 21:1, pp. 19-24.
Paap, Keller D., and Howard D. Paap
2000. *Ishkigamizigewin*: An Ojibwe Rite of Spring, given at The 29th annual Algonquian Conference 24-26 October 1997 in Thunder Bay, Ontario. Published in Papers of the Twenty-Ninth Algonquian Conference, edited by David H. Pentland. Winnipeg:University of Manitoba.
Parkman, Francis
1878. France and England in North America. (A Series of Historical Narratives.) Part Third. Boston: Little, Brown and Co.
1963 [1867]. The Jesuits in North America. Boston: Little, Brown and Co.
2001 [1948]. The Battle For North America. (Edited by John Tebbel.) London: Phoenix Press.
Peacock, Thomas and Marlene Wisuri
2001. Ojibwe—*Waasa Inaabidaa*—We Look In All Directions. Afton: Afton Historical Society Press.
Perry, Richard J.
1997. From Time Immemorial. (Indigenous Peoples and State Systems.) Austin: University of Texas Press.
Peyer, Bernd C.
1998. The Tutor'd Mind. (Indian Missionary-Writers in Antebellum America.) Amherst: University of Massachusetts Press.
Plane, Ann Marie
2002. Colonial Intimacies. (Indian Marriage in Early New England.) Ithaca: Cornell University Press.
Prucha, Francis Paul
1986 [1984]. The Great Father. (The United States Government and the American Indians.) Abridged Edition. Lincoln: University of Nebraska Press.
1997 [1994]. American Indian Treaties. (The History of Political Anomaly.) Berkeley: University of California Press.
Quaife, Milo Milton (Editor.)
1921 [1809]. Alexander Henry's Travels and Adventures in the years 1760-1776. (Edited with Historical Introduction and Notes.) Chicago R. R. Donnelley and Sons, Co.
Quimby, George Irving
1960. Indian Life in the Upper Great Lakes, 11,000 BC to AD 1800. Chicago: University of Chicago Press.
Radisson, Pierre Espirit
1885. Voyages of Peter Espirit Radisson, being an account of his travels and experiences among the North American Indians, from 1632 to 1684. (Edited by Gideon D. Scull.) Boston: Prince Society. Online facsimile at http://wisconsinhistory.org1turningpoints/search.asp?id=12.)
Rasmussen, Charlie Otto
2003. Ojibwe Journeys. (Treaties, Sandy Lake & the Waabanong Run.) Odanah: Great Lakes Indian Fish and Wildlife Commission.
Rathbun, Peter A., and David W. Rathbun, and Mary Yeater Rathbun.
2004. Special History Study: Fur Trade Activity in the Apostle Islands. (This document was prepared by Rathbun Associates, Springfield, Illinois, and Hollandale, Wisconsin, for the National Park Service Midwest Regional Office under Contract No. CX6000-5-0056.)
Ray, Arthur Jr.
1999. Indians in the Fur Trade. Toronto: University of Toronto Press.
Richter, Jeff
2009. Pure Superior. (Lake Superior Photography, with Essays by John Bates, Sam Cook, Justin Isherwood and Howard Paap.) Mercer: Nature's Press.
Ross, Hamilton Nelson
1961. LaPointe—Village Outpost. St. Paul: North Central Publishing Co.
Ross, John F.
2010. War on the Run. (The Epic Story of Robert Rogers and the Conquest of America's First Frontier.) New York: Bantam Books.
Roufs, Timothy G.
1975. The Anishinabe of the Minnesota Chippewa Tribe. Phoenix: Indian Tribal Series.

1978. Nature and the Concept of Power Among Mississippi and Lake Superior Ojibwa: Reflections of Paul Buffalo. (Mimeographed paper in the possession of the author.)

Rowell, Wilfrid A.
1932. The Story of the Old Mission on Madeline Island in Lake Superior. (Pamphlet.)

Satz, Ronald N.
1979. Tennessee's Indian Peoples: From White Contact to Removal. Knoxville: University of Tennessee Press.
1991. Chippewa Treaty Rights. Madison: Wisconsin Academy of Sciences, Arts and Letters.

Schenck, Theresa
1996. "William W. Warren's *History of the Ojibway People*: Tradition, History and Context," in *Reading Beyond Words*, edited by Jennifer S. H. Brown and Elizabeth Vibert., pp. 241-260.
1997. "The Voice of the Crane Echoes Afar." (The Sociopolitical Organization of the Lake Superior Ojibwa, 1640-1855.) New York: Garland Publishing, Inc.
2007. William W. Warren. (The Life, Letters, and Times of an Ojibwe Leader.) Lincoln: University of Nebraska Press.

Schoolcraft, Henry
1878 [1851]. Personal Memoirs of a Residence of Thirty Years with the Indian Tribes on the American Frontier: with brief notices of passing events, facts, and opinions, A.D. 1812 to A.D. 1842. Philadelphia: Lippencot, Grambo and Co. (Reprint by AMS Press, Inc., 1978, New York, N.Y.).

Silver, Peter
2008. Our Savage Neighbors. (How Indian War Transformed Early America.) New York: W.W. Norton and Company.

Skogen, Larry C.
1996. Indian Depredation Claims, 1796-1920. Norman: University of Oklahoma Press.

Skolla, Otto, Fr.
1936. "Father Skolla's Report on His Indian Missions," in *Acta et Dicta* 7, October, pp. 232-234.

Sleeper-Smith, Susan
2001. Indian Women and French Men. (Rethinking Cultural Encounters in the Western Great Lakes.) Amherst: University of Massachusetts Press.

Smith, Alice E.
1985 [1973]. The History of Wisconsin. Vol. 1—From Exploration to Statehood. Madison: State Historical Society of Wisconsin.

Smith, Donald B.
1987. Sacred Feathers: (The Reverend Peter Jones [Kahkewaquonaby] and the Mississauga Indians.) Lincoln: University of Nebraska Press.

Smith, Theresa S.
1994. The Island of the Anishnaabeg. (Thunderers and Water Monsters in the Traditional Ojibwe Life-World.) Moscow: University of Idaho Press.

Soetebier, Virginia M.
1990. Woman of he Green Glade. Blacksburg: the MacDonald and Woodward Publishing Co.

Spielmann, Roger
1997. 'You're so Fat!' (Explaining Ojibwe Discourse.) Toronto: University of Toronto Press.

Steele, Ian K.
1995. Warpaths. (Invasions of North America.) New York: Oxford University Press.

Stephanson, Anders
1996. Manifest Destiny. (American Expansion and the Empire of Right.) New York: Hill and Wang.

Sugden, John
1998. Tecumseh, A Life. New York: Holt and Company.

Tanner, John
2000 [1830]. The Falcon. (A Narrative of the Captivity and Adventures of John Tanner.) New York: Penguin Books.

Taylor, Alan
2006. The Divided Ground. (Indians, Settlers, and the Northern Borderland of the American Revolution.) New York: Alfred A. Knopf.

Taylor, Lolita
1976. Ojibwa, the Wild Rice People and Native American Contributions to Progress. Shell Lake: Wisconsin Indianhead VTAE District.

Thompson, David
1972. Travels in Western North America, 1784-1812, edited by Victor G. Hopwood, Toronto: Macmillan.

Thwaites, Reuben Gold
1896. The Story of Chequamegon Bay, *in* Wisconsin Historical Collections, Vol. 8, pp.397-425.
1911. Collections of the State Historical Society of Wisconsin, edited by Reuben Gold Thwaites, Vol. XX, pp.xi-xxi.
1925. Father Marquette. New York: D. Appleton & Co.

Tinker, George E.
1993. Missionary Conquest. (The Gospel and Native American Genocide.) Minneapolis: Fortress Press.

Titus, Charles H.
1994. Into the Old Northwest. (Edited by George P. Clark.) East Lansing: Michigan State University Press.

Trask, Kerry A.
2007. Black Hawk. (The Battle for the Heart of America.) New York: Henry R. Holt and Company.

Treuer, Anton
2010. Ojibwe in Minnesota. St. Paul: Minnesota Historical Society Press.
2011. Assassination of Hole in the Day. St. Paul: Minnesota Historical Society Press.
2012. Everything You Wanted To Know About Indians But Were Afraid To Ask. St. Paul: Minnesota Historical Society Press.

Treuer, Robert
1998. Voyageur Country (The Story of Minnesota's National Park.) Minneapolis: University of Minnesota Press.

Trigger, Bruce G.
1986. Natives and Newcomers. (Canada's "Heroic" Age Reconsidered.) Montreal: McGill-Queen's University Press.

Trouillot, Michel-Rolph
1995. Silencing the Past. (Power and the Production of History.) Boston: Beacon Press.

Turner, Frederick Jackson
1970 [1891]. The Character and Influence of the Indian Trade in Wisconsin. New York: Burt Franklin.

Upham, Warren
1905. "Groseilliers and Radisson, the First White Men in Minnesota, 1655-56, and 1659-60, and Their Discov-

ery of the Upper Mississippi River," *in* Collections of the Minnesota Historical Society, Vol. X. Part II, February 1905.
Van Zandt, Cynthia J.
2008. Brothers among Nations. (The Pursuit of Intercultural Alliances in Early America, 1580-1660.) New York: Oxford University Press.
Vecsey, Christopher
1986 [1983]. Traditional Ojibwa Religion and its Historical Changes. Philadelphia: American Philosophical Society.
Vennum, Thomas, Jr.
1985. "The Ojibwa Begging Dance," *in* Essays for John M. Ward. Cambridge: Harvard University Press.
1988. Wild Rice and the Ojibway People. St. Paul: Minnesota Historical Society Press.
Verwyst, P. Chrysostomus, O.F.M.
1895. "Historic Sites on Chequamegon Bay," *in* Collections of the State Historical Society of Wisconsin, Vol. XIII, pp. 426-440.
1900. The Life of Bishop Baraga. Milwaukee: M. H. Wiltzius & Co.
Viola, Herman J.
1973. "Introduction," *in* Memoirs, Official and Personal—Thomas L. McKenney. Lincoln: University of Nebraska Press. (Originally published in 1846).
Vizenor, Gerald
1984. The People Named The Chippewa—Narrative Histories. Minneapolis: University of Minnesota Press.
Vizenor, Gerald (Editor).
1987. Touchwood (A Collection of Ojibway Prose.) Minneapolis: The New Rivers Press.
Waddell, Jack
1985. "Malhoit's Journal: An Ethnohistorical Assessment of Chippewa Alcohol Behavior in the Early Nineteenth Century," *in* Ethnohistory 32 (2), pp. 246-68.
Ward, Matthew C.
1988. The Battle For Quebec—1759. Gloucestershire: The History Press.
Warkentin, Germaine
1996. "Discovering Radisson: A Renaissance Adventurer between Two Worlds," in Reading Beyond Words, by Jennifer S. H. Brown and Elizabeth Vibert, pp. 43-70.
Warren, William W.
1984 [1885]. History of the Ojibway People. St. Paul: Minnesota Historical Society.
2009 [1984, 1885]. History of the Ojibway People. (Second Edition, Edited and Annotated, with an Introduction by Theresa Schenck.) St. Paul: Minnesota Historical Society Press.
Weslager, C. A.
1991 (1972). The Delaware Indians—A History. New Brunswick: Rutgers University Press.
White, Bruce
1986. "A Skilled Game of Exchange: Ojibwa Fur Trade Protocol," *in* Minnesota History 50 (6) (Summer 1987), pp. 222-240.
White, Richard
1983. The Roots of Dependency. Lincoln: University of Nebraska Press.
1991. The Middle Ground. (Indians, Empires, and Republics in the Great Lakes Region, 1650-1815.) New York: Cambridge University Press.
Williams, Mentor L., (Editor.)
1992 [1953]. Schoolcraft's Narrative Journal of Travels. East Lansing: Michigan State University Press.
Williams, Robert A., Jr.,
1989. The American Indian in Western Legal Thought. New York: Oxford University Press.
Wilson, James
1997. The Earth Shall Weep. (A History of Native America.) New York: Grove Press.
Woolworth, Allan R.
1977. Editorial Comment in The Minnesota Archeologist, Vol. 36, No. 4, p.161.

### Newspapers

*Ashland Daily Press*, Ashland, Wisconsin.
*Bayfield Press*, Bayfield, Wisconsin.
*The Daily Press*, Ashland, Wisconsin.
*Detroit Daily Free Press*, Detroit, Michigan
*Green Bay Gazette*, Green Bay, Wisconsin.
*Lake Superior Journal*, Superior, Wisconsin.

### Government Publications

Wisconsin Historical Collections, Wisconsin Historical Society, Madison, Wisconsin.
Documents Relative to the Colonial History of the State of New York, edited by Edmund B. O'Callaghan and Berthold Fernow. 15 Volumes. Albany, N. Y., 1856-1887.
Smithsonian Miscellaneous Collections, Smithsonian Institution, Washington, D.C.
The Territorial Papers of the United States: The Territory of Wisconsin, 1839-1848, Volume 27 (1969), Volume 28 (1975), edited and compiled by John Porter Bloom.

### Government and Private Archives and Repositories

Bayfield Heritage Association, Bayfield, Wisconsin.
Northern Great Lakes Visitor Center, Ashland, Wisconsin.
Wisconsin Historical Society, Madison, Wisconsin.

# Index

## A



## B



## C

## D



## E



## F



## G



## H

## I



## J



## K



## L



## M

## N



## O



## P



## Q



## R



## S

## T



## U



## V



## W

# Acknowledgements

When thinking of the persons involved in helping me put this manuscript together the people of Red Cliff, past and present, are the first to come to mind, but there are many others.

Thanks to Steve Cotherman, of the Madeline Island Historical Museum (and The Wisconsin Historical Society) who graciously responded to my request for a few photos. Likewise to Linda Mittlestadt and her staff at the Northern Great Lakes Visitor Center, Ashland, Wisconsin, who were always welcoming during that cold winter when I viewed the many boxes of original personal letters of the Leonard and Harriet Wheeler family.

Thanks also to the Bayfield Heritage Association, and especially Paul Nussbaum and Gary Gaynor, two excellent basement archivists, who helped me immeasurably. Paul's readiness to pour an unbeatable cup of coffee (and willingness to supply its necessary accompaniments), and Gary's intimate knowledge of the Association's holdings are both unsurpassable. And of course, thanks to Spencer Robnik for his archival organizational skills.

When nearing completion of a manuscript of this size and recognizing the length of time involved in such an endeavor, all sorts of influences come to mind. In my case, I acknowledge the effects of the many writers and teachers I encountered along the way. A long list of classes taken at numerous colleges over the years were relevant to this endeavor, and I readily recall several instructors and professors who helped me form pertinent questions and answers. This journey began at Northland College, but soon shifted to the University of Wisconsin-Madison, and in time, the university's campuses at Eau Claire, Milwaukee, and Superior were involved, and finally, the University of Minnesota at Minneapolis. It was at the University of Minnesota, in the 1970s and 1980s, that the culture concept, with its deep importance when studying history, came to the fore. Thanks to Victor Barnouw, John Ingham, Stephan Gudeman, Frank Miller, Janet Spector, Bjore Vahamaki, and several others for their insights into the complexities of the workings of a cultural system such as that of the Ojibwe.

Ron DePerry, of Red Cliff, was very helpful. Ron is a U.S. Army veteran, former teacher, and the only surviving member of the six Ojibwe net-lifters who put their bodies on the line on a cold morning on Lake Superior over forty years ago as they tested treaty rights. His willingness to discuss Ojibwe history and politics continues to help me understand this complex matter.

Once again, thanks go out to Fran DePerry, who responded with willingness and expertise when his uncle was baffled by his computer and errant printer.

Over the years the many readers of the *Red Cliff News*, *The Lake Superior Sounder*, and Ashland's *The Daily Press*, were important in encouraging me to keep writing, and in the case of *The Daily Press*, continue to spur me on today.

Jake Geisler, a friend and neighbor here in Ojibwe Country, never faltered in his willingness to take time for coffee, toast and oatmeal on cold winter mornings. His keen sense of the proper use of English and his interest in literature make for a valued combination.

Thanks also go to Mark Gokee, posthumously, and more recently, to Jason Schlender, whose Ojibwe language classes were, and in Jason's case, continue to be invaluable. Despite my limited linguistic skills and poor study habits, such settings allow an insight into Ojibwe culture that is a must when attempting to understand the history of these people.

Thanks to the good people at North Star Press for agreeing to take this project on, and especially to Anne, who saw it through to completion.

Max Joseph Paap, Beth Marie Paap, and Keller Augustine DePerry Paap have been an inspiration. In their own ways, each carries the torch.

And of course, thanks to Marlene, for her enduring patience and acceptance. Fifty years is a long time no matter how you approach it. My world would have been far different without her.

Lastly, a people can never successfully be separated from the natural place in which they reside, and in this sense the Ojibwe worldview encompasses many persons, both human and, as Alfred I. Hallowell put it, "other than human." These other than human forms of life are also behind a book such as this. *Miigwech* to all.